Cover Photo by C. R. Stecyk III
Skateboarder Jay Smith

Jantzen
MADE IN U.S.A. M

"FASHION IS REALLY ALL ABOUT FADS. FADS COME AND GO.
BUT SKATEBOARDING IS HERE TO STAY!"
- JIM PHILLIPS

SKATEBOARDING IS NOT A FASHION

THE ILLUSTRATED HISTORY OF SKATEBOARD APPAREL

1950s to 1984

2nd edition Hardcover, November 2022

Created and published by
FauxAmi Exhibitions

In association with

GINGKO
PRESS

Conceived by
Jürgen Blümlein,
Dirk Vogel and Cap10

Art Direction by
Jürgen Blümlein

Written by
Dirk Vogel

Apparel pictures by
Cap10

Historical advisor
Todd Huber
SKATEBOARDING HALL OF FAME

Distributed worldwide by
Gingko Press Inc.
2332 Fourth Street, Suite E
Berkeley, CA 94710 USA
gingkopress.com

ISBN 978-1-58423-766-2

2nd Edition

Printed in China

CONTENTS

here it is!
SKATEBOARDER MAGAZINE
T-SHIRT
SKATEBOARDER
magazine

INTRO

INTRODUCTION - WE KNOW FASHION

"It's better to do a dull thing with style than a dangerous thing without it." - Charles Bukowski

Whether they admit it or not, skateboarders have always paid a lot of attention to their clothes. It's a big decision, choosing what to wear before a skate session. Bigger than just picking an outfit for the day, more a question of what kind of vibe and identity our outfits will project into the world as we head out on our boards. If skateboarding is a body language and every skateboard trick performed is a statement, then our clothes are the exclamation points behind our communications with the world at large. There's a fluid aspect to it all, poetry in motion. The graceful posture on a perfectly executed Smith grind enhanced by a white button-up dress shirt and black pants in a form-fitting silhouette; the coattails of an unbuttoned flannel shirt trailing the skater flying eleven feet above the bowl coping like a superhero's cape. The right piece of clothing at the right time can turn the trick volume from ten to eleven. Boom!

When skateboarders engage with skate parks and city architecture, they more than just wear an outfit or a look - they're *rocking* it. "Everywhere we go, we skaters want to look like something! We're not just putting on clothes. Skateboarders are coming correct! I'm gonna show up, grind, and ollie and show everyone what I've got. Head to toe! On and off the board! That's why people care about what they wear," said skateboard icon Christian Hosoi, arguably the most fashionable skateboarder of all time, adding: "Skateboarding separated itself from the rest because it was all attitude. Making your mark - and not giving a hoot about it. That's why it's the coolest activity and art form on this planet. It is gnarly, it is rad, it's dangerous, you could get hurt. All those factors make it exciting and adventurous, and not everybody is going to do it. You gotta fight to even be accepted. All those little criteria sift out all the losers... the posers and the ones that are just hypocritically hanging out, wanting to fit in, but not paying any dues."

With that said, skateboard fashion is only partly something that can be bought - money will just get you clothing - but something that also has to be earned. Dues need to be paid by learning how to hold your own on this incredibly hard to control four-wheeled plank of wood and by taking some heavy slams in the process. In the bigger picture, dressing the part of the skateboarder - typically with skate manufacturer-branded tees and skateboard-specific footwear, and bold messages such as SKATEBOARDING IS NOT A CRIME or SKATE AND DESTROY - immediately connects riders to a larger group. It's a tribal thing, a closely-knit community united by a shared experience. "The first time I saw a group of skaters, it was like looking at a group of soldiers marching by. You know, they had scars and they had weapons and they were marching to certain death or victory - who knows? It sparked something, even if you didn't realize it at the time," said veteran skateboard clothing and denim designer Chris "Slappy" Sutherland, adding: "You were looking at rugged explorers. Men who took control of their environment. And you knew what they were about to do was probably dangerous, and you thought, 'I wanna be like that!'"

FUNCTION VS FASHION: WHAT IS SKATEBOARD STYLE?

Every skateboarder remembers the first piece of "real" skateboard clothing they ever owned, whether it's a T-shirt, a pair of shorts, a hoodie, or just a home-made number with a skate company logo patch on it (because mom wasn't going to throw all this cash at a shirt that's bound to be obliterated within a matter of weeks). And once they own this coveted emblem of belonging, it becomes part of their day-to-day uniform, a way of telling the world what they're all about. "With the first skate shirt you instantly become a part of something," said pro skateboarder and company owner Pierre-André Senizergues, who fondly remembers scoring his first piece of official skate gear in the late 1970s. "At one of the stores in France I found a T-shirt from a skateboard company, Free Former Skateboards. And I thought it was so killer! It was yellow and had a black stripe on it, and I had seen [pro skateboarder] Ty Page wearing one at a demo. It was my first skateboard shirt and I was so excited. I wore it all the time, until it had holes in it." Pro skateboarder and company owner Keith Hufnagel remembers having to resort to DIY-tailoring to make clothes work for him: "I got these crazy SMA pants with a print on the side and when I tried to put them on at home, the bottom opening was so tiny I couldn't fit my feet through it, so I had to cut them off to get in. But that's how it was... you wore what you had and that was your fashion!"

At first, that fashion was for skaters only. While practically everyone today - skateboarder or not - knows what a *Thrasher* T-shirt is, skate clothing still belonged to the initiated few in those early days. "People didn't even know what the hell you were wearing, but skaters would know," said skateboarder and artist Mark Oblow, adding: "That was the cool thing about skateboarding back then, if you met another skater, you recognized it and you were hanging out the next day." Everyone has different memories of how clothes identified people as skateboarders over the years. And that's great, because there is not - and never has been - just one specific "skateboarder uniform" or "skater look." Flipping through the pages of this book, you will see outfits associated with "punks," "surfer dudes," "athletes," and "hippies;" all worn in the act of riding a skateboard. These outside influences - drawing from the realms of music and other subcultures - have been appropriated into skateboarding by ways of diverse looks and outfits. Some of these outfits exploded into full-blown fashion trends within skateboarding - some classic, others better forgotten (think ultra-baggy pants, spandex shorts, and neon-colored nylon jerseys). Pro skateboarder and artist Gary Scott Davis (GSD) sums up dominant fashion trends by decade as follows: "The 1960s were hippies, 1970s surfers, 1980s it was punks, in the 1990s rappers, and the 2000s to 2010s brought a mish-mash of all of these."

On that note, never underestimate the desire among skateboarders to collectively flaunt their feathers as fashion peacocks, even at the risk of crossing into the realm of costumes (paging Simon Woodstock) and ill-advised outfit choices (Goofy Boy pants). As skateboard icon Jeff Grosso famously said on the "Frankly Speaking" web TV show: "I mean, what is fashion, Frank, really? One day's neon is the next day's bad joke!" But although many fashion choices may seem outlandish in retrospect, it all has to be seen in context. Says pro skateboarder and 1990s fashion icon Chad Muska: "Style and fashion are always of the time. Whatever you are doing at the moment is your favorite. And then you look back and they're ridiculous! That's my favorite thing about skateboarding - it's not just one thing, item or style." And no matter how outrageous the outfits have gotten over the years, at the end of the day, it better not get in the way of landing your tricks. "Normally for me as a skateboarder, fashion doesn't come before function. Function always comes before fashion. If it doesn't work good, you better not wear it. If you're uncomfortable and restricted in your body movements, and it's hampering your performance - why wear it?" said skateboard style icon Tony Alva.

CHRONICLING SKATEBOARD FASHION HISTORY

In this book, we set out to explore the storied history of skateboard fashion; a history full of playful experimentation, trend-setting dress codes and the occasional skeleton in the closet. Starting with the culture's strong roots in surfing and beach culture, *Skateboarding Is Not a Fashion: The Illustrated History of Skateboard Apparel* chronicles the evolution of "skate style" over the decades. Along the way, we talk to professional skateboarders and skateboard company owners past and present, and shine the spotlight on numerous style icons throughout skateboard history. These style icons are the pro skateboarders who set the trends and fashion conventions admired and imitated by thousands around the world.

We also implement our personal background as curators of skateboard exhibitions and the Museum of Skateboard History in Berlin, Germany, supplemented by invaluable support from a network of skateboard history buffs and collectors around the world who have already supported our first book, *Made for Skate: The Illustrated History of Skateboard Footwear*. And because skateboard fashion is all about the finer details, we also talk to leading skateboard photographers that have chronicled the culture's many trends, fads, and fashion faux pas over the years.

After all, photographers are the gatekeepers of what is considered "material" for skateboard publications. More often than not they play a decisive hand in what kind of outfits ended up on the glossy pages of *Thrasher, Transworld Skateboarding, Jucie Magzine and The Skateboard Mag*. Quoted in this book, long-time *Transworld Skateboarding* photo editor Skin Phillips even goes as far as saying: "Without skateboard photographers, there would be no skateboard fashion as we know it." And that is probably true today as much as it was in winter 1964 when *The Quarterly Skateboarder* magazine first brought images of skateboard style to newsstands across the US.

ONE STORY - TWO BOOKS

More than 50 years have passed since the first skateboard boom. The skateboard industry has experienced tremendous ups and downs, booms and busts over the decades. So the history of skateboard fashion is not just a roller coaster ride of "In" and "Out" periods, but a rather long story. As we found out while working on this book, it's a story long enough to fill more than just one volume, actually. So in order to give all that style enough room to breathe and the style icons and trend-setters the adequate space to tell their side of the story, we are splitting *The Illustrated History of Skateboard Apparel* in two books: Old School and New School. Starting with the early 1950s roots of skateboard culture, the book you are holding will dive deep into the "Old School" side of things all the way through the early 1980s-when skateboarding found itself after a crucial underground period of soul searching and DIY expressions of individuality.

We're already working on the follow-up volume and will continue the narrative beginning in 1984 with the start of a "New School" marked by the arrival of clothing companies specifically designed for skateboarding. That means not designed for surfing, not as a side product for hardware manufacturers - but its own style of skate clothes. A style deeply influenced by the streets, as skateboard fashion goes from fringe phenomenon to center stage attraction during the big 1980s skateboard boom that brought the world brands such as Airwalk and Vision Street Wear which blew up all the way into the mainstream.

Fast forward to 2018, and skate fashion is still hot. Everyone still seems to want a piece of skateboard style - maybe now more than ever. Luxury fashion labels are hosting runway shows in replica skate parks, while designers like Jeremy Scott unleash the wrath of copyright litigators by "borrowing" iconic staples of skateboard graphic design such as the Jim Phillips "Screaming Hand" for high fashion collections. Marquee rap stars and musicians are gearing up in underground skateboard apparel brands - most notably the hip-hop elite's ongoing love story with New York's SUPREME and London-based label Palace Skateboards - while supermodels recline in *Thrasher* magazine hoodies between fashion shoots. "A lot of highly influential youth culture icons are really gravitating toward the aesthetic appeal of the skateboard industry. If you look at Lil Wayne and the brands that he represents - plus the fact that he is skateboarding and really psyched on it. And Jay-Z is rocking DC beanies. That's really rad and goes to show how influential we can be as an industry," said pro skateboarder and footwear and apparel designer Alphonzo Rawls, while pointing out major trends originated by skateboarders: "From chain wallets to hip sacks to Jason Lee rocking sideburns. We can say, 'We did that!'"

Skateboarders are now the faces of entire fashion campaigns. Influential pro riders such as Dylan Rieder (RIP), Brian Anderson, and Scott Bourne have successfully worked as fashion models for the world's top-grossing designer labels. And today it's no longer just fashion borrowing from skateboarding, but a two-way process. Pro skateboarders are making successful forays into fashion's "in" crowd with their home-spun fashion labels, including the 917 and Bianca Chandon brands by Alex Olson, son of pro skateboarder and style icon Steve Olson.

The fashion and art world is watching for skateboarding's next move. "Many people today that are in the art world are following skating and that is a cool thing," said Mark Oblow, while pointing out: "It's important to harness this back into skating, reminding ourselves that we do lead. We have our own shit. And we need to continue to do that - and not let the outside world come in and take over!"

Keeping that level of control will be crucial. Because any way you slice it - skateboarding is super hot right now. And dressing the part of the skateboarder is not just for practicing members of the tribe anymore; it's no longer just for the ones who in the words of Christian Hosoi have paid their dues. That's just the way the world works, a mixture as explosive and potent as skateboard style is just hard to contain. Then again, rocking skateboard gear will always and forever be a statement, no matter if you paid your dues or not. And while the T-shirts and stickers are perfectly correct in proclaiming that SKATEBOARDING IS NOT A CRIME, it's surely not a fashion trend, either. It´s a life choice.

THE WELL-DRESSED SKATEBOARDER

Photo: Bill Eppridge

Photo: Ralph Morse

THE ROOTS

1

1950s: YOUTH CULTURE AND FASHION

Looking back at the late 1940s, it's hard to believe that there was a time in history when popular culture in the United States was not obsessed with youth. A time before "forever young" became an ideal for entire generations. Before Botox, plastic surgery and "dude speak" for all age groups. When youth culture - not to mention youth fashion - hardly existed and being young was just an awkward, intermediate stage on the way to adulthood. In the aftermath of World War II, young people in the U.S. were raised into strict gender roles - the men as income providers, the women as "homemakers" - and career paths. Fashion styles of the times reflected these norms: Adult men wore grey flannel suits commuting to their jobs in Ford and Cadillac automobiles, while women went shopping in high-heeled shoes and dresses with pinched-in waists to accentuate their feminine silhouettes. Children fit into the picture as "Mini Me" versions of their parents; the boys riding around in miniature Cadillacs and playing with Tonka construction trucks, the girls preparing for their roles as "homebodies" with baby dolls and replica household items.

But luckily, some toys opened up a new world of playful exploration for American "youths" (the term "teen-agers" had first appeared in a 1941 issue of *Popular Science Monthly*, but was not yet commonly used). Some kids found an escape by getting their kicks on early apple crate scooters and skateboards, called "pop-outs." But these homemade thrills required ingenuity - a certain do-it-yourself spirit - because store-bought skateboards were still years away. All across the country, crafty kids built their own skateboards from scratch, using two-by-four planks of wood fitted with trucks and wheels from old roller skates in the late 1940s.

THE KIDS ARE ALRIGHT

America's youth was getting restless, and the 1950s brought changes on a monumental scale. Within less than a decade, young people emerged as a main focus for the targeted marketing of a new wave of consumer goods. Three major factors paved the way for an independent youth culture, replete with its own fashion trends and codes of conduct:

1. The rise of the American middle class. The post-war era brought affluence on an unprecedented scale, characterized by individual home ownership and disposable income spent on consumer products. By 1955, more than 60% of the U.S. population belonged to the middle class with incomes between $3,000 and $10,000 per year. By the end of the 1950s, almost 60% of Americans owned their home, while almost all households owned at least one car and washing machine. This wealth also trickled down to kids and teenagers, who could earn money by working summer jobs or finding after-school employment in the burgeoning service industry.

2. Mass-produced clothing for consumer audiences. Perfected by the U.S. military during World War II, standard sizing (S, M, L, XL) schemes for apparel opened the doors to affordable consumer fashions on a broad scale. The standard-issue white T-shirt brought home by U.S. Navy veterans became a staple in popular culture, immortalized by Hollywood icons including James Dean and Marlon Brando. New materials such as polyester - the Dupont company started commercial production in 1953 in North Carolina - unlocked a new, more youthful color palette, replacing the drab grayish browns of the war years.

3. Radio, cinema and television "mediate" society. Motion pictures (short "movies") exerted a growing influence on popular culture, accelerated by the introduction of color television into American homes in 1951. By 1953, about 53% of American households owned television sets - the number would grow to 90% by the end of the decade - providing a platform for youth culture icons such as Elvis Presley and Jerry Lee Lewis to influence the fashion sense of an entire generation. The pocket radio, brought to market by Texas Instruments in 1954, empowered teenagers to listen to music of their own choosing - mostly the soundtrack of rebellion, rock'n'roll - away from (parent-controlled) living room radio receivers.

Speaking of *Rebel Without a Cause*, the casual dress code introduced by James Dean – whose white T-shirt, blue jeans and red jacket combo remains timelessly chic even 60 years later – had deeper societal implications: Young people were no longer "dressing up" and acting like adults, but gradually beginning to carve out their own place in society while challenging the status quo. The rise of rock music became synonymous with this youthful rebellion, and companies soon noticed a new marketing demographic: teenagers with disposable income.

While parents desperately tried to understand their offspring's growing sense of alienation, teenagers soon enjoyed their own cafés and fast food restaurants. Movies and pop music introduced popular "looks" – or cultural identities – for teens to choose from: The rebellious, leather-clad "greasers," popularized by Marlon Brando in 1953's *The Wild One*, found their counterpart in the neatly-dressed, pleated polyester wearing "preppies." Out in California and Hawaii, another iconic lifestyle had been brewing for decades and was ready to make a big splash: surfing. Much to the dismay of hardcore practitioners, the surf lifestyle received the (superficial) Hollywood treatment in the 1958 production *Gidget*, directed by Frederick Kohner, and was mass-marketed to mainstream audiences with "surfy" outfits sold in department stores across the country.

SURFING'S LITTLE SIBLING

Skateboarding arrived on the heels of surf culture, and the two sports progressed side-by-side for more than a decade. Throughout the 1950s, professional surfers could often be seen fine-tuning their balance and control on skateboards before taking on bigger challenges in the water. In 1958, Carl Jensen of Hermosa Beach, California, produced the first mass marketed skateboards with his company, Humco. The publisher of *Surf Guide magazine*, Larry Stevenson, also began promoting skateboarding as a "natural" extension of surfing culture.

When the infamous bright red Roller Derby Skateboard was introduced at department stores across the country in early 1959 for $12.95 (equivalent of $80.00 today), the skateboard craze hit the mainstream full force, much like previous mass-marketed fads such as Hula Hoops, Hopalong Cassidy guns and Silly Putty. The Roller Derby board featured metallic wheels about two inches in diameter that proved very slippery in contact with concrete. "I hated these boards because they were so damn dangerous. These manufacturers didn't want to create a product that was safe to use to protect people. They just figured how to make skateboards really cheap and sell a lot of them. That was really the worst they could have done to skateboarding," said 1960s professional skateboarder Cris Dawson.

While pundits were quick to point out the dangers of skateboarding – deriding the boards as "bun busters" – a new generation of kids began hitting the streets, not willing to be told where to roll or what to wear. Pleated khakis, checkered button-up shirts or Gilligan's Island-style rugby shirts paired with sailor caps – anything was fair game. Says seasoned skateboard photographer J. Grant Brittain: "You just wore college shirts all the time... That's the way I used to dress when I was a kid growing up in the late 1950s and early 1960s. I pretty much dressed like [the TV show] *Leave It to Beaver*." In those early days, skateboard fashion was a free-for-all. A blank canvas with endless room to experiment, much like the sport of skateboarding itself.

SURF TRUNKS: BORN OUT OF NECESSITY

Surf trunks emerged as the evolutionary predecessor of modern-day board shorts in the mid-1940s, mainly in surf culture hotbeds such as coastal California and Hawaii. Born out of necessity, surf trunks catered to the functional requirements of surfers. They protected surfers from chaffing their legs on the board's surface or scraping coral reefs underwater. Other features included a secure fit around the waist to withstand choppy seas and enough pocket space to store board wax or the occasional tool.

Conventional men's bathing suits at the time offered little functionality from a surfer's perspective, trending towards using minimal amounts of fabric, especially around the legs. Wave riders would fashion their own surf trunks, D.I.Y.-style, by cutting off white canvas sailor pants right above the knees. One such early prototype can be traced to surfboard shaper Dale Velzy and cohorts at the Manhattan Beach Surf Club in Southern California, who hit the waves in home-made shorts before the first commercial surf trunks became available.

CUSTOM-MADE BEGINNINGS

Whereas board shorts today can easily be purchased in even the remotest, land-locked mall stores around the planet, scoring a pair of surf trunks in the 1950s proved challenging. Basically, you had to know the right people. "There was a tailor named M. Nii on Oahu [Hawaii], who made long surf shorts for people," said Jimmy Ganzer, who later started making his own board shorts under the Jimmy'Z brand name in the 1980s. Surf enthusiast and graphic artist Jim Phillips also saw shorts by M. Nii – pronounced "emm-nii" – as hard-to-get items: "I remember they were the hottest thing when I first started surfing in '59. Some surfers brought them back [from Hawaii] to the mainland. M. Nii usually mixed two colors on the quarter panels of the legs and the shorts featured a wax pocket in the opposite color of the panel."

Before long, the first wave of specialized surf shops in California also started offering bespoke shorts as a service. Says Jimmy Ganzer: "You could have shorts custom-made at a store named Ray's Cabana just for you. They used only the best twill and made them just the way you wanted. So early on, surfers understood that you could have your very own style and look different than anyone else on the beach!"

MADE FOR MOVEMENT

With their emphasis on free movement and durability, surf trunks soon became a favorite among skateboarders. "We all wore shorts to skate in," says Jim Goodrich, skateboard photographer and former pro skateboarder, adding: "I can't imagine skating in pants because they are so restrictive. Actually, I still can't!"

But it would take some time for mass-produced shorts to emerge as a product segment in board sports retail. When the world's first skateboard shop, Val Surf in North Hollywood opened in 1962, specialized surf clothing brands were still a novelty. "When we first opened, we had T-shirts and a few surf trunks but there wasn't even anything really designated as a surf brand. When we opened it was companies like Laguna Beach Wear, Zuma Beach Wear, but no Hang Tens, or Jansen," said Mark Richards, owner of Val Surf. As another early surf trunks company, Skateboard photographer J. Grant Brittain remembers: "Schroff, the surfboard company, was the first company making long shorts."

From then on, the floodgates were opened and what had started as a bespoke item became the corner stone of an entire industry for surf- and skateboard-specific apparel, worth a whooping $203 million in 2015. And no need to search high and low for cool shorts. To witness the next step in the evolution of surf shorts, just head down to your local mall.

SURF'S DOWN

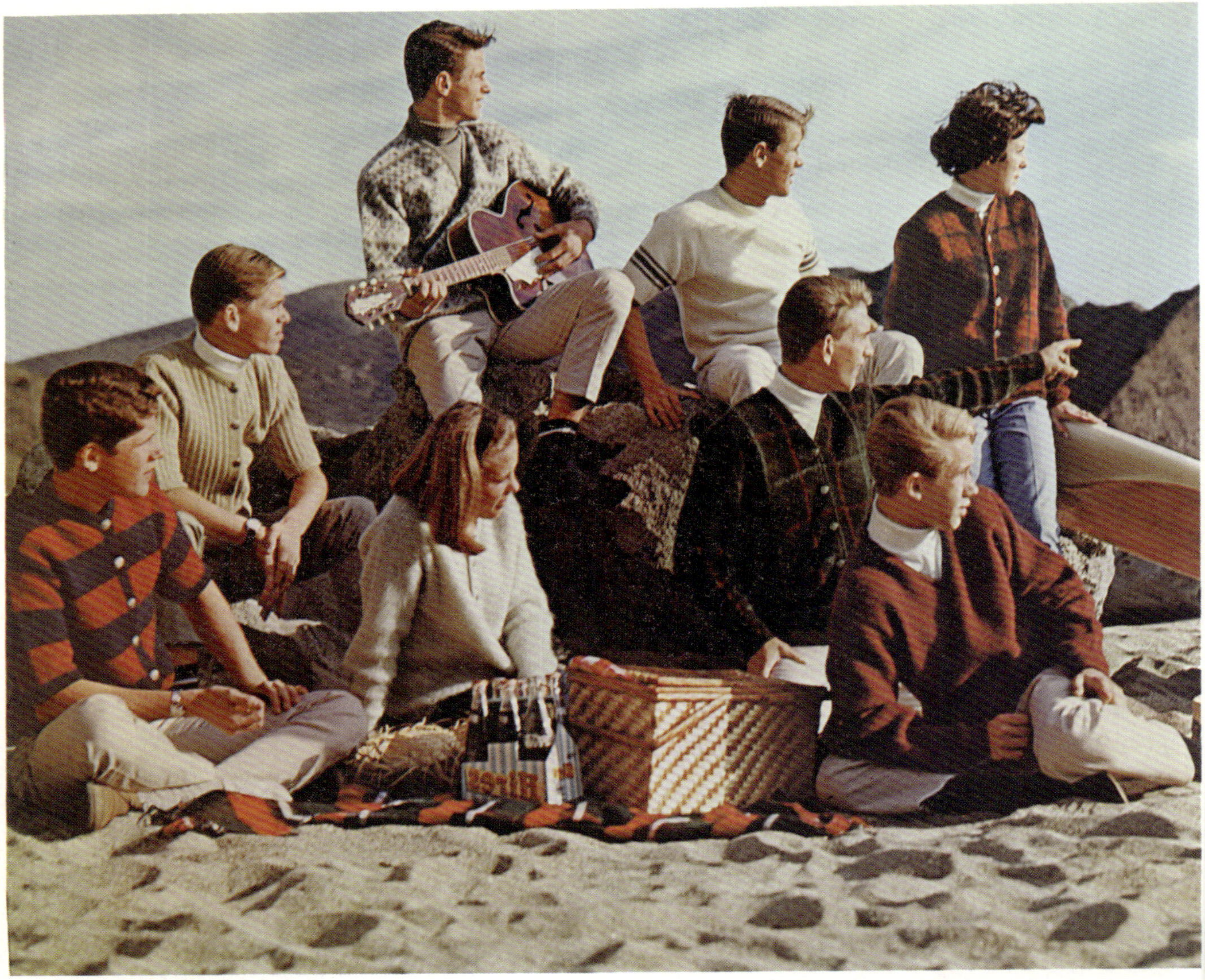

How come all these sweaters and no skateboard?

Well, we figured that skateboarders occasionally want to look at something else, like rear-view mirrors, Mad magazine, or maybe sweaters. Since we make special sweaters for skateboarders, we figured that we'd show them on this page. They're all wearing Big J sweaters, and what they are all doing is looking across the gutter of this great magazine, just like any bunch of skateboarders on a beach. After all, who can skateboard on sand? Now the commercial message: skateboarders, wheel into department stores and Buy Big J sweaters and other* sportswear. There are short sleeves, plaids, mohairs, turtles, shetlands, lambswools, turtle neck tee shirts, and skateboard shirts like the ones the Hobie Skateboard Team is wearing.

This is the Hobie Skateboard Team, all decked out in Jantzen Big J surfshirts.

1965 - Jantzen out of Portland, Oregon, runs the first advertisement from a fashion brand directly aimed at skateboarders.

2 THE SIXTIES

1960s: EVERYBODY'S SIDEWALK SURFING

When surfing caused a big splash around the world in the early 1960s, skateboarding as surfing's "little brother" came along for the ride. Labeled as "sidewalk surfing," skateboarding soon became a favorite pastime for hardcore surfers when ocean waves were flat and sessions in the water proved out of the question. "We called it 'bun boarding' - because you would end up busting your buns. And we really didn't think much of it at first," said skateboard artist Jim Phillips from Santa Cruz, adding: "To go out on the 'bun board' was really only something we did when the surf was flat." Emulating surf maneuvers on concrete also provided easy access to the sport and lifestyle for landlocked enthusiasts. Die-hard surfers often denounced these newcomers as "posers," and the letter pages of publications such as *Surfer Magazine* and Larry Stevenson's *Surf Guide* hosted heated diatribes bashing folks who were calling themselves "surfers," while "only" rolling down the streets on four wheels. The clear verdict among surfing's faithful: Those posers should learn "real" surfing first!

Keeping it "real" in the streets was all about taking inspiration from the ocean. With their bare feet on the concrete and their minds on surfing, early skateboarders closely followed the blueprint developed over decades by surfers in California and Hawaii. Most riders preferred a crouched down, low-to-the ground style adapted from surfing, gliding and turning as much as the rickety trucks and slippery clay wheels allowed. Early skateboarders also adapted the nomenclature for their moves directly from surfing, illustrated in the 1963 hit single "*Sidewalk Surfing*" by pop duo Jan & Dean. According to the lyrics, skateboarders "*can do the tricks the surfers do*," including the "*Quasimodo*" and "*The Coffin*." In search of terrain for performing these adapted moves, sidewalk surfers sought out rounded embankments on schoolyards, reminiscent of ocean waves. Downhill riding also soared in popularity, and one notorious downhill area of San Francisco became known among locals as "*Waimea Bay*," named after a famous Hawaiian surfing spot. Another 1960s hot spot awaited skaters at Los Angeles International Airport; a banked area called "*the Trestle*," named after a famous surfing spot outside camp Pendleton Marine Corps Base on Oahu. Everywhere in the streets, skaters were riding skateboards - but thinking surfing.

THE FIRST SKATEBOARD BOOM

Slowly but surely, skateboarding was building enough momentum to step out of surfing's shadow. Surf enthusiast Bill Richards opened the first specialised skateboard shop, Val Surf, miles away from the beach in North Hollywood in 1962. "The place was full of everything - skateboards, clothing, pads. If you wanted something for skateboarding, you had to go to Val Surf!" said Todd Huber, proprietor of Skatelab in Simi Valley. Joined by his two sons, Richards began selling homemade skateboards assembled from components provided by the Chicago Roller Skate Company. In 1963, surf pioneer Larry Stevenson's company Makaha made history by producing the first-ever pro skateboard. Not for a pro skateboarder, but for a pro surfer: world-famous surf icon Phil Edwards. Business was booming. By the end of the year, Makaha was selling 10,000 skateboards per day at price points between $10.00-13.00, endorsed by an exhibition team of talented riders.

But what about skate fashion? While skateboard hardware progressed, apparel choices remained limited to the occasional graphic T-shirt and windbreaker. "In the early 1960s there was really no skate fashion. We just wore what we had, just jeans and T-shirts. Mostly old clothes to go skating in... nobody really dressed for anything," said skateboard photographer Ted "T-Bone" Terrebonne.

A BUDDING CULTURE

By 1965, surfing's little sibling had grown into a mature, $30 million-per-year market dominated by a handful of early manufacturers. Makaha reported $10 million in revenues from board sales between 1963 and 1965, while Hobie was selling 20,000 of their Super Surfer skateboards per day(!) during peak times. The majority of skateboard companies were based in California, including Hobie, Makaha, Humco, Nash, Roller Derby, G&S, and Hang Ten. Even in 2018, the majority of the skateboard industry still remains rooted in the Golden State. Skateboarding's first boom also elevated the competitive aspect of the sport. The first major international skateboard competition was held in 1965 in Anaheim, California. Broadcast on national television to a broad audience, the International Skateboarding Championships saw 300 competitors from around the world facing off in freestyle and slalom racing events. The event sold out at $5 per ticket (equivalent of $30.00 in 2018), presenting skateboarding as a "real" sport. A brand-new magazine hit newsstands, *the quarterly Skateboarder*, dedicated solely to chronicling the new sport and its heroes.

The teenage skateboard lifestyle became the focus of a critically acclaimed short film written and directed by filmmaker Noel Black. *Skater Dater* chronicles the romantic exploits of a young skateboarder who becomes enamored with a girl from school. Instead of dialogue, the film relied solely on sound effects and a musical score composed by Mike Curb and Nick Venet. Next to film, mainstream television also started a short-lived love affair with skateboarding, and professional riders such as Pat McGee, Danny Bearer, Corky Carroll and John Freis represented the "new fad" on prime time television shows including *What's My Line* and the *Tonight Show* with Johnny Carson. While the youth discovered skateboarding, mainstream culture was enthralled with surf and beach culture, made popular by blockbuster films such as the *"beach party"* movie series directed by William Asher for American International Pictures. Movies like 1965's *Beach Blanket Bingo* taught mass audiences how to dress for the beach, and behind the scenes, an entire cottage industry provided the outfits. "Before there were brands making surf clothing, a lot of the clothing created here in Los Angeles was made in coordination with the *Beach Blanket Bingo* movies. These clothes were made to go into department stores, coordinated with the release of those movies," said Alaric Valentin, who managed a number of surf stores in Southern California throughout the 1960s, adding: "The clothes didn't have a brand logo like Hang Ten, but nevertheless were out for sale at J.C. Penney and other department stores. Before it became specialty, it was already mainstream."

Skateboarders had little use for this mainstreamed "surfer look" and began cultivating a more distinct clothing style. Leaving behind surfing's Tiki vibes and "beachy" garments, skateboarders took to the streets in jeans, T-shirts and canvas pants, while rugby shirts, plaid button-ups and windbreakers also became early skateboard fashion staples. "Music had a big influence on fashion back then," said skateboard photographer J. Grant Brittain. "If the band The Monkees was wearing moccasins, you were wearing moccasins. Or peasant shirts, hippie stuff. There were also these stores called Chess King at the malls selling disco clothing and American flag socks and the like." Competitions were a different story, though. Dressing the part of the professional athlete, company-sponsored skateboard teams wore their own specific team uniforms for competitions and photo shoots. The first screen-printed T-shirts for skateboarders appeared in the mid-1960s, including shirts gifted to *SkateBoarder Magazine* subscribers, and shirts by retailers such as Val Surf.

SWIMSUITS · SPORTSWEAR · SWEATERS · FOOTWEAR
jantzen
International
sports club
sportswear for sportsmen
Jantzen Inc., Portland 8, Oregon
FRANK GIFFORD
BOB COUSY
BOBBY HULL
JERRY WEST
JISC
PAUL HORNUNG
TERRY BAKER
DAVE MARR
JOHN SEVERSON
It is much better to give. That is why Jantzen swimtrunks are made of Chemstrand sharkskin.
The most popular swimsuit in history has always been absolutely perfect, so we thought, but now Chemstrand Blue C Spandex has come along to give something to perfection. Elasticized stretch sharkskin! This splendid blend, exactly right for stretch swimtrunks, is 78% acetate, 16% cotton, and 6% Chemstrand Blue C Spandex. As Frank Gifford, in the $7 webbed belt style, says, it gives more than it gets. Jerry West wears crossed belt loop stretch, about $8. Bobby Hull is in the button tab stretch, about $6. Comfortable, tough, good-looking, and available in the colors shown on the surfboard. All trunks have inside coin pocket, panel supporter. Photo by Tom Kelley at the Hilton Hawaiian Village on recent club outing.
Actionwear
C
SPANDEX
CHEMSTRAND

These early skate tees were mostly manufactured at local print shops and clothing factories. Here's a historic side note: Throughout the 1960s, about 95% of all clothing worn by Americans was still produced in the United States. Thanks to rapid advancements in riding technique, skateboarding on bare feet soon faded, and shoes became the norm. The first-ever skateboard-specific shoe was released by the Randolph Rubber Company in 1965, endorsed in full-page advertisements by Mark Richards, co-founder of Val Surf shop. In 1966, the Van Doren Rubber Company opened the first Vans shoe store in Anaheim, California, with a new concept: Customers were free to choose from three shoe models and a wide range of fabrics and the customized shoes were handmade on-site the same day, as Vans became a staple of the "skater" look.

EARLY OUTLAW IMAGE

Despite the growing number of skateboard enthusiasts - over 50 million boards were sold in the U.S. in 1965 alone - the mainstream media remained critical. A cover article from *LIFE Magazine* in May 1965 - featuring Pat McGee's iconic handstand photo on the cover - portrayed skateboarding as, "Mania - and menace." Next to accident statistics and tales of rebellious misconduct, the article featured pictures of bloody injuries. "It's easier to get bloody than fancy," the article concluded, and upright citizens should leave it alone. Skateboarding, after all, was for punks. Following the *LIFE* article, an editorial in *the quarterly Skateboarder* urged skaters to clean up their act: "Skateboarding is (...) not a sport of destruction - of others or yourself. It's a sport of control. It's up to you to see that skateboarding does not become a sport of rebels and radicals. It's a sport for young sportsmen. We look forward to a great future in skateboarding and we ask you, the pioneers, to make it great."

But the damage was done. By August 1965, skateboarding was banned from the streets and sidewalks of 20 U.S. cities from Rhode Island to California. Medical associations issued safety warnings about the new "dangerous fad," while police officers urged retailers to stop selling skateboards altogether. With hundreds of orders cancelled per day, skateboard companies soon found themselves stuck with skateboard hardware worth millions of dollars. Ultimately, this backlash ushered in skateboarding's first "death" in the public arena, and the "sidewalk surfing" craze came to a screeching halt.

The "menace" of skateboarding was averted - or was it? In 1966, the Canadian short film *The Devil's Toy* depicted throngs of skateboarders on the run from police on the streets of Montreal. After the authorities shut down public skateboarding and confiscate the "devil's toys," the film - dedicated to "all victims of intolerance" - concluded: "The battle was won. For the moment, we are safe." But in closing, The *Devil's Toy* also warned: "Beware! The youth of the world is on the move. And their aim is to take over!" This warning would prove nothing short of prophetic, as a die-hard breed of dedicated skateboarders remained on board. Away from the public spotlight, the sport went through a crucial period of evolution. To be continued...

PAUL
GREG

GETTING RAW: EARLY PIONEERS IN JEANS

The exploration of rugged riding terrain such as streets, school yards, and the first empty swimming pools called for clothes that could take a beating. Durable enough to resist the wear and tear of skateboarding on concrete, denim jeans proved the perfect choice for exploring a whole new world on wheels. Plus, practitioners of the relatively young sport were hard-pressed to find the right clothing options. "There was not much else to wear back then because there was nothing designed for us," said skateboard icon Stacy Peralta, one of the pioneers of skateboarding in empty swimming pools.

Even long before skateboarders adopted jeans as part of their uniform, they were the natural outfit of rugged explorers. Historically, jeans fabric first emerged in the textile mills of Genoa, Italy. During the 16th century, the rugged blue cloth was used in all-purpose pants made for seamen in the Genoese Navy. French sailors labeled the blue pants "Genes" after the French translation of Genoa, which led to the enduring English moniker "jeans".

Jeans also played a major part in the making of America. Popularized in the U.S. by German immigrant Levi Strauss, who patented the copper-riveting process for the sturdy fabric in 1872, true blue jeans soon became a work wear staple in the harsh environments of the American Southwest. Initially called "overalls" – a moniker that stuck until the late 1950s – denim jeans became symbols of Wild West cowboy and Ranch culture. Propagated by a slew of Hollywood movies, jeans emerged as a major fashion fad for all ages that swept America in the mid-1940s, equated with exploration and a pioneering spirit.

CREATING THE SKATEBOARDER LOOK

But not everybody was a fan. Around the time early skateboard pioneers appropriated jeans into their outfits, the pants had already fallen out of favor among American youths – or more precisely, their parents. Although blue jeans briefly enjoyed significant commercial success as emblems of youthful rebellion – preferably in combination with plain white T-shirts – in the image of silver screen icons such as Marlon Brando and James Dean, jeans sales had flattened out in the mid-1950s. The main reason: Schools across the U.S. had outlawed the pants because of their anti-authoritarian implications amidst a backlash from concerned parents who equated jeans with juvenile delinquency.

When San Francisco-based denim company Levi Strauss advertised their jeans as "Right for School" in 1959, an outraged New Jersey mother fired back in a letter: "While I have to admit that this may be 'right for school' in San Francisco, in the west, or in some rural areas I can assure that this is in bad taste and 'not right for School' in the East." Having fallen from mainstream grace, jeans became apparel staples for disaffected subcultures such as bikers, beatniks and hippies, who kept denim alive in the underground.

This cultural vacuum, next to cheap retail prices, made jeans the perfect attire for the budding boardsports culture in California, where surfers and skateboarders embraced the pants as part of their look. Other youths took notice, and Levi Strauss began targeting teenagers and college students with advertisements for their 501 model while officially using the term "jeans" – made popular by teenagers – in ads and packaging.

The company also introduced non-blue options such as White Levis and brown denim varieties. Levis expanded beyond denim, offering jean-styled pants in new materials including twill and the highly popular brown corduroy, while a new breed of synthetics such as Avril rayon and Fortrel polyester found their way into menswear collections.

PART OF THE UNIFORM

At early skateboard contests in the early 1960s, competitors performed wearing jeans in combination with their team jerseys while either skating barefooted or in canvas deck shoes by companies such as Sperry or Vans. Magazine advertisements by brands including the Hobie Skateboards company featured group shots of riders proudly rocking their denim pants paired with Jentzen surf-stripe shirts as one of the earliest "skateboarder looks" in recorded history.

But on the retail side of things, skateboard-specific clothing choices were next to none. "When we first opened our store, clothing was 10% at the most as far as merchandising and allotment of floor space to the product went," said Mark Richards, owner of the world's first skate shop, Val Surf in North Hollywood, adding: "We didn't even hang the garments, they were folded in a display case."

The arrival of denim in skate fashion brought much-needed fresh impulses to the way skateboarders dressed. Even for riders on a low budget, jeans opened up a variety of customization options that added variety to skateboarders' wardrobes. Many riders cut their jeans into shorts in true D.I.Y.-fashion and let the leg openings frazzle out, foreshadowing what would later become a popular women's look in the 1980s heyday of bleached jeans.

And while jeans today reign supreme as the most popular style of pants worldwide – in 2016, U.S. jeans sales accounted for $15.3 billion in the $218.7 billion apparel market – the early 1960s marked a special moment in time when jeans weren't for everybody, and skateboarding and jeans rode together as one.

Photo: Ron Stoner

SURF STRIPES FOR SIDEWALK SURFERS

Widely regarded as the first major fashion craze to sweep the skateboard scene, white T-shirts with broad, horizontal stripes caused a big splash in the early 1960s. Like many trends at the time, the look first caught on among surfers before spilling out into the streets. "We first saw [professional surfer] Phil Edwards wearing a striped shirt in *Surfer* Magazine, and suddenly every surfer just HAD to have one. Plus, the striped tees just looked cool!" said Jim Phillips, long-time surf enthusiast and resident graphic artist at Santa Cruz Skateboards.

Phillips is referring to a photograph in *Surfer Magazine's* April/May 1963 issue: The inside cover fold-out advertisement for Hobie Surfboards featured Phil Edwards - known for endorsing the first pro model skateboard - wearing a black and white broad-striped T-shirt by Portland-based apparel company Jantzen. Also indicating the emerging trend, the issue's second full-page ad by Jacobs Surfboards showed Hap Jacobs, whom Phillips considered "the top surfboard shaper in the world" at the time, also wearing the hot striped shirt. "As young, impressionable surfers we were mightily swayed by such an endorsement, and got the shirts as soon as possible," said Jim Phillips.

D.I.Y. BEGINNINGS

Unable to find a store that sold the coveted shirts near his home town of Santa Cruz, Phillips resorted to D.I.Y. methods to rock the fashionable surf stripes. Using a plain white T-shirt in combination with newspaper and masking tape, Phillips spray-painted his own set of stripes. "It came out great! People asked me where I got the shirt, but I refused to tell them." Emulating the surf stripe pattern proved rather challenging: "The stripes had to have just the right width to get the pattern everyone wanted at the time."

Ultimately, Phillips and crew found a way to get their hands on some original striped shirts, manufactured by Portland, Oregon company Jantzen. "There was a small surf shop more than 300 miles away on Balboa Island near Newport Beach that sold them, so we made the trip and brought back dozens of Jantzen shirts in black-and-white, blue-and-white, and tan-and-white stripes for everyone. We were the only ones in town to have them and were recipients of much envy."

JANTZEN: THE ORIGINAL SURF SHIRT

Ironically, one of the biggest early purveyors of surf-striped shirts hailed not from sunny California, but from the misty coastline of Portland, Oregon. Founded in 1910 as the Portland Knitting company, Jantzen advanced to become America's most popular swimwear brand, known for its evocative logo: a young woman dressed in a bright-red bathing suit assuming a diving position. The company known for functional swimwear landed a smash hit with the "Big J" striped surf shirt during surfing's big wave of mainstream popularity in the early 1960s.

Cementing its status as a leading surf lifestyle brand, Jantzen ran regular advertisements in *Surfer magazine* from 1963 onwards, featuring some of the sport's hottest athletes, including big wave rider Pat Curren together with leading surf stars such as Ricky Grigg, Corky Carroll, and John Severson (later an editor at *the quarterly Skateboarder*). Skateboarders also craved the company's fashionable products, especially when Jantzen enlisted the entire Hobie Skateboards team for an advertisement introducing their "Big J" sweater, a skateboard-specific knit with the slogan: "Skateboarders, wheel into department stores and buy Big J sweaters and other Jantzen sportswear." During competitions, Hobie team riders also wore Jantzen's signature striped Big J surf shirts as part of their official uniform.

"That was pretty much the first BIG fashion trend in skateboarding," said 1960s Hobie team rider Cris Dawson. "It was the Jantzen stripes that were all about surfing, and since skateboarding is a derivative of surfing, Jantzen was the trendsetter for surfing and skateboarding."

NAUTICAL ROOTS

Historically, the connection between striped garments and nautical culture runs deep. Onboard 18th century merchant ships, solid-colored uniforms were the sole privilege of captains and high-ranking officers. Meanwhile, deckhands and common sailors received white sweatshirts with dark, horizontal stripes as their standard-issue garments. More than a matter of distinguishing rank, the contrasting pattern had life-saving properties: In the event of being thrown overboard, sailors floating in the water were much easier to spot bobbing amidst the waves - only a fraction of sailors were able to swim at the time - in their light-colored, striped garments.

Over the years, horizontal stripes remained a standard feature of nautical uniforms. In 1858, "Breton"-style stripes, named after the Brittany region on the coast of France, became the official uniform of French sailors. Originally, the blue-and-white shirts featured the exact number of 21 stripes, each denoting one of emperor Napoleon's victories. In 1917, the "French sailor" shirt outgrew its military roots when it was introduced into the world of fashion by designer Coco Chanel as timeless, leisurely attire.

EVOLVING THE LOOK

Throughout the 1960s, surf companies evolved the striped look, adding more splashes of color and increasingly complex patterns. In the bigger picture, "stripes functioned as a conduit for the introduction of Hawaiian floral prints, and eventually opened a broad spectrum of designs to what was initially a very limited, or it should be said, nonexistent surf fashion market," said Jim Phillips.

In 1965, the Lunada Bay company advertised wetsuits with "competition stripes," while Jantzen introduced stripes in various widths and densities. Another brand, the Laguna Look company, offered striped ensembles of matching tops and shorts famously worn by surfboard company owner Dewey Weber. At Waimea Bay, Hawaii, surfer Greg Noll turned heads by surfing 30-foot waves in his trademark black-and-white striped trunks.

The rest is history: "Hollywood surf movies spread the fad, and the stripes went beyond surfing and became as much of an everyday middle class icon as the stripes on the American flag," said Jim Phillips.

WINDBREAKERS: ENDURING THE ELEMENTS

When the California sun goes down and the soft sea breeze turns into gusty winds, surfers fresh out of water need protection from the elements. In the early days of surf culture, lightweight and water-proof jackets known as "windbreakers" - featuring a soft outer shell constructed from rayon or nylon with a comfortable cotton inside lining - emerged as popular options.

As the perfect choice for budget-conscious skateboarders, generic windbreakers without visible branding were not only widely available at sports retailers and army surplus shops, but notoriously inexpensive. "Windbreakers have always been cheap because they are made from the cheapest materials. Those things are just made out of plastic! Anyone can make that," said skateboard icon Tony Alva from Santa Monica.

At the height of the 1960s skateboard boom, leading skateboard companies including Makaha, Jack's, and Vita-Pakt Hobie Skateboards began offering branded windbreakers. The Makaha Exhibition Team rolled up to competitions and appeared in skateboard films in their signature bright-yellow team windbreakers in a "pop-over" design - the front zipper reaching only slightly below the collar opening - which became coveted items and status symbols equated with company sponsorship.

GENERIC BEGINNINGS

Here's a little known fact: The term "windbreaker" actually started as a trademark, registered by Chicago-based menswear company John Rissman & Son in 1941. The patent-protected design for the boy's and men's jackets featured a zippered front and elastic waistbands, setting the blueprint for what would become a menswear classic. Although John Rissman & Son frequently took legal action against competitors selling jackets under the "windbreaker" name, the term became a genericized tradmark - similar to "Band Aid" or "Kleenex" - associated with this particular style of jacket after the company went out of business in the late 1940s.

The lapse in trademark protection opened the floodgates to a wave of imitators while Nylon, a synthetic premiered at the 1939 Chicago World Fair by chemicals company Dupont, became the material of choice for rain-proof outer shells. Windbreaker sales spiked after Hollywood icon James Dean appeared wearing a bright-red McGregor Anti-freeze style jacket in 1955's *Rebel Without a Cause*, cementing the jacket as a staple in popular culture.

DIRECT SURF INFLUENCE

Before skateboard manufacturers added branded windbreakers to their product line-ups, surf companies had already been putting their own twist on the functional jackets. "The surfing thing always had a lot of influence on the functional side of skateboarding gear. Especially T-shirts and windbreaker jackets or competition jackets with team logos on them," said Tony Alva.

In the early 1950s, California surf trunk company Katin added light-weight jackets such as the Black Diamond windbreaker to their beach wear collection. In 1959, specialized surf tailor M.Nii in Makaha, Hawaii, introduced the light-weight "Surf Club" jacket available in khaki and indigo colorways with contrasting dual-color piping on the front, while surf apparel pioneers Hang Ten began offering windbreakers adorned with their "Ten Toes" logo in 1961. Windbreakers took the industry by storm, and almost every single surf and skateboard company added the lightweight jackets to their line-up.

GENTLEMEN ON SKATEBOARDS

Ignition! Skateboarding's popularity skyrocketed in the early 1960s, as new practitioners hopped onboard by the millions. At the end of 1963, Makaha Skateboards - the company founded by skateboard pioneer Larry Stevenson - was selling 10,000 skateboards per day. And that was just the beginning. Meanwhile, one question kept looming amidst this new-found success: Was skateboarding a "real" sport?

Organized competitions, starting with the first-ever skateboard contest held in Hermosa Beach, California, in 1963 provided an official format for athlete rankings. In a 1965 editorial in Stevenson's new magazine, *the Quarterly Skateboarder*, editor John Severson wrote: "We predict a real future for the sport - a future that could go as far as the Olympics. It's a much more 'measurable' sport than surfing and therefore lends itself more to competition."

But in order to gain wide-spread acceptance as a real sport, the editorial concluded, skateboarders needed act like athletes, not renegades: "It's up to you to see that skateboarding does not become a sport of rebels and radicals. It's a sport for young sportsmen. We look forward to a great future in skateboarding and we ask you, the pioneers, to make it great."

SUIT AND TIE

Dressing the part of the respectable athlete, members of the Makaha Skateboards Exhibition Team such as Danny Bearer, Brad "Squeak" Blank and Woody Woodward rolled up to the airport in dapper business suits when they travelled state-to-state representing the sport. Airplane travel had become increasingly affordable to a growing number of Americans throughout the 1960s, but then again - this wasn't the Big Blue Bus to Venice. Instead of boarding planes wearing scruffy jeans and disheveled surfer hair, professional surfers and skateboarders donned slacks, blazers, and matching ties to emulate Olympic athletes in travel mode.

While skateboard sales reached 50 million units between 1963 and 1965, further cementing skateboarding's "official" status, the skateboard media also proliferated the "gentleman" image: In a Quarterly Skateboarder instructional segment explaining the "kick turn" maneuver, seasoned skateboarder Dave Rochlen wore khakis and the official team blazer for the star-studded Hobie Vita-Pakt Super Surfer Team, for which Rochlen acted as official coach.

HOBIE AND VITA-PAKT: NEW JUICE FOR SKATEBOARDING

Based in Covina, California, the Vita-Pakt Juice Company was owned by entrepreneur Barron Hilton, a member of the Hilton Hotels dynasty. When Barron Hilton began exploring new avenues for promoting his fresh, "Not From Concentrate," orange juice packets to young audiences, he listened to his sons, avid surfers and skateboarders Steve and Dave Hilton, who suggested skateboarding as a vital growth market.

The savvy entrepreneur drove a deep-pocketed, multi-pronged strategy to position Vita-Pakt orange juice as the number one drink for the board sports crowd: Next to running skateboard-specific advertising for juice products, Hilton went the extra mile by barging onto the skateboard hardware market with a substantial investment.

In 1964, Barron Hilton entered into a marketing and manufacturing partnership with skateboard hardware pioneer Hobie Alter – one of the trailblazers of modern skateboard design – to form the Hobie-Vita-Pakt Skateboards company. Their first skateboard, the Super Surfer model, became an instant hit. By the year 1965, Hobie-Vita-Pakt received 20,000 skateboard orders per day and ramped up production to quench the thirst.

"Hobie [Alter] was an amazing promoter and once he decided that skateboarding was cool, he ran with it," said Mark Richards, owner of Val Surf, known as the world's first skateboard shop. But initially, Hobie Alter had some reservations against "sidewalk surfing," Richards said: "We really wanted Hobie surfboards in the shop, we needed a big brand to give us extra credibility. Hobie was only selling his boards in Dana Point, but with the help of John Severson from *Surfer Magazine*, we finally got Hobie to come up here and give us a chance."

But when Hobie Alter made the first surfboard delivery at Val Surf's North Hollywood location in 1963, he was in for a surprise: "We were already selling these hand-made skateboard, rectangular boards with wood screws and Chicago skates on the bottom. When Hobie saw those in our store, he almost didn't want to unload the truck! He basically thought he had opened the door to a toy store," said Mark Richards. As skateboarding caught on in popularity, Hobie Alter soon changed his mind. He returned to form an official business relationship with Val Surf, who helped design Hobie's first skateboard. "We got Hobie involved in skateboarding," said Richards, "and he ended up selling 100% of his rights to Vita-Pakt. They still used his name and called it the 'Hobie Super Surfer'."

SKATEBOARDING'S FIRST SUPER TEAM

The performance-oriented Super Surfer board was endorsed by a heavy-hitting pro team – with big-name riders poached from the Makaha team – including Torger Johnson, Danny Bearer, Danny Schaefer, Ray Flores, Sue Rowland, Cris Dawson, Skeeter Bebe, Colleen Boyd, Tom Waller and Barron's sons Steve and Dave Hilton, who had appeared on the cover of *the Quarterly Skateboarder*'s first issue performing a high jump maneuver. The team also featured two female riders, Wendy (Bearer) Bull – Danny's sister – and Patti McGee, featured on the cover of a 1965 issue of *LIFE* Magazine doing a handstand on a skateboard representing the sport's first "super team."

"With their level of money and promotion, it was very difficult to compete with those guys," said original Hobie team rider Cris Dawson, who held the World Record for spinning 360s on a skateboard. "Compared to Hobie, all the other brands like Banzai, Jack's, and Makaha were just small little fledging companies. Hobie had Vita-Pakt as their sponsor with the Hilton family attached to that, so they were able to promote themselves into fame. And that's how fame happens."

At this point, the dollar amounts Hobie-Vita-Pakt Skateboards pumped into marketing and pro salaries were unheard of in the young sport of skateboarding. As ambassadors of skateboarding culture, Hobie team members appeared on national television, always making sure to cultivate their "gentlemen on skateboards" look with the official Vita-Pakt team blazer, featuring the brand insignia in an embroidered Ivy League-style patch over the chest pocket.

Hobie
SKATEBOARDS
DANA POINT, CALIF.

BIG MONEY, UPSCALE STYLE

Hobie team riders were also known for their elaborate athletic team uniforms worn in competitions. "All of the teams at the time were put together in uniforms, based on the unifying idea that we had to all look alike because we were a team. And it's hard to say who had the most fashionable team in early skateboarding, but the one that got the most promotion was definitely Hobie," said Cris Dawson. On and off their skateboards, members of the new elite team also cultivated a clean, upscale apparel style. "The guys from the North side of town, like Torger Johnson from Pacific Palisades or the Hilton brothers always wore really nice stuff. Nice sporty tennis gear, shorts and jackets with a skateboard company logo on it. That kind of gear was associated with sporting lifestyle and the Hobie team," said professional skateboarder Tony Alva, who cut his teeth skateboarding in the less-affluent Dogtown neighborhood of Santa Monica. "Those guys had a lot of money, so instead of wearing some slummy-scummy stuff given to them for free, they would spend $100 on a sweat suit, which was a lot of money at the time, like the hip-hop kids do nowadays," said Tony Alva, adding: "As kids from the South Side, we just took whatever we could get for free, or in the punk rock heyday, we would go to thrift stores and buy some comfortable but funky second-hand stuff."

THE SHAPE OF THINGS TO COME

For the Hobie Super Surfer team's first national tour, Barron Hilton teamed up with documentary film maker Bruce Brown, who screened his surf film *Endless Summer* at tour stops from California all the way to New York City. Travelling state-to-state in a Winnebago bus branded with the Hobie-Vita-Pakt logo, the team drew crowds up to 10,000 spectators to skateboard demos in parking lots all over the country. Ending the tour with a bang, Hilton arranged a pro skateboard demo during the Thanksgiving game of the San Diego Chargers football team, which he also owned.

When skateboarding's greatest winning streak suddenly ended in late 1965 amidst legal crackdowns and safety concerns, the Hobie Vita-Pakt company was first in line to feel the burn. Thousands of unsold skateboards piled up in warehouses, as pro shops across the country cancelled their orders. Vita Pakt and Hobie continued their marketing all through 1966 as an effort to bring back sales in skateboarding. In 1966 Hobie sponsored a series of contests throughout the southwest, with a final contest culmiminating at the end of the summer of 1966. This final contest was held at one of the first skateparks to open in the world. The park was called SURFERS WORLD located in Santa Ana California. Unfortunately this marked the end of Vita-Pakt's involvement. Skateboarding had officially run out of juice. Nevertheless, Vita-Pakt foreshadowed a legacy of sponsorship by soft drink companies, eager to throw money at athletes and event series during skateboarding's peak times of mainstream fame.

The ultimate goal for mainstream sponsors with deep pockets - then and now - remains the same: getting skateboarding accepted as an Olympics event. More than 50 years after *the Quarterly Skateboarder* editorial predicted a "great future for the sport," the skateboarding is now cleared to make its official debut at the 2020 Olympic Games in Tokyo. Better get ready to bring back those gentlemanly pro skateboard team blazers...

SURFER

obie

RD TEAM

Looking back today, the 1960s may seem like a not very colorful era because many pictures are black and white. This includes the photo on page 50-51 of the Hobie National Skateboards Team at the Santa Monica Civic Auditorium taken in May 1966. Left to right, we see Ray Flores, Sue Rowland, Cris Dawson, Skeeter Bebe, Colleen Boyd, Tom Waller and Wendy (Bearer) Bull. The colorful paisley surf trunks displayed on this page are worn by Ray Flores as well as all his male team members in the picture. Now, despite the black and white, imagine how much color and skateboard action there were on stage!

Hobie
NATIONAL
SKATEBOARD
TEAM

TEAM UNIFORMS FOR "REAL" ATHLETES

Whereas skateboarding today is widely considered the domain of artists, punks, outsiders, and other beautiful losers, the early 1960s presented a different picture. Stepping out of the shadow of surf culture, skateboarding for a brief period toyed with the concept of becoming a team sport, geared around competitive disciplines such as slalom, high jump, and freestyle. "The whole team thing was a period of soul-searching. Other sports were doing it the same way, so skateboarders thought they had to present themselves as a team unit," says professional skateboarder and musician Claus Grabke.

The *Quarterly Skateboarder* magazine, brainchild of surf pioneer Larry Stevenson of Makaha fame, set out to promote skateboarding as a real sport with a bright future. "It's a much more measurable sport than surfing and therefore lends itself more to competition. In the slalom there's no question about who the winner is - the fastest time through the gates," stated an editorial feature, concluding: "Competition should be big in skateboarding, but it's going to take organization and support from the participants."

Professional riders served as important role models in drumming up support for this new, competitive face of skateboarding. Advertisements and editorial photo shoots depicted skateboard company teams dressed in matching team jerseys, significantly shifting the paradigm of skateboard fashion away from its surf-related origins. "Before skateboard teams, we were kind-of grubby, meaning dirty feet and sandy mostly for me. Fashion wasn't an issue," said the world's first professional female skateboarder, Patti McGee, adding: "Before that, I just wore surf shorts and surf club T-shirts, but the teams all wore matching outfits."

SMELLS LIKE TEAM SPIRIT

"Every team had its own unique uniform and a specific colorway," said Michael Chantry, skate photographer, adding: "Everyone on the Hobie team was wearing maroon shoes, mostly Vans, combined with matching striped shirts and maroon shorts. Next thing you knew, everyone in school was wearing striped shirts and plain shorts!" Manufactured by Portland-based outfitters Jantzen, the Hobie team's signature striped shirts soon became bestsellers and emblems of skateboard fashion.

Speaking of "bestsellers" - not all parts of the professional riders' wardrobe were available for sale to the public. Team jackets, mostly windbreakers crafted from lightweight materials such as nylon, could only be earned, not purchased. "Your team jacket was the thing to wear if you were sponsored," said Patti McGee, who made history as the first Women's National Skateboard Champion in 1965 and became a public face of the new sport with appearances in commercials and television shows.

As ambassadors of skateboarding culture, the Makaha Exhibition Team and Hobie Vita-Pakt Super Surfer Team toured the entire United States, staging skateboard demonstrations in mall parking lots in front of thousands of people. Most spectators had never witnessed skateboarding before in their life. Accordingly, skateboard companies took great care in presenting the sport in a favorable light. "It was lots of work!" said Patti McGee. "I traveled as the 'Hobie Skate Demo Girl' from coast to coast and had to practice my signature handstand all the time. I also had to be polite and well-groomed."

The team uniform phenomenon peaked at the first National Skateboard Championships in 1965, broadcast on ABC television's Wide World of Sports program. Leading skateboard companies went the extra mile by commissioning special team uniforms for the contest. The Hobie Super Surfer Team competed in blue-and-yellow shorts and jackets custom-made by surf and swimwear shop Ray's Cabana in the Santa Monica canyon. Meanwhile, the Jack's Banzai Exhibition Team hit the deck in bright yellow, martial arts-style suits - supposedly designed with high jump in mind - while the Tuk 'n' Roller Competition Team appeared in signature red windbreakers featuring a giant embroidered back logo.

CHEESY ATHLETIC UNIFORMS

For better of worse, synthetic materials such as nylon, polyester, and rayon -aided by 1959's introduction of plastic ink for printing company logos onto fabric - became popular choices for team uniforms. However, not every pro rider was in favor of the "sporty" look. "The 1960s style, surf-influenced skateboarding teams would wear the kind of cheesy athletic uniforms made out of really awful materials like polyester. You know, the breathable, plasticky kind of stuff... which I was never into very much myself," remembers skateboard icon Tony Alva.

The heyday of competition-style skateboard apparel ended rapidly when skateboarding's first big wave of popularity crashed in late 1965. As ambitions of becoming a "real" sport washed away, skateboard fashion made way to more free-spirited, individualized styles. "In hindsight, presenting skateboarders as team players was one of the major mistakes of the early years, also from a fashion standpoint," said Claus Grabke.

TUK 'N' ROLLER COMPETITION TEAM TRAINING IN LAGUNA BEACH

Splash! Surfing and "beach culture" reached a new high-water mark of mainstream popularity in the early 1960s. Surfing was everywhere; in commercials, TV series, movies, and department store clothing lines. California surf crooners The Beach Boys barged into #2 on the Billboard charts with their sophomore album. The title song *"Surfin' U.S.A."* called out the fashion elements of quintessential "surfer" style: "Huarachi sandals," a "bushy bushy blonde hair do," and "baggies," meaning baggy shorts.

The hottest innovation in baggies appeared on the beaches of Hawaii in the summer of 1964: Jams World, the company started by surf pioneer Dave Rochlan out of his Honolulu surfboard shop, Surf Line Hawaii, introduced loose-fitting shorts with bright, Pacific Island-style floral patterns. Modeled on cut-down pajama pants - "Jams" is an abbreviation for pajamas - and colored in potpourris of yellows, reds, greens, and magentas, the comfortable shorts became an instant hit on the Hawaiian islands, and soon on the mainland.

Within less than a year, Jams World caught major media exposure by ways of a fashion feature in the June 25, 1965 issue of *LIFE* Magazine. The article's full-page opening photograph depicted young sunbathers, including surfing champion Mike Doyle, frolicking on a lava cliff near Koko Head, Hawaii, decked out in Jams. Another image shows big wave surfing pioneer Butch Van Artsdalen wearing the garish drawstring shorts, holding a skateboard. Caption: "Butch wears his Jams both for surfing and skateboarding."

As it turns out, Jams World had deep hooks into skateboarding from day one, says artist and skateboard visionary Craig R. Stecyk III: "Dave Rochlen's nephew was the manager of the Makaha skateboard team, and later team captain of the Hobie Super Surfer team." Nicknamed "Baby Dave" Rochlen, the award-winning surfer and skateboard coach played a major role in establishing Jams apparel within the skateboard world. "Rochlen gave his clothes to the skaters right away," said Stecyk. "The original Hobie team from the 1960s wore Jams as their team attire. Rochlen was very close to [Hobie's later owner, hotel magnate] Conrad Hilton and the family."

A COLORFUL HISTORY

Upon closer inspection, the history of the man behind Jams World is no less colorful than his garments. Raised on the beaches of Santa Monica, California, Dave Rochlen was a surfer, lifeguard, and dirt bike racer who appeared shirtless on the cover of *LIFE* Magazine in 1949 as an emblem of the California beach lifestyle. "He was a famous surfer and the first to use color in surfboard design in a modern manner. Rochlen worked closely with Bob Simmons, who was the pioneering spirit of surf board design from WWII onwards, and Dave Sweet, who first introduced polyurethane foams," said Craig Stecyk.

In 1954, Rochlen again appeared on the cover of *LIFE* magazine, this time in deep ocean diving gear as the stuntman for Disney's *20,000 Leagues Under the Sea movie.* After a stint as a systems analyst at the military-funded Rand Corporation, the surfing pioneer relocated to Hawaii in 1962 and opened his own surf shop that would serve as the platform for launching the Jams World brand. And what started with a prototype pair of floral-patterned shorts sewn at the kitchen table by Rochlen's wife Keanuenue soon turned into a flourishing business.

Initially sold for $7 to $14 per pair out of the back of Rochlen's car at Makaha Beach, the board shorts crafted from quick-drying cotton with a drawstring enclosure around the waist caught on among local surfers in a big way. The 1965 *LIFE* Magazine story blew Jams World into the stratosphere, propelling Rochlen's start-up from island phenomenon to marquee department store brand available nation-wide at Bloomingdales, Macys and Lord & Taylor as icons of active beach living. "His Jams were originally made for men; girls' were added by demand. Now they are worn day and night for everything but sleeping," the *LIFE* story concluded.

FROM MALIBU TO CAMELOT

Craig Stecyk shares an untold piece of history connecting Jams World all the way to the highest echelons of the American power structure – the Kennedy-era White House. "The connection to the Kennedys was Peter Lawford, an American actor who hung out in Malibu at the beach and was good friends with Rochlen," said Stecyk, adding: "Lawford married Pat Kennedy, the sister of John F Kennedy, the President of the United States."

In the late 1950s when board shorts were only available at select tailors, Rochlen was the inside man whenever JFK and other VIPs wanted to get their hands on authentic surf attire. Says Craig Stecyk: "I have receipts from Hawaiian tailor M.Nii, where Rochlen bought surf shorts for Frank Sinatra and John F. Kennedy, with the items matching the President's size." And when Rochlen started Jams in 1964, he sent clothes to the Kennedy family's Massachusetts beach compound. "So the Kennedys at Hyannis Port were wearing the same clothing that skateboarders like the Hobie team and the Hilton brothers were wearing in California," said Craig Stecyk.

And there's more: From 1947 onwards, Dave Rochlen had also befriended a California beach beauty by the name of Norma Jean Baker, later known as Marilyn Monroe. "When the Kennedys stayed on the beach, [surf photographer] Don James was their next-door neighbor, and he left me a photograph of the Kennedys, with Dave Rochlen in the pool behind them. Some people might think that's how the Kennedys ended up knowing Marilyn Monroe, and they knew Marilyn forever," said Craig Stecyk.

So there you have it, a major chapter of Camelot lore had its start on the beaches of Malibu. In 1969, Dave Rochlen sold Surf Line Hawaii in order to fully focus on building Jams into a global brand. Eventually, the company counted more than 100 employees, selling bright beach wear around the world under various slogans, including "Put some color in your life." Still a family business, Jams World continues its colorful history today under the leadership of Rochlen's youngest son, Pua Rochlen, and the motto "Great Clothes for Real People."

Surf Line HAWAII
ORIGINAL
Jams®

TOP STYLIST: PHIL EDWARDS

Here's a little known fact: The first pro model skateboard ever manufactured carried the name of a professional surfer, not a professional skateboarder. In 1963, Larry Stevenson's surf company Makaha released the first signature skateboard for world famous surf icon Phil Edwards from Oceanside, California. A true cross-over pioneer, Edwards is also credited with shaping and endorsing the first pro model surfboards under the Hobie Surfboards label. And guess who made history as the first board sports athlete with his own signature clothing line? Again, no other than style icon and big wave pioneer Phil Edwards, perhaps single-handedly the most famous surfer of his era. "Phil Edwards was the Kelly Slater of those days. Everyone knew who Edwards was. He was the man!" said Mark Richards, owner of legendary Val Surf skate and surf shop in North Hollywood.

Phil Edwards started surfing in 1946 after moving from Long Beach to Oceanside. Known for his smooth style and progressive riding technique - both in and out of the water - he set the course for a new generation of big wave surfing. In 1951, at the tender age of 13, Edwards began shaping his own boards. While still a teenager, he had already made a name for himself by taking on burly waves otherwise reserved for seasoned riders, including the "Killer Dana" at Salt Creek, California. In December 1961, Edwards made history as the first surfer to ride the dreaded Banzai Pipeline on the North Shore of Oahu, Hawaii, in a session captured by surf movie producer Bruce Brown in the film *Surfing Hollow Days*.

TRENDSETTER AND STYLE ICON

The surf and skateboard icon was also revered as a trendsetter for his clothing style. Anywhere Phil Edwards traveled to attend surf competitions or photo shoots - he even went out of his way to open up new spots on the East Coast, including Virginia Beach - fans recognized Edwards by his signature cotton pants and Hawaiian shirts. In 1963, Edwards made history as the first rider named the "Best Surfer in the World" by *Surfer* magazine's Readers' Poll. Ever the trendsetter, Edwards pioneered a new direction in board sports clothing: In 1964, traditional Hawaiian resort wear company Reyn Spooner started manufacturing a signature Phil Edwards button-front Aloha shirt. The famous surfer thereby became the first action sports athlete with his own signature clothing line; a trend that would only gain serious traction in the board sports industry in the late 1990s, when pro-endorsed clothing lines became a "new" trend.

Tailored in Hawaii from 100% soft cotton, the signature shirt featured a traditional Island Flower Pareu pattern chosen by Phil Edwards from a selection of different patterns presented to him by company founder Reyn McCullough, who started the clothing company in 1949 on Catalina Island, California. Reyn Spooner rose to fame after pioneering "reverse print" Hawaiian pattern shirts, popular for their sun-faded look achieved by applying the print on the shirt insides.

Official recognition for surfing's most dapper pro rider came in 1966, when a cover story in *Sports Illustrated* magazine honored Phil Edwards with the title "Top Stylist." He was inducted into the International Surfing Hall of Fame that same year. After a successful career as an influential board shaper and professional rider for Hobie Surfboards, Phil Edwards retired from the media spotlight and enjoys a reclusive beach lifestyle while remaining an active surfer. And what about the company that started the signature clothing trend in board sports? Under new leadership since 2012, the Reyn Spooner legacy continues today as the "Brooks Brothers of the Islands" sets its sights on building a global brand presence.

HANG TEN: BIRTH OF AN INDUSTRY

Throughout the 1950s, the production of surf-specific trunks was still a cottage industry dominated by a handful of specialized tailors including legendary Hawaiian surf shorts pioneer M. Nii. But that changed forever, thanks to surf enthusiast Duke Boyd, who had picked up the sport in 1957: When the Kansas City native observed fellow surfers on the beaches of Waikiki, Hawaii, hitting the waves in custom-made board shorts, he was staring down a wide open road into a bright commercial future.

Back on the mainland, Boyd approached seamstress Doris Boeck in San Diego to sew a pair of nylon shorts from designs he had sketched out on paper. Rugged enough to withstand the wear and tear associated with surfing, Boyd's shorts offered performance features such as double-stitched seams, heavy woven tie string enclosures, wide leg openings and a reinforced crotch. In search of a brand name, Boyd chose one of the most difficult freestyle surfing maneuvers: The 'Hang Ten' is surf slang for riding mid-wave with both feet parallel on the front end of the surfboard, letting all ten toes "hang" over the edge.

When the first pairs of shorts with the signature "Ten Toe" logo - depicting a pair of stylized bare feet on a yellow background - arrived at surf shops in 1960, they became an instant hot seller among surf practitioners. Struggling to keep up with demand, Boyd and Hang Ten co-founder Doris Moore, an apparel retail expert from New York City, ramped up production. It was a blue sky moment in what would soon become a full-fledged industry, today known as the $19.6 billion per year boardsports lifestyle and apparel market.

MARKETING THE LIFESTYLE

The launch of Hang Ten coincided with a massive surge in surfing's popularity. In the early 1960s, the number of active surfers skyrocketed into the millions while feature films such as the Gidget series proliferated the "beach party" lifestyle. Catering to both types of consumers - the "core" practitioners as well as the interested fans of surf culture - Hang Ten became the original surf and California lifestyle brand.

As the first company to actively market the surfing lifestyle in the media, including full-page advertisements in Larry Stevenson's *Surfguide* magazine, Hang Ten created the blueprint for follow-up surf brands like Ocean Pacific, Quiksilver, and O'Neill. And at a time when surfing and skateboarding were still practically inseparable pastimes, Hang Ten's functional shorts became a favorite among early skateboarders.

Skateboard pioneer Tony Alva said: "My favorite thing to wear in the Seventies were all the different styles of surf-oriented board shorts out there. Hang Ten made some really cool shorts and we all wore them a lot to go skateboarding." Putting the board shorts trend in perspective, Alva said: "Nowadays skateboarding is more technical and people ride a lot more concrete, so you also need more protection. This is why people don't wear shorts as much as we used to back then."

Within a matter of months, Hang Ten's product offering expanded beyond board shorts into T-shirts, sweatshirts and tube socks. Among early skateboarders, the company's trademark horizontal "surf" stripes T-shirts became highly coveted items. "Hang Ten was the shirt to get back then, around 1967 and '68. If you could get your hands on Hang Ten, you were stoked!" said seasoned skateboard photographer J. Grant Brittain. "They were THE hot California thing. Probably one of the first shirts I ever really wanted was Hang Ten. You had to have the little feet!" said skateboard photographer Dave Swift.

THE FULL PACKAGE

Hang Ten not only broke new ground by becoming the first brand to actively sponsor surf events, but the brand also embraced surfing's rapidly progressing offshoot, skateboarding, as a full-fledged sport. In the late 1960s, Hang Ten also began selling complete skateboards, including the 450 SL Wild Wide Ride model, featuring Big Dog wheels. Hang Ten soon introduced its own line of footwear, advertised as "the first shoe designed exclusively for the sport" (although several years earlier the Randolph Rubber Company had already made the first skateboard-specific shoe, the 720 model released in 1965).

Marketed in full-page advertisements as "A California Classic", Hang Ten became deeply engrained into early board sports fashion. "Back then, you had to have the corduroy pants, and you had to have your striped Hang Ten or OP shirt. You also had to have a comb in your back pocket, or a brush. And Puka shells, the little sea shells that all the surfers wore as a necklace. That was kind of the early surfer-slash-skateboarder outfit," said skateboard icon Lance Mountain.

In 1970, the year when retail sales of surf products topped $200 million in the U.S., Duke Boyd sold the Hang Ten brand and started another successful surf apparel company, Lightning Bolt. Over the following decades, Hang Ten rode all the highs and lows of surfing's popularity, always hanging on under changing ownership, while other brands wiped out completely.

Today, the Ten Toes are still kicking, available as a classic brand with an upscale collection, Hang Ten Gold, sold at Bloomingdales, Nordstrom, and specialty boutiques across the world. At the age of 80 years, company founder Duke Boyd resides in Makaha, Hawaii, where he operates his recently launched surf apparel brand, South Shore Traders.

Culottes: Salvador Morrel

A woman's place is in the home

Hosiery: Berkshire

...or somewhere.

THE FIRST COVER GIRL: PAT McGEE!

When skateboarding became the center of national attention as the cover story of *LIFE* magazine's May 1965 edition, the rider depicted on the title page was not one of skateboarding's leading men. Not a top competitor the likes of Danny Bearer or a groundbreaking innovator such as Torger Johnson - but a woman. Performing a rolling handstand on her skateboard, 19-year-old Patti McGee from San Diego, California, represented skateboarding in front of an audience of millions of readers.

In many ways, the iconic photo of the blonde California girl striking a gymnast's pose on a four-wheeled plank of wood foreshadowed the future. At a time when the jury was still out on whether it was appropriate for women to wear pants instead of dresses in many parts of the United States, Patti McGee turned convention on its head dressed in white Capri pants and a bright-orange sweater. Even from a skateboarding perspective, her fashion sense marked a break from the norm.

"This image is really different from others at the time, since there's no competition or skateboard jerseys or team uniform involved. She's not specifically dressed for skateboarding. It's really free-spirited. A woman doing a handstand on a skateboard, boom!" said professional skateboarder Claus Grabke.

And while the debate on whether or not skateboarding was a "real" sport - let alone a women's sport - still raged on at the time, the 1965 Women's Skateboarding Champion paved the way for future generations of female skateboarders. "Some people say girl skateboarders are just a novelty. I myself think that skateboarding is 100 percent just as much for girls as it is for boys," Patti McGee told *Skateboarder Magazine* in October '65.

SKATEBOARDING'S FIRST FEMALE PRO

Having grown up on the beaches around San Diego, Patti McGee started surfing in 1958 and picked up her first skateboard at the Hollywood Teen Fair in 1963. Riding on concrete came easy to her, and by 1964 the teenager already hosted regular skateboard demonstrations at a San Diego store, which led to a spot on the prestigious Hobie-Vita-Pakt Skateboards company team.

That year, she fearlessly set the record for the fastest girl on a skateboard at 47mph, towed behind a motorcycle on clay wheels. In 1965, McGee made history by becoming the first female professional skateboarder and won the women's title at the National Skateboarding Championships in Anaheim, California.

The iconic *LIFE* magazine cover - forever branded into skateboarding's collective subconscious - was shot by staff photographer Bill Eppridge during a promotional outing for Hobie Skateboards in Montgomery Ward, Pennsylvania. Asked about her timeless, feminine outfit, Patti McGee allowed: "I was from Ocean Beach, San Diego and had no idea what other girls were wearing. But I was a surfer first, so that influenced any style I projected. The three-quarter white pants were stretchy Capris and the Orange velour top was the color of the Vita-Pakt company, the distributor for Hobie so to speak, with a large Hobies 'Super Surfer' patch on the back. The pants were my own preference." As an ambassador for the young sport, McGee toured the U.S. to demonstrate skateboarding and, concerns about injuries pervading, appropriate safety practices. Hitting the road also meant looking the part of the professional athlete.

While her male counterparts donned sports coats and ties on outings, McGee went a more feminine route. "For travel purposes I had to wear nice shoes and one time wore lady's golf shorts by Arnold Palmer. Wherever I was on tour, I was always a California girl and as far as my skateboard skills went, most folks had nothing to compare me to."

While in New York City to promote skateboarding at Macy's department store, Patti McGee also donned an evening gown to appear on national television. In the popular CBS Television Network game show What's My Line?, participants had to guess her occupation ("demonstrates skateboards") by posing yes-or-no questions. "Is it this new board... this skating-board that you fly around on?!" the winner beamed, to which a patiently smiling McGee responded, "Yes." The trailblazing female professional also spread the love of skateboarding on the Johnny Carson and Mike Douglas television shows and in commercial work for the New England Bell Telephone company.

In October 1965, Patti McGee graced the cover of *SKATEBOARDER MAGAZINE* skateboarding in front of a swimming pool - another glimpse into the future. "That wasn't just the first time a girl appeared on the cover of a skateboard magazine, it was also the first pool on a cover - water or no water!" In another historic first, Patti McGee became the first female inductee into the International Association of Skateboard Companies (IASC) Skateboard Hall of Fame in 2010. She lives in Glendale, Arizona, helping her daughter Hailey continue the family's skateboarding legacy with the Original Betty skateboard and apparel company.

23" or 24½" board — $8.95 ea.
(check size of board wanted)

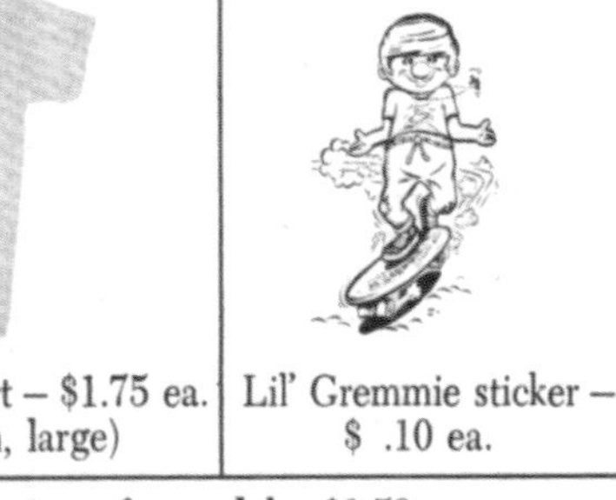

Lil' Gremmie T Shirt – $1.75 ea.
(small, medium, large)

Lil' Gremmie sticker – $ .10 ea.

Lil' Gremmie surfer medal – $1.50 ea.
(wear around neck or on key chain)

Package deal: board, T shirt, medal & decal all for $11.50

Send check or money order.
Dealer & jobber inquiries invited.
Add $1.00 for postage.

Calif. residents please add 4% sales tax.

Products

145 W. 154th Street
Gardena, Calif. 90247
Phone 321-1446 — Area Code 213
a division of Record Pressing Inc.

SKATEBOARDING GRAPHIC T-SHIRTS

Over the years, the graphic T-shirt has evolved into the cornerstone of skateboard apparel. Riders live and breathe skateboarding in their graphic tees. They bust tricks, fail and succeed in their graphic tees; triumph and bleed in their graphic tees. And let the world know they came to SKATE AND DESTROY and RIDE THE FIRE with some DIRTY GHETTO KIDS in a SUPREME manner because SKATEBOARDING IS NOT A CRIME – all through the messages on their graphic tees. But in the early days of skateboard culture, T-shirts commanded no such voice. At the dawn of the 1960s, the former undershirts popularized as menswear by soldiers returning from World War II remained blank canvases. "White T-shirts were all we had back then. It wasn't until J. C. Penney began offering shirts in four different colors that colored T-shirts even became an option," said skateboard graphic artist Jim Phillips, who as a youth would stencil his own "surf stripe" patterns onto blank T-shirts. While companies in other industries already used printed T-shirts as successful marketing tools – including Coca-Cola, Harley Davidson Motorcycles and Walt Disney's Mickey Mouse franchise – the first board sports-themed graphic T-shirts originated in surf culture. In 1961, legendary surfboard maker Floyd Smith, co-founder of Gordon and Smith Surfboards, screen-printed his company logo on blank T-shirts brought in by customers. Soon enough, other surfing brands and competition series emblazoned T-shirts with surf-style graphics, powered by the invention of Plastisol ink in 1959 and mainstream availability of screen printing.

REPRESENTING SKATEBOARDING

Before T-shirts could become walking billboards for skateboard companies, the young sport had yet to cultivate its own distinct graphical style. Some of the earliest artistic renditions of skateboarding included the comic book-style character Murphy, created by influential surf and counter-culture artist Rick Griffin, who during his high school years would pen surf graphics on his friends' T-shirts for 50¢ a piece. As the staff artist of *Surfer* Magazine, Griffin established a zany, skate doodle style inspired by *Mad* Magazine comics, setting the tone for a whole generation of cartoonish art appearing on skateboard decks as well as T-shirts.

Popular graphic themes included cartoon characters "wiping out" on the skateboard, which had become labelled as the "bun buster" in youth culture. "They called it 'bun buster' cause you might bust your buns," said Todd Huber, co-owner and proprietor of Skatelab skate park in Simi Valley. The Cooley brand offered "Bun Buster" graphic skateboards and matching T-shirts, while characters such as "Lil' Gremmie the Sidewalk Surfer" endorsed skateboards priced at $8.95 and T-shirts at $1.75 (equal to $69.00 and $19.00, respectively, in 2018). Leading brands, as well as the National Skateboard Championship series, also offered sew-on patches embroidered with skateboard graphics. Specialized retailers, including the world's first skateboard shop Val Surf in North Hollywood, lead the charge in bringing skate T-shirts to the masses. "We never had skateboard T-shirts back in the day, but Val Surf probably made some of the earliest shirts," said skateboard photographer J. Grant Brittain. When Val Surf opened in 1962, color options for T-shirts were still limited, remembers store owner Mark Richards: "When we opened it was almost exclusively white shirts, and there weren't a lot of good quality T-shirts available at a wholesale level. So we would go to J.C. Penney [department store], who had the really beefy tee's that everyone wanted, and they wouldn't even give us a discount. We had to pay full retail for the shirts and take them to our screener and print our logo on them."

"It had to be mid-to-late 1960s before we even started offering color shirts," said mark Richards. "But even today, white is still one of the most popular options. Classic designs just pop better on a white t-shirt!" Although *Skateboarder* Magazine and skateboard companies such as Makaha, Hobie, and Native Custom Skateboards also offered graphic tees from the mid-1960s onwards, they would remain a fringe phenomenon during skateboarding's first wave of popularity. "In those days, printed T-shirts were still really new on the scene," said Patti McGee, 1965 Women's Skateboard Champion.

BUN
BUSTER
skateboards
by cooley

SKATEBOARDING'S FIRST WORLD CHAMPION: DANNY BEARER

Every generation has its hero. That one skateboarder every young kid wants to be like, skate like, dress like. For many riders catching skateboarding's first wave of popularity in the early 1960s, that role model was Danny Bearer. With his flawless riding style, and even more flawless competitive track record - crowned by a first place in the Flatland Slalom event at the 1965 International Skateboard Championships in Anaheim - the teenager from Santa Monica, California, was perfection personified, also in the way he dressed.

"Danny Bearer didn't look like the typical skateboarder, he was always dressed to the T! Obviously he was a good-looking guy, he had the image," said Mark Richards, owner of Val Surf skate and surf shop, opened in 1962. In those days, spectacular aerial stunts on ramps and burly leaps down massive stair sets - now the benchmarks of leading professionals - were still decades away. What defined a great skateboarder, above all, was a combination of style and control. Also a good amount of flow and fast turns - all of which came natural to Danny Bearer, having picked up surfing in 1963 at the age of 12.

"He was a good all-around skater and came from the beach. He had a good style in surfing, the way he was able to keep power in the water and all that combined," said skateboard pioneer Craig R. Stecyk III. "I surfed effortlessly. One could often find me lingering about the blue green see-through water dangling my toes over the front of the surfboard during the early glassy mornings of the day," he wrote in his unpublished autobiography, *Defence Above All*. When ABC television's Wide World of Sports aired an interview with the freshly crowned world champion in his white turtleneck T-shirt and neatly sideways-parted blond hair, Danny Bearer became the poster boy for California skateboarding culture for millions of viewers.

Before young Danny Bearer discovered skateboarding, he was already turning heads as a roller skating prodigy at the Pacific Palisades skating rink. Then "sidewalk surfing" hit, opening up a whole new world to be explored on miniature surfboards on clay wheels. As the natural terrain for turning tricks, Bearer and friends scoped out concrete embankments at L.A. schoolyards, which they nicknamed after famous surf locations; Bellagio Road Elementary ("Waimea Bay"), Marquez Elementary ("Banzai Pipeline"), and Paul Revere Elementary ("Sunset Beach") schools.

"The asphalt-paved banks were very much the same shape as the waves we used to surf!" he wrote. "To us, it resembled Hawaii!" Together with riders such as Torger Johnson, David and Steve Hilton, and Woody Woodward, Bearer became part of skateboarding's avant-garde; the innovators that laid down the blueprint for early skateboard maneuvers recreating the flow of wave surfing on concrete, including 180s, 360s, hang tens, kickturns, and tic-tacs. And nobody made it look easier than Danny Bearer. He rose to fame just as effortlessly. At the age of 13, Bearer became sponsored by Larry Stevenson's Makaha Skateboards company, only to be poached onto Baron Hilton's elite Hobie Super Surfer Team less than a year later. Team riders worked without compensation, but Bearer was grateful to receive free supplies of, "surfing and skateboarding equipment and all clothing such as blue Vans sidewalk surfing shoes, one pair a week, red, white and blue striped t-shirt uniforms, wet suits, surfboards, bathing trunks."

In 1964, Bearer won the first National Skateboard Championship at Covina Skate Park on a Hobie Fiberflex board at the age of 14. That summer, the Hobie team embarked on a two-week tour of 25 states, spreading the gospel of "sidewalk surfing" to crowds of up to 5,000 spectators, most of whom had never witnessed skateboarding before. With his winning smile and flashy bag of tricks, Danny Bearer brought thousands of new kids on board, all wishing they could skate with the natural ease of the quintessential California Kid with the sun-bleached hair.

Unfortunately, soon after Bearer's 1965 International Championship title, skateboarding's first big wave of popularity hit its high-water mark, crashed and rolled back. The child prodigy returned to his surfing roots, winning championship titles and promoting the sport across the world in places such as Mexico, Morocco, and France. Before his untimely passing in 2009, Danny Bearer became instrumental in realizing a public skateboard park in his hometown, Santa Monica. In 2012, Danny Bearer was posthumously inducted into the Skateboarding Hall of Fame in Simi Valley as skateboarding's first world champion, and an untiring champion of skateboard culture.

BIG TIME: SKATEBOARDING ON NATIONAL TV

Skateboarding's rapidly expanding media presence peaked in 1964, when Hobie team rider Corky Carroll appeared on the Tonight Show with Johnny Carson. Dressed-to-impress in slacks, sports coat, and dress shoes, the young pro surfer represented skateboarding in front of a national audience of over 8 million viewers. But an incident during Carroll's skateboard performance foreshadowed how quickly public perception of the new sport could, quite literally, take a nose dive: The combination of clay wheels and slippery broadcast studio floors sent Carroll's board flying into the bleachers on his first kick turn, hitting an audience member in the third row. Needless to say, the King of Late Night TV was not amused, and neither were his viewers.

While the cover of *Surf Guide* magazine's May/June 1964 edition proclaimed "SKATEBOARDING GOES WILD!" the sport was gaining a reputation as a safety hazard in the mainstream media. Sponsored by the National Safety Council, an article in *Good Housekeeping* magazine warned that skateboarding may cause facial fractures, stunted bone growth in adolescents, and possibly death. The Washington Post quoted the chief of radiology at a children's hospital in Washington, DC, saying: "The skateboard should be outlawed." The medical community identified a new, skateboard-specific injury: The term "skateboard elbow" - soon spread by the media - denoted a fracture of the olecranon, the tip of the elbow. "There was a lot of talk about kids getting hurt and how it was dangerous for kids and they would all end up with 'skateboard elbow,'" said skateboard graphic designer Jim Phillips.

LIFE MAGAZINE DELIVERS DEADLY VERDICT

Delivering a deadly blow to skateboarding's public image, the cover story of *LIFE* magazine's May 14, 1965 edition exposed, "The craze and the menace of SKATEBOARDS." Accompanied by photos of adolescents skateboarding through Manhattan traffic and speeding down hills in Central Park ("they take over paths made for peaceful strollers"), the article branded the new sport as "a menace to limb and even to life." In support, the story cited a Los Angeles hospital treating 25 skateboard injuries per month, and the deaths of two young skateboarders in traffic one month before publication.

"It's easier to get bloody than fancy," the *LIFE* article concluded, and cities in Massachusetts, New Jersey, New York, and California began enforcing bans on skateboarding in public. Skateboard manufacturers saw their sales dwindling and for damage control, Larry Stevenson's *Quarterly Skateboarder* magazine printed an editorial to set the record straight. Discussing the question "Why Speed?" editor John Severson warned: "Like skiing and surfing, skateboarding is excellent for anyone - if he uses a little common sense. But speeding out of control on a skateboard is just inviting an accident."

Because a growing number of accidents were caused by beginners losing control on downhill runs, Severson advised skateboarders to make their descent with controlled turns: "Don't go straight down the hill - you'll only hurt yourself." Severson also pointed out that, for ultimate rider safety, "the skateboard should never travel faster than a slow run," concluding: "This isn't a sport of speed - it's a sport of skill. [...] Why race downhill on skateboard? In the end speed only hurts - you." In response to mounting safety concerns, companies in the skateboard industry founded S.A.F.E., the Skateboard Association for Education.

Official large 1969 National Skateboarding Championships patch.
The portrayed skateboarder is Mark Richards from Val Surf store in North Hollywood.

In the summer of 1965, S.A.F.E. launched a public safety campaign under the motto "NO STREETS, NO HILLS, NO SPEED, FOCUS ON KNOW HOW," encouraging skateboarders to wear safety helmets and practice safe riding. Participants in safety training sessions were awarded a woven patch with the cross-shaped S.A.F.E. emblem. Manufacturer Nash Sidewalk Surfboards printed safety rules on skateboard products and also introduced the Nash Skateboard Helmet as the official safety gear of the National Skateboard Championships in Anaheim, California.

S.A.F.E. NATIONAL CHAMPIONSHIPS

Broadcast live on ABC television's Wide World of Sports to a national audience of millions of viewers, the 1965 National Skateboard Championships required all competitors to wear the officially sanctioned Nash helmets. In an effort to display skateboarding as a "real" sport, the championships featured events such as freestyle, high jump, and for the grand finale, head-to-head downhill slalom racing. For the first time in history, viewers across America received a glimpse into California's skateboard-specific fashion, with competitors wearing slacks, shorts, and jeans, paired with T-shirts, official team jerseys and the ubiquitous of-the-moment trend item, surf-striped shirts by companies such as Jantzen and Hang Ten.

And here's a little-known NSC fact: the skateboarder featured on the official patch for the National Skateboard Championships is no other than Val Surf shop co-founder Mark Richards. "But they inverted the image! I'm regular-footed in real life, they flipped me and I'm goofy-footed. And they stuck a number on my T-shirt and made me the symbol of the NSCs," said Mark Richards. Speaking of the T-shirt number on the patch, some versions feature the number 5, while others feature the number 69. Nevertheless, the patches were popular among young skateboarders, as they offered a chance to add skateboard-specific style to plain T-shirts or shorts.

The Nash helmet, however, stood out like a sore thumb in all its bulkiness. During 13-year-old Dave Hilton's freestyle run, an ABC commentator pointed out: "The helmet's almost bigger than he is!" Skateboard-specific protective gear such as knee or elbow pads would only be introduced years later, and skateboard photographer Jim Goodrich mentioned: "A lot of people still skated barefoot at the time," including a substantial amount of competitors. Despite the NSC's focus on safety and accident prevention, the motorbike-style helmet with its wrap-around design, front visor, and molded chin cup remained the only piece of safety equipment on the competition circuit. TV commentators called it the "Crash Helmet," as words such as "bail" or "slam" - or the concept that falling down is part of the sport - were years in the future.

In the bigger picture, the helmet and corresponding safety campaign merely treated superficial symptoms, not root causes of the problem. The culprit behind the escalating number of skateboard accidents was not lack of skill, but inferior equipment. Throughout the 1960s, product innovation had focused on the skateboard's top deck - with advancements such as fiberglass and laminated wood - while the undercarriage remained practically unchanged: Rudimentary trucks adapted from roller skating, paired with steel or clay wheels. Says skateboard icon Stacy Peralta: "Remember that we were riding clay wheels, which were the equivalent of skating on round pieces of ice!" Ultimately, the S.A.F.E. campaign only forestalled skateboarding's inevitable death. It also may well have backfired among core enthusiasts: To a growing number of disenchanted practitioners, "NO STREETS, NO HILLS, NO SPEED," also equaled NO FUN. Without these elements, the sport lost its attraction, and rising prosecution from municipalities and police departments - confiscating skateboards in the streets in some towns - only accelerated the downward spiral.

CHARTER MEMBER

NSC NATIONAL SKATEBOARD CHAMPIONSHIPS, INC. 1965

Scott Zwolenkiewicz

Member # 814

President

As a member of National Skateboard Championships Association I pledge:

1. To practice safety at all times
2. To work for the betterment of skateboarding
3. To compete cleanly and fairly always
4. To wear recommended safety equipment when competing
5. To help build this association for the benefit of all skateboarding

Accepted

Signature of Member

NATIONAL SKATEBOARD CHAMPIONSHIPS ASSOCIATION

Interim

RULE BOOK

(Official Rule Book will be published January, 1966)

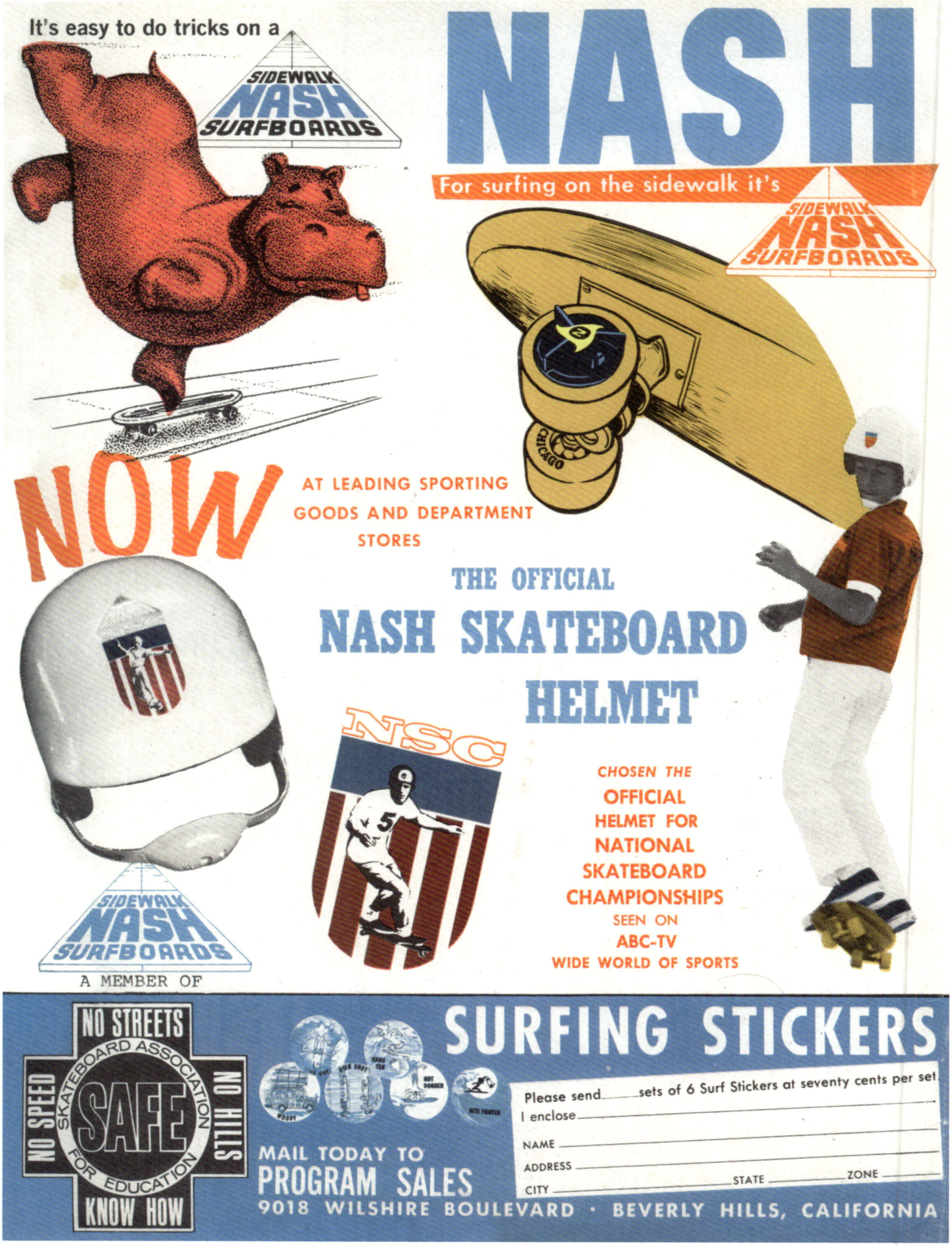
It's easy to do tricks on a
SIDEWALK NASH SURFBOARDS
NASH
For surfing on the sidewalk it's
SIDEWALK NASH SURFBOARDS
CHICAGO
NOW
AT LEADING SPORTING GOODS AND DEPARTMENT STORES
THE OFFICIAL
NASH SKATEBOARD HELMET
NSC
5
CHOSEN THE OFFICIAL HELMET FOR NATIONAL SKATEBOARD CHAMPIONSHIPS SEEN ON ABC-TV WIDE WORLD OF SPORTS
SIDEWALK NASH SURFBOARDS
A MEMBER OF
NO STREETS
NO SPEED
NO HILLS
KNOW HOW
SKATEBOARD ASSOCIATION FOR EDUCATION
SAFE
SURFING STICKERS
Please send ______ sets of 6 Surf Stickers at seventy cents per set.
I enclose ______
NAME ______
ADDRESS ______
CITY ______ STATE ______ ZONE ______
MAIL TODAY TO
PROGRAM SALES
9018 WILSHIRE BOULEVARD · BEVERLY HILLS, CALIFORNIA

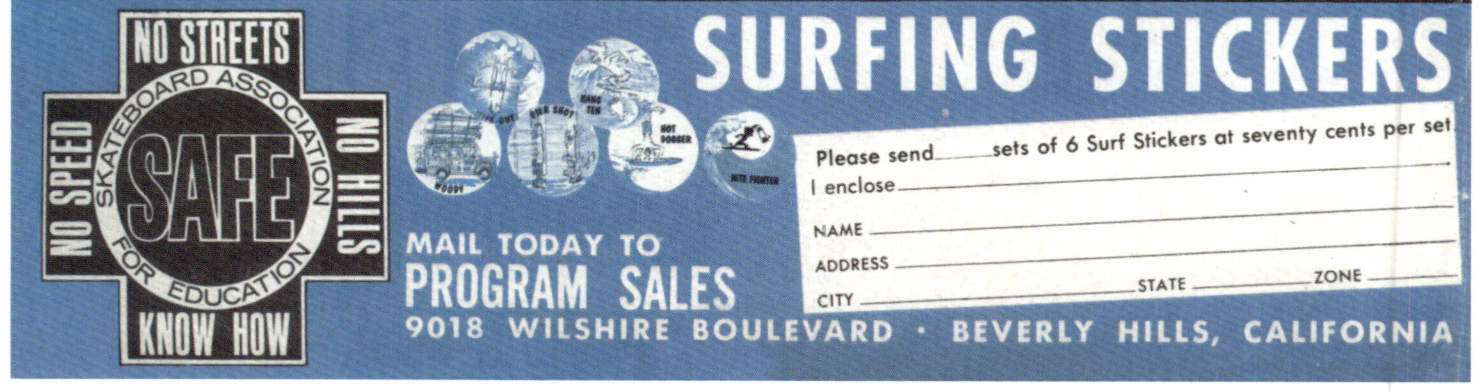

By late 1965, skateboarding had been outlawed in 20 cities across the U.S. as well as the entire country of Norway. Planting the final nail in skateboarding's coffin, the California medical association branded the sport as the "newest medical menace," warning that the board on wheels was just as dangerous as the bicycle. Experts agreed that skateboards were unsafe, kids should not ride them and stores better refrain from selling them. Case closed.

Sports shops and department stores cancelled their holiday orders, leaving manufacturers with ten thousands of unsold skateboards. Allegedly, Larry Stevenson's Makaha skateboards received 75,000 cancellations within one day in late 1965. Practically over night, sales came to a grinding halt, and the industry hit rock bottom. Skateboarding seemed destined for the graveyard, where previous youth culture fads such as the yo-yo and hula hoop loomed.

"Is the skateboard going the way of the hula hoop?" asked a 1966 article in the *Los Angeles Times*. Within one year, the sport had gone from prime time television to relative obscurity. As a member of the Studio City Recreation and Parks Department told the 'Times: "To our knowledge, nobody is manufacturing skateboards any more." And that was almost true, as only a handful of companies held on until the end of the decade, determined to bring back skateboarding better, safer, and most importantly, faster. Also way more fun...

Hobie

Cooper
HOBIE

Op
sunwear
Made to Fit
the way you ride.
TEAM ocean pacific
Steve Sherman
rides G&S
Peter Reese
Mike Jenks
the difference is
TREVIRA
Mainland office
14312 Chambers Rd.
Tustin Calif. 92680
Ocean Pacific (NZ) Ltd.
P.O. Box 30065 Takapuna 9
4 Silverfield Takapuna
Auckland, New Zealand
Japan Surfing Promotions
3-1-7 Hatori, Fujisawa City
Kanagawa Pref, Japan 251
for free Op decal or information on the Op Skateboard Team write dept B. Tustin address.

3 THE SEVENTIES

1970s: OUT OF THE WATER, INTO THE AIR

As the saying goes: You can't make an omelette without breaking a few eggs. Skateboarding had officially crashed and burned. The industry was flattened by the major drop in mainstream popularity in 1965. The hype was over, public interest at an all-time low. But the crash had also left a clean slate, a blank canvas for a new generation of innovators to unfold their own vision of what skateboarding was and how it could progress on its own unique path into the future.

In order for skateboarding to mature into a sport and culture of its own, it had to sever all ties to surfing. It was time for skateboarding to grow beyond "sidewalk surfing" and all its beach movie giddiness. Skateboarders turned away from the beaches – away from their surfing roots – to focus on what the urban environment had to offer. Exploring this space, skateboarding evolved into a distinctly landlocked practice. Ultimately, it would even learn how to fly.

Rolling into the 1970s, three major factors supported skateboarding's emancipation from surfing into a full-fledged culture, replete with its own heroes, dress codes and rules of conduct. These three deeply interconnected factors were:

1. Advancements in skateboard hardware. The arrival of the urethane wheel, mass-produced by professional surfer Frank Nasworthy under the "Cadillac Wheels" label from 1972 onward, proved nothing short of revolutionary: With their smooth riding surface and maneuverability, urethane wheels opened up new terrain previously unskateable with clay or metal wheels, including the vertical walls of empty swimming pools. Skateboard icon Lance Mountain remembers: "I started skateboarding in 1974, right when the urethane wheel came out and there was a huge boom. All of a sudden there were all these kids skateboarding with urethane wheels."

Skateboard decks offered riders additional control with the kicktail, the angled back-end of the board invented by Larry Stevenson in 1970. For added traction, sandpaper-like "griptape" coating across the riding surface of skateboards became standard in 1975. Around the same time, skateboard company NHS from Santa Cruz, California, introduced the first precision bearing wheel, the Road Rider, for a significant speed increase, while a new generation of skate-specific trucks including Tracker, Gullwing and Independent unlocked a new level of turning. Kicktail and griptape featured prominently on one of the most popular skateboards of all time, the Stacy Peralta Warptail model by Gordon & Smith (G&S) released in 1976.

The width of the average skateboard progressed from 6 to around 10 inches throughout the 1970s, while manufacturers experimented with alternative board materials, including fiberglass (Santa Cruz Skateboards and G&S) and colored plastic (Zephyr Shop), ultimately settling on 7-ply Canadian Maple constructions (Willi Winkel for SIMS) as the enduring gold standard in board constructions. These advancements offered a faster, more stable and responsive ride, directly reflected in a rapid influx of new skateboard maneuvers and a radical new direction for the entire practice of skateboarding.

2. Rapid progression of riding technique. With the grip and control afforded by urethane wheels, skaters were ready to step to new kinds of terrain and finally move out of the shadow of surfing. Leaders of this new school included skaters on the Zephyr Team from "Dogtown" Santa Monica, California, such as Jay Adams, Tony Alva, Stacy Peralta, Wes Humpston, and Jim

Muir. The "Z-Boys" took influences from short board surfing into the streets, for example the "Bert slide" named after Hawaiian short board pioneer Larry Bertleman, and pioneered an aggressive riding style based on speed and velocity.

Speaking of velocity: Riding the rounded walls of empty swimming pools, popularized during the 1976 drought in Southern California, led to the invention of countless new maneuvers, most importantly aerials, inverts (handstands on the edge of the pool) and "grinding" the trucks along the lip of the pool, called "coping." Meanwhile, a style of skateboarding on flat ground called "Freestyle" developed, incorporating elements from gymnastics such as handstands and musically choreographed contest routines.

"So much happened in so little time and as such none of the manufacturers knew where skateboarding was going or what it was going to become. Would skateboarding become a sport dominated by freestyle or slalom? Downhill or long jump? Bank riding or pool riding? No one knew," said professional rider and skateboard evangelist Stacy Peralta, adding: "The only thing the manufacturers did know is that skateboarding had the potential to be a far larger and far more profitable business than surfing." And indeed, profits soared to new heights in 1975, when a total of 150 manufacturers on the booming skateboards market accumulated over $250 million in annual sales.

3. Dawn of the skate park era. The new breed of trick-oriented skateboarding soon needed a new home. This became painstakingly clear in light of regular police crackdowns on skateboarders practicing their moves by the hundreds on the inclined embankments of popular Los Angeles schoolyards such as Paul Revere Junior High School or Kenter Canyon Elementary School in the 1970s. Purpose-built skateboard facilities, or "skate parks" offered a legal alternative, and a new platform for the evolution of the sport.

The heyday of concrete parks began in February 1976 with the opening of the first facility, Skate City, in Port Orange, Florida, closely followed by Concrete Wave skate park in Anaheim, California. Soon hundreds of concrete skate parks shot up all across North America, offering ditches, slalom tracks and downhill runs with curved walls, called "snake runs," as well as areas of smooth flat ground reserved for freestylers. Although the majority of these new parks were hampered by major design flaws - ultimately sealing their fate - they became the stomping grounds for a new generation of pioneers progressing the sport to new, unseen heights.

On the fashion side of things, the dawn of the skate park era also marked a paradigm shift from early 1970s surf fashions: "I grew up in San Diego around a lot of surfers, with surf fashion like OP shirts and Hang Ten shorts. Wearing shorts and Vans shoes for skating to school - that became the popular 1970s surfer look," said professional skateboarder Dave Duncan. With skate parks, the style changed towards wearing full pads - knee, elbow, wrist guards, and helmet - combined into color-coordinated outfits. "As a skate park kid, you had to get the blue or yellow Rectors and you would wrap up your helmet so it looked perfect in shiny black or red. It was important to me as a skate park kid to have rad looking pads," said skate photographer Dave Swift.

RAPID EVOLUTION

Powered by more advanced hardware, a growing repertoire of cool new tricks and challenging terrain promising all kinds of riding thrills, skateboarding was once again hot in the public spotlight. By 1975, there were an estimated 2 million skateboarders in California alone – over 10 million across the U.S. according to a UPI article – served by a new wave of skateboard manufacturers including Banzai, Free Former, Variflex, Mad Rats, SIMS and Santa Cruz skateboards, among others. A complete skateboard retailed between $60 to $90 in 1975, the equivalent of $200 to $300 today.

Professional skateboarders including Stacy Peralta and Tony Alva became important brand emissaries for their companies and professionally endorsed skateboards provided a lucrative revenue stream for riders and manufacturers alike. In less than two years, Peralta's "Warptail" pro model on Gordon & Smith sold more than 100,000 units. Soon enough, every skateboard hardware company began offering pro-endorsed models.

Providing a new voice for the movement, skateboard pioneer James O'Mahoney published *Skateboard* magazine as the official magazine for skateboarding's second wave. A year earlier, O'Mahoney had also published a detailed index of maneuvers, the Handbook of Skateboard Tricks with pro rider Russ Howell. Although O'Mahoney, who also founded the United States Skateboard Association and the World Skateboard Association, applied the same diligent focus to the new magazine, Skateboard only published one issue due to distribution problems.

Carrying the torch, *the Quarterly Skateboarder* returned under the name *Skateboarder Magazine*, after it had been discontinued in 1966. In 1975, *Skateboarder Magazine* published 75,000 copies per issue; a number that would increase to 200,000 copies in 1976 when the magazine went bi-monthly. With an emphasis on street and skate park riding, captured in era-defining photographs by editor-in-chief Warren Bolster, the articles by contributors such as Craig Stecyk equally observed and defined the new culture: "Two hundred years of American technology have unwittingly created a massive cement playground of unlimited potential. But it was the mind of 11 year olds that could see that potential," Stecyk wrote in a highly influential 1975 article.

That same year, *Downhill Motion*, a documentary film by Spyder Wills and Greg Weaver documented the diversity of skateboarding's new wave, showing a broad range of terrain such as street, ditches, school yards, pools, freestyle and skate parks. The footage exerted a captivating effect on young people everywhere, propelling skateboarding into an international phenomenon: Around the globe, from Brazil to Great Britain to Japan, concrete skate parks began popping up, offering a new generation of riders a chance to get radical.

STYLE, ATTITUDE AND... SAFETY

By 1977, there were more than 20 million skateboarders in the United States. Mainstream attention was at an all-time high, with millions of spectators following events such as the Pepsi Cola skateboard team's national tour featuring a portable half-pipe made from transparent Plexiglas. And nothing fascinated the masses more than the sight of skateboarders "catching air," pioneered by reigning world champion Tony Alva, who landed the first frontside air during a pool session in 1977.

AFTER 6 MONTHS OF PRACTICE, THE MOST-SKATED PARK IN THE WORLD PRESENTS THE THINGS TO SKATE ON, AND WITH . . .

Introducing SKATOPIA Skateboard Products

painstakingly developed on our runs since we opened in June

***SKATOPIA ONE**
The laminated park board, 3-color logo, 27" 30", $24.95**

***SKATOPIA TWO**
The oak park board, 27" 30", $21.95

***SKATOPIA STRONG TRUCK**
If it breaks, we'll replace it, $6.50

***SKATOPIA ROUNDABOUTS**
Freestyle wheel & park rider wheel, yellow & orange, 2¼ x 2 & 2⅜ x 2⅜

***SKATOPIA HARD HATS**
Great-colored sparkling helmets, $21.95

***SKATOPIA SOFT HATS**
Visors in all colors with black logo, $4.95 (not shown)

***SKATOPIA GOLD**
Our famous logo on a real-gold plated necklace or key chain, actual size 1" diameter, $4.95

***SKATOPIA SKINS**
Men's long sleeve, men's short sleeve & women's cap sleeve silk-screened T-shirts, all colors, 3-color logo on men's, $7.95 $5.95 & $5.95

***SKATOPIA TATOOS**
3-color decal and embroidered patch, $.50, $2.50

STOCK ON HAND FOR IMMEDIATE DELIVERY. DEALERS CALL COLLECT (714) 630-4742

**all prices retail

VEGA

SKATEBOARD INDUSTRY NEWS

THE ORIGINAL MAGAZINE OF THE SKATEBOARD AND SKATEPARK INDUSTRY

Vol. 1, No. 5 June/July, 1978

Fashion Market Develops

As skateboarding matures and broadens its base of consumer support, more and more retailers across the country are reporting a growing awareness on the part of skaters with regard to clothing.

This awareness is manifesting itself in several ways: color coordination of outfits, greater demand for shorts and shirts to wear out of the skatepark and away from skating, and a general demand for a more attractive and unified appearance seems to be steadily increasing in most areas of the country. And the retailer response to this demand is to either expand their original inventory, or to take a serious look at including some fashion items in their store's stock.

Doug Davenport, of Dynamic Skateboards in Bellflower, California, reports that his store sold over $800 in clothes in just one week. "We only have an 840 square-foot store, but the demand for clothing is incredible. And it's not just safety equipment. We sell pads and shorts, but we also sell shirts and clothing items that you can

(Cont. on pg. 9)

Roller Skates Show Revival

By Jonathan Miller

Angel Kate Jackson does it.

John Travolta grooves to it.

And Cher Bono Allman rents the entire rink so she and her entourage can swing along with the gathering craze of . . . ROLLER SKATING.

That's right, roller skating, the born-again leisure activity that has the stars grooving, 25,000 amateur skaters competing and some leaders in the skateboard industry betting it could be their ticket to ride in '79.

"I see it as a strong source of revenue that I didn't have before," says California skatepark owner Sandy Saemann, one of the first to actively court the new generation of outdoor skater. "I see it definitely growing as do some of the leading (skateboard) manufacturers. I'm just in on the ground floor."

Saemann, the president of the Runway in Carson, has instituted a reduced-price, week-night program, as has a San Diego skatepark operator, to woo the swelling legions of outdoor skaters, many of whom are cramming the beach strands from San Diego to Los Angeles.

It is this market, coupled with potential ones at disco and family-oriented roller rinks, that has manufacturers like Oakstreet, Z-Products, California Free Former and the Mattel Athletic Group tooling up to cash in on what many hope will be a spring '79 boom.

"I think it's ready to explode," says Ed Gottschlisch of Oakstreet, the company that feels it has the best and only bona fide outdoor roller skate now

(Cont. on pg. 24)

SUMMER SALES HEAT UP

The most groundbreaking maneuver of the skate park era, however, was the Ollie air, named after its inventor, 15-year-old Alan "Ollie" Gelfand from Florida. In 1977, the scrawny teenager figured out how to "pop" no handed airs above the lip of a pool by hitting his tail on the way up. The Ollie not only dazzled outsiders – "Look, dad – no hands!" – but emerged as the new benchmark for separating the boys from the men.

But while riding technique progressed at an unprecedented pace, skate park construction faced the challenge of keeping up with rider demands. Soon enough, hardcore skateboarders protested the lack of deeper pools with steeper transitions leading all the way up to vertical walls – a necessity for catching air. This led to a second generation of skate parks featuring "vert" pools and even full pipes, including the infamous Pipeline Skatepark in Upland, California.

This rising popularity of pool skating, which became a fixture at a new generation of skate parks such as Marina Del Rey, Del Mar Skate Ranch and Winchester, also added an extra element of physical danger to the game. Injury levels were up again – also due to the often harebrained and dangerous designs prevalent in "old school" skate parks – and once more, the mainstream media jumped on the "dangerous fad" angle, portraying skateboarding as a reckless and dangerous craze.

In response, skate park owners went to great lengths in safeguarding their facilities. Park hours were divided by sessions according to skill level, while protective gear and helmets became mandatory at skate parks. Hard shell knee and elbow pads, introduced by Mike Rector's safety gear company in 1977, added a new level of safety to pool riding: With their slick plastic surface, the pads enabled riders to dismount from their boards – even in mid-air after a failed aerial attempt – and slide safely down the pool surface on their knees. Rector's new generation of pads instantly replaced volleyball-style pads as the new state-of-the-art in safety gear.

THE LOOK: REBELS VS. PARK RATS

Keeping up with safety demands, the standard "look" of the prototypical 1970s "park skater" was characterized by wearing full pads, helmet and other protective gear – including padded shorts by brands such as Mad Rats. Skate park or manufacturer logo T-shirts became a staple. Must-have flair items for "park rats" included headbands and bandanas – made iconic by Dogtown skate legend Shogo Kubo – while safety gloves emerged as the single most popular accessories of the skate park era. Park skaters also embraced tube socks and high top sneakers, again for safety reasons, and color-matched their outfits and protective gear from head-to-toe.

The resulting "skate park look" pulled skateboarders closer into the realm of performance-oriented sportswear. Wearing argyle socks or cut-off T-shirts became a popular way to inject the safety-oriented uniforms with some personal style and attitude. Overall, many a pro skater felt left in the middle, said Lance Mountain: "It was weird, we were very rebellious against the hippies, so we didn't want to wear what they were wearing. But we were rebellious against the jocks at the same time, too."

With a more rebellious take on skateboard fashion, the vibrant subculture of Venice Beach and Santa Monica – celebrated in the iconic artwork of hardgoods company Dogtown Skateboards started by Jim Muir in 1977 – provided an alternative to the sporty "park skater" aesthetic. Dogtown legend Tony Alva made history as skateboarding's first rock star by entering contests and appearing in photo shoots in black leather jackets, jeans and T-shirts, preferably with cut-off sleeves.

When Alva started his own company, Alva Skateboards, his choice of artwork and riders further solidified this new, "punk" look. In 1978, the *BBC* documentary *Skateboard Kings* even went as far as portraying Tony Alva at the forefront of a new cult of masculinity. "How do you prove you're a man?" the documentary asked, answering: "If you're a Maasai tribesman in Africa, you kill a lion. If you live in Dogtown, Los Angeles, you ride a skateboard." Skateboarding's new-found sex appeal was also picked up by men's periodicals: Several covers of French *Lui* magazine (French for "Him"), the European pendant to *Playboy*, featured semi-nude models frolicking about on skateboards.

THE SKY IS THE LIMIT

Skateboarding also featured prominently on popular TV shows, including *Charlie's Angels*, remembered for Farrah Fawcett's famous skateboard chase scene. Pursued by a hoodlum in a stolen ice cream truck through Griffith Park, Fawcett rides to safety dressed timelessly chic in bell-bottom jeans, a red windbreaker and low-top Nike sneakers. A few episodes later, pro skater Stacy Peralta made a cameo appearance on the show. In 1978, Universal Pictures releases *Skateboard: The Movie*, the first major big-screen production devoted entirely to skateboarding. Starring Tony Alva and Leif Garrett, who allegedly did all of his own stunts, the movie tells the story of a down-and-out hustler who starts a skateboard team as a get-rich scheme (life would imitate art on several occasions in the years to come).

Any way you slice it, skateboarding was hot again. In 1978, the United States was home to around 40 million skateboarders, joined by millions and millions of like-minded practitioners all around the globe. The skateboard apparel market, mostly based in California, was also booming. The June issue of Skateboard Industry News spotlighted the booming skateboard "fashion market," with retailers selling over $1,000 worth of clothing in one weekend in a market dominated by, "color coordination of outfits, greater demand for shorts and shirts to wear out of the skatepark and way from skating."

As skate fashion spilled out into the streets - and the mainstream wanted a slice of "skate cool" - retailers in the *Skateboard Industry News* article expected up to 40% sales increases for the 1978 Holiday season, with one store owner from North Carolina saying: "I'm optimistic as hell about the growth of this aspect of the market." The rest of the industry shared this sense of optimism in what is remembered as a new Golden Age for skateboarding. In the late 1970s, skateboarding had become bigger than ever, and a new generation of skate parks provided a permanent home for the booming sport. The sky was the limit, and for a brief moment in time, it seemed like skateboarding might have just become too big to fail...

Photo: Warren Bolster

WEARING NEXT-GENERATION BRAND LOGOS

While the mass extinction event that wiped the dinosaurs off the planet remains a mystery, the culprit behind skateboarding's sudden death in 1965 is well-known and documented: Inferior equipment – slippery clay and metal wheels on rickety roller skate trucks – had rendered skateboards dangerous safety hazards at worst, mere children's toys at best. Abandoned by an entire generation of disenchanted riders, millions of skateboards ended up in attics and garages, where previous youth fads had found their final resting place. "I first started skating in 1969 on steel wheels, but it was considered just playing with a toy. As kids in America we had seen trends like the yo-yo and the hula hoop, and a skateboard was just another thing in the garage that young kids pulled out and fooled around on when they were bored," said pro skateboarder Dave Duncan.

This period of fooling around ended in the early 1970s when a series of milestone technical innovations in skateboard hardware appeared. Advancements like the urethane wheel, skateboard-specific trucks, sealed precision bearings, and wider boards with kicktails not only brought skateboarding back from the dead and into the public spotlight. These mutations also shattered skateboarding's close ties to surfing and started a new evolutionary bloodline that marked the dawn of modern-day skateboarding.

"In the three-year period from 1974 to 1977 we saw the evolution of the skateboard truck go from the roller-skate designed Suregrip to the skateboard-designed Tracker Fultrack. This was the evolutionary human equivalent of a ground squirrel evolving into a tree monkey in three years!" said 1970s pro skateboarder and visionary Stacy Peralta, adding: "It was a hurricane of change that affected every aspect of skateboarding; equipment, terrain, contest formats, and fashion."

FLYING THE REVOLUTIONARY FLAG

From a skateboard fashion perspective, the major innovative push in skateboard hardware profoundly impacted the way skateboarders dressed, especially in the professional ranks. From 1974 onwards, pro riders started signing separate endorsement deals for either boards, trucks, wheels, and safety equipment with a new wave of specialized manufacturers. Consequently, every skateboard pro's outfit became prime advertising real estate for brand logos and corporate artwork, displayed visibly in photo shoots and competitions as part of professional contract duties.

Much like Formula 1 racers, pro skateboarders signalled allegiance to their sponsors from head-to-toe, displaying brand logos from their helmets down to their shirts, shorts, socks, and even their decks. "We spent a lot of time on stickers. Sticker placement was important for sure," said 1970s pro skater Steve Olson, one of the first riders to endorse the revolutionary Road Rider wheel from Nor-Cal company NHS. As an interesting side note, Olson added: "When I rode for them, I was kind of dumbfounded because they told me, 'You can't make any money on clothing.' I just thought, 'Wow, that's an interesting approach. Why can't you?' But they said there was no money in clothing."

Cadillac Wheels
Cadillac Wheels
TM
Big Wheel

RESIN CRAFTS
NAGS HEAD, N.C.
Skating away

Back in those days, skateboard hardware manufacturers still regarded T-shirts as mere giveaways for brand promotions, a practice that started around 1938 with motorcycle companies such as Harley Davidson and Indian Motorcycles, said skateboard artist Jim Phillips. "These brands began printing their company logos on T-shirts, handed out for free to customers as swag," said Phillips, known as the creator of iconic brand icons such as the Screaming Hand for Speed Wheels. "But the shirts soon became sought-after items among bike enthusiasts who wanted to display their passion for the sport in public."

The same thing happened in skateboarding: While hardgoods companies dismissed apparel as a mere merchandising platform or marketing expense, wearing a brand logo T-shirt from one of the innovative new companies held tremendous cultural value in the mid-1970s skateboard scene. For every skateboarder - professional or not - it was a chance to fly the flag of a revolutionary style of skateboarding that was fast, aggressive, and definitely not just for kids anymore.

ROLLING INTO THE SPACE AGE

In the blink of an eye, skateboarding went from innocuous beach-side cruising to adrenaline-charged shredding on new types of dangerous terrain, including the vertical walls of empty swimming pools. Among all the groundbreaking inventions leading the way toward this new frontier, one clearly stood out: "What changed everything was the urethane wheel," said 1970s pro skater and influential graphic artist Wes Humpston of Dog Town Skateboards fame, adding: "I don't care at what time somebody first skated a pool, and I have total respect for dudes doing it on clay wheels. Because you know what... I wouldn't! I wouldn't even think about it! I'd say 'fuck you!'"

In a *SkateBoarder* Magazine editorial, the inventor of the urethane skateboard wheel, professional surfer Frank Nasworthy, concluded: "If one needs a comparative analysis to understand its impact on the sport, try driving your car with wooden wheels." As legend has it, Nasworthy first came across urethane wheels in a backyard shop named Creative Urethane in Virginia in 1970. Applying his technical design chops from college, he then proceeded to create his own blend of skate-specific urethane wheels, mass-produced under the "Cadillac Wheels" label in 1972.

The new wheels were off to a rough start, mainly due to their relatively high price at $8.00 per set (equivalent to $35 today). But once skaters experienced the difference, they never went back to clay or steel wheels. Nasworthy also seeded his wheels to speed-oriented skateboarders at spots like legendary downhill run La Costa near Encinitas, California, which led to endorsements from A-list riders like Bruce Logan, Ty Page (creator of the four-wheeled "Ty Slide" maneuver), and Gregg Weaver aka "The Cadillac Kid." After Nasworthy sold the Cadillac Wheels brand to Bahne Skateboards in 1974, sales took off while other manufacturers pushed onto the wheel market.

The future had officially landed. Compared to the previous generation's clay and steel wheels, the semi-translucent, precision-molded urethane wheels looked so futuristic, they might as well have been dropped by aliens from a UFO. Accordingly, advertising and branding for the new generation of wheels - taking skateboarding from the Stone Age into the Space Age - emphasized technical performance and futuristic art styles, introducing technical terms such as traction, durometer, and heat-injection molding into skateboarding vernacular.

Mail Order: send $3.25 for each Califlex or Califlyer (2"): $1.75 for each California Regular (1½"), to California Wheels, 113 Main St., Seal Beach, Calif. Terms available for wholesale distributors.

Hot New Skateboard T-Shirt designs from California T-Shirts printed on quality Hi-Crew shirts in multicolor inks.

If you would like one of the above designs, send $5.25 check or money order, design number, color preferences, list 3. Send to California T-Shirts, 113 Main St., Seal Beach, CA. Include your name and address.

THE WHE

EL HOUSE

Introducing the orange wheels with juice..

OJ's

MANUF DISTRIBUTOR:
RICHARD METIVER
P.O. BOX 665
APTOS, CA. 95003
(408) 462-1474

SOUTHERN CALIFORNIA:
KEITH HAGEN
CARDIFF, CA. 92007
(714) 225-9272

OJ
Superjuice

OJ's
OJ WHEELS
OJ WHEELS

RISE OF THE LOGO T-SHIRT

On the pages of *SkateBoarder* Magazine, Cadillac Wheels drove an ad campaign with graphics created by influential skateboard artist Jim Evans, whose signature blend of candy-colored airbrush realism presented urethane wheels as the pinnacle of hardware innovation. In several advertisements, Jim Evans dreamed up Formula 1 race cars equipped with oversized Cadillac Wheels accompanied by the tagline: "If they could... they would." Evans and other influential artists - including Griffin, Dennison and Sharp - also offered their artwork on T-shirts sold by Adventure Design out of Long Beach, California for $5.75 per full-color printed tee.

But not all of the new upstart wheel companies flooding onto the market - and their numbers were legion - had the necessary funds for full-color prints or artistic graphics by renowned artists. "When you see a logo on the shirt and only the logo, it's because the company was working from a very small budget. And they know that the most important information to have on a T-shirt is their logo, not necessarily a concept," said Cris Dawson, 1960s Hobie pro skateboarder and graphic designer (Zephyr, Powell Peralta Skateboards).

Despite budgetary constraints, the days of white or black as the only available fabric colors in T-shirts were finally over, and wheel manufacturers printed their designs on shirts in all colors of the rainbow. Primary colors - yellow, red, blue, and green - emerged as powerful choices, while T-shirt designs advanced with pocket T-shirts, V-Necks, and so-called "ringer" T-shirts with elastic sleeve bands in contrasting colors. Wearing a bright-yellow T-shirt with the Cadillac Wheels logo printed over the chest pocket, Gregg 'The Cadillac Kid' Weaver appeared carving the deep end of a swimming pool on the cover of the freshly resurrected *SkateBoarder* Magazine in 1975. At that point, Cadillac Wheels had already sold over 120,000 wheels, signalling the start of a new boom period for skateboarding.

SPINNING INTO HIGH GEAR

Skateboarding was back on top, and wheel companies deserve major credit for attracting an entire new generation of skaters, including some of the most iconic pro riders of all time. "I started skateboarding in 1974, right when the urethane wheel came out. There was a boom, all of a sudden there were all these kids skateboarding with urethane wheels," said Lance Mountain. The same goes for pro skateboarder Christian Hosoi: "When I really got into it was when the urethane wheel came out. And then it was like, 'Wow! Riding smooth on cement! Skateboarding is insane!!!'" said Hosoi, who would move on to break the 11-foot barrier for highest air on urethane wheels.

Within a matter of years, urethane wheel manufacturing grew from a cottage industry into the biggest cash cow in professional skateboarding. The highest-paying competitive event of skateboarding's Second Wave was presented by a wheel company: The 1975 Bahne-Cadillac National Championships in Del Mar marked the dawn of a new era. At the contest, the legendary "Z-Boys" team from Zephyr skate and surf shop in Santa Monica, including riders like Tony Alva, Jay Adams, and Stacy Peralta, introduced a new, aggressive riding style - made possible by urethane's increased traction. Everybody wanted a piece of the wheel business and skate enthusiasts embraced the new urethane wheels with open arms. "After the Del Mar event skateboarding blew up, and new skateboard companies mushroomed up and down the coast of California hoping to cash in on the new sport," said Stacy Peralta.

DON'T CONFUSE
IMITATION WITH INNOVATION

IMITATION IS A COMPLIMENT. OJ'S ARE THE MOST COMPLIMENTED WHEEL IN THE WORLD. BUT JUST BECAUSE A WHEEL LOOKS LIKE OJ DOESN'T MEAN IT WILL PERFORM LIKE AN OJ. SOME THINGS CAN'T BE COPIED.
HERE ARE JUST SOME OF THE FUNCTIONAL DESIGN ELEMENTS THAT HAVE MADE OJ'S OJ'S: HIGHLY ENGINEERED OJ CURVE (PAT PENDING); TRI-BLEND URETHANE (A COMBINATION OF SPEED, TRACTION AND DURABILITY); AND THE OJ LIP DESIGNED FOR GRIP
EACH OF THESE AND OTHER FUNCTIONAL INNOVATIONS SUCH AS DURABILITY THAT SURPASSES ALL OTHER WHEELS, RACE WINNING SPEED, AND A TRUE BEARING SEAT, MAKES OJ'S THE BEST RIDING WHEELS IN THE WORLD OF SKATING. SO DON'T SETTLE FOR AN IMITATION — GET REAL OJ'S AT YOUR SKATE SHOP DEALER.

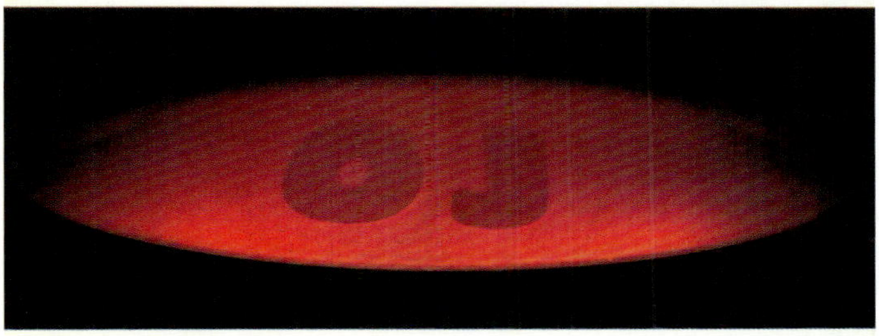

P.O. BOX 665
APTOS, CA. 95003
(408) 462-1474

Photos J. Cahoon

My Weed's Legal

Not only are my wheels legal, they're the hottest way possible to handle coping. So if you're into front and back-side kick turns, rock walks or any type of coping maneuvers the Weed Wheel™ works. Here's why:

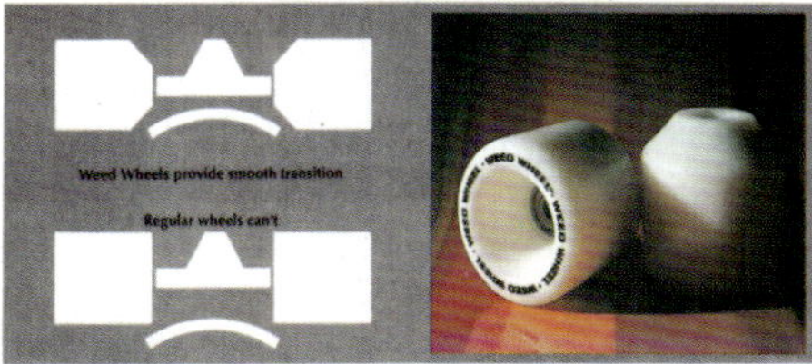

Weed Wheels™ even come with super-hard cores so your bearings will stay where they're supposed to. When you smoke with Weed don't worry about a bust, just worry about 1st, 2nd, or 3rd.

Available in stark white and green.

Weed

WEED WHEELS™ · 641 N. Poplar · Orange, CA 92668 · Ring: (714) 997-4224

Our thanks to the Placentia City Police Dept., Placentia, CA
© 1979 Pro Class Inc., Orange, CA. World Rights Reserved.
© 1979 Bad Co., Orange, CA

"Many of these companies were run by young entrepreneurs that owned small surfboard businesses." Early skateboard retailers, The Frog House Surf Shop in Newport Beach, even ran an advertisement depicting urethane wheels stacked from wall-to-ceiling, changing its name to "The Wheel House."

SKATEBOARDERS ON WINGS

Despite the enthusiasm, one key innovation was still missing for the ultimate smooth ride: "The first Cadillac Wheels still had loose-ball bearings. I fell so many times on those fucking things! We used to ride the big banks at Paul Revere [school], and suddenly, all the bearings would fall out," said Wes Humpston. "And you'd be walking around trying to find them. You'd find these little stones, thinking, 'Is that a bearing or a rock?"

All that digging in the dirt came to an end when Quality Products, Inc. out of Rhode Island introduced the Road Rider Wheel in 1975. The first skateboard wheels to feature sealed precision bearings, Road Riders barged onto the market with distribution on the West Coast by NHS, the company behind Santa Cruz Skateboards, co-founded in 1973 by Richard Novak, Doug Haut, and Jay Shuirman. Advertised as "20% faster on downhills" and "dirt-resistant," Road Riders introduced a new, smooth riding experience.

"Then the sealed bearing came in… and they were quiet. That was revolutionary! You're like, 'What, it's quiet? No RRRRRHHHHHRRRR and the bearings would fall out?!'" said Christian Hosoi. The next generation had landed. Practically over night, Road Rider Wheels replaced Cadillac Wheel as the market-leading manufacturer. While the "skateboard wheel on wings" logo created by artist Jim Phillips became a popular design on T-shirts, long-sleeves, and collared jerseys, Road Rider sold 6 million wheels by 1976, establishing precision bearings as the industry standard in an increasingly crowded marketplace.

Fighting for market share, wheel manufacturers engaged in a fierce innovative arms race, promising customers the best urethane formula - also called "juice," as in OJ "Super Juice" and SIMS "Pure Juice" Wheels - for optimal traction and turning abilities on slalom and downhill runs. Catering to the budding skate park scene, Road Rider introduced the Park Rider wheel series in 1976 with higher durometer urethane for more grip on vertical riding terrain. But for every new innovation, countless imitations popped up. The market became overrun with copycats, literally struggling to re-invent the wheel. In 1977, OJ Wheels declared in a print advertisement: "DON'T CONFUSE IMITATION WITH INNOVATION."

ALL THE COLORS OF THE RAINBOW

In order to stand out from the rest of the pack, wheel companies embraced image marketing, sugar-coating near-identical products in the wildest varieties of themes and art styles, including: proven performance (Variflex, Road Rider, Kryptonics Star Trac Wheels, Stroker "Hill Hugger" Wheels), futuristic technology (UFO Saucers, YoYo Wheels, Gyro Hub Wheels, Astral Wheels, Dyna Star Wheels), rebellious rockers (Dog Town Rock'n Rollers Wheels, Zephyr Skateboard Wheels), straight from the animal kingdom (Tiger Trak Wheels, Spider Wheels, Panther Radial Wheels), all the way to psychedelic (Bennet's green "Hot Pot" Urethane, California "Blue Streak" Wheels, and "SMOKES!" by Weed Wheels). Far out!

ROAD RIDER WHEELS
SKATEBOARDS
ROAD
RIDER

GYRO
HUB WHEELS

New Gyro
GYRO
HUB WHEELS
15558 GRAHAM ST. HUNTINGTON BEACH
CALIFORNIA, 92649 PH. 714-891-2653

All these wheel companies offered branded T-shirts in their respective art styles, adding new variety to the stylistic vernacular of skateboard clothing, as well as plenty of color options. In 1977, the urethane wheels themselves expanded their color spectrum when SIMS launched the "Pure Juice" line of solid-colored radials. This marked a paradigm shift, especially since only two years earlier, Cadillac Wheels had been advertised as, "only available in clear, because color pigments tend to reduce the holding traction." With the arrival of new varieties of wheel colors, skateboarders were able to match their color-coordinated outfits – leading 1970s pro skaters wore meticulously color-matched helmets, pads, t-shirts, shoes, and socks – with their wheels.

Kicking the color-matching craze into high gear, "SIMS came out with sets of wheels in different colors in one pack, so you could have red and black wheels, for example. And then you could match your clothing. I remember tube socks in matching colors were a big fashion thing at the time," said skateboard photographer Ted "T-Bone" Terrebonne. Around the same time, an engineer by the name of George Powell approached leading pros like Steve Olson and Ray Rodriguez to test his latest invention: solid-white colored wheels, called "Bones." Total. Game. Changer.

While innovation in the wheels segment propelled skateboarding into a bright future, skateboard trucks remained stuck in the past. Ever since the early 1960s, when the first hand-made skateboards sold at stores including Val Surf in North Hollywood, trucks had been provided by roller skate truck companies like Chicago Trucks. But these inherently narrower – measuring less than two inches in width – and stiffer trucks were reaching their limits as skateboard wheels and riding surfaces (or "decks") started trending towards wider shapes.

SIMS
PURE JUICE

SIMS
PURE JUICE
WHEELS
SKATEBOARD
TEAM

SIMS
GYRO

SIMS

The original floating power
TRACKER TRUCKS
are the finest trucks available Period. Trackers are incredibly strong and they will compliment any skateboard used. The width of the Tracker is engineered for optimum use of today's super wheels. The Tracker low-mount trucks enable the modern skateboarder to tune his vehicle to whatever he needs, whether they are mounted on a cushion or rigid spacer, or a wedge which changes the geometry for quick steering, or just plain low for a low center of gravity. In short the Tracker Truck offers the finest ride available Period. Featured with Tracker Trucks are the precision bearing O.J. wheels, a high traction and super quality wheel.
TRACKER TRUCKS
per pair $20.00 (add $1.00 for shipping). T-shirt $4.50 (specify size) sticker .25 cents — free brochure. Send cashiers check or money order ONLY: Tracker Trucks P.O. Box 217, Cardiff-by-the-Sea, California 92007

When the Road Rider Wheel hit in 1975, old-fashioned trucks required inserts over their seven-millimeter axles to accommodate the new precision bearings, which resulted in a shaky ride. Something needed to be done. And the man to do it was a marine engineer with a love for Hot Rod cars by the name of Larry Balma. Familiar with the physical dynamics of a stable ride, Balma knew that the natural counterpart for the revolutionary urethane wheel was a wider skateboard truck.

Joining forces with Gary Dodds (metal working) and Dave Dominy (sales) with offices in Oceanside, California, Balma incorporated Tracker Designs – the name inspired by railway car assemblies – in 1975. Their first truck, ultimately known as the Fultrack model, hit the market that same year. At more than double the width of roller-skate trucks – the hanger measured 4.25 inches – the Fultrack defined the blueprint for skateboard specific-trucks with a four-hole mounting pattern on the base plate, stationary kingpin, and Chromalloy axles. Once the day's leading pro skateboarders got a hold of the new trucks, milestone trick innovations like the first aerials or grinds followed. Check the historic photographs and see, most of these tricks happened on Trackers.

Much like the Cadillac Wheel, the Tracker truck marked a blue sky moment in an entirely new market segment. A fresh wave of skateboard-specific truck manufacturers set up shop, including Bahne and Bennett, who were still banking on the old paradigm of narrower trucks around two inches in width. But next-generation skateboarders, especially the pros, wanted the controlled turn and wider surface only offered by Tracker trucks. "You can't point to any pro skater and say they never skated Trackers. Everybody skated Trackers back then. They were the truck, they were the best!" said skateboarder and rapper Gerry "Skatemaster Tate" Hurtado.

THE YIN AND YANG OF SKATEBOARD TRUCKS

Similar to wheel companies, truck manufacturers relied on building recognizable brand identities to differentiate their products. Tracker was marketed as the leading pros' choice, endorsed by A-listers such as Stacy Peralta, Tony Alva, Gregg Weaver, and Alan "Ollie" Gelfand in ads titled, "In the spirit of competition". Trucks by Bennett, Logan Earth Ski, and ACS Trucks were advertised as offering the best turning capabilities. Truck brands with futuristic names such as Lazer, Megatron, Energy, and Stroker Trucks promised cutting-edge technology, with advertisements asking, "Are you still using prehistoric equipment? Or are you into the future?" For riders set on catching high airs in pools and ramps, Gullwing Trucks was the only logical choice with their motto: "More Pros are Flying on Wings".

The powerful combination of urethane wheels plus new trucks changed everything. It allowed skateboarders to hoist aerial maneuvers – in short "airs" – several feet above pool coping. Thanks to new technologies in trucks and wheels, skateboarding – initially the landlocked descendant of surfing – had finally learned how to fly!

ALAN GELFAND
POWELL/PERALTA Winner of SkateBoarder Magazine's "Most Spectacular New Maneuver" of 1978 for his "No Hands Ollie Aerial"
Tracker congratulates Alan for his award and his choice of trucks.
TRACKER TRUCKS
For brochure, order form and a sticker, send 50¢ to: Tracker Trucks, P.O. Box 398, Cardiff-by-the-Sea, California 92007 Dealers call (714) 481-9551
Haftracks (2⅝"), Gnarly Midtracks (3⅜"), Gnarly Fultracks (4¼"), Gnarly Extracks (5"), and Copers Gnarly Magnesium Trackers, too

GNARLY
TRACKER
T-SHIRT
TRACKER TRUCKS

GET THE PICTURE?
TRACKER TRUCKS
Greg Ayres:
6'4½" tall
195 pounds
GNARLY EXTRACKS
with COPERS
Bert La Mar:
4'9" tall
75 pounds
GNARLY
MAGNESIUM
EXTRACKS
with COPERS.
HAFTRACK, MIDTRACK, FULTRACK, EXTRACK, coming soon SIXTRACK
2⅝" 3⅜" 4¼" 5" 6"
For a sticker, brochure and order form send 50¢ to: Tracker Trucks,
P.O. Box 398, Cardiff-by-the-Sea, California 92007. Dealers call 714-481-9551.

TRACKER

MEGATRON

MEGATRON™... AN EXPLOSION UNDER YOUR FEET

You are looking at the newest top-of-the-line truck, engineered for a superior new feel in skateboard riding. Innovative, solid design by a quality manufacturing system puts you in touch with a balance and feel you have never experienced from a truck before.

Megatron™ trucks are available in three sizes:

130mm Freestyle
150mm Bowl Rider
170mm Slalom

more **structural strength** engineered into the **hangers** for greater shock abuse

high alloy steel axle made to take all the free falls and flyaways you can dish out

nylon hanger **swivel cup** for long lasting fast response

strong space age metal goes beyond the T-6 toughness rating other manufacturers try to reach

guaranteed against defects and breakage

steeper hanger angle for more radical stick maneuvers in high performance riding

lower suspension nut for no-snag lip riding

high alloy steel suspension pin tested to last no matter how tough the terrain

superior **memory rubbers . . . suspension** you can feel the difference from bowl riding to tight free style maneuvers

Megatron™ trucks shine like no other trucks with a **lightening brilliance** sure to blind your competition

"high-riser" base eliminates need for riser pad . . . quicker more stable response due to one piece construction

old Only At Your Local Megatron™ Truck Stop™,
o Shop Or Sporting Goods Store

atron Corp., P.O. Box 1782, York, PA 17405, (717) 843-9024

MEGATRON™
"Engineered For The Feel Of It"

UCKS
by
BANZAI

COPYRIGHT 1977 ACS

STAR TRUCK™

Skateboard Trucks by ACS

Against all competition, ACS has become the world's largest manufacturer of premium skate-board trucks. Number one in the world. The Star Trucks.

The reasons why are basic.

ACS has capacity. As the country's largest producer of aluminum hubs for bicycles, ACS has many years of experience in precision machined castings—and the ability to deliver them in quantity. (ACS hubs are used exclusively by major bike manufacturers in their top-of-the-line MX models.)

ACS has quality. ACS is the only manufacturer of premium trucks that produces castings within its own factory—to the same high standards laid down by the U.S. Consumer Products Safety Commission for critical bicycle parts. All ACS trucks are certified 356 aluminum-magnesium alloy heat treated to the T-6 condition.

ACS has the line. Five models are offered to meet every condition—a big reason why ACS trucks are used by so many pro riders. ACS. Don't settle for anything less beneath your feet.

American Cycle Systems, 1449 Industrial Park St., Covina, California 91722

ACS TRUCKS

PHOENIX TRUCKS
MIKE WILLIAMS
PHOENIX
BELAIR
Flight of the
PHOENIX

TEAM
TRUCKS

Taking the level of attitude in the truck segment to new heights, the Independent Truck Company, co-founded in San Francisco by Richard Novak, Jay Shiurman, Fausto Vitello, and Eric Swenson, released its first skateboard-specific truck, the Stage 1, in May 1978. With a logo often mistaken for the German Wehrmacht's Iron Cross – it's actually the papal Alisee Cross – the Independent Company cultivated a more aggressive, punk rock-inspired counterpoint to the clean-cut, performance-oriented truck companies. A Nor-Cal Yin to the Southern California Yang that was Tracker – a duality that ultimately saw both camps launch new skateboard magazines for championing their respective causes; *Thrasher* and *Transworld Skateboarding*.

In the bigger picture, designated truck companies completed the holy trinity of every pro's skateboard hardgoods sponsors. Riding for separate deck, truck, and wheel companies became the norm, and so did cross-promotions, including products like the Logan 5 wheel manufactured by Road Rider, "tested and approved by the Logan Earth Ski Team." And by printing their logos on T-shirts and team jerseys, the new wave of skateboard truck companies further expanded the variety of skateboard apparel, to a point where branded skateboard apparel slowly but surely became more than just a merchandising gimmick, but a lucrative market segment.

BEYOND HARDWARE

Branded skate clothing was booming. In the late 1970s, market leader Tracker Trucks not only sold massive amounts of hardgoods, but also shipped up to 50,000 branded T-shirts per month, said Louise M. Balma, wife of Larry Balma and in charge of Tracker's marketing department during peak times of the brand's popularity. What started with a basic yellow Tracker tee featuring the black Wing Logo as a back print soon expanded into an ambitious T-shirt offering geared around recognizable brand insignia designed by prominent artists such as Chuck Edwall (created the Tracker Wing Logo and Circle Star), and Craig Stecyk (created the Tracker Man).

As customers demanded more and more branded clothing from hardware companies, the overall shelf space dedicated to apparel increased at surf and skate shops. This marked a paradigm shift in what had traditionally been a hardware-dominated industry. Pioneering retailer Mark Richards of Val Surf estimates the initial ratio of hardgoods over softgoods at 90/10 in the mid-1960s. Suddenly, the scales began to shift towards equilibrium between clothing and equipment at many stores. And since hardgoods companies became the main drivers of this change, many started re-thinking their initial stance: Maybe there was money to be made in skateboard clothing after all?

In the case of Tracker Trucks, initially a hardgoods-only company, the success of their branded apparel line led into a flourishing textiles business, manufacturing clothing for several successful hardgoods brands as well as designated apparel lines: "We also made clothing for Skate Rags, Street Rags, Street Rod, Limpies, Blockhead, Invisible, Sixteen, Neighborhood, Stamina, Orion, and of course Transworld," said Laura Balma.

With this in mind, it's safe to say that hardgoods innovations like the urethane wheel, precision bearing, and skateboard-specific truck not only pushed skateboarders into a new age of radical riding technique and up into the air. But with a variety of styles and far-out flavors – we're talking to you, Weed Wheels! – the 1970s evolution of hardgoods also made skateboard fashion a whole lot more fly.

THE GULLWING CLASSIC

"Gullwing covers all my needs, and Baby, they're covered!"
Bobby Piercy

B.P. holding the new Gullwing Classics.

HPG IV Corp. • 1126 Pioneer Way, El Cajon, CA 92020 • Phone (714) 440-0116

Manfredo
INDEPENDENT
INDEPENDENT
TRUCK COMPANY

THEY'RE #★X⚡!!! HOT!

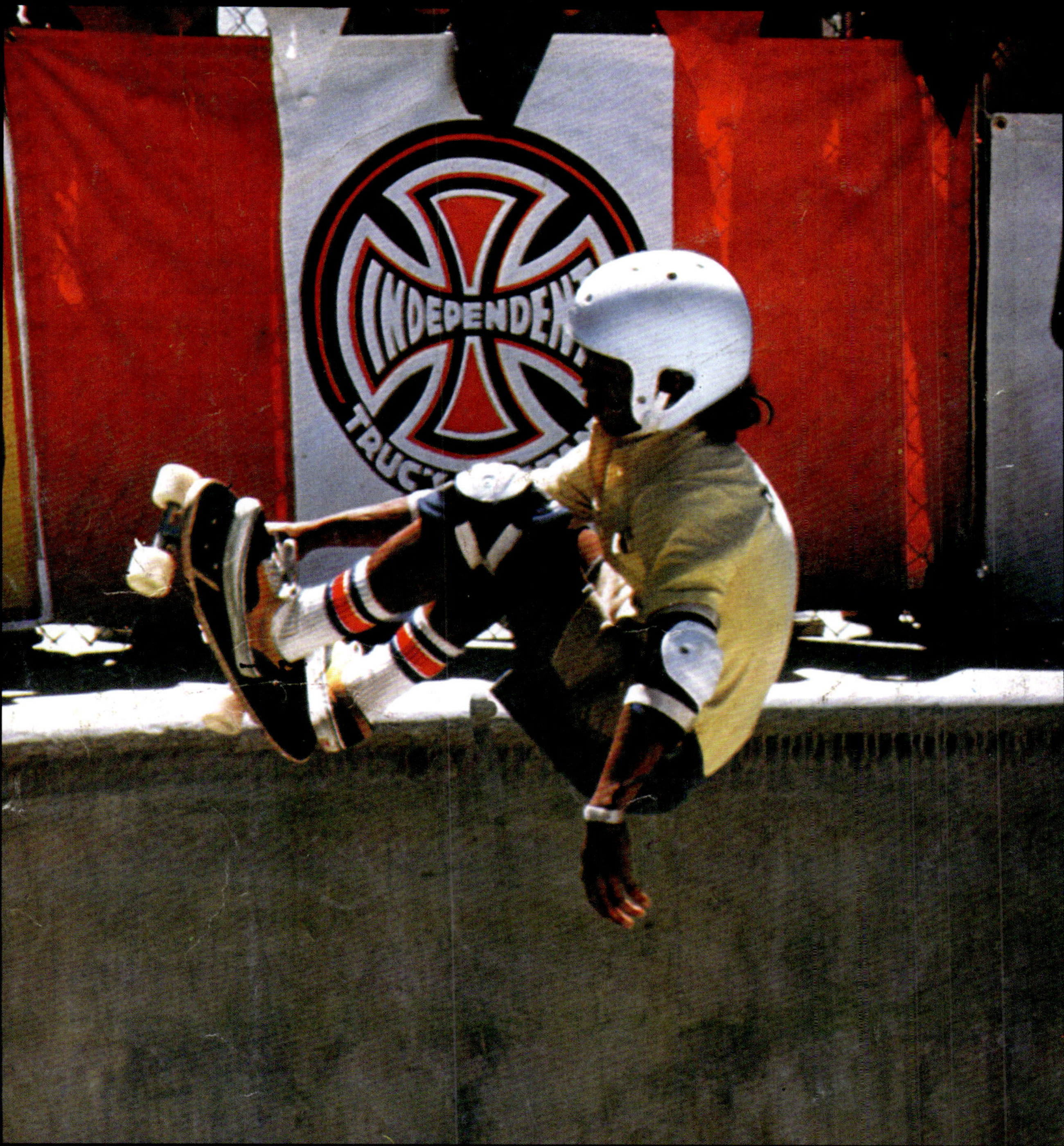

Bobby Valdez, Powerflex Team, Hester/ISA Pro Bowl #3, Newark, Ca.

AVAILABLE IN 77MM AND 88MM.

"FLASH" 4 OUT OF THE TOP 8 FINALISTS AT THE HESTER ISA PRO BOWL#3 IN NEWARK, CA, RODE INDEPENDENT TRUCKS, INCLUDING WINNER BOBBY VALDEZ AND 2ND PLACE RICK BLACKHART.

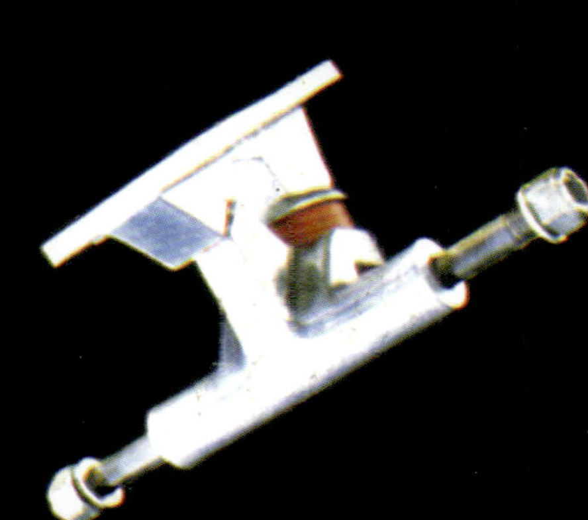

Available thru **NHS**, Inc. 825 41st. Ave. Santa Cruz, Ca. 95062 408-475-9434

Bahne skateboards are precision tuned to challenge the professionals and built strong to withstand the punishment of the Competition Circuit. We guarantee it. We make skateboards the way all professional sporting gear should be made.

The streamlined outline of a Bahne is wide for stability, to give you that extra edge of confidence. Experts and skiers can ride parallel stance. High jumpers and free-stylers know a wide board is a must.

The Bahne 150 truck has a quick turning action for slalom; we made it wide to grip the road. The hollow tube steel axle has amazing lightweight strength. The outer axles are removable for quick wheel changes between races. You may never need to know how easy it is to replace these axles because they are much stronger than any standard axle.

Some freestyle riders may prefer the Bahne 110 truck. The narrower track makes 360's and spacewalks easier. The 110 has the quick reflexes that free-styles want.

Hand poured urethane Cadillac wheels with sealed precision bearings complete the board. DK 38's turn and pivot quicker for freestyle. The DK 51 is fast becoming a favorite of many pro racers.

Add gripdeck and shockpads and a warranty card, and you have all you need.

But remember, it's not a toy.

CONGRATULATIONS TO ALL OUR GREAT RIDERS

Northern California Pro-Am
Cow Palace, San Francisco

Paul Engh — 1st Pro Men's Slalom
Davey Andrews — 2nd Amateur Men's Slalom

North County YMCA Contest, Carlsbad

Patrick Flanagan — 2nd Men's Pro Giant Slalom; 3rd Men's Pro Cross Country

Ellen Berryman — 3rd Women's Pro Freestyle

Davey Andrews — 1st Amateur Men's Cross County; 2nd Amateur Men's Slalom; 2nd Amateur Men's Giant Slalom

Dale Dobson — 2nd Amateur Men's Cross Country

Richard Boyden — 3rd Amateur Giant Slalom; 3rd Amateur Freestyle

Karen Knox — 1st Women's Amateur Giant Slalom; 2nd Women's Amateur Slalom; 2nd Women's Amateur Freestyle

Julie Flanagan — 1st Junior Women's Slalom; 2nd Junior Women's Freestyle

Kim Taylor — 2nd Boy's Cross Country

BAHNE

Products of Bahne and Company. Dealers welcome. For further information call or write:
Bahne Skateboards, Post Office Box 326, Encinitas, California 92024; (714) 753-0255.

BAHNE
SKATEBOARDS

BAHNE: PUSHING THE LIMITS

Asking around about the "Greatest Early 1970s Skateboard Brands" inevitably brings up the usual suspects; brands like G&S, Hobie, SIMS, Santa Cruz and Logan Earth Ski. But asking around among the era's core riders and company owners, another name always enters the conversation about who did it best - or even who did it first - in those early days: Bahne Skateboards. "I believe that Bill Bahne is the single person who started the new era of skateboarding, bringing it from the Sixties into the modern day," said Jeff Ho, co-founder of LA-based Zephyr skateboards, which is in turn a leading name on the list of Greatest Mid-1970s Skateboard Brands. "With his insight, he was the one who made the first fiberglass production skateboard featuring the urethane wheel."

Started in the early 1970s by brothers Bob and Bill Bahne out of their surf fins manufacturing business Fins Unlimited, Bahne skateboards took the market by storm with the right product at the right time. The Bahne brothers drew on their expertise in fiberglass manufacturing to design skateboard decks with the right amount of flex demanded by the day's leading downhill and freestyle riders. The company was also first to realize multi-colored logos and elevated graphics in an era when the aesthetics of most skateboards still resembled ski equipment. And through strategic partnerships with urethane wheel pioneers Cadillac Wheels and the Chicago steel truck company, the Bahnes were able to make a strong push into retail by offering ready-to-ride complete skateboards at competitive price points.

But Bahne Skateboards did more than just design next-level sports equipment. The San Diego-based company also sponsored a team of style icons and notorious risk takers that were pushing the aesthetics and dangerousness of skateboarding to new heights. An iconic Bahne advertisement shows a motion-blurred photograph of Dennis Shufelt charging down the legendary La Costa hill run - riding shirtless, feet improperly close to the nose - at breakneck speed under the headline "Clocked at 40 m.p.h." Skateboarding was definitely not child's play anymore and the new combination of flair, thrills, and performance sent sales into overdrive. At the high-water mark in 1975, Bahne was cranking out 1,000 skateboards per day and co-sponsored the Bahne Cadillac National Skateboarding Championships in Del Mar, remembered as the competition that ushered in skateboarding's next big wave.

ATTITUDE MEETS PERFORMANCE

The impact of Bahne's complete boards - especially at a time when serious, performance-built products were scarce commodities - can hardly be overstated. "Bill is way overlooked in the history of skateboarding. They give Frank Nasworthy credit for discovering the urethane wheel but Bill Bahne took that over and distributed the wheels and also mounted Chicago trucks on his complete skateboards," said Jeff Ho. At a time when skateboard manufacturing was a high-touch industry, Bahne had his hands on all key components of skateboards, which ultimately unlocked an entirely new generation of riding. "They don't give Bill Bahne the proper respect for the person that he was, which was a designer and engineer," said Jeff Ho, adding: "He was also the first one to develop the mono ski - before there was even snowboarding!"

Bahne's new generation of skateboards were no longer toys and the company sponsored the best riders of the day to prove it. The revolving door of Bahne team riders included Bob Mohr, Dennis Shufelt, Danny Trailer, Neil Graham, Paul St. Pierre, Karen Knox, Ellen Berryman, and Chris Yandell.

One of the most stylish riders on the Bahne team was Freestyle Champion Bob Mohr from Cardiff, California. Known for gymnastics-inspired moves such as rolling headstands, one-footed wheelies, and sideways-rolling planks, Mohr also played saxophone in a funk band known as Heat Treatment and defied common sports etiquette by showing up to compete with his arm in a full cast (still winning 1st place). Bob Mohr also made a mark on skate fashion with his signature faded denim poor boy hat, accompanied by team jerseys and a full mane of hair and mustache. Speaking of team jerseys, Bahne also created the paradigm for skateboard teams with some of the first recognizable branded uniforms out on the circuit.

The physical proximity of Bahne's company to the La Costa downhill run and the Carlsbad Skatepark at the time was also key. Bill Bahne was witnessing the evolution of skateboarding - plus getting direct feedback - on a daily basis, which helped open the doors to modern-day skateboarding in so many ways. As company history maintains, Tony Hawk's first skateboard was a blue Bahne complete board handed down by his older brother Steve. In 2013, Tony Hawk donated said board to the Smithsonian National Museum of American History in Washington D.C. where it is now part of a permanent U.S. heritage exhibition. Meanwhile, the story of Bahne continues as the company is now serving the hungry market for longboards and cruisers with its unique blend of performance-built complete boards.

MEET KRYPTO MAN - BUILT FOR SPEED!

Photo: Glen E. Friedman

FASTER THAN A SPEEDING BULLET
KRYPTONICS
KRYPTONICS INC., 5660 Central Avenue, Boulder, CO 80301 (303) 442-9173

KRYPTONICS
65MM
GREEN WHEELS
This reusable package contains four Kryptonics C-series skateboard wheels. Each wheel includes two special low-torque bearings that are sealed on the outside and shielded on the inside. The bearings are seated in a rigid plastic core that is molded into the wheel. The core improves performance by assuring precise alignment of the bearings. Flex and distortion that normally occur in and around urethane bearing seats are eliminated. Specific information about the wheels contained in this package can be found in the box below.
GREEN FORMULA
DUROMETER–94A
DIAMETER–65mm WIDTH–50mm
RECOMMENDED USE:
Skateparks, pools, pipes and freestyle. Very hard and fast for easy sliding on smooth surfaces.
KRYPTONICS
KRYPTONICS INC.
5660 CENTRAL AVENUE
COLORADO 80301

NO SKATEBOARD FOR EVERYONE

The 1970s were the golden age of mega skateboard companies that covered it all: Wheels, trucks, decks, apparel, safety gear and accessories were marketed by super brands like Hobie Gordon & Smith as part of their comprehensive offering. Looking back, it's a little-known fact that the list of uber-brands also included – if only for a brief period of time – the Colorado-based skateboard wheel specialists at Kryptonics.

Kryptonics first emerged on the scene in 1976, right when the invention of urethane wheels sparked an explosion of new wheel brands selling their own unique compound formulas. As one of the most recognizable brands of that era, Kryptonics carved out a niche by selling 'resilient skateboard wheels' that were immune to flat spots and chipping. Known for providing a smooth riding experience, the 76A durometer wheels instantly caught on with downhill racers, and Kryptonics became the preferred wheel label on the 1977 championship circuit. "They were the first wheels that you could really run over ANYTHING! Huge cracks, boulders, whatever. You could just mow them on those red Kryptonics and I loved those wheels," said pro skateboarder and Kryptonics team rider Dave Hackett.

With close ties to competitive skateboarders and a sizeable pro rider team on payroll, Kryptonics decided to take the leap to become an all-inclusive skateboard brand in the late 1970s. The release of the C-Wheels series in 1978 not only introduced innovative packaging in a tube-shaped container, but also added pre-installed precision bearings into the product offering. At the same time, Kryptonics also fired shots at its biggest rival, the OJ Wheel company, in competitive ads asking: 'Tired of the same old juice?' With new-found swagger, the brand boldly announced an innovative milestone: The Kryptonics Skateboard. Made from foam and fiberglass instead of wood, the new product promised an evolutionary upgrade. It also featured a bumper crafted from urethane 'to increase durability as well as performance'. As the advertisements concluded: 'The new Kryptonics Skateboard is not for everyone.'

NO SKATEBOARD FOR EVERYONE

On the strength of a performance-driven marketing campaign, Kryptonics presented itself as the skateboard brand of the future. As brand ambassadors, the brand signed vertical skateboarding siblings Steve and Micke Alba, who endorsed signature pro model boards featuring K-Beam construction, advertised under the slogan 'Beam me up'. By the time Micke Alba won the day's biggest vertical pool competition event in skateboarding, the 1979 Hester Series, the Kryptonics product portfolio had expanded to include complete set-ups that featured the latest innovations from the brand based in Boulder, Colorado. But in a case of inopportune timing, the brand's product innovation peaked right at the same moment when skateboarding as a whole took a dive into the early 1980s crash.

As skate culture retreated to underground spots and backyard halfpipes, Kryptonics ditched the futuristic vibe for a punk-inspired graphics style on a new wave of pro models for vertical riders such as Ken Block as well as Art and Steve Godoy. After some hard yards, Kryptonics found success around 1987 with a rediscovered focus on its core competency: wheels. A Thrasher magazine advertisement for the new Pro Series wheel series featured Brian Brannon, Team Captain of JFA (punk rock band Jody Foster's Army). But right when things got rolling again, the skateboard industry hit another wall in the early 1990s crash, and Kryptonics retreated from the scene in 1991. End of story? Not so fast! The early 2010s and the rise of retro cruiser boards generated renewed interest in classic wheel brands. Kryptonics returned as part of the Dusters California family of brands, replete with 1970s style icon Dave Hackett and vert skater Cindy Whitehead as brand ambassadors. The future is now!

KRYPTONICS

KRYPTONICS
SKATE TEAM

THE OUTER LIMITS

When it comes to high technology and proven performance one name stands out, Kryptonics. We pioneered the development of high rebound urethanes, precision hubs, composite decks and high technology wood boards. We were the first to explore the outer limits, now we control them.

COMPETITION SERIES WHEELS – The 64MM Double Conical and 60MM Freestyle are highly specialized, professional quality wheels. Both feature Dupont Zytel ST super tough glass reinforced nylon cores. The new black core is used only with the ultra-resilient 92A formulation developed after thorough testing during the Hester Series. The newly designed 64 is the lightest and fastest competitive bowl wheel we have ever produced.

RACING SERIES WHEELS – The 62MM Slalom and 70MM Downhill have no competition when it comes to street racing. Both designs have been refined and improved after years of testing and development. Both the Orange 88A Formulation and Red 78A Formulation feature the precision molded black core and a smooth, fast ride. The soft red formula delivers the highest rebound of any wheel made, an incredible 80%.

HIGH PERFORMANCE DECKS – Kryptonics offers an extensive line of high quality skateboards including three Krypstik Models, two K-Beam 2 Models including a new Micke Alba Signature Model, two Freestyle Decks designed by Stuart Singer and two Foam/Fiberglass Composite Decks.

THE PROVING GROUNDS – When we're done with a product in the lab it goes to the team for testing. While testing and developing the 1980 product line, the Kryptonics Skate Team happened to win the Prestigious Hester Series, the East Coast Amateur Championships at Cherry Hill, and the Florida Team Challenge. Results say a lot about the limits of both riders and equipment, those results speak for themselves.

When you're ready to explore the outer limits of your skill and equipment, stay on course. Follow the leader, Kryptonics.

Micke Alba winning at Boulder on his way to winning the 1979 Hester Series.

KRYPTONICS, INC.
5660 Central Avenue, Boulder, CO 80301
(303) 442-9173

Val Surf
The Skateboard Capital

In the skateboard universe, authentic skateboard retailers have been the salt of the earth – the evangelists spreading skate culture, missionaries bringing new converts on board – since day one. Throughout skateboarding's peaks and valleys, a few die-hard skate shops have always provided skateboarders with a place to stock up on new gear, catch up on the latest trends, and meet fellow enthusiasts. And in order to spread the gospel of skateboarding, graphic T-shirts with skateboard-inspired designs have proven a powerful medium ever since the world's first skate shop opened for business in 1962: Val Surf in North Hollywood, California.

"As young skateboarders we never had T-shirts, but Val Surf probably had some of the earliest shirts in skateboarding," said skateboard photographer J. Grant Brittain. In the big picture, the influence of specialized retailers goes even further: Next to pioneering graphic T-shirts as wearable pieces of skateboard culture, Val Surf also introduced "skateboard clothing" as an attractive product category; attractive to both shoppers and brands in the boardsports industry. Ultimately, this progression saw skateboard-related apparel advance from sideshow act to headline attraction in the retail product mix. "When we first started out, there weren't even clothing racks at Val Surf, just surfboards. But by the time we moved the shop [in 1973], clothing had grown to probably taking up 35–40% of the sales floor," said co-founder and current owner of Val Surf, Mark Richards. "It became apparent that clothing was going to be what would keep us in business. The margins on clothing were much better than in hardgoods... it's like that to this day. So we offered as much as we could while maintaining our credibility as a skate and surf hardware store."

PIONEERS OF SKATEBOARD STYLE

The credibility never suffered. Opened by surf enthusiast and former record producer Bill Richards and his two sons Mark and Kurt on October 6, 1962, Val Surf remains the oldest family-owned boardsports shop in the world today. Asked about the origin of the store's name, Mark Richards explained: "'Val' stands for 'Valley.' A lot of people these days don't know that. We still have solicitors call up and ask for 'Val'. At the time there were businesses in the valley that used it, like Val Beauty. That was how my dad came up with it." From the start, the Richards' store was dedicated to supporting the thriving inland surf scene: "Obviously you have to go to the beach to surf, but you shouldn't have to go to the beach just to get your surfing product," said Mark Richards. The landlocked surf community also embraced the new practice of sidewalk surfing quite early on. "People in the valley saw skateboarding as very compatible with surfing. If there wasn't anywhere to surf, you went skateboarding."

But most skateboards at the time were still either crude homemade contraptions or poorly designed commercial offerings. This inspired Val Surf to bring into retail a legitimate alternative: "When we opened our doors, we thought, 'What the heck, let's offer some really good skateboards unlike what was available anywhere else at the time,'" said Mark Richards, who designed and assembled the first Val Surf skateboards from rectangular wooden boards supported by trucks purchased from the Chicago Roller Skates company.

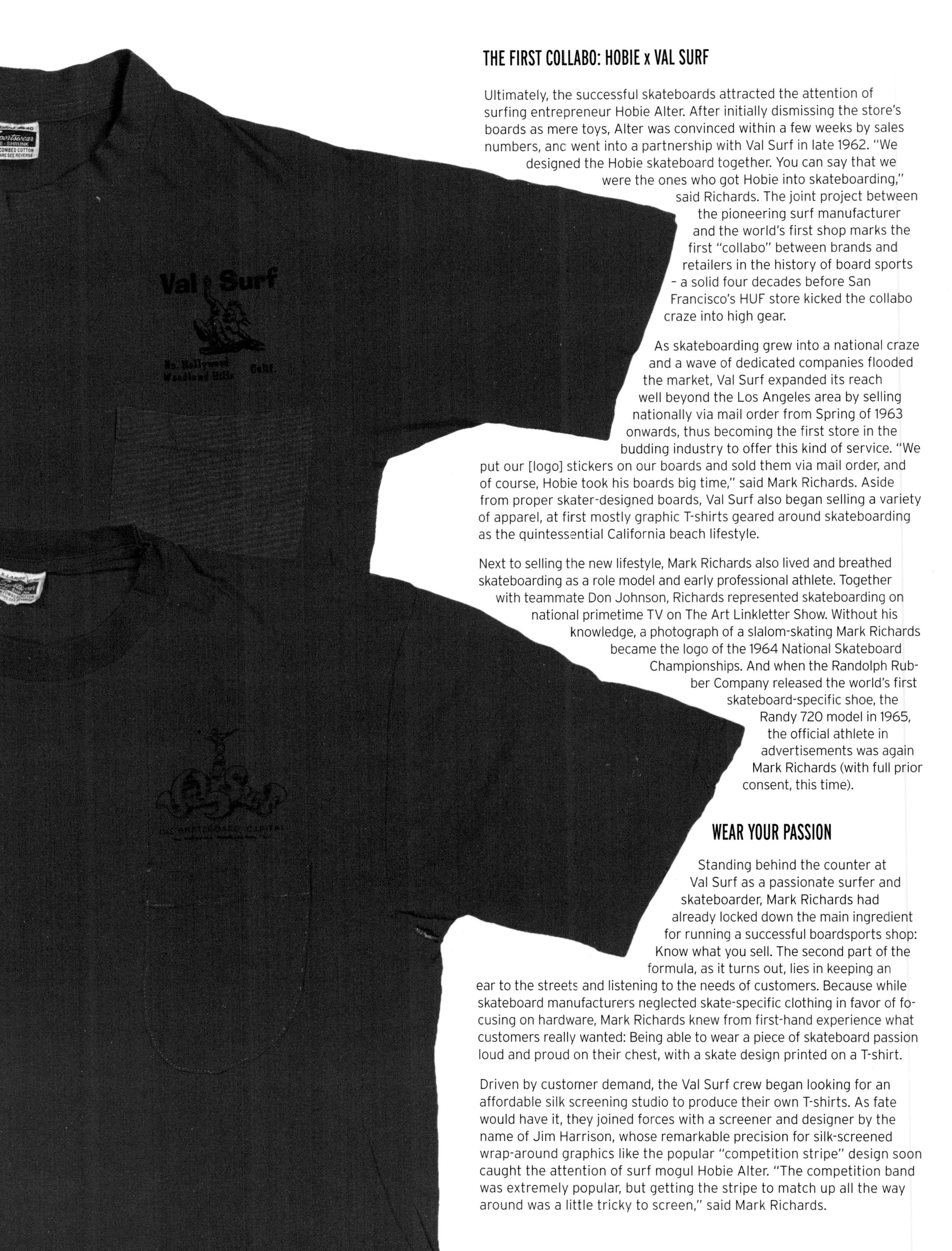

THE FIRST COLLABO: HOBIE x VAL SURF

Ultimately, the successful skateboards attracted the attention of surfing entrepreneur Hobie Alter. After initially dismissing the store's boards as mere toys, Alter was convinced within a few weeks by sales numbers, and went into a partnership with Val Surf in late 1962. "We designed the Hobie skateboard together. You can say that we were the ones who got Hobie into skateboarding," said Richards. The joint project between the pioneering surf manufacturer and the world's first shop marks the first "collabo" between brands and retailers in the history of board sports - a solid four decades before San Francisco's HUF store kicked the collabo craze into high gear.

As skateboarding grew into a national craze and a wave of dedicated companies flooded the market, Val Surf expanded its reach well beyond the Los Angeles area by selling nationally via mail order from Spring of 1963 onwards, thus becoming the first store in the budding industry to offer this kind of service. "We put our [logo] stickers on our boards and sold them via mail order, and of course, Hobie took his boards big time," said Mark Richards. Aside from proper skater-designed boards, Val Surf also began selling a variety of apparel, at first mostly graphic T-shirts geared around skateboarding as the quintessential California beach lifestyle.

Next to selling the new lifestyle, Mark Richards also lived and breathed skateboarding as a role model and early professional athlete. Together with teammate Don Johnson, Richards represented skateboarding on national primetime TV on The Art Linkletter Show. Without his knowledge, a photograph of a slalom-skating Mark Richards became the logo of the 1964 National Skateboard Championships. And when the Randolph Rubber Company released the world's first skateboard-specific shoe, the Randy 720 model in 1965, the official athlete in advertisements was again Mark Richards (with full prior consent, this time).

WEAR YOUR PASSION

Standing behind the counter at Val Surf as a passionate surfer and skateboarder, Mark Richards had already locked down the main ingredient for running a successful boardsports shop: Know what you sell. The second part of the formula, as it turns out, lies in keeping an ear to the streets and listening to the needs of customers. Because while skateboard manufacturers neglected skate-specific clothing in favor of focusing on hardware, Mark Richards knew from first-hand experience what customers really wanted: Being able to wear a piece of skateboard passion loud and proud on their chest, with a skate design printed on a T-shirt.

Driven by customer demand, the Val Surf crew began looking for an affordable silk screening studio to produce their own T-shirts. As fate would have it, they joined forces with a screener and designer by the name of Jim Harrison, whose remarkable precision for silk-screened wrap-around graphics like the popular "competition stripe" design soon caught the attention of surf mogul Hobie Alter. "The competition band was extremely popular, but getting the stripe to match up all the way around was a little tricky to screen," said Mark Richards.

CALIFORNIA

The rest is history: Hobie and Harrison went into business as H&H Graphics, producing Hobie's heavily distributed line of branded softgoods - kicked into high gear once Hobie formed a skateboard venture with hotel magnate Conrad Hilton's Vita-Pakt juice company - as well as Val Surf's growing T-shirt offering. Jim Harrison also created Val Surf's popular "Surf Wheeler" design, blending the acts of surfing on concrete and water, while the original Val Surf logo saw the light of day as water-transfer decals created by Art Decal in Los Angeles. "That was before stickers, these were water transfer decals. They had an in-house artist and we just made the 'S' [of the word 'Surf'] into a breaking wave. It's still our number-one selling logo today," said Mark Richards.

EARLY CROSS-PROMOTIONS

In what turned out smart business foresight, Val Surf also printed cross-promotional T-shirts in cooperation with leading skateboard hardware brands in the early 1970s; some of which could not be bothered to make T-shirts of their own. "When clothing became more and more popular, we went to all the different companies like Kryptonics and screened shirts where we typically put our logo on the front and their logo on the back," said Mark Richards. "This was our attempt to disassociate surf a little bit from our name to be able to capitalize on the fact that we were the original skateboard shop - even though 'skate' wasn't part of our name. We also kept changing our logo and put a skater in there."

The cross-branded T-shirts, featured prominently in full-page *SkateBoarder* magazine ads for Val Surf's mail order service, turned out to be major sellers. Most of conveniently, Val Surf had no licensing obligations to any of the featured brands, fully cashing in on the profits. "The brands were thrilled because it was free advertising for them. I don't think I gave them a dime, we just got the signed authorization. They knew they were going to be in every skate magazine on the mail order ad with all their competitors," said Mark Richards. Powered by surging T-shirt sales, the share of clothing in Val Surf's line-up grew within less than a decade from 10% in the mid-1960s to almost 40% by 1973. At that point, a men's short-sleeved tee sold for $5.50 (equivalent to $29.99 in 2018), kid's shirts for $4.50 ($24.00), and long-sleeved shirts for $6.95 ($39.00).

As the mid-1970s rolled around, Val Surf shirts diversified in terms of colors and designs. Next to corporate artwork from skateboard brands such as Bahne and Cadillac Wheels, photographs of the Val Surf skateboard team - including heavy hitters such as Brad Bowman, Jerry Valdez, and Kent Senatore - also featured heavily on tees and long-sleeved shirts. "Val Surf had these shirts with a photo called 'Three Wheels Out,' and it was a photo with ornate 1970s drawings. There were several shirts. There was one with Kent Senatore, that was the shirt I had to have," said pro skateboarder Lance Mountain, who cut his teeth as a skateboarder riding pools and ramps in the valley.

A LOCALS THING

Wearing a Val Surf shirt gained a political edge - at least within the tightly-knit L.A. skateboarding community - as skateboarding's second wave of popularity hit. Surf culture's undercurrent of hostility between the valley and the beach - epitomized by Val Surf on one hand, and Zephyr shop in Santa Monica on the other hand - came to a head as both local skateboarding scenes locked horns.

"There was a big thing going on between Dogtown and the valley. 'Locals only' type stuff, but some of the best guys came out of there... Kent Senatore, Brad Bowman. I say these 'Val' guys ripped!" said skateboarder and rapper Gerry "Skatemaster Tate" Hurtado. On the streets of Venice Beach and Santa Monica, being called a "Val" ranked as a major insult. The major prejudice at work was that 'Val' skaters had no direct beach access and therefore no respect for skateboarding's surfing roots.

Speaking on the rivalry, Mark Richards said: "The surfing image with the valley has had issues for quite some time. 'Val' had some negative connotations to it. But surfing was growing through leaps and bounds, and it wasn't just growing through the residents of beach communities, it was inland surfers just as well." Turning the perceived weakness into a strength, Val Surf provided land-locked surfers and skateboarders with access to their lifestyles right where they lived. "No matter what you needed in surfing - even if it was just a simple bar of wax, you had to go to the beach to get it. So we based our entire concept around that. And of course it worked, there's plenty of inland surf shops today."

STARTING A LEGACY

While chalking up an impressive number of historic firsts - including first legitimate store-bought skateboard, first stickers, and cross-branded shirts - Val Surf started a legacy of specialized retailers that would leave their own indelible mark on skateboard culture. Standouts include Zephyr (founded in 1972), Rip City (1978), and X-Large in Los Angeles (1991); SHUT (1986) and Supreme in New York City (1994); Skates on Haight (1974), FTC (1986) and HUF (2002) in San Francisco; all the way to distant relatives such as Canada's PD's Hot Shop (1976), Germany's Titus and Holland's Rodolfo's (both 1978), as well as London's Slam City Skates (1986).

And as we all know, some of these skateboard stores grew into influential brands with deep hooks into fashion and streetwear; just consider SUPREME, X-LARGE and HUF, for instance. In that light, core skateboard shops have not only spread the love, but added a few crucial chapters of their own to the gospel of skateboarding. Up in Santa Barbara, there's even a store called the "Church of Skatan," worshipping the devious arts in an actual former Baptist church with 100-year-old stained-glass windows since 1997. So whatever floats your boat, you'll find it at the local skate shop.

BING CROSBY HALL
TIMING
ZEPHYR
ZEPHYR

Photo: C. R. Stecyk III

JEFF HO SURFBOARDS
ZEPHYR PRODUCTIONS
JEFF
慧
智
何
NATHAN
SKIP
JOHN
2003 MAIN STREET, SANTA MONICA,
CA 90405
HAWAIIAN SHIRTS
BODY GLOVE WETSUIT
SUMMER GIRL SWIMM WEAR
OCEAN PACIFIC SUN WEAR
75¢ DECAL
SURF LESSONS
COMPLETE ACCESSORIES
& CLOTHING
(PLANTS too.)
AT ZEPHYR JEFF HO SURF-SHOP TIME AND CARE ARE OUR TRADE MARKS. PRECISION MADE SURF-BOARDS THE RULE. STOP BY AND GET ONE OF OUR FINALLY SET JEWELS. 7 YEARS IN THE SHAPING ROOM. 8 YEARS IN THE WATER WERE IT COUNTS. STOP BY AND CHECK US OUT.
ART-WES HUMPSTON 10/73
(213) 396-3221

Forget surf dreams of golden-haired teenagers catching waves on pristine beaches. The early 1970s brought a harsh reality check, a plunge into the needle-infested waters of Dogtown, California, where only the toughest surfers dared to show their faces in the line-up, and the toughest of them all gravitated around one surf and skateboard shop that became the nexus of a new hardcore aesthetic: Jeff Ho Surfboards and Zephyr Productions. Opened in 1971 by surfboard makers Jeff Ho (shaper) and Skip Engblom (sander) with stylistic and philosophical oversight by artist, photographer, and co-founder Craig R. Stecyk III (airbrusher) on a run-down strip of Main Street in Santa Monica, the Zephyr shop created the template for modern-day skate and surf stores while injecting board sports culture as a whole with a new level of attitude.

More than just a storefront selling boards, wheels, and apparel, Zephyr evolved into one of the most recognized brands in skateboarding, mostly thanks to a high-profile skate and surf team. The latter actually came first, as Jeff Ho points out: "All of the kids that were on my team were surfers first and then I started a skate team." On and off their boards, the Zephyr riders became notorious for a hardcore lifestyle loosely geared around surfing and skateboarding, infused with a healthy dose of street culture and rock 'n' roll. And that lifestyle wasn't for everyone, as countless stories of co-owner Skip Engblom keeping shop doors closed to outsiders, whom he scolded as "kooks" and "Vals" (short for "valley surfers"), will attest. Much like the Zephyr team's home surf spot, the disheveled Pacific Ocean Park Pier between Santa Monica and Venice Beach, the shop was "Locals Only" territory, reserved for those in-the-know. Posers and kooks not welcome.

"There was so much aggression... they were more like a street gang than a skate team," wrote editor Kurt Lederman in a 1975 issue of *SkateBoarder* magazine, right after the Zephyr Competition Team stole the spotlight at the Del Mar National Skateboard Championships with their attitude, dress code, and low-to-the-ground riding style. The contest marked a changing of the guard. "It changed everything in 24 hours. This contest was the first gathering of everybody. The next day, everyone was in the parking lot going, 'What the fuck happened there yesterday?!'" said Alaric Valentin, who managed a number of surf stores in Southern California throughout the 1960s, adding: "They had a swagger and attitude that no one had seen before. It was like when the Beatles went on the Ed Sullivan Show in 1966. Nothing was the same after that!"

The Del Mar event turned the twelve skateboarders on the team - nicknamed the "Z-Boys" after the contest announcer tired of repeatedly saying "Zephyr Competition Team" - into international household names: Shogo Kubo, Bob Biniak, Nathan Pratt, Stacy Peralta, Jim Muir, Allen Sarlo, Chris Cahill, Tony Alva, Paul Constantineau, Jay Adams, Peggy Oki, and Wentzle Ruml looked different - dressed in Levi's with matching competition T-shirts and deck shoes, paired with street gang-influenced bandanas and flannel shirts - and skated different from the rest. Soon, riders across the globe wanted a piece. "That Z-Boys style and West Coast cool was the first thing every skater wanted to look like. And these guys laid the foundation for what skateboarding is now," said skateboard photographer Skin Phillips, who became fascinated with the Dogtown legend as a youth growing up in the UK.

STRAIGHT OUTTA DOGTOWN

Every legend has a beginning, and Zephyr's story was epic from the start. True to the shop's larger-than-life aura, the Zephyr name was part mythology, part local pride. "Zephyr was the wind god, and at one point we were at Zephyr Court in Venice, where I had an art studio for a second," explained Craig R. Stecyk III, adding: "When Skipper and Jeff and I decided to make surf boards together, I had a building in Downtown that was going to be the manufacturing building. But we got the opportunity to be on the corner of Bay and Main Street in Ocean Park. These were all places nobody cared about." What's more, the area where Zephyr set up shop 1971 was regarded as downright sketchy. "Dogtown was rugged at the time," said surf apparel designer Jimmy Ganzer of Jimmy'Z fame. Zephyr team rider Nathan Pratt recalls: "There were hookers on Main Street back then. There was nothing nice about it."

Contrary to popular belief, the area known as "Dogtown" did not include Venice Beach. To hear 1970s pro skateboarder and Dogtown local Wes Humpston tell it: "Dogtown was [Southside] Santa Monica, around Ocean Park. [Zephyr rider Bob] Biniak was right at the edge of Rose [Ave], I was on Ocean Park. We figured Dogtown went up to the [Zephyr] shop on Main [Street] and east all the way to Lincoln [Boulevard]. Because [Jim] Muir lived on the other side of Lincoln, we told him he was a Val." Being called a Val ranged as a major insult in Dogtown, and perhaps the clean-cut, athletic style of the valley surf and skate scene represented by Val Surf shop in North Hollywood served as the Yin to Zephyr's Yang; the antithesis to Dogtown's rugged, street and motorcycle gang-inspired art style.

"Our vibe was… we were rocking and rolling. That was our whole deal. San Diego [skateboarding] wasn't like that," said Nathan Pratt, while putting things in perspective. "We weren't the only ones around here. You went to a Venice High party, you weren't the toughest guy. There were tougher guys than us. Full-on, real deal!" Some of the Dogtown skaters, including Jay Adams, rolled with notorious street heavyweights, also reflected in clothing choices such as gang color-coded bandanas, flannel shirts, and deck shoes that presented a harsh contrast to the sports-inspired apparel styles endemic to skateboarding at the time. "We were influenced by the street. Street style in LA has always been Chicano-influenced, Mexican-influenced. LA style in general," said Tony Alva, who also brought music and rock culture into skateboard attire, including fedora hats, boots, and leather jackets.

STREET-STYLE AESTHETICS

Aside from a unique style, Zephyr's success also resulted from having a winning product at the right time: The Zephyr Skateboard checked all the boxes for what a next-generation skateboard needed: Most of all soft and grippy urethane wheels, which Jeff Ho first saw when he visited his friend, skateboard manufacturer Bill Bahne in his workshop in La Jolla near San Diego. "I used to go down to his factory and the first time I saw the wheel, he said, 'I got this new thing and just made this. Why don't you try the skateboard?' So I rode his skateboard and said, 'We have to have these!'" The rest is history. Jeff Ho brought the urethane wheels back to his team riders and almost instantly decided to manufacture his own line of boards while introducing some technical improvements. "Riding Bill's skateboard, I discovered a design flaw that I could take and make better. That's when I came up with the design for the Zephyr skateboard, which then became the EZ Rider and then became a Z-Flex."

ZEPHYR
COMPETITION TEAM

Custom cars and surf culture influences collided when the Zephyr collective created their first line of T-shirts. "I had watched my dad make Customs America shirts with George Barris. I knew about the process of making T-shirts because the car guys had the best T-shirts. The surfboard shops and Ed Roth had a huge thriving business between them with him painting on T-shirts. Presumably I was aware of it when we screened the first Zephyr shirts with Skip and Jeff, or later when we did multi-print T-shirts," said Craig R. Stecyk III.

THE "MUST HAVE" SHIRT

Before elaborate multi-prints and colorways raised the level of flair and finesse, Zephyr's apparel offering was pedestrian at best. The very first item of clothing ever produced under the Zephyr name originated not from an artist's studio, but a high school graphic arts class. The Zephyr team's first competition T-shirt was designed by 17-year-old surf shaping apprentice and Zephyr team rider Nathan Pratt: "That shirt was produced because we were going to have a surf contest against Eddie Talbot's team, ET Surfboards. So we all had the same competition team T-shirts, they didn't say 'surf' or 'skate.' I made the graphics in graphic arts class in high school and then we had them printed. And the colors are Venice High School colors - navy and white. The shirts were printed over on Rose [Ave in Venice]."

In the bigger picture, the simple white-on-navy print design was emblematic of Zephyr's underlying philosophy. "There's a concept behind the one-color screen and that is something Jeff Ho believes in thoroughly: Don't complicate your message. Be simple, clear and straight to the point. A lot of the time when you see a skateboard Jeff Ho designed, it's white type, blue board, really simple and very straightforward. And his mantra is not to get things complicated," said 1960s pro skateboarder and graphic artist Cris Dawson, who worked on Zephyr's advertisements and T-shirt graphics, adding: "Using one color on the T-shirt is also the fastest way of getting shirts produced."

Printed in a highly limited run and handed out exclusively to team riders, the shirts could only be earned, not bought. To no surprise, the Zephyr Competition Team tee punched far above its weight for a plain cotton T-shirt. Charged with the exclusive representation of the day's hottest skate team, the navy-colored shirts became coveted items out on the streets; emblems of initiation into an exclusive circle, similar to the elaborate, members-only jackets worn by motorcycle gangs. "You could never buy it. There were no copies, no knock-offs, no mainstream model. There was only one team shirt and that was it!" said Nathan Pratt, adding: "It was the real deal!" According to contemporary witnesses, the team T-shirts were the keys to a world of benefits, from sessions in exclusive empty swimming pools, to women, weed, and parties - none of which the Z-Boys were known to turn down.

SMELLS LIKE TEAM SPIRIT

Adding to Zephyr's notoriety, the team's bad boy antics on the contest circuit soon became the stuff of legend in the skateboarding scene. Team manager Skip Engblom would appear at competitions dressed like a beachside hustler in Hawaiian shirts paired with snow-white dress shoes, oversized sunglasses, and a fedora. Pulling the team's registration forms and entry fees from a black suitcase, he would demand organizers flat-out hand over the trophies to Zephyr, as their skateboarding style represented the kind of new level none of the established riders could compete with. Which was kind of true. "Earlier skating had no flow. It was all about mechanical moves, while we were continuous motion. All of us were driving into the maneuver, accelerating into the tricks. It was carving versus tick-tacking. We were surfing versus the guys doing stationary handstands," said Z-Boy Nathan Pratt. Behind the scenes, the presentation of the Zephyr team as disrupters with a rebellious image was part of a master plan laid out by Jeff Ho: "What I was trying to do was bring this whole new sport. I could tell that it could blossom and there would be pro riders and it would become something that could be an industry." In order to achieve this goal, the surf and skate pioneer mentored his riders in regular sessions on their role as brand ambassadors. "I used to train these kids in, like, a skate camp and there was skate practice and team gatherings. These are things I also did for my surf team. I organized the skate team so they could be a presence as a team and not just individuals," said Jeff Ho, adding: "I gave them a sense of identity with the shirts, which are kind of a uniform, but not really, with the Levi's and Vans shoes."

The 1975 Del Mar Nationals marked the culmination of Jeff Ho's plan, and he prepared his team accordingly. "I wanted to make sure that we were ready. This was like the first X-Games. It was all about the idea of the team, when you see twelve or 15 guys come down with the same team." And it worked - the combination of team spirit, attitude and progressive riding caused the perfect storm that shook up the established order in the skate/surf industry. "It was all those nice blonde kids from good families and all of a sudden you released a prison population inside the sport! It scared the living shit out of a lot of people," said Alaric Valentin. Company owners such as Larry Stevenson and Bill Bahne openly voiced their concerns about the Zephyr team's radical image. "Bill and I were friends but he was a bit upset about what happened at Del Mar and what we were doing. But I had an idea and a sense of what the big picture was going to be," said Jeff Ho.

From a marketing standpoint, the Zephyr team presented the shape of things to come for an entire industry. "That was the first time anyone saw that surfing could become skateboarding and take it to that level of consciousness. This was what I saw at the Del Mar Nationals - the beginning of a culture," said Jeff Ho, adding: "Skateboarding itself as we know it today is a worldwide culture. But back in that time period, riding was frowned upon like, 'You are a surf bum! Look at that toy skateboard! Look at what you are doing, you're never going to make a living of that! You are never going to be anything! You can't make surfboards! You can't... do this!'" Well, over forty years later, Jeff Ho is still doing it, working as a surfboard shaper and company owner in Venice Beach. "It has given me a living and I still do what I did back in the day. And I have helped many other young people become businessmen in the surf skate culture in what it is today."

OUT WITH THE OLD

On a technical level, the Z-Boys' radically new skate style, influenced by the low-charging moves pioneered by Hawaiian surfing legend Larry Bertlemann, blazed a new trail for riding streets, school yards, all the way to empty swimming pools. Meanwhile, the emphasis was on style as much as on technical difficulty. As C. R. Stecyk III wrote in *SkateBoarder* magazine: "It's not what you do, it's how you do it. True progression results not only from where you go, but from how you get there. A gram of push is always worth a ton of holding back." And push they did. "When Jay and Tony and those guys showed up at La Costa, you could see the level of skateboarding rising. You could see the level of skateboarding rising every week, it was palpable," said Alaric Valentin. Tony Alva, Jay Adams, Bob Biniak and their cohorts soon became notorious for their trailblazing stunts in empty swimming pools - the new frontier in skateboarding's progression

ZEPHYR

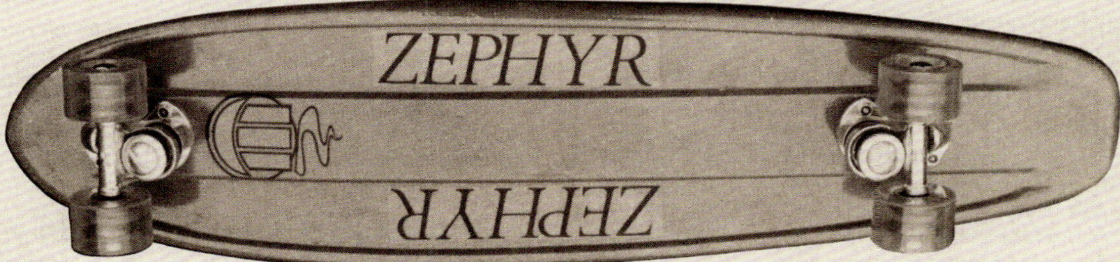

The Zephyr Skateboard

The most functional, fast, stable skateboard available. Designed specifically for professional slalom and freestyle skateboarding.

100% uni-directional, heat and pressure molded fiberglass chassis. 27″ long and 6½″ wide.
Natural rocker for lower center of gravity and more leverage in tail.
No-skid deep textured deck.
Center beam for controlled flex, added strength and extra wheel clearance.
Recessed wheel wells to accept wider, larger wheels.
Reinforced nose, tail and rails.
Wide blunt shape, no dangerous sharp edges or points.

All Zephyr Skateboards are equipped with X-Caliber trucks and Roller Sports wheels. To order your Zephyr Skateboard by mail, send your name, address, zip and $36.95 (Calif. residents add 6% tax) in check or money order, plus $2.00 for postage and handling.

For Getting RADICAL!

Jay Adams
1st Free Form (Kate Sessions), 1st Boys' Slalom (Santa Barbara Contest), 2nd Boys' Free Form (Santa Barbara Contest), 3rd Jr. Men's Freestyle (Del Mar-Ocean Festival Contest), 3rd Boys' Freestyle (Huntington Beach Contest)

Nathan Pratt
4th Jr. Men's Slalom (Del Mar-Ocean Festival Contest)

Peggy Oki
1st Girls' Freestyle (Del Mar-Ocean Festival Contest), 1st Girls' Slalom (Santa Barbara Contest), 4th Girls' Free Form (Santa Barbara Contest)

Tony Alva
2nd Jr. Free Form (Santa Barbara Contest), 4th Jr. Men's Freestyle (Del Mar-Ocean Festival Contest)

Dennis Harvey
2nd Jr. Men's Slalom (Del Mar-Ocean Festival Contest)

Stacy Peralta
2nd Jr. Men's Slalom (Santa Barbara Contest), 3rd Jr. Men's Freestyle (Huntington Beach Contest)

Wentzle Ruml
3rd Jr. Free Form (Huntington Beach Contest), 3rd Super Heat Slalom (Huntington Beach Contest)

Bob Biniack
3rd Jr. Men's Slalom (Santa Barbara Contest)

Paul Constantineau
1st Boys' Slalom (Huntington Beach Contest), 2nd Boys' Freestyle (Huntington Beach Contest), 4th Boys' Slalom (Santa Barbara Contest)

Jim Muir
1st Jr. Men's Slalom (Huntington Beach Contest), 3rd Super Heat Slalom (Huntington Beach Contest)

Photos: C. R. Stecyk III

Remember the last time you skated that special place? The one you know you could rip, except it ripped you, because that old skate had so much flex it bottomed out and you had road rash for two weeks? Well, cheer up, bud, now you too can ride the skateboard of the pros, proven in flat-out everyday hard skating by the Zephyr Skateboard Team, the hottest young skaters in California. Young dudes who go for it at some of the heaviest spots around demand the best, and get it. Get yours.

P. S.: Watch for the Zephyr Team to come to your town, or drop us a line for bookings.

Dealer Inquiries Requested

Available at finer surf shops everywhere.
Watch for the Zephyr Skateboard wheel. Coming Soon!

ZEPHYR **12530 Yukon Ave.**
Hawthorne, CA 90250

ZEPHYR
productions, factory team
ZEPHYR
productions, factory team

The team's forays into riding vertical pool walls also called for more rugged, protective attire than the "beachy" board shorts prevalent on the competition circuit at the time. Among the Dogtown skaters, "no one wore shorts!" said original Zephyr team rider Stacy Peralta. Instead, the team adopted a household brand name as their pants of choice. "We all wore Levi's. And all those white pants are corduroys, not jeans," said Nathan Pratt, pointing out the famous Zephyr skate team photo taken at the 1975 Del Mar Nationals, adding: "Everything in the photo is Levi's, either jeans or cords. They were the original skate pants. The only uniform was the shirt. We had blue shoes, deck shoes, but we bought our own shoes."

Speaking of shoes in the mid-1970s, some riders still refused to wear shoes for skateboarding for fear it would ruin the "soul" of riding. Jeff Ho remembers some of his team riders taking an anti-footwear stance: 'They all loved to skate but some of them wanted to skate barefoot. And I said, 'No, no! You're not gonna have any toes left!" Soon enough, the Zephyr riders saw the light, with the technical pioneers leading the charge: "I never skated barefoot," said Stacy Peralta, who was known for skating in Wallabees. "I couldn't stand skating barefoot as I felt it held me back and gave me no control." Looking back on the skate scene at the time, Peralta adds: "Jay Adams is the only person I remember ever skating barefoot and he only did it once in a while. No one I skated with back then preferred skating without shoes – it was too hard on the feet when you came off the board, which was all the time."

BIRTH OF A LEGEND

While the Zephyr team's spectacular live appearances would turn heads, their media presence created a mystique that reached audiences across the globe. In the freshly re-launched *SkateBoarder* magazine, Craig R. Stecyk III wrote a series of "Dogtown articles" from 1975 onwards – under various aliases including John Smythe and Carlos Izan – exalting the idea of skateboarding as art form and signifying practice. The underlying Tao of Stecyk, a heady new skateboarding philosophy with Dogtown as the epicenter, presented skateboarding as a way to make sense of otherwise barren urban environments, offering riders "esoteric rewards" unattainable through the established corporate order in the process. "Two hundred years of American technology has unwittingly created a massive cement playground of unlimited potential. But it was the minds of 11 year olds that could see that potential," Stecyk wrote in Vol.2 1975 of *SkateBoarder* magazine, predicting the rise of what would become modern-day street skating.

Foreshadowing the future , Zephyr's advertisements in skateboarding magazines broke the rules of sports products marketing by featuring no skateboarding whatsoever, shifting the focus on the team riders with personality-driven ads instead. "I was just trying to do stuff that was interesting. Skipper and I and Jeff were not very interested in what other brands were doing. That's the reason why we started our own brand. I think we viewed the riders as empowered individuals. I think people were recognizing who they are as creative individuals," said Craig R. Stecyk III.

The formula worked, as orders for Zephyr's latest innovation started gaining momentum: The next level in hardware technology was a fiberglass skateboard, designed by Jeff Ho and Nathan Pratt. "It was basically just an updated version of the old 1966 Super Surfer," according to Pratt. Produced in partnership with Jay Adams's stepfather, fiberglass technician Kent Sherwood, the new Zephyr board exceeded the wildest expectations in terms of sales.

Jay Adams Bob Biniak Shogo Kubo

Z BOYS are back

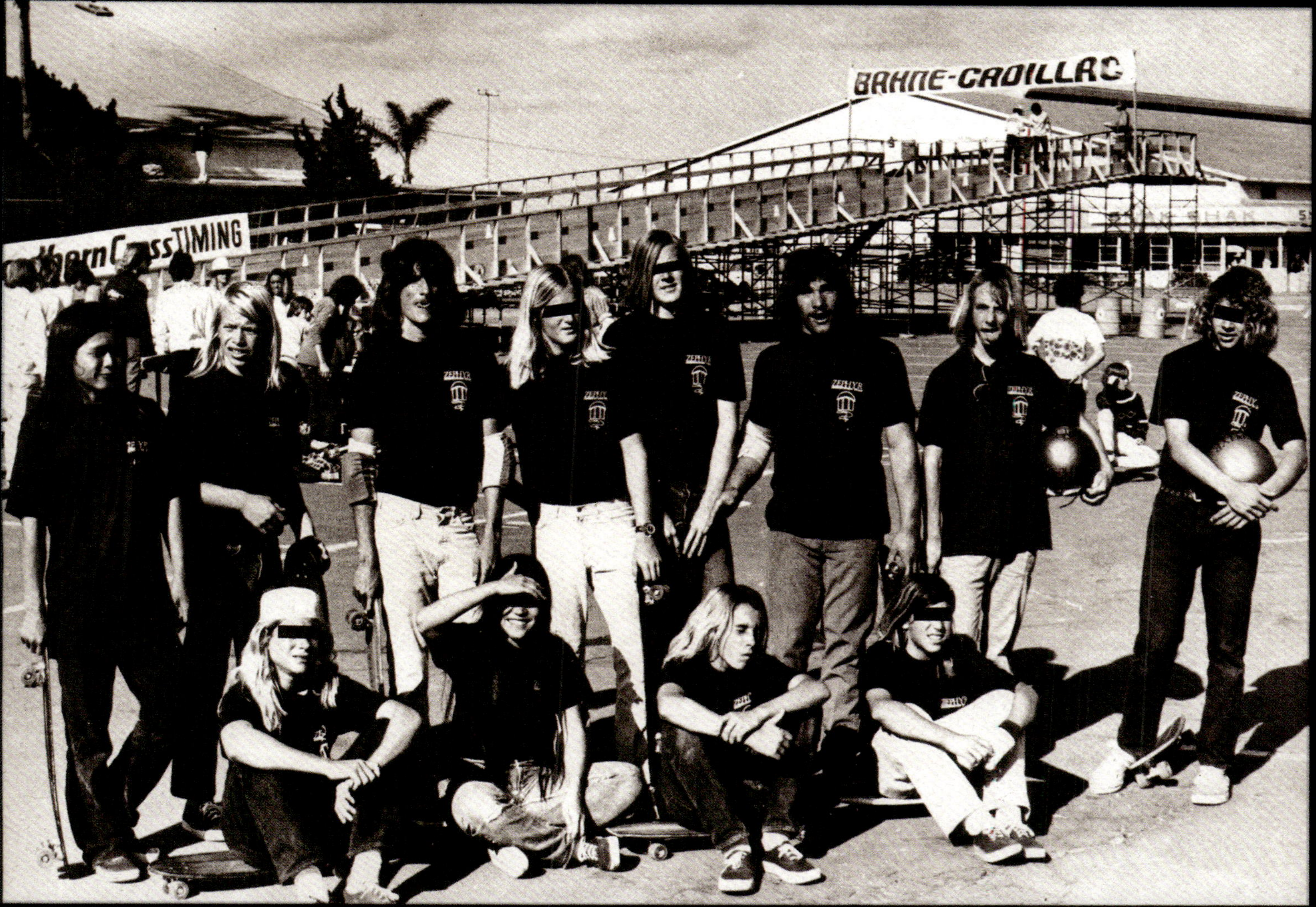

The original Zephyr skate designed by Jeff Ho is a landmark in the evolution of the sport. Pick one up, feel the weight, check out the width, rocker and bottom configuration. See who was five years ahead of everyone else back then. Carefully examine this team photo from the '74 Del Mar Nationals. (Due to ego and legal trips certain highly recognizable persons have been obscured.) The Z boys created the revolution that the rest are still following. Now go to the source. No matter what some dogs tell you, it's clear where they stole "their" tricks. Examine one of the new Zephyr skates and see why history repeats itself.

Kanvas by Katin
CUSTOM SURF TRUNKS
SURFSIDE, CALIF.
ZEPHYR
factory team
ZEPHYR

Asked about the secret to Zephyr's sweeping success, Cris Dawson, team rider and designer some of Zephyr's key advertisements, offered: "Be original. That's the most important thing. You don't have to try to do something that catches on. If it's powerful enough for the time, it will catch on." And catch on it did, as every issue of *SkateBoarder* featured a new Stecyk story on the exploits of Dogtown riders, forever embedding the new style of bank and pool riding into skateboarding's collective consciousness. Dogtown had become more than an area, but a global movement, an icon sprayed on ramps and skate park walls across the planet. "'The whole thing has been going on up here for a long time, now the trip is out of the bag, and the influence is spreading," said Tony Alva in 1976's article on The Westside Style.

FASHION APPEAL

With its revolutionary edge and progressive attitude - including never-before-seen maneuvers captured by photographer Glen E. Friedman - the "Westside Style" of skateboarding caught on in a big way. The skateboard business, powered by the thrills of vertical pool skating - where the Dogtowners led the charge - rose again. In late 1975, skateboarding was on the fast track to becoming a $400 million per year industry by the end of the following year. Bolstered by skyrocketing sales, Zephyr expanded its apparel offering, creating new shirts with full-color print designs - including Pacific Island-style flower ornaments and surf scenes - in new colorways such as purple and orange. "The shirts went from blue to orange with purple-ish ink. More like a Buddhist style," said Craig R. Stecyk.

The reasoning behind the orange shirts, according to Skip Engblom, was Zephyr's earlier commissioning of track suits for competition use. "The reason why we got the orange suits and shirts is I went up to this company called White Stag up in Oregon, and convinced them they needed to sponsor the team. And they gave us all the sweats and everything. So we ordered the orange T-shirts to go with the sweat pants and shirts, branded in the back 'White Stag from Oregon.' Stacy was wearing one at the Long Beach contest." Another T-shirt design, created by Cris Dawson, took the Zephyr logo into the realm of corporate insignia: "It looked like a rubber stamp, which was a joke," said Stecyk.

Despite their popularity, Zephyr shirts and other apparel never figured prominently in the overall product line-up. While brands such as SIMS, G&S, and Logan Earth Ski went all-in with their apparel offerings by producing elaborate jerseys and entire team uniforms, Zephyr kept operating as a hardgoods manufacturer. Asked about the Zephyr shop's spread between soft and hardgoods, Nathan Pratt said: "It was all hardgoods! And one rack of t-shirts, one rack of trunks, one rack of girl's bikinis, one case with sandals, and wax and leashes."

TOO MUCH OF A GOOD THING

Ultimately, this focus on hardware proved Zephyr's downfall. In late 1975, the house that Jeff Ho, Skip Engblom, and Craig R. Stecyk III built tumbled, not for lack of success, but too much. When order numbers for Zephyr skateboards skyrocketed into the five-digits, manufacturing capacities could not keep up with demand. Plus, the board factory was allegedly selling identical boards under a brand name of their own, funneling profits away from Zephyr. "By Fall '75 it was over. Skip went to Hawaii by Christmas 1975, and Jeff struggled with the shop for the rest of 1976. Then he closed in Fall 1976," said Nathan Pratt, who took over the Zephyr store and opened his own surf and skate company in the same location in Spring 1977, branded Horizons West. The Zephyr fallout left some of the day's hottest pro riders in skateboarding in the market for sponsorship, as all leading skateboard manufacturers wanted a piece of Dogtown's edge - and star power - for their rosters. When the music stopped, leading Zephyr riders found a chair with companies such as Logan Earth Ski (Jay Adams, Tony Alva, Bob Biniak), Gordon & Smith (Stacy Peralta, Paul Constantineau), and SIMS (Shogo Kubo, Jim Muir). "A lot of these kids that I had on my team have become men in the industry. That is one of the things in this whole deal that was good," said Jeff Ho. Meanwhile, the implosion of Zephyr also left a vacuum for companies capitalizing on the Dogtown image, such as Z-Flex and Dogtown Skates; all staffed by Zephyr alumni and not exactly on speaking terms with one another.

Hostilities between former team riders came to a head in 1979, when Jeff Ho resurrected the Zephyr company with Jay, Shogo, and Biniak as team riders, firing shots at defected team riders in a magazine ad with their faces blacked out in the famous team photo from the 1975 Del Mar Nationals: "Due to ego and legal trips certain highly recognizable persons have been obscured. [...] No matter what some dogs tell you, it's clear where they stole 'their' tricks," the ad read, while proclaiming that, 'The Z boys created the revolution that the rest are still following." According to an insider, this advertisement marks "the first usage of the term 'Z Boys.' It had never been copywritten but Jeff Ho was the first one to use it."

DOGTOWN REALTY INC.

The 'Dogtown' phenomenon has since been commercialized, commodified, and marketed to infinity. As Craig Stecyk III already observed in a 1979 *SkateBoarder* magazine article: "The name Dogtown is now 'trademarked.' The skaters, instead of walking, now drive imported cars. Some carve for currency. [...] Dogtown has gone uptown or, more precisely, Uptown has gone Dogtown." Today, Dogtown and the Stecyk-designed cross logo advertise everything from Yoga classes, real estate agencies, hotdog vendors, all the way to household cleaners and auto repair shops. While popular belief now equates Dogtown with Venice Beach, the actual birthplace of skateboarding's hardcore movement in Southside Santa Monica has lost much of its edge from the days of hookers on Main Street. Surrounded by coveted beach view condos, Jeff Ho's former Zephyr store is now home to a cozy cafe, Dogtown Coffee (DTC), serving fairly traded coffee specialties and brunch. Walls lined with vintage skateboards and photographs of the Zephyr team keep the memories alive.

Some things never change, though. Out-of-towners still get robbed in broad daylight on the Venice Beach ocean front walk. And although some surviving members of the tribe are still not on speaking terms - "Jeff Ho and I don't talk," Skip Engblom told us - the Legend of Zephyr lives on today. In terms of stylistics and fashion appeal, Adams, Alva, Biniak, Cahill, Constantineau, Kubo, Muir, Oki, Peralta, Pratt, Ruml, and Sarlo have successfully introduced a template into skateboarding apparel that will forever remain relevant. Says 1970s pro skateboarder Brad Bowman: "Dogtown has always had its own look. [The Z-Boys] always had those canvas shoes with rubber bottoms, and plain front khakis and tank tops. Plus, the Suicidal Tendencies look. That look has been around for 40 to 45 years. And even today, anyone who wants to be represented as a hardcore-looking dude still dresses like that."

Photo: Glen E. Friedman

BOARD PARKS

SKATE PARK SHIRTS: REPRESENT YOUR TURF

Hardware innovations such as the kicktail, urethane wheel, and skateboard-specific truck propelled skateboarding into the Space Age. As skateboards evolved from dangerous toys on rickety clay wheels into performance-engineered assault vehicles, the only thing missing was the kind of innovative terrain commensurate with the wild imagination of a new wave of riders. Something more futuristic than wiggling through a slalom course, catching a downhill run, or spinning 360s on flat ground. Something straight from the future, like skating a crater on the moon, or flying through the air with all four wheels lifted off the ground, weightless. Something, in the parlance of the times, far out.

Those (half)pipe dreams became reality with the dawn of a new era of skateboarding terrain: In February 1976, the first modern skatepark opened in Port Orange, Florida. A sprawling wonderland of moon-like craters and basins poured from the smoothest concrete, Skateboard City offered next-gen riding thrills such as bowls, moguls, and winding snake runs. One week later, Carlsbad Skatepark in California opened as the first commercial concrete wonderland on the West coast. And like popcorn rattling in a kettle, hundreds of skateparks began popping up all over the U.S., Europe, South America, Australia, and Asia, as a new generation of skateboarders rose to the challenge.

Riders such as Duane Peters, Tony Alva, Steve and Micke Alba, Eddie Elguera, Rick Blackhart, Stacy Peralta, and Steve Olson built the foundations of their influential pro careers as skatepark locals on their respective home turfs. "Concrete Wave [in Anaheim] was my skatepark. My brother worked there and I skated it every single day. That's where I honed all my shit at," said 1970s pro skateboarder Steve Olson, proudly adding: "We helped build that pool, that was the first pool in a skate park!" Local pride ran deep among park regulars, and graphic T-shirts with park-specific logos and artwork became a popular way of representing their home turf while celebrating the fresh new way to skate. The T-shirt for Cosmic Waves skatepark in Kalamazoo, Michigan, featured a stylized image of a skateboarder floating through space, Silver Surfer-style, catching a moon-shaped wave. The logo for Moon Dust Skateboard Parks in Sheboygan, Wisconsin depicted a gravity-defying frontside air under the moon and stars. The future had arrived, and it was groovy.

UNIQUE BY DESIGN

From 1976 until the end of the decade, specialized skatepark construction firms such as Campo Constructions, Skatepark Constructors, and American Recreational Properties ran full-page advertisements in skateboarding magazines to draw riders to their parks. Advertised as, "The Sport of the Future, The Future in Sports," the Skater Cross facility in Reseda, California offered "swimming pool-type bowls, tubes, jumps, vertical walls - all in one continuous downhill course!" This super-charged mash-up of completely unrelated terrains may sound crazy, mostly because it was. Nevertheless, many riders enjoyed the new flavor: "Skater Cross was kind of cool, it was like a motorbike track and had a vert corner around the side," said 1970s pro skateboarder Wes Humpston.

But whereas skatepark designers today are creating new parks from similar templates, their mid-1970s counterparts were marching to their own drummer. "Each skatepark had a different design. Each was like a different kind of skating," said Wes Humpston. For maximum allure, every skatepark needed a centerpiece attraction; a unique design feature offering maximum stoke factor that could be found nowhere else.

ROACH
M
apple
Skateboard Park – Columbus Ohio
SIERRA
WAVE
SKATE PARK

THE CONCRETE WAVE
SKATEBOARD PARK

Now the best skatepark membership program is even better. New features like monthly passes, tourist and birthday specials, contests with great prizes and – the big bonus – sessions at the WILD WILD WET – the world's largest water slide – only the CONCRETE WAVE gives you the hottest skating and the coolest slide.

Send today for your membership kit. You'll also want the official CONCRETE WAVE T-Shirt.

Order now for holiday gifts.

I'll see you at the Concrete Wave.

Don't miss our first anniversary celebration Thanksgiving week – Enter the biggest amateur contest ever held. Thousands of dollars in prizes plus one of the biggest displays of equipment you've ever seen.

COSMIC WAVES
SKATEBOARD PARK

WHITTIER
Skate City
CALIFORNIA

COSMIC
WAVES'
SKATEBOARD
TEAM
Kalamazoo, Mich.

STAFF

"Skatetopia was a classic park because it had the first half pipe in a park. Upland because it was the first full-pipe in a park. Marina Del Rey because it had the Dog Bowl. And they had the big contests. These were places where tricks were invented and monumental events happened that defined competitive skateboarding and vertical skateboarding," said skateboarder and rapper Gerry "Skatemaster Tate" Hurtado.

In the search for marketable attractions, everything was fair game to skatepark operators: Anaheim's Concrete Wave bordered on the Wild Wild Wet water park, thus the owners advertised the park as offering, "the hottest skating and the coolest slide." Other parks kept it "real" by drawing on actual skate spots discovered out in the wild: The Pipeline Skatepark in Upland, Northern California, became notorious for its enormous full-pipe, modelled on the legendary Mt. Baldy pipeline in the Badlands. "We used to skate these places that they eventually duplicated in the park. Like the L-pool or the Mount Baldy pipeline," said Gerry Hurtado, pointing out that the legacy of Upland's legendary Combi Pool endures today in Orange, California, as a truthful replica in the Vans Skatepark.

Spilling out into skate fashion, these marquee park attractions also featured prominently in the official skatepark logos and artwork, available on T-shirts, hats, and stickers. Designed by 1960s pro skater and graphic artist Cris Dawson, the logo for the Marina Del Rey Skatepark prominently rendered the park's signature audio speakers blasting music over the skaters' heads. The logo for the Del Mar Skateboard Ranch - designed by legendary skate artist Pushead in return for a free one-year park pass - featured the park's legendary keyhole pool, while Upland's logo showed the Pipeline with the word "Badlands" signalling local pride.

"I always loved wearing shirts when there was a local element, like the Del Mar or Upland skatepark shirts. Those were legendary and a lot of it had to do with the quality of the logos," said skateboard photographer Jim Goodrich, adding: "And if people liked the logo, that went a long way for the parks." At the height of the park era, official skatepark T-shirts from some of skateboarding's landmark facilities - including Hester pro contest series stops such as Big O., Upland, Winchester, Hi Roller, Del Mar, Whittier, and Spring Valley - became coveted souvenirs among visitors. Experience marketing at its finest, the shirts emerged as tokens of been-there-done-that skatepark tourism.

EXIT THROUGH THE PRO SHOP

For traveling skateboarders, picking up a skatepark shirt at the pro shop became a rite of passage; a notch in the belt; memories of where they skated. "When you were from out of town, that's what you got. I always got the shirts and even went and got the stickers from the park," said Gerry Hurtado, whose first paying job was doing chores and park patrol at Skatopia skatepark. When Hurtado was promoted to Skatopia's pro shop, he sold quite a few park shirts to visitors. "I remember we had a team come all the way from New Zealand, and they all got shirts and hats, and stickers." On that note, Hurtado pointed out that stickers were rare collectibles, because "the sticker runs at a skate park were 50% less than any company, and they were out of a garage done by the skaters themselves." Although graphic tees provided a welcome revenue boost to pro shops - a tough market overall, Val Surf pulled out of running Endless Wave's shop in Oxnard after a year - their overall sales share was negligible in what was still mainly a hardware-driven market. "Back then it was 75% boards, trucks and wheels. Very little clothing, and the only clothing people bought back then were T-shirts and hats," said Gerry Hurtado.

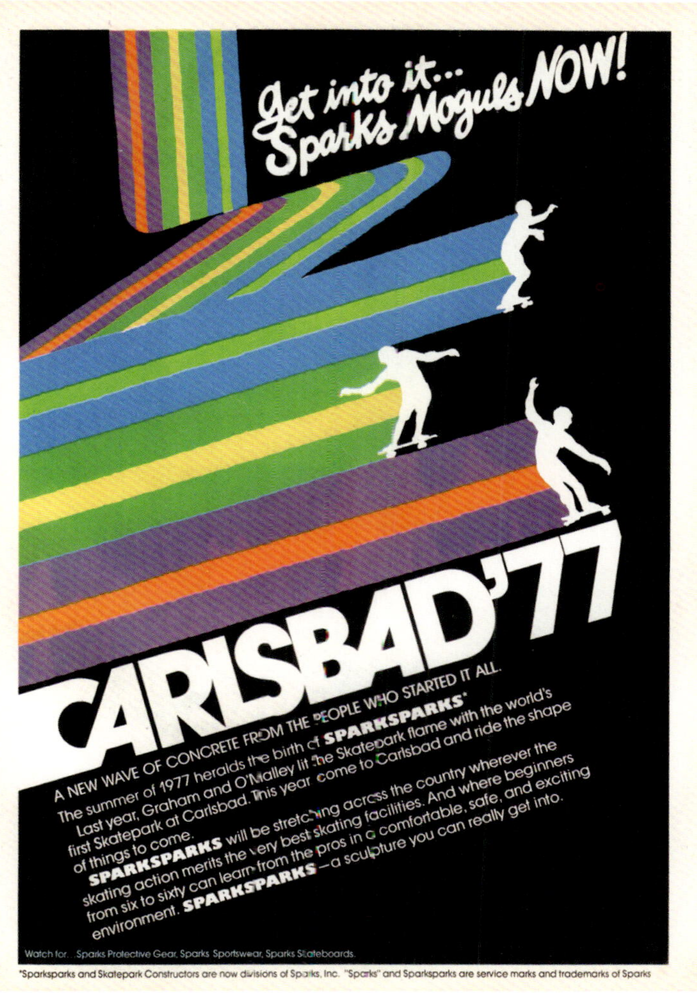

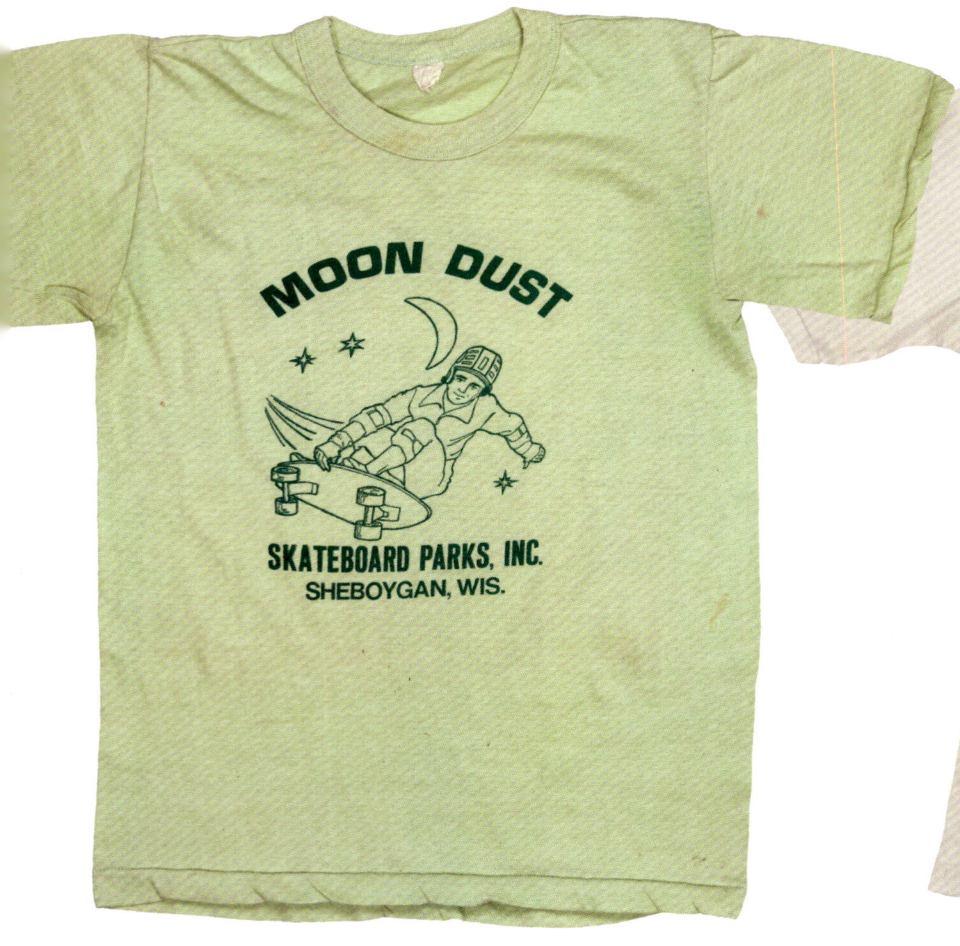
MOON DUST
SKATEBOARD PARKS, INC.
SHEBOYGAN, WIS.

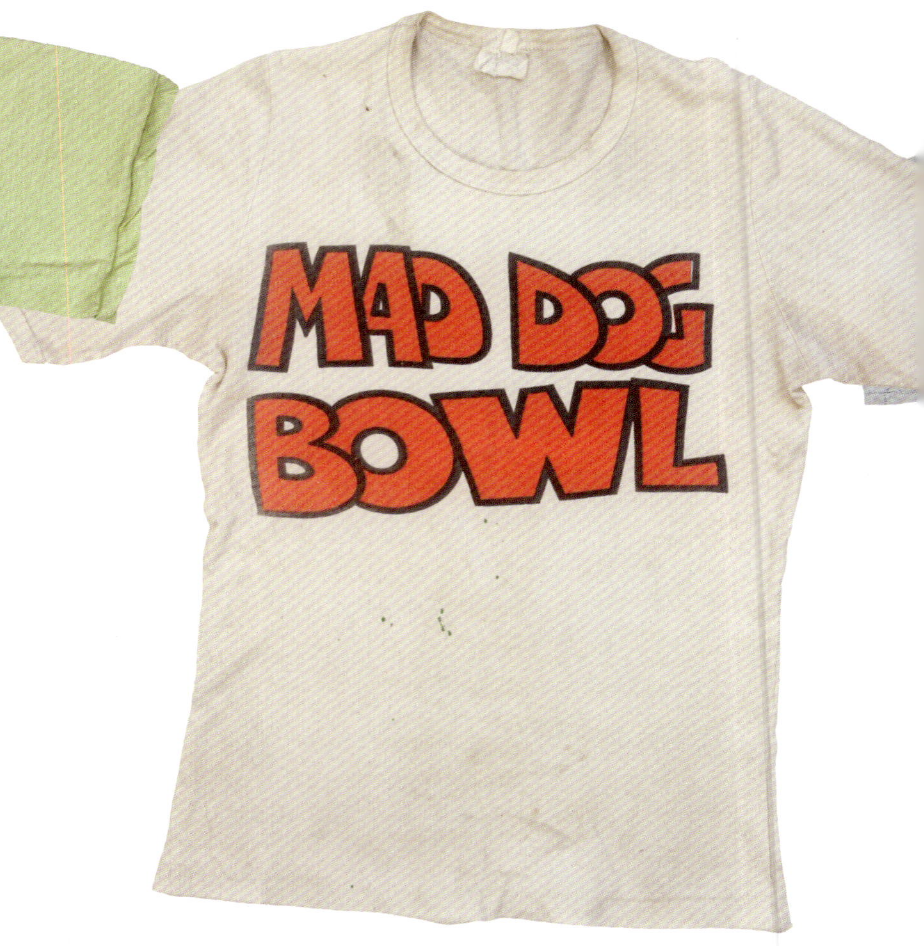
MAD DOG
BOWL

Winchester
Skate Park

SKATEBOARD
SAFARI
West Palm Beach,
Florida

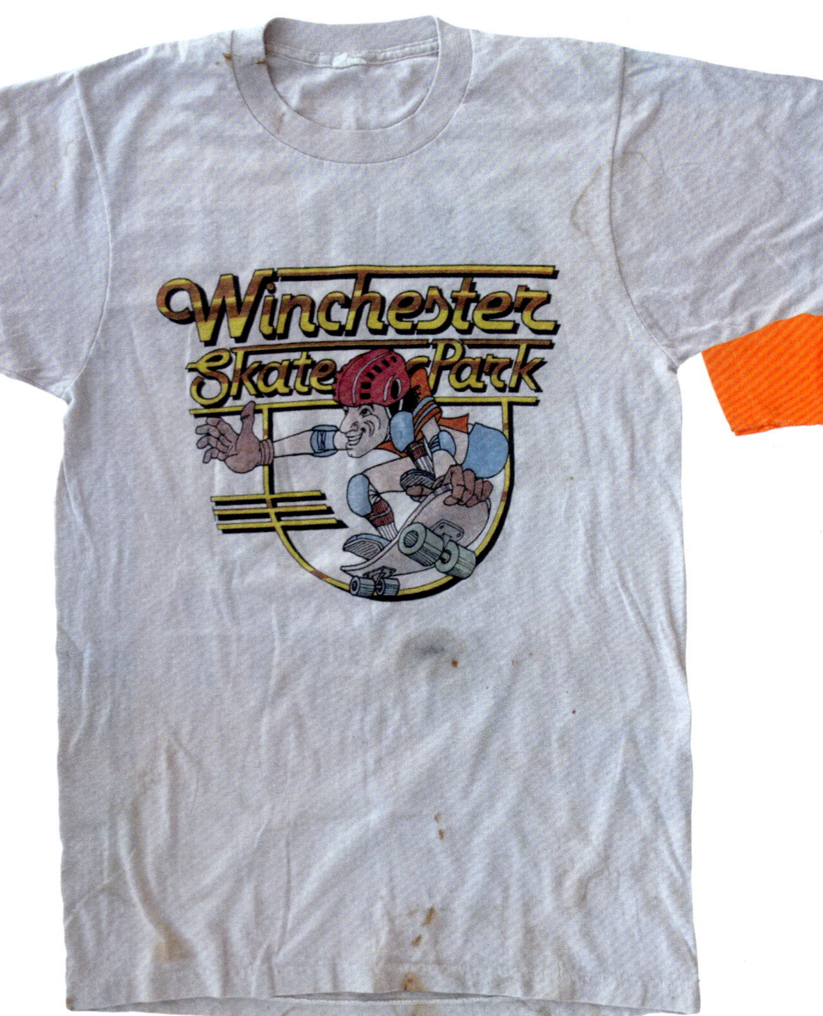

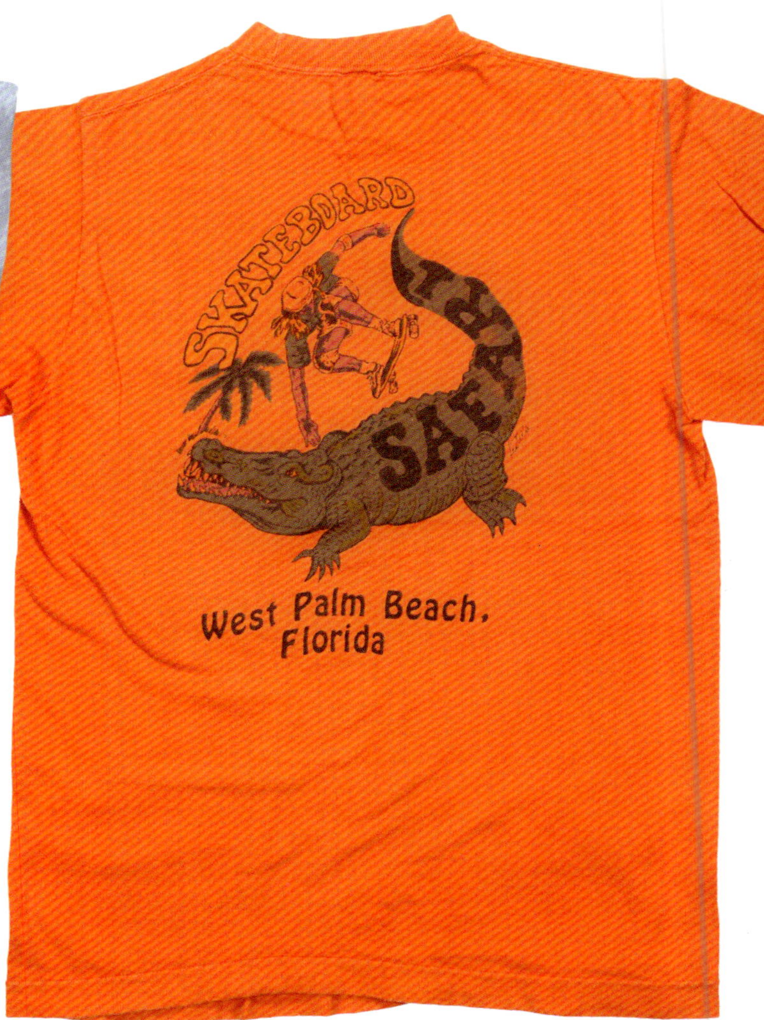

SKATEBOARD
WORLD

Winchester
SkatePark

DEL MAR
SKATEBOARD
RANCH
CALIFORNIA

big
O
SKATEPARK

big
O
SKATEPARK

Photo: Jim Goodrich

OFF THE WALL
THE PIPELINE
UPLAND, CA.

Photo: Thib[illegible]aux

On top 1970s THE PIPELINE team rider shirt, botton row 1980s team rider shirts.

MARINA DEL REY
SKATEPARK
MARINA DEL REY
SKATEPARK
"Home of The New Dog Bowl"

Some fortunate skaters did not have to spend their own money on buying skatepark tees. "I was pro so whenever I went to a new park, they gave me a new shirt. And throw in a key chain and some stickers," said pro skateboarder Eddie Elguera, adding: "When you signed up for the contests like the Hester series, you also got a free park shirt." Michael Chantry, skate photographer and part of the original Hobie team in 1965, also remembers: "Everywhere we went, I always tried to get a skate park shirt to take with me. And I never had to pay since I was pro, so that was cool."

TURF WARS

Aside from the pros, the only other people eligible to receive free skatepark T-shirts were staff members - clearly identified by STAFF printed or embroidered on the sleeves or back of the shirt - and also the amateur team riders. "The people on the amateur circuit were mostly the ones wearing the skatepark shirts. The pros already were already sponsored, so they had their company shirts," said Steve Caballero. "I had my Campbell skatepark shirt with my name, Steve. The shirts were important for parks to advertise and also because the parks had their own teams." Skateparks also served as launch pads for successful pro careers.

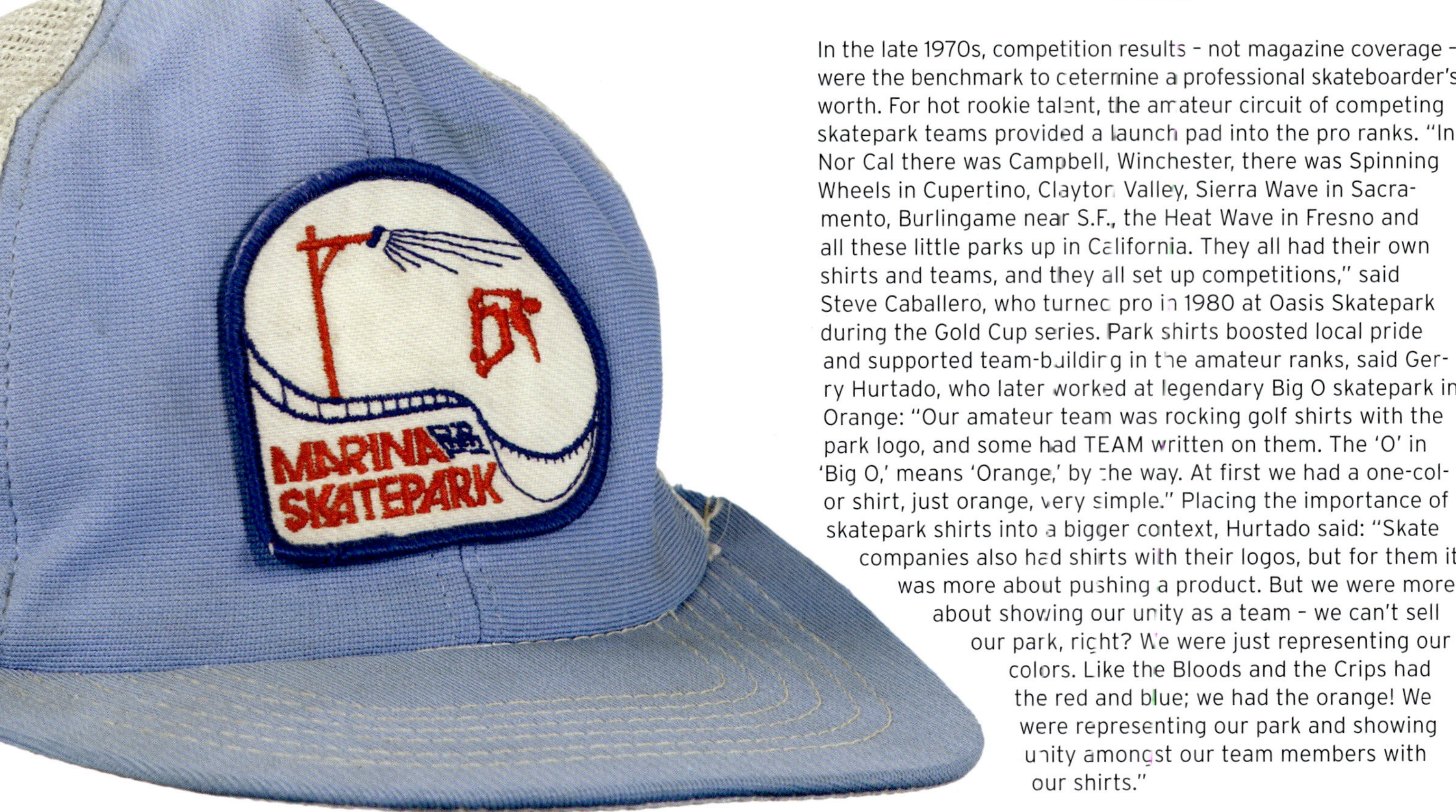

In the late 1970s, competition results - not magazine coverage - were the benchmark to determine a professional skateboarder's worth. For hot rookie talent, the amateur circuit of competing skatepark teams provided a launch pad into the pro ranks. "In Nor Cal there was Campbell, Winchester, there was Spinning Wheels in Cupertino, Clayton Valley, Sierra Wave in Sacramento, Burlingame near S.F., the Heat Wave in Fresno and all these little parks up in California. They all had their own shirts and teams, and they all set up competitions," said Steve Caballero, who turned pro in 1980 at Oasis Skatepark during the Gold Cup series. Park shirts boosted local pride and supported team-building in the amateur ranks, said Gerry Hurtado, who later worked at legendary Big O skatepark in Orange: "Our amateur team was rocking golf shirts with the park logo, and some had TEAM written on them. The 'O' in 'Big O,' means 'Orange,' by the way. At first we had a one-color shirt, just orange, very simple." Placing the importance of skatepark shirts into a bigger context, Hurtado said: "Skate companies also had shirts with their logos, but for them it was more about pushing a product. But we were more about showing our unity as a team - we can't sell our park, right? We were just representing our colors. Like the Bloods and the Crips had the red and blue; we had the orange! We were representing our park and showing unity amongst our team members with our shirts."

RAMPAGE
DEL MAR OPEN
PRO/AM
RAMPAGE
DEL MAR OPEN
PRO/AM
RAMPAGE
HESTER SERIES
N.S.C.F.

Get off on the RAMP-AGE

RAMPAGE has been on top of the ramp scene since the first lofty tracks were explored. We at RAMPAGE have put a lot of time and energy into the ramp-riding concept (see "On The Rampage", SKATEBOARD, Oct. '77, Vol. 4 No. 3) and now feel confident in bringing the results to you. We offer a simple, do-it-yourself design package for one of three hot RAMPAGE ramps. Included in the package is the critical curvature template which gives you the most desirable transition for your skating surface, and blueprints rendering Tom Stewart's ramp designs in easy to read form to make it easy, yet exact, to build your own RAMPAGE. You also receive a full materials list with each ramp plan package. Now you can have your own RAMPAGE ramp to expand your abilities with unlimited time, and no crowds....maybe. Be the first in your area to build your own RAMPAGE. Start a team, have a contest, the possibilities are in your own hands. There's no hassle with OFF LIMITS skate terrain because you build RAMPAGE where you want it. We make it easy and inexpensive to build a professional-style skating surface. So go with a proven winner - after all, there is a little RAMPAGE in all of us.

Tom Stewart on the original Rampage. Photo: Warren Bolster

Please send mail orders to: RAMPAGE, INC. P.O. Box 226, Encinitas, CA 92024

Ramp Plan Packages Include: blueprint plans, curvature template, full color poster, 2 stickers - $12.50. Plan A - ¼ Pipe ☐ Plan B - ½ Pipe ☐ Plan C - Lip Slide ☐.

Rampage "Eagle" T-Shirts: SS - $6.50 sm ☐ med ☐ lg ☐ xl ☐; LS - $7.50 sm ☐ med ☐ lg ☐ xl ☐; Ladies - $7.50 sm ☐ med ☐

Circle two color choices: orange, yellow, natural, green, burgundy, red, lt. blue.

Full Color Poster: 17"x22" - $2.50 ☐

Stickers: Rampage Logo - $1.00 ☐ Rampage Eagle - $1.50 ☐.

Postage & handling add .75 (U.S.A.), $1.50 (foreign). California Residents add 6% sales tax.

Enclosed $ ____________

Name ____________

Address ____________

City ________ State ________ Zip ________

Dealer/Demo/Pack Design/Consulting inquiries invited.

Poster Design: Norm Vitale

UNDERCOVER BROTHERS - INOUYE'S POOL SERVICE

Photo: Sharp

Get it while you can. The severe 1975 drought had unlocked a wealth of empty swimming pools across Los Angeles County, single-handedly establishing the area as the new frontier of vertical skateboarding. Pool riding pioneers such as Tony Alva and Stacy Peralta would cruise affluent neighborhoods in their cars - with Jay Adams on the roof on lookout - in search of tasty transitions and tiled walls in those days before Google Maps and widely available satellite imagery. But once skaters found a pool, one key challenge remained: Located on private properties, pools were essentially forbidden fruit, with neighbors less than welcoming to hordes of skateboarding hoodlums in their backyards. Complicating matters, most pools - even without fresh water - still held residual liquid, requiring hours of draining, enough for Neighborhood Watch to call the police.

Enter Tom "Wally" Inouye from Los Angeles. As one of the era's most popular pool skaters - the "Wally" nickname reflects his ability for high turns on vertical pool walls - Inouye firmly believed that the future of skateboarding would lie in riding the rounded terrain of skate parks, banks, and empty swimming pools. And to access those pools - even if it meant hopping a white picket fence - Inouye found a way to hide in plain sight: In 1976, he started his own company, Inouye's Pool Service (IPS), as a cover operation for his crew's nefarious pool hunting antics.

"We started IPS so we could get into people's backyards to drain their pools. We were getting caught draining people's pools all the time, so we came up with a fictitious pool company," said Tom "Wally" Inouye. The rest is history: Wielding professional pool draining equipment, the crew would pull up in an IPS-branded truck wearing IPS T-shirts and getting to work before the skate session could commence. True heist movie material, but true. In the late 1970s skateboarding scene, Tom "Wally" Inouye and company partner Chris Strople became legends, their IPS T-shirts and stickers adopted as emblems of hardcore pool riders.

GUERRILLA STYLE

Historically, the use of outward appearances as distractions from underlying motives has been documented since the days of the Trojan Horse. Known in military circles as "ruses de guerre" - literally meaning "ruses of war" - examples of deceptive tactics include the British ocean liner RMS Lusitania's attempt in 1915 to escape German submarine fire by flying the neutral American flag (thus spawning the term "false flag" operation). Outside the military domain, one of the biggest robberies of all time - the 1950 Brinks Armored Car depot heist in Boston - was carried out by men wearing Brinks company employee uniforms to haul in a stunning $2.7 million in bank notes undetected. Not stealing any money, just a few hours of sessioning otherwise off-limits pool terrain, Inouye's Pool Service became a Robin Hood figure of the budding pool skating scene. Leading manufacturers began making IPS-branded products, including skateboards (Caster Skateboards) and trucks (Gullwing Truck Co.). Meanwhile, the company's own marketing materials started rather grassroots: "Of course we needed an official company shirt, but when we made the original IPS shirts, we only made two of them," said Tom "Wally" Inouye about the first run of tees, which have since become collector's items.

INOUYE'S
POOL
SERVICE

INOUYE'S
POOL SERVICE

As a constant advocate of pool riding, Tom "Wally" Inouye encouraged skatepark owners to involve skateboarders more closely in the design process: "I think skating could advance a lot faster if they would just start building better skateparks," he said in his 1978 Skateboard World interview. Putting his money where his mouth is, Inouye expanded IPS into full-fledged park design company, whose early projects included design of the famous Del Mar Skate Ranch, conceptualized by Inouye and Chris Strople in 1978 with design input from Curtis Hesselgrave. How many pools and parks has "Wally" built since then? "I can't count! I need more than my fingers, probably hundreds," he said.

Today, Tom Inouye runs a skate shop under the IPS flag in Hood River, Oregon, also offering T-shirts, wheels, and skateboards. Speaking of his influence, Wally noticed: "Nowadays every [skate] company has a pool service [T-shirt], like 'Foundation's Pool Service.'" With thousands of pools drained and hundreds of new ones built, IPS is charging ahead while looking back on a storied legacy. Sitting next to pool skating legend Steve Alba at a recent Vans Pool Party contest, Wally said: "We even taught this guy right here how to find and drain pools. Right, Steve?" To which Salba replied: "I learned from the fucking best!"

HANDY ACCESSORIES: SKATEBOARD CARRIERS

From a product marketing perspective, the Skate Park Era proved one of the biggest windfalls in skateboarding history. Now that skate parks strictly enforced wearing a mandatory armor of pads, gloves, and helmets, sales for safety equipment were soaring. And as the next logical innovation, a wide number of equipment manufacturers offered specifically-designed board bags for lugging around all that extra gear on the way to the skate park. "These skateboard carrying cases will provide an attractive alternative for transporting your skateboards and protective gear from home to safe, well managed skateparks and other supervised skateboarding areas," read a Skateboarding magazine advertisement for OMAC skateboard cases.

In the same vein, most marketing initiatives for skateboard carriers focused on the fact that skateboarding was now a"real" sport, exercised in the safe confines of purpose-built skate parks. What's more, youngsters had limited access to cars, and skateboarding on sidewalks was outlawed all across the U.S. in the late 1970s. So young skateboarders had to rely on bikes or public transportation in order to get to their nearest skate park. This made bags a logical necessity - at least in terms of marketing logic - justifying premium price points.

DIFFERENT DESIGNS

The most minimalist carrier was marketed by LA-based company Rainbow Blaze: The SkateSling consisted of a nylon shoulder strap connected to a canvas harness that wrapped around the middle of the skateboard. The contraption allowed for slinging the skateboard over one shoulder, much like a guitar strap. Marketed as a "lightweight, durable, washable skateboard carrier," the SkateSling could be folded into a satchel worn around the hip during skate sessions. Launched in 1978, the SkateSling was available in different versions for wood, aluminum, or fibreglass skateboards from 24 inches to 33 inches in length at $13.95 retail (equivalent of $45.00 in 2018). A Buyer's Guide in the 1978 edition of *Skateboard Industry News* magazine suggested: "The SkateSling is especially useful while riding a bicycle, and the skateboard is in the SkateSling, it can be hung up, for safety and convenience." Equipment company OMAC out of Los Alamitos, California, introduced Great Cover Ups, protective board sleeves reminiscent of tennis racket covers. The protective skateboard carriers offered a zipper opening in the middle for easy access to the skateboard and accessories. The lightweight bags were available in a variety of materials including top-grain leather, canvas and vinyl. For added mobility, Great Cover Ups incorporated a "unique strap" that "allows you to carry the case over your shoulder, on your back, or in your hand." Bike-mounting options for skateboard bags were offered by the Merrick Skateboard Products Division, which sold a specific Skateboard Carrier rack for the Pro Pack series, compatible with any style of bike.

Skateboard hardware manufacturers such as Santa Cruz skateboards and Powell-Peralta also launched their own skate bags in the late 1970s. Designed in the style of military-issue duffel bags – a cylindrical canvas bag that derives its name from cloth produced in the Belgian town of Duffel – these affordable carriers proved a big hit with the skate park crowd. Many park skaters took to adorning their skate duffels with marker pens and patches embroidered with skateboard company logos. And even when novelty designs such as the SkateSling ultimately went the way of previous fads, the trusty duffel bag remained a staple in the skateboard scene.

OJ WHEELS
ROAD RIDER
ACS
TRUCKS
makaha
SKATE BOARD CLUB

SANTA
CRUZ

SANTA CRUZ
SKATEBOARDS

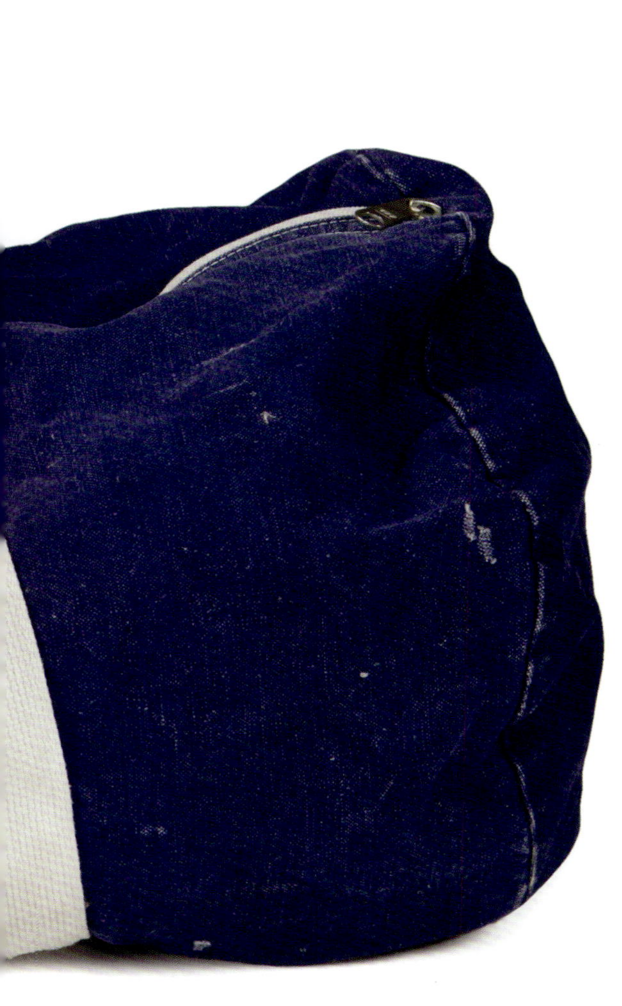

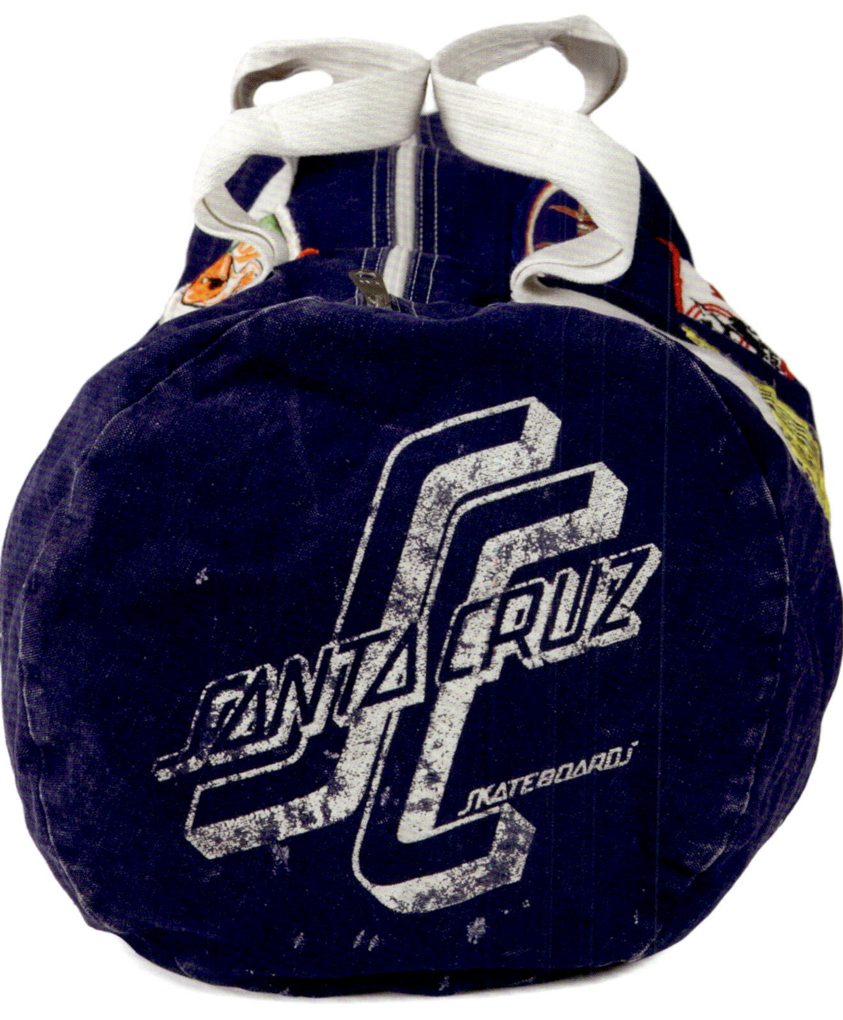

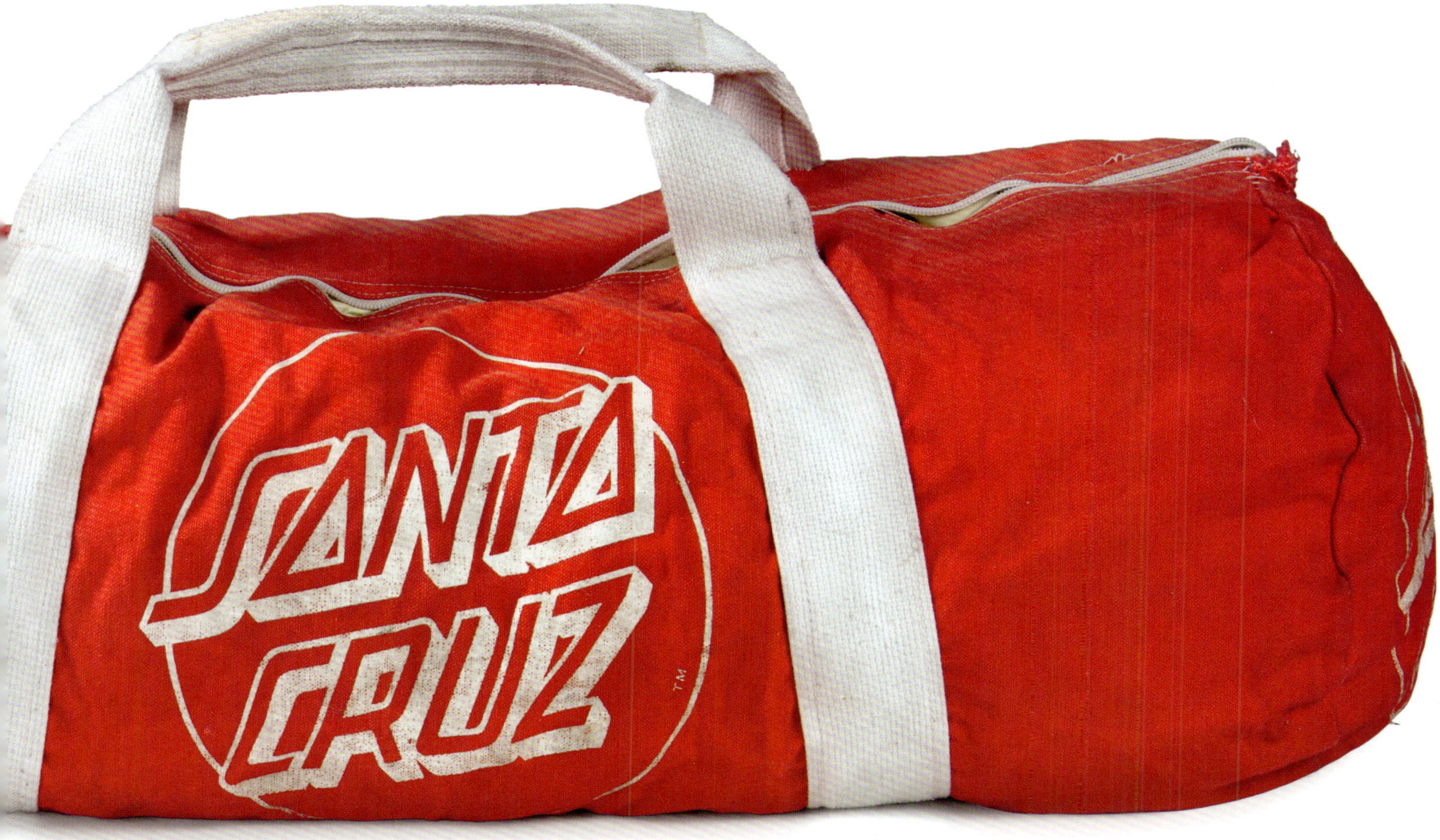
SANTA CRUZ
TM

THE PRO'S CHOICE: ROBINAK PACKS

Marketed under the slogan "Keep it all together," Robinak Packs out of Santa Barbara, California, set the gold standard for professional-grade skateboard carriers. Sold at premium price points, the brightly colored nylon bags were highly coveted items, endorsed by an A-list professional skate team including SIMS riders Frank Blood and Lonnie Toft, among others.

"Everybody wanted one, because Brad Bowman and Doug de Montmorency rode for them. Robinak Packs were one of those cool things you just wanted to have, and really neat to put all your stuff in," said 1980s pro skateboarder Eddie "El Gato" Elguera. Fellow pro skater Lance Mountain agrees: "Robinak Packs were the most popular packs. Those were the ones all the pros had - so that's what everyone wanted. You wish you had it!"

Wishful thinking is what owning a Robinak Pack remained for many skateboarders, due to the high retail price of $17.00 (equivalent to $59.00 in 2018). For perspective, a complete pro model skateboard such as the 27-inch Stacy Peralta Warptail model by G&S Skateboards retailed for $17.95 in 1977. So it's no surprise that Robinak Packs remained highly coveted items, and in many cases, for pros only. Or as advertisements said: "Designed by the Pros/Built by the Pros/Used by the Pros."

KEEPING IT TOGETHER

Available in four colors - red, green, royal blue and navy - the Robinak "Skatepack" was the company's flagship product. Designed as a backpack with adjustable shoulder straps featuring nickel-coated buckles, the Skatepack was constructed out of durable six-ounce two-ply nylon, waterproof from the inside. The main compartment held a skateboard - keep in mind that late-1970s skateboards were highly compact at an average 27 inches length, 7 inches width - held securely in place by three draw cord locks. The front of the Skatepack featured an 8-by-11 inch zippered pouch for storing tools and spare parts.

According to advertisements in premier skateboard magazines, Robinak's Skatepack was "just right for packing away your board when bicycling to your favorite spot or park." For advanced riders, the company introduced the Pro Duffle in 1978; a duffle bag-style skate carrier with a horizontal zipper opening, large enough to hold a full array of pads, spare wheels, and a helmet for the small price of $33.00 (equivalent to $109.00). For extra safety points, Robinak's official First Aid Kit - a zippered nylon pouch with a belt loop - sold separately for $8.00 holding ACE bandages, plenty of BAND AIDS for "covering small cuts," and "first aid cream for minor cuts and bruises."

When the Skate Park Era came to a grinding halt in 1979, advertisements for Robinak Packs disappeared from skateboarding magazines. Today, all that's left are a few mint-condition pro bags floating around on eBay, while the company's origins remains shrouded in obscurity. But there are theories: Behind the scenes, Robinak Packs may have been a joint venture between SIMS Skateboards and a NorCal luggage company. "I think it was connected with SIMS. They licensed it out. Whenever they did ads, they had SIMS riders in it. It was not a skateboard brand, but they licensed it for skateboarding," said pro skateboarder Steve Caballero.

ROBINAK PACKS

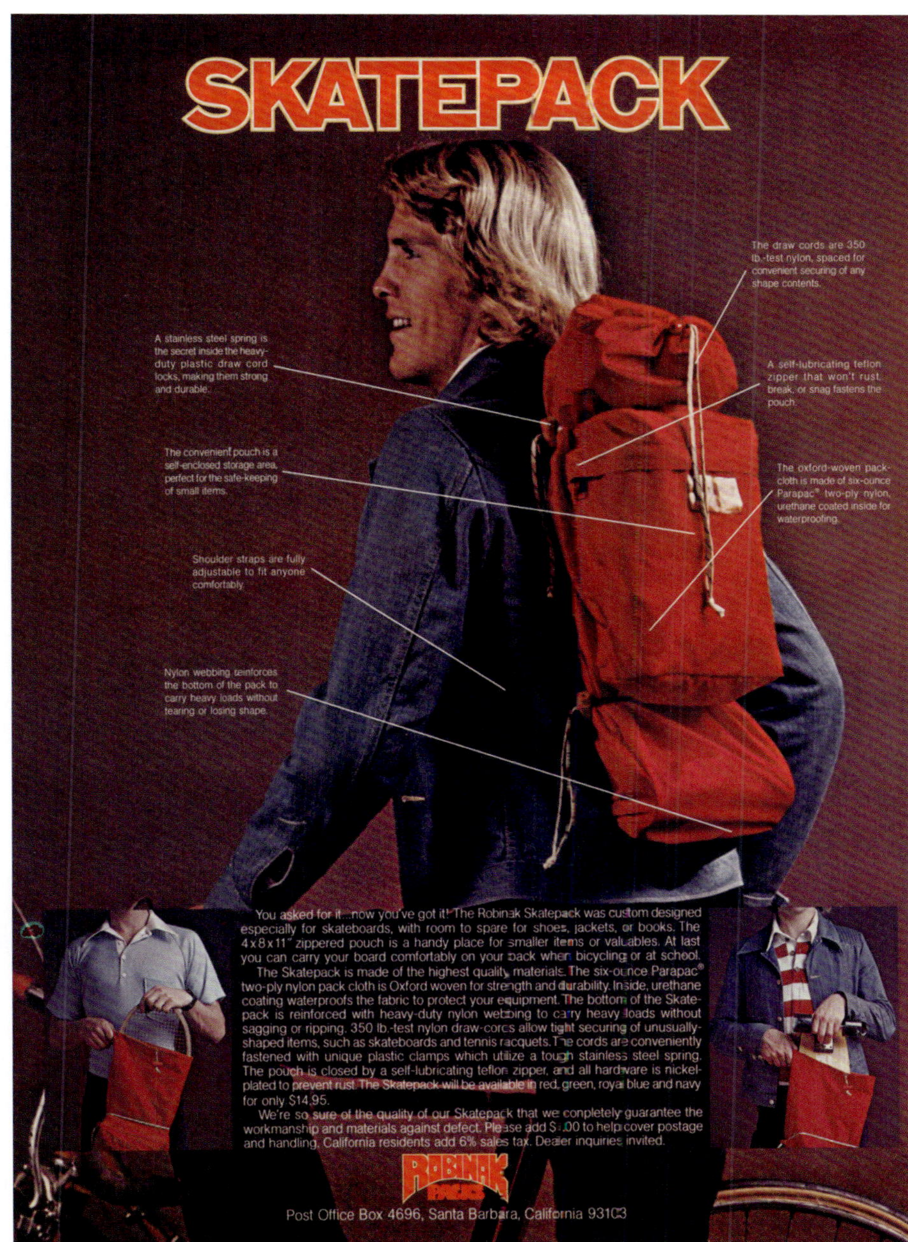
SKATEPACK
The draw cords are 350 lb.-test nylon, spaced for convenient securing of any shape contents.
A stainless steel spring is the secret inside the heavy-duty plastic draw cord locks, making them strong and durable.
A self-lubricating teflon zipper that won't rust, break, or snag fastens the pouch.
The convenient pouch is a self-enclosed storage area, perfect for the safe-keeping of small items.
The oxford-woven pack-cloth is made of six-ounce Parapac® two-ply nylon, urethane coated inside for waterproofing.
Shoulder straps are fully adjustable to fit anyone comfortably.
Nylon webbing reinforces the bottom of the pack to carry heavy loads without tearing or losing shape.
You asked for it...now you've got it! The Robinak Skatepack was custom designed especially for skateboards, with room to spare for shoes, jackets, or books. The 4 x 8 x 11" zippered pouch is a handy place for smaller items or valuables. At last you can carry your board comfortably on your back when bicycling or at school.
The Skatepack is made of the highest quality materials. The six-ounce Parapac® two-ply nylon pack cloth is Oxford woven for strength and durability. Inside, urethane coating waterproofs the fabric to protect your equipment. The bottom of the Skatepack is reinforced with heavy-duty nylon webbing to carry heavy loads without sagging or ripping. 350 lb.-test nylon draw-cords allow tight securing of unusually-shaped items, such as skateboards and tennis racquets. The cords are conveniently fastened with unique plastic clamps which utilize a tough stainless steel spring. The pouch is closed by a self-lubricating teflon zipper, and all hardware is nickel-plated to prevent rust. The Skatepack will be available in red, green, royal blue and navy for only $14.95.
We're so sure of the quality of our Skatepack that we conpletely guarantee the workmanship and materials against defect. Please add $ .00 to help cover postage and handling. California residents add 6% sales tax. Dealer inquiries invited.
ROBINAK PACKS
Post Office Box 4696, Santa Barbara, California 93103

ROBINAK PACKS

THE SANTA CRUZ SKATEBOARD TOP IS LAMINATED UNDER EXTREME HEAT AND PRESSURE USING KILN DRIED HARDWOOD AND EPOXY GLASS PRODUCING MAXIMUM STRENGTH AND FLEX RETURN. AVAILABLE IN STANDARD W/CAMBER, CUTAWAY W/CAMBER, AND KICKTAIL, FLAT W/KICK. SEE YOUR SKATEBOARD DEALER FOR MORE INFO, T-SHIRTS AND DECALS.

BEARINGS

Photography: Dan Devine

NHS INC. • 825 41ST AVE., SANTA CRUZ, CA 95062 • (408) 475-9434

SCS: FULL SPEED AHEAD

In skateboarding culture, some company logos become more than just brand insignia. Some logos evolve into charged cultural symbols, displayed on shirts and skateboards - sometimes even inked into the skin to last forever - and worn with a sense of pride and belonging. Over the years, no other company has branded the collective skateboarding psyche with more high-profile insignia than NHS, the skateboard manufacturing outfit founded in 1973 by Rich Novak, Doug Haut, and Jay Shuirman (NHS is an acronym of their last names) in Santa Cruz, California. Logos for NHS-owned brands - including the red-and-yellow Santa Cruz Skateboards "Capsule" logo, the Road Rider Wheels "Wings" logo and the Independent Trucks Cross - have since become the skateboard equivalent of the Nike Swoosh: Instantly recognizable works of corporate art and representative of skateboard culture as a whole.

Asked about the secret behind these high-impact logos, NHS co-founder Rich Novak pointed out a visual approach dating back to the days of late 1970s pool skateboarding competitions. These contests were heavily covered by magazines - so a well-placed banner advertisement would find its way into contest articles, which meant free advertising. "We used to stand in a pool to test out banners, to see which one would have the best 'jump' on a photograph. And we learned that literally a spray can with black paint on white was the best jump you had in a magazine photo. The jump was great on [the] Independent [Cross], and Santa Cruz was a bit more complicated because it had the three colors. But all our stuff was based on how it would jump in a magazine photo," said Rich Novak, adding: "A lot of people get very exotic in their graphics, but then all of a sudden they just bleed into the surroundings. You can't see it - you can't read it. We wanted to make sure that if we were going to this, we wanted to be seen."

Turns out that the brands were seen, and then some, as Santa Cruz Skateboards and its sister labels emerged as global phenomena during the mid-1970s skateboard boom, recognized by skateboarders the world over. In the big picture, Santa Cruz Skateboards also owes its impact to industry-changing product innovations - including the Road Rider wheel that pioneered sealed precision bearings - and a pro team stacked with world champion skateboarders the caliber of slalom racer John Hutson, female slalom and pool pro Judi Oyama, and the three horsemen of the punk rock apocalypse; Steve Olson, Duane Peters, and Steve Alba. Over the years, tees and sweatshirts adorned with the Santa Cruz Skateboards logo have become part of the "skateboard wardrobe" with deep hooks into the mainstream, much like *Thrasher* magazine apparel. But it wasn't always like that...

WE NEED SOME SHIRTS?!

When the company first started gaining traction on the skate market, Santa Cruz was 100% focused on manufacturing skateboard hardware, mostly boards and wheels. T-shirts were far from anyone's mind, so when the emerging skateboard competition circuit started kicking into gear in early 1975, the Santa Cruz Skateboards team took a rather unconventional approach to get some team T-shirts made, pronto. "Our first team shirts were airbrushed by hand by an artist called the Great Bernero here at the local theme park in Santa Cruz. He was a very famous and talented artist," said Tim Piumarta, original Santa Cruz Skateboards team rider and Director of Research and Development at NHS (SCS, Independent Trucks, Bullet Wheels).

The local artist was even willing to strike a deal: "He said, 'I agree to do your shirts for free, since you kids have no money, but you have to let me advertise on your shirts as your sponsor.' said Tim Piumarta. As part of the deal, the front of the shirts featured the silhouette of a skateboarder and the "co-branded" insignia of "The Shirt Factory" - a real win-win situation. "He included his insignia and we had our first team t-shirts," said Piumarta.

"MIKE"
THE SHIRT FACTORY
SANTA CRUZ

"STEVE"
THE SHIRT FACTORY
SANTA CRUZ

TEAM
SANTA CRUZ

TEAM
SANTA CRUZ

John
SHIRT FACTORY
Scott
SHIRT FACTORY
Tony
SHIRT FACTORY
NTA CRUZ

Anvil
SANTA CRUZ
SANTA CRUZ
SKATEBOARDS

Keep on
Boarding

IRON-ONS: HOT NEW TEES

The late 1970s made history as the Golden Age of the Graphic T-shirt. New textile printing techniques conspired with a cultural climate of free-spirited creativity, resulting in a new wave of graphically inspired T-shirts with artwork and slogans projecting the wearer's stylistic preferences and opinions ("MAKE LOVE, NOT WAR!") into public space. The phenomenon expanded into DIY-territory with the arrival of iron-on transfers, a technique allowing consumers to apply graphics - printed as reverse, "mirror image" versions on heat-sensitive polymer foil - onto garments at home with a simple iron.

The first iron-ons worn by skateboarders came from Hollywood movies and super hero comics, not skateboard brands. "Iron-on was really popular in the 1970s," said skateboard icon Steve Caballero, adding: "I always wore *Star Wars* iron-ons. When I showed up at the skateboard park I had *Star Wars* iron-on shirts and *Star Wars* socks, like Chewbacca." Official *Star Wars* iron-ons were produced under license by a company called Factors, Etc. Inc. in Bear, Delaware, at the time the second-largest purveyor of iron-on graphics next to Roach Studios out of Columbus, Ohio.

Literally putting the heat in the hands of the people, iron-ons proved the perfect merchandising opportunity for skateboarding's blossoming (and strapped-for-cash) print media. Basically, iron-ons allowed skateboard magazines to give away free branded clothing by including iron-on film inside their print editions - and all readers needed was a blank T-shirt or sweatshirt, and their mom's iron. Brilliant! Following its resurgence in 1975, *SkateBoarder* magazine on several occasions included iron-ons featuring its logo and customized artwork, and follow-up publication *Action Now* continued the tradition.

HOT OR NOT?!

Skateboard companies such as Powell-Peralta also relied on the heat transfer process to create last-minute artwork for photo shoots. In a 1980 Powell advertisement, Steve Caballero is depicted rocking a rare T-shirt - featuring a photo of himself floating a backside air, shot by Ted Terrebone. As it turned out, the shirt was created on the same day, just for the photo shoot: "Craig Stecyk made the heat transfer graphic just for the ad, a self-made iron-on transfer. I kept one of those shirts because it was cool," said Steve Caballero.

Not so cool, was the fact that the novelty of iron-on graphics attracted hordes of corporate businesses looking to get "on board" with the skateboard demographic. Unfortunately, these companies were not very on board with skateboard-appropriate artwork, which led to many fashion and style failures that should never have seen an iron, or shirt. "There was a lot of horrible looking shit out there," said Skip Engblom of Zephyr and Santa Monica Airlines fame. The iron-on graphics Hall of Shame includes clumsy skateboard cartoons, 1960s-style "Bust Your Buns" motifs, and, powered by a new method known as litho transfers, countless photo-realistic variations of teenage Leif Garret's mug from the *Skateboard* movie. Not to forget shameless appropriations of action photos from magazines into corporate logos for dubious companies, including Tom "Wally" Inouye's frontside kickturn mashed up with Tom Sims into a Concrete Glider iron-on artwork (all SIMS Skateboard logos from original photos conveniently glossed over, of course.)

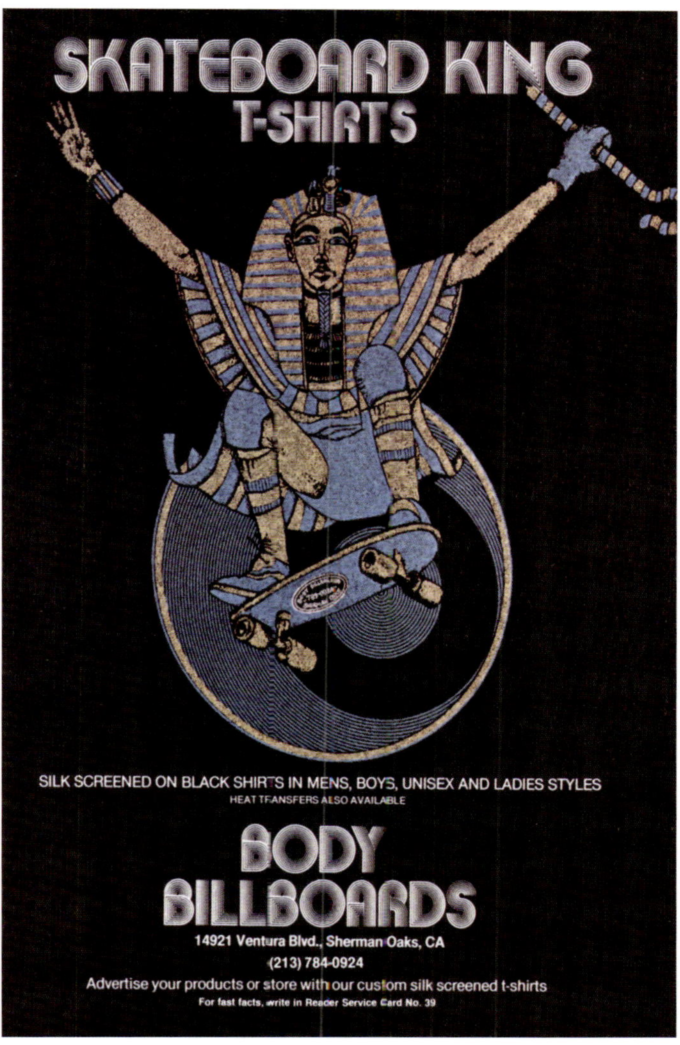

Today, only very few iron-on graphics remain. The reason is simple: The novel, adhesive polymer printing process tolerated machine washing very poorly. Even turned inside-out before washing - as per the instructions - the shirts lost their graphics after a few cycles as the thin plastic print coating peeled and faded into oblivion. Then again, considering the quality of most iron-on artwork, maybe that's not such a great loss after all.

FREE SKATEBOARDER MAGAZINE IRON-ON T-SHIRT TRANSFER
(See instructions below)

cut along dotted line

SkateBoarder
MAGAZINE

cut along dotted line

DIRECTIONS:
The ink for your SKATEBOARDER transfer has been specially formulated for use on Permanent Press T-shirts of 50% polyester/50% cotton. Shirts with this fiber content hold the transfer colors through repeated machine launderings. We do not recommend using 100% cotton T-shirts because most of the transfer ink washes out in the first laundering.

1. Set a dry iron at "medium" temperature setting.
2. Center transfer page ink-side down on upper part of T-shirt.
3. Apply very firm and even pressure on all parts of the design for 20 seconds on each section. DO NOT MOVE IRON BACK AND FORTH.
4. CAUTION: If using steam iron with holes, do not position holes over color transfer area.

SkateBoarder
MAGAZINE

L (42-44)
Healthknit
50% COTTON
50% POLYESTER
MADE IN U.S.A.
FOR CARE SEE REVERSE
BUST
YOUR BUNS
©vortex 76
Hank...

Leif Garrett
IN
SKATEBOARD
TM*
© 1977 Boulevard Associates

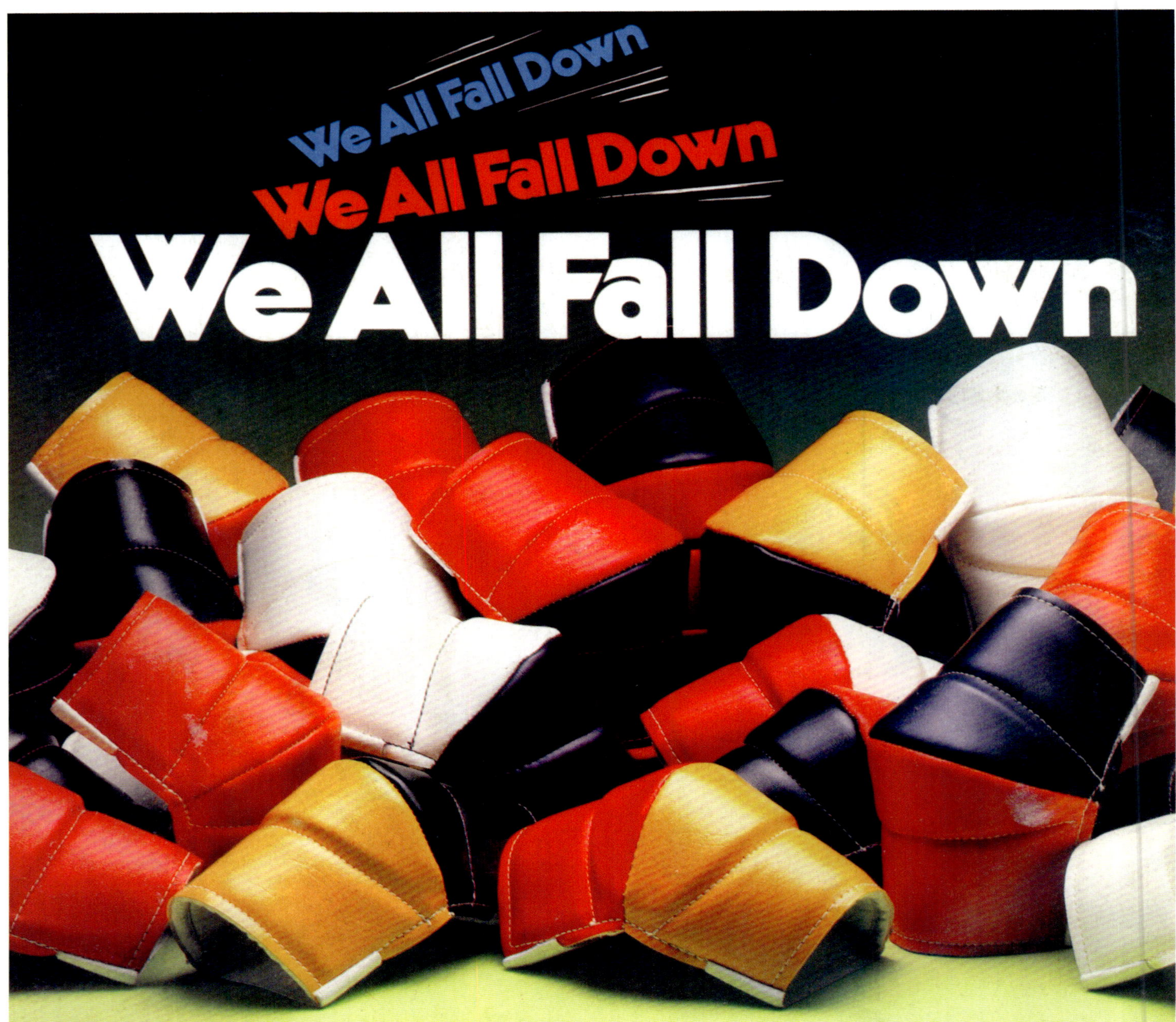

It's a fact of life.
Someday you're going to fall off your skateboard.
When it *does* happen, you'll be glad you chose Clo-Mat.
The elbow pad that's actually shaped to fit your elbow.
In two-tone leathercloth with an indestructible expanded polyethylene liner,
Clo-Mat pads will take the rough with the smooth.
And keep on taking it.
Now for the good news.
Clo-Mat pads won't cost you the earth, they're British made,
and you can choose from 24 exciting colour combinations.
See them at your local dealer or, for dealer enquiries, contact
American Grafitti, 3 Bell Street, Reigate, Surrey. (Tel. Reigate 41657)

Clo-Mat. Give your elbows a treat.

Real skaters wear protection. When skateboarding met its first sudden death in the mid-1960s, safety concerns had proven the final nail in the coffin. Now that skateboarding was once again hot - a $300-million-dollar market fuelled by 20 million participants in 1978 - the industry had learned its lesson. "Yes there are safety problems involved with skateboarding - the usual assortment of cuts, bruises, and sprains that go with just about any adolescent sporting activity," wrote Phillip Missimore in the February 1978 issue of Skateboard Industry News. "But even these problems can be alleviated or strongly curtailed by the proper use of full safety gear - helmet, gloves, knee and elbow pads, and shoes - by all riders, and by the availability of proper surfaces for riding," the article titled "Selling Skateboard Safety" concluded.

As the "proper surfaces for riding," industry organizations such as the American Skateboard Association (ASA) promoted concrete skate parks that mushroomed all over the United States in the mid-1970s. "Get Off The Streets... and into ASA!" became a catchphrase for attracting kids into parks, where park operators mandated all riders to wear shoes - a big surprise for the barefoot "concrete surfer" crowd - and full safety gear. "No pads, no shoes, no helmet - no session!" became the norm at skate parks all over the U.S. together with signing a waiver to free park owners from any liabilities in the case of an injury. "Skate parks had to be insured at the time, so everyone had to wear pads, even the pros. And of course, the pros had to promote safety gear, so all the kids would wear it as well," said skateboard photographer Ted "T-Bone" Terrebonne. The skateboard media played a major part in promoting skate parks and "proper" use of safety gear. "When parks boomed they were everywhere. That's all the mags covered, so people equated parks with skateboarding," wrote Don Redondo in the 1986 *Thrasher* magazine article "The Last Ride."

From a skateboard fashion perspective, this new focus on skate parks resembled a paradigm shift. "Skateboard clothing went from the whole surf look to the 'skate park look.' Everyone had beat-up [safety] gear, and [pro rider Brad] Bowman and these guys had matching pads," said professional skateboarder Lance Mountain. In the process, skate parks not only became the new focus for the evolution of riding technique, but the runway for parading the latest fashion styles, including the era's trending outfit of soft pads, jersey shirt, padded shorts, Vans shoes, tube socks, skate gloves and helmet.

Speaking of helmets, the first wave of head protection came from the world of competitive cycling: Soft-shell, "hairnet"-style helmets constructed out of padded leathers by manufacturers such as Brancale and L'Eroica soon became the norm among pros. For added flair, skateboard teams would commission customized helmets in brand colors - like the red, white, and blue of the Pepsi Team - and add company logos to the front or side of the helmet. Sponsored skateboarders, including Tracker Trucks team riders Stacy Peralta and Tony Alva also added brand logo stickers to their helmets, with sticker placement behind or above the ear a key spot for nailing the "pro look."

FASHION OVER FUNCTION

At the height of the skate park craze, wearing the right combination of gear could be the make or break of a professional skate career. "Everyone dressed real fancy for the parks, and the photographers liked color. Everyone knew that if you

SKATEMATES

Knee and Elbow pads

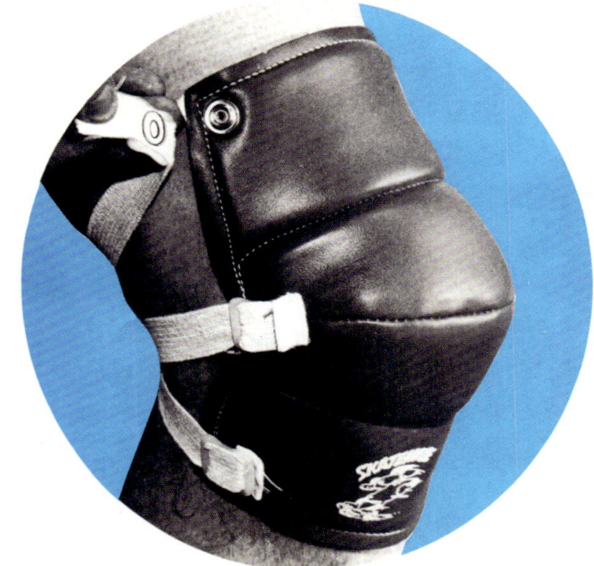

- **Knee Pads**
- **Easy on snap fit** – ***No need to remove your shoes to put on***
- **Special Foam Padding inside**
- **Plastic Cup to disipate shock**
- ***Reviewed and recommended in the February issue of Skateboard***

Skatemates the protective gear people

14 St. Leonard's Terrace, Londo

wanted to get into the magazines, you had to look good and ride good as well," said Ted "T-Bone" Terrebonne. According to *Thrasher* magazine's Don Redondo, magazines "even banned all cover shots where the rider didn't have full pads and a helmet, thereby cutting out 95% of all non-park skating." Meanwhile, skateboard magazines significantly grew their page counts (and revenues), supplemented by full-page advertisements for safety gear by brands such as Hobie, Rector, Cooper, and Sure Craft.

Magazines spread the new "skate park look" all across the world as the new de jour outfit for skateboarders. "There was an American skateboard style with Vans shoes, tube socks, and Rector [pads] that you saw in all the skate magazines. We didn't have that yet, so we tried to get whatever we could get our hands on. It was a really organic skate fashion that caught on in the skate world," said UK-born skateboard photographer Skin Phillips. In terms of colors, primary colors were all the rage in those halcyon days of neon and Day-Glo. "In the 1970s everyone dressed really colorful, in bright T-shirts and all the safety equipment was really bright as well. Pads, gloves and helmets came in colors like red, blue and yellow," said Ted "T-Bone" Terrebonne.

Among active skateboarders, wearing the right safety gear in the right colors was a major source of confidence. A sense of pride of being part of a movement; the future of skateboarding. "As a skate park kid, you had to get the blue or yellow Rectors and you would wrap up your helmet so it looked perfect in shiny black or red. It was really important to me as a skate park kid to have rad looking pads," said skateboard photographer and Del Mar Skate Ranch local Dave Swift. Speaking of helmets, skateboard-specific head protection was still in its infancy in 1978, and many young riders resorted to appropriating gear from other sports, including Steve Caballero, who "always wore a CCM hockey helmet for skateboarding."

Despite hitting high marks in the fashion department, the first generation of safety gear struck out in terms of functionality. Most of all, the "soft pads" such as the Sure Craft elbow protectors (suggested retail $7.49 in 1978) with their three layers of foam provided some degree of impact protection, but proved no match to the harsh realities of concrete skate parks. "The early pads just came right off your body. They were made from foam and elastic materials, so as soon as you hit your knees or elbows [on the surface], they came off. Some guys would even double-up the elbow pads because they were getting all these injuries," said 1970s Hobie team rider Jim Goodrich.

NECESSARY EVIL

So despite these major shortcomings, why did skate park riders even bother with protectors in the first place? "The only reason why people wore them was because the parks made you wear them. Although they weren't that functional. They would help a little bit," said professional Eddie Elguera, adding: "In [backyard] pools I wouldn't wear safety equipment, only when the parks made us." Many riders considered pads as a necessary evil, imposed on them by the powers that be: "It made skateboarding look a little goofy, with helmets, and elbow pads, knee pads. Especially because they were these soft, basketball-type pads at first. Skateboard pads with plastic caps had not been developed yet," said pro skateboarder Dave Duncan.

Further hindering the acceptance of protective gear was the fact that many skateboarders refused to spend their own money on pads.

THE Sanjon SYSTEM

From the people that brought you the first wrist support...

Now another first! The "park pad". All the high quality characteristics found in our shock absorber. The park pad has abrasion resistant vinyl covers and a unique laminated cushion that won't bottom out! Unlike the basketball pads used as safety equipment for skateboarding, it will take the punishment other pads won't. The SANJON system...get with it and stay with it. Available in red, blue, black and orange. Sizes: small, medium, and large. Also look for our helmets and gloves coming soon.

SANJON ENTERPRISES, INC.
P.O. Box 57099 Los Angeles, California 90057 (213) 483-2762 Order by mail

"PARK PAD"

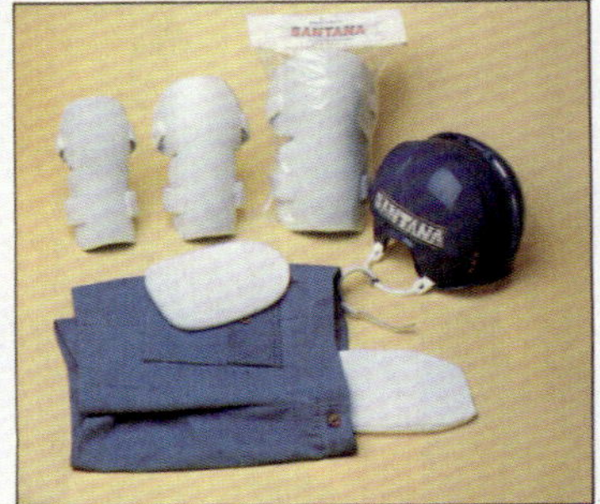

The Santana Skateboard System gives me the deep carving feeling that I enjoy in surfing and skiing.

Mike Doyle

Innovator of the single snow ski and the soft surf board.

For information on all Santana Skate Products contact:
Dick Abrams or Phil Stubbs / Leisure Specialties
17895 Sky Park Circle / Suite J / Irvine, CA 92714
Phone: (714) 546-6290

A complete pro system at a price everyone can afford.

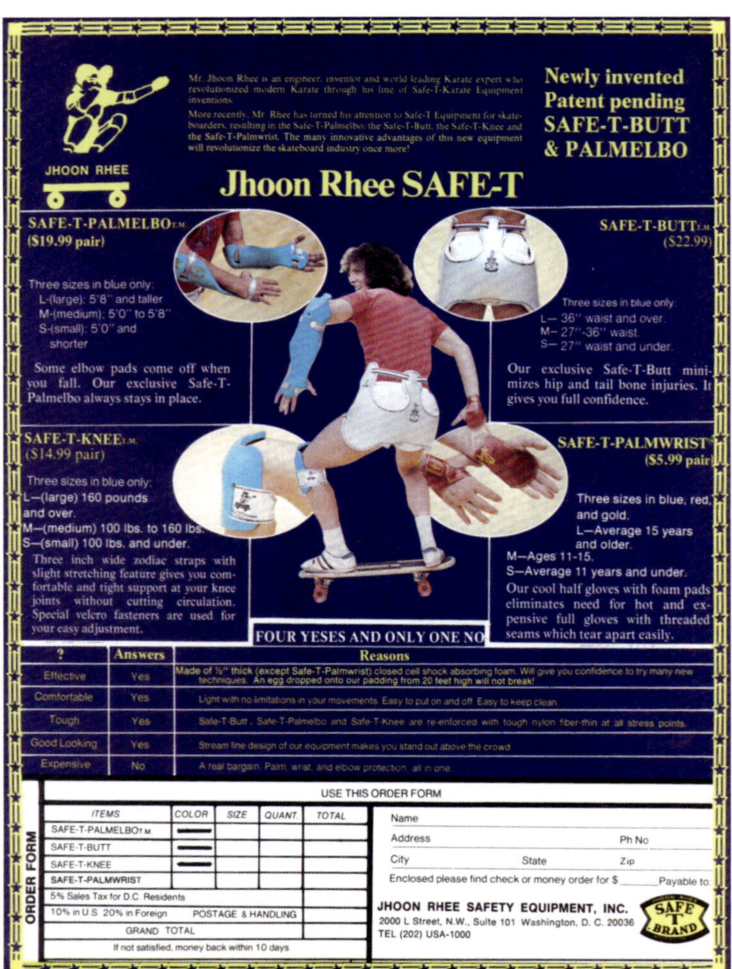

?	Answers	Reasons
Effective	Yes	Made of ½" thick (except Safe-T-Palmwrist) closed cell shock absorbing foam. Will give you confidence to try many new techniques. An egg dropped onto our padding from 20 feet high will not break!
Comfortable	Yes	Light with no limitations in your movements. Easy to put on and off. Easy to keep clean.
Tough	Yes	Safe-T-Butt, Safe-T-Palmelbo and Safe-T-Knee are re-enforced with tough nylon fiber-thin at all stress points.
Good Looking	Yes	Stream line design of our equipment makes you stand out above the crowd
Expensive	No	A real bargain. Palm, wrist, and elbow protection, all in one.

ORDER FORM

USE THIS ORDER FORM

ITEMS	COLOR	SIZE	QUANT.	TOTAL
SAFE-T-PALMELBO T.M.	—			
SAFE-T-BUTT	—			
SAFE-T-KNEE	—			
SAFE-T-PALMWRIST				
5% Sales Tax for D.C. Residents				
10% in U.S. 20% in Foreign POSTAGE & HANDLING				
GRAND TOTAL				
If not satisfied, money back within 10 days				

Name

Address Ph No

City State Zip

Enclosed please find check or money order for $ ______ Payable to:

JHOON RHEE SAFETY EQUIPMENT, INC.
2000 L Street, N.W., Suite 101 Washington, D. C. 20036
TEL (202) USA-1000

SAFE T BRAND

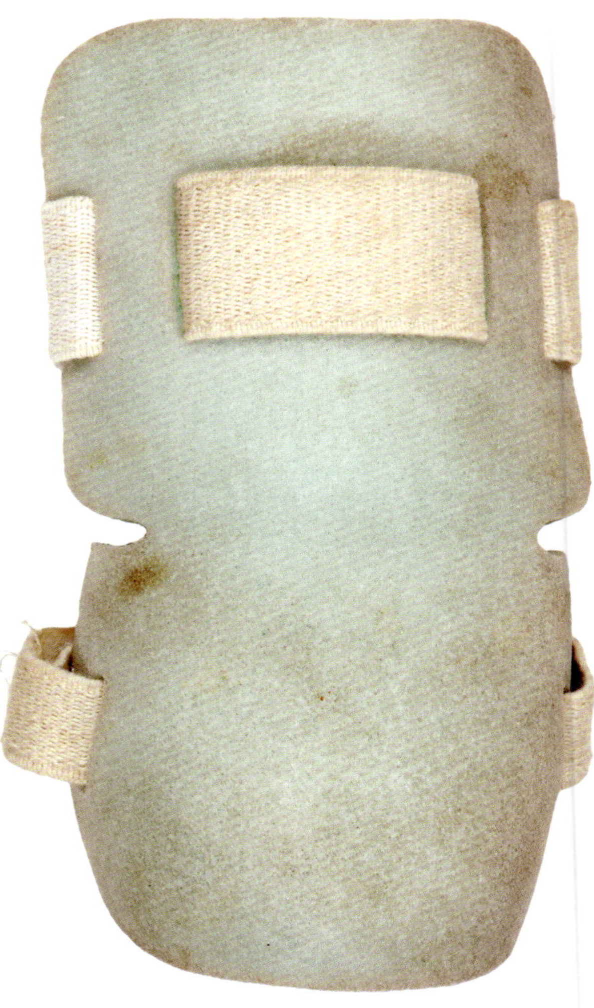

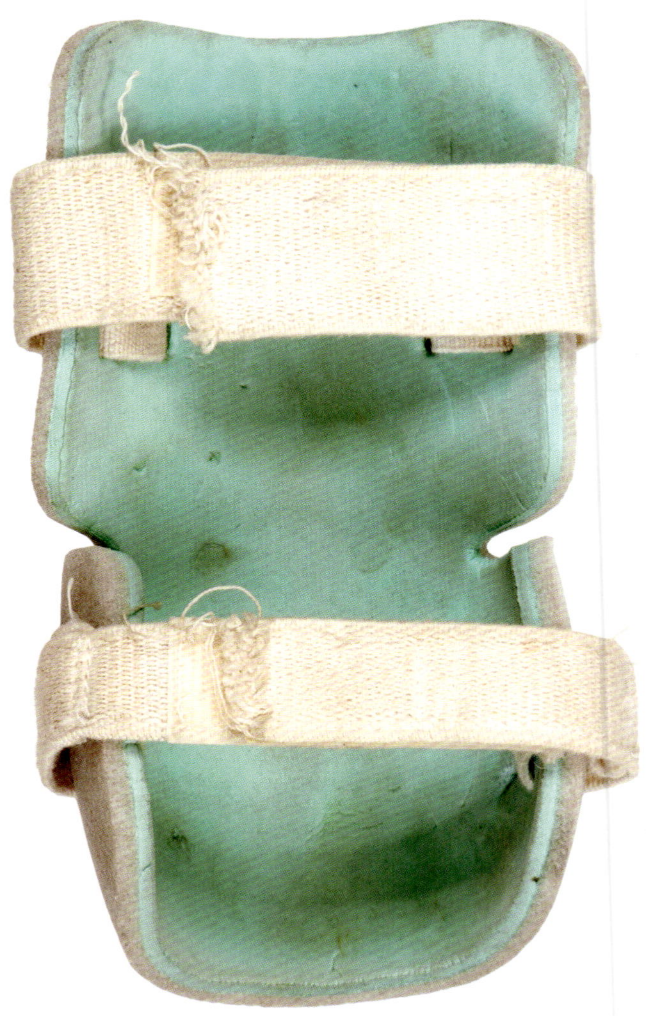

Most riders relied on rental gear from the skate park, where pads were cycled out after each one-hour session and kept in wire baskets like shoes at the bowling alley. "When you would go into a session and got the pads, they were all stinky and wet from the session before. And they sprayed them with Lysol," said Eddie Elguera. Fellow pro skateboarder Steve Olson also remembers: "It was disgusting! Wearing these rented pads, all sweated. Totally disgusting!"

Acceptance of safety gear took a quantum leap when protector design finally caught up to the demands of park riders in late 1978. Manufacturers such as Hobie and Rector introduced hard-shell plastic caps to their knee and elbow pads that allowed for safely sliding down the concrete walls of skate park pools and bowls. This technique paved the way for taking aerial maneuvers higher above the lip, and every pro rider found ways to pad up with plastic caps. "The Hobies first had caps on them," remembers Eddie Elguera, "so we would take the Rectors with no caps and put the other caps over them and then we could knee-slide [down the transition]." At this point, however, Eddie Elguera had already learned not to depend on pads at all, earning him the nickname "El Gato," meaning "The Cat" in Spanish: "They called me 'El Gato' because you always had to land on your feet because you couldn't knee slide."

Some pros never fully warmed up to pads and the entire "skate park look," cultivating their own aesthetic away from the skateboard media's focus instead. "In a lot of magazine photos from that era you will see that skate park look. I used to skate a lot of backyard pools so we didn't wear pads," said Dave Duncan, adding: "It was kind of a cool style skateboarding just raw with shorts and whatever normal clothes in a pool with no pads." The schism between "pads" and "no pads" still runs deep within the skateboard scene, said skateboard pioneer Mark Richards of Val Surf skateboard shop: "Even to this day, safety gear has not really been accepted. Especially in street skating, they just will not wear it. It's never been cool. The only thing that made it viable is when skate parks back in the day would require it, and rightfully so."

SURFERS
DO IT IN THE TUB
PURE
JUICE

Photo: Craig Fineman

THE „BRAIN BASKET": CHECK YOUR HEAD

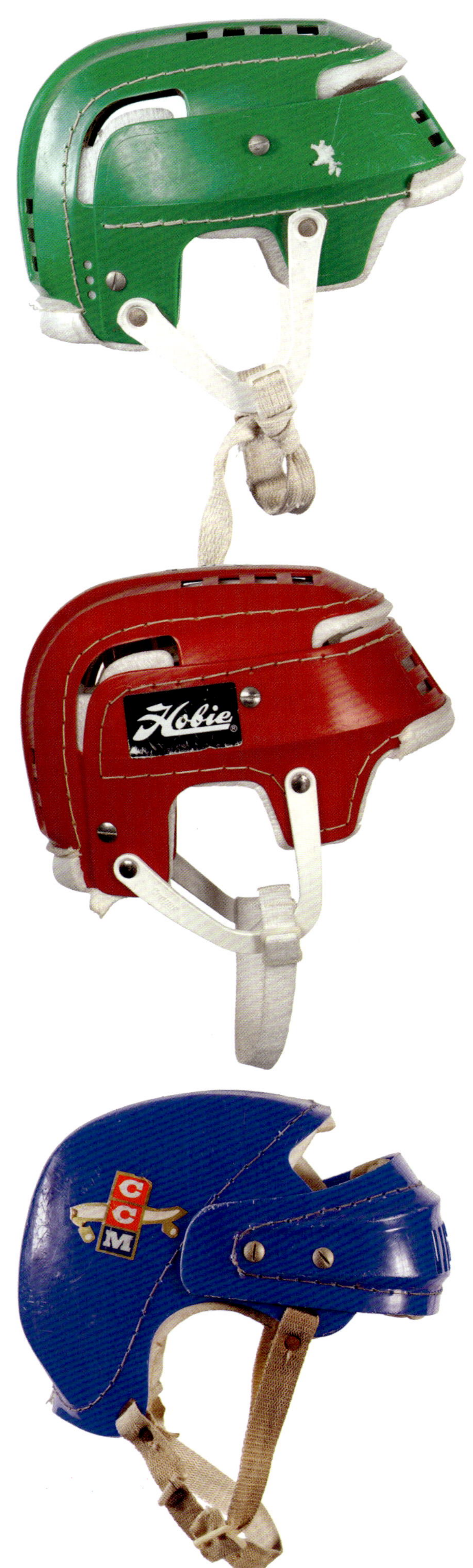

Go fast, go big, go over the edge – but always wear a helmet! Hundreds of concrete skate parks across the US offered the kind of thrills depicted in movies and magazines, where the likes of Brad Bowman, Tony Alva, and Jay Adams pioneered a new style of upwardly mobile skateboarding on vertical terrain. But right at the door, skate parks also posted a series of stringent safety rules, including mandatory safety gear to be worn by all riders at all times. Which also meant "No helmet, no session." The only problem facing both riders and park operators: In 1977, when the Skate Park Era was starting to gain momentum, not a single manufacturer had brought to market a helmet specifically designed for the requirements of skateboarding.

In search of alternatives, skateboarders began rummaging through head protectors used in other sports. They soon found suitable helmets in the adrenaline-fuelled world of automotive racing, where the legacy of American auto racer and safety equipment evangelist Roy Richter loomed large over helmet designs. "Helmets go back to Roy Richter, who is regarded as the godfather of helmets and introduced them to competitive car racing," said skateboard graphic artist Jim Phillips from Santa Cruz, adding: "Before skateboard helmets were around, skaters would wear helmets from Richter's company, Bell Helmets, for protection." Originally started in 1946 after Richter's close friend was killed in a car racing accident, Bell Helmets created the blueprint for hard-shell wrap-around helmets still worn by race car drivers today.

Originally designed for motorcycle racing, the Magnum model from Bell Helmets became a major seller among race and downhill skateboarders. This sub-specialty of skateboarding garnered national attention in 1975 when ABC television's "Wide World of Sports" covered the inaugural Signal Hill Speed Run downhill race. Competitors attacked the 30-degree incline on customized longboards – called Luge Skateboards – protected by full racing leather suits and Bell Helmets. Clocking in with a 50.2 mph top speed, local skateboarder Guy Grundy advanced into the Guinness Book of World Records as the world's fastest skateboarder (today's world record is slightly above 80 mph).

"It was all about speed and performance and testing the boundaries of how fast you could go on a skateboard," said Todd Huber, proprietor of Skatelab skate park and museum in Simi Valley, home to the world's largest exhibit of historic Luge skateboards and even faster Skate Cars. From a style perspective, speed racers made sure to color-match their helmets with their leather racing overalls, oftentimes in the colorways of their sponsors. The race skating era also started the tradition of customizing helmets with stickers and hand-painted artwork in Sharpie pencils – also a nod to the All-American outfits worn by motorcycle stunt pioneer Evel Knievel – which carried over into skate park riding.

HOCKEY HELMETS TO THE RESCUE

Motorcycle helmets proved ideal for pushing the limits of speed racing, but their bulk and weight limited the free movement required in skate parks. As a new generation of park riders pioneered aerial moves in concrete bowls and vertical pools – requiring fast reflexes and constantly shifting the body's center of gravity – the top-heavy motorcycle helmets had to make way for a lightweight alternative. From cycling, skateboarders had already adopted the soft-shell, leather "hairnet"-style helmets by manufacturers such as Brancale and L'Eroica.

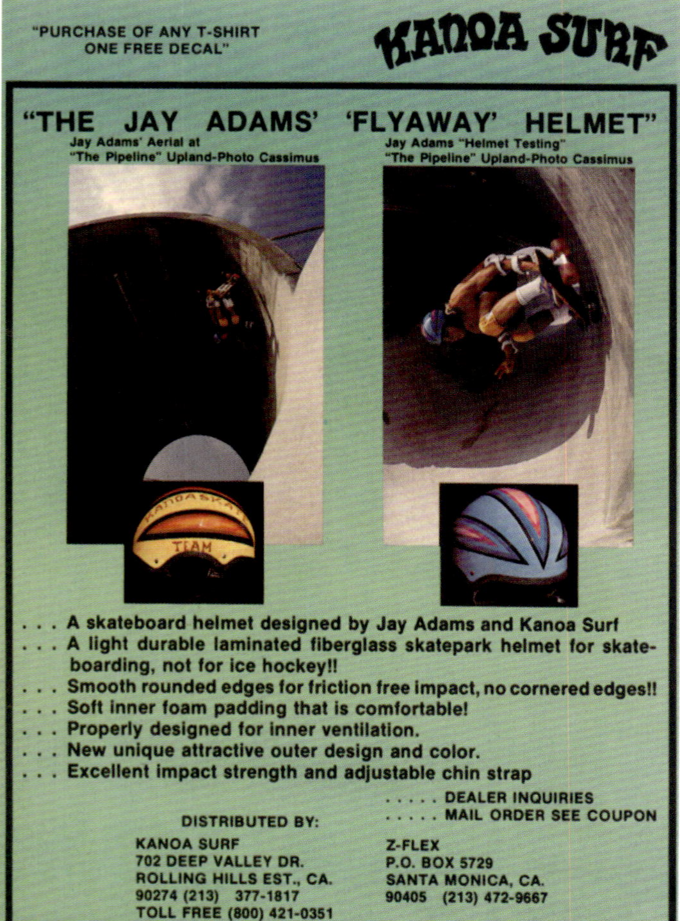

But these helmets proved no match for the harsh realities of crashing on hard concrete. How about helmets that could handle the blow of crashing on unforgiving ice surfaces – or the occasional assault with a hockey stick? "My first skateboarding helmets were rudimentary ice hockey helmets made by companies like Cooper and Norcon. Mostly because there were no helmets made for skateboarding, and these were light and relatively inexpensive," said pro skateboarder Steve Caballero, whose first helmet was manufactured by Canadian company CCM, short for Canada Cycle & Motor.

Hockey equipment companies like CCM and Minnesota-based Norcon soon noticed the surging interest among skateboarders and proceeded to market their helmets in skateboarding magazines – but entirely without adapting their original helmet designs to the new demographic. Nevertheless, hockey-style helmets struck a nerve with the skate park crowd and became major sellers, with hockey company Cooper International out of Lewiston, New York, emerging as the new market leader. Cooper's SK100 Hockey Hurling Helmet, rebranded as the "SKB100 Skateboarder Helmet," created the mold for the short-lived hockey helmet era: Poured from polyethylene, the outside shell featured multiple ventilation ports for air circulation and vinyl foam padding together with chin straps from molded Geon.

In a 1978 advertisement entitled "What to wear to a wipeout," the company explained: "Cooper learned all about protective equipment in tough, hard-hitting sports like hockey. So when it comes to protection know-how, you know Cooper's got it." The company's offering also included elbow and knee pads of the "soft" variety; without the plastic caps later popularized by Rector. Several skateboard manufacturers, including Hobie and Free Former skateboards, released their own branded versions of hockey-style helmets. And because imitation is the sincerest form of flattery, British company Skatemates released their own Faux-Cooper helmet – shamelessly sold as the "SK100" model – for the competitive price of £4.50. But as it turned out, the entire hockey helmet trend was riding on thin ice. Before Cooper could fire back with a copyright lawsuit, the industry was leveled by a landmark invention: the world's first skateboard-specific helmet.

FLYAWAY: DESIGNED FOR SKATEBOARDING

In late 1978, Kanoa Surf Shop out of Rolling Hills, California, shook up the safety equipment industry with advertisements for "the first skateboard helmets designed for skateboarders – not hockey players!" Crafted from high impact aircraft fiberglass, the company's Flyaway model, endorsed by pro skateboarder Jay Adams, as well as the Airborne and Kanoa Pro helmet stood out from the rest of the pack with their aerodynamic shape and sleek paint coating. Functional features included soft vinyl nitrite inner foam padding and adjustable D-ring chin strap, but the helmets' main impact was in the realm of aesthetics. Where standard hockey helmets looked boxy and clumsy, Kanoa helmets looked "spacy" and futuristic with their rounded edges and streamlined silhouette. Practically over night, the Flyaway became the helmet for serious park skateboarders.

"When the Flyaway helmets came around, everyone wore them. They were just the ultimate, they were spacy, modern looking with their airbrushed colors. They were cool – unlike any other safety gear at the time. They were stylish when other things were just practical," said skateboard photographer Jim Goodrich. "When the Flyaway helmet first came out, I just had to get one," remembers pro skateboarder Steve Caballero.

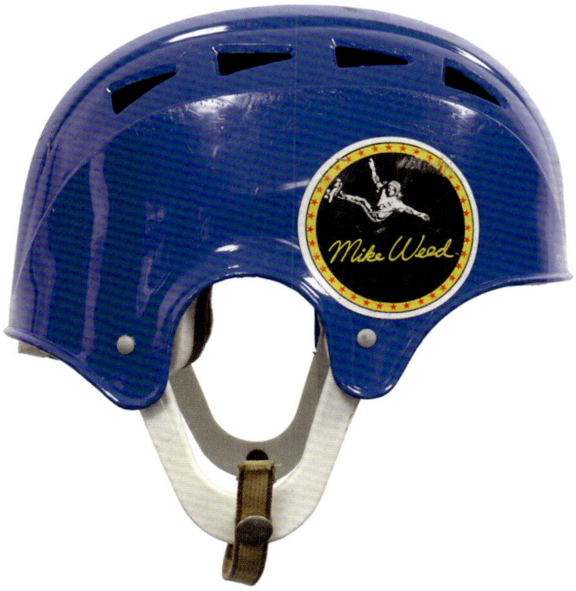
Mike Wead

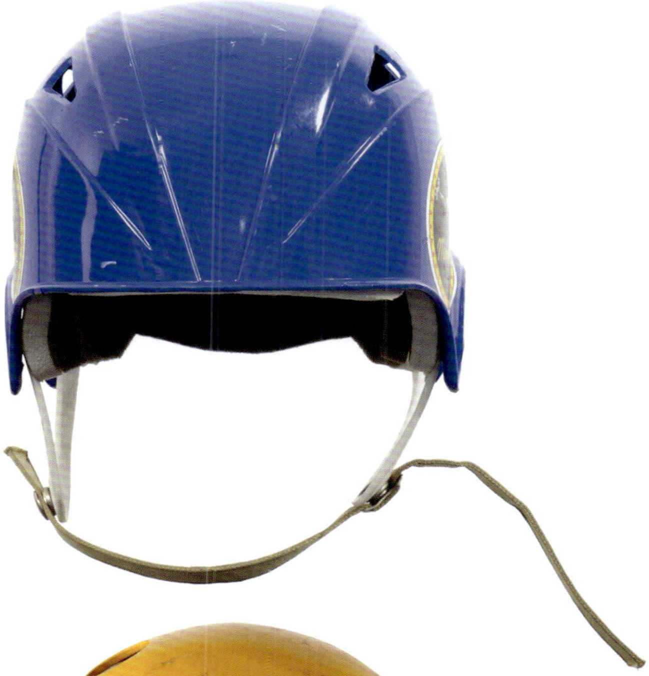

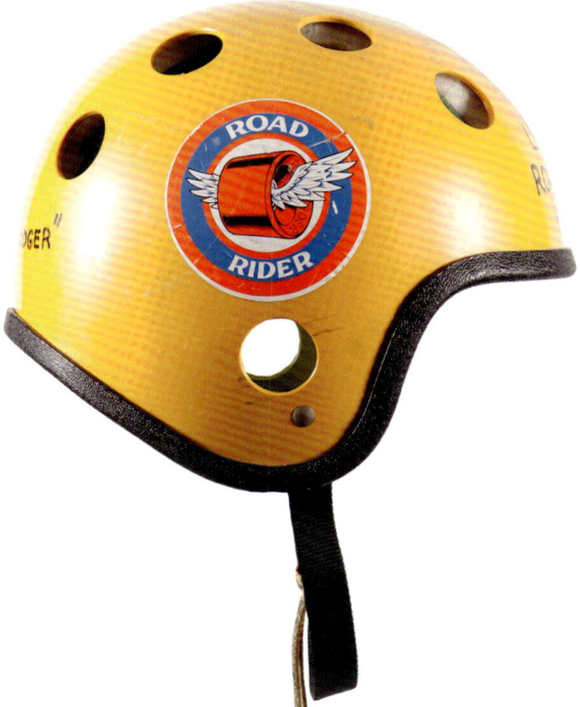
ROAD
RIDER

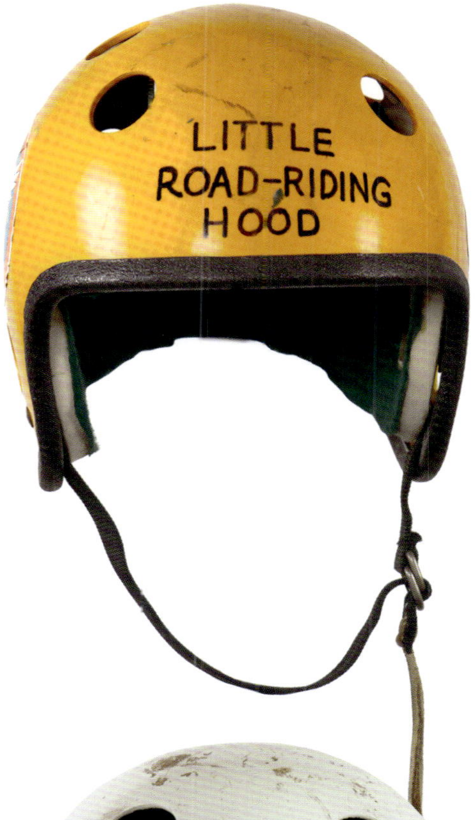
LITTLE
ROAD-RIDING
HOOD

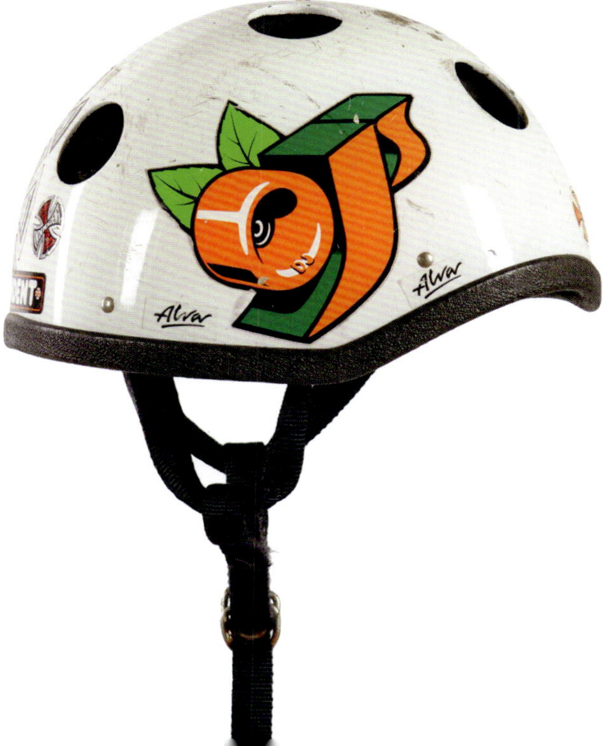
Alva
Alva

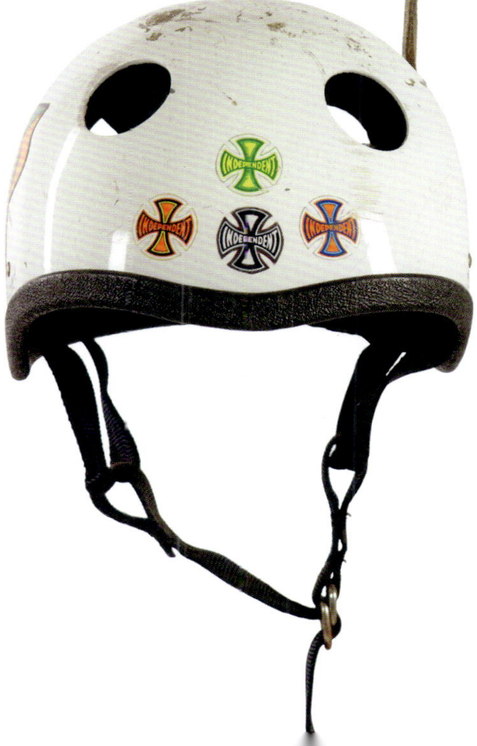

SANTA CRUZ
INDEPENDENT
TRACKER
TRACKER
TRACKER
TRACKER
TRACKER

"It just had a cool looking style to it, really sleek and the colors looked cool!" With their professional endorsements and next-level design, Flyaways signaled the end of the hockey helmet era. "The Flyaway was Jay Adams' helmet, that was his influence. Cooper helmets just became rental helmets and were made fun of," said skateboard photographer and Del Mar Skate Ranch local Dave Swift.

"So you want protection, huh? My Flyaway's got you covered," beamed the founder of Kanoa surf shop in a 1978 *Skateboarder* magazine advertisement. The helmets proved a major seller for Kanoa surf shop - the store also sold its own line of complete skateboards and padded shorts - especially when airbrushed limited edition colorways with stars and other customized designs came to market. Within months of their market launch, the Kanoa helmet line spawned countless imitators, including the "Z" skateboard helmet sold by the International Sports Products Corporation with an almost identical design, enhanced by a detachable hard plastic visor. But nothing came close to the cool aura of the original Kanoa collection, poised to take over the safety equipment industry by storm. If only the helmets had lived up to their promise...

FASHION OVER FUNCTION

As it turned out, the helmets fell short of delivering on the "friction free impact" and "excellent impact strength" promised in advertisements. This was mostly due to their half-shell, cut-above-the ears design and loose fit. As one of the major downsides, the outside fiberglass shell extruded beyond the foam padding, directly pushing into the wearer's skull on impact at a certain angle. "They were definitely dangerous helmets. A lot of guys cut their eyebrows on the fiberglass. They just looked good, though," laughed Steve Caballero. "It cuts you right above the eye! I saw it happen to so many people," said pro skateboarder Eddie Elguera.

The streamlined design of the helmets' outer shell also left the base of the skull exposed to impact, and sideways collisions also proved problematic as the forces of impact transferred directly inwards. "Flyaway was a dangerous helmet," said skateboard photographer J. Grant Brittain. "The part that comes down at the side of your head would press into your temple and people would clonk out. I saw a lot of people knocked out wearing Flyaways." Pro skateboarder Steve Olson said: "I cracked my skull with a Flyaway helmet on! Cracked the helmet and cracked my head! Because it really didn't protect it." Eddie Elguera relates another high-profile: incident involving a Flyaway helmet: "Salba fell at Pipeline [skate park in Upland] during the Hester series [contest] cut his eye and ever since then wore Pro-Tec helmets."

PRO-TEC: THE NEW GOLD STANDARD

While Flyaway helmets dominated the spotlight with their futuristic, aerodynamic helmet designs, the Pro-Tec helmet company in Orange County embarked on a search for the perfect skateboarding helmet design. Revisiting the wraparound style of earlier hockey helmets, but in a more form-fitting, rounded overall silhouette, Pro-Tec introduced the Full-Tec helmet model in 1978 as the new state-of-the-art in safety equipment: For a major improvement, the hard-shell polyurethane helmet featured Velcro-attached foam liners on the insides in four different sizes - thereby maintaining a secure fit and preventing injuries from "rocking" the helmet's shell.

Available in five colorways - black, red, white, blue, and gold; as well as green for skate park rental versions - Pro- Tec helmets blew up as the new pro's choice. They became the must- have helmets of the skate park era.

"When Ray Bones had ads in the new Full-Tec helmet, everyone wanted one of those!" said Dave Swift. "He was doing a tail tap with a yellow board and that full Pro-Tec helmet. And everyone, almost overnight, had to get Pro-Tecs! Those are the kind of things that changed skate fashion!" As Swift points out, Pro-Tec also ran a licensing agreement with Powell-Peralta skateboards to produce a cross-branded Powell x Pro-Tec helmet: "Alan Gelfand did the first ollie in the big red Pro-Tec Full-Tec helmet. All the Powell guys had Full-Tecs." Steve Caballero, as the new amateur on Powell-Peralta, also started wearing Pro-Tec by default: "We would get our Pro-Tec helmets through Powell, and Powell would just put their logo on them!"

As an organic upgrade to the full-wrap helmet, Dave Swift recalls skaters "cutting off their full Tecs into half-shell helmets, with straps from rental helmets. We would take straps from Norcon helmets after we saw Duane Peters cutting off his Full-Tecs." During this period, the customized DIY-half shells became the calling card of punk rock-minded skateboarders such as Duane Peters and other pioneers. And in a twist similar to the genesis of the Half Cab shoe that started with 1990s skateboarders cutting off their high-tops into low-tops, the DIY-helmets inspired the manufacturer to revise the design. "Six months later, Pro-Tec also started making half-shell helmets," said Dave Swift.

Whether pros preferred half-shell or full helmets, their head pieces became a major part of their outfit, customized with paint and sticker jobs. "Sticker placement was planned in a major way! Helmet sticker placement could take forever to do. Because it's gotta be perfect, or else," said pro skateboarder Christian Hosoi, adding: "It's like hanging a painting on a wall. Where would you hang it? Up high? Down low? Close to the wall? My dad was an artist and he hung art as part of his job, so he knew where something would look aesthetically right and I would always sit there and watch him do it." Look at any photo from the height of the skate park era, and chances are pro skateboarder outfits are color-matched and brand-coordinated from the sticker on their boards all the way to the logos on their helmets.

As the 1970s wave of skate parks broke into the 1980s era of backyard half pipes, both Pro-Tec and Flyaway helmets came along for the ride. Neither brand managed to dominate the market, both remained equal choices. Next-generation vertical riders such as Steve Schneer and Peanut Brown made Flyaway their calling card, while others including Neil Blender, Lance Mountain, and Jeff Grosso swore by Pro-Tec as their helmet of choice. "It was really a question of faith. Flyaway was always the helmet for the style riders, the dudes who only rode frontside. And Pro-Tec has always been more for the punk rock guys," said pro skateboarder Claus Grabke, adding: "With Pro-Tec you had a whole different world of options when it came to sticker placement, while Flyaways kind of pigeonholed you as a '70s skater. But ultimately, Pro-Tec pretty much was always the better helmet."

SkateBoarder
MAGAZINE

Photo: Craig B. Snyder

Power Gloves™

Take a close look...

then you'll see why Power Gloves are the top skateboarding gloves made.

Power Gloves 1 (the original)
Extra rugged for long lasting protection. Features include reinforced suede leather on back and tips of fingers, double on palms, nylon stitching, 100% leather (no pigskin)

Power Gloves are used exclusively by Skateboard World, Torrance, Calif.

E.T. Ripstix & Power Gloves
Available at finer pro shops everywhere.
Mail order send $16.95 plus $1.50 postage and handling
Calif. Residents add 6% sales tax
Send tracing of hand or XS, S, M, L.
We invite dealer inquiries

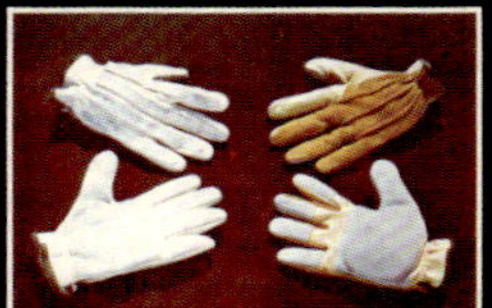

"The original skateboarding gloves"

Power Gloves 2
Provides the ultimate palm protection. Features include high density foam pad plus reinforced suede leather on palms and fingertips. (A lot more padding for the thumpers.)

Power Gloves 3
You'll see, it will blow ya all out!

"For concrete comfort"

E.T. Company, 916 E. Aviation Blvd., Hermosa Beach, CA 90254 (213) 379-7660

SKATE GLOVES: FOR CONCRETE COMFORT

Under immense pressure from liability insurance companies, almost all U.S. skate parks from 1976 onwards started requiring skateboarders to wear full safety gear, including gloves on both hands for extra protection. But when gloves first became mandatory safety attire, the skateboard industry had little to offer by ways of skateboard-specific glove designs. This led an entire generation of skaters into DIY-territory, or to be more specific, the sprawling aisles of their closest Home Depot store. "Before skateboard companies offered professional gloves, everyone would wear gardening gloves to protect their hands," said seasoned skateboard artist Jim Phillips of Santa Cruz Skateboards.

PROTECTION FROM CONCRETE AND BOLTS

Professional skateboarder Steve Caballero has vivid memories of touching up his own DIY-gloves as a young Nor Cal skate park local: "For my first gloves I went and got gardener gloves and wore those at the park. People would always rip the fingers off the gloves from getting caught on the bolts of their trucks, like when they did tail taps. If your glove was stuck, you would go down with the board and slam. So a lot of guys would cut the finger tips off because we would do a lot of tricks where we would touch the nose."

Once protective products manufacturer Mike Rector designed – and patented – the first skateboard-specific gloves in 1978, he opened the floodgates to an entire cottage industry of "performance" glove companies. Advertised in leading skateboard magazines with heavy endorsements from top pro riders, skate-specific gloves became a hot fashion statement and coveted status symbol with often ludicrous price tags, including SIMS gloves for over $49.99 retail (about $120.00 in 2018). "When you saw pictures of Brad Bowman and Steve Olson wearing those gloves, you were like, 'Man I have to have those!'" said skateboard photographer J. Grant Brittain.

THE ORIGINAL: RECTOR GLOVES

Brought to market in mid-1978, the PALM PADS GLOVS [sic] designed by Mike Rector created the blueprint for skate-specific hand protection. "He calls his line Rector Skatewear and you're going to call it unreal," said the magazine advertisements for Rector's gloves, also promising: "Protection, durability, and style combined with a sense of freedom and confidence that you'll find out about the first time you land on them. Mike [Rector] is serious about his sport and about providing you with the protective clothing that meets your demands."

Built for "serious" park shredding, Rector's patented design incorporated high-density foam pads sewn into the palms of both hands for impact protection, supported by double-layer reinforced finger tips. The gloves' palm segments consisted of pig skin, while the outside layers had been crafted from cowhide suede. Securing a tight fit around the wrists, the gloves were held in place with a rainbow-colored elastic band featuring Velcro enclosures, trademarked as the Rainbow Wriststrap. In terms of colorways, Rector Palm Pads Glovs came in red and tan, or blue and tan at $19.50 (equivalent to $59.90 in 2018) per pair.

Photo: James Cassimus

DIY GLOVES: HOME-SPUN INNOVATION

But not every skateboarder was able to afford a spanking new set of gloves. Professional skateboarder Lance Mountain remembers showing up at the skate park as a young grommet. "I have this one photo were everything is the worst. I have these earth-colored shoes with white knee-high socks with no stripes on them. Levi's shorts that are cut off – and not even Levi's, probably J.C. Penney. And garden gloves, because you had to have garden gloves at the parks. Oh, and the worst skateboard," said Mountain, adding: "I love that picture, because I had all the wrong stuff. But I was dreaming I had all the right stuff!"

Elaborating on the issue, Lance Mountain said: "As a skateboarder, you just want better stuff. Because you are having more fun. That is all part of it. The dream if it all." For most cash-strapped skateboarders, professional gloves remained an elusive dream. "A lot of guys kept wearing gardening gloves and sliding padding into them," said J. Grant Brittain. But creativity in DIY glove designs also led to new, more functional mutations such as the "slide gloves" featuring hard plastic inserts on the palms for safely sliding the hands along the pavement on high-speed downhill runs. Later made popular by Stacy Peralta's high-octane downhill racing segment in 1984's *The Bones Brigade Video Show*, the first "slider gloves were self-made. They made them from [hard] plastic rails," said Lance Mountain.

sims

INTRODUCING

Newly invented • Money saving • Pat. Pending Safe-T-Palm with tight wrist enforcement

ONLY $4.99 plus 50¢ shipping

$5.99 with protective padding

Do you really need full gloves in hot summer? Not anymore!!!

Try our Safe-T-Palm. If you are not satisfied, we will return your money if you send them back within 10 days.

Safe-T-Palm is made of metallic design, and durable plastic material. They will match with your colorful skateboard beautifully. Available colors are white, gold, blue, and red.

Safe-T-Palm comes in three sizes as follows:

- ML—Medium Large for medium and large adults.
- S —Small for age 12 (average) and above, ladies' and small men's.
- JR—Junior for age 11 (average) and under.

Return for exchange in case of improper fit.

Roller Athletics Company, Subsidiary of
Jhoon Rhee Safety Equipment, Inc.
2000 L Street, N.W.
Washington, D.C. 20036 Tel. (202) USA-1000

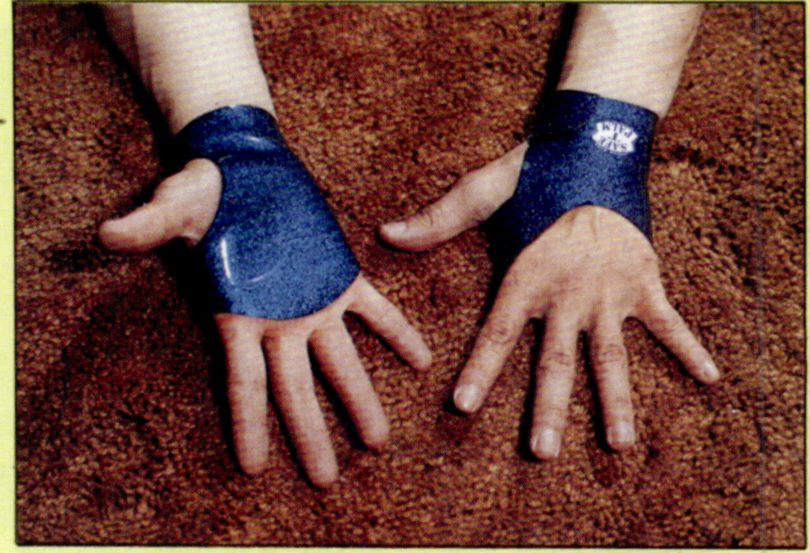

ROLLER

Enclosed is $__________. D.C. residents add 5% sales tax

$__________, plus shipping 50¢. Total Amount $__________.

Size:______ Color:________ Padding ($5.99)________

Name ____________________

Address ____________________

City __________ State ______ Zip ______

DEALER INQUIRIES INVITED

Another variation on the theme of crouching low and sliding both hands across the concrete originated in Hawaii, said Dave Duncan: "A lot of guys still skated barefooted with their sandals on their hands, like when they were skating ditches. The surfers in Hawaii always wore flip flops so you took your sandals off and used them like gloves to put your hands down." Throwing all low-budget skateboarders a bone, the ROLLER skateboard company introduced entry-level gloves: With their metallic surface and minimalistic, fingerless design, the Roller Safe-T-Palm plastic protectors were available in white, gold, blue, and red at the low price point of $4.99 ($5.99 with protective padding).

SIMS GLOVES: THE PRO'S CHOICE

Then again, who wants the budget option when the Ferrari of skate gloves – the SIMS Gloves in all their neon green and blue high-tech glory – is right out there in every issue of every magazine? Introduced in late 1978 by the SIMS Skateboards company, the gloves retailed for more than double the price of Rector's. "They lasted about five days and they were around 50 bucks!" said Dave Swift. But despite the high price point, they proved a major hit. "I would buy them although they were expensive," said pro skateboarder Eddie Elguera, adding: "I used to love them because they were leather, nice and soft. And they had that nice glossy blue top made from synthetic materials, and urethane tips which were good for grabbing."

Open any magazine from the halcyon days of late-1970s skate parks – and pros will be riding SIMS Gloves. "Everyone wore SIMS gloves back then. Especially everyone riding the parks had them," said skateboard photographer Michael Chantry. Several decades later, Nike SB paid homage to the SIMS gloves with a Dunk sneaker in the classic colorway of neon green and blue in a 2009 collaboration with Hollywood-based skate shop Brooklyn Projects. The enduring legacy is even more surprising given the fact that the gloves were plagued by several shortcomings. "Everybody had those gloves. But they would break if you slid them on the ground," said 1970s pro Wes Humpston.

What's more, SIMS safety gloves could prove a severe safety hazard under certain conditions: "The material was prone to getting caught in the protective netting they had surrounding the pools. So if you weren't careful, you would catch your fingers riding by and get stuck in the netting and slam or even dislocate your shoulder or the like. So I preferred to cut mine off," said skateboard photographer Michael Chantry. Soon enough, cutting the finger tips became a rite of passage among serious park skaters: "The first step would be for people to cut the fingers off, but then they would totally rip!" said Dave Swift. Steve Caballero also remembers: "Cutting the fingers off SIMS Gloves was huge at the time. The gloves were super big on me, so I had to cut them off anyways so they fit better. Even when they were not mandatory at the park people wore them, just for style."

Speaking of style, gloves with cut-off fingers also became the darlings of punk rock-minded skateboarders such as Duane Peters, while 1980s style icons such as Christian Hosoi and Tommy Guerrero would flaunt their street moves wearing only a single glove on one hand. Historically, finger-less gloves have always been a fashion statement. The practice dates back to 16th century Eastern European aristocracy, who wanted to show off fancy jewelry in cold weather by exposing their fingers. So it's no surprise that hand protection and extra points in skate style – even at ludicrous price points –have always fit together like hand in glove.

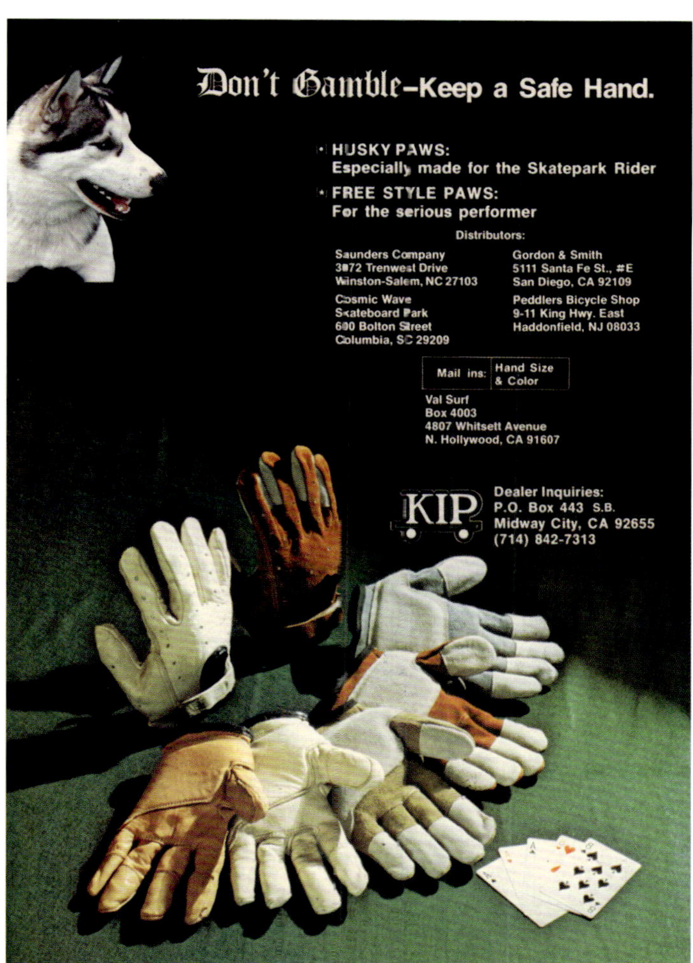

Photo: Glen E. Friedman

WOMEN'S SKATE FASHION: DO IT YOURSELF

During the first major boom in the 1960s, skateboarding had been embraced by boys and girls alike. Active participation reflected an equal share of male and female riders, as skateboarding still underwent a period of playful experimentation in terms of riding technique and aesthetics. That changed in the mid-1970s, when skateboarding blew up for a second time, this time focused around high-risk stunts on vertical terrain. Suddenly, skateboarding had become the domain of 'real men,' and the attitude toward women changed accordingly. "We used to call all the girls 'betties.' We used to ask them, 'Hey Betty, give me a spit-shine on my helmet,' and all that nasty stuff," said 1970s pro skateboarder and graphic artist Wes Humpston.

It was a man's world, and only few girls could hang in such an environment, not to mention deal with the blows of riding vertical concrete pools. Standout female pro riders of the era include Dogtown's Peggy Oki, Laura Thornhill and Robin Logan of Logan Earth Ski fame, vertical pioneer and Hobie teamrider Brenda Devine, Marina Del Rey local Cindy Whitehead, and Judy Oyama from Santa Cruz. The late 1970s competitive female skateboarding circuit was a tightly-knit group, rife with heated rivalries. "Terry Brown was the premier girl skater, Judi [Oyama] always tried to beat Terry. But Terry was just a natural athlete. You could do anything you want and train as hard as you want – you couldn't beat her. Kind of like Steve Olson," said Richard Novak, co-founder of NHS Skateboards in Santa Cruz.

But from a business perspective, women fell short of constituting a large enough demographic to warrant specialized products. "There was no women's skateboarding, they were only 1% of the market," said Richard Novak, at NHS Skateboards (Santa Cruz, Flip, Creature, Road Rider etc.). Accordingly, the industry's female-oriented offerings were practically non-existent. "Girls just weren't going to buy a lot of stuff in that era. They could have anything the guys wanted," said Richard Novak. While skateboard hardware proved compatible, the shortage of female-appropriate products became especially problematic in the apparel segment. "They never really had any clothing for girls... you had to customize everything to make it work," said Judi Oyama, original Santa Cruz team rider and one of the first female pro pool riders, whose tailoring skills earned her a reputation in the 1970s skate parkscene.

Some of Judi Oyama's original pieces include a denim button-up shirt with a red Santa Cruz Skateboards patch on the back, created by surf artist Jeff McKormack, who had a short-term stint at the company before Jim Phillips took over as resident artist. It was Phillips who created the famous Santa Cruz capsule logo, which Judi Oyama implemented on a customized white and blue women's track suit jacket. The active pool and slalom rider also offered customized board shorts with padding for fellow female riders upon request, replete with fashionable accents such as leopard patterns and corduroy paneling. Further fashion staples of the time, according to Judi Oyama, included "soccer-type uniforms, lots of collared shirts, and also wide-wale corduroy."

Other female pros also took the DIY-route to stay fashionable on and off the board. Robin Logan of San Diego's storied board sports dynasty would turn heads with her customized jackets, made in Europe. When Brenda Devine picked up a new board sponsor – the trailblazing vert skater became the first woman on the acclaimed Powell-Peralta team – she received limited edition runs of girl-sized T-shirts featuring the company's popular skeleton graphics. And while girl's skate apparel would become a standard category in the late 1980s, female skateboard fashion in the 1970s was still as underground as it gets.

SANTA CRUZ
SKATEBOARDS
SANTA CRUZ
SKATEBOARDER
LOGAN EARTH SKI
TEAM
LANE CHANGER
beach skatewear

The Solid Professionals

Two time WORLD CHAMPION Bruce Logan, skatin' Carlsbad Skatepark, polishing his innovative skills. Bruce is riding his new DURA-LITE shape which he designed to compliment his championship style. Bruce is a major contributor to Logan Earth Ski's extensive research and development program, which is constant in its efforts to bring you the most sophisticated equipment any pro could ask for. Bruce, along with the entire Logan family, is dedicated to providing you with equipment you'll have to live up to. Please send for our new brochure and discover all the fine professional components Logan Earth Ski has to offer you. Thanks.

742 Genevieve, Suite Q, Solana Beach, California 92075, 1-714-755-5452

Every era in skateboarding needs its super brand, that larger-than-life company selling the hottest gear endorsed by pro team riders with the biggest names in the sport. During skateboarding's second big wave of mass appeal, that super brand was Logan Earth Ski out of Encinitas, California. Built on an entire family's passion for skateboarding, the company was started in 1974 by "skateboarding's first family": Brian, Brad, Robin, and Bruce Logan together with their mother Barbara Logan. With an emphasis on using only top-shelf components and the highest-quality wood for their skateboards - all the while other manufacturers relied on plastic or Plexiglas - Logan Earth Ski set the paradigm for a company run by skateboarders, for skateboarders.

But wait a second - how does "skiing" factor into the brand name for a skateboarding company? "The Logan Earth Ski name came from a gentleman named Jeff Turnbull, who was a friend of our family in North County San Diego. He figured that Logan was a skateboard you rode on the earth not unlike a ski, and so he pulled it all together," said Robin Logan, a champion freestyler in the 1970s who is credited as the world's first woman to ever land a kickflip. Speaking of credited achievements, the rest of the Logan family also scored big on the competitive circuit: Brad Logan brought home the family's first national championship title before Bruce Logan, aka "King of the Nosewheelie," won the first of three World Freestyle Championship titles at the 1975 Bahne/Cadillac National Championships in Del Mar, where Robin took second in the women's division. Meanwhile, Brian Logan handled team management and product development, where Logan was in a league of its own.

In magazines and on the contest circuit, the Logan Earth Ski team's signature red jerseys became emblems of an elite squad, worn by team riders such as Torger Johnson, Bob Biniak, Jay Adams, Danny Bearer, Woody Woodward, and Eric Dressen as well as women's champion Laura Thornhill. Much like the shirts, the company was red-hot in 1976. And when the notorious Zephyr Skateboards Team disbanded that year, and brands stood in line to steal some of the shine by signing one of the high-profile "Z-Boys" to their roster, there was only one logical place to go for the highest profile rider of them all: In late 1976, Tony "Mad Dog" Alva signed onto Logan Earth Ski - following his childhood idol Torger Johnson - and proceeded to win two Skateboard World Championship titles in his bright-red Logan Earth Ski team T-shirt.

"When the Z-Boys split up, SIMS and Logan were the biggest companies because they had the most money. So [Bob] Beniak skated for SIMS for a little while and then went off to Logan. And Jay [Adams] and Tony [Alva] went straight to Logan," said 1970s skateboard pro Wes Humpston, while adding a little rock'n'roll lore to the mix: "The Logans were big partiers at the time, that's why everyone wanted to ride for Logan."

HARD MONEY IN SOFT GOODS

Another reason for the company's appeal was simple - Logan had the best boards. Bruce Logan and the family diligently tested their prototypes at 1970s hot spots including the notorious La Costa downhill run outside of San Diego. On the strength of performance-tested product, Logan Earth Ski grew from a backyard operation cranking out 50 boards per week in 1974 to a full-fledged production powerhouse selling 5,000 boards per week by 1976.

Swingster
World of Wearables
SIZE S
LOGAN EARTH SKI
TEAM

LOGAN EARTH SKI
TEAM

LOGAN EARTH SKI* TEAM

LOGAN EARTH SKI
LOGAN EARTH SKI
LOGAN EARTH SKI
LOGAN EARTH SKI
BRUCE LOGAN
BRUCE LOGAN

JOGGING STYLE: SWEAT THE TECHNIQUE

Before skateboarding caught its second wave of mass popularity in the mid-1970s, another quintessentially American sports trend spread across the globe like wildfire: Low-impact running, also called "jogging", became the latest craze for the Baby Boomer generation after U.S. marathon runner Frank Shorter won Olympic Gold in 1972. More than 25 million Americans, including President Jimmy Carter, took up jogging in the 1970s, and annual sales of sportswear such as jogging pants and tracksuits surpassed $8 billion by the end of the decade.

Inexpensive, comfortable, and widely available, jogging and track suit pants also became a fashion staple among 1970s skateboarders. One particular pro rider of the skate park era, all-round ripper Kevin Reed of Haut Skateboards fame, made full-length athletic pants his signature style. "Kevin Reed always wore long pants when he skated. He thought his legs were too skinny and always hid them," said skateboard photographer Ted "T-Bone" Terrebonne.

When Kevin Reed skated a pro demo at Campbell Skate park in Northern California, he made a lasting impression on a young Steve Caballero: "The first skateboard fashion I ever saw was when Kevin Reed came to our park. They called him Mr. Radical. He was wearing full sweats - sweatshirt plus long sweatpants under his knee pads," said Caballero, who commenced to stock up on sweat suits at the local athletic goods store that same day. "Because Kevin Reed was a pro and I thought that's what you were supposed to look like," said Steve Caballero.

LEGEND OF THE SWEAT SUIT

Long before skateboarders embraced comfortable athletic wear, the sweatshirt had its start in the year 1920 in a place where people were known to break a sweat. One particularly humid summer in Alexander City, Alabama, the son of underwear manufacturer Benjamin Russell was looking for a more comfortable type of football uniform than the standard-issue wool jerseys that chaffed and itched players in the balmy Southern climate. On a visit to Russell Senior's factory, he discovered the lightweight cotton jersey fabric worn by seamstresses and asked for a football top crafted from the same material: Enter the world's first sweatshirt, initially worn by the University of Alabama football team.

Soon enough, the long-sleeved jersey tops became so popular among college and high school athletes all over the U.S. that Russell started a new division dedicated to sportswear: Russell Athletic. Around the same time across the Atlantic, in France, entrepreneur Émile Camuset introduced the first athletic pants made from knitted gray jersey through his company, Le Coq Sportif: Enter the world's first sweatpants, an instant hit among runners and gymnasts. And once sweatshirts and sweatpants made sweet, steamy, intercontinental love, the result was the sweat suit, solving the question of what to put on before leaving the house for entire generations of leisurely-minded gentlemen.

Photo: Jim Goodrich

End of story? Not quite, as the late 1960s brought revolutionary material innovations into athletic sportswear, including flexible blends of nylon, polyester, terry cloth, and cotton in bright colors. These advanced materials spawned the rise of the sweat suit's upscale blood relative - the so-called tracksuit - which soon spilled into the streets as a major fashion item. While the sweatshirt owes its status as a fashion icon to actor Steve McQueen's sweater-clad performance in 1963's thriller The Great Escape, the tracksuit also became en vogue thanks to a big screen performance: After martial arts legend Bruce Lee adopted bright yellow track suits as his signature outfit in 1970s martial arts flicks such as Game of Death, men around the world followed "suit" and zipped up in sportswear.

Sportswear was everywhere in the early 1970s. At Olympic Games and major sports events, national sports teams competed wearing track suits as their official uniforms. Designed in the colorways of each country's national flag, a majority of these suits were made by the market leader in sports equipment, Germany-based Adidas. But slowly, a company founded in 1964 by Phil Knight together with the author of Jogging, the bible of the running movement, Bill Bowerman, started to gain traction. Initially focused on producing running-oriented footwear under the name Blue Ribbon Sports, the company changed its name to Nike, after the Greek goddess of victory, in 1971, and made major forays into athletic wear with sales reaching $3 billion in 1973.

HATE IT, LOVE IT

Worn separately, track suit pants and jackets became menswear staples, especially after Adidas released a new nylon and polyester blend suit in 1975. Cuban President Fidel Castro began an ongoing legacy of welcoming visiting heads of state dressed in a three-striped Adidas track suit jacket. Jogging pants became the staple of active lifestyles such as jogging and later aerobics, worn in and out of the gym. Naturally, this kind of success is bound to draw some flack, and haute designer Karl Lagerfeld famously noted: "Sweatpants are a sign of defeat. You lost control of your life so you bought some sweatpants."

Then again, skateboarders can't be expected to care about Karl Lagerfeld, so they adopted sweatpants with a vengeance. The mid-1970s marked a peak in athletic wear in the pro skateboarder ranks: In his 1975 *SkateBoarder* magazine "Who's Hot" checkout, the founder of Logan Earth Ski and multiple world champion Bruce Logan is depicted breaking the 40mph downhill speed barrier dressed in sweatpants, cut into shorts. On the 1976 cover of *SkateBoarder* magazine, pool riding pioneer Mike Weed can be seen mid-kickturn at the newly discovered Mt. Baldy pipeline, rocking bright red Adidas tracksuit pants with the signature three stripes. Subsequently, red track suits officially became a thing in skateboarding.

TRACK SUITS ARE RED HOT

The new generation of skate park riders like Steve Caballero jumped on the red hot fashion trend: "On my first cover of *Skating News* magazine, I'm wearing full red sweats doing bank slalom. If you look at early photos of me, I'm always wearing red sweatpants underneath my pads. Even if it was over 100F outside, I wore full sweats - for style!" said Caballero. For skateboarders in places without regular access to apparel from California-based skateboard companies, the adaptation of athletic gear into skate style proved a life-saver.
In Europe and even Florida - where Vans shoes and apparel weren't available until the late 1970s - track suits, jogging pants, and athletic shoes became the norm at skate parks.

SKATIN WITH KATIN
PHOTO: GRANNIS
« The Perfect Combination »
Dealer Inquiries Invited.
KANVAS
BY KATIN, INC.
Send 50 cents for
decal and 76 brochure.
16250
PACIFIC COAST HWY.
SURFSIDE, CA 90743 (213) 592-2052
katin

SKATEBOARDER MAGAZINE: CALI DREAMING

Every culture needs a forum, a platform for the shared visions of its participants, a voice of inspiration to keep things moving forward. After *the Quarterly Skateboarder* magazine had ceased publication following its Christmas 1965 issue, skateboard culture had gone quiet and almost ceased to exist. But when the magazine returned in 1975 under the name *SkateBoarder* – with doubled page count and full-color photographs on glossy paper – skateboard culture also came back swinging: Featuring a photo of Gregg Weaver carving barefooted in an empty swimming pool, the cover of *SkateBoarder*'s first new iteration presented the shape of things to come, promising "HOT ACTION, HIGH SPEED, RADICAL RUNS." All of which the *Surfer* magazine offshoot delivered, and then some: "When *SkateBoarder* magazine started republishing, it blew the whole scene up! They were really good about covering everything – they covered slalom, banks, parks, bowls, and all the new things that were coming out," said 1970s pro skateboarder Brad Bowman.

Edited by influential skateboard photographer Warren Bolster, *SkateBoarder* would showcase the day's hottest talent as the official voice of skateboarding's rise from the ashes. Next to the writings of Craig R. Stecyk III, responsible for putting the new Dogtown skate style on the map, and the larger-than-life persona of assistant editor Kurt "Mellow Cat" Ledterman, the magazine established the visual blueprint for skateboarding's new wave. Captured in wide-angled "fisheye" splendor against the backdrop of endless blue skies and palm trees, SkateBoarder brought readers California dreams of pools, banks, skateparks, and endless downhill runs courtesy of photographers such as Glen E. Friedman, Jim Cassimus, Jim Goodrich, Michael Chantry, and Ted Terrebone. In those days before constant visual overload via the Internet, a single photographic image – Tony Alva's first-ever frontside air at the Dog Bowl or the first full pipe sessions at Mt Baldy – could have earth-shattering effects on skateboard riding technique and fashion sensibilities.

"For me as a kid, a picture would just speak to you. I would look at skate photos in magazines for hours. And you would be like, 'Whoa! I gotta get those shorts!'" said skateboard photographer Dave Swift. Speaking of shorts, next to sponsored advertisements for the day's leading apparel, hardware, and safety equipment brands, *SkateBoarder* also offered its own collections of branded merchandise. Modelled by top pros such as Tony Alva, Gregg Weaver, and Tom "Wally" Inouye, the magazine advertised T-shirts, long-sleeved shirts, windbreakers, trucker hats, striped tube socks, headbands, and day packs bearing the magazine logo paired with competition-style stripes and photographic screen-prints, including the iconic silhouette of slalom rider Chris Yandell's downhill run. The advertisements encouraged readers to "JOIN THE TEAM" – make themselves known as skateboarders – and "Put SkateBoarder T-Shirts, Skatebreakers, headbands and day packs on your body." In the bigger picture, *SkateBoarder* magazine exerted an even more profound influence on the era's fashion sense. As part of a partnership with skatepark operators and safety equipment manufacturers – which happened to be major advertisers – the magazine would only feature photographs of riders wearing full safety gear, especially on cover shoots.

SkateBoarder

SkateBoarder
MAGAZINE
SkateBoarder
MAGAZINE

In their role as gatekeepers of skate style, the magazine's photographers decided what was trending and worth covering – not just in terms of riding technique, but also from a skate fashion standpoint. "Color-coordination was important and all the pros tried to match their pads with their shoes, wheels and clothing. We photographers liked it as well and encouraged skaters to wear colorful gear," said SkateBoarder photographer Ted "T-Bone" Terrebonne. In other words, skaters had to look fresh to get coverage. When Terrebonne shot Christian Hosoi's first photo for *SkateBoarder* magazine, the 11-year-old prodigy was wearing yellow knee pads to match the yellow wheels on his board. Well played. Other riders took some strong-arming: When his sponsors flew pro skateboarder Alan Gelfand out from Florida to premiere his new "ollie" aerial, the magazine's photographer had the last word on outfit choices. "I wore long pants my entire life skateboarding, and in order for me to be in the magazine they said I had to wear shorts!" said Alan Gelfand.

In that sense, the late 1970s established the ground rules in the complex relationship between riders and skateboard publications: The skaters with the most coverage would always be the ones who knew how to play the game. Skateboard photographer Skin Phillips, longtime photo editor of *Transworld Skateboarding* magazine even goes as far as saying: "Photographers and photo editors were the ones who got to decide what to put into magazines. They chose all the right people and that made all the difference. Without them choosing what to put into magazines, there wouldn't even be such a thing as skateboard fashion!"

MELLOW CAT: PATRON SAINT OF SKATE STYLE

Sometimes there's a man, and you know, he's just the man for his time. In mid-1970s skateboarding, that man was writer, cultural icon, and *SkateBoarder* magazine editor Kurt "Archie" Ledterman from La Jolla, whose alter ego Mellow Cat became a larger-than-life symbol of skateboarding lifestyle. Known for taking it easy, living the dream, and enjoying the stoke of a good session with the bros, the bearded, long-haired personification of a "surfer dude" starred in a series of Ted Richards-designed cartoons on the pages of *SkateBoarder* magazine in 1978 that turned Mellow Cat into a household name among surfers and skateboarders across the US. Also in 1978, Mellow Cat took the leap into skateboard apparel when Skateboarder began marketing trucker hats, T-shirts, and sweatshirts featuring Mellow Cat's stylized comic book likeness. "Woah, Hey, We're almost out!" Mellow Cat barks in an advertisement for the bubble-lettered T-shirts bearing his character. A "far out" Ted Richards shirt design shows Mellow Cat zipping out of the earth's stratosphere on his board, saying "RAD-E-KAL MON!"

Expanding his legend status to international audiences, Mellow Cat appeared in 1980's road movie *Skateboard Madness* playing a motivationally challenged photographer herding a gang of pro skaters including Stacy Peralta, Gregg Ayres, Alan Gelfand, Kent Senatore and Dan "Mini Shred" Smith on an odyssey in search of "killer" skate photos. His publisher breathing down his neck, demanding photos, Mellow Cat takes the time to smell the roses and explore new terrain off the beaten track. Shouldering the Halfpipe dreams of an entire generation, Mellow Cat represented the underlying message that skateboarding really is all about the journey, the perpetual quest for fun. "Mellow Cat was an imaginary figure that was made up, a fictional character in skateboarding," said Ledterman's co-star, professional skateboarder Alan Gelfand from Florida, adding: "He was almost like [enigmatic Powell video character] *Animal Chin* when they had him in the '80s. 'Have you seen him?' Mellow Cat was the *Animal Chin* of the 1970s."

In real life, Kurt Ledterman remained an active advocate of surf and skateboard culture. A passionate surfer throughout his life – his local spot in La Jolla Shores is called "Archie's Lefts" in his honor – he played an integral part in defining the voice and character of *SURFER* magazine, as well as sister publication *SkateBoarder* magazine after its re-launch in 1975. Upon his passing in 2015, the surf and skateboard scene responded with fond memories of "Archie" and his lasting influence as a style icon and historian of board sports culture.

mellow cat
RAD-E-KAL MON!
mellow cat

El Gato
VARIFLEX®
THE EDDIE ELGUERA
"SUREFOOTED" CONCAVE MODEL
□ 30.5" x 10.75" □ 6 PLY ROCKHARD MAPLE CONSTRUCTION □ TOUGHSKIN TOP AND BOTTOM □ ROUTED UNDERSIDE □ CONCAVE DECK □ TAPED □ PREDRILLED.
NEW C-3 WHEELS: (64mm, Cone & Conical). Don't let the winners of the Hester Upland Contest be proof—try them for yourself—Fast, fast and durable. Available in a 91A yellow and a 94A red. Ride the winners!
CONNECTION TRUCKS: Two functional sizes with the 8.5" and the new 9". Both with hardened axle. 356-T6 aluminum and CLOUDS® suspension cushions make the connection on Variflex's—no hang-up trucks!
26CM DECK: 31" x 10.5". 7 ply bi-directional maple construction with top and bottom black piles complete with clear 3M tape.
DENNIS MARTINEZ MODEL: 29.5" x 10" smoother transition with this "4-slide" 6 ply hard rock maple deck. TUFSKIN top and bottom. The four air-slide bars insure strength and control and does not sacrifice lightness.
ERIC GRISHAM MODEL: 29.5" x 10.25" multi-channel, multi-functional. Strong and light 7-ply hard rock maple. TUFSKIN top and bottom with unmistakable inlayed bottom graphics.
VARIFLEX® NINE: 28.5" x 9" superlight deck with six ply unidirectional construction. TUFSKIN top and bottom, complete with 3M® tape and predrilled.
VARIFLEX® TEN: 30.5" x 10" same construction as "THE NINE" just wider and longer!
BILL HANES SLALOM MODEL: 29" x 8" more snap, positive footing and pre-drilled. U.S.A.S.A. National Champion designed and tested. Black hand-layed fiberglass over dence foam—complete with grip tape. ..The Racer's Choice!
9644 LURLINE, CHATSWORTH, CA 91311 (213) 341-7301
NOW AVAILABLE—THE NEW VARIFLEX® PRO-WRIST GUARD
PHOTO: RUIZ

Don't be fooled by the perfect image of sportsmanship and athletic-looking professional skateboarders competing for championship titles in their company's branded team jerseys. Behind the facade of sportsmanlike conduct and fair play, a number of heated battles raged deep within the late 1970s pool competition circuit. It was a bonfire of the vanities, an epic clash of Punk VS. straight-edge, Nor Cal VS. So Cal, Vals VS. Dogtowners – and the punk rock-minded Santa Cruz Skateboards team against the clean-cut, contest-winning technicians on the Variflex team. The gloves came off during the 1980s Gold Cup pool contest series, said Variflex professional skateboarder Eddie "El Gato" Elguera: "When I came up on the bowl, they would spit at me during my contest run. And they would yell, 'FALL! FALL! FALL!' And they always called us 'Varibots.'"

At the bottom of this animosity lies a fundamental schism in the late 1970s, from which two rival schools of skateboarding emerged: While Variflex blazed a trail based on trick difficulty and technical progression, companies such as Dogtown Skates and Santa Cruz – with team riders Salba, Duane Peters and Steve Olson – went the power and style-driven route. "The name 'Varibots' was what Salba and the [Santa Cruz] guys called us," said Elguera. "During the first Hester Series [in 1978] it was still all about surf style with guys like Gregg Weaver and carves and reverts. And when I came in, I started doing a lot of different tricks and they called this 'robot style' because it was more technical." On the competition circuit, the clash between the two schools – radical style VS. technical style – was epitomized in the rivalry between Elguera and Duane Peters, with the mainstream media fanning the flames. Asked in a 1980 television interview whether he was afraid of competing against reigning pool champ Elguera, a nonchalant Peters said: "I'm not scared or anything... he doesn't bother me."

Despite their clashes at contests, Santa Cruz and Variflex were in entirely different leagues in terms of target demographic. While Santa Cruz prided itself on brand-name performance products, Variflex catered to mass-market consumers with affordable equipment. "It was one of those companies that were more in department stores, for the kids that wanted a cheaper skateboard," said Eddie Elguera. Nevertheless, the Moorpark-based company at one point in time sponsored some of the most influential riders and trailblazers of modern-day skateboarding, including Eric Grisham, Steve Hirsch, Pattie Hofman, Allen Losi, Dennis Martinez, Eddie "El Gato" Elguera, Lance Mountain, John Lucero, and Jeff Grosso.

VARIFLEX: TECHNICAL EDGE

Big-name pro riders figured prominently in the marketing of Variflex skateboards right from the start in 1977, when the father of pro skater Allen Losi, Raymond H. Losi, established the brand as a family business. "They started with making Variflex trucks and also wanted to do a pro line. So they got some already established pros on the team, like Dennis Martinez and then started building from there with Eric Grisham and Allen Losi," said Eddie "El Gato" Elguera. Magazine advertisements for Variflex were a classic case of "The future, imagined in the late 1970s" with lots of neon, polished metal, plastic – the technical performance look, backed up by affordable boards and equipment that, also resonated with core skateboarders.

"By 1980 they were making really good boards and had built a strong brand with Lance [Mountain] coming on," said Elguera, adding: "But by 1981 they were already back to the department stores and cheaper boards because they could make more money that way - selling more to the masses." Regardless of the brand's marketing tactics, the Variflex team riders proved strong competitors on the pool riding contest series. Dressed in their team jerseys and Variflex safety helmets, the riders built a reputation for pioneering never-before-seen tricks and unleashing them at contests for an extra edge, including Allen Losi's airs to fakie and Elguera's varial inverts. Although the two diverging schools of skateboard style would never reconcile their differences - in a way, the battle between tech VS. hesh still rages on - approval for technical pioneer Elguera came later, from the most influential technical skateboarder of all time, Tony Hawk. "In his book and interviews he said he looked up to me at the time, because he didn't have that much style but he could do a lot of tricks. For me that's a compliment because Tony is probably the most recognized skater of all time and an ambassador for skateboarding."

Variflex endured as a company at a time when other skateboard brands went under: Variflex reported $1.5 million from skateboard sales in 1983 - when skateboarding was practically dead - only to reach $30 million and a 37% market share in 1987 by selling 1.9 million skateboards. In the early 1990s, the company banked heavily on the inline skating trend and sold $100 million worth of product in 1995, as inline skates became 90% of Variflex's business. But when the inline skateboarding bubble burst, Vari ex hit some hard yards, but still held on until the early 2000s by marketing board sports brands such as Static Snowboards, as well as trampolines and Quik-Shade beach canopies.

THE VARIFLEX AMATEUR TEAM

"...HERE TODAY, PRO TOMORROW"

Success is attributed to many things but most of all enthusiasm. Skateboarding is no different The success that Variflex has experienced stems from not only the research and development on the manufacturing level but most important it comes from the skaters themselves: pro and amateur, the Variflex teams and their friends have supported not only the team but the sport itself. Enthusiasm and hard work demand responsible and dependable equipment. Variflex thanks "the skaters" for their assistance in helping to develop top equipment in a competitive sport.

A WINNING TEAM!

VARIFLEX AMATEUR TEAM: PATTI HOFFMAN—1st Van's California State Championships ☐ GIL LOSI—1st Coulton ASPO Bank Slalom ☐ FREDDIE DESOTA—1st Van's California State Championships ☐ MIKE HIRSCH—1st USASA Championships ☐ ALLEN LOSI—1st Van's California State Championships ☐ MIKE SIEGFRIED—1st Reseda Pro-Am ☐ KY LAMBERT—1st Van's California State Championship ☐ LANCE MOUNTAIN—1st Van's Marina ☐ DANNY JORGENSON—1st Van' California State Championships.

VARIFLEX PRO TEAM: Eric Grisham ☐ Eddie "El Gato" Elguera ☐ Bill Hanes ☐ Dennis Martinez ☐ Steve Hirsch.

DANNY JORGENSON

LANCE MOUNTAIN

9644 LURLINE, CHATSWORTH, CA 91311 (213) 341-7301

VARIFLEX
VARIFLEX
VARIFLEX

MAD RATS.

Photo: Jim Goodrich

Lightning Bolt

the symbol of that full juice feeling!

Red hot Bobby Piercy off the lip in his contrast panel Bolt "Action Wedge" shirt.

Mike Williams wheelies in his striped "Action Wedge" shirt.

Tom Padaca, suited for W
Jamming.

Choice threads and fine bangles for Bolt gals.

"The Source"—black magic energy.

Action photos at Concrete Wave, Anaheim, California.

Bolt energy for your feet.

These are pure Bolts—beware of imitations.

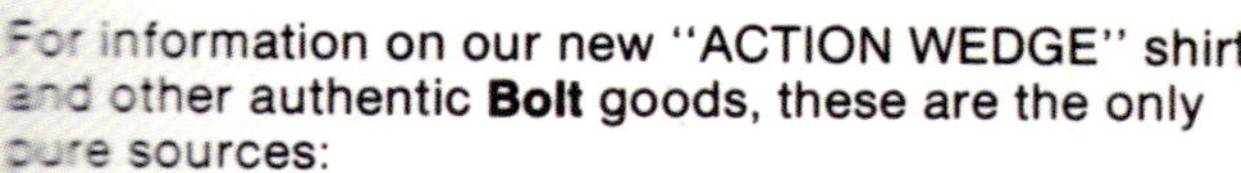

For information on our new "ACTION WEDGE" shirt and other authentic **Bolt** goods, these are the only pure sources:

BOLT Skateboards, 618 East Sunny Hills Road, Fullerton, CA 92635 **BOLT For Gals,** 14223 Bessemer St., Van Nuys, CA 91401 **BOLT Sportswear,** 6415 DeSoto Ave., Woodland Hills, CA 91367 **BOLT Surfboards,** 1503 Kapiolani Blvd., Honolulu, HI 96814 **BOLT Jewelry,** P.O. Box 1323, Newport Beach, CA 92663 **BOLT Wax,** P.O. Box 601, Cardiff-by-the-Sea, CA 92007 **BOLT Surf and Ski Suits,** 530 6th St., Hermosa Beach, CA 90254 · **BOLT Fin Leash Connection,** P.O. Box 163, Huntington Beach, CA 92648 **BOLT Surf Leash,** 2603 Duson, Simi Valley, CA 93065 • **California/BOLT Surfboards,** P.O. Box 216, Dana Point, CA 92629 **BOLT Wave Jammer/USA,** 724 N. Poinsettia, Santa Ana, CA 92702 **BOLT Sandals/USA,** 1005 Mark Ave., Carpinteria, CA 93013 • **Japan/BOLT Surfboards,** 3-9-25 Motomachi, Tsjuido, Fujawa-shi, Kanajawa-Ken **New Zealand/BOLT Sportswear,** P.O. Box 41179 St. Lukes, Auckland • **Australia/BOLT Sportswear,** 112-142 Trennery Crescent, Abbotsford, Victoria 3067

As skateboarding progressed away from the beaches and into concrete skate parks throughout the 1970s, the classic "surf stripes" pattern came along for the ride. "Surfing fashion became a thing and we started wearing striped shirts and striped socks. And then we would get laughed at in school by the jocks!" says skateboard photographer Ted "T-Bone" Terrebonne, adding: "This was also the time for bleached, long hair. But it was already considered long when it touched your ears."

For 1970s skateboarders, wearing stripes became a way of standing out from the masses, foreshadowing the later adoption of the pattern into punk rock attire. Says skateboard photographer Dave Swift: "Crew socks were kind of nerdy, so skateboarders wore tube socks and if they didn't have stripes, they were definitely uncool." Todd Huber at Skatelab skate park and museum remembers cross-over apparel brand Hang Ten as one of the first skateboard-oriented companies to capitalize on the trend: "They were both a surfing and skateboarding company and known for skinny stripes, mainly in green and white."

The pattern's major push into skateboarding happened in 1978 when bad boy skateboarders Steve Olson and Duane Peters released striped and checker patterned pro model boards on Santa Cruz Skateboards and appeared rocking striped shirts and socks on the cover of *SkateBoarder* Magazine. "Duane Peters and Steve Olson were the first punks in skateboarding," said Ted "T-Bone" Terrebonne. "Duane Peters made stripes punk rock, without a doubt," said Jim Phillips.

Across the Atlantic in Germany, young skateboarder Claus Grabke emulated the look in true D.I.Y. fashion: "My first home-made boards all had stripes, carefully done with masking tape and spray paint. I had a black board with silver stripes, really hot shit back then!" Grabke, who later turned pro on Santa Cruz Skateboards with a board graphic designed by Jim Phillips, added: "The stripes came from motor bikes, that was before I knew there were other skateboarders out there."

Since then, stripes have remained a classic element of skateboard graphic and apparel design. As a little-known fact, Jim Phillips revealed the impact on one of his best-known skateboard deck graphics: "I think there is a graphic link to the Rob Roskopp 'Target' graphic owing to the power of the stripes, because the target is simply stripes arranged concentrically." Today, surf stripes have come full-circle: Buoyed by the trend towards retro styles in skateboard apparel, their prominence in current collections is second only to the most ubiquitous of graphic patterns, camouflage.

SIMS
Competition
SKATEBOARDS

SIMS: ATHLETIC CHAMPION STYLE

According to industry insiders, short company names with one or two syllables prove the most effective when it comes to marketing skateboard brands. Names around four to five letters translate into compact, symmetrical logos ideal for display on branded skateboards and apparel. In that light, world champion freestyle skateboarder Tom Sims chose wisely when he went with his last name to launch SIMS Skateboards in 1975, selling state-of-the-art skateboard hardware and apparel with the recognizable, bold-lettered SIMS logo designed by graphic artist Rick Sharp.

In a little-known aside, instead of going into business for himself, SIMS almost landed a spot on the coveted team of Jeff Ho Surfboards and Zephyr Productions in Santa Monica. "Tom Sims almost rode for Zephyr. He was a really great longboard skater," said Zephyr co-owner Skip Engblom. Blazing a trail of his own, SIMS trusted his status as a high-profile, contest-winning rider to get his company up and running. "If you follow the history of Tom Sims, he won a lot of championships in '75 and '76... a lot of them freestyle, some slalom. He originally came from surfing," said SIMS team rider Ed Economy, who also helped manage the company with Tom Sims' father while Tom Sims focused on the team.

Speaking of the team, Tom Sims recruited an elite selection of the day's best riders to represent his brand, including Brad Bowman, Bert LaMar, Lonnie Toft, Doug de Montmorency, Tom 'Wally' Inouye, Marc Hollander, and Dave Andrecht. Out at skateparks and competitions, the more than 15 members of the SIMS Skateboards team turned heads when they rolled up in their branded van wearing matching team jerseys in SIMS' signature red, white, and blue color scheme. "I thought those shirts were cool. When I saw them I thought, 'That's a team!' It made them look like a full-on team," said pro skateboarder Steve Caballero. Adding to the brand's reputation, Tom Sims pioneered some of the day's most groundbreaking advancements in skateboard equipment. "SIMS was like the Powell of the '70s. I was very aesthetically attracted to them. They were very advanced," said pro skateboarder and former SIMS team rider Pierre André Senizergues.

STATE-OF-THE-ART DESIGNS

In the long run, SIMS Skateboards owed its success to a constant commitment to product development. Equal parts talented skateboard athlete and tinkerer, Tom Sims pioneered the world's first longboard skateboards – with decks sourced from old water skis – which he began marketing in 1975. In search of lightweight alternatives to conventional solid wood or fiberglass decks, Sims teamed up with a water ski manufacturer to develop multi-ply laminated wood decks from Canadian maple in 1977. Nothing short of a complete game changer, 7-ply maple boards created the mold for the future of skateboard construction.

Early test pilots for the new boards included Jim Muir, who spent a short stint on the SIMS team right after Zephyr had disbanded. "When Tom Sims made the first laminated skateboards, he gave one to Bob Biniak, one to Lonnie Toft, and one to me. They were half an inch thick and half the weight of all these solid wood skateboards," said Jim Muir, who unwittingly ended his tenure when he showed up at the SIMS factory with a classic Makaha Skateboards team patch on his shorts.

"When Tom Sims saw the Makaha Club patch on my shorts, he freaked out and started yelling at me. Because at the time, the guy from Makaha, [Larry] Stevenson, was suing everyone for the kicktail [board construction he had patented]. So he kicked me off the team!"

But for Jim Muir, experiencing the next-level performance offered by SIMS' breakthroughs provided the impetus to start his own company, Dogtown Skates. "I still had that laminated skateboard, and Biniak quit SIMS and gave his board to [Dogtown co-founder] Wes Humpston. He and I were skating pools and these two boards were the best we had ever ridden, so we decided to recreate these boards." Tom Sims also pushed the boundaries in urethane wheel formulas. "The best wheels were SIMS Gyro chronicles. They were the top of the line in 1978 – that was the cutting edge. That was the wheel to have!" said Ed Economy. Having built the world's first precursor to the snowboard – 1963's "skiboard" created in seventh grade woodworking class – SIMS also turned his innovative pursuits towards snowboarding, again pushing the boundaries. In 1983, SIMS Snowboards marketed the first snowboards with metal edges, backed by Tom Sims himself winning the World Snowboarding Championship that same year.

SPORTY FASHION

In an age when athletic, sports performance apparel was all the rage in skateboarding, SIMS raised the bar with its head-to-toe clothing collections. The company's patented skateboard gloves became equal parts mandatory protective gear and hot fashion item. Released in 1977, the lightweight nylon sports jerseys – with horizontal color-blocking in red, white, and blue stripes plus the winged SIMS logo on the chest – became a major hit after team rider Ed Economy made the pages of a popular magazine. "I got the center spread of Wide World of Skateboarding in army pants and a SIMS jersey that Tom gave me. And I was the only one to make the magazine, so Tom was really stoked on that!" said Ed Economy. Word of the sporty shirts traveled all the way to the UK: "Looking through the magazines, I would always see the long-sleeve SIMS shirt that everyone used to wear. We couldn't get them [in the UK], but I always wanted one... I dreamed of that shirt!" said pro skateboarder Don Brown, who ultimately became sponsored by SIMS in 1984.

Not everyone was singing the team jersey praises, including SIMS team rider Brad Bowman. "I really liked the jerseys, but for me it was a bit too much of a high school sports team – football or baseball. I really liked the short-sleeve shirt in red, white, and blue with the collar and the logo on the left pocket. Those I wore a lot," said Bowman, while offering the inside scoop on the collared shirt. "Looking back at photos today you realize how giant the collars on these polo shirts were. But that was the Seventies. I liked it, though, because I was a big Elvis fan." Nevertheless, the shirts had their shortcomings in a performance setting. "After a while, you would sweat so much that the collar would just stick to you, so we started cutting the collars out of our shirts.

Mike
Folmer
SIMS
TEAM
Ed
Economy
SIMS
TEAM
SIMS
SIMS
Ultimate Equipment

That's when Sims said, 'We're not gonna make them anymore, the guys are just ruining their shirts!' So the collared shirts went the way of the dodo." On that note, Tom Sims always kept an open ear for suggestions from team riders, including 1980s freestyle pro Steve Rocco: "For my SIMS board with the checkered design, I had graph paper and filled in every other square and sent it to them - and they made it exactly!" Next to its punk rock-inspired checkerboard design, the SIMS Steve Rocco freestyle board would become iconic for breaking the monotony of wide-bellied skate park shapes with a slim, street-oriented design complemented by a responsive Steve Rocco wheel that struck a note with the freestyle crowd. Equally pioneering, SIMS also became one of first companies to offer full-fledged sponsorship to female skateboarders, including vert pro Cindy Whitehead from Huntington Beach.

LEADING THE CHARGE

Some say that imitation is the sincerest form of flattery, which would make SIMS Skateboards one of the most highly complimented companies of the late 1970s. All across the world -especially in Brazil with its self-sustained, bootleg-driven skate economy - blatant SIMS knock-offs appeared, from skateboards to all manner of apparel. Lots of shirts featured variations of a photo depicting SIMS rider Tom 'Wally' Inouye performing a kickturn. "Wally is on a lot of rip off stuff," said Ed Economy, looking through counterfeit SIMS apparel. "You see the SIMS one on the V-neck shirt? We never had the shirt like that! And this one's a SIMS [logo] shirt but it doesn't say SIMS, so it's a rip off."

By 1981, SIMS had grown into one of the leading brands in the skate business. Always on the lookout for fresh talent, Tom Sims recruited top pros such Steve Rocco, Todd Swank, Pierre Andre, Brad Bowman, Dave Andrecht, Chris Strople, and Wally Inouye, while also enlisting a wave of upcoming amateurs including Kevin Staab, Tony Hawk, and Christian Hosoi. As Hosoi recalls: "Tom Sims called me, saying 'SIMS is going to give you a [pro] model!' These are guys I grew up idolizing for their style - Brad Bowman, Doug de Montmorency." Hosoi said yes, and although his model's release suffered a slight delay when Tom Sims licensed his company to Brad Dorfman of Vision Industries in 1981, the rookie ultimately entered the pro ranks in harness for SIMS. "They made the Rising Sun board, which was a pretty good deal," said Hosoi, who sold up to 20,000 boards per month at peak times.

Unfortunately, the skateboard industry entered another major slump in the early 1980s, and major companies such as SIMS faced enormous difficulties collecting open payments from struggling skate shops. Nevertheless, SIMS Skateboards continued its run through the highs and lows of the business all the way until today. Maintaining an interest and active reign in the company until his passing in 2012, Tom Sims remained an outspoken advocate of skateboarding and snowboarding - the two sports on which he left a tremendous mark, both on and off the board.

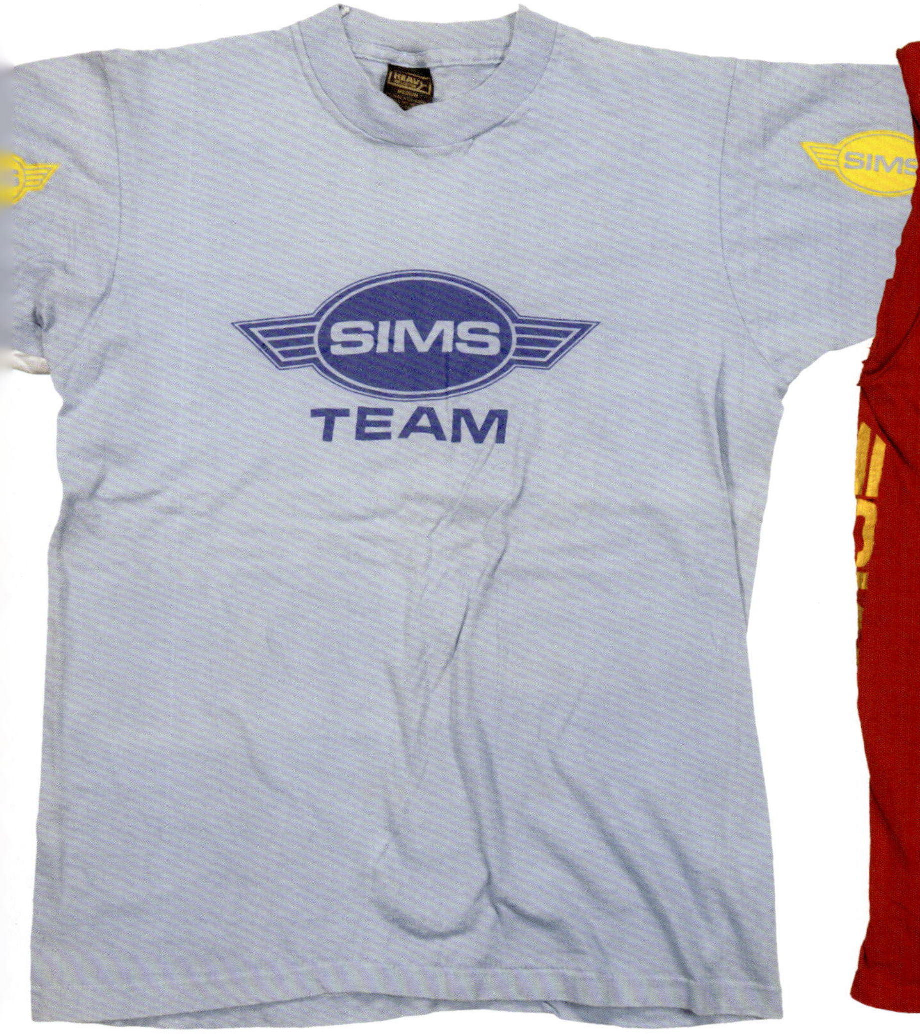
SIMS
SIMS
TEAM

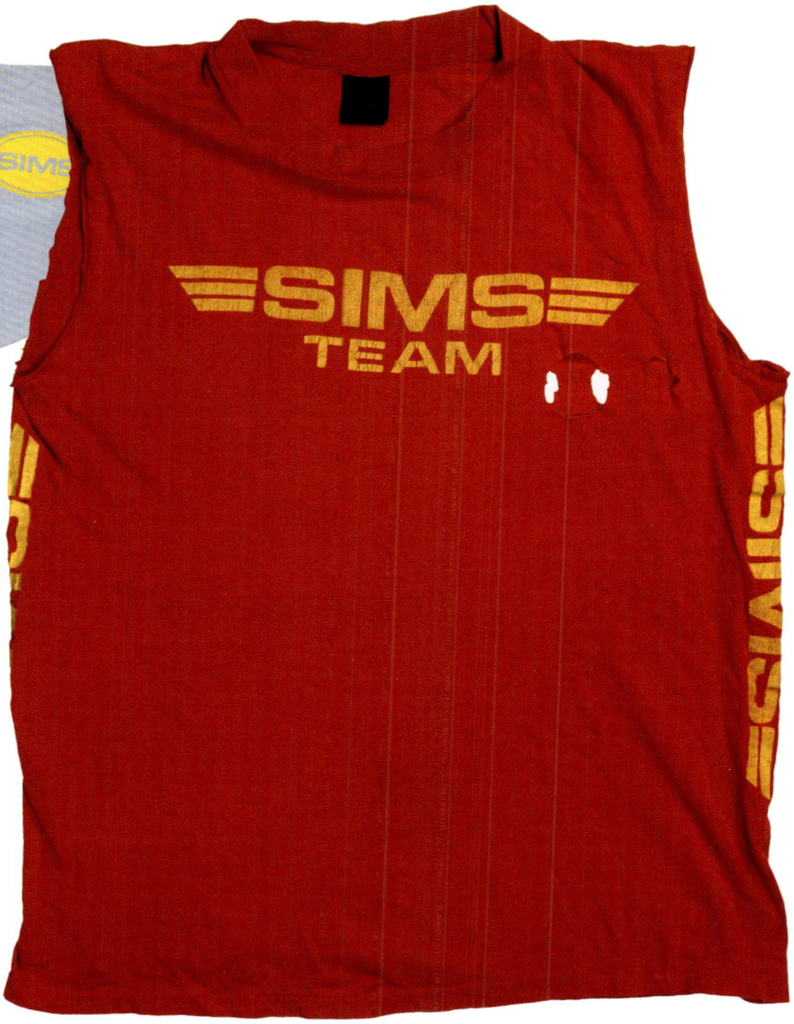
SIMS
TEAM
SIMS

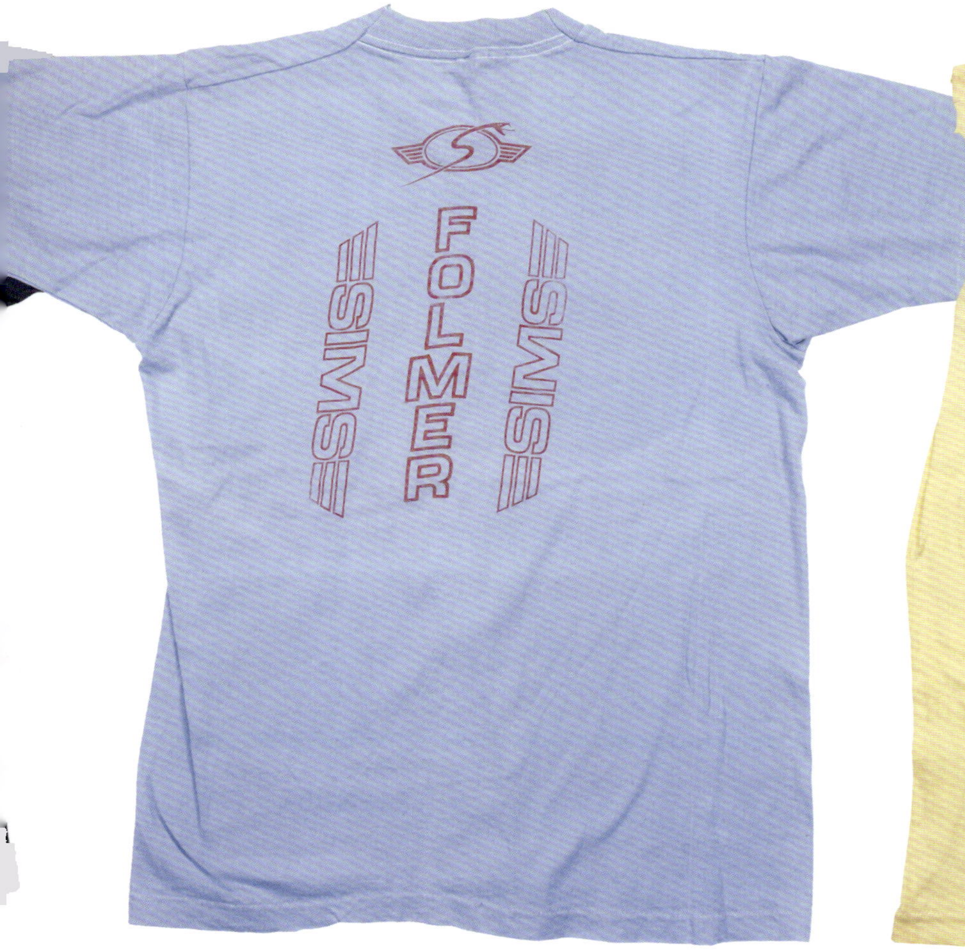
SIMS
FOLMER
SIMS

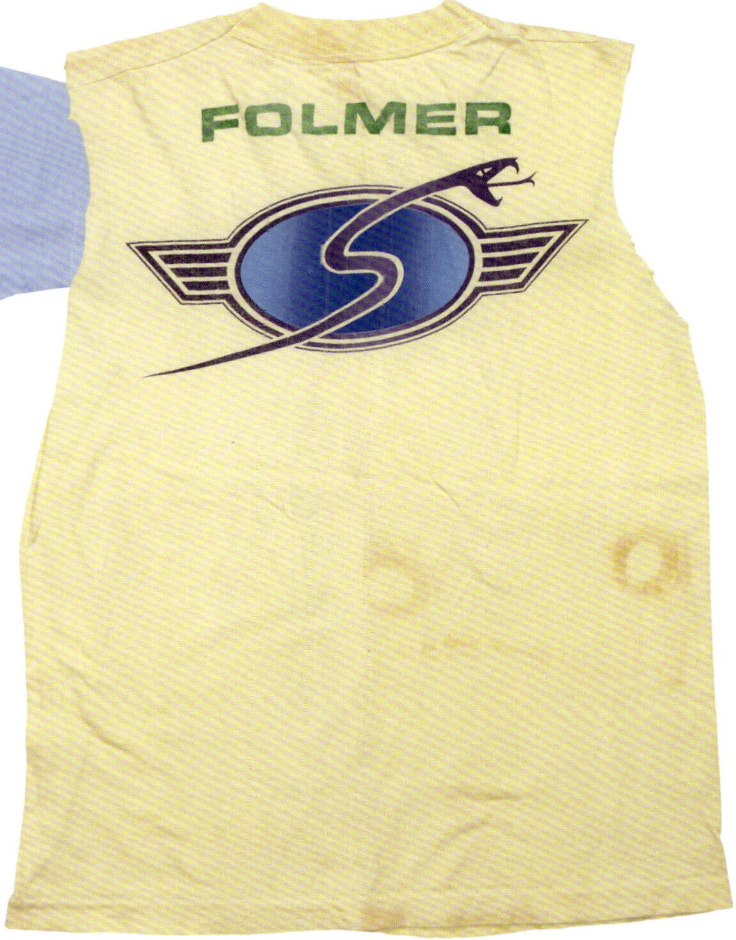
FOLMER

SIMS
SIMS
SIMS
SIMS
SIMS
SIMS
SIMS PURE JUICE
SIMS PURE JUICE
PURE JUICE

Photo: Tom Sims

SIMS

Photo: Craig Fineman

BUSHWAKKER®
SPORTSWEAR
Endorsed by the pros:
Logan Brothers
Ty Page
Denis Shufeldt
Curt Lindgren
Robin Logan
Laura Thornhill
Tony Alva
Torger Johnson
Chris Chaput
Steve Cathey
Bryan Beardsley
Gregg Weaver
Mike Weed
Pro Skateboard Jerseys
Logan Earth Ski
GT Grentec
Thunderboards
Weber
Freestyle
Hobie
Wayne Brown
Kona
G & S
Spinnin' Wheels
Bahne
Makaha
Ty Page
Santa Cruz
Banzai
Sims
Photo: Pro skater Curt Lindgren
Pro Jerseys
100% vented nylon, long sleeves, crew neck.
Sizes 12, 14, 16, S, M, L.
Buy Direct $14.95. California residents add 6% sales tax.
Add $1.00 for shipping and handling. All orders prepaid by
money order only.
California residents add 6% sales tax.
Add $1.00 for shipping and handling. All orders prepaid by
money order only.
BUSHWAKKER®
1466 Pioneer Way, Suite 1,
El Cajon, CA 92020
(714) 444-4424

A second wave of mass popularity rolled across the globe, as the skatepark era sent the number of active skateboarders skyrocketing. In a matter of two years, active participation in the United States doubled from 10 million riders in 1975 to a whooping 20 million in 1977, while hundreds of new skateparks popped up across the country. But unfortunately, participation was not the only statistic soaring to new heights: In a 1977 report quoted in the Chicago Tribune newspaper, the U.S. Consumer Product Safety Commission counted 106,000 skateboard-related injuries treated at emergency rooms across the country that year; "approximately 30 times the number treated in the same period in 1973."

As several counties and municipalities across the U.S. banned skateboarding in public areas, the mainstream media jumped back on the "dangerous fad" angle from the 1960s, pointing a finger at the risky sport. "Skateboarding was so new that the public thought it was tremendously dangerous and many consumer advocates warned parents not to allow their children to skateboard because they would end up broken to pieces," said 1970s pro skateboarder Stacy Peralta. Ultimately, this kind of negative press was bound to be bad for business. Although the industry was booming like never before - skateboard equipment sales climbed to $400 million in 1977 according to the Chicago Tribune - memories of skateboarding's first sudden death in 1965 over safety concerns still lingered. The industry needed to address the safety issue. And quickly.

As an antidote, skateboard companies began presenting professional team riders as role models for safe conduct on the board, while suggesting skateparks as the safest environment for skateboarding. And to dress the part of legitimate professional athletes, skateboard teams adopted a "professional look," said Stacy Peralta: "That 'professional look' resulted in one of skateboarding's worst fashion trends of the 1970s - the long-sleeve, pinned-holed, polyester, multi-colored and brightly colored team shirts."

Around 1977, all major skateboard manufacturers began decking out their riders in mesh nylon team jerseys, designed in corporate colorways with prominent brand name placement: Bahne, Hobie, G&S, Logan Earth Ski, Makaha, SIMS - every major skateboard team jumped on the trend. The market for these "competition team long-sleeve nylon jerseys" was cornered by two California-based manufacturers producing the jerseys under licence for skate brands: Bushwakker Sportswear out of El Cajon - they also produced motorbike jerseys for Honda, among others - and United Skateboard Products out of La Costa. The next level of skateboard fashion was here. If skateparks represented the riding terrain of the future, nylon team jerseys paired with helmets and protective gear provided the official high-tech uniform to match.

SMELL YOU LATER, SKATER

As is often the case with "skateboarding's worst fashion trends," team jerseys were considered the best thing, like, ever at the time. "There was something cool about the jerseys. I don't quite know what it was. A mesh jersey. It had a cool aesthetic to it, I thought as a kid," said 1970s pro skateboarder Steve Olson, adding: "When I got a Quiksilver team jersey, I was stoked." Pro skateboarder Lance Mountain is on the same page: "All the teams had jerseys, like the Pepsi team and the G&S team. It was really goofy, but back then, you were like, 'This is cool!!!'"

Flow Motion
skateboard team
progressive

Hobie
HOBIE SKATEBOARDS
GLOVES
HOBIE SKATEBOARDS

NICE LEGS?
Keep them that way!!
Gnarly® Skate Pads are built to take punishment—your knees and elbows are not! Like the Hobie Wrist Guards they give the added protection a Hot Skater needs. Gnarly® Skate Pads were developed by Bob Skoldberg and the Hobie Pro Team to "TAKE THE GRIEF OUT OF YOUR BEEF!" Stronger and Tuffer yet Lighter and more Flexible—Gnarly® Skate Pads for your knees and elbows.
HOBIE
GNARLY!
SKATE PADS
Foreign Dealers Contact:
Hobie Skateboards
P.O. Box 812
Dana Point, California 92629 714/646-2404
Skaters:
Send $1.00 for 3 Decals and "Hot News From Hobie."
Darrell Miller rock'n at the Big "O" in his argyle socks
Photo: Jeff Ruiz
gnarly
gnarly

Hobie
PRO-GEAR

"The most rapid growth in skateboard sales is in the top-quality merchandise," said a *SkateBoarder* magazine ad for Hobie's new line of complete boards and safety equipment. Equally progressive, Hobie Sportswear raised the bar for functional skateboard fashions by incorporating new school materials such as nylon and rayon into rainbow-colored team jerseys with breathable mesh inserts and circular color-blocking around the neck opening. Other fashion-forward items included yellow long-sleeve pocket team shirts screen-printed with the blue Hobie Skateboards logo, as well as Hobie's popular protective gloves.

Special clothing perks went to the team in the shape of not-for-sale fashion items. "We all had a blue Hobie jacket with red stripes, a jumpsuit like the [California] Free Former [skateboard team] guys," said former Hobie team rider Eddie "El Gato" Elguera. At competitions and demonstrations, the team rolled up in matching team jerseys and jackets, complemented by color-coordinated Hobie safety gear and helmets, another carryover from the way skateboard teams had been marketed in the 1960s. "They were all in the same uniform. That's what they were dictated to wear, I guess," said skateboard photographer James Cassimus. Putting the underlying marketing strategy in perspective, pro skateboarder Claus Grabke said: "In the Hobie team, the emphasis was on the team as a whole, not so much the individual rider. Much like the Makaha team, or the notorious [California] Free Former team, where the only guy people really knew was Ty Page. And why? Because he was the one with the fucked-up haircut."

STEP INTO A HOBIE!!

In 1978, the company entered the shoe market by launching Hobie Athletic Footwear, advertised under the slogan: "IF THE SHOE FITS... WEAR IT!" Designed in the brand's signature rainbow color scheme, the shoes were crafted from blue suede with yellow and red paneling, replete with a plastic-protected toecap. Functional features included a reinforced padded ankle section with the company's signature "H"-logo on the heel tab and a flexible, grippy sole built for pool skating. Due to growing popular demand, the Hobie shoe was also available as a high-top model, which more and more skaters realized was the way to go for skating large pools.

But right around the time of the shoe release, the company was already losing footing on the market – although quietly and behind the scenes at first. When amateur bowl riding champion Eddie "El Gato" Elguera skated his first pro contest during the 1979 Hester Series at Hi-Roller skatepark in Boulder, Colorado, the brand – despite the flashy marketing – had hit a rough patch: "Hobie were already going out of business, so they sent me and Duane [Peters] and Darrell [Miller] out there with one-way tickets. We really had to win some money [in the contest] to get a ticket home. They also said the guy at the skate park had a place for us to stay, but when we got there, the guy said we could stay on the roof of the pro shop, where we stayed for a couple of nights." It was the beginning of the end. Both Duane Peters and Eddie "El Gato" Elguera soon traded in their rainbow-colored team jerseys and moved on to greener pastures. The second run of Hobie Skateboards lost its steam soon afterwards and when the skateboard industry as a whole collapsed in 1980, the brand's new tastemakers got out of the kitchen.

HI CRU
by STEDMAN
100% COTTON
LARGE (42-44)
Hobie
SKATEBOARDS

Hobie®
SKATEBOARDS
Hobie

ALWAYS RADICAL

Z-FLEX

P.O. BOX 5397 SANTA MONICA CA. 90405 • RING (213) 822-9988

• NOW PLAYING • JAY ADAMS/SKATECROSS – RESEDA • PHOTO • STAN SHARP • DESIGN • DON SHERIDAN •

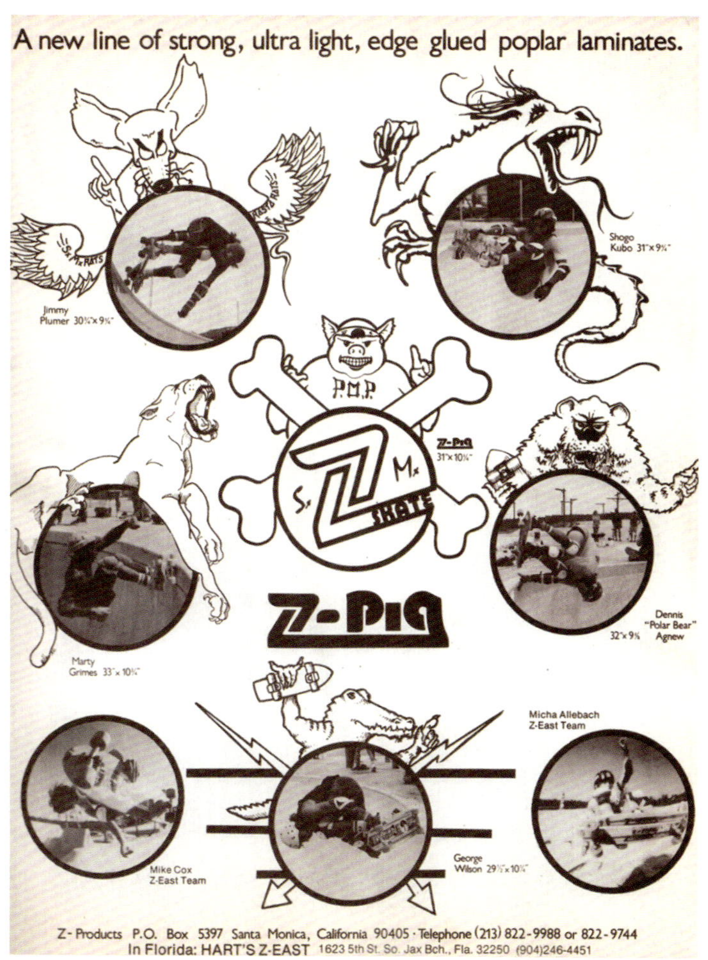

Z-FLEX: PERFORMANCE-DRIVEN TECHNOLOGY

The skateboard industry has always relied on passionate individuals who turn their favorite pastime into thriving businesses. But when passions run high, alliances can prove fragile, as business partners turn into rivals, friends turn into enemies, and technical breakthroughs into contested intellectual property. It's a recurring pattern, dating all the way back to the mid-1970s, when the masterminds behind Dogtown's notorious Zephyr surf and skate shop - surf shapers Jeff Ho, Skip Engblom and Craig R. Stecyk III - commissioned the production of Zephyr-Flex fiberglass skateboards from an expert mold maker by the name of Kent Sherwood. "Kent was [Zephyr teamrider] Jay Adams' stepfather and an expert in designs and materials. He came up with the materials to fabricate our first skateboards," said Craig Stecyk.

Shaped in the image of the popular Hobie and Bahne competition boards, the Zephyr-Flex complete skateboards outpaced the competition with their horizontal beam construction and advanced fiberglass blend. Fiberglass looked like a winning ticket in an age of see-what-sticks experimentation among manufacturers, a few years before laminated maple wood became the material of choice in skateboard decks. But right when order volumes started taking off, Sherwood decided to go it alone, producing his own fiberglass boards under the EZ RYDER name in late 1975. Further twisting the knife, Sherwood poached a good chunk of Zephyr's high-profile team riders - this would become another recurring pattern in the skateboard biz - including Jay Adams, Tony Alva, and Jim Muir, before changing the company's name to Z-FLEX in 1976.

With its team roster of Zephyr alumni and "Z"-derived moniker, Z-FLEX raised some heated questions in the scene. Was this brand related to Zephyr? Did it come out of Dogtown? Was there beef between the two camps? Z-FLEX took out an ad in *SkateBoarder* magazine's 1976 Spring issue, stating: "You can call them what you like - Zephyr, EZ, The Original, E-Z Rider, but we are calling them Z-Flex! The reason is the original company that conceived and manufactured them wants to eliminate the confusion of WHO, WHERE and WHY...We are WHO, Skatetown is WHERE and Quality is WHY." The tension became palpable when the remaining Zephyr team competed against the Z-FLEX defectors in the 1976 Hang Ten World Pro-Am Championships in Carlsbad, which answered the question about beef between both camps in the affirmative.

TECHNICAL EDGE

Right from the start, Sherwood differentiated Z-FLEX Skateboards by emphasizing technical innovation and manufacturing expertise in marketing communications: *All Z-Flex boards are made from unidirectional hand-laid-up and pressure-molded fiberglass for unbelievable strength and durability.* Out in the streets, the advanced boards - also endorsed by new team riders Dave Hackett and Marty Grimes - set a new benchmark for performance-enhancing innovation. "Kent Sherwood was an extremely influential designer and fabricator. He later built the wings on the Pegasus missile which went eight-times the speed of sound. And he did it using composite constructions, already developed in surfboard building technology." said Craig Stecyk

In a little known twist of history, a fundamental chapter of 21st-century drone warfare was written in mid-1970s California surf shaper workshops. According to Craig R. Stecyk III, leading shapers received special attention from the US government, keen on leveraging light-weight composite materials into unmanned aircraft for military purposes. Some of Stecyk's surf-shaping mentors consulted on what would ultimately evolve into remotely controlled drones deployed in overseas war zones. "[Influential surfboard shaper] Dave Sweet also did some interesting glider and drone work early on," said Craig Stecyk.

And the rivalry with Zephyr? Ultimately, Z-FLEX would have the last word by means of sheer staying power, as the Zephyr team disbanded in late 1976. Z-FLEX continued churning out technical innovations such as Z Smooth and Z Grooves urethane wheels and various board constructions, supported by a revolving door of team riders including the likes of Jimmy Acosta, George Wilson, Butch Sterbins, George Watanabe, and Jimmy Plumer. Under the name Z-Products, the company turned heads in the 1980s with their Z Roller trucks - equipped with revolving hanger inserts - and continues to offer a range of decks, wheels, cruisers, and longboards today.

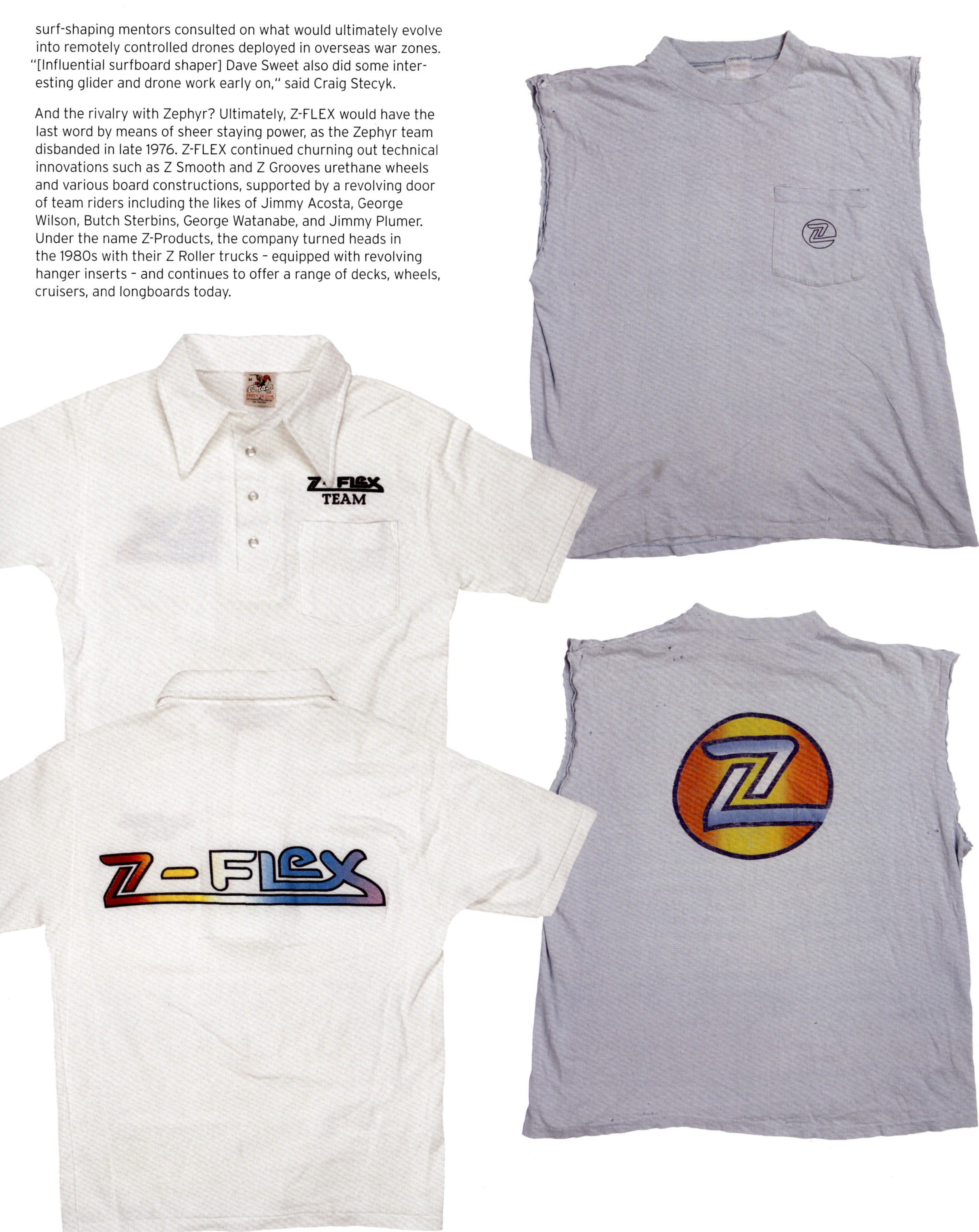

JAY ADAMS: THE BIRTH OF HARDCORE

Child prodigy, trailblazer, renegade, dropout, convict, reformed man – Jay Adams wore many hats throughout his skateboarding career, always with an insistence on doing things his own way. Jay's laminated 1976 skate park ID card from Skatopia says it all. The photo shows a wild-eyed teenager with shoulder-long surfer hair flipping the middle finger into the camera. Beneath, scribbled in bold ink letters is the name that would personify rebellion for a generation of skateboarders: JAY ADAMS.

Raised on a steady diet of surfing and skateboarding from the age of 4 by his stepfather, influential surfboard shaper Kent Sherwood, Jay Adams is celebrated by his peers as one of the most naturally talented riders to ever set foot on a board. By the time he joined the legendary Zephyr shop team in 1974 as its youngest member, the child prodigy – mentored by surfing's most infamous in the waters beneath LA's Pacific Ocean Pier – had already mastered the established blueprint of surfing and skateboarding. Time to tear up the rule book and blaze a new trail. "Jay would blast off aerials and hit parts of the skate park where nobody else was going. He would figure it all out by himself. He would just see something and go for it," said former teammate Wes Humpston.

This radical, no-holds-barred approach made Adams a leader for a new generation of skateboarders. But what made him a style icon, emulated by thousands of skateboarders across the world in terms of riding style and attire, was another quality. "Jay had charisma. He was Mr. Cool. When he walked into a room, it would light up," said Nathan Pratt, who rode with Jay on the Zephyr team, adding: "Tony [Alva] had presence, but Jay had charisma. He would just dominate, naturally." And just as naturally, the skateboard world would follow, whether it was long blond surfer hair, fedora hats, "Skate Nazi" insignia, bandanas and flannels, Flyaway helmets, or a bleached Mohawk – if "Jay Boy" was rocking it, people knew it was hardcore.

AGAINST THE GRAIN

Often painted as a poster boy of the Dogtown skate style, there is a part of Jay Adams that is forever Venice Beach (although Dogtown is technically part of Santa Monica). Many of Jay's fashion choices, including Latino gang-inspired chino pants, bandanas, and flannel shirts in turf-appropriate colors, reflect a sense of pride in the neighborhood. "Skateboard fashion changed in the early '70s when Jay and Shogo [Kubo] came in. They started caring about what they wore and why they were wearing it. They wore blue Vans, because it was part of their neighborhood. And it was who they represented as a group," said pro skateboarder Christian Hosoi, adding: "Pride is a huge part of your look, your fashion. It's about who your family is, who your close friends are, where you are from. People who don't care about it are about as boring as can be."

Far from boring, Jay always stayed on the wilder side of life, on and off the skateboard. "Jay never cared about the money. All he wanted to do was surf or skateboard. And now he's the most idolized of the original group," said Nathan Pratt. Competitive skateboarding was never Jay Adams' world, although he dominated from an early age onward. When punk rock hit, Jay's world became the raging parties and concert mosh pits that marked the start of his transformation into hardcore skate icon. Christian Hosoi remembers early 1980s punk concerts at Marina Del Rey skate park: "Jay Adams went from surfer guy to a Mohawk, doing backflips into the slam pit. And you would just go, 'This guy is crazy!'"

Eventually, Jay's complete disregard for consequences – arguably the key to his trailblazing progression on a skateboard – would backfire in real life. Battles with addiction, violence, and incarceration left their indelible mark on Adams. The sun-kissed surfer kid grew into a burly, scarred man with heavy neck and facial tattoos – the evolution of skateboarding from surfing roots to hardcore aesthetic literally etched into his body – but he never lost his passion for riding. Drug-free and reformed after his imprisonment in 2005, Jay Adams walked the line providing outreach to troubled youths and remained an active part of the skateboarding scene to the very end. He passed away from a heart attack while surfing in Mexico in 2014, never to be forgotten.

Photo: Grant Brittain

UNLEASHING THE STOKE: PHOTO PRINT TEES

Some action photos are far too radical as to be confined to the pages of skateboard magazines. They need to run free and be released into the wild. Printing these images on T-shirts offers a way to bring their stoke value out into the world, perhaps even add a dose of inspiration to the next skate session. That's why photo prints enjoy a long tradition in skate fashion, and the origins could hardly be any more classic: When new printing techniques met the photographic talents of one 15 year old Glen E. Friedman and the hard-charging skate style of original Z-Boy and DogTown local Jay Adams, the iconic long-sleeved shirt with the slogan "PUSHING THE LIMIT" presented the next level in T-shirt design upon its 1977 release.

Glen E. Friedman vividly remembers the genesis of the image: "Jay is hitting the last wall at Reseda's Skater Cross, laying out a "Bert", one of the earliest skate parks built in the LA area. It was out in the Valley, We had to take a long long bus ride to get out there." The influential photographer, known for capturing era-defining images of 1970s skateboarding as well as the trailblazers of hardcore punk rock and hip- hop, actually traces the early roots of his professional career to photo shoots like this one, at out of the way "bizarre" skate parks and of course illegal back yard pools. "I made some cool photos at that former drive-in restaurant, and it was where I met [skateboard photography pioneer] Warren Bolster in person for the first time at their grand opening," said Glen E. Friedman, adding that Bolster gave him an important jumpstart: "He gave me three rolls of film! Kodachrome 64 - the first time I ever got free film. And I was beyond stoked, made a full-pager of [Tom] Wally Inouye that day, my third photo ever published."

The long-sleeved T-shirt bearing the photo of Jay Adams, framed by surf-style ornaments in primary colors, hit stores in the summer of 1977. As a commission, Friedman received "$50 and a dozen shirts for my friends and I." The rest is history: Photo-realistic prints became a staple in skate fashion and the day's leading photographers found their images transferred to textiles, including Warren Bolster, Wynn Miller, "King James" Cassimus, and others. Photo prints have remained an ongoing trope in skateboard T-shirt designs ever since, featured heavily over the years by many brands, as well as all prominent skate magazines.

"Pushing The Limit"

HORIZONS WEST
BY NATHAN PRATT

It's a widely known part of skateboard lore that once the Z-Boys team disbanded in 1976, their legendary hangout, the Jeff Ho and Zephyr Productions surf and skate shop in Santa Monica, went under soon after. Many people are also aware that today, the former Zephyr storefront on 2011 Main Street near Ocean Park is home to a neat coffee shop, Dogtown Coffee, paying homage to the former heart of Dogtown skate and surf culture. But, it is lesser known to the general public that the store continued to operate as a surf and skate shop for decades under the direction of former Zephyr team rider Nathan Pratt, who carried the torch right after Jeff Ho and Skip Engblom closed their shop. In Spring 1977, Nathan Pratt reopened the store under the name Horizons West, making hand-shaped surfboards, skateboards, and apparel in true West Side surf/skate style.

"When I opened Horizons West I had five surfboards, five cases of wax, and three dozen T-shirts. That was my opening inventory," said Nathan Pratt, who originally started working at the shop in 1971 at the age of 14 before joining the Zephyr team as the first Z-Boy. "For a while, when Arthur Lake was riding them, we were the number one selling skateboard in LA. We made them in Mike Davis' dad's garage up on 21st Street." For artistic support, Nathan Pratt enlisted original Zephyr artist Craig R. Stecyk III. Continuing the gritty aesthetic laid down by Stecyk's Dogtown articles in *SkateBoarder* magazine, one of the first magazine advertisements for Horizons West skateboards featured a black-and-white Stecyk photograph of team rider Arthur Lake riding beyond vertical on the roof of a full pipe with the slogan: Skates that take you where you've never been before.

Horizons West adopted a sunset arc as the logo, which some think was in homage to Zephyr's Crescent Moon logo printed on team shirts by Nathan Pratt in 1975, but as Pratt explains: "I came up with the Horizons West logo one night when I was shaping. It is the shape of the sunrays coming off of the setting sun when it is a little over halfway down over the horizon, which is in the west; hence Horizons West. Kind of the idea of limitless possibilities." In the bigger picture, the new brand did not miss a beat in carrying on the Dogtown legacy. Nathan Pratt, as the first Z-Boy, shaped his own surfboards, drawing on what he learned as an apprentice of Zephyr's Skip Engblom and Jeff Ho. "I hand-shaped the boards and did my own airbrushing and we also printed our own T-shirts," said Nathan Pratt, who is credited with introducing the "Bert" slide - inspired by surf legend Larry Bertlemann - into the skateboard repertoire when fellow Z-Boy Stacy Peralta commented at one session that the slide Pratt was doing looked like Bertlemann. As one of the first skate and surf shops with its own line of branded hardware and apparel, Horizons West would continue - with a single change in management to Randy Wright in the mid-1980s - providing a home to board sports in the old Zephyr location until the year 2008, when it became a casualty of the Great Recession.

BIG IN JAPAN

Designed by Nathan Pratt and Craig Stecyk, the shop's clothing line pursued a graphically-driven direction, mostly geared around logo tees screen-printed in the back of the store. "Clothes were just T-shirts at first, after that came sweatshirts, and trunks and walkshorts," said Nathan Pratt. Standout designs include an "Explosive" Haz-Mat warning sign, the "California Gun" with M-16 machine gun design and the surf-inspired Maltese Cross and a graffiti "Water Ratz" stripe.

California Gun
HORIZONS WEST
2011 Main Street
Santa Monica
CA 90405
213-392-1122
CLARK FOAM

HORIZONS WEST
California Gun

But the one design that has stood the test of time is the "Pig & Crossbones" logo, which is Pratt's longtime trademark: "The Pig & Crossbones was the original symbol from when we surfed at POP Pier. Stecyk used to hand paint it on my board, so I asked him to do a graphic of it for shirts and boards. The Pig & Crossbones had never been printed on anything before. That was in 1982 and it's still going today. There have been knock-offs, but this is the original."

Next to success on Horizon West's home turf, Nathan Pratt positioned the brand on the lucrative Japanese market. "We were all making all our money in Japan. The 'big in Japan' thing was strong in the '80s. They loved California and they wanted California brands," said Nathan Pratt, who even ended up starring in Japanese TV commercials at the time. "I did a TV commercial for Samsung. It was one of these 60 second product endorsements, featuring me shaping surfboards and talking about surf culture. And the tagline was, 'The wind has a way.' They ran the spot wall to wall for an entire summer in Japan." Speaking of television, Nathan Pratt also created and produced the popular Nickelodeon show, Sk8-TV, bringing Stecyk and Stacy Peralta on board as creatives.

Ultimately, Horizon West's run ended when the U.S. economy hit another downward economic spiral in the mid-2000s. "Horizons West was the oldest shop in Santa Monica, but it couldn't survive the recession. And my manager ran it for over 20 years until 2008. 1977 to 2008 wasn't a bad run," said Nathan Pratt, who afterwards operated the Z-BOY footwear and apparel brand in Los Angeles and most recently has revived Horizons West and a Pacific Ocean Park/POP line.

Horizons West ©82
Horizons West
Championships
'82

DOGTOWN SKATES: ORIGINAL INFLUENCE

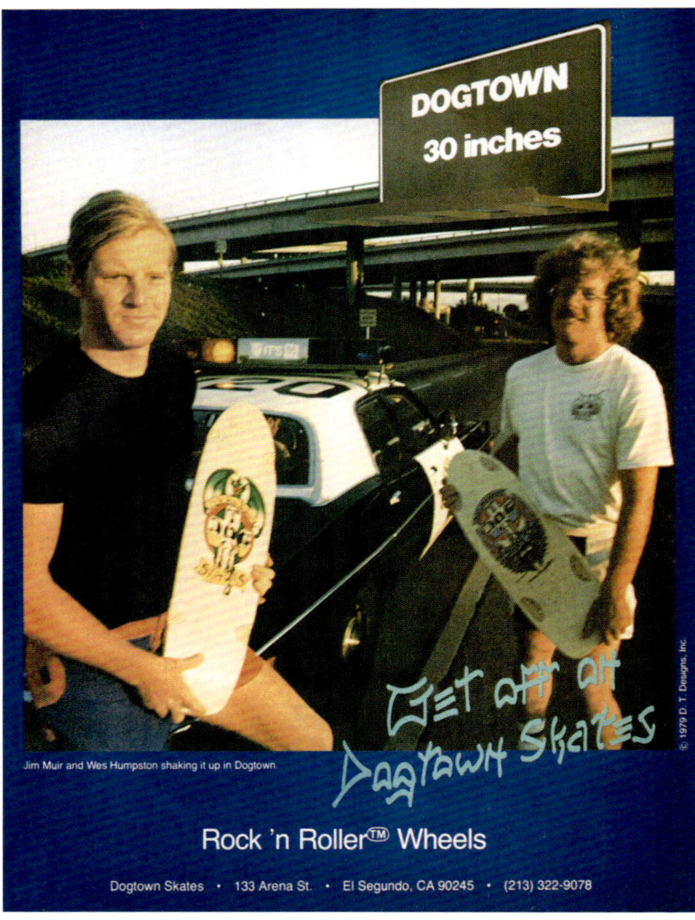

If the founders of Dogtown Skates received a dime every time the Dogtown name or iconic Dogtown Cross logo are used to advertise business ventures as obscure as hot dog stands, yoga studios, or professional dog training services, they would be billionaires. Still, the rich influence of the company started by pro skateboarders Jim "Red Dog" Muir and Wes "Bulldog" Humpston in 1976 can hardly be overstated. Deeply rooted in the Los Angeles hardcore skateboarding and music scene, Dogtown Skates revolutionized the way skateboards are designed and marketed, while elevating the status of professional skateboarders from token athletes to cultural icons. It all started in the run-down patch of coastal Santa Monica known as Dogtown, where resident surfer and graphic artist Craig R. Stecyk III spray-painted decrepit building walls with the same blend of street-inspired graffiti applied to custom-made surfboards sold at Zephyr surf shop, which he co-owned with Jeff Ho and Skip Engblom. "I probably might have been the first person to put DOGTOWN on a surf board or a skateboard," said Craig R. Stecyk III, adding: "This went back to a conversation I had with Skipper where I said, 'It's a dog's life in a dog's town.' Which is the kind of stuff you said all day over silver satin and Kool Aid..."

The Dogtown legend grew wings through Craig Stecyk's series of attitude-driven articles in *SkateBoarder* magazine, highlighting local riders and their antics: "When Stecyk did that article with [Zephyr rider] Nathan [Pratt] dressed like a cholo with sunglasses and the headband, and on the wall it said 'Dogtown' with the cross... Well, that was when we started going like, 'Fuck yeah!'" said Wes Humpston, who had been crafting home-made skateboards with former Zephyr rider Jim Muir at the time. "We called our boards DTS, Dogtown Skates. And then I asked Craig, 'Can we use that cross? Is it cool if we call it Dogtown? Dogtown Skates?' And he goes, 'Yeah, do whatever!'" said Wes Humpston. Stecyk confirms: "One day Jim and Wes asked if I had any problem or wanted to go into business and I said, 'I don't want to go into business but you guys should do whatever you want with it.' I knew those guys well, they were from the neighborhood."

Stecyk's blessing marked the beginning of Dogtown Skates, initially a backyard operation offering custom skateboards handcrafted and hand-painted by Jim Muir and Wes Humpston, who also endorsed the boards as the company's first team riders next to Paul Constantineau. Within one year, the start-up brand grew into a full-fledged board company - adding big name riders such as Bob Biniak and Shogo Kubo along the way - taking out full-page ads in *SkateBoarder* magazine to announce their line of pro model skateboard decks: "From the boyz who brought you skateboarding... Skateboards. Dogtown Skates. The Originals." The rest is history, as Dogtown - through a 1978 licensing deal with deep-pocketed New York investors - blew up as a major cultural force in late 1970s skateboarding and beyond.

THE NEW ORDER

At a time when vertical skateboarding in backyard pools - mostly accessed illegally - emerged as skateboarding's next frontier, Dogtown's skateboards offered a more stable ride due to their above average length and width. At 9 inches width and 30 inches length, Jim Muir's 1978 pro board created the template for modern-day pool riding shapes. What's more, the board was crafted from 7-ply hardrock maple that would soon replace fiberglass as the industry standard for board construction. But that's not the only way in which the company predicted the shape of things to come. Here are three ways in which Dogtown Skates changed the skateboarding industry forever:

1. Pro model graphics. The day's leading companies such as Bahne, Gordon & Smith, and Logan Earth Ski were already selling signature pro model skateboards endorsed by their top riders. But they were just that: Wooden boards bearing a pro's name and signature, next to the company's logo. With the introduction of signature graphics for each pro model – featuring a recognizable multi-colored graphic associated with the rider's name – Dog Town took skateboard graphic design into the realm of conceptual art and pop culture. Says Jim Muir: "In the late 1970s when Dogtown Skates started, the focus shifted to the rider and the [pro] model. We started the basic system of professional models, which is still how most companies run their teams today."

Setting the tone for the rest of the skate industry, pro model artwork served as a reflection of each team rider's personality and image. "Each of the graphics gave an idea of the pros. They were personally involved with the graphics. They would come up with the concept and would have either Kevin Ancell or Wes Humpston draw the graphics or give them a rough. So our riders had input from concept to final production," said Jim Muir. Famous Dogtown graphics include the red-and-white Rising Sun/Kamikaze design for Japanese-American pro rider Shogo Kubo, "the Humpston Bigfoot" model, or the original Jim Muir Bulldog graphic originally created by Wes Humpston in 1972.

2. Pro apparel and streetwear. Dogtown's personality-driven approach extended beyond the realm of hardware, as pro model graphics found their way into apparel and accessories. "I can't say what the ratio was between softgoods and hardgoods, but back then if you had a board graphic, you received a T-shirt graphic and a sticker. It always came as a package. That used to go on until the '80s. No one gets stickers for their board graphics anymore," said Jim Muir, adding: "For instance, when we did an Eric Dressen graphic, Eric Dressen also got a board, a sticker and a T-shirt." Asked about the scope of Dogtown's apparel output, Wes Humpston said it was mostly controlled by the company's licensing partners: "We did a lot of shirts, but they didn't really give us numbers." Dogtown also made early forays into streetwear, starting off the "collabo" trend with collaborators including "The Godfather of Streetwear," Shawn Stüssy. "We made Dogtown team jackets that were made out of Stüssy Garage jackets. And Stüssy would sponsor a lot of our team riders in the '80s, so we would embroider our team riders' names on it and add *Thrasher* patches and customize them and all that," said Jim Muir.

3. A new way to get paid. Putting their money behind their pro team, Dogtown pioneered an incentive system similar to the music business, where artists receive royalties based on record sales: "When we ran the program of board, T-shirt graphic and sticker, the pros got paid for their T-shirt and sticker as well. Anything with your name on – you got paid for. Which is how a professional should be paid appropriately. It's a system that still works to this day," said Jim Muir. Delving deeper into the issue, Muir said the approach stemmed from his own dissatisfaction with the state of the industry at the time: "Our riders got paid three to four times as much for their boards [than other companies], and it was a much better way to compensate the riders. Because those other guys were getting ripped off at 50 cents a board. And they sold hundreds of thousands of certain models back in the day – so the company was making a lot of money. But it wasn't the company pushing the sales, it was the rider."

From the boyz who brought you skateboarding . . . Skateboards.

Dogtown Skates • The Originals

Paul Constantineau . . . Gettin down at a home town pool.

Photo: Glen Friedman

Paul Constantineau, P. C. Tail Tap Design/8¼" wide
Jim Muir, Red Dog Design/9" wide
Wes Humpston, Bulldog Design/10" wide

Each model available in:
Hotline/7-ply hardrock maple
Proline/10-ply
Fibreply/glass and wood

Dogtown Skates • *11711 Santa Monica Blvd.* • *West Los Angeles, CA 90025* • *1-800-421-6631* • *Local Tel. 213-477-4808*

BuLL DoG DesiGn
DOG
SKATES
©1978 D.T. DESIGNS, INC.
TM

BULLET
DESIGN
DOG
SKATES
© D.T. DESIGNS, INC.
TM

SIGNATURE PRO BOARDS

One of the first Dogtown Skates riders to get his own signature cross was Bob Biniak, one the day's biggest stars who quit big-money label Logan Earth Ski in 1978 to join the underdogs on LA's Westside. Known and respected as one of the original Z-Boys skaters sponsored by Jeff Ho's Zephyr label, Biniak earned the nickname "The Bullet". That's because at a time when the invention of the urethane wheel put wings on skaters, Biniak was among the fastest and most fearless riders in backyard pool sessions, enormous full pipes and riding downhill. Plus, with his insistence on skipping safety equipment and riding shirtless, he had the swagger and persona to match his aggressive riding skills.

"Tony Alva was the first real rock star. But there were a couple of them. Biniak was a rock star, too. When the Z-Boys split, they all went straight to the biggest companies. Biniak skated for SIMS for a little while and Logan [Earth Ski]. We would go over to Biniak's house and party. And you would stay the night and leave the next day and be like, what happened?" said Wes Humpston. Allegedly, Biniak was also a regular on the Hollywood party scene and would be seen hitting the town with actor Charlie Sheen.

For Biniak's pro model, Wes Humpston added the word 'Bullet' in stylized typeface to the original Dogtown Cross design. Supplemented by wings carrying bullets and bombs, the graphic immortalized Bob Biniak as part of the day's most notorious pro team. Compared to the competition, Dogtown Skates really stood with the four-color graphics on their pro models: "Before we gave our riders custom graphics, teams would just have the company name on their boards, like G&S or Santa Cruz or Bahne. So in the magazines you would see Shogo Kubo, Jay Adams, Bob Biniak and myself riding these multi-colored full-bottom boards," said Dogtown Skates co-founder Jim Muir, who also created customized team jackets for his riders. Based on Stussy garage jackets, the exclusive apparel items were embroidered with each rider's name and decked out in patches.

Famous for doing things his own way, Biniak pursued a career as professional golfer after his skateboarding career ended in the early 1980s and began touring Europe and South Africa. This marked a stark contrast to most of his cohorts, who either took on industry roles in the skate and surf business or kept involved on a cultural level as artists or filmmakers. Although he remained somewhat absent from the spotlight - also widely overlooked in documentaries and skate history books - Bob Biniak was mourned upon his passing at an early age in 2010. With a gathering at Venice Skate Plaza, his peers remembered Biniak for his pioneering legacy, never to be forgotten.

Photo: Glen E. Friedman

TOP OF THE LINE

By the end of 1978, Dogtown had become a major player in the booming skateboard industry, and the founders and team riders started reaping serious rewards. "Everyone had BWMs, Beniak had a Bavaria, I had a 1600, and a lot of people had 2002s," said Wes Humpston, describing the company's investors as having, "bucks out the ass. One of the guys had the biggest diamond store in New York." Dogtown's success and fair treatment of riders helped attract an elite team, including names such as Tim Jackson, Scott Oster, and Duane Peters. "Gator was on for a moment, and we were Hawk's and Hosoi's first sponsor when they were amateurs," said Jim Muir.

In a little known twist, Christian Hosoi had quit the elite Powell-Peralta team in 1981 over having to wait to a couple of years to turn pro. "Couple of years? I'm turning pro now! Dogtown approached me and offered to give me a model. These guys were all my idols. So of course I quit Powell, and Dogtown immediately goes out of business. Bankrupt," said Christian Hosoi, adding: "My graphic was already done and everything... samurai swords, yin and yang, Christian Hosoi model, Dogtown skates."

Jim Muir attributes the company's downfall to the overall challenges in the skateboard business: "The whole industry died. There was just nothing going on. When they were no longer making money, [the New York partners] shut it down in 1981." Wes Humpston remembers: "They dumped everything we made at the swap meets and ran back to New York."

The end? Not quite, as Jim Muir was not ready to let go: "We brought it back in 1982 and I got the Dogtown trademark back in my name." Since Wes Humpston pursued his own graphic design career - he still sells custom painted boards under his Bulldog Skates label - Jim Muir brought his brother on board: Mike Muir of hardcore band Suicidal Tendencies fame. "We started SUICIDAL SKATES and ran ads in *Thrasher*, and in 1984 released a T-shirt called BORN AGAIN because Dogtown was being born again," said Jim Muir.

The combination between hardcore skateboarding and music still runs strong today: Almost 40 years after the company's backyard beginnings, DOGTOWN X SUICIDAL skateboards keeps the Dogtown vibe alive with quality skateboards and constant collaborations with riders and artists such as Lance Mountain and Mike Vallely - true to Dogtown's founding idea of elevating the riders as creative individuals, and pushing the culture forward.

ALBA
DESIGNS
DOG
TOWN
BULL DOG ART
SKATES

SHOGO KUBO: SMOOTH OPERATOR

One of the most stylish individuals to ever set foot on a skateboard, Shogo Kubo's approach can best be described by the old adage: "Speak softly, and carry a big stick." Without his skateboard, the Japanese-American from Los Angeles exuded a quiet, unassuming presence without the slightest hint of aggression or destructive attitude. But once he set wheels on a backyard pool or skatepark, all bets were off. "Shogo Kubo rides with an authority and aggression that generally blows minds," wrote skateboard artist Craig R. Stecyk III in the 1979 *SkateBoarder* magazine article "Dead Dogs Never Lie."

Powerful and effortless at the same time – a Zen-like manifestation of explosive physical energy without strain – the original Dogtown local's style has often been likened to martial arts. Actually, without practicing judo at a dojo in Culver City, Shogo Kubo may have never discovered skateboarding, or become part of the legendary team of Jeff Ho Surfboards and Zephyr Productions in Santa Monica. But in 1971, the stepfather of surfing and skateboarding prodigy Jay Adams was looking for ways to help young Jay stay out of trouble. "Jay was totally out of control, so Kent [Sherwood] wanted to take him somewhere he could work off some of his energy," said Dogtown pro skateboarder Wes Humpston. "So Jay met Shogo at the dojo where he was taking judo, and that's how they started skating together."

Photo: Glen E. Friedman

Photo: Glen E. Friedman

The rest is history: Bonding with Jay Adams like brothers from different mothers, Shogo Kubo took to skateboarding and surfing naturally. The two would hit the waves at Santa Monica's Pacific Ocean Pier in the mornings before skating concrete banks on local schoolyards such as Kenter and Paul Revere in the afternoons. When Zephyr started a skateboarding team in 1975, Shogo and Jay were both natural fits. Documented in leading international skateboarding publications, Kubo's groundbreaking antics in empty swimming pools - including frontside grinds and signature layback moves such as the underplant - turned the wiry, long-haired teenager into a style icon idolized by skateboarders from the US, to Brazil, Australia, Europe, and Japan. What's more, he was also the strongest competitor on the Zephyr team. "Shogo Kubo was a stylist and he was the one out of the group who kept that competition thing going throughout the entire time while everyone else went into the lifestyle." said Shogo's former sponsor, Jeff Ho of Zephyr fame.

LOUD STYLE

Although Shogo Kubo preferred to let his skateboarding do the talking, he knew how to spice up his act with plenty of fashion flair. Never afraid of loud outfits, Shogo showed up at sessions rocking home-made headbands with Japanese kamikaze-style lettering paired with Hawaiian print shirts and the two-toned corduroy shorts that were all the rage in the late 1970s. After appearing in the internationally acclaimed Skateboard Kings documentary in 1978, Kubo embarked on a national demonstration tour - titled "Skate America" - introducing the new sport to the masses together with Tony Alva, Dennis Martinez, and Russ Gosnell. Shogo's low-crouching, energetic style earned him the title "Layback Master" and kids around the world wanted to skate like him.

In 1978, Shogo Kubo joined the LA-based Dogtown Skates label to release his iconic pro model: The Wes Humpston-designed graphics featured the Dogtown Cross over Japanese-themed Rising Sun artwork, double-headed snakes and skulls, also printed on stickers and T-Shirts. Unfortunately, the timing coincided with the skateboard industry's sudden bust. "The Shogo board came out in the late 1970s right when shit died down. So Shogo ended up being probably the best skateboarder at that time period out of all of us, but too late. There was no money in it then," said Dogtown Skates co-founder Jim Muir, adding: "Everyone's used his original graphic from [Christian] Hosoi to Santa Cruz [Skateboards], again and again."

After ending his pro skateboarding career, Shogo Kubo relocated to Hawaii to start a family and follow his lifelong passion for skating and surfing - quietly and in private. Even when 2001's Dogtown and Z-Boys documentary brought long-overdue recognition to his Zephyr cohorts, he chose to stay out of the spotlight. When Shogo Kubo passed away in 2014 at age 54 while surfing in Hawaii, the global skateboard community responded with anoutpouring of stories of the many lives he had touched with his skateboarding and his down-to-earth demeanor. In an era when far less talented pro skateboarders embarked on raging ego trips, Shogo Kubo was living proof that it's possible to be the world's best skateboarder - blessed with beatific style and grace - while still remaining a humble and positive individual.

INTERNATIONAL WATERS
777
Surfing Machines
NO SURFING!

13
WAIKIKI
GREMLIN
SOCIETY
BA 69
VERBOTEN
Machines
PHILLIPS

Photo: C. R. Stecyk

It's a story as old as Adam and Eve in the *Bible*: Give a bunch of teenagers the freedom to do whatever they like, except for one rule they absolutely must not break. One single thing that's absolutely taboo, totally off-limits. For Adam and Eve, it was the apple in the Garden of Eden that got them into a world of trouble. For hardcore 1970s skateboarders like the raucous Dogtown crew, it was the swastika - the "hooked cross" associated with the German National Socialist regime's mass genocide and ideology of racial superiority - that became the symbol of their authority-defying race against social norms, the fire brand of their teenage rebellion. When skateboarding rock stars such as Tony Alva, Jay Adams, and Wes Humpston showed up at skate parks and competitions with swastikas branded on their helmets and the words SKATE NAZI emblazoned on their boards and clothing, it was a heavy statement, even for skateboarding's lenient, counter culture standards.

To hear 1970s pro skateboarder and influential graphic artist Wes Humpston tell it: "I would put on swastikas, sure. This was before punk rock. We all used to do it on our boards and shit. And on those helmets made for bikers. Like, 'Look! I got a badass German helmet!'" Meanwhile, swastikas were not regarded so "bad ass" in post-World War II Germany, where public display of "unconstitutional symbols" such as the swastika or lightning bolt "SS"-runes remains strictly verboten and punishable by law. "Americans tend to have a rather relaxed attitude towards using these symbols, because the whole thing is rather 'remote' for them compared to us," said German skateboard distributor and magazine publisher Jörg Ludewig.

At the height of the Skate Nazi craze, Tony Alva - the day's most successful rider on the contest circuit - competed wearing a black WW II German military helmet with a red with golden glitter swastika during the 1977 California Free Former contest held at the Long Beach arena. Soon afterwards, the executive director of the International Skateboard Association pointed to Alva as the representation of everything that is "vile" in skateboarding. Meanwhile, most of the hardcore skate scene at the time clearly sided with the young rebel, at least in the US. "A stunt like Alva rocking a swastika on his helmet would definitely create some pushback here in Germany. Using these symbols outside of a historical, documentarian context is against the law here, so he would have gotten in trouble for it," said Jörg Ludewig, adding: „It's also disconcerting because it could lead some unsuspecting young blokes to wear these symbols under the guise of coolness without really knowing what they are actually doing."

SHOCK VALUE OVER POLITICS

Naturally, the skate Nazis knew very well that brandishing symbols of Nazi ideology meant playing with fire. But their motives were not political. For die-hard skate Nazis, the whole thing mostly reflected a 100% devotion to skateboarding. "I don't hate Jews or nothing like that. It's no political trip. A skate Nazi is dedicated completely to skatin'. It's not about killing," said pro skateboarder Jay Adams, who was known to draw swastikas on female autograph seekers' breasts at contests, in his 1982 *Thrasher* magazine interview.

In the bigger picture, skateboarders adopted the swastika in a similar fashion as British punk rock band The Sex Pistols later did in their 1979 documentary *The Great Rock 'n' Roll Swindle*.Mainly for shock value. Scribbled on skateboards in awkward paint marker ink, the swastika flipped a middle finger to society as an emblem of revolt against being told by the powers that be what was permissible behavior, and what was condemnable. Most of all, as is almost always the case with teenage rebellion, the end game was pushing buttons and getting a reaction. "It was about being radical! It was doing something people normally don't do. It's a risk... wanting to cause waves. Put a swastika on it, you're gonna get some waves!" said pro skateboarder Christian Hosoi on the issue.

Arrow
KENT
SKATE
NAZI
SUICIDAL SKATE

Photo: Jim Goodrich

XL
SALBA

In the 1980s, Salba created a hand-drawn board graphic featuring the swastika, "made it into a shirt to carry on the DogTown surf skate Nazi tradition."

Photo: Stan Sharp

As a major figure in the movement, Jay Adams can be seen wearing a hand-painted SUICIDAL SKATE NAZI shirt by Rick Clayton depicted in this chapter: Painted with black Sharpie marker pen on white cotton, the short-sleeved button-up shirt features a skull and crossbones graphic accompanied by the number "13," as well as the anarchy "Circle A," and the word "Cult" next to the Z -FLEX skateboards logo. If the late-1970s hardcore element in skateboarding had a discernable peak, this Skate Nazi shirt rocked by Jay Adams was probably it. Asked why he painted swastikas on his skateboards despite drawing outrage in public, Adams explained in *Thrasher*: "I guess it looked cool... I did notice that [swastikas] did sort of upset some people. We just like the way they looked. It's sort of like a tradition."

SURF NAZI TRADITION

The tradition referenced by Jay Adams goes back a long time. In 1914, a home building company by the name of Pacific System Homes from Los Angeles was inspired - the founder's son was an avid surfer - to start producing surfboards. This marked the start of the Swastika Surf Board Company, known for advanced boards hot iron-branded with the hooked cross a symbol for good luck. Skateboard and surf artist Jim Phillips from Santa Cruz even goes as far as saying: "That Swastika was really the first surf logo that was really burned into your brain." Enjoy the Thrill of a Swastika, announced an advertisement featuring a stylized thin line graphic of a surfer - sporting what looks suspiciously like a Hitleresque moustache - catching a wave with a large Swastika looming on the horizon. Combining laminated redwood with balsa, the Swastika Surf Board Company made history as the first manufacturers of commercial surfboards - competing with small shaping workshops that had been the industry norm - while the logo was widely deemed inoffensive. In those days before WW II, even produce companies - including L.V.W. Brown Estate out of Riverside, California - innocuously used the hooked cross design to advertise their goods: "Swastika - Fine Eating California Fruit," read a commercial for oranges. But in 1938, when Adolf Hitler's National Socialist Party prepared for global conquest wielding the Swastika as its official banner, the "Swastika" surf line changed its name to "Waikiki" surfboards.

In the 1950s, after the horrors of WW II had become common knowledge, the "surf Nazis" emerged as a pack of surf rats with a fanatical devotion to surfing. Some of the more hardcore Southern California surfers, including Malibu legend Miki Dora aka "The Black Knight," started painting SURF NAZI lettering on their boards, next to other WW II symbols such as the Iron Cross. "For them it was a sign of rebellion, the entire 'Surf Nazi' thing. People didn't get it and thought, 'Are surfers Nazis?' But it wasn't that, it wasn't about Hitler," said Jim Phillips, adding: "I never heard of any anti-Semitism in surfing connected to that, it was always just rebellion." A 1958 photograph depicts bare-chested surfers posing with a vintage 1939 Plymouth "surf wagon" automobile, hand-painted with swastikas and the Reich's Eagle emblem of the Nazi era. The popular early 1960s Beach Party movie series - featuring Miki Dora next to some of the day's leading surfers - also gave a nod to surf Nazis in the shape of a leather-clad Malibu biker gang. Says Wes Humpston: "The surf Nazis were the bad guys in the movies. There was a biker and he was all dressed in black leather. That was kind of a joke off the Nazis, they made them look like a bunch of goofballs." As an ongoing inside joke, the use of swastikas and surf Nazi attitude continued to bubble as a pungent sub cultural stream beneath the vanilla-flavored "Beach Boys" image of the California surf lifestyle. "I've always done the 'SS' [rune symbol]. I took that right off the Waffen SS," said Wes Humpston, who would paint these icons on his friends' boards and clothes with Sharpie pens. Regarding his usage of the swastika, influential skateboard artist Craig R. Stecyk III pointed out: "That's a hakencross by the way, we don't use the word swastika.

Photo: Wynn Miller

SHOGO
1976
DOG
TOWN
OG's

DOG
SKATES

There is no German word for swastika! It's a Hakenkreuz, meaning a hooked cross." Going deeper into the issue, Stecyk allowed: "It's an Indian symbol going far back, arguably the oldest symbol with consecutive meaning, [aside from] maybe a dot. It meant balance and harmony in the universe."

But out in the waves, among surfers in the lineup, the swastika and other Nazi emblems did not resemble balance and harmony at all. Far from it. Once the 1970s rolled around and everybody wanted a slice of surf cool, Nazi era symbols became the calling card of die-hard surf locals. These roughneck crews of surfers were marked by extreme territorial behavior, culminating in LOCALS ONLY spray-painted across hot surf spots such as the Pacific Ocean Pier in Dogtown as a warning to outsiders trying to snake into their sessions. "The surf Nazis were hardcore surfers. They're the kind of guys, if you are out there – you don't wanna surf next to them! They'll run you over or kick your ass or whatever!" said Wes Humpston. By extension, the skate Nazi movement shared the same element of LOCALS ONLY, the same in-group VS. out-group discrimination and territorial attitude. Jay Adams and the Dogtown crew of skateboarders became notorious for banning outsiders from "their" skate spots, including the famous Dog Bowl, thereby pushing their fanatical devotion to skateboarding into street gang territory.

KAMIKAZE PILOTS

Expressing an equally fanatical devotion to skateboarding, although with somewhat less controversial symbols than Nazi-era runes and swastikas, some 1970s skateboarders took to wearing the regalia of Japanese kamikaze pilots from World War II. Riders including Dogtown style icon Shogo Kubo brandished headbands with "Rising Sun" imagery and militaristic Kanji lettering. With these charged symbols, the Japanese-American skateboarder gave a nod to the suicidal tactics of kamikaze warplane pilots who would consciously accept their own death, crashing their explosive-laden planes into enemy lines or warships to inflict maximum damage. Shogo Kubo's pro model graphic on Dogtown Skateboards, created by Wes Humpston as one of the early graphic designs for a professionally endorsed board in the history of skateboarding, also featured red-and-white "Rising Sun" artwork to match the no-holds-barred attitude.

"Why did we use it? It was kamikaze!!! It was straight up, until you die!!! I will crash and burn with this!" said Japanese-American professional skateboarder Christian Hosoi, adding: "It was an almost innocent motif, but symbolically, it does more than what we think. It's like the number 666, which on some level is just a number. But if you've never felt it and experienced it, you wouldn't know it."

Never known to shy away from making a strong statement, Christian Hosoi used the Rising Sun symbol as his signature graphic for Hosoi Skates at the height of his 1980s fame. He also competed in contests wearing sleeveless T-shirts featuring the confederate flag, despite controversial connotations with the Southern States of the US along with racism and slavery. "It was a rebellious thing!" said Hosoi, allowing that times have changed. "Now with the Internet everybody's got a voice. And now it's a big deal." Even Hosoi's "Rising Sun" graphic is under fire, associated with the Japanese occupation of Korea in 1910. "In Korea they're coming down on me. It's like the swastika to them! I can't use it anymore," said Hosoi, adding: "I've had that graphic since 1982. All the while I lived in Korea Town, in LA. And no one said a thing! There was no Internet for them to say it."

HOT-BUTTON ISSUE

In today's Internet-connected, social media-policed cultural landscape, it's safe to say that swastikas and SS-runes on skateboards and helmets would not be well-received. The powers that be already came down like a ton of bricks on Germany-based skateboard distribution company Urban Supplies for selling a line of controversial skateboard decks in 2008: As the bone of contention, the decks released by US-brand Mystery Skateboards featured a single "S"-rune in the lightning bolt-style of the Nazi Era "SS"-symbol. "It was a single rune in a circle, and although we had mixed feelings about it, we figured one rune would probably be okay. Obviously, two runes would have been out of the question," said Urban Supplies co-owner Jörg Ludewig. But trouble started brewing when an alarmed citizen sued a skate shop in the town of Nuremberg for selling the decks, inciting a federal investigation.

As it turned out, the rune-and-circle symbol used by Mystery Skateboards originally belonged to the Nazi regime's "Jungvolk" organization; a recruitment tool for funneling adolescents into the Hitler Youth movement in the years before World War II. Although German authorities refrained from confiscating the controversial boards – ownership is okay, only distribution is punishable –they made an example of the distributor. "We were ordered to desist from selling the boards in Germany and sentenced to pay over €10,000 in fines. But they reduced it to €1,000 apiece [for Ludewig and his business partner] with a three-year probation period, during which we were super careful about this kind of thing. I still have some Chet Childress [pro model] decks by Black Label [skateboards] in my office with two SS-runes in his name that we couldn't sell. And we also stopped selling decks by [death metal band] Slayer," said Jörg Ludewig. During the investigation, the German State Office of Criminal Investigation also sent Urban Supplies an entire catalogue filled with imagery defined as "unconstitutional symbols" – including various Nazi flags and insignia – that may under no circumstances be legally distributed in Germany. "We sent copies of the catalogue to all the American skateboard brands that we carried at the time," said Jörg Ludewig. But whether these graphic examples were received as warning shots or sources of inspiration for even more controversial skateboard graphics, will forever remain a mystery...

SIMS
KAMIKAZE
SIGNAL
SIMS
KAMIKAZE

Photo: Glen E. Friedman

Alva
SKATES

ALVA SKATES
714/957 0971

The world of professional skateboarding can be divided into two eras: Before and after Tony Alva. In the pre-Alva days, professional skateboarders were clean-cut surfers with sun-bleached hair, gymnasts performing choreographed routines, and "real" athletes representing their "sport" on national television with proper gentlemanly demeanor. Tony Alva – or just T.A. – changed all that, injecting skateboarding with attitude, swagger, and a rock star wardrobe. Nicknamed 'Mad Dog' by his peers for his aggressive riding style, Alva made the pages of skateboarding magazines wearing fedoras and leather jackets, flipping the bird into the camera, pioneering aerial moves over the edge of backyard pools in a whirlwind of stardom that sent a shock to the system, changing skateboarding culture and fashion forever.

"Alva was just Mad Dog. Back then he was gnarly, aggressive. He had the long hair, and he was kind of surf punk-ish. He would terrorize sessions and go to clubs. It was really before its time, people just couldn't relate to it," said skateboard icon Christian Hosoi, who joined Alva's skateboard team at a young age. Going against the grain, Alva and his entourage began dressing in the vernacular of rock and roll at a time when skateboarding was wrapped in surf style. "I always liked Tony's whole scene. He always did his own thing and dressed the way he did. He had the fedora hats. He was influential, for sure, because he just had his own style," said 1970s pro and early punk rock adopter Steve Olson.

And by bottling his boundary-pushing swagger into an eponymous skateboard brand, Alva Skates, skateboarding's resident bad boy opened the door to an entirely new way for pro skaters to present and market themselves. With attitude-driven advertisements and rock 'n' roll-inspired imagery, Alva Skates proved that skateboarders could be more than talented athletes. They could be heroes, rebels, and fashion icons – larger than life. "He was the first real rock star in skateboarding! To me, he blazed the trail and showed people how to do it," said 1970s pro and influential Dogtown graphic artist Wes Humpston, adding: "He probably got more people off their ass, off their couch, and on a skateboard than anybody else!"

BIRTH OF A LEGEND

Tony Alva's skateboarding journey started in 1967 when he discovered "sidewalk surfing" at the age of 10. Born and raised in Santa Monica, California, as the son of a Dutch mother and Mexican-American father, Alva learned how to surf on the beaches down the street from his house: "The North Side [of L.A.] is where I grew up surfing. I caught my first couple of waves down there," said Tony Alva. Skateboarding and surfing went hand-in-hand in those days, and Alva's early role models included pro surfers/skateboarders from Santa Monica and Pacific Palisades such as Hobie team riders Danny Bearer, Torger Johnson, and the Hilton brothers.

"All our heroes were professional surfers. Everyone we looked up to in the sense of trying to emulate them were all professional surfers, not skateboarders," said Tony Alva. In terms of skateboard apparel, the close ties to surfing also carried over into wardrobe choices. "Our deal was to emulate surfing on land. So we just wore whatever the surfers were surfing in," said Tony Alva, who would skateboard the concrete embankments of local school yards such as Kenter and Paul Revere wearing the "surfer look" of the time: deck shoes and tube socks paired with board shorts and a T-shirt bleached by the California sun. But as Alva's riding skills progressed, the young prodigy gravitated towards a grittier, more aggressive style of surfing pioneered by the locals in the harsh waters of Santa Monica's "Dogtown" neighborhood on the border of Venice Beach. In the shadows of the defunct and rapidly decomposing Pacific Ocean Park Pier, Alva became part of a tightly-knit gang of outsiders with a "Locals Only" attitude, including Jay Adams and Shogo Kubo. "It takes a while before you become accepted as a transplant in Venice," said Tony Alva. "I'm from the other side of the tracks, the North end of Santa Monica. My dad used to think he could take me away from the riff-raff and bad influences by moving me to a nice neighborhood. And that wasn't necessarily true."

WRONG SIDE OF THE TRACKS

In 1972, Alva joined the junior surf team of legendary Jeff Ho & Zephyr Productions Surf Shop, located close to the beach on Main Street and Ocean Park Boulevard in the heart of Dogtown. Together with fellow "Z-Boys" - short for Zephyr - including Jay Adams and Stacy Peralta, the wild-haired rebel brought the low-gravity, aggressive surf style cultivated in the wreckage of the Pier into the streets, replacing the upright, somewhat stiff riding style of the time with a healthy dose of attitude and danger. Ultimately, Alva and his cohorts graduated from the junior surf team to form the Zephyr Competition Skate Team, a force to be reckoned with on the competition circuit; equally feared and revered in their matching navy blue Zephyr team T-shirts and torn-up jeans.

In the streets and school yards, Alva and the Z-Boys soon became notorious for their reckless antics and trailblazing stunts, adapting low-slung surf maneuvers like the Bertlemann slide, named after surfing pioneer Larry Bertlemann, into the streets. Their early forays into riding vertical pool walls also called for more rugged, protective attire than "beachy" board shorts. Says original Z-Boy and professional skateboarder Stacy Peralta: "Skateboarding was an offshoot of surfing and as such anyone back in the 1970s or prior who rode a skateboard dressed like a surfer with baggie and scruffy Levi's or pinwheel cords, T-shirt, Vans deck shoes and if needed a Pendleton over shirt. No one wore shorts! When you look at the now famous [1975] Del Mar skateboarding [championships] event, you can see that virtually every competitor is dressed like this and it all came from surfing which was all based around looking scruffy and unkempt."

The 1975 National Skateboarding Championships in Del Mar is also remembered as the point in skateboarding history when the counter-cultural edge proliferated by Alva and the Z-Boys collided head-on with the old, gymnastics-driven style of skateboarding. In the burgeoning skateboarding scene - skateboarding had just caught its second major wave of popularity - the new "Dogtown" style effected a radical paradigm shift. "When you saw pictures of them in magazines, you just wanted to skate like those guys. Like, 'Oh fuck, I could do that!'" said Wes Humpston. Former Alva Skates team rider Dave Duncan also recalls the profound stylistic influence of Alva and the Z-Boys: "I just loved Tony Alva in the 1970s and how he brought this aggressive, gnarly way into skateboarding. All the Dogtown guys had this amazing style and image, whether it was Jay Adams, or Shogo Kubo, or Bob Biniak... That gnarly style from the 1970s!"

THE FIRST PIECE OF SKATEBOARD FASHION

The key enabler to this new, gnarly style of skateboarding had been the urethane wheel, unlocking a new world of sharper turns and previously unrideable terrain. As one of the key pioneers on the forefront of skateboarding in empty swimming pools, Tony Alva realized that it was time for another innovative step in skateboard equipment: padded, skateboard-specific shoes built tough enough to withstand the wear and tear of pool skateboarding, which had received a major boost in popularity during the 1976 drought in Southern California that left a world of empty pools open for exploration from Beverly Hills all the way to San Diego.

BRAD BOWMAN
A Tastefully Punk Interview

BATTLING IN THE BADLANDS '79
The Heaviest Pro Bowl Yet
SNOWBOARDING
A Perfect Winter Alternative
THE STREET EXPERIENCE
Curb Grinding And Other Joys
FOCUS
Hester Series Portfolio
SKATEBOARDER OF THE YEAR BALLOT

With a design for a new, more rugged shoe in mind, Alva called on Vans, his shoe sponsor from 1974 onwards, and sold Vans founder Paul Van Doren on an adaptation of the classic Vans Authentic deck shoe. Replete with a grippy, waffle-patterned rubber sole, collar padding and supportive heel cup, the Vans Era model, co-designed by Tony Alva, made history as the world's first skateboard-specific shoe, featuring the classic "Off The Wall" slogan above the heel.

In the world of skateboarding, previously a mere shadow phenomenon of surfing, the arrival of the Vans Era marked the dawn of skateboard fashion as we know it, says Stacy Peralta: "The very first fashion element that came into skateboarding in the 1970s – the very first fashion element that skateboarding can claim as its own, free from the surfing world, was the custom-colored Vans deck shoe made popular by Tony Alva in *SkateBoarder* Magazine. His Vans shoes were blue and red and the store could not stock enough of them after he was pictured in the magazine skating in them."

ROCKING AND ROLLING

The Vans deal put rocket boots on Tony Alva's popularity. Out of all the hard-charging Z-Boys, who all went separate ways after the Zephyr team disbanded in 1976, it was Alva who would ultimately take skateboarding into rock star territory. And while Alva already knew how to roll, he learned how to rock with best of them from jet-setting millionaire and surfer, Bunker Spreckels. "He was a surfer and heir to the Spreckels Sugar fortune, and the godson of Clark Gable. He would get flown in on helicopters to go surfing and knew Hawaiian royalty. Alva was hanging out with him a lot and that's how he got into the whole rock 'n' roll lifestyle," said skateboard photographer J. Grant Brittain.

Coming from money, Spreckels stylized himself into a larger-than-life surfing super star, known as The Player, dressed in leather jackets and fur coats, surrounded by a never-ending maelstrom of parties and chicks and weed and coke and orgies. Alva lived with Spreckels in Los Angeles and Hawaii for a period, during which he crafted his own bad boy persona and wardrobe. "Bunker Spreckels was a full-on multi-million dollar playboy jet-setter. He had a lot of rock 'n' roll influence on our style when we were off the board," said Tony Alva, while pointing out: "But on the board we mostly wore stuff that was associated with sporting lifestyle. Like what Torger [Johnson] used to wear, cause he was from the Palisades and Malibu… nice sporty tennis gear and shorts and jackets."

Off the board, Alva would take to wearing leather jackets and night club outfits, and a famous Art Brewer photograph depicts T.A. next to Spreckels in an all-white suit with his lion's mane hair tucked under a wide-brimmed sun hat. Swagger. At high-profile skateboarding events, Alva would show up in competition suits covered in decorative rhinestones, custom-made by celebrity tailor Nudie Cohn. "Alva won the combined World Championships in a Nudie Suit that Bunker Spreckels had commissioned," said skateboard artist and writer Craig R. Stecyk.

After Bunker Spreckels passed away at the age of 27 in 1977, Alva carried the rock 'n' roll torch in skateboarding, taking super stardom to new heights.

Alvar

Photo: Jim Goodrich

"Alva was most definitely skateboarding's rock star. He was a world champion skateboarder, and he wanted to prove to the world that he was the best - and he did! He had the ego to go with it and say, 'Hey, I'm a skateboarder!' He was proud to be a skater and make skateboarding famous in the eyes of the rock 'n' roll world, and was also hanging out in Hollywood with rock stars," said Dave Duncan.

L.A. STREET STYLE

As Alva's popularity soared, the Los Angeles native became an internationally recognized style icon, touring from London to Germany to Tokyo as skateboarding's most recognized ambassador. "Everyone wanted to look like Alva, and wear the hat like Tony Alva - but you couldn't wear that stuff year-round," said skateboard photographer Skin Phillips, who grew up skateboarding in Wales, UK. Alva's signature "hat" - a slim fedora with tapered brim - would become his calling card accessory, deeply ingrained into the collective skateboarding psyche. "Alva wore a Fedora and rode backyard pools," said 1980s pro skater Neil Blender in summarizing Alva's stylistic legacy. "The fedora hat was a subversive statement - an independent statement and a statement of 'screw convention, we're doing this our way,'" said Stacy Peralta. "The fedora hat was made popular by Tony Alva and Jay Adams. Many other pro skaters and many skateboarders all over the world embraced this look."

Asked about the inspiration for the fedora - previously known as an "old man's hat" - Alva allowed that it originated, not from stylistic escapades into rock 'n' roll couture, but from his Hispanic roots and Los Angeles street culture. "We were influenced by the street. That's how we started to wear fedoras. And that's also how we wore the kind of chinos, the khaki pants the Mexican kids were wearing. Street style in L.A. has always been Chicano-influenced, Mexican-influenced," said Tony Alva, adding: "On the far West Side, Venice had a lot of Chicano influence because there were a lot of Mexican kids that grew up there. But if you went over to East L.A. - Boyle Heights or you went to Lincoln Heights - those kids were wearing the same thing, except the guys at the beach were skateboarders and surfers, while the skaters from the inner city were just skateboarders."

THE NEXT BIG THING

The year 1977 proved a banner year for skateboarding - revenues from skateboard products topped $400 million according to The Chicago Tribune - and Tony Alva cemented his title as the world's best skateboarder on the competitive circuit as part of the Logan Earth Ski team. Next to winning the Men's Overall Professional World Championship title in 1977 - although Wes Humpston insists that Alva "never practiced, he just went down there and kicked everybody's ass" - Alva also set the Guinness Book of World Records for jumping 17 barrels (he cleared 19 barrels later that year). Much like his idol Torger Johnson, Alva evolved into an all-terrain skateboarder - riding freestyle, slalom, banks, pools - and strived to be the best at everything, with the swagger to back it up, always surrounded by autograph-seeking admirers and a clique of fan boys.

Outside the competitive arena, where champions are crowned, Alva earned respect where it counted - in the backyard pools where legends are born. In the summer of 1977, all the stars of his stylistic legacy aligned - the fedora, the wild hair, the lofty style - when Alva landed what is credited as the world's first frontside aerial in a pool, captured in a Glen E. Friedman photograph at L.A.'s Dog Bowl.

You look at it and go, 'Orange, really!? Only TA could do that!' I love it, that's what it takes to make you be you." Ultimately, Alva Clothing's mainstream success also proved its downfall. "I think they just couldn't fill the orders. That was the problem. It was popular at Macy's in New York. But I don't think they were ready for the production," said Steve Olson. In hindsight, Tony Alva has mixed feelings about his clothing line. "If you wanna know the truth, I thought it was a mistake. But you have to make mistakes in order to make progress and to see what works and what doesn't. To take a skateboard company and a brand that represents hardcore attitude towards skateboarding and try and go into some big clothing company, I would never do that again."

STAYING PUNK

The financial fallout from Alva Clothing also marked the death of Alva Skateboards, a high price to pay for Alva at the time. Then again, his company had set a new benchmark for how high a personality-based brand could go in skateboarding. "He was big and we was the first one who knew where you could go with it. And unless you go and try, you're never gonna know if it's gonna work or not," said Wes Humpston. After Alva Skates went out of business, T.A. focused on skateboarding and the emerging punk rock movement: "All that fashion stuff to me seemed like a bit of a waste of time. Cause I figured I would rather be skating, I'd rather be surfing. I'd rather be doing like things I thought were more hardcore."

Alva fondly remembers the changes effected by punk rock in skateboarding as a golden era. "I think the best time for me was the late '70s and into the early '80s. There was a transition that happened then. The surfer, street, low-rider style went to a full-on hardcore rock'n roll punk rock style. Music has always been a big influence when it comes to fashion. Because it goes hand-in-hand with attitude," said Tony Alva. "Punk rock had a lot of fashion going on, whether it was considered fashion or not. But it was excellent. And New Wave was New Wave with suits and everything and rockabilly and everything had a sense of style behind it," said Steve Olson. And once again, Alva was not just following a movement, but leading the way in skateboarding together with other punk-minded pioneers.

"When punk rock came in, it started to become the B52s, the Clash and all guys like Tony Alva and [Steve] Olson and Jay Adams started shaving their heads and playing rockabilly. Being punk rock. And Fear and Circle Jerks came out and it was just this whole style of spiked bracelet, bowling shirts, cut-off sleeves. Beat-up Levi's with boots. It was Doc Martens, it happened quick. Boom! Skaters took it on fast. Because it was rebellious! It was something that was just not normal," said Christian Hosoi. Not everybody in skateboarding was a fan of punk rock, and Alva and cohorts caught some flack at the time, says Steve Olson: "Other skaters were also like, 'These guys are not good for our sport!' Everyone is entitled to their opinion. Little did they know, the kids were gonna dig it too, though!"

Even company owners were worried, especially when Olson took the stage at the 1979 Skateboarder Awards wearing leather bondage pants. "It really tripped the people out in the industry, they were like, these guys are NOT what we want our sport to be. No way. This punk rock stuff is no, no, no! It's a bad scene! Our two top dudes Alva and Olson are deeply into this whole movement and bla, bla, bla..." Ultimately, the rejection created a strong bond between Olson and Alva. "That's when I became friends with Tony, we both enjoyed this music world. It was fun and it was happening and wild and brand-new to us."

But as fate would have it, the rise of punk rock in skateboarding also coincided with the downfall of skateboarding's second wave of mass popularity. Skate parks, the focus of 1970s skateboarding, shut down by the hundreds and skateboard participation contracted to grass roots levels. Alva's company was out of business, but he still reigned supreme in both worlds - skateboarding and music. Together with Mike Ball of Suicidal Tendencies fame and "Rico" Reid Rolan on drums, Alva formed punk rock band The Skoundrelz, while remaining a force to be reckoned with on a skateboard. "At all these big rock shows there were halfpipes and he would go out there and be the king of the halfpipe and be the star of the show. He had the attitude and all the photos in the mags," said Dave Duncan.

OUT OF THE DARK

But although Tony Alva brought back Alva Skates in 1982 with young prodigy Christian Hosoi as their next-generation team rider, the punk rock years marked a dark time for skateboarding's first rock star. With punk rock came parties and booze and drugs, and over the years, Alva watched some of his closest friends in skateboarding and music lose the battle against their inner demons. In 2007, T.A. came out on top, found spirituality and became clean. That year, he founded the band G.F.P. (General Fucking Principle) with seasoned punk rock musicians Tom Paul Davis from DFL, Greg Hetson from Circle Jerks and Bad Religion, and Amery Smith from Suicidal Tendencies.

"The whole punk rock thing can be done sober," said Tony Alva. "If I kept doing what I was doing, I would either be in jail, or dead, or in an insane asylum. That's where drugs and alcohol take me." Getting deeper into the issue, Alva points out: "I'm one of the few guys in the skateboarding and punk rock world that is, first of all, still here. And second of all, still alive. And third, I'm sober. That in itself is miraculous and it's from having a higher power in your life and a connection with God. God's got your back."

In 2018, Alva enjoys skateboarding and surfing, and working on the perfect hybrid surfboard shape with his company, Alva Surfcraft. In the fashion department, the style icon nowadays likes to "keep it clean, not too soiled. The dreadlocks and the beard don't necessarily enhance your fashion credibility when you're wearing dirty clothes." As his favorite brands and designers, Alva listed "vintage pieces from the '70s and '80s, like Paul Smith or jackets by Yves Saint Laurent, old vintage Lacoste jackets, Marni sunglasses."

All of which he has access to through his girlfriend of eleven years, Katie Rodriguez, who runs L.A. fashion boutique Resurrection Vintage. "My closet is a mixture of action sports meets rock'n roll, nice khakis, flannels. I'm a jacket junkie so I have too many jackets, about 20 jackets." Having recently appeared in a *Playboy* magazine fashion shoot wearing a Ralph Lauren Purple Line suit, Alva stated, "I wouldn't really recommend going skating in a $6,000 suit."

As one of the skateboarders forever ingrained on skateboarding's Mount Rushmore, Tony Alva continues to travel the globe as one of skateboarding and punk rock's international ambassadors. At the age of 60, skateboarding's original Bad Boy still assaults pool coping on the regular, but has found his inner peace. "The credit goes to God, because God gave me the grace to walk through a lot of gnarly things in my life and still be here. Now I can help others by telling my story. Whether it be surfing, skateboarding, music, fashion, art – you name it. I have a connection to all those things because of the fact that I have lived long enough to enjoy it." And when it comes to putting on a show, skateboarding's first rock star still knows about the importance of dressing the part. "You want to show people a good time and you want to look good and connect to people. When you are up on stage under the lights, you got to have a little extra flair to keep that attention."

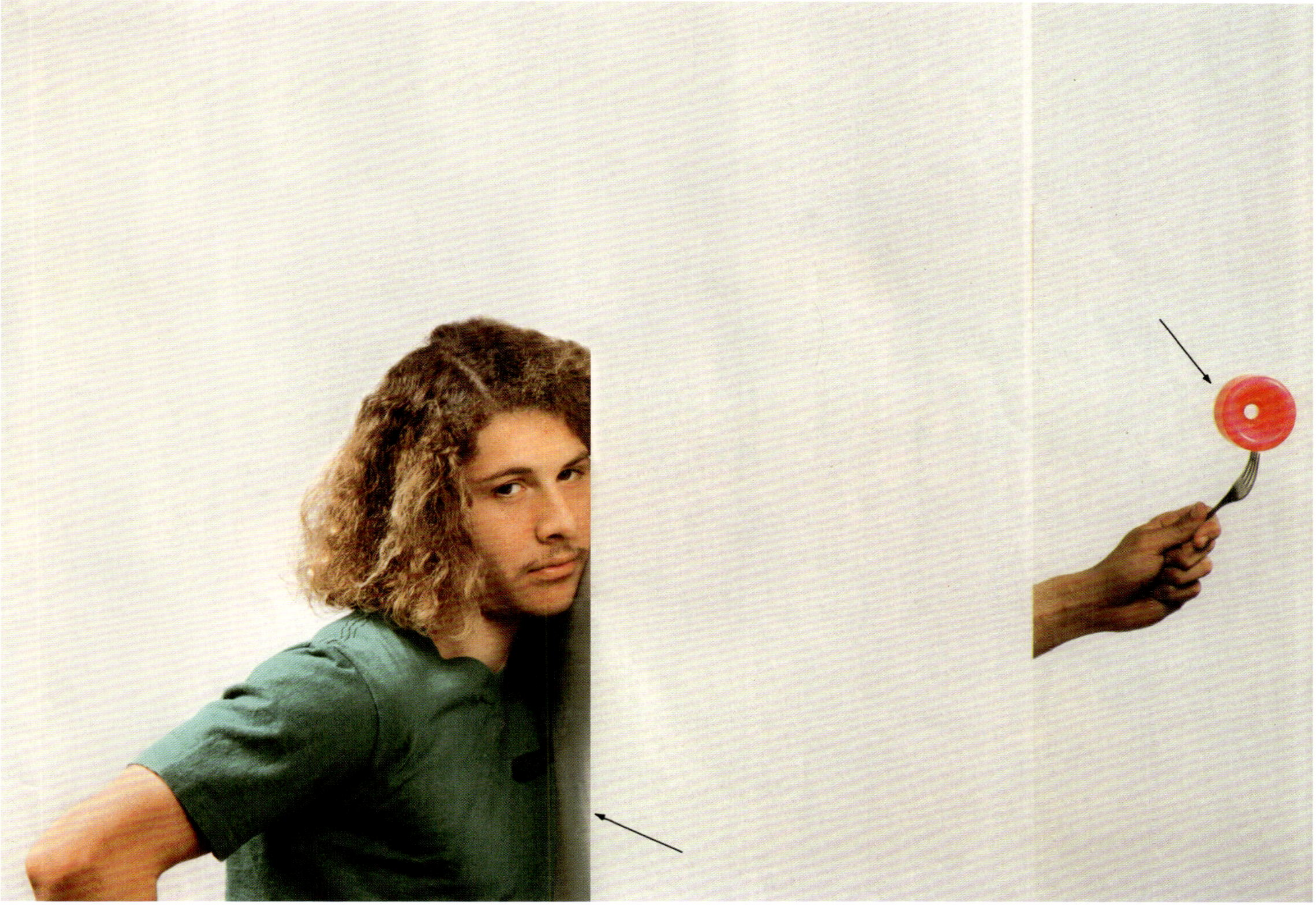

FEDORAS: STREET STYLE FLAIR WITH AN EDGE

The physical act of skateboarding holds the power to elevate everyday experience into the sublime. In the same vein, skateboard fashion can elevate even the most common and unassuming pieces of attire into of-the-moment fashion items. This is exactly what happened to the humble fedora hat, basically a dented felt hat with a wide brim, in the late 1970s. In the hands of skateboarding's premiere fashion peacocks - Dogtown's Tony Alva and Jay Adams - the classic menswear staple became transformed into an emblem of rakish masculinity, embraced by skateboarders the world over as a sizzling hot trend.

Owing its name to Fédora, an 1882 play by playwright Victorien Sardou, the hat was associated with 1920s Prohibition-era gangsters, and later picked up by singer Frank Sinatra as an emblem of male swagger. Actually, make that "older male" swagger. "This was a hat originally designed in the '40s or '50s for older men who might be going out on the town," says 1970s pro skateboarder Stacy Peralta.

But it was the Dogtown skateboarders who injected the fedora with youthful energy. "Tony and Jay made it into a fashion statement and accessory for teenagers while doing a subversive activity like skateboarding illegally in someone's backyard pool," said Peralta. Despite its casual appeal, the hat - preferably worn with a flower or bird's feather in the headband for extra style points - rebelled against skateboarding's sports-driven, safety-oriented public image. And it's significant that the most competitive skater at the time, 1977's World Champion Tony Alva, was leading the charge in this rebellion. "Tony was the first guy in skateboarding to wear a hat all the time. Not a helmet, but a hat!" said fellow Zephyr team rider Nathan Pratt.

What's more, Adams and Alva not only said "shine" to the safety gear prescribed at official skateboarding facilities, they also imported an element of flair into the world of board sports. "They were not only wearing a hat instead of a helmet but they were wearing a dinner hat, a dress hat, an older men's fashion hat," said Peralta. The broader context was one of subversion and rebellion, as the rise of fedoras in skateboarding around 1977 also signaled an attitude that would later come to full bloom in the shape of punk rock culture. Says Peralta: "What was so important about this look also is that it presaged the whole punk revolution that would hit skateboarding just a few years in the future."

Asked about the origins of the fedora look, skateboard icon Tony Alva said: "In the punk rock heyday, we would go to thrift stores and hand-me-down second-hand stores. We would buy the really comfortable but durable funky stuff that was from the '50s and '60s, including fedoras."

Once photographs of Alva's first successful frontside aerials in a backyard pool - wearing a fedora, of course - hit magazines in 1977, the look spread like wildfire. First, it was adopted by pro skateboarders such as G&S team rider Dennis Martinez and Brad Bowman. Next, teenage skateboarders across the world embraced the look as one of skateboarding's first global fashion trends. From England, to Japan, to Australia, every skate crew had a coolest guy; and that guy wore the fedora. And while the hat still looms large over hipster chic today, the same rule applies as it did back then: For every crew, only one guy with fedora allowed. Thanks.

Photo: Glen E. Friedman

Photo: Glen E. Friedman

RAINBOW STRIPES: CALIFORNIA LIFESTYLE

To borrow from a Rolling Stones song, skateboard fashion in the mid-1970s came in (primary) colors everywhere, like a sparkling rainbow. Introduced into skateboarding by 1960s hardware and clothing brand Hobie, the rainbow pattern - color-blocked stripes of blue, red, yellow, and green - proved a popular ornament on everything from shorts, to shirts, and outerwear. In 1975, surf apparel company Ocean Pacific landed a major hit with hooded nylon windbreakers, available in white and navy blue as base colors paired with rainbow stripes across the chest. Surf and skateboard hardware manufacturers also implemented rainbow colorways, including 1976's fiberglass completes by Jupiter Skateboards from Bellevue, Washington, as well as Rainbow Surfboards, the company started by Mike Hynson of Endless Summer fame out of La Jolla, California. "Rainbow was hot! Everyone in California had rainbow stickers on their car, or rainbow wallets. We called them 'surfer wallets' with Velcro closure," said skateboard photographer Dave Swift. And while the Rainbow Flag has since become the symbol of gay pride and equal rights, the design did not yet hold any LGBT connotations in the mid-1970s. "Rainbow colors were this hippie thing. Everyone was into it, even before it was embraced by the gay community in San Francisco," said skateboard photographer Ted "T-Bone" Terrebonne. Skateboard photographer Michael Chantry also traces the rainbow's origins to 1960s counter-culture: "I think it was a hippie thing at the time... like, being real mellow and all that."

SURGING POPULARITY

Protective skateboarding equipment specialists, Rector Skatewear, equipped their Pro Series knee and elbow pads with rainbow-patterned "elasticated" straps held by Velcro fasteners. The company's highly popular skateboarding gloves also featured two-inch rainbow-colored wrist straps, adjustable with Velcro. In 1977, co-owner and designer Mike Rector even went as far as filing a patent on his Palm Pads Gloves and rainbow-patterned fasteners, marketed as Rainbow Wriststraps, in response to copycats flooding the protective gear market with rainbow-inspired designs.

But it was too late. One particular company, California Rainbow, built its entire corporate identity around the popular design while building strategic partnerships with high-profile skateboard teams, including the Pepsi exhibition team. Behind the scenes, California Rainbow was part of Imperial Century Inc. in San Diego, whose director John Baron also owned the Pepsi team's clothing sponsor, 360 Sportswear. An early 1978 Skateboarder magazine advertisement for the California Rainbow Skateboard Company, announced: "Good enough for the Pepsi Skateboard Team? We are. California Rainbow (manufacturer of the Pepsi Skateboard Products) is the same high quality safety gear worn by the members of the Official Pepsi Skateboard Team. Our Rainbow design is the only difference. The product is the same." Bringing the rainbow theme full-circle, the Pepsi team also rode bright yellow skateboards with rainbow decals. Produced in partnership with Rainbow Surfboards, the Pepsi boards included safety instructions such as, "always wear long-sleeved shirts, long pants and sneakers."

The Hobie Skateboards team toured the entire US with rainbow colors as their official team regalia. The year 1978 marks Peak Rainbow in skateboard culture, as magazine coverage and skateboard films attest. "All the skaters around the world were rocking it, especially freestylers. Rainbow really became a freestyle thing," said 1980s pro skateboarder Claus Grabke. Ultimately, the rainbow design became the official symbol of the gay and lesbian community during the San Francisco Gay Freedom Day Parade on June 25, 1978, when the first rainbow flag designed by artist Gilbert Baker flew over the Castro district. The rest is history, and the primary colors still represent freedom and inalienable rights today.

SKATEBOARD PROTECTIVE ELBOW PADS
PRICE
STYLE NO. EPA-201
SIZE
S
california rainbow
T.M.
AND OTHER PATENTS

MAD

RATS

RECTOR: NEXT-LEVEL PROTECTION

Evolution never happens overnight. It's a long process marked by trial and error, success and failure, rewarding the ultimate feats of adaptation to changes in the environment. The evolution of skateboard safety equipment proved no different. When concrete skate parks offering pools, bowls, and vertical riding terrain in the mid-1970s called for a whole new generation of pads and safety gear, one company set out to raise the bar with next-level solutions: Rector, a brand name conveniently rhyming with "protector," stepped to the plate in 1977 as the one-stop provider for all things skateboard safety: "Concentrate on your skating. Rector's got you covered," read the company's full-page ads in skateboarding magazines, promising "safety for the new wave of skaters and skateparks."

Started by engineer-slash-skateboard-enthusiast Mike Rector together with seasoned entrepreneur Bob Wolfe in 1977, Rector Skatewear barged onto the market with its patented design for skateboard-specific safety gloves that set a new industry standard and sold thousands of units. But in the bigger picture, the company based in Santa Rosa, California, owes its major breakthrough to constant adaptation and improvements of product designs in another crucial segment: Rector kneepads, available in primary colors such as red, yellow, and blue - paired with white plastic knee caps - became a must-have item of the Skate Park Era.

"Rector was it!" said skateboard photographer Jim Goodrich. "Rector was THE safety gear just like Vans was THE shoe!"

A LEADER IN SAFETY GEAR

Admittedly, Rector's smash hit came on the heels of a few strikeouts. Their first line of kneepads, introduced under the name Flex Line in 1977, may have offered key performance features such as high-density foam, robust nylon coating, and anatomically correct fit. But what looked perfect on paper proved deficient in skate park practice: "Their first kneepads sucked! They would stick to the ground if you fell on them and they didn't last long, either. You would fall on them once or twice, and the velcro would break," said 1970s skateboard pro Wes Humpston, adding: "So the ones with the cup on them, that's what you needed."

As it turned out, it was what everyone needed. When Mike Rector added a riveted hard plastic cup to his company's kneepads - introduced and patented as the Rector Kneeguard in late 1978 - the design single-handedly propelled skateboard riding technique into a new era. Says professional skateboarder Lance Mountain: "Kneepads are one of the biggest inventions in skateboarding. They changed skateboarding! They allowed people to go out of the bowl. Before, you were skating inside the bowl. They allowed people to go really high and come down safely by knee-sliding. And try it over and over and over again to really to push the limits of how high you can go. It was all thanks to having pads with a [plastic] recap. That was a huge change from a kneepad without a recap."

When Lance Mountain and the new guard of progressive park skaters embraced Rectors as their go-to pads, the company emerged as a leader in the protective-equipment market. At the height of the skate park boom, when full protective gear became mandatory at all skateboarding facilities, Rector Skatewear's offering included padded shorts, wrist guards, gloves, helmets, elbow pads, as well as branded apparel. So it's safe to say that Rector literally kept skaters "covered" from head to toe.

Rector
Skate Boarder MAGAZINE
Rector

RECTOR DRAWS THE LINE,

YOUR LINE OF SKATEBOARDING APPAREL

t's happening, skateboarding is the hottest, nost radical new sport around. What you're seeing in this magazine are some of the best iders in the world ripping up the hottest spots to skate. You can be sure that these skaters are taking their skating to the limit, with style, and with the best equipment available.

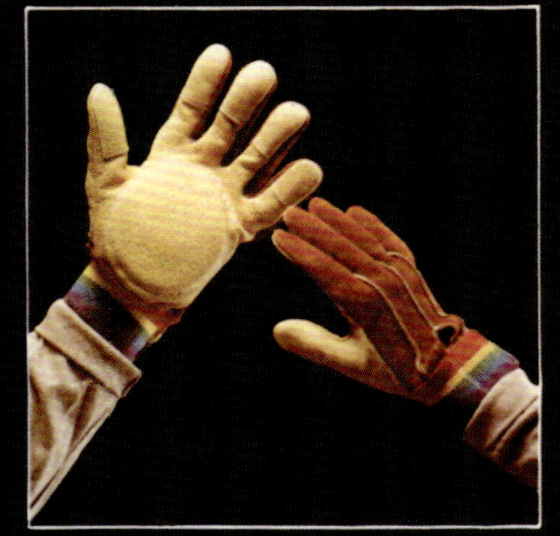

That's why he Rainbow Wriststrap™ of the Rector Palm Pads Glovs™ has become a familiar sight on so many of hese top riders. They have heir choice of equipment and hey choose Rector Palm Pads Glovs™ because they work. Isn't that the way it should be? We sure think so.

SKATEWEAR™ CONSCIOUSNESS

Most sports develop and become popular in basically the same way. First, the idea. Next, enthusiasts pioneer the sport until it matures with equipment and clothing which develop through the technology and demands of the sport. This is happening to skateboarding, and it's happening fast.

Whether you're a pro or just getting started with skateboarding, the flow is on and you're a part of it, with Skatewear from the ones who invented the word and the equipment. Rector draws the line, your line of skateboarding apparel.

FORM FOLLOWS FUNCTION

GLOVES. Your hands and wrists usually have to take the initial impact when falling or sliding, so we gave you the PALM PADS GLOVS™. They work the best, so far. PALM PADS™ are designed to be the all-around glove, but you might need a more specialized glove to suit your particular style. We have them. The **Skatepark Specials™**, a complete line of gloves designed for skatepark use. The **'Signature™'** freestyle glove. And the totally radical new **Palm Pads U-2™.**

SHORTS. "These shorts are outrageous!" That's the overwhelming response to the new Rector PROTECTIVE SKATE SHORTS™. Two styles to choose from with a choice of colors and fabrics, all with exclusive **'REMOVABLE'** Rector hip and tail pad system. We should add that "removable" means the whole pad comes out easily, not leaving wet pockets to make you uncomfortable. Stylish on or off your skateboard, these revolutionary shorts may well be the most comfortable pair you've ever had.

ELBOW AND KNEE PADS. We spent a lot of time working on pads that will really work. We could have put our name on pads designed for another sport (everyone else has), but we're not trying to fool you we're trying to protect you. So we took the time and came up with a line of pads for the sport.

SHIRTS. Open collar, lightweight Skatewear Tops in a variety of styles and colors. Full cut in the right places for action and freedom of movement.

SOCKS. Skatewear socks, developed exclusively for skateboarding; these knee high, reinforced socks stay knee high and give your ankles all the support they've been needing.

WE'LL MAKE YOU AN OFFER

On page 104 you'll find the information on how to order all the RECTOR SKATEWEAR™ products plus a chance to help us get RECTOR SKATEWEAR™ in your local stores. And you'll make money doing it TURN TO PAGE 104 FOR DETAILS.

RECTOR SKATEWEAR™
RECTOR AND WOLFE INCORPORATED
P.O. Box 371, Graton, California 95444
Phone (707) 823-9267, (707) 546-0255
DEALERS CALL COLLECT

Gregg Weaver at Reseda SkaterCross

Rector Skatewear Protective Shorts™ RS-2

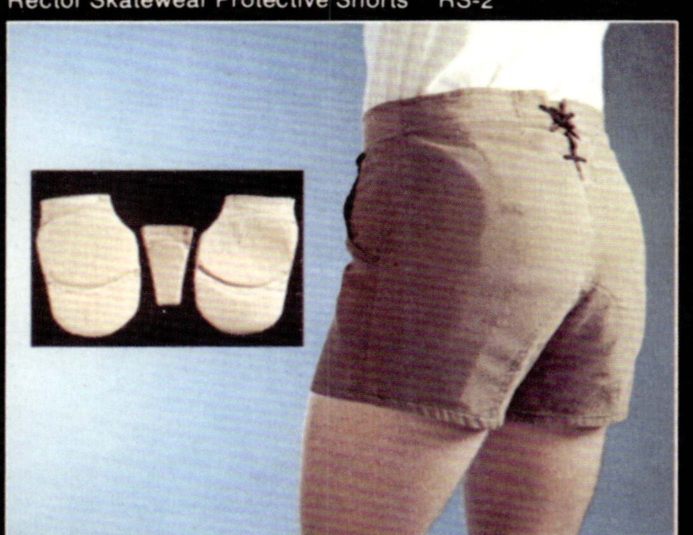

RS-1

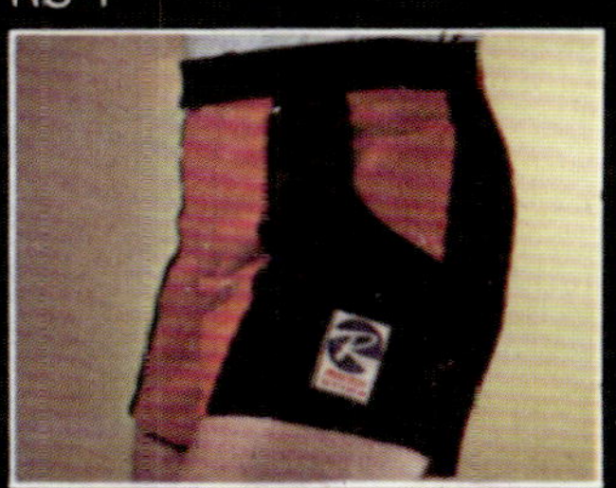

Denim

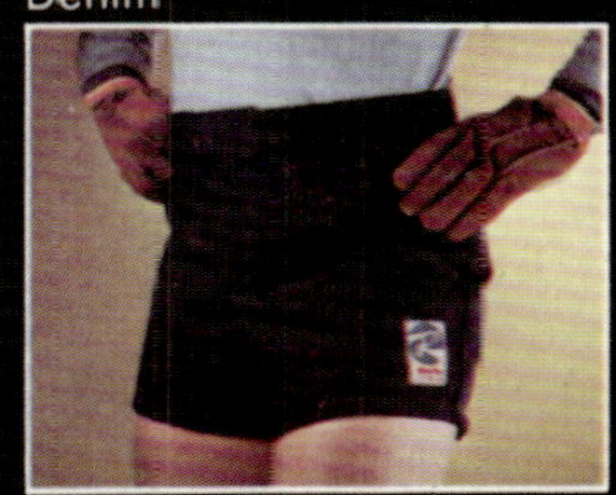

Rector™

Aector
Aector
Aector

CONSTANT EVOLUTION

Contrary to popular belief, Rector did not invent protective plastic caps on knee and elbow pads. That was done by other companies such as Hobie or Norcon, who introduced plastic caps as early as 1976 – but as part of pad designs that proved far too fragile for the skate park era. "At the time Rectors came out there was already a company called Norcon that had plastic caps on their pads, but the padding was super thin. Like the ones you would find at Toys"R"Us," said skateboard icon Steve Caballero.

Combining the padding offered by Rector kneepads with the plastic knee caps from competing brands, Caballero and fellow park skaters would double-up on pads in true DIY-fashion. "I would put on Rectors first and then Norcons on top, so I could do knee slides. Before that, I never saw anyone doing a knee slide, ever. Everybody was running out of their tricks." Pro skateboarder Eddie Elguera, nicknamed "El Gato" for always landing on his feet like a cat, was on the same page: "The Hobies had [plastic] caps, so we would take the Rectors with no caps and put the other ones with caps over them. And then we could knee slide!"

SUCH GREAT HEIGHTS

The knee slide, a calculated fall to safety by way of sliding down the transition of a ramp or pool on plastic-capped kneepads, proved a game changer in the exploration of aerial skateboard tricks. In the late 1970s, skateboarders took their aerials to new heights, soaring several feet above the pool's coping – and it was all thanks to the safety afforded by a new generation of kneepads: "The first gear was primarily made for impact. And then the second generation with the plastic caps allowed skaters more to be able to slide," said 1960s pro skateboarder Cris Dawson.

Speaking on the evolution of the knee slide, Steve Caballero credits hard-plastic knee pads as the main catalyst: "It was just natural. When I put them on, this was the way I bailed… that I would just knee slide out of everything. And I swear, a few months later I open up Skateboarder magazine and I see this article with Brad Bowman about 'The Art of Kneesliding.' I was like, 'That's crazy! I'm already doing that!' We can't really say who did the first knee slide, but it seemed like a natural progression."

And although Rector was not the first company to add plastic caps to their pads, they were the first ones to get it right. "Knee sliding allowed you to skate on another level, so Rectors were really the key to that. Even more than shorts or other protective gear, the knee pads were really the key," said Eddie Elguera. Fellow pro Steve Caballero agrees to the game-changing impact of "when Rector came out with the [plastic] cap," while admitting that regular-sized kneepads proved too large for him as a pint-sized teenager: "In my first Tracker ad I'm actually wearing big Rector elbow pads on my knees!"

DESIGNED FOR SKATEBOARDING

Rector's skateboard-specific pads not only took riding technique to a whole new level, but also helped legitimize safety equipment in front of a mass audience. "We're originating products as we go. The basketball pads idea just won't work. We're trying to design gear that will help popularize the sport in the mass market," said Mike Rector in a 1977 newspaper interview. And it worked: Whereas early park skaters had grudgingly worn "soft" protectors offered as rental equipment at skate parks, owning a pair of Rectors now became the calling card of progressive-minded park skaters.

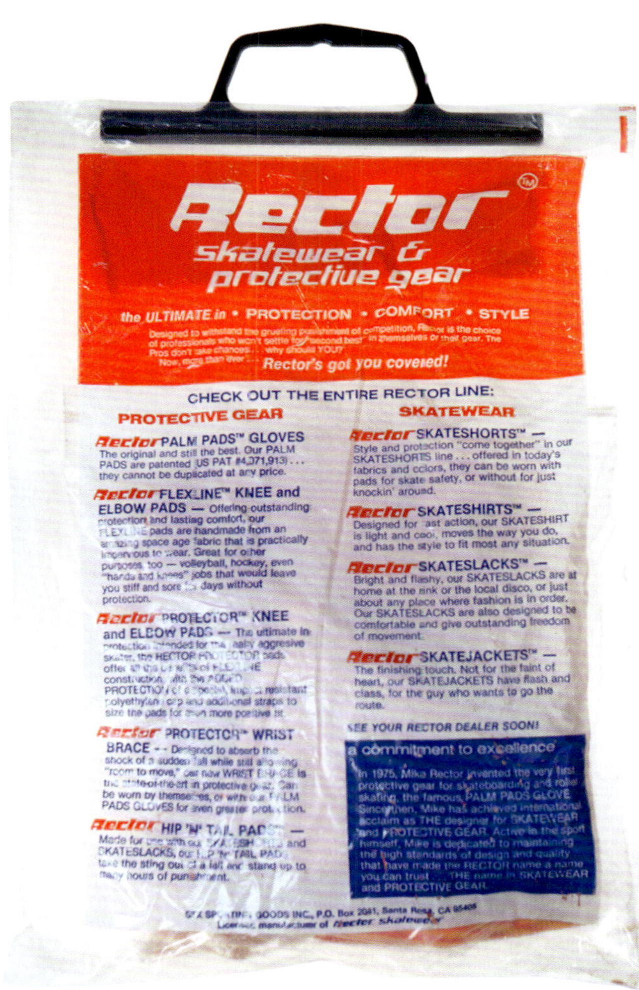

"All the vertical skating at the time took off because people could now learn new things thanks to the new safety equipment," said Lance Mountain, adding: "All the things people are doing today are here because people learned them thanks to pads."

Listening to the trailblazers on the new frontier of park skateboarding became the cornerstone of Rector's research and development efforts. "My involvement with a lot of the skaters you see in the magazines has a lot to do with the directions I am taking as a designer. I feel that these athletes are the real innovators expanding the sport for all of us to enjoy," said Mike Rector in a 1978 interview with Skateboarder magazine.

Examples of Rector's innovative approach include knee pads mimicking natural body lines with three separate panels filled with foam, while the back section behind the knee consisted of elastic material creating a "suction" fit. The popular Rector Skateshorts could be customized with the Curtis Hesselgrave "Hip'n Tail" Pro Skateboarder Pad System, a set of removable pads offering "maximum protection for the radical skater." As a special design twist, the pads connected to the waist band of the shorts with velcro strips. "This enables the pads to move with the skater, not the pants," explained Mike Rector in Skateboarder magazine, adding: "I can't over-emphasize the importance of the non-restricting qualities I am stressing. It is of the utmost importance that the wear must not cause the fall by restricting the skater's motions."

SAFE GEAR, RISKY FASHION

Next to allowing free room for movement, Rector Skatewear also cultivated its own signature aesthetic. "The equipment should look as good as it works; it is very important that the wear must not distract from the beauty of the sport," said Rector in Skateboarder magazine. From a fashion standpoint, Rector stood out by offering head-to-toe pads and clothing in signature colorways, blending neon yellow and bright tones of blue and red in their multi-paneled skate shorts and open-collar Rector Airborne design shirts and jackets.

But let's not pigeon-hole Rector as sole purveyors of flashy neon. Quite early on, Rector also embraced the darker, more rugged aesthetic of punk rock. In a 1979 advertisement, pro skateboarder Rick Blackhart is depicted under the headline "Rector Punk Protectors." That year, the famous "Freedom of Choice" video from New Wave pioneers DEVO - widely credited with setting the stage for the punk rock revolution in the late 1970s - also prominently featured Rector safety gear. Says pro skateboarder and early punk adopter Steve Olson: "When we did the DEVO video we all had the Rector shirts and shorts and pads. It was me, Jay Smith, Daryl Miller, and Dave Andrecht did the channel jump."

When the skate park era - and skateboarding as a whole - suffered a sudden fall from glory in late 1979, Rector Skatewear also went down - but not down for the count. As backyard vert ramps became the new focus of progressing skateboard riding technique, demand for functional pads and safety gear remained intact, and Rector rode along as the trusted brand in skate protection. Beyond the realm of skateboarding, Rector's Proformer line of pads emerged as a popular choice among construction workers and SWAT teams, thereby continuing the constant evolution of safety gear in new environments.

Rector
SKATEWEAR

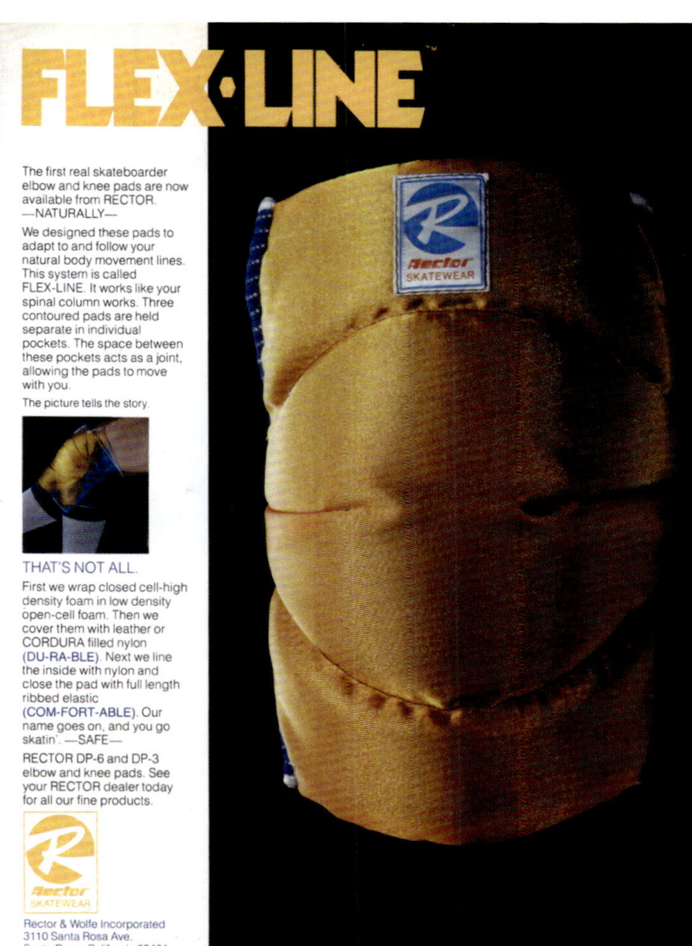
FLEX·LINE
The first real skateboarder elbow and knee pads are now available from RECTOR.
—NATURALLY—
We designed these pads to adapt to and follow your natural body movement lines. This system is called FLEX-LINE. It works like your spinal column works. Three contoured pads are held separate in individual pockets. The space between these pockets acts as a joint, allowing the pads to move with you.
The picture tells the story.
THAT'S NOT ALL.
First we wrap closed cell-high density foam in low density open-cell foam. Then we cover them with leather or CORDURA filled nylon (DU-RA-BLE). Next we line the inside with nylon and close the pad with full length ribbed elastic (COM-FORT-ABLE). Our name goes on, and you go skatin'. —SAFE—
RECTOR DP-6 and DP-3 elbow and knee pads. See your RECTOR dealer today for all our fine products.
Rector
SKATEWEAR
Rector & Wolfe Incorporated
3110 Santa Rosa Ave.
Santa Rosa, California 95401
(707) 823-9267
Rector
SKATEWEAR

New products from Rector
Safety
for the new wave of skaters and skateparks. Concentrate on your skating. Rector's got you covered.
The NEW RECTOR PROTECTOR WRIST GUARD™ with removable palm pad fits over the RECTOR PALM PADS GLOV™ for the ultimate in hand and wrist security.
RECTOR'S NEW KNEE GUARD™ extra long, extra thick, slide and impact cap that really works.
Rector Protector
Rector
Available soon — RECTOR PROTECTOR SKATESHORTS WITH EXTRA DURABLE NYLON. CURTIS HESSELGRAVE HIP AND TAIL PADS. RECTOR HELMET. RECTOR EQUIPMENT BAGS.

Before skateboard manufacturers adopted the fashion craze, generic tube socks from sports retailers offered affordable, one-size fits all alternatives. "I just went and bought them at the sporting goods store. I always made sure to get the high socks, pretty high," said pro skateboarder Steve Caballero.

Skateboard brands soon jumped on the trend, offering their own branded versions of tube socks. In 1977, Hang Ten clothing introduced "Lifestyle Hosiery," including the "Skateboard Sock" featuring red and yellow horizontal stripes and the company's "Ten Toes" logo. Skateboarder Magazine released its own branded tube socks – featuring the mag's logo on the ankle, a placement known as the "clock" in the socks business – under the slogan: "You'll always have the best foot forward in the NEW Skateboarder Magazine Socks!" And for the ultimate in style, pro skateboarders matched the stripes on their tube socks to the rest of their outfits. "Tube socks in matching colors were a big fashion thing at the time," said skateboard photographer Ted "T-Bone" Terrebonne.

ARGYLE: YOUNG REBELS IN OLD MEN'S SOCKS

As tube sock mania soared to new heights at skate parks and competitions, some of skateboarding's more non-conformist pro riders decided to say "shine" to the whole trend. Riders such as Jay Smith, Brad Bowman, Steve Rocco made argyle socks their calling card. "Around 1978, that's when skateboarding was going from 'surfy' towards punk. That was when DEVO came out and this kind of stuff was really cutting edge," said pro skateboarder and entrepreneur Steve Rocco. The argyle socks phenomenon can be traced back to pro rider Darrell Miller from Del Mar, inventor of the Miller flip, who wore the socks in a late-1970s Hobie Skateboards advertisement. "There were always certain skateboarders that wore argyle socks, even when the whole striped tube socks thing was going on. Like Darrell Miller with his gnarly argyle socks," said pro skateboarder Lance Mountain who also wore the socks with riders of his generation such as John Lucero, adding: "You were supposed to wear tube socks as a kid, and argyles were like old men socks. But we would always wear argyle socks because of a couple of guys. That was a skateboarder thing."

Originally, the diamond-shaped knit pattern goes back to the highlands of Western Scotland, worn by the tartan clan known as the Campbells of Argyll in custom-made kilts and plaids in the 17th century. Early on, the Campbells also wore argyle-patterned socks known as "tartan hose." In the 1970s, the pattern became a staple of "old men" clothes frequently used in sweaters and socks, before being adopted by members of the early punk rock movement. When skateboarders like Mike Smith began wearing argyle sweaters and socks, it was a break from the norm that caught lots of attention in the skateboard scene, said Dave Swift: "As kids we spent a lot of time just looking at photos [of pro skaters]. What they were wearing, the haircuts – the whole kit!"

Fast-forward to 2018, and "old school" tube socks and argyle socks remain relevant fashion choices in skateboarding. "Tube socks are still a big thing today, people still wear those with their Vans. That is still a trend that is relevant today," said skateboard photographer Skin Phillips. Over the years, skateboard-specific socks have grown into a viable market segment spearheaded by brands such as Stance, HUF, and NEFF that have proven big sellers at skate shops. Then again, skateboarders on a tight budget can always find a cheap pair of tube socks at the next sporting goods store.

HEADBANDS: FUNCTION MEETS FASHION

At a time when a skateboarder's greatness hinged on the number of 360s he could spin, shoulder-long surfer hair was à la mode hairstyle among trend-savvy riders. Ultimately, a clash between the two was inevitable - only so many 360s you can spin before your mane gets in the way. Enter the headband, a humble accessory with a functional twist that turned into a global skateboard fashion craze in the mid-1970s. However, function came first, said skateboard icon Stacy Peralta: "Headbands weren't really a fashion as more a function. We all had very long hair back then and there was no such thing as skateboard safety equipment, including helmets, so we needed something to keep the hair out of our eyes when we skated pools. So headbands and hats were our only option."

Function versus fashion aside, several 1970s skateboarding greats single-handedly owned the hairband look: 'Mad Dog' Tony Alva rocked headbands with a haphazard afro mane, Stacy Peralta with straw-blond surfer hair, freestyle Russ Howell with no shirt and a mustache, while Dogtown's Jim Muir brought in the low-slung tied bandana, and Shogo Kubo restrained his hair with added Kamikaze insignia on the headband.

Historically, headbands go back to Greek antiquity as trophy-pieces worn by victorious Olympic athletes. When skateboarders began appropriating headbands into their wardrobes, inspiration came from different areas, also including mainstream sports. Athletic riders such as Russ Howell and Stacy Peralta opted for workout-style jersey headbands from the sporting goods store. "Sweatbands were originally worn by professional tennis players like Bjorn Borg. And we looked at it as skateboarders and said, 'We sweat, let's get a sweat band in!' It was just natural progression," said 1970s pro skateboarder Cris Dawson.

Street kids such as Dogtown's Tony Alva also drew on natural influences from their surrounding culture: "We wore mostly tied-down bandanas that came from the street. The street culture has always been big with the Chicanos wearing the basic bandanas like bikers and low-rider kids. Americana kind of style," said Tony Alva, adding: "Bandanas have always been a big part of American culture even in the '40s and '50s." Meanwhile, Alva's teammate on the Zephyr team, Shogo Kubo, introduced Kamikaze-style headbands into the mix, which he often hand-made himself. Tony Alva remembers backing the style: "I used to rock the Kamikaze headbands. I knew a Japanese import store in Hawaii that I used to pick up stuff from. This lady imported genuine Japanese Kamikaze headbands."

Other skaters went the DIY-route, including SIMS rider Ed Economy, who cut one arm off a long-sleeved team jersey for a one-of-a-kind headband that read TEAM. "It was really hot and I had my team jersey skating the bowl with three other people - and it was 100 degrees! So I cut the sleeves off and made a headband out of it, that was just something we would do back then," said Ed Economy.

Encouraged by the popularity of DIY-headbands, commercialized versions by leading skate brands soon hit retail. Z-Products released the Z-Band ("Keeps your eyes dry"), while SMILE Products out of Glendale, California struck gold with cross-branded headbands featuring the insignia of skate hardgoods brands such as G&S, Logan, Star Trucks, and Kryptonics for $1.25 (around $4.99 in 2018). Despite their cheap, flimsy construction, the Velcro-fastened headbands proved quite successful. "There was a craze, those head bands were just as cheesy as can be with foam material," said Mark Richards at original skateboard store Val Surf in North Hollywood, adding: "But we did sell a load of them, primarily through the mail order." A lucrative business while it lasted, the hairband trend proved short-lived and faded out together with long surfer hair when the 1980s arrived.

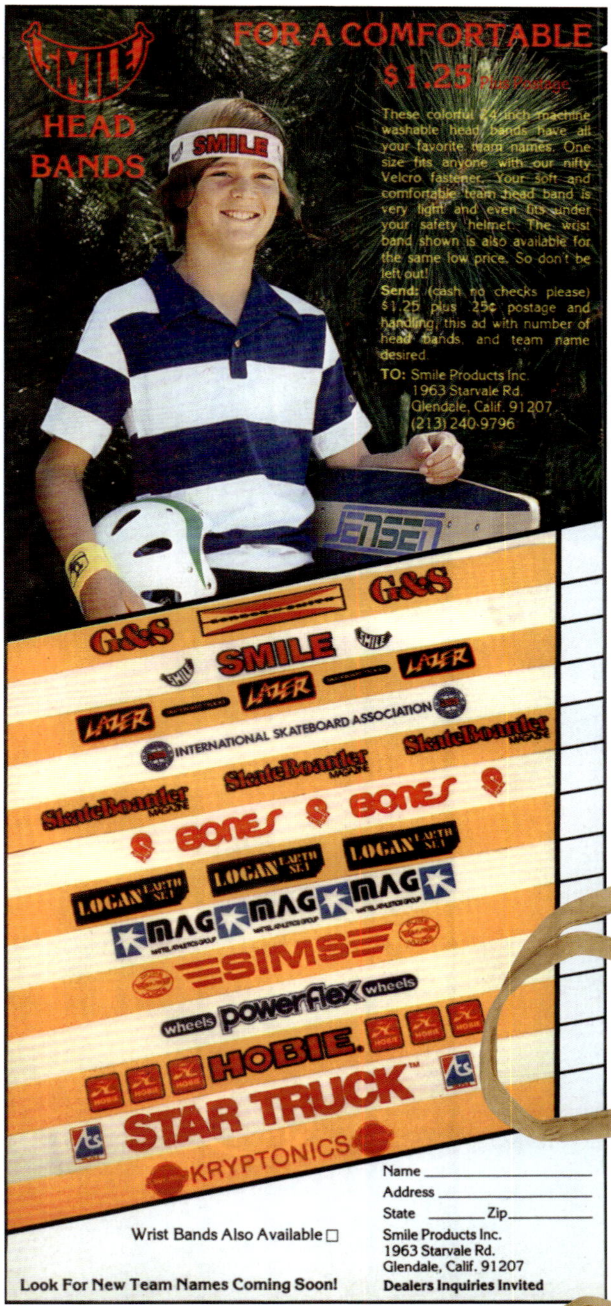

SMILE HEAD BANDS

FOR A COMFORTABLE

$1.25 Plus Postage

These colorful 24-inch machine washable head bands have all your favorite team names. One size fits anyone with our nifty Velcro fastener. Your soft and comfortable team head band is very light and even fits under your safety helmet. The wrist band shown is also available for the same low price. So don't be left out!

Send: (cash no checks please) $1.25 plus 25¢ postage and handling, this ad with number of head bands, and team name desired.

TO: Smile Products Inc.
1963 Starvale Rd.
Glendale, Calif. 91207
(213) 240-9796

G&S
SMILE
LAZER
INTERNATIONAL SKATEBOARD ASSOCIATION
SkateBoarder MAGAZINE
BONES
LOGAN EARTH SKI
MAG
SIMS
powerflex wheels
HOBIE
STAR TRUCK™
KRYPTONICS

Name ______________
Address ______________
State ________ Zip ________

Wrist Bands Also Available ☐

Smile Products Inc.
1963 Starvale Rd.
Glendale, Calif. 91207

Look For New Team Names Coming Soon!

Dealers Inquiries Invited

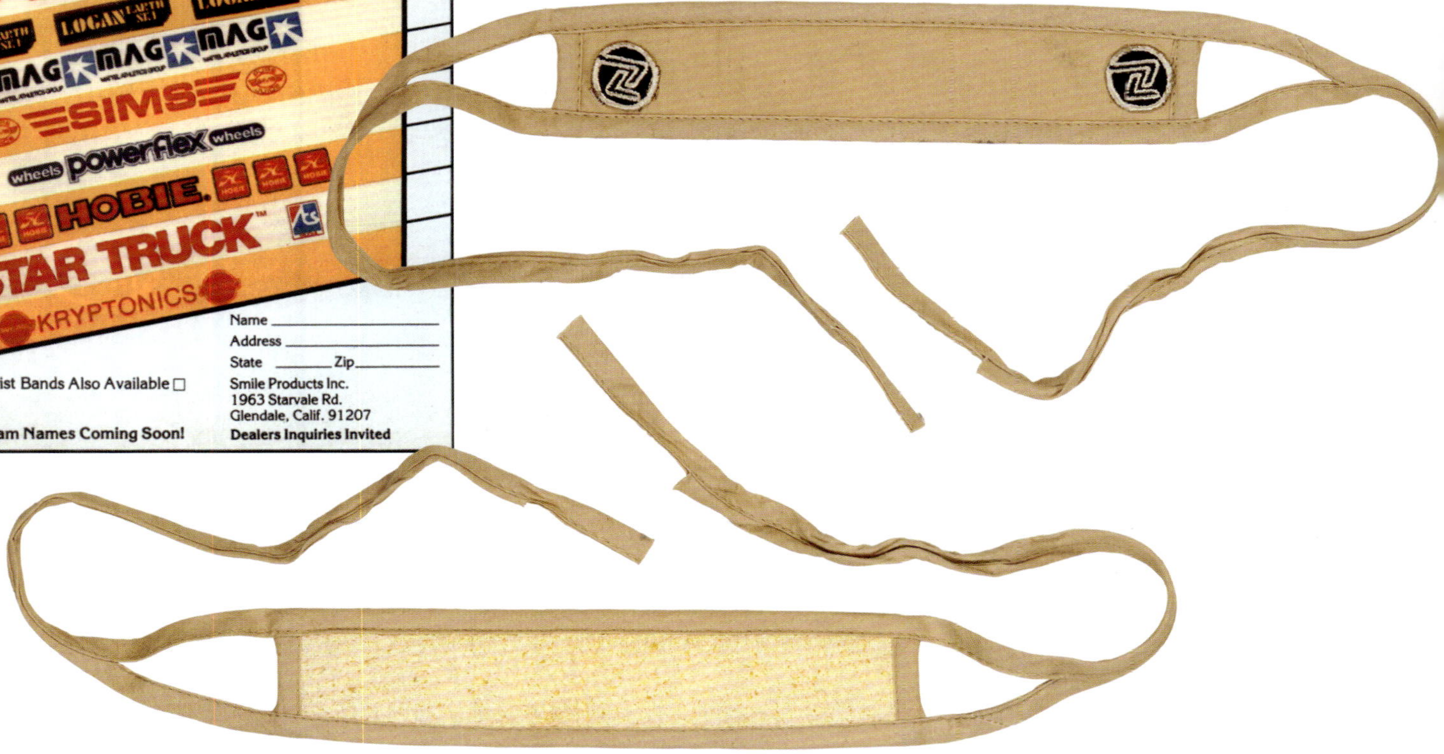

SkateBoarder MAGAZINE SkateBoarder MAGAZINE SkateB

BONES

BONES

STAR T

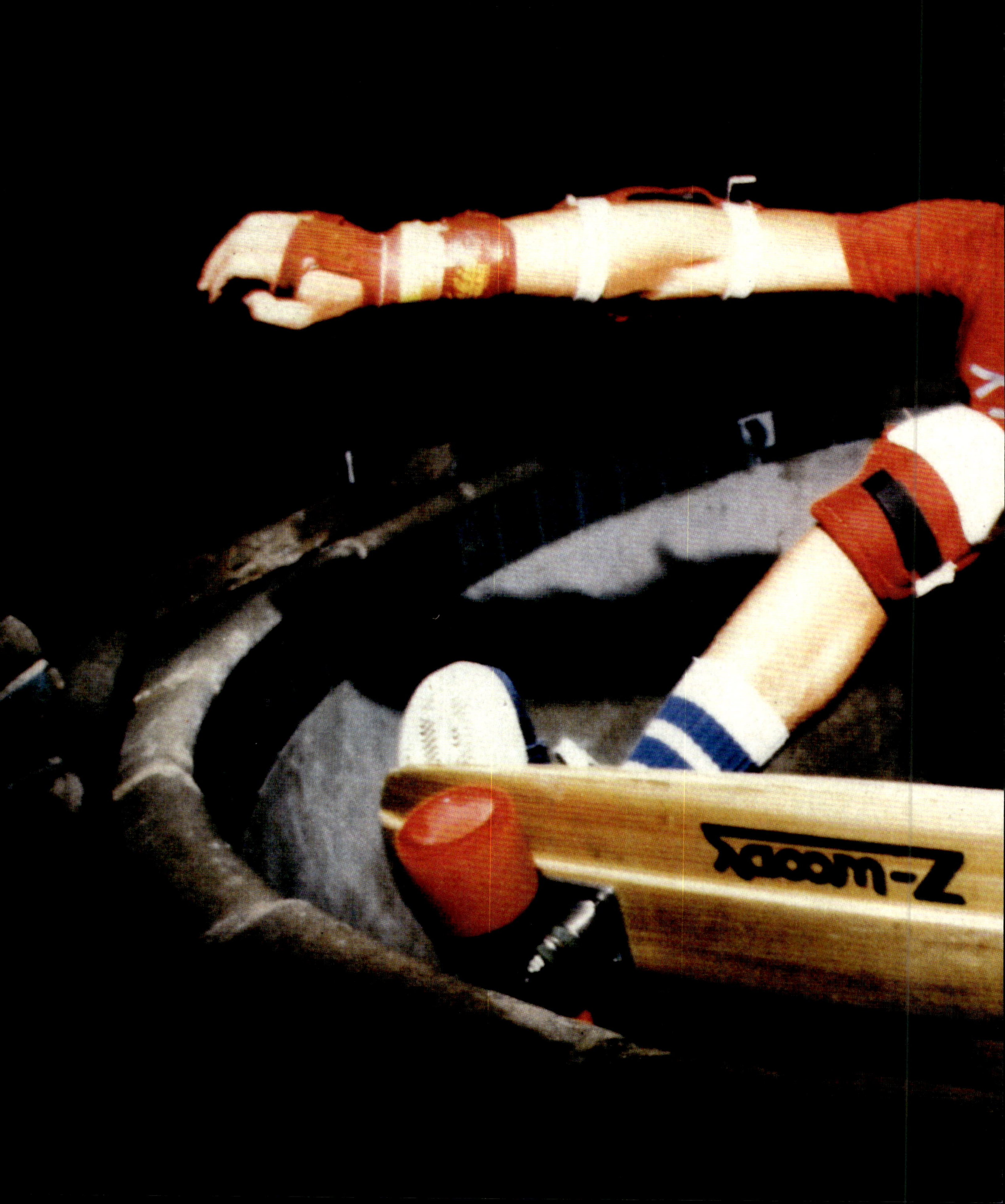

RUCK™

360°
California
360°

Don't believe the hype. Whenever skateboarding catches a wave of mainstream popularity, it's bound to draw some sharks in the water. These include, but are far from limited to, mass-market department store brands selling watered-down iterations of 'skateboard cool' to broad audiences. The pattern, built on hot pros peddling lukewarm products, goes back to the late 1970s skateboarding boom when skateboarding exploded into a $400 million-per-year business. Launched in 1977 by John Baron of Imperial Century Inc. in San Diego, also manufacturers of California Rainbow safety gear, 360 Sportswear secured endorsements from some of the day's top pros, including Jerry Valdez, Dave Hackett, and Tony Alva for collections of shorts, T-shirts, and jerseys sold at JC Penney department stores across the US. "It was new – a skateboard company that offered only clothing, something Brad Dorfman later did with Vision Street Wear," said skateboard photographer Jim Goodrich, who shot most of 360 Sportwear's ads.

For maximum audience appeal, the 360 company name was a rather safe bet, chosen after the most popular skateboard maneuver of the pre-kickflip era. "It was all about how many 360s you could do on your board," said original Hobie pro skateboarder Cris Dawson from Los Angeles, who in his prime set the world record at 35 consecutive 360-degree spins on flat ground. Asked whether 360 Sportswear was representative of the day's skateboard fashion styles, Dawson said: "I look at these jerseys and think it's European motocross or French bicycle racing!" Echoing the athletic, team sports aesthetic prevalent at 1970s skate parks, 360 Sportswear offered color-coordinated outfits consisting of shorts with matching short-sleeved collared shirts and long-sleeve jerseys, all crafted from "gutsy poly-cotton jersey" in color-blocked horizontal stripes of yellow, orange and red.

As part of an ongoing partnership with Pepsi, the clothing brand also offered cross-branded Pepsi x 360 Sportswear jerseys. Meanwhile, 360's sister company California Rainbow produced the Pepsi team's official safety gear. Designed in the cola company's signature red, white, and blue colorway, these were the official jerseys worn by the Pepsi team on skateboard safety demonstrations all over the country, as well as in advertisements in mainstream media. "Laurie McDonald and Jerry Valdez look good in their safety equipment. [...] As seen worn by the Pepsi Team, now at your local department store. HAVE A PEPSI DAY THE SAFE WAY!" Together, Pepsi and 360 brought a new level of big-budget marketing into skateboarding: In April 1978, 360 Sportswear raised the bar for prize money in skateboarding competitions with a $10,000 purse in the 360 Sportswear Easter Classic at Oasis Skate Park under a freeway overpass in Mission Valley, where Dave Hackett won first place and joined team 360.

TAKE THE MONEY AND RUN

In a smart marketing move, 360 Sportswear sponsored two separate pro skateboarding teams; one from the LA area, the other from Southern Cali. This strategy resonated with end consumers, who strongly preferred one team over the other, depending on where they lived. "We hated those guys from San Diego, they were like the surfer kooks to us. We liked the Dogtown crew, those were our guys!" said Todd Huber at Skatelab skate park and museum in Simi Valley. Headlined "DO A 360 IN STYLE," the Skateboarder magazine ad for 360's Los Angeles team showed Tony Alva, Lonnie Toft, Ray Flores, David Hackett, Kirk Talbot, Doug "Pineapple" Saladino, and Shogo Kubo wearing matching 360 T-shirts.

"Trying to get them to pose together was almost impossible," said Jim Goodrich about the photo shoot, "because they all wanted to be tough guys. So they didn't want to seem like they're models, posing for photos. None of them wanted to seem like pansies because they were posing. And skaters weren't used to that sense of fashion." Goodrich also shot a 360 advertisement showing Steve Cathey and mini ripper Bela Horvath at Upland skate park, while yet another ad depicted Steve Olson - not even a 360 team rider - receiving a $1,000 award presented by 360 Sportswear for "Park Rider of the Year" at a Hester Series contest.

Milking big name pros for endorsements was emblematic of the way corporate sponsors approached marketing at the time. "Back in the day, those companies, all they did was get a bunch of pros in front of the camera and give them some gear, give them some money and take pictures for ads - and the companies would be off to make their money," said 1970s pro skateboarder Wes Humpston. Behind the scenes, even the heavily marketed 360 Sportswear riders were only loosely organized and barely compensated. "They'd give the riders some stuff to wear and that was it. There wasn't a team!" said Wes Humpston. Then again, the riders were far from loyal - or exclusive - in their choice of sponsors and product endorsements, said Wes Humpston: "Everybody was just whoring out. Everybody was just whores!" And while the getting was good, 360 and Pepsi were some of the biggest sugar daddies in town. Until skateboarding's big wave crashed and the sugar rush was over.

SAY 360°

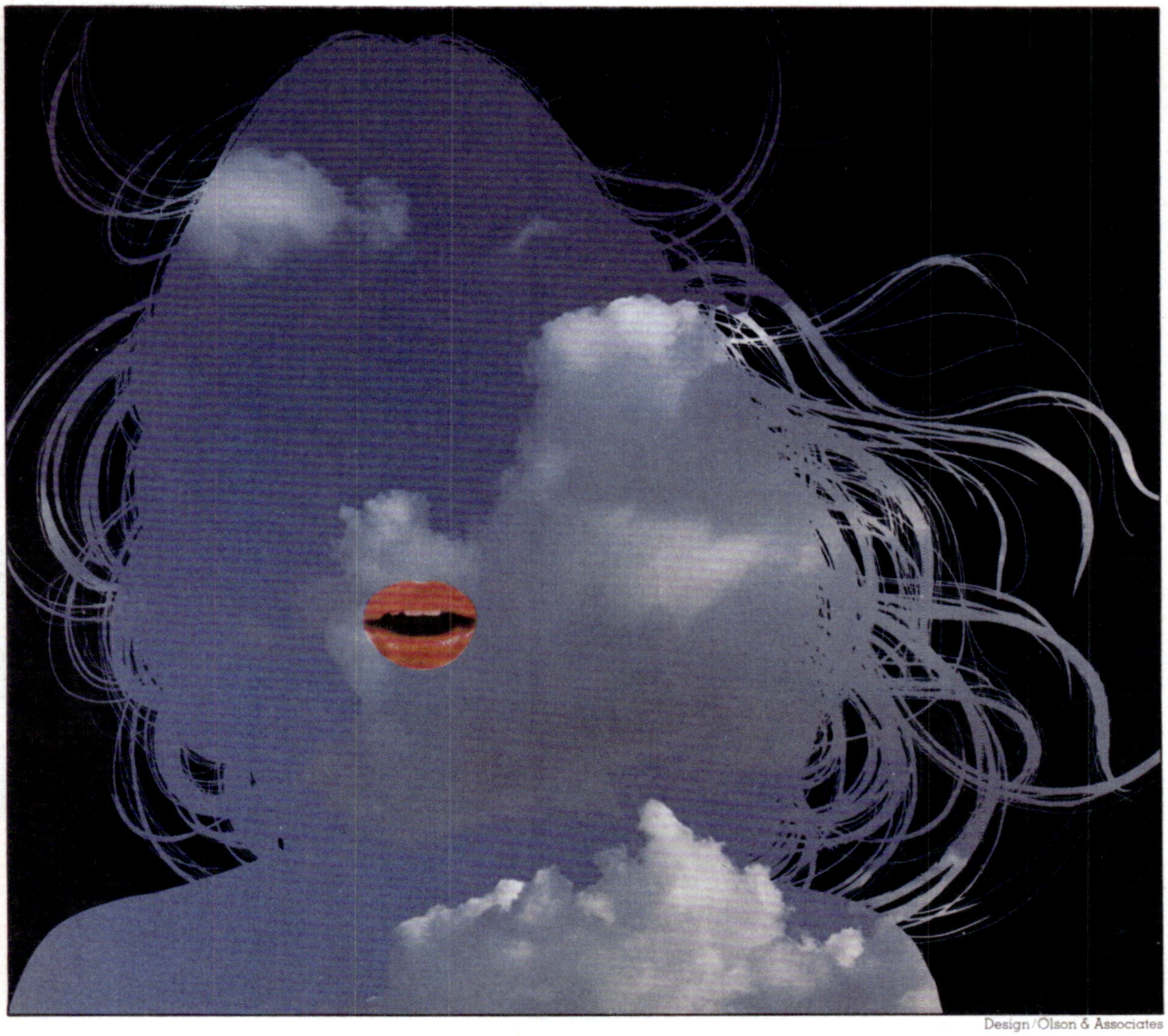

Design/Olson & Associates

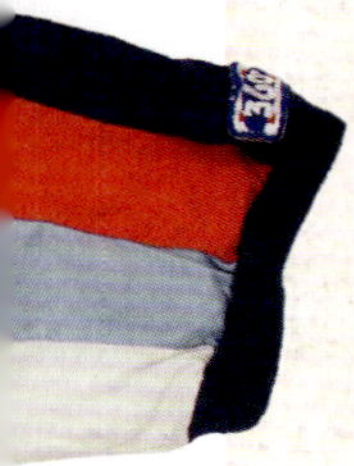

FOR A COMPLETE REVOLUTION IN SPORTSWEAR

360 Sportswear, 9455 Cabot
Drive, San Diego, California
92126 (714) 566-4500

DIRECTOR
INTERNATIONAL SKATEBOARD ASSN.
isa
MEMBER

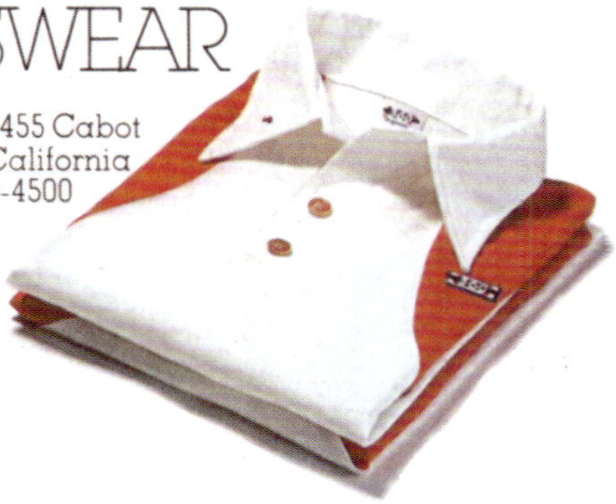

PEPSI: SKATEBOARDING'S NEW DREAM TEAM

PEPSI
G&S

PEPSI'S WINNING 'EM OVER!

The Pepsi Skateboard Team is spreading the word about skateboarding – and winning new converts as fast as the Pepsi Challenge is winning over Coke drinkers!

For three years now, the Pepsi Skateboard Team has been showing thousands of kids around the country what this exciting new sport is all about.

We're stressing safety as much as fun. (In fact, the team was organized originally to give safety demonstrations at schools.) And so far, in addition to hundreds of junior and senior high schools, our talented Pepsi Skateboarders have performed at Knott's Berry Farm, the Pasadena Tournament of Roses Parade, Long Beach Grand Prix, Hanna-Barbera's Marineland, Los Angeles Scout-O-Rama, in a variety of auto shows and many other events nationwide.

PEPSI

Look for the Pepsi Skateboard Team coming to your area. And whenever you work up a big thirst from a hot session, reach for an ice-cold Pepsi. It's Pepsi. Taste that winning taste!

Bottled by Pepsi-Cola Bottling Co. of Los Angeles under appointment from PepsiCo, Inc., Purchase, N.Y. Coke is a registered trademark of the Coca-Cola Company.

Blame it on the cola, but judging from TV commercials and documentary films, 1970s youth culture appears as one big, giddy sugar rush. As kids dosed with caffeinated soft drinks playfully channeled their superfluous energy into new sports and fads like skateboarding, youth marketing efforts from soft drink conglomerates kicked into high gear. In 1976, the Pepsi-Cola Bottling Company of Los Angeles sponsored a national TV commercial filmed at Carlsbad Skatepark to boost skateboarding – and Pepsi Cola – in the youth market. "From an age standpoint, these [skateboarders] are the Pepsi Generation, and we want them to think favorably of us," said Pepsi's director of marketing, Jim Davie, in an industry publication at the time.

The timing was perfect: Skateboarding had evolved into a "real sport" with hundreds of concrete skate parks offering the proper terrain for exciting new riding techniques. But these new challenges also brought a new level of risk. Amidst reports of surging skateboard-related injuries, the mainstream media reverted to portraying skateboarding as a "dangerous fad" again. PEOPLE magazine called skateboarding "a sport that caused a reported 335,000 injuries" in an article deriding World Champion Tony Alva for his reckless behavior. "At this time skateboarding was so new that the public thought it was tremendously dangerous and many consumer advocates warned parents not to allow their children to skateboard because they would end up broken to pieces," said 1970s pro skateboarder and Pepsi team rider Stacy Peralta.

To set the record straight – and make skateboarding marketable to mass audiences – Pepsi's Los Angeles branch launched an educational program on skateboard safety, coordinated by John Baron of Imperial Century Inc. from San Diego, makers of 360 Sportswear and California Rainbow skateboards and safety equipment. In late 1976, Baron began assembling an all-star cast of the day's top pros into the Pepsi Skateboard Team, including Stacy Peralta, Ray Flores, Gordy Lieneman, Jerry Valdez, Russ Howell, Gregg Ayres, Lonnie Toft, Waldo Autry, Wink Roberts, Paul Hoffman, Dave Hackett, and Steve Rocco. "They were big. There were actually two different groups [one West coast, one East coast], and they were all great skaters!" said SIMS team rider Ed Economy. By 1977, the Pepsi team had grown to include over 40 members staging skateboard demos at schools and events across to United States accompanied by marketing collateral with subtle product placement: "And whenever you work up a big thirst from a big session, reach for an ice-cold Pepsi. It's Pepsi. Taste that winning taste!"

SAFETY FIRST

Speaking of winning taste, the formula of mixing skateboard safety lessons with demos by leading pros had audiences across the country thirsting for more. By Fall 1977, the Pepsi Team had clocked in over 170 exhibitions at public schools and more than 20 major demos at car shows, shopping malls, and fairs according to a Skateboard Industry News article. Big outings included skateboard demonstrations at family destination Knott's Berry Farm and the Long Beach Grand Prix, accompanied by Pepsi's marketing push to become the leading cola company with a blind taste test known as the Pepsi Challenge. "PEPSI'S WINNING 'EM OVER! The Pepsi Skateboard Team is spreading the word about skateboarding – and winning new converts as fast as the Pepsi Challenge is winning over Coke drinkers!" read a 1977 Pepsi advertisement.

Skateboard retailers also had the option of booking the team for demos, said Mark Richards at Val Surf in North Hollywood: "We used the Pepsi Skateboard Team at a lot of our demos. They had that Plexiglas ramp they would bring out."

Have a Pepsi day
The Safe Way!

THE CHOICE OF
A NEW GENERATION.

PEPSI
PEPSI
©PepsiCo

BELIEVE IT OR NOT

Dennis Martinez made this new maneuver and others just like it with his G&S Fibreflex Teamrider model. It's just another radical maneuver that is a part of progressive skating.

The G&S Fibreflex Teamrider, designed by Dennis Martinez and Doug Saladino, is our most popular and versatile board.

Doug, Dennis and many others use this model for every type of radical skating including their professional freestyle routines.

If you weigh between 70-180 lbs. • if you're from 10 to 30 years old • if you skate everyday • if you're into ripping parks and pools but still do freestyle, we know you'll appreciate and love this board.

For skating excellence, we recommend the Team-riders use with YoYo or Wonker wheels.

Gordon & Smith Skateboards, A Christ Centered Company, 5111 Santa Fe Street, Suite E, San Diego, California 92109, (714) 483-3230.

G&S

G & S PRODUCTS GUARANTEED AGAINST FAULTY MATERIALS AND WORKMANSHIP

Innovators, trailblazers, visionaries: The list of industry-first inventions championed by San Diego-based surf and skateboard company Gordon and Smith is without parallel in the boardsports business. Started in 1959 by surf enthusiasts Larry Gordon and Floyd Smith in the latter's Pacific Beach garage, Gordon and Smith changed the industry one invention at a time. From the first polyurethane foam surfboards (1959), to plastic and Maple wood Fibreflex slalom boards (1965), all the way to the world's first pro model skateboard to break the 100,000 unit sales barrier – the Warptail model endorsed by Stacy Peralta (1977) – G&S charged ahead where other brands would follow.

But while the company is mostly known for hardware innovations, G&S proved equally revolutionary in the world of boardsport apparel: According to Matt Warshaw's Encyclopedia of Surfing, Floyd Smith also invented the surf company logo T-shirt when, in 1961, he set up a screen printing press at his shop, inviting local surfers to bring their own plain T-shirts, on which he printed the Gordon & Smith company logo, free of charge. In one fell swoop, Smith laid the foundation for three major skateboard fashion trends: DIY screen-printed apparel, company logo shirts – with a small logo on the chest, large logo on the back – and skateboarding's ongoing love affair with plain white tees featuring minimal artwork. It's all there, more than 55 years ago.

Equally trailblazing in the world of skate fashion, the 1977 Gordon and Smith Skateboards team turned heads on the competition circuit with their eye-catching team uniforms: "The G&S team's colors were red and gold, and they were very vibrant. Everyone got the jersey and matching shorts with the red and gold stripes, and the same went for the socks," said 1970s pro skateboarder Brad Bowman. Branded G&S garments such as bright yellow polo shirts with the imprint COMPETITION TEAM, or the red-and-yellow nylon mesh jerseys produced under license by equipment manufacturers Nor Con became emblems of elite pro skater status, worn in magazines and at pro competitions by A-list team riders including Stacy Peralta, Dave Hackett, Paul Constantineau, Dennis Martinez, Doug Saladino, Bobby Garcia, Chuck Webb, and Chris Yandall. The younger team riders got an extra boost on their garments with the Ichthys symbol, commonly known as the "Jesus fish", for extra spritual protections. Also to make sure that G&S would get the blessing from parents when asked if their kids were okay to go on tour. With the innovative products and team to boot, Gordon and Smith was serious when a 1977 Skateboarder magazine advertisement announced the company as, "BEST IN THE COUNTRY."

LAST OF THE MOHICANS

Arguably, Gordon and Smith was not the first surfboard company to try its hand at designing and marketing a line of skateboards. But without a doubt, the brand is the longest-running surf and skate hardware manufacturer – still standing with a full line of retro skateboards and new decks available at gordonandsmith.com – in the history of the sport. Innovations such as the Fibreflex board – a sandwich composite of polyurethane layered around a Maple wood core – and the addition of wheel well groves over the trucks for wider turning angles would become familiar touches in the industry.

GORDON & SMITH

FIBREFLEX
SKATEBOARD
by
G & S
Marty Schaub

FIBREFLEX
SKATEBOARD
by
GORDON & SMITH

COMPETITION TEAM
G&S
FIBREFLEX
SKATEBOARDS
G&S

G&S
G&S
G&S
FIBREFLEX
SKATEBOARDS
G & S

Although G&S produced a line of surfwear sold exclusively in surf shops in 1981, the brand operated mostly as a skateboard hardware manufacturer. Long-time G&S team rider, Neil Blender, insists that clothing "was separate. We didn't think about it much. The surf trunks were always available." Speaking of Neil Blender, the artist was also behind another industry-first courtesy of G&S when he drew his own pro model graphics - also featured on T-shirts - in 1982: "It was fine with G&S, they encouraged it," said Blender about the graphic that single-handedly opened the floodgates to an ongoing wave of skateboard artwork penned by the pro riders themselves.

The secret of Gordon and Smith's longevity - the company weathered every single bust period in skateboarding's turbulent history without going under - lies with the hands-on approach and constant commitment to innovation maintained since the early days. Founder Larry Gordon still surfed and maintained an active role in the business right until his passing in 2016. "His ability to stay true to his vision of 1959 by perpetuating innovation and staying relevant to today's lifestyle, is one reason Gordon and Smith has stood the test of time," said the company website. A true trailblazer and pioneer of surfing and skateboarding culture, Larry Gordon was remembered with a paddle-out at his local spot Tourmaline, Pacific Beach, attended by G&S team riders Steve Cathey, Dennis Martinez, Stacy Peralta, Jim Gray and Neil Blender, together with hundreds of others honoring his legacy. It's a legacy so vast and influential, it will be revisited in volume two of *Skateboarding is Not a Fashion*. Stay tuned.

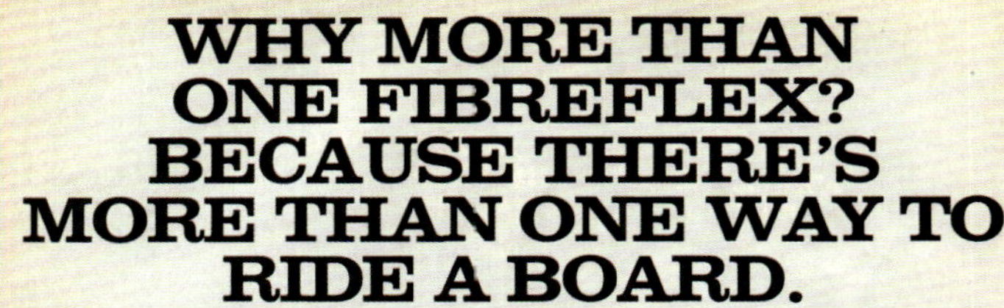

You're looking at four boards from the 1978 Fibreflex series. The boards that scream performance from the first turn of the wheel. It's the superior "strength to weight" construction that gives advantage to a variety of designs, used for a variety of functions, by a variety of people. Whatever your age, size, ability, style or skating preference, there is a Fibreflex for you. Outside of your own ability and time spent skating, your equipment is the single most important advantag factor in safe, progressive, high performance skating.

Test the Fibreflex advantag yourself. Available at reputab dealers and pro shops every

Footnote: G&S Team memb from left to right, Masami Countryman, Bobby Garcia Webb and Doug "Pineappl Saladino.

FIBREFLEX

G&S 5111 Santa Fe St., Suite E, San Diego, Ca. 92109 (714) 483-3230 A Christ Centered Company

COMPETITION TEAM
G&S
FIBREFLEX
SKATEBOARDS

Photo: Jim Goodrich

STACY PERALTA: ALL-AMERICAN ICON

One of the most iconic late-1970s skateboarding photographs captures Stacy Peralta spinning continuous 360-degree turns in front of a concrete backdrop gloriously speckled in psychedelic twirls of yellow, blue, and red. Shot by artist Craig R. Stecyk III from a bird's-eye perspective, the image encapsulates all the elements of Peralta's signature style: Long blond surfer hair whirling in a hurricane spiral, arms poised at balanced angles in a bright-yellow long-sleeved tee complemented by red shorts and signature red Vans deck shoes with a white side stripe worn with white ankle socks.

"That was all part of Stacy's persona. He always liked his red trunks and his long blond hair and red tennis shoes and white socks," said Cris Dawson, 1960s professional skateboarder and art director for Peralta's sponsor, G&S Skateboards. Internationally known for his flawless style and professional product endorsements – his Warptail skateboard by G&S became the world's best-selling skateboard with 100,000 units sold within a year of its 1976 release – Stacy Peralta ranks among the most revered skateboarders of his era, with thousands of skateboarders worldwide emulating his iconic dress code and professional demeanor.

"Stacy was an icon for me growing up in the '70s," said pro skateboarder Steve Caballero, adding: "He was one of the top guys who were always in Skateboarder magazine. He always traveled and entered contests, and he also starred in a couple of movies, like *Freewheelin'* and *Skateboard Madness*." And when Peralta, at the height of his fame as a leading athlete, retired from professional skateboarding to become a partner in Powell-Peralta Skateboards in 1978, his influence as the creator and ringleader of the legendary Bones Brigade team as well as pioneering skateboard filmmaker ultimately changed the entire culture of skateboarding forever.

DOGTOWN ROOTS

Born and raised in Venice, California, as the son of Mexican and Irish parents, Stacy Peralta developed a love for surfing at an early age. And with surfing came an early passion for skateboarding, which Peralta shared with fellow surfers in the "Dogtown" neighborhood of Santa Monica. Together with local surfers/skateboarders including Tony Alva, Shogo Kubo, and Jay Adams, Peralta began testing the limits of riding and turning on primitive clay-wheeled skateboards, a sensation Peralta describes as "riding on ice." The crew's antics on concrete embankments in local schoolyards soon caught the eye of the most hardcore surf retailer in Dogtown, Jeff Ho Surfboards and Zephyr Productions, who put them on the newly-formed skateboarding team – initially the "B-team" to Zephy'rs surf team – in 1973.

The rest is history, as the "Z-Boys" helped to emancipate skateboarding from surfing as its own radical urban practice. They changed the paradigm from emulating surfing on the street towards a new, aggressive style of riding that spearheaded the second big wave of skateboarding's mass popularity. In the process, Peralta and the Z-Boys replaced the old, surf-driven blueprint with a more rugged approach; also in terms of dress code. While some surf-minded riders still refused to wear shoes for skateboarding – for fear it would ruin the "soul" of riding – the Z-Boys begged to differ. "I never skated barefoot," Stacy Peralta remembers. "I couldn't stand skating barefoot as I felt it held me back and gave me no control."

STACY PERALTA
warptail
GORDON & SMITH

G&S
SKATEBOARD
TEAM
Stacy Peralta
G&S
SKATEBOARD
TEAM

STACY PERALTA
Warptail
GORDON & SMITH

Photo: C. R. Stecyk III

Looking back on the skate scene at the time, Peralta adds: "Jay Adams is the only person I remember ever skating barefoot and he only did it once in a while. No one I skated with back then preferred skating without shoes - it was too hard on the feet when you came off the board, which was all the time. And remember, we were riding clay wheels, which were the equivalent of skating on round pieces of ice!" The conflict between the old guard and the dawning modern era came to a head at the 1975 Skateboard World Championships in Del Mar, where the Z-Boys famously introduced their attitude-driven style to a broad audience. Skateboard magazines spread the legend of the new "Dogtown" movement, launching Peralta and his fellow Zephyr Skateboard Team members into the spotlight as the hottest pro riders on the circuit.

COLOR-CODED PROFESSIONALISM

The eyes of the skateboarding industry rested on Peralta and his fellow Z-Boys when the Zephyr team disbanded in a bonfire of conflicting egos in 1976. Every company wanted a piece of their revolutionary spirit. While reigning World Champion Tony Alva became a marquee pro on the attitude-driven Logan Earth Ski brand, Stacy Peralta signed with the sports performance-oriented G&S Skateboards label. As the perfect skateboard for the emerging skate park era, Peralta's Warptail I and later also the Warptail II professional skateboard became the biggest-selling boards of their time, immensely boosting Stacy Peralta's fame.

Hollywood soon came knocking. At the age of 19, Peralta starred in the biggest skateboarding motion picture to date, the Scott Dittrich-directed *Freewheelin'*. Released in 1976, the story centers on Peralta as an upcoming skateboarder on the make - but still working kitchen jobs, a true biographical fact - who ultimately steals the girlfriend of a Porsche-driving high roller: "Skateboard meets sports car, and the skateboard won," said Peralta's movie girlfriend, played by Camille Darrin. With a supporting cast including some of the era's hottest skateboarders such as Russell Howell, Tom Sims, and Mike Weed, *Freewheelin'* propelled Stacy Peralta into a worldwide household name.

As the headline professional for G&S Skateboards, Peralta traveled the world, representing skateboarding from England to Japan, all the way to Australia. And wherever Peralta went, skateboarders recognized - and copied - his perfectly color-coded outfit and matching safety gear. "Stacy came around with his yellow and red socks - one yellow, and one red - and red shorts, yellow-and-red shirt and red headband. Everyone really liked to copy that look," said professional skateboarder Claus Grabke from Germany. Speaking of headbands, fellow Z-Boy Tony Alva sees them as part of Stacy's athletic persona: "The sports sweatbands were mostly worn by the more conservative guys. Guys like Stacy Peralta and some other more sporty looking dudes. We wore mostly tied-down bandanas that came from the street."

ATHLETES VS. REBELS

This conflict of "street" style versus "conservative" athletic sportsmanship in skateboarding escalated in 1977, when former Zephyr teammates Tony Alva and Stacy Peralta found themselves cast to personify opposite sides of the spectrum: athletes VS. rebels. Injecting skateboarding with new levels of swagger and rebellious rock star attitude, Tony Alva started his own eponymous brand Alva Skates that summer and appeared in magazines flipping the bird into the camera as skateboarding's new resident Bad Boy. Representing the clean-cut, role model athlete type, Peralta demonstrated proper use of safety equipment on television and visits to high schools, promoting skateboarding as a safe and healthy lifestyle. In the process, Peralta and Alva became a new Yin and Yang - of the growing lifestyle.

As a film director and screenwriter, Peralta worked this rivalry into his feature film treatment of the Zephyr era, 2005's Lords of Dogtown. In the film, Peralta's character (played by John Robinson), asks Jay Adams (Emile Hirsch): "So what's up with Tony [Alva]? You guys still skate with him?" Response: "He's competing with the sun for the center of the universe!"

The clash between rock star antics and drama-free professionalism also plays into Peralta's documentary Dogtown and Z-Boys, released in 2001, which has earned the criticism of some of his peers. "There were some pretty big egos in Dogtown and Z-Boys. Tony was pretty bad, but then again, what did that do? Stacy wanted to make himself out as being the good guy, 'I'm the good skater. Tony's the evil one,'" said 1970s pro skater and artist Wes Humpston.

Putting things in perspective, professional skateboarder Mike Vallely said: "I like Stacy Peralta and I like Tony Alva and I have so much respect for all those guys that came before me. All those different styles and all those different approaches and energies. But comparing somebody to somebody, that doesn't make any sense! It's more: Does it speak to you? Do you like it?" Ultimately, not one single approach - rock star VS. athleticism - would become a dominant force in skateboarding, as both continue to coexist as the two major polarizing factions in skateboard culture.

POP CULTURE ICON

Nevertheless, a 1978 advertisement campaign for the G&S Skateboards Warptail II model saw Peralta poking fun at Hollywood rock star style. The two-part advertisement first depicted a "Hollywood" version of Peralta, rocking a Hawaiian shirt and thick-rimmed aviator shades, followed by Peralta's regular athletic persona dressed in pads and skate shorts. "We made him go Hollywood, and in the second ad he is back to his original self. It was all about getting him to be Hollywood. But the message was, 'Stacy is the same guy he's always been!'" said Cris Dawson.

Speaking of the "same as always," Peralta's shoe endorsement deal with Vans became a major part of his iconic style. Peralta was always seen skating Vans, and as the skate park era saw skateboard riding technique soar to new heights, Peralta's signature red Vans shoes were due for an upgrade. The first Vans Skate-Hi model, introduced as the Style #38, was released in 1978. "I was skating at the Skatopia Skatepark in Orange County one day and was shocked when I saw Chris Strople wearing high tops. It was a revelation. That was it! The next day I had a pair of them and so did everyone else. One day we were all skateboarding in low tops, the next day virtually every pro skater was in high top shoes, said Peralta, adding: "This was a very important fashion trend not only because it was functional, but because it lasted for at least for the next ten years."

DEFINING A LEGACY

In a 1978 advertisement for the new "Hi-Powered Hi-Tops,' Peralta is quoted saying: "I wear nothing but VANS, they're dependable for critical situations." And critical situations were aplenty for Peralta, who starred in the music video for New Wave pioneers DEVO's song *"Freedom of Choice"* as well as a 1978 episode of the year's most prominent television sitcom, *Charlie's Angels*. Riding down the streets on his board in his signature shorts and headband outfit, Peralta even has a few lines promoting his sport when the actor asks him: "What is that?" To which Peralta replies: "It's a skateboard, what does it look like? Pretty far out, huh?" As the highest-grossing pro on the circuit, Peralta also appeared in Hal Jepsen's feature film *Skateboard Madness*, all the while planning to shock the world with a major plot twist.

In a decision that sent shockwaves around the skateboard industry, Peralta quit Gordon & Smith Skateboards at the peak of his career in order to partner with Santa Barbara-based engineer George Powell, who had pioneered a number of promising skateboard hardware innovations but needed someone with a finger on the pulse of skateboard culture. And that man was Stacy Peralta, who co-founded Powell-Peralta in 1978, setting a new paradigm for a skateboard brand with a quasi-military aesthetic and the iconic skull and sword graphics created by artist Vernon Courtland Johnson (VCJ).

Adding to the industry's confusion, Peralta refused to issue himself a pro model on his new company – he still won SkateBoarder magazine's 1979 Skater of the Year award – while taking a backseat to the new generation of talent he hand-picked for a new kind of team which he dreamed up and headed: the Bones Brigade. "Stacy was in charge of the team. He was smarter than the average bear, because he knew that being in the position of making decisions was more important in the long run than being a skater. So he had that extra level of push that a lot of these guys don't have," said Cris Dawson, who followed Peralta from G&S to become Powell-Peralta's lead designer.

Under Peralta's visionary direction – using his own professional experience as guidance for his young pros – the Bones Brigade emerged as skateboarding's new professional dream team; a band of clean-cut, ultra-talented riders documented in highly influential skateboard films starting with 1984's The Bones Brigade Video Show, which also marked the start of Peralta's career as a filmmaker. Stacy Peralta also laid out a new vision of what skateboarding was all about: Centered around Tony Hawk, Steve Caballero, Tommy Guerrero, Lance Mountain, Rodney Mullen, and Mike McGill, the Bones Brigade videos painted a fun, family-friendly picture of skateboarding that helped usher in a new skateboarding boom in the mid-1980s, with Powell-Peralta skateboards as one of the main drivers.

Peralta also exerted a profound influence on skateboard clothing styles, as the company's iconic VCJ-designed imagery featured prominently on T-shirts, sweatshirts, and pants. And with a focus on camaraderie and progression, Peralta's vision of skateboarding left an enduring legacy that inspired entire generations of skateboarders to go out in search of fun; in the pursuit of happiness on four wheels. "Stacy Peralta is my all-time skateboarding hero. To me, he is the most influential skater of all time," said pro skateboarder and Bones Brigade alumni Mike Vallely, adding: "Because if it wasn't for Stacy and his sensibilities and his vision for skateboarding, we would not have those videos. And we would not have a real formed identity as skateboarders."

POWELL

Photo: Glen E. Friedman

Powell Peralta
© 1978 POWELL ®

What's the secret behind building a new kind of skateboard brand, capable of forever changing the face of an entire industry? In the words of revolutionary American architect, philosopher, and inventor R. Buckminster Fuller: "You never change things by fighting the existing reality. To change something, build a new model that makes the existing model obsolete." That's exactly what happened when Stanford-educated aerospace engineer George Powell joined forces with accomplished professional skateboarder Stacy Peralta to form the Powell Peralta skateboard company in 1978. With creative direction from surf and skateboard artist Craig R. Stecyk III - the street-savvy instigator behind the Dogtown movement - Powell Peralta commenced to create a new model for marketing best-selling skateboard products, super-charged with the halo of must-have cool.

"The objective was to create a mystique, rather than just pushing product. And that is a culture-defining environment, rather than just having a logo on a shirt or advertisements showing product. That's why they were so successful - it was a creative concept and a leap beyond merchandising," said former Powell-Peralta graphic designer and pro skateboarder Cris Dawson.

Leading where others in the skateboard industry would follow, Powell-Peralta challenged the established order with a barrage of what-were-they-thinking moves: Full-page advertisements devoid of depicting the act of skateboarding? Going all-in on urethane wheels in pale enamel white - marketed as "Bones" - when everyone was selling mass amounts of neon red and yellow wheels? Printing images of skulls, swords, snakes, and tanks, straight from the morbid imagination of artist Vernon Courtlandt Johnson, on skateboards and T-shirts sold to kids? Dressing the skate team, a quasi-military "brigade" replete with its own ranking hierarchy, in camouflage-patterned shorts and yellow tees adorned with bombs and military airplanes? Powell-Peralta definitely marched to its own drummer - but the new model worked! Within a matter of months, the Santa Barbara-based brand emerged as the preeminent voice of skateboard style and culture - with the Bones Brigade riders as poster boys for next-level skateboarding under the banner of skull-and-bones pro model graphics - in a reign that would last well into the late 1980s.

BALANCE OF OPPOSITES

As far as personalities go, Powell Peralta's two namesakes could not have hailed from more opposite ends of the spectrum. Known as an equally brilliant but reclusive tinkerer, George Powell had advanced quickly from building homespun skateboards for his son in 1974 to marketing his advanced Quicksilver slalom boards with skate manufacturer Tom Sims. Although hailed as major improvements on the state-of-the-art, the "silver torpedo" boards had a slow start when Powell took marketing efforts into his own hands in 1977, also making a first foray into skate apparel with Quicksilver T-shirts (not to be confused with the Quiksilver surf brand). Something was amiss in Powell's product-driven marketing; something called "street cred" or "core spirit" in the parlance of our times. "George was a very interesting person. I never met anybody like George before or since," said Craig R. Stecyk III, who worked with Powell for years, pointing out their radically different backgrounds: "I was an exhibiting artist, I grew up skating and surfing. You might look into what George did growing up." However, the stars aligned when Powell's brains and engineering skills found their counterpart in Stacy Peralta's super star status as one of skateboarding's top-selling professionals, paired with an unfailing eye for new, undiscovered talent.

When Peralta left G&S Skateboards at the height of his fame - his G&S Warptail 2 model remains among the best-selling skateboards of all time - to form Powell Peralta, the product innovations continued. Only this time, the audience was listening thanks to Stacy's input and super star halo. Released in late 1978, Powell-Peralta's Beamer board catered to a new generation of pool skaters with a wider riding surface (up to 10 inches), reinforced beams crafted from aerospace materials, and light-weight laminate maple construction. Next to an action shot of Stacy Peralta, the introductory ad in SkateBoarder magazine's January 1979 issue said: "Stacy has joined POWELL CORPORATION. Together we have created a new line of strong, light, high performance decks: BEAMER." For an extra futuristic edge, the board was also available with Brite Lite paint coating that came to life under black light.

Most notably, the highly popular Beamer board featured Bones wheels, a George Powell innovation that would figure front-and-center on all levels of marketing."George's first urethane wheel that he created was white colored. He made the first white urethane wheels in the skate industry - back then most wheels were colored red. Being that they were white, they looked like bones so he ended up naming them Bones wheels and the name stuck," said Stacy Peralta. On stickers and T-shirts worn by team riders Ray Rodriguez, Tay Hunt, and Harvey Hawks, the Bones logo created by graphic designer Michael Burridge in a bold typeface with rounded edges became one of the era's most recognized brand insignia. Burridge also designed the company's circular "Triple P" logo, which would remain Powell-Peralta's main emblem for decades and is still used today. Although Craig R. Stecyk remarks: "The 'Triple P' logo was something reminiscent of the Continental Can [Company] logo. There were a number of concentric circle logos around. Unless they invented a time machine and came forward and stole George's design."

SKULL AND BONES

The Bones theme kicked into high gear when George Powell brought his brother-in-law, graphic artist Vernon Courtlandt Johnson, into the fray to handle a special request: For his first pro model board graphic, team rider Ray Rodriguez requested a skeleton wielding a medieval sword, similar to the cover of a popular Grateful Dead album. The resulting artwork, known as the "Skull and Sword" graphic, proved so powerful that skulls in all kinds of iterations remain a continuing theme for Powell-Peralta's line of pro model boards, similar to the manifold variations on "Dogtown crosses" created by Wes Humpston for Dogtown Skates. Although initially, the idea of selling products with this kind of macabre imagery to minors raised red flags for Stacy Peralta. "I was actually very concerned in the late '70s when we came out with the original Skull and Sword graphic for the Ray Bones model, as I thought we were going to get a lot of angry mail from parents - but as it turned out we didn't."

Minor complaints came in from Southern religious groups threatening to boycott Powell Peralta products over their "satanic" imagery and the Triple P-logo, which according to urban legend resembled the Number of the Beast '666' when viewed upside-down and in a mirror. But that only added to the company's legend. Widely undeterred, Powell Peralta stayed the course by making Vernon Courtlandt Johnson' fine line drawings of skeletons its signature aesthetic on skateboards and apparel. "He had a better way of presenting skulls and shit. His art was way more serious than other graphics. It made you stare and wonder more. I'm not into skulls, but the Ray Rodriguez graphic is very memorable," said pro skateboarder and artist Neil Blender.

BONES
BONES®

POWELL PERALTA
POWELL CORPORATION FOUNDED·MCMLXXVI
19©81
POWELL PERALTA

Club
Powell Peralta
POWELL PERALTA
QUARTERMASTER

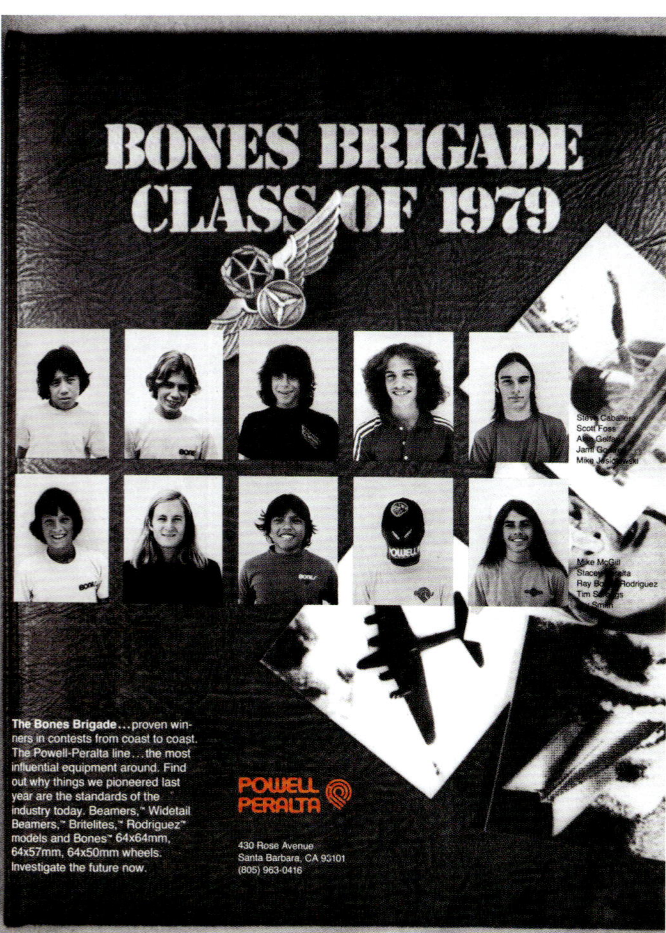

Next to the Ray Rodriguez model, ultimately earning the pioneering pool rider the nickname "Bones," popular examples of VCJ graphics forever burned into skateboarding's collective subconscious included the "Ripper" graphic, Mike McGill's "Skull and Snake" model, Tony Hawk's "Bird Skull," the Per Welinder "Nordic Skull," and the "Canadian Mounties Skeleton" for Kevin Harris. "The [Bones] name obviously lent itself to the entire skeleton library of images which is what he went off of. It seemed the more graphics we came up with the more people responded positively and the entire skull-bones-art-trend took off," said Stacy Peralta.

Adding fuel to the flames, a controversial Powell-Peralta advertisement showed Ray "Bones" Rodriguez flashing his Skull and Sword board into the camera in front of a burning limousine and the slogan: Avoid Obsolete Technologies. True to Powell-Peralta's mystique, the ad was part of a larger, image-driven campaign. While conventional skateboard advertisements relied on the proven formula of action photos and what Craig R. Stecyk III calls "over-lit hardware point blank, and on-center," Powell Peralta's ads went a different route. "There was never a picture of skateboarding! That was the whole thing Craig Stecyk brought in. There would be fights about that kind of stuff, but Stecyk was a genius and I went along with him," said team rider Alan Gelfand. During the 1979 economic crisis, another legendary Powell-Peralta ad depicted Stacy Peralta and his team riders manning a gas station decked out with the company's innovative skateboard products, next to the slogan: Energy in an empty tank world. "It was during a year that gas rationing was horrible. And Powell Peralta had the energy. We just had the shit," said Cris Dawson, whose driveway in Los Angeles served as the location for the photo shoot. Oozing with confidence, advertisements for Powell Peralta equipment boasted: "Find out why things we pioneered last year are the standard of the industry today."

BONES BRIGADE: CLASS OF 1979

Next to high-end products courtesy of George Powell's R&D lab, Powell Peralta's most valuable asset was their legendary skate team, introduced in a military academy yearbook-themed ad under the title: Bones Brigade – Class of 1979. Next to the obvious product-placement angle, the moniker also broke with the team sports-oriented phase of 1970s skateboard marketing, replacing the athletic overtones with the ethos of a tightly-knit military unit. Says Stacy Peralta: "When I was putting the team together, I was adamant about not calling it a 'team.' I didn't want the name 'team' in the title of this group of skaters and I didn't want the word 'skateboarding' in it either," said Stacy Peralta, adding: "I was tossing this around with Stecyk one day and he just blurted out 'Bones Brigade' – and it stuck. 'Bones' being a reflection of the products we made and 'Brigade' being a reflection of the 'One for all, all for one' ethic."

Speaking of ethics, instead of stealing established pros from other companies – a common practice in the industry at that point – Stacy Peralta hand-picked relatively unknown riders in whom he saw the potential to change the sport as leading stars with their unique individual skills and personalities. The Class of 1979 featured riders such as Stacy Peralta, Ray "Bones" Rodriguez, Mike McGill, Alan Gelfand, Tim Scroggs, Scott Foss, Jay Smith, and a young Steve Caballero. "Stacy could see people who had a passion for skateboarding and knew that they could go somewhere with it. He had a good eye for talent," said Caballero, who was asked to join the Brigade after Peralta had watched him place fifth in a pool contest, looking past the prodigy's contest result at the pure potential. Peralta's faith in the rookie would prove one of many winning bets on the talent front when in 1981, Caballero invented the Caballerial – a 360-degree ollie from fakie – as only one of many groundbreaking trick innovations courtesy of Powell-Peralta team riders.

BONES BRIGADE
BONES BRIGADE
POWELL PERALTA

POWELL PERALTA
QUARTER
POWELL PERALTA
POWELL PERALTA
BONES BRIGADE

CABALLERO
MCGILL
MCGILL

On that note, the company's groundbreaking product innovations would always find their match in contributions to riding technique by Powell-Peralta team riders, including Alan Gelfand (inventor of the Ollie air), Steve Caballero (the Caballerial), Mike McGill (the McTwist), Tony Hawk (the 720, Ollie McTwist, most of modern vertical skating), and Rodney Mullen (The foundations of modern-day street skating). Laser-focused on progressing the state-of-the-art – and with Stacy Peralta drawing on his own pro experience and artistic vision to groom riders into icons – the Bones Brigade forever changed skateboarding with their innovative maneuvers, as they rolled as one unit, inspiring the imaginations of entire generations of skateboarders.

TEAM RIDERS ONLY

Surprisingly, Powell-Peralta's progressive edge did not extend into the apparel segment. I would say that we were not innovators in the early-to-mid-1980s with our garments. We watched what our team liked to wear, and then put our amazing graphics on them, but in the late 1980s we did create a full line of clothing designed for active skaters, which included a number of innovations," said George Powell. In the early days, Powell Peralta operated primarily as a hardware manufacturer and even at the height of the company's popularity, clothing only played a negligible role. Asked about the share of apparel at peak times, George Powell estimated: "Probably about 15–20 percent of sales."

Released in 1979, the first line of Bones Brigade T-shirts never even become available for sale to the public, said Craig Stecyk: "Cris Dawson and I made those Bones Brigade shirts. It was not something commissioned – just something I did. The night before the contest. And then we sent them to Stacy for the guys to ride." The bright yellow team T-shirts featured a bomber plane with the Triple P logo on its wing next to the words BONES BRIGADE in military stencil lettering on the back, accompanied by the wearer's rank – for instance Quartermaster – indicated by the number of bomb icons on the left sleeve. "The bombs stood for how long you were with the team. It was like a rank. Stacy had five and George had five," said team rider Alan Gelfand, adding: "The Bones Brigade shirts weren't for sale back in the day. I was so excited when I got my shirt with my fourth bomb on it!" Gelfand also pointed out that the team-only shirts and other garments attracted plenty of attention as the mark of a sponsored skateboarder – sometimes too much attention. "I sometimes liked to take my team jersey off and hide in the corner and skate a pool in a rental helmet. Just to go skate, you know?" said Gelfand.

In skateboard retail, the yellow Bones Brigade T-shirts soon became highly demanded items, also due to their rarity. But nevertheless, Powell-Peralta only printed occasional runs at random intervals – often handed out for free at contests – while keeping the focus on hardgoods. "The Bones Brigade shirts were primarily just team shirts and then they became popular and they changed some words on them," said Cris Dawson. Most of the company's apparel output revolved around Vernon Courtlandt Johnson board graphics screen-printed on bright orange and yellow T-shirts. "Stacy and Craig designed a number of pieces, and had ideas for others. Some I designed. Most of our apparel was oriented around our team members, using their graphics," said George Powell. But there was also a dark side: At one point, the Ray "Bones" pro model graphic started being used on shirts and boards without the rider's name – thereby cutting off Ray's apparel revenue stream – and became simply known as the "Skull and Sword" design. "They took his name off the logo and cut his name out – and he was out. He never received any royalties," said an anonymous pro skateboarder. Completing the Bones Brigade outfit, Stacy Peralta commissioned a run of shorts with military-style camouflage paneling, custom-made by skateboarder and musician Gerry "Skatemaster Tate" Hurtado.

EXTEND YOUR RANGE

Tap the unrealized potentials of the global cement playground. The Street Issue is Powell-Peralta's armament for the total annihilation of all street-style and freestyle environments. This maximum feedback vehicle is an updated version of *the* classic era skate. The lost art is found again with its 28" length, 7½" width and natural, full rocker. This combination provides an ultra responsive, quick-turning performance package. The Street Issue's smaller dimensions allow you to rip a sidewalk where a wide board would just hang up and track. Don't be misled by the hypesters and ego merchants; street riding is the basis for all progressive skateboarding. Don't get hung up in some limited trip. Expand your horizons. Let your mind run free. The Street Issue will keep you ultra tuned and greatly multiply your fun coefficient. Check one out and add it to your quiver. It's currently available at the ridiculously low price of $16.50 (tape included) due to our scoring a surplus lot of quality pre-inflation hardwoods. They're already going fast, so get on it and take it where you want it.

"Stacy asked me for these shorts. I borrowed the design from the original Mad Rats shorts. Me and my girlfriend Tammy at Big O [skatepark in Orange] made them and I presented them to Stacy," said Gerry Hurtado, adding: "I made enough for the core five guys and then later I made another dozen, maybe 25 pairs overall." Working from the blueprint of Mad Rats shorts, consisting of four panels, waist band, and pocket panels, Hurtado inserted camouflage-patterned canvas into the side panels, paired with orange nylon inserts in the front. As an interesting side note, the nylon panels – stuffed with insulating material in the style of a micro puffer jacket – were sourced by cutting up pieces of the most ambitious apparel collection at the time, Alva Clothing. "Then I put the camo in and came up with a combination of colors, and it worked with the whole Bones Brigade thing. The look was definitely Bones Brigade," said Hurtado.

Maintaining a consistent Bones Brigade "look" and image in public was important to Powell-Peralta. But keeping the troops in line, sometimes required involvement from the company's "generals," especially when the rebelious influence of punk rock impacted skateboarding in the early 1980s. Several team riders, including Steve Caballero and Lance Mountain would get "the talk" from their team captain for falling short of wearing Powell Peralta's branded clothing, instead rocking band T-shirts or comic hero logos. Hair styles could also be problematic, said Cris Dawson: "The biggest change I remember was Jay Smith. He was a young guy when he came in. In the gas station ad he sat in the background and was pretty quiet. And one day he showed up at a contest and had cut off all his hair. That was not the Powell Peralta look! And that led to some friction. There was definitely a certain brand they wanted to promote."

Behind the scenes, rumors of a secret guide book – the Bones Brigade Style Manual – circulated in the skateboard scene. Allegedly, the manual provided the protocol for how Brigade members should dress and conduct themselves in public. Although he had personally not seen such a document, graphic designer Cris Dawson did not rule out its existence. "I could imagine that George, as smart as he was, would be concerned about the overall image of the company and they were definitely taking into account the brand experience that was happening." On the other hand, artist Craig Stecyk III claimed: "I have never seen it! I would tell you. I certainly never had one in my possession and cannot recall having seen such a document." As the source of the rumor, team rider Steve Caballero said that Craig Stecyk maintained a folder of team photographs, which Stacy Peralta would consult before scolding riders over brand-agnostic wardrobe choices. So perhaps that folder started the legend of the Bones Brigade Manual? To which Stecyk replied: "I just took pictures of people doing what they were doing. Or maybe I wrote the Style Manual and just forgot about it?!"

Regardless of brand-appropriate dress codes and top-notch team riders, Powell-Peralta's business success took a major hit when skateboarding as a whole fell out of style in the year 1980. With sales down a whooping 60 percent, the company downsized to a skeleton crew in order to weather the economic storm. It would take almost four years for skateboarding to rebound, as the sport went from spectacular contest series and a wealth of over 400 concrete skateparks across the U.S. to private competition events at a handful of backyard halfpipes, where skateboarding's faithful survived the fallout. In the meantime, Stacy Peralta added a few promising riders to the team, including Rodney Mullen, Lance Mountain, and Tony Hawk, whose groundbreaking trick innovations he filmed for 1984's revolutionary skateboard video, The *Bones Brigade Video Show*. When the video became a smash hit across the world, the Bones Brigade returned to the spotlight as Powell-Peralta reemerged as a global phenomenon without precedent in the skateboard industry. But that's a chapter for a different time. To be continued...

ACTION NOW
19
CUP SERIES '80
GOLD CUP
VANS

Bones Brigade member Lance Mountain's special Italian leather jacket with custom-made Powell-Peralta dragon embroidery.

TRACKER
MAD RATS

Photo: Ted Terrebonne

THE PRO'S CHOICE: MAD RATS SHORTS

Padded skateboard shorts are perfectly safe and practical, but how about something with a little more edge, a little more swagger? Enter Mad Rats Skatewear, the attitude-driven and pro-endorsed protective shorts brand launched in 1979 by Vision Industries out of Newport Beach, California. "Mad Rats was when the whole punk rock thing came into skateboarding. You can tell right away by the logo – dirty with the rat. And with terms like 'mad' and 'radical' it definitely wasn't aimed at the mainstream. It was a whole different story with a more punk look, and that resonated with skateboarders," said pro skateboarder Claus Grabke.

At skate parks across the US, Mad Rats shorts became signifiers of a new generation of hardcore skaters. "Back then there was really no designated clothing geared towards skateboarding that made you a skater. Mad Rats was the first article of clothing like that," said Mark Oblow, skateboarder, photographer, and former Vision employee. The street slang name and punk rock-inspired checkerboard graphics separated Mad Rats from the athletic, performance-oriented protective shorts on the market. "They definitely weren't considered as dorky as Rectors," said Todd Huber at Skatelab skate park and museum. Endorsements by leading pros such as Eddie "El Gato" Elguera and Bert Lamar added to the company's street cred.

Behind the scenes, Mad Rats also resembled a new breed of skateboard company: A nimble, core-focused start-up company, Mad Rats operated out of the home of Lou Anne Dorfman, the sister of Vision founder Brad Dorfman. "Lou Anne made Mad Rats mostly in her home. That's why Vision Industries was the distributor of Mad Rats. It was just a small company that ran little ads in magazines," said former Mad Rats team rider Eddie Elguera. But once next-generation riders such as Steve Caballero wore the shorts in high-profile photo shoots – including customized camo versions made by Gerry "Skatemaster Tate" Hurtado – Mad Rats emerged as an international household name, all the way to the UK. "We would see the magazines and go, 'I gotta get those Mad Rats camouflage shorts Caballero is doing a frontside invert in at Winchester!'" said 1980s pro skateboarder Don Brown.

MAD PROGRESSION

From a design perspective, Lou Anne Dorfman advanced the tailoring of skate-specific shorts by leaps and bounds. Improvements included a new enclosure system and details like different-colored inner lining. "The first shorts didn't have buttons, just the pull-open rubber strap in the waistband. And on the inside they were orange," said Eddie Elguera. In stores, Mad Rats retailed at premium price points, with the first pairs advertised for $26.50 in 1978 (equivalent of $79.90 in 2018). From the start, Mad Rats focused marketing efforts on key technologies such as the removable, half inch high-density foam pads protecting the hips and tailbone. "You could take them out and wear the shorts without the pads," said Eddie Elguera, who began endorsing his own signature pro model Mad Rats shorts in 1979 with checkerboard-patterned waistband and lining."The checkers were New Wave and Punk back then, Steve Olson had them on his board. My signature shorts also had the green, red, and white Mexican flag because I was Hispanic," said Eddie Elguera, adding: "I think I got the pro shorts because when I turned pro on Hobie [skateboards], I was already wearing Mad Rats all the time.

Velcro removable padding

MAD RATS
MAD RATS

Photo: Jim Goodrich

And I was at the top as a pro and they wanted to capitalize on that. I earned a little royalties from them, like 50 cents per pair. It wasn't much, but back then it was just cool to have your own shorts."

Additional functional features included large front pockets and a 'failsafe' rear seam, together with two-toned, heavy duty "Godzilla Skin" nylon that proved perfect for rugged skate park riding. "They came at a time when people were in-between bailing out of tricks by knee slides or going down on their ass, and these shorts just slid on concrete, like weehee," said skateboard photographer and Del Mar local Dave Swift.

MAD POPULAR

In 1981, Mad Rats hit their prime as the hot shorts on the market. "We probably sold thousands of pairs of these at the skate park shop," said skateboard photographer J. Grant Brittain, who manned the pro shop at Del Mar Skate Ranch from 1978 to 1984. Despite their commercial success, not all retailers sang Mad Rats praises. "It was a terrible product. Inconsistent in the way they fit and the quality control was terrible," said Mark Richards at Val Surf shop in Hollywood, adding: "But then again, safety was never a major part of the market. And Mad Rats were the ones who really took the padded short and ran with it. They successfully created a following with kind of a catchy name, but the product was pretty cheesy."

Mad Rats was discontinued in 1983 after the big 1970s skateboarding boom had gone bust. But ultimately, the experience and design expertise from Mad Rats planted the seed for Brad and Lou Anne Dorfman's next endeavor, a little company called Vision Street Wear. But that's a skateboard fashion story for another chapter...

The end? Not quite. Apparently, Mad Rats is alive and well in Brazil, where the local skate scene - after decades of trade embargos and high mark-ups on US products - revolves around affordable, homegrown brands. Throughout skateboard history, these locally manufactured brands have "borrowed" names, artwork, and logos from popular American brands. "Mad Rats is still huge in Brazil!

But it's not the same company, they had fake everything, knock offs. But it still has the same rat logo and is a huge company there," said Eddie Elguera. In the bigger picture, Mad Rats is not the only US brand to take on a life of its own after the original was discontinued, as Brazilian versions of Alva Skates - endorsed by local skateboarder Beto Alva - as well as Tracker, Sims, and Vision will attest.

MAD
RATS

Eddie “ElGato” Elguera Mad Rats signature shorts

MAD RATS
MAD RATS
MAD RATS

LOOK SHARP: CUT YOUR SLEEVES

Skateboarders have always found ways to turn even the most fun-damental wardrobe staples into hot fashion trends. Even the humble graphic T-shirt could become the next big thing – after applying some well-placed scissor cuts, that is. For pro skateboarders in the late 1970s, the way to look cutting edge at skate parks and competitions was cutting the sleeves off their T-shirts for a rugged, frazzled appearance that became all the rage when magazines brought the practice to a wider audience. While some neat-minded pros asked their mothers to stitch the cut, the most nonchalant way to rock the style was to let the cut sleeves frazzle out and roll over on the next machine wash. Of course, this look sent the underlying message, at least in the pro ranks, So what? *I get my clothes for free – who cares?!*

"In the late '70s, it was all about cut-off shirts, even cut-off shorts. That's just the way the style was," said pro skateboarder Eddie Elguera. In hindsight, pro skateboarder Steve Caballero first noticed the trend as a young rookie during the 1978 Hester Series contests: "One of the first guys I saw with cut T-shirts was Bert LaMar. All the guys in the Hester Series. Even [Eddie] Elguera had some pretty short tees, basically just half shirts. Him, Micke Alba, and Brad Bowman." After magazine coverage of the Hester Series contests hit newsstands, the trend spread like wildfire – to a point were regular, uncut T-shirts just wouldn't cut it anymore. "The earliest skateboarding fashion trend I can recall was in the 70's – the half-cut T-shirt!" said 1980s pro vert skater Steve Douglas.

According to pro skateboarder and style icon Brad Bowman from Los Angeles, the look was all about function, not fashion – at least initially: "We used to cut our shirts up a lot, mostly because of the heat exhaustion from skateboarding for six or seven hours during competition days. So we would cut the sleeves off and make a little tank top." This "function over fashion" angle is also supported by 1970s pro skater Stacy Peralta: "I think the person who began the most primitive form of the cut-off shirt movement was Steve Alba. He used to cut just the bottom of his shirts off, I think for ventilation – but then it morphed when the 1980s skaters started doing it.'

HALF SHIRT, FULL FLAVOR

Peralta mentions an important variation on the theme: The "half T-shirt" style – later famously rocked by 1980s pop music icons such as Prince or Wham! – also originated from DIY skateboard fashion. "We would also leave the sleeves on and cut the belly off, so it was right under our ribs, which looking back is a bit Rod Stewart for me – but it's what we did back then," said Brad Bowman, who later actually met Rod Stewart at a bar, "and he bought me a drink! Rod Stewart ran with the half-shirt look for a long time." Meanwhile, pro skateboarder Lance Mountain presents his own radical theory: "Everyone wonders why we were all wearing cut-off shirts? I know where that came from! Back then in college football, when they wore the shoulder pads, their jersey would come up. And so everyone started to cut their t-shirts off to have that style."

Regardless of the origins – fashion or function – the late 1970s became a period of playful customization in skateboard fashion. Skateboarders approached their wardrobe choices as creative, empowered individuals, cutting their own styles instead of looking cookie-cutter. "It was a good time because it was really experimental," said Brad Bowman, adding: "We went through a four-year experimental prototype phase. It was exciting because every time you went to the skate park or a contest you saw guys you hadn't seen in four or five months – and they looked completely different! Their clothes looked different, and generally the boards and wheels were different because the product was moving just as fast as the fashion."

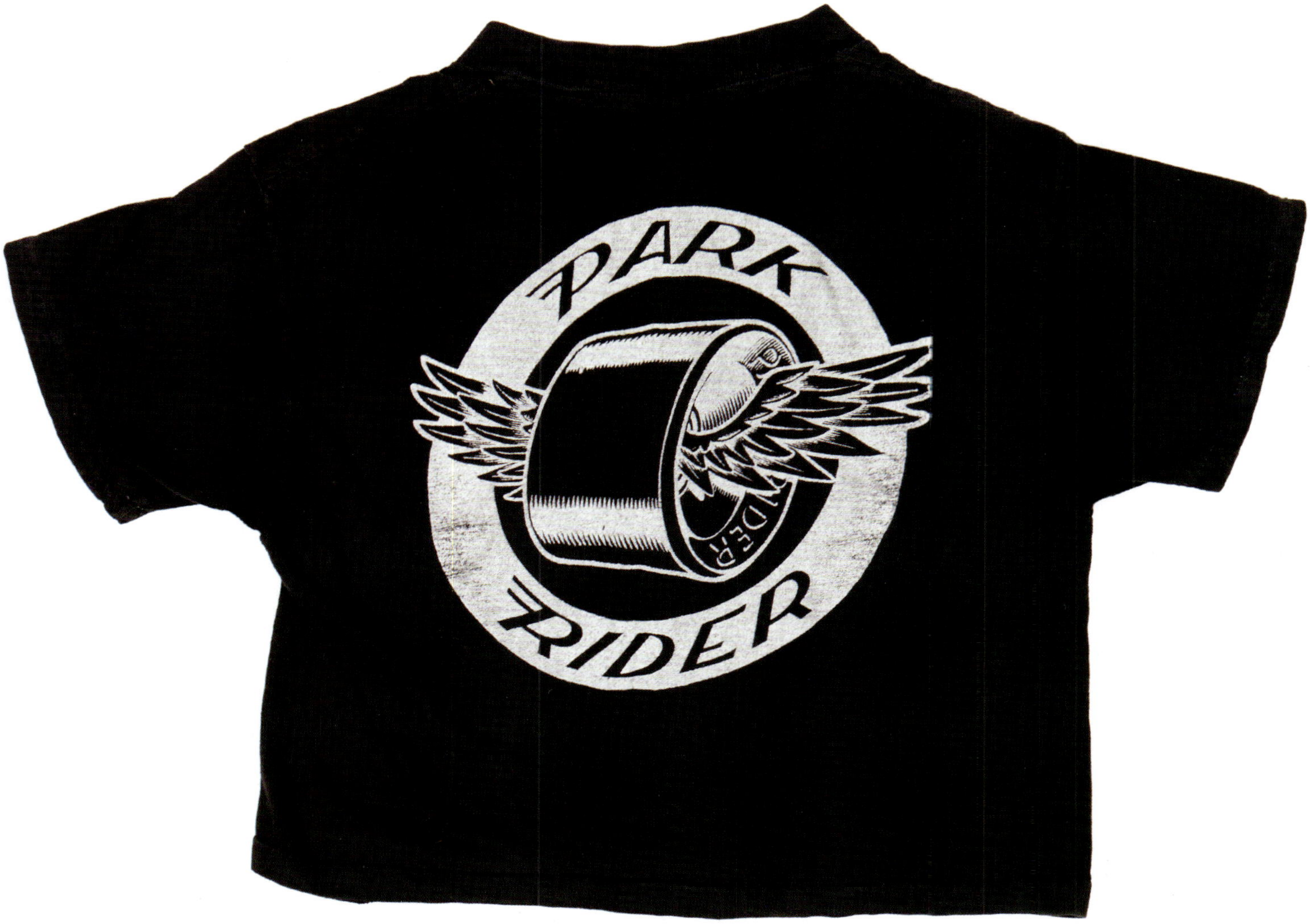

THERE IS ONLY ONE
INDEPENDENT
TRUCK COMPANY
TRUCK LINE
88mm
109mm
121mm
131mm
151mm
169mm
NEW! 151mm Stg. II
169mm Stg. II

INDEPENDENT
INDEPENDENT
INDEPENDENT
INDEPENDENT
INDEPENDENT
INDEPENDENT
INDEPENDENT
INDEPENDENT

J. BARBERI
SANTA MONICA
AIRLINES

INTRODUCING SCRATCH PATCH.

Only $4.95

In the spirit of competition, have the confidence to go for it. Scratch Patch saves the hide on your tail and adds a lifetime to the seat of your pants. The White Lightnin' Scratch Patch is a tough, top grain, rough-out leather, and can be applied easily with a special bonding Stick-Um-Aid glue, also included. Scratch Patch is guaranteed for the life of your pants. If you can wear it out we'll send you a new one!

WHITE LIGHTNIN'

Be the first Hot Dog in your area to sport a Scratch Patch behind. Dealer Inquiries Invited.

Send cash, check or money order to: White Lightnin', P.O.Box 11414, St.Louis, Mo. 63105

☐ Here's $4.95 for the Scratch Patch and $1.00 for handling.

☐ Here's an extra $1.00 send me the matching knee patches.

To assure a custom fit specify pants size ____

Name ____

Address ____

Zip ____

Glue

White Lightnin St. Louis, MO.

WACK PRODUCTS: FAD FAILURES

Every hit record has its B-Side, and for every game-changing innovation on the scale of the urethane wheel or kicktail, skateboarding saw a dozen obscure novelties that never caught traction. When skateboard product sales soared into the stratosphere - breaking the $300 million per year barrier at the end of 1976 - any number of outside companies began looking to hitch their wagons to skateboarding's rising star. Hell-bent on "innovating" new groundbreaking gadgets or contraptions, these non-endemic companies began flooding the market with random products that skateboarders never knew they needed - but just had to have.

"There were all kinds of fads on the market when skateboarding was hot," said skateboard artist Jim Phillips at Santa Cruz Skateboards. "Things were happening so fast that all the companies were groping for the next new invention, the next new thing to sell. Obviously, this meant a lot of fad failures that never took off."

Setting their minds on innovating skateboarding's next technical breakthrough - but unable to think like skateboarders - outside companies produced some rather amusing novelty products, which generally fell into the following categories:

1. **"Alternative" skateboards.** Instead of innovating for the needs of skateboarders, why not just create the next fun pastime? Exactly what Mark 10 Industries out of Madison must have thought upon introducing the Sit-Skate; an illegitimate lovechild between an oversized plastic shoe horn and roller skate trucks for seated downhill racing. "The newest most exciting fun sport on wheels that's like owning your own roller coaster!" Equally trailblazing California-based Snowcrafters launched SKEETER - The Skateboard for the Snow - featuring a plastic deck mounted on split skies. Both inventions went downhill fast, and not in a fun way.

2. **Bags and carrying solutions.** Because tennis players need nice bags or shoulder straps for carrying their rackets, let's throw skateboarders some rope. Building on the tennis-approved concept, the SkateSling from Rainbow Blase combined a canvas skateboard holster with a nylon carrying strap. Also great for displaying skateboards as wall ornaments, and quite a bargain at $17.95 (equal to $59.95 in 2018). Reduced to the max, the Skate Mate allowed for "Freestyle Carrying" the board on your hips by connecting the truck to a belt latch.

3. **Novel protective gear.** Just when you thought Rector, Norcon, and SIMS had the safety gear market cornered, White Lightnin' from St. Louis dropped the Scratch Patch. Applied to the butt end of shorts and jeans with Stick-Um-Aid glue, this top-grain leather patch put an end to bustin' one's buns. "Scratch Patch saves the hide on your tail and adds a lifetime to the seat of your pants."

4. **Wack T-shirts.** Who doesn't like Manfred the Skateboarding Cricket? Let's put the cuddly green character on a ringer shirt, and let's sell shirts with Buck Rogers-style astronauts spinning 360s while we're at it - it's the trending radical skateboard move. Unfortunately, these were often the shirts unsuspecting moms would pick up, thinking they scored a "real" skate tee for their young ones. "Thanks for getting me a poser shirt, mom." Heartbreaking.

5. **What-the...?** This last category really took out-of-the-box thinking to new heights. How about a Skate-Board Tow Rope, similar to a water ski line for hitching a ride on your buddy's bike? (Actually, this one may need revisiting.) Also, never perform maintenance on your skateboard without wearing the Norton Inc. Eye Shields; it's just not safe!

And if you wear prescription frames during exercise, make sure to opt for Skateboarders frames from Univis, "rugged as the skateboarders they're named for."

Shunned by skateboarding's hardcore practitioners - always able to smell a wack fad from miles away - some of these companies saw considerable success by preying on unsuspecting newcomers with inferior beginner-grade products. "Those were just companies trying to make money. Also because there were so many new people coming in that didn't know about skateboarding," said 1970s pro skater and Dogtown Skates co-founder Wes Humpston. Fortunately, the "innovation" stopped when skateboarding entered another downward cycle and the shakeout knocked imitators off the bandwagon.

©A&PU
EZ RIDER

BOARD SPIN
© By Allison N.Y.

VANS: OFF THE WALL, INTO SKATEBOARDING

What's the secret behind building the world's longest-running skateboard brand, recognized around the globe as the epitome of classic skateboard style? For California footwear company Vans, co-founded in 1966 by brothers Paul and James Van Doren, the way to the top was paved with always keeping an ear to the streets. At a time when no other company offered shoes specifically designed for skateboarding, Vans took inspiration from its pro team – and that has made all the difference. "The reason why I'm glad to be sponsored by Vans is that they were the one company out of action sports, and the sporting industry in general, that would listen to the input we had as skateboarders," said pro skateboarder and Vans team rider Tony Alva, who first adopted Vans shoes in the early 1970s and single-handedly put the brand on the map as the day's hottest skateboarder on the pro circuit.

To hear Alva's teammate, pro skateboarder Stacy Peralta, tell it: "The very first fashion element that came into skateboarding in the 1970s – the very first fashion element that skateboarding can claim as its own, free from the surfing world was the custom-colored Vans deck shoe made popular by Tony Alva in Skateboarder Magazine. His Vans shoes were blue and red and the store could not stock enough of them after he was pictured in the magazine skating in them. Vans was the first and only company back then to embrace skateboarding." Adding to the brand's fashion appeal, Vans offered a special service: "Skateboarders were allowed to go to the Vans shop in Santa Monica and custom-order their own color patterns for their shoes. The custom Vans shoe was the first way we as skateboarders could express any kind of personal fashion statement in skateboarding," said Stacy Peralta.

The rest is history. "Vans became THE shoes for skateboarding," said skateboard photographer Jim Goodrich, who captured the who-is-who of 1970s skateboarding for the day's leading publications. Hardcore skateboarders gravitated towards Vans as the only shoe offering the perfect combination of ultra-grip soles and flexible uppers. As the shoes of choice for skateboarding's boundary-pushing pioneers, Vans became more than just sport-specific footwear, but charged cultural signifiers, recognized by those in the know. "When you saw people wearing Vans, you knew they skated. This wasn't a fashion shoe, but a shoe for insiders – for people who actually skated in them," said pro skateboarder and Vans team alumni Claus Grabke. Over the years, Vans maintained close ties to skateboarding's core contingent, which helped create milestones such as the first skate-specific shoe design – 1975's Vans Style 95 – as well as the first high-top skate shoe, first royalty payments for pro shoe contracts, and the longest-running signature shoe line; to mention just a few industry-firsts in a legacy spanning over 50 years of brand history, and counting.

CUSTOM-MADE BEGINNINGS

Skateboarding was hitting an all-time low when The Van Doren Rubber Company set up shop on March 18, 1966, in a small store front in Anaheim, California. The mid-1960s skateboarding boom had just crashed and burned, leaving skateboarding practically dead as a market segment. What's more, many of the few remaining skateboarders had little use for shoes and preferred to ride barefooted, leaving Vans shoes as fashion staples among surfers, tennis players, and yachtsmen. Nevertheless, the Van Dorens were busy keeping up with demand right from day one when they opened their small store entirely without any finished shoes available for purchase.

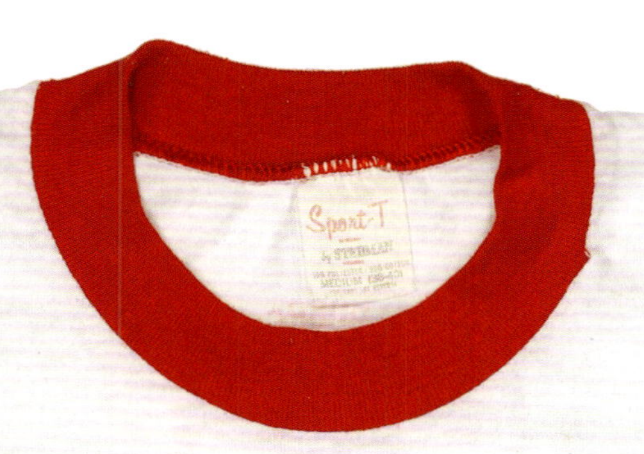
VAN DOREN RUBBER COMPANY
HANDCRAFTED, AMERICAN-MADE, ATHLETIC FOOTWEAR
704 E. Broadway, Anaheim, CALIFORNIA, U.S.A.

Only a few display models of Vans shoe styles lined the shelves, next to loads of branded cardboard shoe boxes, as every single pair was made-to-order at customers' request, available for pick-up the next day. On that note, it's worth pointing out that Vans, with their focus on built-to-order footwear, preceded modern-day shoe customization programs by several decades. Right from the start, customization was not just a service for Vans – it was the entire business model. "Vans had their own little shops which were only 8 meters by 10 meters in size. They displayed six different kinds of shoes and you could order them in any color you wanted and any size," said 1970s pro skateboarder Brad Bowman. "You could pick any color combination you wanted at the store and pick up your finished shoes later," said Jim Goodrich.

Customers were also free to add their own sense of flair to their pairs of Vans. For a small surcharge, they could bring in their own fabric – and the Van Dorens would turn it into Vans shoes. Corduroy, suede, or leopard fur found their way into legendary one-of-a-kind orders. "We always left it up to the customers. They could make their own clothes, bring the fabric in and we would make shoes for them," said Paul Van Doren's son Steve Van Doren, who headed Vans retail operations between 1976 and 1988 and retains an active role in the company.

A NEW WAY TO ROLL

Skateboarders' attitudes towards shoes finally changed in the early 1970s with the introduction of griptape – a sandpaper-like coating on the skateboards' riding surface – offering the kind of traction needed for more radical maneuvers. Early on, the new, attitude-driven style of skateboarding cultivated on schoolyard embankments and in empty backyard swimming pools gravitated towards so-called "deck shoes;" canvas boating shoes with rubber soles in the style made by Sperry and a slew of other companies for maritime use. Skateboard pioneer and ringleader of the Dogtown skateboarding movement, Craig R. Stecyk III said: "I grew up skating in canvas deck shoes that were thrown out by the yachtsmen down at the marina. They would go out and crew for uber-wealthy customers and because proper yachtsmen could not have dirty deck shoes – they would come in and throw the greasy shoes away. And that's how we all had an endless supply of free shoes."

For those skateboarders without hooks into free shoe supplies, Vans deck shoes emerged as the new way to roll. "Vans became really popular here in southern California in the '70s. They had really good soles with good grip and they were cheap and available. It became a really popular skate shoe," said 1980s pro skateboarder Dave Duncan. But what ultimately attracted hardcore skateboarders to the kind of deck shoes sold by Vans was not only their customization options, their roots in surfing, or their inexpensive price points. "You could even buy only one shoe at a time, which was really good for skateboarders, because usually your back foot was the one that always wore out first. So you could just go into Vans without spending money on a whole pair, but just get one new back foot shoe," said pro skater Brad Bowman, who rode on the Vans team in the mid-1970s.

The "buy one single shoe" trend did not go unnoticed at Vans stores, especially once high-profile pros, including Dogtown riders such as Tony Alva, started putting their own personalized spin on the theme. "Tony [Alva] and those guys would go in and get navy blue shoes and once they wore out one shoe, they would go in the store and get another single shoe for half price, around $4 or so. After a while that turned into, 'I'll just get a red one!' So they wore one shoe in navy blue, and one in red," said Steve Van Doren.

Before long, Vans began offering pairs of shoes in the Alva-approved navy-and-red color combination - which began flying off the shelves. Buoyed by the incredible response from core skateboarders, Vans was ready to take the next step: It was time to make the connection to skateboarding official, build a team, and invite skateboarders to design the kinds of shoes they always dreamed about. It was time to go off the wall.

OFF THE WALL

As the first order of business Vans commissioned California skateboarder Scott Senatore to round up a skate team in 1975. "Scott was [pro skater] Kent Senatore's younger brother. He spoke to the Vans manager and had us doing contests and demos at shopping malls," said pro skater Brad Bowman, who rode on the first Vans team next to leading bowl and pool skaters such as Jerry Valdez, Tony Alva, and Stacy Peralta. Regarded among the most marketable pros of his day - and perhaps the one with the best work ethic - Peralta made skateboarding history by receiving the first royalty payments from a shoe sponsor. "Stacy was the very first person Vans ever paid money to wear its product. It was $300 per month, and he says he still has that original check!" said Steve Van Doren. "That's the kind of person he is. If I had 300 bucks and I'm 18 or 19, I'm cashing that mother! But not Stacy."

The new focus on vertical riding also inspired the classic Vans slogan, "Off the Wall" in reference to the vertical walls in empty swimming pools, the new benchmark of getting "radical." Drawn by Steve Van Doren's cousin Mark, the 'Off the Wall' logo featured a stylized skateboard that would become the mark of the brand-new line of skate-specific Vans products rolled out in close conjunction with the team. At this point, it's worth pointing out that such a commitment to skateboarding was not without risk. Skateboarding had crashed severely in the mid-1960s - the majority of big-name brands expired - and was only slowly starting to prove itself as a real culture with real staying power when Vans started their skate team. "The thing everyone needs to know about the Van Doren Rubber Company is that that family was the first to stand up and see any worth in skateboarding. Before that skateboarding didn't exist. It was a Frisbee, a yo-yo, a toy a fad. But the Van Doren family was like, 'What these kids are doing is cool and somebody should back their play.' They put a skateboard in their fucking logo that's how much they believed in us!" said Vans team rider Jeff Grosso.

Vans also trusted Stacy Peralta and Tony Alva to design a shoe that would cover all the functional requirements of modern-day skateboarding. It was a chance skateboarders had been waiting for - but had never been offered. "It really took a while for us to really get shoes designed specifically for skateboarding," said Tony Alva. Based on the classic Style 44 deck shoes naturally adopted by skateboarders, Alva and Peralta's creation became known as the Style 95, or the Vans Era model. Released in 1976, the Era featured a padded collar to protect the heel together with the sure-grip Vans waffle sole and the Alva-designed wildly trending red-and-navy colorway. The first in an ongoing series of Off the Wall-branded shoes, the style #95 became an instant bestseller, especially with the budding bowl and pool riding scene. Skateboarders across the globe embraced the shoe, and did whatever they could to get their hands on a pair. "Even when I smell a pair of Vans shoes today, it totally takes me back to when I received my first box back in the day. Mine came from England at the time. They were handmade back then, and they had this rubber stuff on the sole you had to skate off first," said 1980s pro vert skater Claus Grabke from Germany.

m m

m m !
NS

OLD SKOOL STYLE

The next Vans shoe bearing the Off the Wall logo released in 1977: The Style 36, also known as the Old Skool, enhanced the deck shoe build of the Style 95 with more rugged materials such as suede in critical areas of the upper. "It had the same waffle sole and the same No.10 duct materials, our patented heel collar, and the Off the Wall on the shoebox and heel label," said Steve Van Doren. From then on, logo placement on the rubber heel tab would become an ongoing tradition in skate-specific Vans shoes. The Old Skool also introduced the iconic Vans "sidestripe" logo – often called a "jazz stripe" or "leather racing stripe" in advertisements. Created by Paul Van Doren, the wave-shaped leather stripe connecting heel tab and lower eyelets would evolve into a branding staple, the Vans counterpart of the Nike "Swoosh" and adidas "Three Stripes" insignia. "My dad always doodled and that's where the sidestripe came from," said Steve Van Doren. "The shoe added leather reinforcement at the toe and the heel, and the sidestripe was introduced right there in 1977."

The Old Skool's leather reinforcements catered to the needs of pool skaters, who at the time began "knee-sliding" to safety on their plastic-capped knee pads – putting tremendous strain on the toe section of the shoes. When aerials and over-the-edge maneuvers became the new frontier in pool riding, skaters increasingly asked for more support and ankle protection than low-top deck shoes could offer. Again listening to its team riders, Vans developed a new accessory: the Van Guard, a velcro-fastened ankle guard constructed from heavy-duty vinyl with padding on the inside. It was specifically designed to complement Vans low-top models such as Style 36 and Style 95.

Advertised as "A safety product specifically for ankle protection," the Van Guard resonated with the avant-garde of progressive pool skaters, including a young Steve Caballero: "When I saw the advertisement, I instantly went out to the Vans store in San Jose and bought some Vans low tops first and then bought the Ankle Guard for protection," said the pro skateboarder, whose line of Vans signature shoes – started in 1989, still going strong in 2018 – made history as the longest-running pro shoe franchise in the industry. But despite backing from top pros, the Van Guard would only prove a short-lived workaround on the way to the next step. For a short blink-it-and-you-missed-it moment, Vans offered a mid-top shoe, the enigmatic Style 37: "We built the ankle guard into the Style 37 as a mid-top, but we only did that for around nine months before we moved on to the next thing," said Steve Van Doren about the shoe that has since become a hot collectors' item as the missing link in the evolution of skateboard-specific footwear.

HIGH ON HIGH TOPS

For the next big thing in skateboard style, the stars aligned in 1978 when pool skateboarding kicked into high gear with the Henry Hester contest series at skateparks all over California, and Vans released what would become the shoe for progressive pool riding: The Style 38, also known as the Sk8-Hi, expanded the performance features of the Old Skool into a high-top silhouette with extra layers of padding around the ankles. The extra durability and padding proved beneficial because skateboarders were constantly experimenting with new maneuvers, often sending boards flying around the park or shooting into the riders' ankles on failed attempts. Replete with the Vans sidestripe, vulcanized outsole, and signature sure-grip Vans waffle sole, the Sk8-Hi offered an unprecedented blend of free movement and durability. "The Sk8-Hi was bullet proof, it wore a long time because it had leather on it," said Steve Van Doren.

Photo: Mello

Within weeks of its release, the Sk8-Hi became part of the trending "skatepark look," composed of color-coordinated safety gear, padded shorts, and matching T-shirts or company-branded team jerseys. Stacy Peralta remembers the shift in skate fashion: "The High Top Vans shoe! I was skating at the Skatopia Skatepark in Orange County one day and was shocked when I saw [pro skater] Chris Strople wearing high tops. It was a revelation. That was it! The next day, I had a pair of them and so did everyone else. One day we were all skateboarding in low tops, the next day virtually every pro skater was in high top shoes.

This was a very important fashion trend not only because it was functional, but because it lasted for at least the next ten years." Fellow Vans pro Alan Gelfand confirmed: "High top Vans is what we wore. And we tore them up like it was nobody's business." Looking back at magazine photos of the Hester Series events, the majority of competitors - Vans team riders or not - are attacking the pools in Vans Hi-Tops with white sidestripes. Throughout the mid-1970s Skateboard Boom, Vans shoes featured prominently in era-defining magazine photos that ingrained the shoes into the collective skateboarding psyche: There's Jay Adams crouching low, one electrified hand on the pavement, into a high-speed downhill Bert slide in his Vans "authentic" Style 44s, captured by Craig R. Stecyk III for Skateboarder magazine in 1975.

The Vans Era model's waffle sole and white foxing tape shine in Tony Alva's boundary-pushing frontside air - the Glen E. Friedman photo is considered the world's first documented aerial on a skateboard - at the legendary Dogbowl in 1977. The white sidestripe glistens on Stacy Peralta's ultra-rare and bright-red Style 37 mid-tops as he spins 360s, blond surfer hair spiraling over color-splashed concrete, in the iconic Craig R. Stecyk bird's eye shot featured in Skateboarder Magazine. And Vans Hi-Tops paired with striped tube socks appear in Jim Goodrich photos documenting team rider Alan Gelfand's groundbreaking ollie aerial - the first-ever no-handed aerial off the wall of a pool - that changed skateboarding forever upon their publication in 1978.

Speaking of the ollie maneuver, when people first saw Gelfand soaring into the air without the use of his hands to secure the board, many simply could not believe it. Some even suspected foul play, and like spectators peaking behind a magician's stage, scrutinized Gelfand's equipment, zeroing in on his Vans. "They used to steal my shoes! I was sponsored by Vans, and they used to steal my shoes because they were looking for glue, hooks, et cetera. So I would go on tour and bring two or three pairs of Vans, and when I left I was lucky if I still had shoes on my feet. I was lucky if I had sandals!" said 1970s pro rider Alan Gelfand, who toured the U.S. in 1978 to debut his trick invention at skate parks across the country. "I must have had 50 pairs of shoes stolen," said Gelfand.

As the 1980s approached, everybody - not just hardcore skateboarders - wanted to get their hands on a pair of Vans shoes. At the end of 1979, Vans had expanded its waffle-patterned footprint across the globe, reaching 70 U.S. stores and several international distribution outfits. And that was just the beginning. The 1980s would take the brand's fame to new levels, as Hollywood soon wanted a piece of California cool, courtesy of the Van Doren Rubber Company. To be continued...

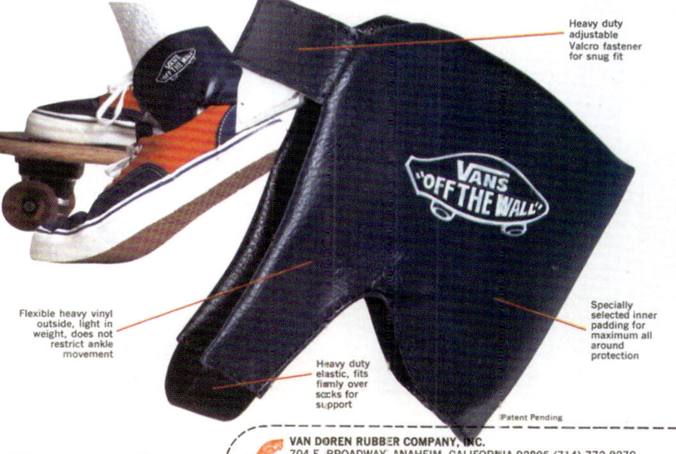

DESIGNED FOR MAXIMUM ANKLE PROTECTION
VANS "OFF THE WALL" T.M.
VAN ANKLE GUARD
PROVIDES MAXIMUM ANKLE PROTECTION
Patent Pending
WEAR VAN ANKLE GUARD AS PICTURED
Wear Van Ankle Guard over socks
COLOR Blue
SIZE XL
ONE PAIR

Specially
selected inner
padding for
maximum all
around
protection
Heavy duty
adjustable
Valcro fastener
for snug fit
U. S. PATENT
VANS T.M.
"OFF THE WALL"
Flexible heavy vinyl
outside, light in
weight, does not
restrict ankle
movement

BRAD BOWMAN: SKATEBOARDING'S MR. STYLE

Nowadays, it's perfectly acceptable for professional skateboarders to present themselves as more than just highly talented athletes but also as artists, fashion models, and full-blown rock stars. This wasn't always the case, and it took a number of courageous individuals to break the mold – individuals such as pro skateboarder Brad Bowman from Los Angeles, whose 1980 Skateboarder interview shocked the skateboarding scene: In a magazine otherwise filled with sporty-looking riders wearing athletic gear, Bowman strikes a punk rock pose in black leather pants and biker jacket, paired with a leopard print top, oversized shades, and leather boots. "Brad is a full-on New Wave fan. He's even known to wear a genuine artificial leopard skin coat and a cheap crop-top, and is said to be a mean pogoer," read the intro to the interview accompanied by Jim Cassimus photography.

Famous for his 1978 signature pro model skateboard on SIMS, featuring the initials 'BB' in a shield modelled on the Warner Brothers film company logo, Bowman became a figurehead of progressive vertical skateboarding in the late 1970s. This new type of skating in skate parks and empty swimming pools would cut skateboarding's close ties with surfing once and for all, so it was only logical for dress codes to follow suit. "We started needing to segregate ourselves from the whole surfing thing because we were skateboarders. The music scene came in around the same time with punk rock and all that," said Brad Bowman, adding: "People really started grabbing onto it and that took us skaters out of the corduroy shorts and collared shirts, and into pointy-toed leather shoes with stove pipe pants, and narrow collared jackets. Everything went - it was a free-for-all!"

Injecting skateboarding with a fashion sense inspired by punk rock and the Hollywood club scene, Brad Bowman became one of the first pros to take ownership of their entire public persona, also by meticulously choosing his color-coordinated outfits for competitions and product endorsement photo shoots. "I would think that Brad was the best-dressed skater around back then. As for me, all I cared about was skating. But Brad was really into fashion with the sunglasses and all the other stuff," said professional skateboarder Alan Gelfand from Florida, adding: "Brad was the style master. He was Mr. Style!"

RISE OF A FASHION ICON

Raised as the son of a funk drummer father and entertainment industry mother dialed into the Hollywood scene, Brad Bowman grew up under stylish stars. "My father was a very fashionable man and always wearing really nice clothes along the lines of Miles Davis and all those jazz guys. Tight. Really sharp. I picked up a lot of my fashion influence between him and my mother," said Brad Bowman. "All their friends were Hollywood people who dressed great in the '70s. It really rubbed off on me. I was kind of a shy kid but very observant about how people presented themselves. I would see a lot of their friends on TV and how great they looked. I just knew, 'I wanna dress like that!'"

Bowman's deeply ingrained fashion sensibilities were matched by his smooth riding style, which his early sponsor Mark Richards at Val Surf skate shop in North Hollywood attributes to surfing. "Brad was always a great stylist, because he was a fantastic surfer, too. You can tell if a skater is a good surfer as well. Their styles are different." In an ironic twist, Bowman made his big break into skateboarding not because of his style, but by beating the clock in the downhill race event at the 1977 Catalina Classic. "That got me sponsored on the G&S team. Had I not been a downhill and slalom rider, I may have never been sponsored. But the stars were really aligned for me," said Bowman. But most of all, his talent really shone in backyard pools, where he perfected the kind of cutting edge maneuvers that would make him a top competitor on the pool riding circuit. As Skateboarder editor Sam Slash wrote: "The kid obviously had the moves, classy style and some weird pale blue eyes that seemed to glow when the strobe hit them just right." Ready to look the part of the pro skateboarder when the limelight hit, Bowman spearheaded the late-1970s trend of matching his apparel, skateboard hardware, and protective equipment into a complete look.

BJB
BRAD ALAN
action wear

SkateBoarder

A SURFER PUBLICATION

AUGUST 1979 VOL. 6, NO. 1 $1.50

Curt Kimbel "It's hard to just 'play' — I want to win."

A New Pro-Bowl Elite Winchester and Marina Results

The Most Outrageous Contest Yet

Winners and Losers in the Great Signature Model Hunt

"Brad Bowman is very iconic in the way he color-coordinated his stuff. He was the best, so amazing! He would match blue shirt, blue wheels with yellow shorts, yellow helmet. And it looked so good on photos," said pro skateboarder Lance Mountain. At a time when a pro's net worth largely hinged on contest results, Bowman elevated the importance of also making sure to represent his sponsor's products in a favorable light in advertisements and editorial photo shoots. And it worked, turning products like the SIMS skateboard gloves into hot sellers. "When you saw pictures of Brad Bowman and Steve Olson wearing those gloves, you were like, 'Man, I have to have those!'" said skateboard photographer J. Grant Brittain.

CONTROLLING THE IMAGE

Behind the scenes, Bowman would invest considerable time and effort into art-directing his photographs. For a nighttime action shoot at Oasis Skate Park that ran as a double-page spread in Skateboarder magazine, he combined a neon orange nylon vest from Tony Alva's short-lived fashion label with a purple-striped Flyaway helmet, blue-and-yellow knee and elbow pads plus gloves, blue Converse Chuck Taylor high-top shoes and matching laces. "I thought it would be cool to have shoelaces matching the top, but it took me three stores and two-and-a-half hours to find those shoelaces! The argyle socks took only five minutes to find," said Bowman, adding: "With argyle socks, I wanted to bring a bit more street wear into skateboarding. The knee-high tube socks [that were popular at the time] were cool – but I had worn them my entire life." Among upcoming pros, this commitment to stylistic details did not go unnoticed. "I was heavily influenced by seeing that. I just think it looks better in a photo – a bright shirt or striped shirts," said Lance Mountain, adding: "I still recall what a photo made me feel like, so when I shoot now, I go more for what it will make people feel like." Next to meticulous color-coordination, Bowman's signature look also featured a different kind of appendage: "In 70 percent of the photos taken between '78 to 1980 I have a cast on one of my wrists. I was always breaking my wrist and still skating," said Brad Bowman.

As another signature trait, Bowman always wore high-top shoes to withstand the wear and tear of pool skating. When his mother grew tired of paying $30 for shoes every other week, Bowman wrote a letter to then-CEO of Nike, Phil Knight: "I sent this handwritten note as a 17-year-old precocious kid. I basically told him that he needs to sponsor me, because I can sell a lot of shoes for him and I'm going places!" Bowman said with a laugh. After two months passed without word from the Portland-based company, Bowman returned from tour one day to find a huge package waiting at home. The contents: dozens of high-top Nike sneakers and apparel – making Bowman the first unofficial Nike-sponsored skateboarder – which he matched for photos including a 1980 Skateboarder cover of an ollie air wearing a yellow Nike tank top with matching pads and high-top Nike Blazer sneakers.

PUNK ROCK AND DIY

When the punk rock movement hit, Brad Bowman become an early adopter of punk rock acts like The Clash, Dead Kennedys, 999, The Ramones, and Buzzcocks. "It's really good for skating – get's [sic] you pumped up," he said in his Skateboarder interview. Although at the time, punk was not for everyone, Bowman remembers: "Only a handful of skaters really got it. The ones who really got it right away and ran with it were Steve Olson, myself, Salba, Mickey Alba, Bert LaMar, Jonny Ray Bartel, and Skate Master Tate.

There were 20 to 25 of us that really got into it." Consequently, Bowman's fashion sense – pre-disposed towards leather by 1970s acts such Queen, Elton John, Ted Nugent, and Aerosmith – took on a rougher edge especially when he moved to the world's epicenter of New Wave style, Hollywood. "When I moved to Hollywood with my girlfriend and her gay brother, there was a leather gay bar two blocks away from his apartment. These guys would always walk by our house on their way to the club, and I was checking their outfits thinking they looked pretty raw and cool. They looked like Queen, Judas Priest or somebody," said Brad Bowman. For his milestone Skateboarder interview, Bowman searched Hollywood thrift stores for the right kind of leather pants, but when he finally found a pair, made a rookie mistake: "I put Armor All on it, this kind of spray you put on your tires to make them shiny. And the pants got this brilliant shine that I didn't want. I was all, Oh no!'"

The rest of his outfit also came from thrift and Army/Navy surplus stores, where he and like-minded professional skaters such as Steve Olson, Eric "Shreddi" Repas, and Kent Senator salvaged most of their outfits. "We pretty much made up the looks all by ourselves. And the coolest thing was, all that stuff would be three bucks at the thrift store. The whole outfit!" said Brad Bowman. "You could literally go and get four outfits for twelve bucks and wear that for three months and be the most fashionable guy in your neighborhood." The underlying do-it-yourself mentality would become the driving aesthetic of early 1980s skateboarding style. As skateboarders explored their individuality, Bowman and cohorts would also print their own T-shirt graphics, using the screen-printing set-up at the factory of his board sponsor, SIMS. "Once the graphics and DIY artistic mentality came in – it exploded. Skateboarding turned the page on a chapter," said Bowman. "All the old, matching team stuff was out – and every skater, even on the same team, was trying to look different than his teammates."

BRAD ALAN ACTIONWEAR

In a little-known historic side note, skateboarding's Mr. Style even started his own apparel label at one point. After missing the top three at a Del Mar Skate Ranch pool skating competition in 1982, Brad Bowman chose to end his pro career: "I felt I had reached my zenith in skateboard vertical competition. I applied pressure on myself to figure out what was to come of me after pro skateboarding." In search of his next venture, Bowman found the perfect fit: "I had always liked fashion, art and music. Ah! Was there something I could create within these realms either together or separate that was compelling and financially worthwhile?"

In search of an answer, Bowman zeroed in on the idea of creating sports apparel "geared towards surfers & skateboarders." But looking around what was on the market, Brad Bowman saw a lot of same-same collections and approaches from different brands. "Everybody was doing a 'sportswear' line or a loosely based line marketed to 'the sporting of mind.'" So in order to offer his own take on the theme, Bowman decided to create a line of "actionwear," because "action was far superior to sports in the title description as action meant actually doing something."
This marked the beginning of Brad Alan Actionwear, whose name was inspired by Bowman getting a speeding ticket in his red 1959 Porsche 356 A-type. "I had pulled out my wallet and looking down at my full name on the drivers license brought the idea of using my first and middle names in tandem. I thought it had a memorable ring," said Bowman. After soliciting advice on how to screen print graphics onto T-shirts from the production crew at his board sponsor SIMS, Bowman set up his own print operation.

As a first step, he printed the Brad Alan logo on plain T-shirts as well as a Sims Brad Bowman "BB Shield" shirt. "I wore that shirt to skate in as often as possible. Shogo Kubo even commented that Sims wasn't paying me because every time he saw me skating, I had that same shirt on," said Bowman, adding: "Always the commenter he was. I loved skating with Shogo as it was always a silent fight to out skate each other." Ultimately, Brad Alan Actionwear proved short-lived. "I never did get Brad Alan off the ground as I lost the initiative once I enrolled in college and was distracted by the workload it produced," said Bowman. "It was a fine, fleeting dream for a couple minutes there in the dawning of the 1980s."

LIFE AND STYLE

Never missing a beat, the style icon went all-in on the fashion business. "I went from skateboarding to hair styling, to make-up, to photography in that whole advertising, fashion, and celebrity world." In a career as a hair and make-up artist spanning over 20 years, Bowman lent his stylistic talents to photo shoots for publications such as Elle, Vogue, Rolling Stone, and Vanity Fair, getting up close and personal with celebrities including Rod Steward, Aerosmith, Robert Downey Jr. and Angelina Jolie in the process. "It was a great run and also really fun to meet every major celebrity from the '80s, '90s, and 2000s while seeing how it all operates." Today, Brad Bowman lives happily in the Basque Country near San Sebastian, Spain, where he surfs and runs his own skateboard and apparel company Bowman Boards. Asked about fashion sentiments in the current scene, skateboarding's original Mr. Style said: "Kids take it for granted now. They can walk into a skate shop and get outfitted from head to toe. Deck, helmet and gear – everything. And they look great! We really had to seek it out and find it and actually put together the outfits back then, because there was no one to show us or tell us how to do it."

USA
ALVA MODEL S.A.

Photo: Craig Fineman

Hanes
BEEFY-T
SALBACLAUS

The mid-1970s marked a deep schism within the skateboarding scene, caused by an influx of riders hailing from landlocked communities. These new skaters did not surf or claim roots in surf culture, as had been the rite of passage for decades, but solely focused on skateboarding. Battle lines were drawn, not everyone was a fan. "In the Seventies, people started to become skaters. Suddenly you had these guys living up in the fucking Badlands. Those shitheads didn't even know where the fucking ocean was!" said a member of the original Dogtown skate and surf crew from Santa Monica. But as history would prove, this new type of skateboarder was here to stay, perfectly exemplified by the enduring professional career of Steve Alba from Upland, California, who put the Badlands on the map with style, skills, and swagger.

After winning the first-ever pool skateboarding contest - held at Spring Valley during the 1978 Hester Series - Steve Alba commenced to become a fierce competitor on the circuit, nicknamed "Le Machine" for his unfaltering consistency. But underneath his technical perfection and competitive success, "Salba" had a different side. A raw edge that would earn him a new, musically-inspired nickname: "Screaming Lord Salba." An early adopter of punk rock, he cultivated a signature look composed of dark-tinted wayfarer sunglasses, massive knee pads - preferably with tiger or leopard patterns - red helmet, and shorts from pro skater Steve Olson's company Molly's, together with cut-off band T-shirts by the likes of the Sex Pistols and the Ramones. "[Steve] Olson and I and a few others, including Salba, went deep into the punk scene. When the Ramones hit - that was us!" said skateboard icon Brad Bowman.

A rugged explorer of unknown terrain, Salba is known to have unearthed hundreds of backyard pools all over California and counts among the first riders to session the humongous transitions of legendary Mount Baldy full pipe. After a revolving door of sponsors including Kryptonics, G&S, and Tunnel skateboards, Salba finally found the attitude-driven skateboard company commensurate with his edge: As a professional rider for Santa Cruz Skateboards and Independent trucks, he became a regular on the pages of *Thrasher* magazine in the 1980s and inspired entire generations to search for new rideable terrain and skate hard with aggressive energy.

SCREAMING LORD SALBA

Born, raised, and still residing in Upland, about 30 miles from the ocean, Steve Alba never had direct access to the beach. But after stepping on a skateboard in third grade, he soon became hooked on another kind of natural terrain: backyard pools. Under the mentorship of Tom "Wally" Inouye, who started the undercover pool-draining operation Inouye's Pool Service (IPS) in 1976, Salba became an expert at scoping out new pools to ride. "We taught Steve how to find and drain pools," said Tom "Wally" Inouye. To which Salba replied: "I learned from the fucking best!"

Next to his signature skill of riding even the most unwieldy backyard pools, Salba's talents shone bright at the Upland Pipeline park - featuring a replica of the Baldy full pipe - where he and his brother Micke were the eminent locals. The local spirit would flame up during competitions, when out-of-town teams came to Upland for a rude awakening. "Salba and the guys... when I came up on the bowl they would spit at me during my contest run and yell, 'FALL! FALL! FALL!'" said Eddie "El Gato" Elguera, who was pro for Variflex skateboards at the time, which the Uplanders loathed with a vengeance. "They thought they were all punk rock and called us the 'Varibots' because we did a lot of tricks."

Actually, Steve Alba and his punk rock-inspired cohorts took less offense in the Variflex team's penchant for tricks than their clean-cut, goody-two-shoes image. It was not Salba's vision of skateboarding, so together with Steve Olson - who introduced him to UK punkers The Buzzcocks - he carved out a new niche: Thrift store outfits, stencilled lettering, bleach, cut-off sleeves, and bondage pants became emblems of their rebellion. Taking things beyond skateboarding, Salba played guitar in punk bands including Screaming Lord Salba and his Heavy Friends, who contributed songs to two Santa Cruz Skateboards videos, and today plays in So Cal band Powerflex 5. Having celebrated his 50th birthday in 2013, Steve Alba can still be found riding new pools and was inducted into the Skateboarding Hall of Fame in 2016 as a trailblazing pioneer. He remains a prolific artist and musician, while his son Jesse Alba is one of today's most talked about new street skaters, as the Badlands legacy continues.

EXTRA PROTECTION: PADDED SKATE SHORTS

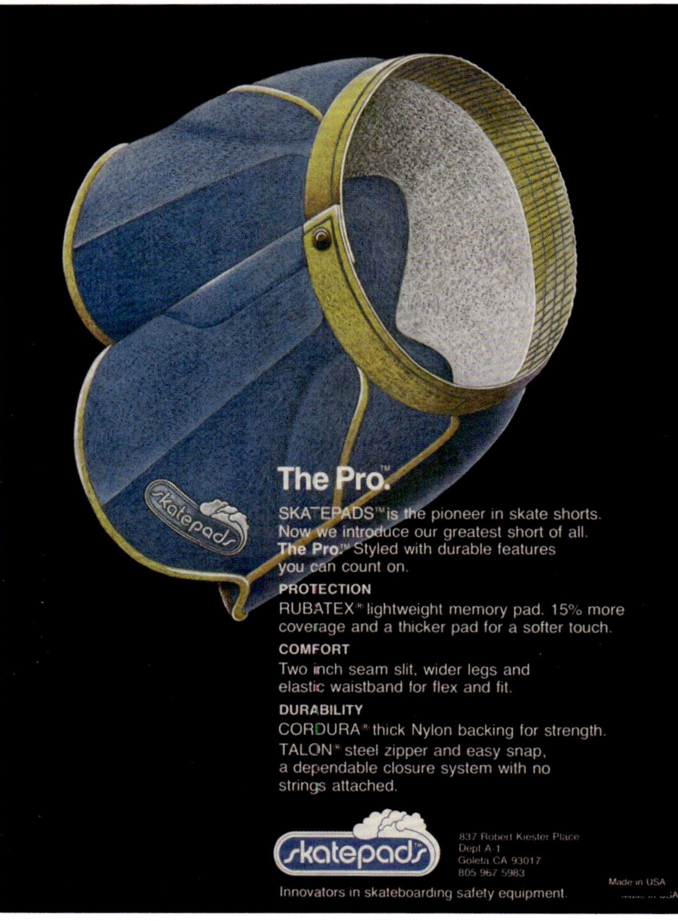

Following the invention of the frontside aerial by Tony Alva in a backyard pool in 1977, the evolution of skatepark riding took a quantum leap. Pools became the focus of a new wave of concrete skateparks such as Pipeline in Upland, California - labelled "The World's First Vertical Skatepark" - as well as Big O in Orange, Del Mal Skate Ranch, Marina Del Rey, and countless others. Despite the obligatory knee pads and helmets, this push into aerial moves and vertical terrain added a considerable element of danger. "We were riding some big concrete back then, like a 15-foot pool with 7 feet of vert on little skinny boards, so we could use all the protection we could get," said pro skateboarder Alan Gelfand, known as the inventor of the Ollie air maneuver. As a way to prevent the dreaded "hipper" - painful swelling from taking a slam to the hip - skateboarders began adding foam padding to their shorts. Offered as a commercial product by category starters Rector Skatewear in late 1977, nylon shorts with padded hip and tailbone pads offered the extra protection skateboarders needed.

Between 1978 and 1981, protective skate shorts made from durable nylon with foam polyurethane inserts by brands such as Mad Rats, Molly's, Skatepads, SIO, and others became the dominant look at skate parks and in magazines. What's more, skateboard publications all but enforced padded shorts as "proper" attire for pro skaters. When Alan Gelfand's sponsor, Powell-Peralta Skateboards, flew the Floridian to California to show the world his Ollie Air maneuver, he was in for a big surprise: 'They made me wear short pants to be in the magazines! I wore long pants my entire life skateboarding, Toughskins jeans from Sears because you just could not destroy them. I had the whitest legs of any person being from Florida. And they said, 'You can't have a kid skateboarding in long pants on the cover of a magazine.'"

THE MISSING LINK: SURF SHORTS

Only a few years earlier, the majority of the skateboard community would have shared Gelfand's animosity towards short pants. But then a cataclysmic event altered the course of skateboard fashion forever: The 1975 Bahne/Cadillac National Skateboard Championships in Del Mar, California, became the defining moment for a new breed of skateboarding. And many leaders of this new school, including freestylers such as Russ Howell and Ty Page, entered the widely televised event in shorts. "Prior to the Del Mar event almost everyone skated in long pants, no one skated in shorts," said 1970s pro skateboarder Stacy Peralta. "After the Del Mar event, almost everyone skated in shorts and the red corduroy Katin short was the most popular at that time - the most hard to get and the most coveted. You were someone if you wore the red Katin shorts."

The Katin brand started as a family business in 1954, when watersport enthusiasts Nancy and Walter Katin opened Kanvas by Katin, a shop specialized in boat covers in Surfside, California. In 1957, Katin became one of the first stores to offer custom-ordered surf trunks, which soon became the Katin family's primary line of business when the 1960s surf and skateboarding boom hit. During the second major skateboard boom, Katin sponsored freestyle skateboarder Russ Howell, who made the red shorts - worn without a shirt, just beard and long hair - his calling card. Headlined S'KATIN, Russ Howell's 1975 ad in Skateboarder magazine read: Katin's are made with the best materials money can buy. If you're into skateboarding, get into KATIN'S. Judi Oyama, original Santa Cruz Skateboards team rider, remembers the shorts for their quality: "Katin shorts were really durable and strong."

SAFE
SKATE

SIO
SIO
© DIRT SHIRTS INTL.

Next to Katin's esteemed corduroy shorts, shorts by original surf brands such as Hang Ten, Ocean Pacific, and Town and Country also became trending skate wear - especially combined with knee pads at skate parks. Some brands even formed their own skate teams: "We wore Hang Ten a lot when we skated, and eventually Jay [Adams], Shogo [Kubo], and I all got sponsored by Town and Country. So we used to wear the Yin-and Yang design T&C board shorts a lot," said skateboard icon Tony Alva. From a fashion perspective, 1978's rise of padded shorts in cuts and lengths mimicking surf shorts presented a logical evolution on a familiar theme. "They weren't too different from what we were already wearing. We were already wearing tight little OP shorts," said 1970s pro skateboarder Brad Bowman.

RECTOR SKATEWEAR SHORTS: THE ORIGINAL

Designed by engineer Mike Rector for freedom of movement and protection, Rector Skatewear Protective Shorts created the blueprint for a new generation of skate park shorts. "Rector was probably the first skate company to put padding into the shorts," said Judi Oyama, original Santa Cruz team rider and one of the first female pro pool riders and slalom racers. Endorsed by a pro team consisting of Curtis Hesselgrave, Wentzle Ruml IV, Bobby Piercy, and rookie Frank Blood, Rector shorts featured a "lace-up expansion waist" - laced in the back of the waistband - and double-thick fabric in the seat. Speaking of fabric, Protective Shorts were available in nylon and corduroy replete with Rector's signature blue and yellow colorway.

Stylistics aside, the major innovative leap consisted of the removable FLEX LINE pad system with foam pads covering the hips and tail bone. "The whole pad comes out easily, not leaving wet pockets to make you uncomfortable," promised Rector's 1978 Skateboarder magazine advertising. Wearing the shorts without padding was an option, but not without risk. "I got some Rector shorts for my twelfth birthday and my mom dropped us off at the Endless Wave [skatepark] in Oxnard. I didn't put the pads in because they made me look fat. And I slammed so hard, I got this huge hipper and limped around for two weeks. I couldn't even tell my mom because she bought me these pants to be safe," said Todd Huber, proprietor of Skatelab park and museum in Simi Valley.

Rector Skatewear marketed the shorts as part of a head-to-toe protective outfit, introduced as "The New Age" of park attire in a 1978 advertisement featuring Frank Blood. Stylish on and off your skateboard, these revolutionary shorts may well be the most comfortable pair you've ever had. But when it comes to style, not everyone considered padded shorts as an improvement. "The hip pads were just ridiculous, they made a lot of guys look like girls. When you had the shorts all padded up, they gave you girlish hips, especially the younger guys who had no chest yet," said skateboard photographer Jim Goodrich.

DIY SAFETY GEAR

Taking the DIY route, Judi Oyama tailored her own shorts with Rector pads added on the inside, "because they didn't make girl shorts." Rector's sizing also proved prohibitive to younger skaters, including teenage Steve Caballero: "My first pair of shorts were Rectors, but they were way too big for me. I tried to tie them in the back, but they would snap!" Caballero received help from Judi Oyama, whose DIY padded shorts soon became coveted items in the Nor Cal skate park scene. "I would make my own shorts and also customize them for other people, like Steve Caballero, because he was 14 years old and super small."

As requests for homemade shorts gained momentum, Oyama also liked to spice up her designs with details such as leopard prints and tiger stripes. One particular pair of shorts caught the interest of skateboarding's original punk rock bad boy, Steve Olson. Judi recalls: "I made these shorts with red hearts and black hearts, which closed up with Velcro because I didn't know how to make zippers. They were kind of big and Olson wanted to wear them, so I gave him a pair."

The outcome turned out classic skateboard lore: "Olson was doing this frontside grind in the corner where [pro skater] David Hackett and his girlfriend were sitting. And then - swish - the shorts came off, and he had no underwear! So later he came over and said, 'Judi, you need to put a strap into these.' I'll never forget that!" said Judi Oyama. Whether or not the incident inspired Olson to start his own protective shorts brand, Molly's, remains unknown. But beyond a doubt, the padded shorts market exploded in 1978 as countless new brands flooded the market.

TINY SHORTS, MAJOR TREND

The first brand to hop on the bandwagon, Skatepads out of Goleta, California marketed padded shorts as "the pioneer in skate shorts" (sure, if launching half a year after category starters Rector Skatewear still counts as "pioneering"). Advertised with the claim, "confidence to go for it," the company's "Pro" short piled on technical advancements. RUBATEX™ lightweight memory pad. 15% more coverage and a thicker pad for a softer touch. CORDURA™ thick Nylon backing for strength. TALON™ steel zipper and easy snap, a dependable closure system with no strings attached. The latter obviously constituted a stab at Rector's lace-up harness closure.

As protective shorts gained momentum, another major trend rocked the shorts segment: Color-blocked two-tone colorways - either contrasts of two primary colors such as Rectors' yellow and blue, or monochromatic shades of the same color - became all the rage among skate park riders. And while most nylon shorts featured this trending color combination, the most stylish skateboarders knew that corduroy was the way to go.

"The two-toned-colored corduroy skateboard short was a giant fashion trend in skateboarding in the '70s that would carry into the early '80s. It was to the best of my knowledge made popular inside of the skateboarding world. I believe it was a fashion trend that was indigenous to skateboarding," said skateboard icon Stacy Peralta.

SIO SHORTS: EAST COAST STYLE

Out in Florida, where skateboard fashion trends could take a while to arrive, the Tallahassee Skate Club ranked among the pillars of the local skate scene. In 1979, the club's founder Barry Zaritzky launched clothing company SIO (Skateboards Inside Out) SKATEWEAR to offer protective clothing in fashion-forward colorways. Straight out the gate, SIO released trendy two-tone shorts with foam padding, endorsed by pro riders such as Chris Strople, Dennis Martinez, and Shogo Kubo. Slogan: "SIO PROTECTS THE BOTTOMS OF THE TOPS!" SIO flow riders also included rookie pro Steve Caballero: Barry Zaritzky was friends with Mike Mc Gill and gave me some shorts. I think you could take out the padding and they had a butt patch out of corduroy, so they seemed more sturdy than thinner shorts like Mad Rats."

Another grateful SIO rider included Alan "Ollie" Gelfand, who mainly wore the shorts for practical reasons: "I was never much into fashion, I just wore the shorts Barry from SIO gave me. I always wore hip pads and no one really knew it. It made me feel better when I skated. My knees were always bad, so it was hard to run out of anything. So I always slid to my sides." In order to keep bulking around the hips at a minimum, Gelfand would cut down the foam in his shorts: "I cut my hip pads up, totally. And I only wore the padding on my hips, not on my butt." So, did SIO shorts live up to the bold slogan "TO HELL WITH HIPPERS"? Definitely, says Gelfand: "Barry invented this foam named Ensolite. You could drop a 4 x 4-inch foam square with an egg wrapped inside from a building and it wouldn't break. It was the best foam. I probably wouldn't be walking today if it wasn't for Ensolite, and Berry was the innovator behind it."

For added flair, SIO shorts shipped with embroidered patches featuring the brand's logo. "They were super generous and SIO shorts always came with tons of patches so you could customize your shorts any way you wanted," said said 1980s skateboard pro Claus Grabke. But despite their fashion edge, the short leg length on SIO shorts - and other shorts at the time - could prove challenging. "They were super tight, and so short, they barely reached beneath your balls when you wore them," said Grabke.

In hindsight, padded shorts may have added safety from injuries, but it sometimes came at a price. "If you did a frontside grind sometimes your wang would come out of the shorts, or your sack," said pro skater Brad Bowman, adding: "I'm sure countless photographers have shots that are unbelievable but that they can't use - because someone's wang is hanging out in the picture."

SIO
SIO
SIO
SIO SIO
SIO SIO

Photo: Ted Terrebonne

When the free-wheeling spirit of skateboarding collided with the rebellious energy of punk rock, sparks went flying. It was a match made in heaven – love at first sight. Except, that's not entirely true. Because initially, skateboarding's reigning champions – role model athletes in matching team jerseys endorsing skateboard safety and their sponsors' products – wanted little to do with the aggressive new blend of music washing in from the UK and New York City around 1977. "We were all into mellower bands at the time and punk really was a departure from that," said Hobie team rider and skateboard photographer Jim Goodrich, adding: "A lot of us looked at punk as something cool, but not a lot of people embraced it at first."

Then something extraordinary happened. The era's hottest newcomer, 1978 Hester Series winner and Skateboarder Magazine Reader's Poll Award recipient Steve Olson from Long Beach, California, went off the deep end, diving head-first into punk rock. Hyped on bands such as Mink DeVille, The Ramones, and the Sex Pistols, Olson felt the natural connection between skateboarding and punk rock culture. "I always thought the energy was kind of like when you're mackin' a grind. There was some parallel to it. And it was fun. And it was really fun to shock people! That was part of the whole thing. And I dyed my hair and they really flipped out," said Steve Olson. When he accepted his Reader's Poll Award wearing a white blazer with bondage pants, pointed toe boots, and a polka dot tie, flinging insults and buggers at the crowd, the skateboard industry felt a shock to the system. "Even other skaters were like, 'These [punk] guys are not good for our sport!' Little did they know, the kids were gonna dig it, though," said Steve Olson.

Punk rock changed skateboarding's new leading man – the music, the attitude, the not-giving-a-fuck about what other people think or say – but skateboarding also changed with him. "Steve Olson introduced the whole punk era. After that, they were all searching for something and that's when punk fully came in with Duane Peters and all the other guys," said Olson's board sponsor, Rich Novak at Santa Cruz Skateboards. Posing for magazine photos in leather jackets, stove pipe jeans, and outrageous outfits sourced from thrift stores, Olson became a role model for punk and New Wave dress code: "In those days, Steve Olson was Mr. Fashion," said pro skateboarder Alan Gelfand. Always backing up all the flair with his skating, Olson laid the foundation for a school of skateboarding where it not only mattered how difficult your tricks were – but how you looked doing them. "Without a doubt, Olson has always been a style god," said pro skateboarder Claus Grabke. And by starting his own skateboard companies – Molly's Shorts and Steve Olson Skates (SOS) – Steve Olson forever transformed the image of pro skaters from uniform-wearing brand mannequins into artists and empowered creative individuals.

RISE OF A STYLE ICON

Steve Olson first stepped on a skateboard in 1966, right at the point where skateboarding had hit its high water mark of mass popularity, and finally the wave broke and rolled back. Not like he cared. Steve skated occasionally, and spent most of his time surfing with his older brother Bucky. "My brother is four years older so I was influenced through my older brother, mostly. Older brothers always know what's going on, because they have their finger on the pulse. And he was very much in tune with what was happening." In true DIY-spirit, Olson's brother built his own surfboards, worked on airbrush graphics, customized his own clothing, hunted for cool music – all of which Steve soaked up like a sponge.

Steve Olson

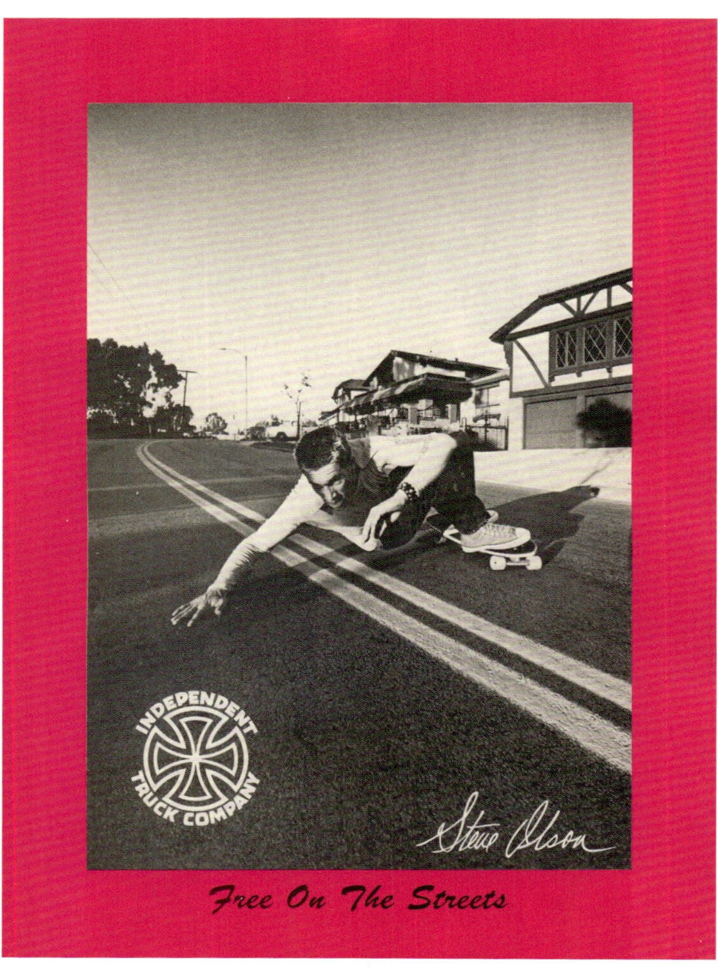

ANYBODY, ANYWHERE

STREET SKATE, OLSON MODEL, BEVEL, WIDEPLY, STINGER, GRAPHITE SLALOM

MANUFACTURERS OF: SANTA CRUZ SKATEBOARDS, INDEPENDENT TRUCKS, PARK RIDER, ROADRIDER, BLACKHART, RHYTHM, OJ WHEELS, MOLLY SHORTS, AND MIGHTY MITTS.
DISTRIBUTORS OF: ALVA, ACS, AZF, CASTER, DOGTOWN, GYRO, G&S, GULLWING KANOA-FLYAWAY HELMET, KRYPTONIC, NORCON, NTN BEARINGS, RECTOR, TRACKER, 3M AND Z-FLEX.

TELEX 171030 825 41st AVE. SANTA CRUZ, CALIF. 95062 408-475-9434

"Olson is lucky because he had an older brother who was really into music and fashion. So he got a lot of stuff given to him from his brother that I wished I had," said 1970s pro skateboarder Brad Bowman. When the urethane wheel unlocked a new way to ride in the mid-1970s, Steve Olson joined Southern California's budding bank and pool riding scene. Idolizing Tony Alva and the Zephyr team, he became a local at Carlsbad skatepark, where his brother picked up vertical roller-skating. With skateparks as the new focus, skateboarding was hot again. Olson progressed at skateboarding fast, winning a few amateur contests and picking up his first sponsor, Wayne Brown Skateboards. When Concrete Wave skatepark opened in Anaheim, it put rocket boots on Steve's progression. "That was my skatepark! My brother worked there and I skated it every single day. That's where I honed all my shit at. We helped build that pool, that was the first pool in a skatepark," said Steve Olson. Rubbing elbows with the era's best riders at Concrete Wave, Olson exhibited a unique sense of fashion style at a young age. "I had a leopard skin swimsuit that I loved and wore to skate. Guys like [pro riders] Gregg Ayres and Rod Saunders were always making fun of me. I was like 14 or 15. 'Why do you wear those?!' I was like, 'They're cool man!' It was all about cool, that was all there was to it," said Olson.

Undeterred, Olson stuck to his guns – even when Dogtown's Jay Adams called him a "fag" for wearing his animal print shorts – and progressed from really good to straight-up dominating. After winning the amateur division in skateboarding's first major pool riding tour, 1978's Hester Series, leading brands wanted a piece of him. "In the pool you could do what you wanted and work out as hard as you wanted, but you probably couldn't beat him. Nine times out of ten he's a better athlete," said Rich Novak at Santa Cruz Skateboards, who signed Olson in 1978. That year, Olson doubled down on punk rock, which was only gradually making a mark in skateboarding. "I remember hearing some of the early stuff at the first Hester contest. Like Mink DeVille, '*Cadillac Walk*.' There were some songs that were slid in. You had Aerosmith and '*Toys in the Attic*' – they were a blues-based bar band and '*Cadillac Walk*' was like a hopped-up '50s song. It all goes hand-in-hand... Ted Nugent, Black Sabbath, and then my brother was blasting Iggy Pop, T REX, Bowie, Sweet, Slade, all of it." Pro skateboarder Lance Mountain also remembers the sea change in musical influences: "[Pro skater] Doug Saladino skated to Blondie at a contest and the music changed overnight."

NEW WAVE STYLE

The paradigm shift went beyond musical styles and into fashion choices. The new batch of punk bands cultivated eccentric dress codes, which was right up Steve Olson's alley, especially since he had always idolized athletes with flamboyant lifestyles. "We grew up with dudes like Joe Nameth wearing mink coats. And that was a football player! And Cassius Clay – Muhammad Ali – who was very outspoken and then there were dudes like [Hawaiian surfer] David Nuuhiwa and the whole glam scene going on, along with T REX and Iggy and Bowie." At competitions, Olson would spice up outfits with flair items such as argyle socks or striped tops, gradually breaking the mold of matching team jerseys and safety gear. "It was Olson! He was the first to introduce people to wearing checkers and stripes," said Lance Mountain. To hear Steve Olson tell it: "Skateboarding was like shorts, sneakers, your safety gear – and then it was like, 'Yo, you don't have to dress like that anymore!'"

Off the board, Olson took to wearing rockabilly outfits with greased hair, and scouting thrift stores for leather jackets, fur coats, and the kind of larger-than-life get-ups worn by glam rockers. "Within the glam world, they dressed kind of outrageously, so that made sense. And I always liked dressing up for Halloween.

So this was fashion. It was interesting and fun," said Steve Olson, adding: "I didn't think, 'I'm a skateboarder, I can I pull it off.' It was more, 'I can dig it.' Punk rock had a lot of fashion going on, whether it was considered fashion or not. But it was excellent. And New Wave was New Wave with suits, and rockabilly, and everything had a sense of style behind it." Speaking of style, Olson lists punk rock musician and underground cultural icon Terry Nails – later also one of the creatives behind Independent Trucks and an avid downhill racer in the Stroker car scene – as a major influence: "Terry Nails really is one dude that flipped up the whole fashion thing for me and is really important to talk about. He was a musician and played in bands, he was dressing in the new style that was happening within New Wave and punk rock. He comes from a musician's family and played with the Pointer Sisters and Ozzy Osbourne, and he was very important to changing the way it was," said Steve Olson.

Thrasher shirt with Mofo photo of JFA frontman Brian Brannon in Olson homage checker style frame.

Terry Nails would also lend Olson a hand in customizing his punk-inspired outfits. "I remember Terry Nails did some clothes for him. They didn't make those in mainstream fashion until much later," said skateboarder and musician Gerry "Skatemaster Tate" Hurtado, adding: "Olson started it all in skate fashion!" And that's not an understatement, because what Olson started would become a defining cultural current of skateboarding from the late 1970s onwards. When fellow pro skateboarders such as Tony Alva, Brad Bowman, and Duane Peters openly flew their punk rock flag at competitions and in the skateboard media, the punk phenomenon took on a life of its own. "And then the movement started and they said, 'You started it!' But I just did what I wanted to do. It was fun to go and dress up," said Steve Olson, who also played bass in numerous punk bands in the late 1970s, including stints with The Hoods, The Jones, and CASH.

THE FULL PACKAGE

By the time Santa Cruz Skateboards decided to turn Steve Olson pro in 1979, he had become notorious for his antics and Hollywood-style partying at concerts and skateboard events, much like his teammates Duane Peters and Steve Alba. Speaking on the issue, Rich Novak at Santa Cruz described his line-up of pros as a cultural counterforce to the clean-cut, 'goody two-shoes' aesthetic portrayed by Powell-Peralta's new elite skateboard team, the Bones Brigade. "They were a bunch of pussies. Look at the movies, look the pictures. And then look at my guys – Olson and them were fucked up! They were tough! And the Bones Brigade were just a bunch of kids. Their balls hadn't even dropped yet." Asked about Steve Olson's influence, Novak also pointed out: "As a matter of fact, Olson did this first street skate punk ad. No one even came close to street skating when we did the first ad, I think around October 1979. It was a layback on the curb kind of punked-out and his girlfriend was standing next to him. That was the first street ad that anybody put out."

In 1980, Santa Cruz Skateboards released the punk-inspired Steve Olson Checkerboard model, one of the most iconic pro graphics of all time. Together with Duane Peters' Hazard Stripes pro model, the board brought punk rock style into the hardware segment, establishing Steve Olson as one of the top-selling riders of his day. "The Checkerboard was a board graphic that I came up with together with my brother. There was a company called Bardahl Racing that had the checkered flag in a logo on the Indy 500 [racing circuit]. My brother was an artist so he did the graphic, and we were kind of coming into the punk rock New Wave thing so it made perfect sense."

JAMS

Photo: Glen E. Friedman

That same year, Olson starred in the music video for "Freedom of Choice" by influential band Devo, next to Tony Alva and Stacy Peralta and other leading pro riders. This also launched Olson's career as a model and actor; he would star in advertisements in Harper's Bazaar magazine and Times Square billboards, as well as numerous movies including 1986's *Thrashin'* as part of the Daggers skate gang. "People like Steve Olson and Dave Hackett stood out because they looked really clean, just models on a skateboard," said pro skateboarder Don Brown.

At the height of his pro career, Steve Olson also decided to bank on his marketable persona by starting his own line of padded skateboard shorts, Molly's, in partnership with automotive customization pioneer and designer Molly Sanders. As an inspiration, Olson pointed out the DIY-spirit instilled by his older brother: "He could paint and build surfboards, and build single-skis. That's what I grew up on. So to do Molly's shorts made perfect sense, channeling my older brother's influence. He also did all my graphics." Although the functional and fashion-forward shorts were distributed by NHS, the company behind Olson's board sponsor Santa Cruz, the enterprise turned out short-lived, as skateboarding entered another massive downward spiral in the year 1980. "Olson was really gifted but he happened to have picked the wrong timing. He got in right at the collapse in the late '70s and didn't take advantage of the '80s when it came back in," said Rich Novak.

KEEPING THE FAITH

Suddenly and irrevocably, skateboarding was dead in 1980. The major US economic crisis, marked by gasoline rationing at gas stations throughout the country, and the mass closing of skateparks due to insurance woes had dealt a double punch. It was harsh, especially for top pros like Steve Olson. "One year you're World Champion – the other year you're thinking, 'What am I gonna do with the rest of my life?' It's not like it is now where you have 15, 20 year careers. Everyone went out and had to do things and get jobs and become different people. It was a harsh reality check in '79 to '80," said Steve Olson, who was also dealing with a major injury at the time. "I had messed up my ankle and there was a huge progression that happened right then. 'Olson, you're done!' I'm just injured. 'Well, let it go. Now it's Duane [Peters].' Thank god, I won a contest after the fact."

Picking himself up, Steve Olson kept skateboarding, and in Spring 1980 beat the day's best vert skaters – old and new generation – at the Big O pool contest in Orange. And while skateboarding was down, Olson still had one of the most marketable names on the circuit, so he approached his board sponsor about launching his own eponymous company: "It was SOS, Steve Olson Skates. Surf Or Skate. Save Our Souls. Whatever it was, it was short-lived," said Steve Olson, who had big plans for SOS, including a clothing line. "But we did just the SOS board and the sticker, but never any clothing." SOS launched in 1980, and the rugged, hand-painted lettering created by NHS artist Jim Phillips on Day-Glo neon boards resonated with punk rock fans. Dreaming big, Olson already had the entire SOS fashion line mapped out in his head, inspired by the punk rock uniforms of the Clash, the Ramones, and Johnny Thunders and the Heartbreakers: "I wanted black-and-white ads with this chick in front of beat-down, post-apocalyptic areas. Definitely [Craig] Stecyk-influenced and Robert Frank."

But NHS would not budge on producing SOS-branded clothing, even when a buyer from Nordstrom's department stores signaled strong interest at a tradeshow. "The projections at Nordstrom's were huge, which I found interesting, because the guys [at NHS] had told me I couldn't make money with shirts.

Then it got crazy and I quit. It was sad. I was pissed. I wanted to create, but I let my emotions get involved." With his namesake brand discontinued, Olson moved to San Francisco where he stayed with *Thrasher* magazine's Kevin Thatcher and Eric Swanson, working in a punk store on Haight Street and playing in a band named Cowboy Zero. Ultimately, SOS would find a new home in 1986 with board brand Skull Skates, who announced the launch with an ad featuring Olson doing a bert slide on New York's Brooklyn Banks in a leather jacket, riding his new SOS checkerboard-patterned model, still keeping the faith.

ENDURING LEGACY

Keeping the faith has made all the difference, because here's the thing: Steve Olson never quit skateboarding and being punk, during the dark years when he oscillated between New York City, San Francisco, and Los Angeles while the skateboard industry flat-lined. Even when Skateboarder magazine became the watered-down *Action Now*, Steve Olson would have coverage, ripping with the best and influencing the rest of the scene with his fashion choices. "Check out issues of Skateboarder Magazine back then and *Action Now* magazine, you can see pictures of Steve and Duane and other pros dressed in checkered shorts, black leather, and you can see the re-introduction of wearing pants while skateboarding. Prior to the '80s, all skaters in the late '70s wore shorts while skateboarding," said Stacy Peralta about Olson's influence.

Also in *Action Now*, Steve Olson wrote and starred in full-on fashion spreads, including "THE ROCKABILLY LOOK." Supplemented by James Cassimus photography, the story explained the historic origins of rockabilly as follows: "The look included a really spectacular hair style - a high front pomp with slicked back sides to a DA (Duck's Ass for those who don't know)."

Olson advised skateboarders to rock pegged pants with pleats or tight stove pipe Levi's, easily found at thrift stores: "You should be able to do the whole thing, from shoes on up, for as low as $15." On that note, Olson spearheaded the trend towards thrift-store hunting that would remain fundamental to skateboard fashion, especially at a time before skateboard brands produced punk-themed clothing. Most of all, Olson encouraged a sense of individual style in his *Action Now* column: "What you need is the clothes mentioned here and your own feel for what you think is cool." By following his own sense of cool, Steve Olson transformed the look and attitude of an entire generation of skateboarders, all the way into hairstyles. As Lance Mountain pointed out, "around 1981, you had to cut your hair to say that you're punk and it was Olson who brought that look into skateboarding with Black Flag and short cut hair."

Today, Steve Olson still skateboards - he appeared on the cover of *The Skateboard Mag* skating doubles with Lance Mountain in 2015 - and makes a living as an artist in Los Angeles. "People don't look at it as a successful choice of living. Not everyone can pull it off. Most can't. But I make art and create things from nothing. The word artist is so overused, but you gotta follow what your heart tells you," said the Skateboard Hall of Famer, who avidly chronicles skateboard culture through interviews with skateboard icons for Venice-based *Juice* magazine. Next to his own stylistic legacy, Olson's greatest gift to skateboarding is his son Alex, also a professional skateboarder and the mastermind behind successful fashion label, Bianca Chandon (talk about the apple not falling far from the tree). Reflecting on his career, Steve Olson offered: "I helped influence a whole new movement. And without a doubt, I took mad shit from people. I was skating and I was also down with this whole new movement of New Wave - and no one else was. Just a couple of people, not the dudes who claim it now. Come on, at least be honest now, okay?"

MOLLY

MOLLY'S SHORTS: FLAIR AND PROTECTION

When it comes to designing products for skateboarding's highly demanding audience, one formula has always proven to work best: Designed by skateboarders, for skateboarders. In 1979, reigning Skateboarding World Champion Steve Olson from Los Angeles took a look around the market for protective gear, and saw the need for skater-designed protective shorts. "I always wanted to build things that had pads in them to offer protection. We would always smash our tailbones and our hips. I looked at motocross and motorcycle racing - and they already had pads. So I knew there was a demand for it."

As it turned out, a friend of Olson's father had deep hooks into the motorcycle world: The highly influential customized motorcycle pioneer Rollin "Molly" Sanders of Molly Designs in Newport Beach, California. "Molly was right with it, he was a great motorcycle enthusiast and picked up on skateboarding right away. I was in graphic design and he was into motorcycles and we worked together a lot," said Dave Olson, Steve's father, who also worked on customized car detailing, including surf-style stripes for Volkswagen cars. As Steve Olson tells it: "Molly was my dad's business partner. Molly Designs. I helped him design the shorts, and because he was in the car and motorcycle world, he produced the shorts with all the different materials."

"It took us a while to find the right fabric that lasted. Molly understood skateboarding because of his motorcycling background and him and Steve talked about designs. So they put the pads into the shorts right where skateboarders would take a beating when they landed," said Dave Olson. Right from the start, the advanced fabrication garnered significant attention for Molly's Shorts in the skateboarding world. "It was all high-end motorcycle racing material. All the other stuff that came out at the time was just shit. But those were the first real skate shorts that came out," said Olson's former board sponsor Richard Novak, co-founder of NHS Skateboards in Santa Cruz, who distributed Molly's Shorts.

RIDER-INSPIRED PROTECTION

Adding to Molly's marketing buzz, Steve Olson, credited with introducing punk rock into skateboard culture, took it upon himself to represent the brand on the contest circuit, where he dominated. In 1979, Olson won the highly acclaimed Skateboarder Magazine Skater of the Year Award and appeared on stage wearing, not Molly's skate shorts, but leather bondage pants while raining insults on the crowd for shock value. Olson's notorious edge also influenced the design of Molly's Shorts, injecting punk rock-style checkerboard patterns into the logo and pants lining. "The checkers pattern was totally Steve Olson," said Richard Novak, who released Olson's iconic Checkerboard pro model on Santa Cruz Skateboards in 1980.

In terms of colorways, Molly's offered riffs on the popular "two-tone" style of the late 1970s era, combining color-blocked panels of different materials such as nylon and corduroy. Speaking on color variations, Steve Olson offered: "There was a little bit of red-white-and blue in there, a little Americana. And there were lots of red, and dark and light blue." As for cuts and silhouettes, Molly's echoed the "short shorts" style that dominated skate parks at the time. "They were a little short but that was just the era," said Richard Novak. Olson's shorts instantly struck a note with the day's leading pro riders, including Brad Bowman: "Molly shorts were really snug, tight shorts with pads around them. Which was great. It really felt like you were wearing underwear. And they were padded."

Out on the pro circuit, Steve Olson - working on a tight budget for his start-up apparel brand -resorted to grassroots marketing tactics. "Steve gave his shorts to the top guys at contests because he wanted to get publicity. And they were great," said Brad Bowman. Other early adopters included a young Steve Caballero: "I wore Molly's for a while. There's also a famous photo of [Santa Cruz pro] Steve Alba doing a frontside edger at Upland in a blue Flyaway [helmet] wearing Molly's shorts." But despite its promising start, the company was unable to maintain its momentum. "It went on for a year or two at the most. Somewhere down the chain they couldn't produce the shorts anymore," said Steve Olson, adding: "They were not very easy to get, anyway. And I never made a penny off of Molly's shorts."

Photo: Craig Fineman

MOLLY
MOLLY

SkateBoarder
A SURFER PUBLICATION
VOL. 5, NO. 3 OCTOBER 1978 $1.50
UK90p
RICK BLACKHART INTERVIEW
"Vertical riding can go much further."
HESTER PRO—THE BIG "O"
Alba-Olson Showdown
SUMMER COMPETITION WRAP-UP
Vail, Akron & Oceanside
BILL BAHNE INTERVIEW
'You can't b.s. those kids.'

Let San Diego and Los Angeles keep the year-round sunshine and skate sessions in breezy beach outfits. Up in Northern California, fashion styles have always followed a different route than the brightly colored surf shorts and tank tops portrayed in leading skateboard magazines. One of the first riders to put Nor Cal style on the map, Rick 'Rubberman' Blackhart - also known as 'Dr. Blackhart' - from San Jose barged onto the scene in 1976 as the polar opposite to the prototypical LA-surfer dude. Rocking a somber color palette of blacks, browns, and grays instead of SoCal's neons, Blackhart famously hated surfing - another thing San Diego and Los Angeles could keep for themselves - but loved partying and living the life of a rolling stone, which he would proliferate as an integral part of *Thrasher* magazine from 1981 onwards.

According to legend, Blackhart first stepped on a skateboard in 1969 but really got hooked in 1973 when his neighbor brought home an Excalibur, one of the first boards featuring urethane wheels. As he said in a Juice magazine interview conducted by pro skater Steve Olson, Blackhart traded seven joints of brown Columbian weed in return for borrowing the board - and turned pro one year later. As a professional for Nor Cal board company Tunnel Skateboards from San Mateo, Rick Blackhart raised the bar for aggressive skating in drainage ditches, full pipes, and backyard pools. A long-time local at Upland Skatepark, he also showed an interest in skateboard hardware design, tinkering with board constructions with fellow Tunnel pro Kevin "KT" Thatcher. Innovations included early longboard constructions and downhill racing boards. Blackhart also had a hand in designing the original Stage 1 Independent Truck.

Most of all, Blackhart made style and aggression the focus of riding. "Blackhart had a definite style of his own, a power style," said skateboard photographer James Cassimus. With a persona too loud to be ignored, Blackhart put an end to the skateboard media's biased focus on solely covering the Los Angeles scene: "A lot of the early stuff in Skateboarder was a lot of shit from LA, much like in surfing, because the guys who were doing the magazine didn't wanna drive north or south," said Rich Novak, co-founder of Santa Cruz skateboards and Independent Trucks, which Blackhart endorsed as the first team rider. Next to the design for 1978's original Stage 1 truck, Blackhart also came up with the brand's slogan: "They're fucking hot!"

NOR CAL STYLE

In one of the Independent Truck Company's first ads - headlined THAT WAS THEN... THIS IS NOW - Blackhart models the blueprint for what became known as Nor Cal skate fashion style: trucker hat, black sweatshirt, and work wear chino pants. Back then as much as today, the Nor Cal Look consisting of flannel shirts, windbreakers, sweatshirts, chinos and jeans, paired with beanies and trucker hats is a direct response to the region's brisk climate.

With his hardcore aesthetic and penchant for exploring new terrain such as Nor Cal's many hidden full pipes, Rick Blackhart paved the way for generations of skateboarders, to whom he offered advice in his equally humorous and insightful *Thrasher* magazine column, Ask the Doctor with Dr. Blackhart. Asked about the best way to prepare for a tense contest situation, the Doctor - also one of the main proponents of *Thrasher*'s Skate Rock movement - offered: "Always skate to loud rock 'n' roll as this simulates a contest situation." In 1983, the Dr. Blackhart logo also became available on official *Thrasher* T-shirts, available for $9.65 (postage and handling included). As Blackhart wrote by ways of endorsement: "Don't be a common twid like everyone else. Get one now and be a happening twid!"

OCEAN PACIFIC: BEACH TO CONCRETE

In the image-driven world of board sports apparel, so much depends on the concept of "perceived value." When consumers perceive a brand to be highly valuable, it can charge premium prices for products well above the industry standard. In the mid-1970s, no surf and skateboard apparel brand played perceived value like Ocean Pacific Sportswear – in short "Op" – from San Diego. Sold exclusively at specialty surf shops, the full line of OP-branded apparel such as shorts, tees, sweatshirts, windbreakers, and knits with their primary color schemes and surf-themed stripes sold at top-shelf price points. And every skateboarder wanted a piece. "When I was a 13-year-old, it went from Hang Ten to Op. 'Mom, can you buy me Op?! 'You would really cry to get that shirt!" said skateboard photographer Dave Swift.

Originally started as a surf apparel company by North County surfboard shaper Jim Jenks in 1972, Ocean Pacific managed the rare feat of building a credible following in the skateboard community just in time to catch skateboarding's second major wave of popularity. "The name is based on 'Pacific Ocean' – and Jim just flipped it," said Mark Richards at original skateboard shop Val Surf in North Hollywood, one of the first resellers of Op. Advertised to surfers under the slogan "For watermen the world over," Ocean Pacific also formed its own skateboarding team. It was stacked with pro freestyle world champions Ellen Berryman and Bob Mohre, among others. In a 1978 SkateBoarder Magazine advertisement, the two pro riders model Op's corduroy shorts, tropical print tees, and collared long-sleeve striped shirts with the message: "Radical designs, outrageous colors, and performance. That's why more pros are into Op."

Behind the scenes, Op's connection to skateboarding was a family affair. "[Pro skateboarder] Steve Sherman had a best friend – and his dad was the owner of Op! That's why Op got involved with Del Mar skate park," said SIMS team rider Ed Economy. Sold at the Del Mar Skate Ranch's pro shop and other specialty retailers, Ocean Pacific emerged as the leading clothing brand for discerning skaters. "Around 1977, Op was the top. Every skater wore Op," said Del Mar park local and skateboard photographer J. Grant Brittain, who became directly involved with the company. "I worked for Op driving a truck so I was there when they made $1 million in one month. They were the biggest surfwear company." And as is often the case when core boardsports brands catch a big wave, Ocean Pacific soon expanded their distribution channels, becoming even bigger in the process. "Op also went to malls and department stores, so inland skaters could get it in those days before you had mail order," said Dave Swift.

PART OF THE LOOK

Next to Hawaiian-print shirts and rainbow striped colorblocking, Ocean Pacific's biggest contribution to the "boardsports look" lies in their high above the knee corduroy "walkshorts."With an inseam length around only four inches, these "short shorts" became a quintessential part of the California Beach Lifestyle proliferated through surf movies and magazine fashion spreads around 1974. When skateboarders jumped on the trend, short lengths would evolve into slightly longer territory around six inches and Op took over the scene. Asked about the first "skateboard fashion" outfit he remembers people wearing, pro skateboarder Mark Gonzales said: "Op shorts and Lightning Bolt shirts." Propelled by sales of shorts, graphic tees in colorways such as rust and powder blue, as well as sweatshirts and windbreakers with rainbow stripes, Ocean Pacific raised the bar for how large a boardsports apparel brand could grow. At the end of 1979, Op raked in $40 million in annual sales according to *The Encyclopedia of Surfing* – and the brand was only getting started.

Following a period of international expansion and mainstream marketing, Op rode the wave as the biggest, most popular brand in surf apparel. Sales peaked at $370 million in 1987, but the big company also paid a big price. Along the way, Ocean Pacific lost touch with its core consumer base. Like many a brand in skare history, it had become too big to be cool. Establishing a pattern that would become familiar in the boardsport business, the brand entered into a series of big-time licensing agreement and partnerships, reporting sales of $170 million and licenses in 83 countries in 2000.

Op sold "back to the roots" products, but dropped the "short" style cord shorts. "The essence of cool in the surf industry has been the length of the shorts," Ocean Pacific Chief Executive Dick Baker told the LA Times in 2002. "The antichrist of that has been the Op cord short." In 2007, owners Iconix Brands Group signed a direct-to-retail license agreement with U.S. retail chain Walmart. As of 2018, Walmart markets a full line of Op apparel as well as Op-branded skateboard shoes, bringing the brand's evolution from the beach to the street full circle.

MAGNUM DEVELOPMENT: BUILT FOR SPEED

As the mid-1970s skateboard boom took the industry to new heights, companies were still fighting a major political battle: The mainstream media, municipalities, and society at large still needed convincing that skateboarding was not a toy. Not a short-lived kid's fad like the Hula Hoop, Yo-Yo, or Frisbee – but an actual sport with a bright future. Ironically, one of the biggest advocates of skateboarding as a "real sport" was the world's number one manufacturer of children's toys, the Mattel Corporation. In 1977, the toy company launched a new brand, the Magnum Skateboard Division based in Hawthorne, California, with a focus on downhill racing and slalom; arguably rather mainstream-compatible aspects of skateboarding given their race-against-the-clock format.

Previous to launching Magnum Development, Mattel had already tried – and failed – to gain a foothold in skateboarding. In the early 1970s, the brand produced Mattel Sizzler Plastic complete skateboards, using the Sizzler brand name from their line of popular Hot Wheels Cars toys. So in a way, the authentic, skateboard-driven marketing approach behind Magnum was Mattel's Trojan Horse into the skate biz. With advertisements in major skateboard publications, Magnum Development drove a marketing campaign centered on performance technology, using the brand's pro team riders as evangelists. THE MAGNUM TEAM TALKS RIDER TO RIDER, said a 1978 Skateboarder magazine ad depicting the team hosting a safety clinic at a Southern California skate park.

But beneath the surface, a lot of the marketing promises did not hold up. The company's Hi-Velocity Wheel system is a prime example. Featuring wheels with flashy names such as Banana Jammers and Blue Streakers, Hi-Velocity wheels were designed around a removable center bearing insert, adjustable by ways of a futuristic tool. M.A.G. makes 'em fast and makes 'em last, promised the advertisement. But in a 1978 article on the state of the skateboard business, skateboard industry spokeswoman Sally Anne Miller gave the products a scathing review, suggesting: "Go back to making Barbie dolls."

THE FUTURE OF SKATEBOARDING?

During its short-lived involvement in skateboarding, however, Magnum Development went all-in, offering everything from complete skateboards, wheels, racing overalls, helmets, all the way to branded clothing and accessories. In terms of apparel, Magnum Development offered a full clothing collection in brand colors black, baby blue, and white and the company's "Magnum Star" logo. Magnum's fashion-forward team jerseys were crafted from nylon, featuring a black sleeve on one arm, contrasted by white on the other, together with futuristic color-blocking and the brand's logo across the chest.

Catering to the budding downhill racing and slalom scene, Magnum produced full-coverage, visor racing-style helmets in brand colors. Accessories included a Magnum-branded carrying case with a zippered side pocket and inside compartments large enough to accomodate complete skateboards. But despite significant marketing expenditure, the brand failed to gain traction and disappeared during the major consolidation period on the skateboard market in 1981.

The end? Not for Mattel, because as every skateboarder knows, the brand does, in fact, own the future as the official makers of Marty McFly's Hoverboard from the *Back to the Future* movies. Initially set for release in 2015, the free-floating hover skateboards – just don't try to ride them across water – will be coming to a skate shop, not a toy shop, near you really soon.

MAGNUM™

STEVE

MAGNUM™

MAGNUM™
MAGNUM
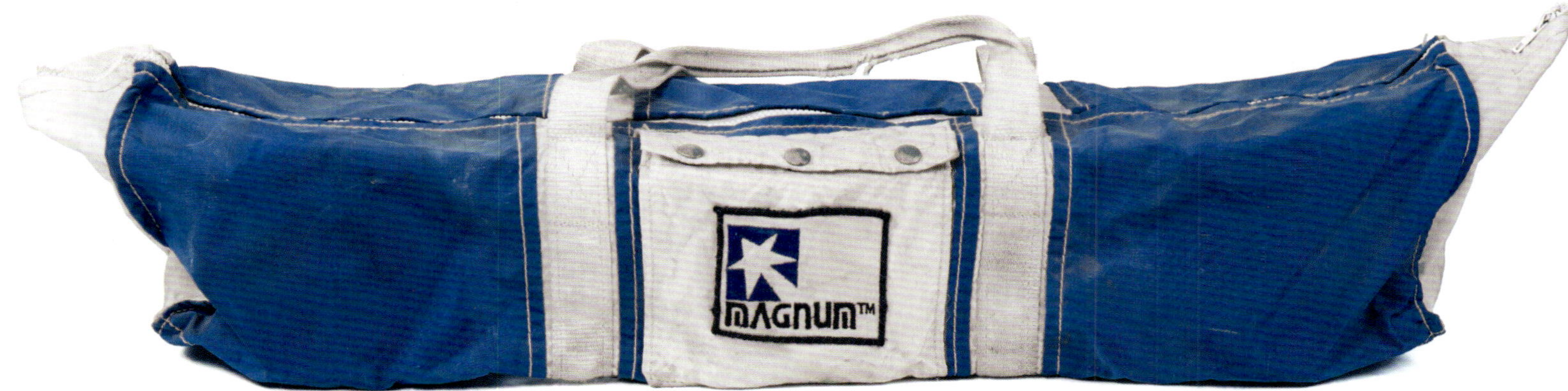
MAGNUM™

HESTER SERIES
HESTER SERIES
WINCHESTER
HESTER SERIES
SHOOTOUT
WINCHESTER
SHOOTOUT
HESTER SERIES
WINCHESTER SHOOTOUT
BOULDER CUP
DEL MAR OPEN PRO
WHITTIER CLASSIC
UPLAND FINALS
HESTER SERIES
HESTER SERIES
SKATE CITY
SUMMER PRO
CLASSIC POOL
WHITTIER
CALIF
HESTER SERIES

HESTER SERIES: THE FUTURE HAS LANDED

Sometimes the future arrives with such sudden force, it might as well have landed overnight. Within a matter of a few months in the mid-1970s, skateboarding cast off its surf-related origins, and entered a new evolutionary trajectory. The paradigm shift affected all areas, including skateboard hardware (urethane wheels, precision bearings, 7-ply boards, skate-specific trucks), safety equipment (skateboard helmets, gloves, knee- and elbow pads with plastic caps), and riding technique (vertical grinds, aerials, edgers). All of these changes compounded in 1978 at the start of the Henry Hester Pro Bowl Series, the world's first vertical pool skateboarding contest tour at parks throughout California. From a history perspective, the Hester Series presented the shape of things to come in terms of vertical maneuvers, skateboard hardware, and dress code.

The future had landed. And it unfolded in skateparks, or more specifically, the kind of vertical pools first introduced into the vernacular of skatepark design at parks such as Concrete Wave in Anaheim and Pipeline in Upland. Organized by professional slalom racer and namesake Henry Hester in cooperation with the International Skateboard Association (ISA), the 1978 Hester Series kicked off in March at Spring Valley's Skateboard Heaven skatepark. With the notable absence of big-ticket names such as Alva, Biniak, Kubo, and Adams, the contest saw 34 contestants square off in four pool skating events: consecutive one-wheelers, longest carve, doubles riding, and freestyle. After Steve Alba won $1,000 in freestyle at the first stop, the series continued at Pipeline skatepark in Upland, Ride-On skatepark in Newark, and ended with Steve Olson winning the overall title at Big O skatepark in Orange, California.

The progression was staggering: At the first stop, standout maneuvers included 360 wall slides, kickturn grinds, edgers - all tricks below or at the edge of the pool. By the time the fourth stop rolled around, the organizers had added a high air event, as aerials and inverts - also called "handplants" - had already gone from cutting edge to status quo. All within a few months! Setting the blueprint for the future of skateboard fashion, the Hester Series introduced the "pro look" of color-coordinated tube socks, padded shorts, pads, gloves, shirts and helmets, proliferated by magazines as the new "fresh" way to dress the part of the progressive professional skateboarder. Behind the scenes, leading pros went out of their way to plan their outfits for the big events: "I laid out all my gear for those contests. It was definitely an effort, a conceptualized effort to put something that would pop at the contests but still work for me and help me win," said pro skateboarder and top competitor Brad Bowman.

More than just color-coordinating their outfits with their pads and skateboard hardware, professionals such as Brad Bowman even cultivated their own signature color patterns. While Bowman was known for rocking blue and yellow and white, skateboard photographer Jim Goodrich noticed that "Steve Cathy took it to extreme with red and yellow." For young amateur skateboarders at the time, the "pro look" became a coveted fashion style, said Steve Caballero: "Steve Olson had that look, Brad Bowman had that look - so I wanted to have that look, too! At one point, I had a Flyaway [helmet], and I had the SIMS gloves, and the Molly's shorts."

SKATEBOARD CLUB OF AMERICA
This club is for you – the skateboard rider of America. SCA, in order to help and promote the art of skateboarding, is offering you the opportunity to buy the Product of the Month® Top performance products including wheels, boards, shorts, helmets, pads and other safety gear – all at reduced prices!
Other benefits available to SCA members will be discounts at local skate parks, discounts at contests and movies. Send $7.00 and we'll rush you your SCA Membership Card. And for joining now, we'll send you a beautiful SCA Color T-Shirt, plus an SCA Decal. Buy the SCA Product of the Month shown in the box below.
THE SCA PRODUCT OF THE MONTH®
A plastic adjustable safety helmet in 5 colors: white, red, blue, orange and yellow. Made of polycarbonate with front to back reinforced recess for maximum strength, protection and style, it has 10 holes allowing free flow ventilation while decreasing helmet weight. The chin strap allows easy size adjustment and is made with double D-rings for positive strap positioning. The interior is shock resistant with comfort pads of urethane foam comfortably conforming to the head and absorbing impact. This is the first of many great products to be offered as the Product of the Month by the SCA. Only $7.95
Suggested Retail $14.95
SCA Member $7.95
Skateboard Club of America
Box 9344, Marina Del Rey, California 90291
☐ Yes, I want to be in the SCA. Enclosed is $7.00 for my Membership. And since I joined now, please rush my SCA Decal and Color T-Shirt. Small ☐ Medium ☐ Large ☐
☐ I am enclosing an additional $7.95 for the SCA super Product of the Month (Calif. residents add 6% sales tax). Helmet Size: Small ☐ Medium ☐ Large ☐ Color: White ☐ Yellow ☐ Orange ☐ Red ☐ Blue ☐
name
address/city
state/zip
circle card used
Cash, check, money order Master Charge B of A (Visa)
Card # Expires
Signature
Postage not incl. Color subject to availability
Skateboard Club of America
Box 9344, Marina Del Rey, California 90291
☐ Yes, I want to be in the SCA. Enclosed is $7.00 for my Membership. And since I joined now, please rush my SCA Decal and Color T-Shirt. Small ☐ Medium ☐ Large ☐
☐ I am enclosing an additional $7.95 for the SCA super Product of the Month (Calif. residents add 6% sales tax). Helmet Size: Small ☐ Medium ☐ Large ☐ Color: White ☐ Yellow ☐ Orange ☐ Red ☐ Blue ☐
name
address/city
state/zip
circle card used
Cash, check, money order Master Charge B of A (Visa)
Card # Expires
Signature
Postage not incl. Color subject to availability
SCA
SKATEBOARD CLUB OF AMERICA®

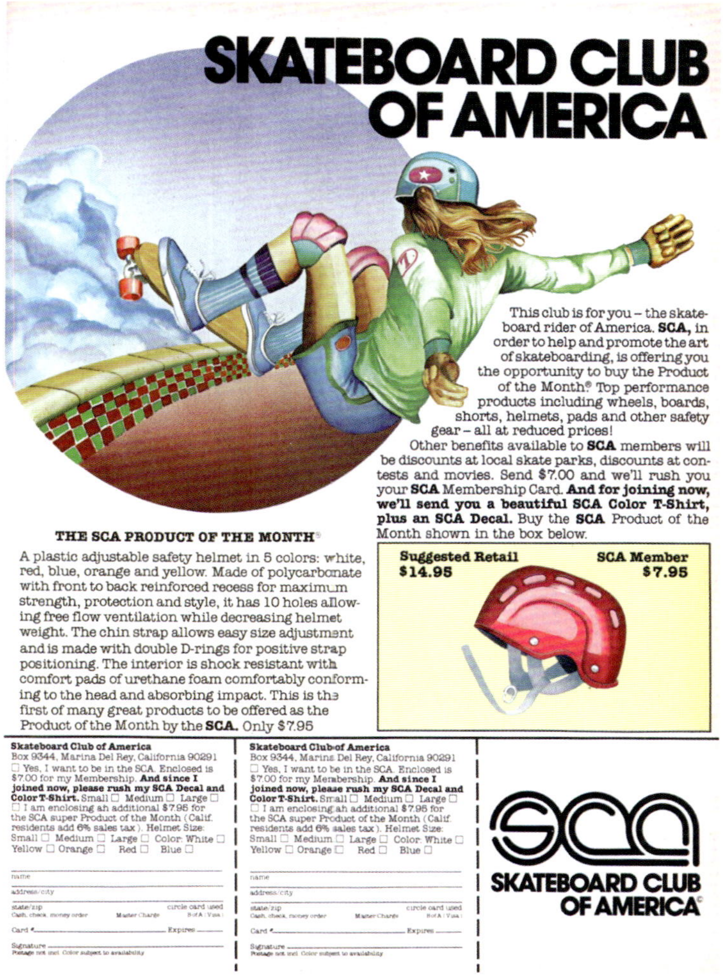

COLOR-MATCHED FROM HEAD TO TOE

The color-coordination craze went deep into detail, all the way to matching the color of wheels with the rest of the outfit. "Sims [skateboards] came out with sets of wheels in different colors at the time, so you could have red and black wheels, for example," said skateboard photographer Ted Terrebonne. At the same time, small touches like sticker placement and the way riders color-matched their outfits also added a sense of individuality. "It was really uniform back then," said pro skateboarder Christian Hosoi, pointing out the message behind cultivating a personal look: "Mine isn't uniform, mine is planned and looks color-coordinated. That is different from a uniform. Color-matched down to the sticker on the tail!"

In its first year, the Hester series still experienced some growing pains on the way to finding the right contest format. As Tom "Wally" Inouye said in his 1978 Skateboard World interview: "They called it a Pro Series, but they turned around and let anybody with 50 bucks enter." Wally also pointed out that, "there were better parks it could have been held at," but nevertheless conceded that the contests "got the ball rolling." The Hester Series would return for a second round in 1979, this time adding stops all over the US, including New York and Colorado, followed by the Gold Cup Series.

For participating pros, the new organized contest format brought an entirely new set of responsibilities and expectations when it came to performing and behaving like "real professionals." Says pro skateboarder Alan Gelfand: "I have these letters from [my board sponsor] telling me I gotta learn inverts and have a compulsory run for the series. And they were saying, 'Alan you can't fool around with a girl under the ramp anymore.'" The times, they were really a-changing...

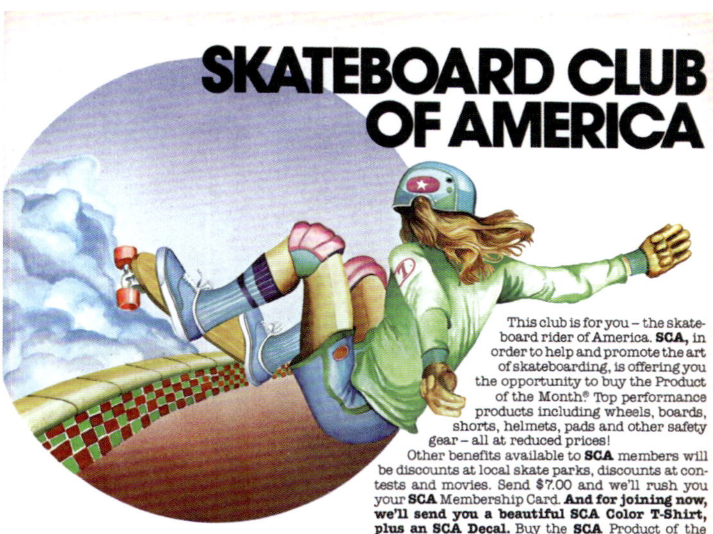

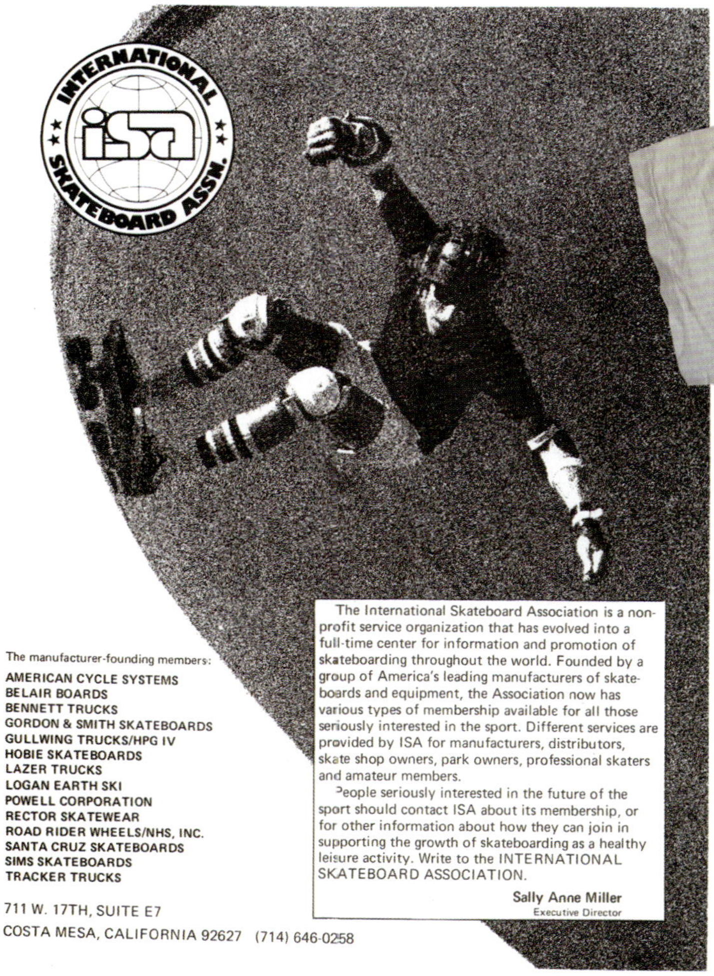
INTERNATIONAL isa SKATEBOARD ASSN.
The manufacturer-founding members:
AMERICAN CYCLE SYSTEMS
BELAIR BOARDS
BENNETT TRUCKS
GORDON & SMITH SKATEBOARDS
GULLWING TRUCKS/HPG IV
HOBIE SKATEBOARDS
LAZER TRUCKS
LOGAN EARTH SKI
POWELL CORPORATION
RECTOR SKATEWEAR
ROAD RIDER WHEELS/NHS, INC.
SANTA CRUZ SKATEBOARDS
SIMS SKATEBOARDS
TRACKER TRUCKS
711 W. 17TH, SUITE E7
COSTA MESA, CALIFORNIA 92627 (714) 646-0258
The International Skateboard Association is a non-profit service organization that has evolved into a full-time center for information and promotion of skateboarding throughout the world. Founded by a group of America's leading manufacturers of skateboards and equipment, the Association now has various types of membership available for all those seriously interested in the sport. Different services are provided by ISA for manufacturers, distributors, skate shop owners, park owners, professional skaters and amateur members.
People seriously interested in the future of the sport should contact ISA about its membership, or for other information about how they can join in supporting the growth of skateboarding as a healthy leisure activity. Write to the INTERNATIONAL SKATEBOARD ASSOCIATION.
Sally Anne Miller
Executive Director

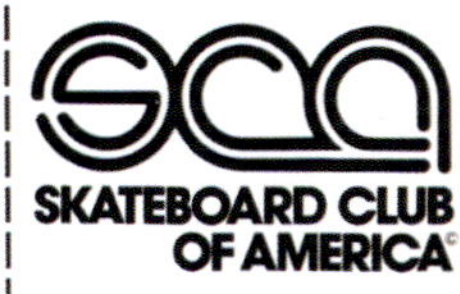

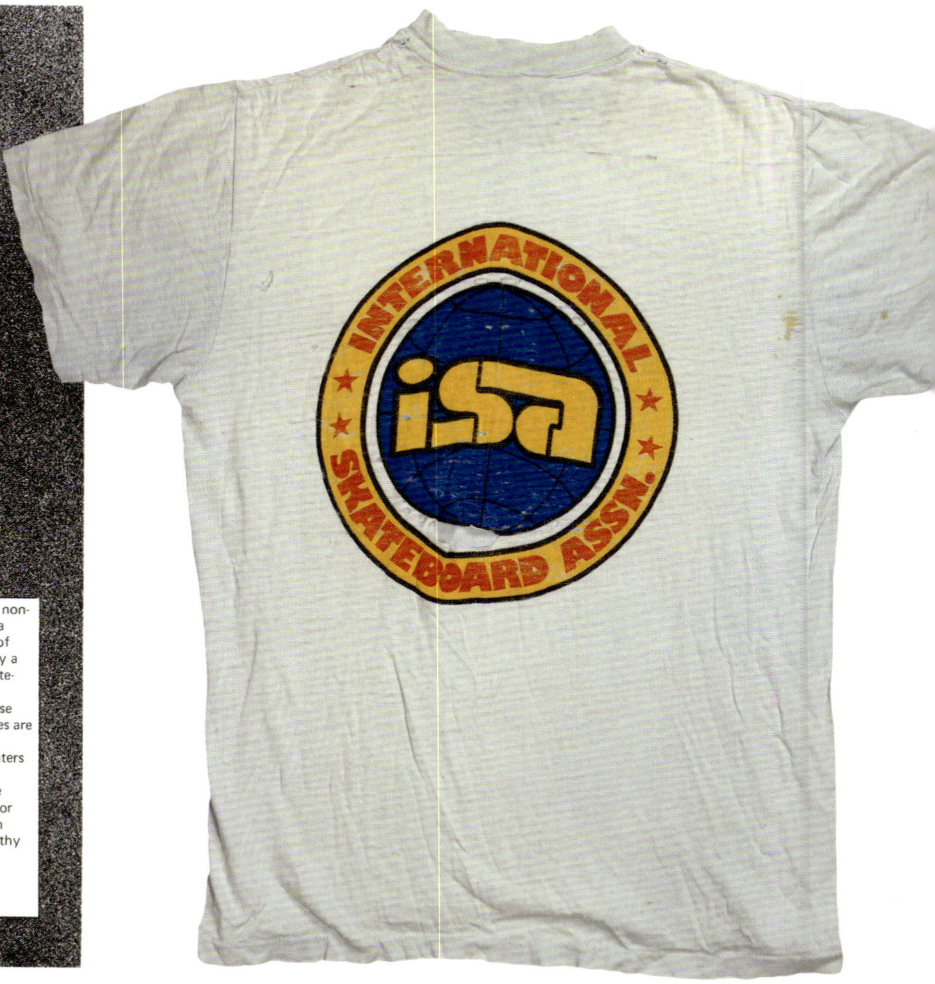
INTERNATIONAL
isa
SKATEBOARD ASSN.

Hester-I.S.A
PRO BOWL
series
Hester-I.S.A
PRO BOWL
series

THIS IS THE END: BYE, BYE SEVENTIES

For the record: Skateboarding would not be what it is today without the 1970s. While most histories of skate culture will point to the 1980s as the period where skateboarding "found itself," the Seventies really created the mold for a self-sustained aesthetic and industry, bigger and better than ever before. The skate business soared to unseen heights during the mid-1970s skateboard boom, as skateboarding enjoyed its second wave of mainstream fame. Early manufacturers like Logan Earth Ski went from backyard tinker shops cranking out handmade boards by the handful to full-fledged production outfits shipping upwards of 5,000 boards per week. Innovations like the urethane wheel, skate-specific truck, precision bearings, and 7-ply boards with kicktails not only created the now-familiar blueprints in skateboard hardware design, but also jumpstarted a cottage industry of specialized parts manufacturers. By the year 1977, skateboarding had come full circle: The business went from dead in the water after the mid-1960s skate boom to resurrecting as a buzzing $650-million-per-year business at peak times.

As the driving force behind it all, skateboarding had something everybody wanted: Style, thrills, an esprit-de-corps among participants, a lifestyle, a sense of progression, and a mentality of pushing the limits. At the height of the 1970s boom, around 40 million people skateboarded across the world, inspired by images of energetic teenagers rolling across California beaches, empty swimming pools, and sprawling concrete wonderlands called skateparks, where hardcore riders commandeered the new frontier of riding technique dressed in matching team outfits and proper safety gear. Because if the 1960s crash had taught the industry one thing, it was that safety had to come first if skateboarding was to win over parents as a "real sport" for their kids to enjoy. The formula was working: Pro rider Stacy Peralta appeared on the day's biggest TV show, *Charlie's Angels*. Hollywood produced the skate epic Skateboard, while Vans shoes emerged as de rigueur footwear for the counter culture movement. Countless TV commercials used skateboarding to push products with an extra edge of California cool, and the Pepsi Cola company sponsored a team of top-notch riders, touring the country as evangelists for skateboard safety and sportsmanship.

Speaking of sportsmanship, skateboarding's athletic progression between 1976 and 1979 can hardly be overstated: Within a number of years, the avant-garde of pool skating laid the foundation for modern-day vertical riding, practically in the blink of an eye. In 1977, Tony Alva landed the first documented aerial on a skateboard in a backyard pool, opening Pandora's Box for the rest of the skate world. Soon after, the first skateparks included pools into their range of riding terrain. One year later, the first pro pool riding competition – 1978's Henry Hester Series – saw competitors roll out newly invented trick creations at every stop. By 1979, the modern day version of skateboarding had landed: aerials, grinds, inverts and slides had become the state-of-the-art in pool riding. "It was a good time because it was really experimental. Like a four-year experimental prototype phase," said pro skateboarder Brad Bowman, revered as one of the most stylish and fashionable riders of his era. On that note, amidst all this progression, skateboarding was not just growing by leaps and bounds in terms of athleticism, but also found its swagger on the fashion and attitude front.

And the attitude was – for the most part – exclusive, even hostile to outsiders. Skateboarding was for skateboarders, not for everybody. Against the grain. The mid-1970s marked the start of an ongoing subversive, rebellious streak in skate culture, pioneered by the likes of LA's Dogtown skateboarding movement and its gritty, street style aesthetic fostered by underground artist Craig R. Stecyk III. Revolution, counter culture, Zen, and so much style – the late Seventies unleashed the powers of rock 'n' roll into the skate arena, transforming everything from skate advertising to product design. Pointing out the Tony Alva "Leopard" graphic skateboard, former Zephyr teamrider Nathan Pratt said: "The leopard board with the triple Alva [logo] deck, that's maybe the best board ever made, graphically. That is the apex. No one has made better stuff than that." And perhaps, no one has lived it up and struck poses like skateboarders in the 1970s – at least no one before in history ever had – who rubbed shoulders with the biggest music and film celebrities of the day on nights out in Hollywood to party like rock stars, rock like party stars.

REBEL YELL

Aside from skateboard pros turned into fashion peacocks and nightlife legends, the 1970s brought a major discernible shift on a cultural level: A schism between skateboarding and surfing. The old rules were crumbling. Before the late 1970s, all of skateboarding's pioneers had been surfers first, and skateboarders second. The pioneers hit up concrete waves on their skateboards with a head full of surf moves and a layer of sea salt caked on their skin from their morning session in the line-up. And that influenced everything, from the maneuvers all the way to dress codes. "In the beginning, skateboarders were dressing like beach people, the way surfers dressed. Because we were all coastline dwellers," said Brad Bowman. "Then we started needing to segregate ourselves from the whole surfing thing because we were skateboarders, and the music scene came in around the same time."

The shift was hard to accept for some of the day's pros. "It all started at the beach. Skateboarding came from surfing and everything came from that. At least for us. But in the seventies, people started to become skaters," said 1970s pro and graphic artist Wes Humpston, adding: "Anywhere away from the ocean where you could buy a skateboard and go skate. They didn't have the surf culture anymore, they just had the skate culture." Pro skateboarder Christian Hosoi, arguably the most fashionable skateboarder of all time, also remembers the response to the shift in skate demographics: "It was the transition from surfers from the '60s to the '70s to having people who didn't surf, but who skated. Kooks! Those guys were like idiots. They don't even know anything. Don't forget your roots, where did it come from? That just goes with the things that have rich value to it."

BROKEN BONES

Once manufacturers began putting skulls on skateboards, the industry was definitely not in surf land anymore. In 1978, Powell-Peralta Skateboards started a new trend by introducing the first skeleton-themed artwork on a pro board for Ray "Bones" Rodriguez: The iconic skull and sword graphic created by artist Vernon Courtland Johnson (VCJ) became a big hit with consumers and radically contrasted what other companies were offering in terms of graphic designs at the time. Screen-printed on T-shirts, VCJ's morbid graphics soon became a calling card of the company, made famous around the world by the "Bones Brigade" team, an elite line-up of the world's best skateboarders handpicked from 1979 onwards by Stacy Peralta and business partner, influential skateboard engineer George Powell. Meanwhile, broken bones continued to be a problem – just like in the 1960s. The United States Consumer Protection Agency reported 325,000 skateboard-related injuries at the end of 1978.

As the mainstream press rekindled its "dangerous fad" portrayal of skateboarding, skate park operators found it increasingly hard to secure liability coverage. "Insurance rates started going high. What we had to do at Big O - and they also did at Skateopia - is we joined up with the Boy Scouts and combined memberships. So when you signed up for the skate park, you were a Boy Scout now. That way, we had that multi-million dollar insurance for the Boy Scouts of America covering us skaters. It was a good idea but i don't know what happened to it," said skateboarder and rapper Gerry "Skatemaster Tate" Hurtado, who worked at Big O skatepark in Orange, California in the late 1970s.

But it was a losing battle. Many skate park proprietors found themselves pressured by liability lawsuits from angry parents and injured riders. Most of the over 400 skateparks operating in the U.S. in the late 1970s were forced to shut down, with few exceptions including Marina Del Rey, Del Mar and Upland Pipeline. As the bulldozers rolled in to eradicate thousands of square miles of concrete wonderland, skateboarding hit a new low. "It just died. I know people sued skateboard parks. But it became that you needed a skateboard park or a pool [to skate], so when skateboard parks started shutting down, the sport was losing momentum. But there was also the economy - a recession had hit. People were trying to keep their head above water and that probably had a lot to do with it. So the skateboard parks were done and so was skateboarding," said pro skateboarder Steve Olson, one of the most progressive pool riders of his era.

ROCK BOTTOM

The mass extinction of skateparks is considered the final nail in the coffin for skateboarding's second wave, at least in the official version. But some sources suggest a different scenario: While skateboarding's core participants had their eyes on the stellar progression of park skating - progressing to all-new heights around 1978 - the skateboard industry, according to statistics quoted in a 1978 *Los Angeles Times* story, may have already been a dead man walking. The numbers provided by Money magazine suggest that the industry may have peaked in 1977 at $650 million in annual sales, and year-on-year sales had already dropped a devastating 50 percent by mid-1978. These numbers suggest: The mainstream had turned its back on skateboarding. Why? Perhaps the rapid progression of riding technique at skateparks had raised the bar too high, and many newcomers found skateboarding too difficult as to warrant continued interest. Visualizing this twisted correlation in a graph, the LEVEL OF RIDING TECHNIQUE shoots up in a steep curve, while LEVEL OF MAINSTREAM interest plummets at a dramatic rate.

So while the evolution of skateboard tricks continued, only a small, core circle followed the trajectory. Park skating garnered a negative reputation for being "elitist" - not to mention expensive because of park fees and required equipment - so average consumers moved on to BMX or roller skates as their next big thing. (Business lesson for the future: Always keep it fun.)
In the process, skateboarding's dress code - the shorts, the graphic tees, the "California look" - had fallen out of fashion among the broad public. "My take is that skateboarding had not yet become mainstream enough so that the fashion was able to survive. It must have completely crossed over into a mainstream environment to fully take off. Skateboarding is a small niche environment," said 1960s pro skateboarder and Powell-Peralta graphic

designer Cris Dawson. As the market entered a downward cycle, leading skateboard manufacturers found themselves strapped with unsold inventory and stunted demand from shops. In 1979, Santa Cruz Skateboards went from $20 million in annual sales during the previous year to a mere $400,000. The same happened to other top brands, and the resulting belt tightening encompassed all levels of the industry. Companies downsized, laid off staff, cut back production. The skateboard media also consolidated and cut back. "In late 1979, Skateboarder magazine cut the regular salaries for photographers. So we were only making money off published photos," said skateboard photographer Jim Goodrich.

When the music stopped, many of the day's big ticket pro skateboarders found themselves without a chair. "You're World Champion and Skater of the Year and suddenly it doesn't matter. 'Now what are you gonna do?!' And you're like, 'Maybe I can enjoy it for a little bit?' But no, you weren't allowed to enjoy it," said Steve Olson. Dealing a double punch, the severe crash of the skate business coincided with an all-out economic crisis. "Everything went down when [President] Jimmy Carter came to office. They started rationing the gas, so you could only fill up your car on alternating days. Gasoline prices went from 16 cents to over a buck a gallon. It killed the car industry and the skateboard industry went under as well," said Steve Olson's father, Dave Olson, who helped his son start the Molly's shorts brand.

BACK TO THE UNDERGROUND

But no matter how severe skateboarding's fall from grace had been, those involved in the industry knew: This was NOT a case of history repeating. This was not the 1965 crash all over again. Because this time, skateboarding had already gone viral across the globe. And as opposed to the mid-1960s, when skateboards were still rickety toys on steel wheels, skate hardware had advanced into the space age, into radical territory. And some riders were way too hooked to let it go. Everywhere around the world, skateboarders had caught the bug, pushing the limits of how high and fast they could go on a skateboard - and none of them cared whether their sport was "trendy" or "popular." As parks closed down, wooden half pipes in backyards became an underground refuge and the new frontier for riding. On that note, it's worth noticing that the first plans for skater-built halfpipes were distributed by the thousands starting in 1975 by Tom Stewart's company Rampage Ramps. After the great skatepark purge, these Rampage blueprints became survival aids for a new underground vert scene.

Meanwhile, in Hermosa Beach, California, another phenomenon started brewing around 1979: On the sidewalks along the beach promenade, a young skateboarder by the name of Steve Rocco was rubbing shoulders with some of the era's most innovative riders, including Ty Page, Chris Chaput, and Curt Lindgren, who invented the kickflip. Out of this innovative climate, and the lack of skatepark terrain, Rocco threw together his own style of riding, soon to be known as street skating. "There were no pools or ramps around here, so I started doing pool skating tricks on curbs and benches here in Hermosa Beach around 1979," said Steve Rocco, who would gather large crowds of onlookers with home-made obstacles like the Rocco Ramp. "We had a four-by-four plank of wood leaned against the wall to ride up in front of a huge crowd by the Hermosa Beach Pier." True to the nature of street skating, this takeover of public infrastructure soon attracted attention from the police, who informed Rocco: "We are enforcing the No Skateboarding law." To which Rocco replied: "Good, tell me about the other laws you are not enforcing - so I can break those!"

The new anti-establishment, underground aesthetic of skateboarding also marked the end of the flashy, athletic dress codes of the 1970s. "From 1979 onwards, they just killed off the team uniforms and the whole thing stopped where all skaters had to look alike. It became more self-governed from there. Plus, the entire idea of presenting skaters as a team was the single biggest mistake of the early years anyhow, also from a fashion perspective!" said pro skateboarder Claus Grabke. As a side effect of the downturn, the economic crash wiped the slate clean for a new style of skateboard apparel to emerge. "In the 1970s, it was all disco and people dressed up like *Saturday Night Fever*. In the 1980s, it was the exact opposite.

You were not trying to pick up on chicks, you were just trying to hang with your buddies and be gnarly. That's where a lot of punk fashion came from," said pro skateboarder Dave Duncan. Initially rejected by the majority of pro skaters, the rugged vibe of punk rock became one of the defining aesthetics as skateboarding turned a page on the glamorous Seventies, and rolled into an uncertain future, flipping double middle fingers at the world.

Photo: Christian Lepanto

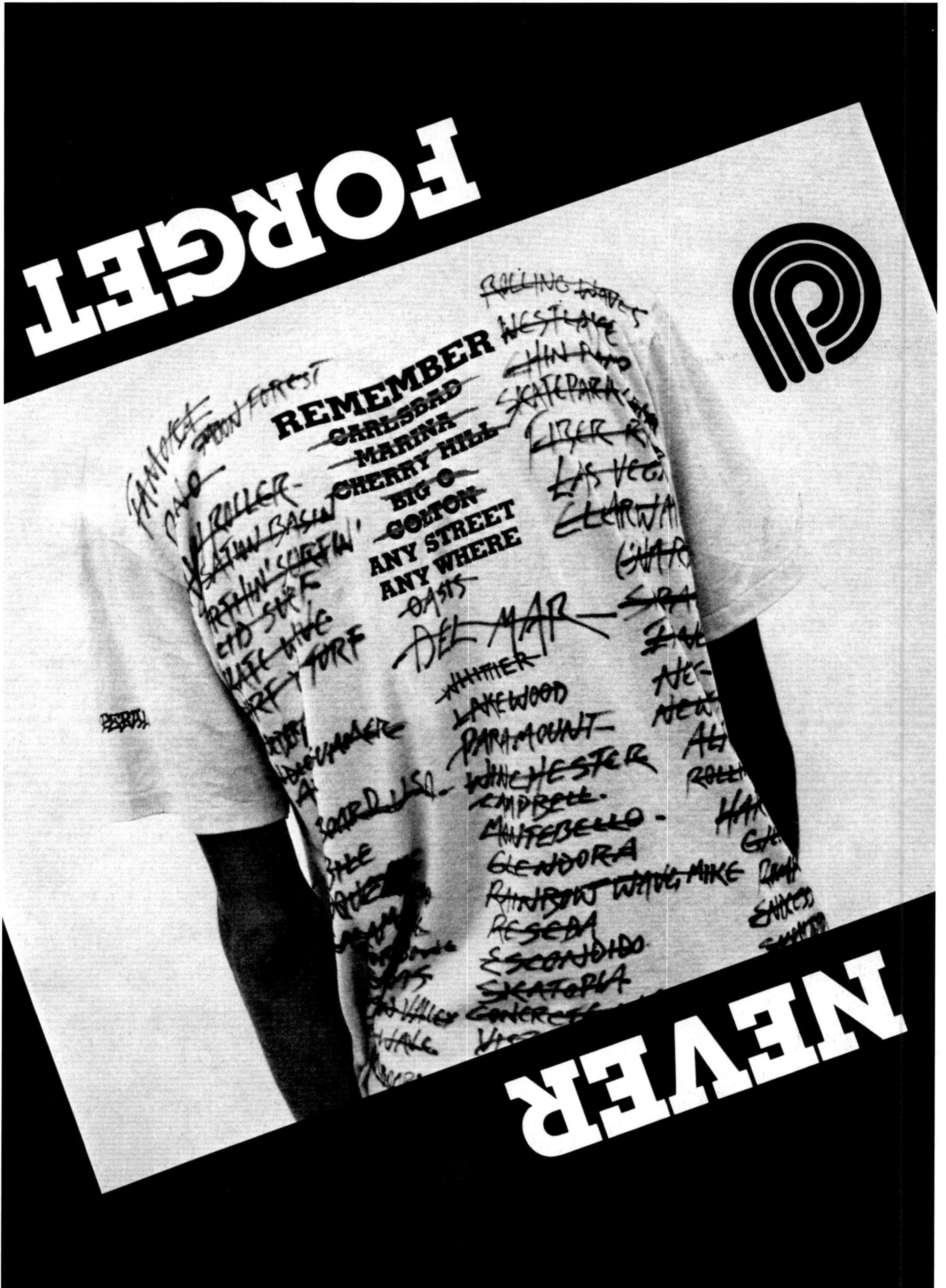
NEVER
FORGET
REMEMBER
CARLSBAD
MARINA
CHERRY HILL
BIG O
COLTON
ANY STREET
ANY WHERE
OASIS
DEL MAR
LAKEWOOD
PARAMOUNT
WINCHESTER
MONTEBELLO
GLENDORA
RESEDA
ESCONDIDO
SKATOPIA

3 THE EIGHTIES

1980s: BACK TO THE UNDERGROUND

Ask anyone who was there: The 1980s were a magical time to be alive, especially as a youngster. Every day brought new toys, trends and fads for kids to get into, including Rubik's Cubes, BMX, karaoke, Pac-Man, Swatch watches, breakdancing, MTV and not to forget a slew of crazy new hair care products for even crazier hairstyles. Technological progress kept unlocking magical new gadgets and milestone inventions – including home video, portable audio players, home computers, and video games – that would transform popular culture forever. Skateboarding was about to join the party, but first needed to pull itself out of the gutter. The late-1970's death of the skate park era had left skateboarding in a slump. Attendance numbers were down from the millions into to the six-digits again. Manufacturers had abandoned the sport, and the number of paid professional skateboarders had dropped from 175 at the height of the 1970s skate boom to only 15 pros at the start of the 1980s.

As skate park after skate park was bulldozed into oblivion, skateboarding shifted from concrete pools into wooden backyard half-pipes. Legendary backyard ramps, where skateboarding not only survived but thrived in terms of riding technique, included Mike Chantry's halfpipe in Tahoe, California. "We built the Tahoe halfpipe in 1982 and I had 20 to 30 people staying over every weekend, everyone skated the ramp. It featured the first escalators ever seen on a vert ramp and over-the-channel coping," said skateboard photographer Mike Chantry. Private ramps popped up all over the U.S., many built from "borrowed" materials. Says Chantry: "The local lumberyard didn't have a fence, so you would always see kids by the side of the road carry two-by-fours."

It turned out, this low-key aesthetic would make skateboarding more approachable, and in the long run more attractive to mass audiences than the elitist arena of concrete skate parks. Street skating, in particular, would help democratize skateboarding into something that kids could enjoy anytime, anywhere – even if the next ramp or skate park was miles away. Backyard pools remained in high demand, shared within the close-knit skateboard scene like buried treasures. Speaking of close-knit, pro skateboarder Brad Bowman looks back fondly on the camaraderie in those days: "It was such a small community at that point that if someone was riding a backyard pool, you wanted to be their friend. Because number one, they had a skateboard. And number two, they might know of some more pools you didn't know about." Skateboard clothing designer Chris "Slappy" Sutherland, who started skateboarding in 1981, remembers: "Being a skateboarder and having a skateboard meant something at the time. It made me realize that I was different from the general public... heck, we even used to get beat up for it!"

BACK IN THE PUBLIC EYE

On its way back into the public spotlight, skateboarding received a considerable boost from Hollywood film studios. In 1980, cinemas around the world began screening the late 1970s production Skateboard Madness directed by Julian Pena. The plot follows skateboard photographer "Mellow Cat" on a magazine assignment to chronicle the antics of skateboard greats such as Tony Alva, Stacy Peralta und Alan "Ollie" Gelfand. Next to documenting spectacular moves such as the first aerials and full-pipe rides, the film succeeded in capturing the carefree and dynamic lifestyle behind skateboarding; including pro tours, backyard pool sessions and the constant hunt for new, skateable terrain. By portraying skateboarding as more than just a sport, but a unique and fun-loving culture, *Skateboard Madness* inspired an entire new generation to get on board. The movie also featured California punk band, The Surf Punks, and foreshadowed the rise of punk rock in skateboarding. New wave pioneers Devo enjoyed a healthy following among skateboarders, and in 1980, pro skater David Hackett appeared in Skateboarder magazine carving a pool in full Devo-style overalls and sunglasses.

The prototypical "skater dude" of the time was epitomized on the silver screen by Sean Penn's character Jeff Spicoli in the 1982 smash hit *Fast Times at Ridgemont High*. Spicoli's slacker cool and fashion style instantly struck a nerve as a "look" that people liked to emulate – whether they skated or not. The checkered Vans slip-on sneakers worn by Spicoli would become the company's best-selling shoes of all times after *Fast Times* hit cinemas, and board sales at skate shops also began picking up again, as skateboarders kept experimenting with DIY-clothing designs, screen printing, and looks borrowed from punk and rock 'n' roll culture.

THE NEW BIBLE OF SKATEBOARDING

Two new skate-specific magazines broadcast the latest developments in riding technique to readers around the world: The attitude and style-driven *Thrasher* magazine – nowadays often called the "New Testament" of skateboarding – was founded in 1981 by Eric Swenson and Fausto Vitello in San Francisco. Initially started to promote Swenson and Vitello's company Independent Trucks, *Thrasher* would grow to become a defining force in hardcore skate culture under the ethos "Skate and Destroy." When skateboarding started trending again around 1984, the magazine became the cultural blueprint for the movement, combining skating, lifestyle, and music into one gnarly package. "There was an explosion of skateboarding, and *Thrasher* was supplying a vision of what skateboarding looked like to millions around the world," said pro skateboarder Don Brown.

But the gnarly vision also found its critics. As a counterforce to *Thrasher's* aggressive vibe, *Transworld Skateboarding* magazine was started in Southern California in 1983 by Larry Balma, owner of Tracker Trucks, together with Peggy Cozens. The first issue featured an article titled "Skate and Create," in which Cozens noted: "I have become increasingly concerned about a new skate attitude being pushed on skaters: Skate and Destroy." In response to the rebellious lifestyle advocated by *Thrasher, Transworld* emphasized the athletic, creative aspects of skateboarding.

The cultural significance of skateboard magazines, together with their impact on skateboard apparel styles, can hardly be overstated. Photographers exerted an immense influence on what riders would wear on magazine photo shoots, which then in turn influenced readers to wear the same. "I'd see photographers like Grant [Brittain] tell skaters, 'Can you wear a red shirt today?' Because of the sky and the way the colors popped," said photographer Dave Swift. Speaking of color-pop, the brightly-colored Eighties found their perfect medium in a style of 35mm film from Japan: "Fuji Velvia overtook Kodachrome, once I discovered how good Fuji Velvia was I shot that all the time. It was just so accentuated, the colors were just so exaggerated. The colors would pop, and for printing it was perfect," said Grant Brittain, who in 1983 contributed skateboard photos to the premiere issue of *TransWorld SKATEboarding* magazine and would serve as Photo Editor and Senior Photographer for decades.

Progressive sports, people, music and way more
ACTION NOW
$2.00
OCTOBER 1981
VOL. 8, NO. 3
SkateBoarding:
WHAT HAPPENED?
WHO'S TO BLAME??
CAN IT SURVIVE???
Inside:
FREEBOARDING GETS WILD!
Fashion: THE CHIC "G.Q." LOOK
Supercross: BARNETT TAKES L.A. AND THE SERIES
Skate Contest: EAST MEETS WEST AT FLORIDA'S KONA PRO

SOUL SEARCHING

On a cultural level, skate magazines helped the growing skateboard community build an identity. "As a skater, you dressed a little bit differently than everyone else, and all of a sudden you saw someone in a magazine that was similar – you felt like you were part of something!" said Chris "Slappy" Sutherland, adding: "Skateboarding was a shift, you said, 'Now I'm in control! If I fall down, I pick myself up.' And that's vastly different from being raised to be a society of good consumers. It's about being creators, producers – people who take charge!" As far as skateboard style went, the period marked a free-for-all; a time of undiluted experimentation and soul searching. Pro skateboarder Gary Scott Davis aka GSD remembers: "I introduced fashion concepts from inside my head into my own personal world of skateboarding, which definitely never started any trends! Around 1980, I wore a long sleeve sweatshirt with one arm cut off completely at the shoulder. I don't know what the hell I was thinking. 'Hey, look at me! I'm different!'"

The skateboard industry offered little by ways of skateboard apparel in those hunger years, when most of the companies still standing after the economic crash focused on producing hardgoods such as decks, trucks, and wheels to keep the culture rolling. "For the first couple of years in the 1980s, there wasn't really any specific skate fashion. You either had old Mad Rats [shorts] or you found stuff at a thrift store," said J. Grant Brittain, whose long-time colleague Dave Swift agreed: "Around the time skate fashion was kind of coming into punk rock, which was clothes brought in from thrift stores, or Duane [Peters] wearing bermudas."

But regardless of what style skateboarders were rocking, what mattered most was that they kept the faith, and kept skating. The rest was yet to be decided. "People were trying the right look and what skateboarding was about. Whether it was a surf thing, or a punk thing, or street or vert," said pro skateboarder and Alva Posse member Dave Duncan, adding: "It was cool to see all the fashion trends as skating grew in the 1980s."

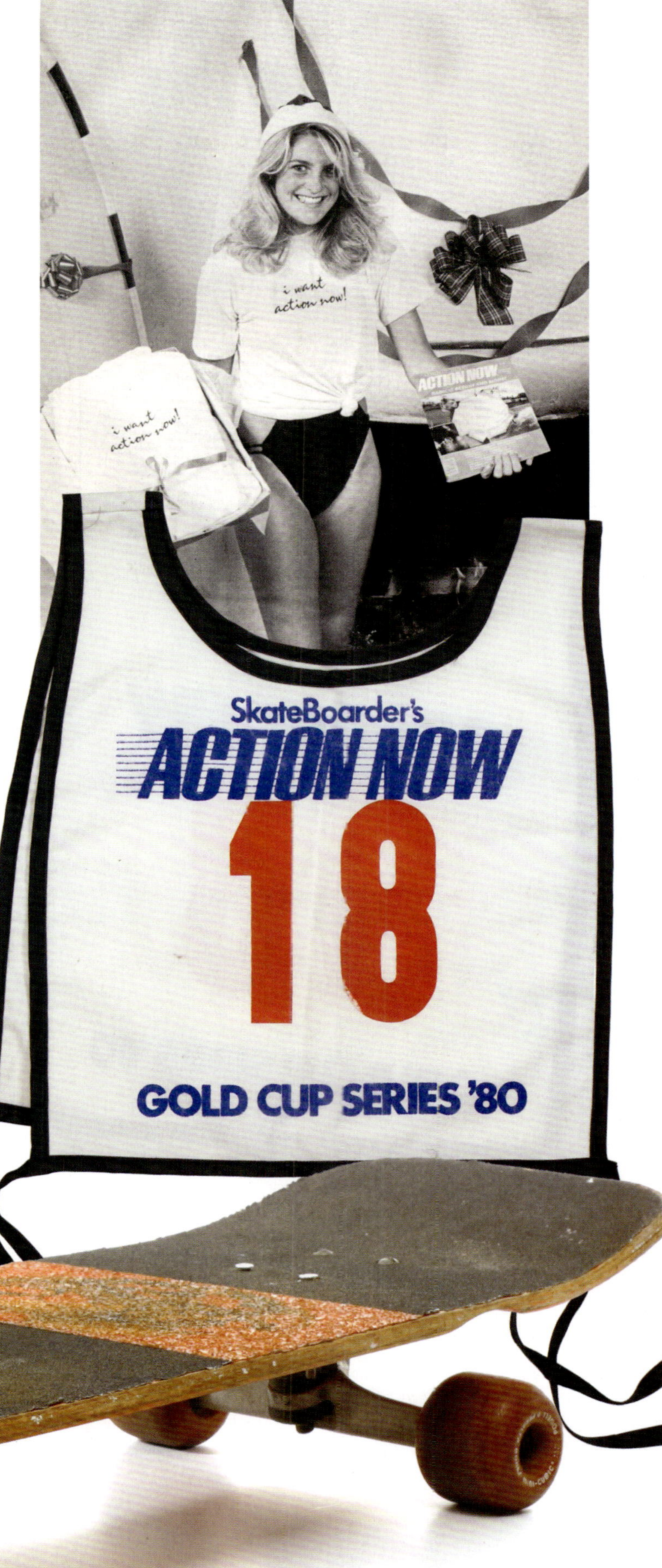

ACTION NOW: WHOLE WIDE WORLD OF SPORTS

Desperate times call for desperate measures. Magazine advertising budgets were first to feel the burn when the skateboarding sales market imploded in 1978. At first, *SkateBoarder* Magazine as the day's largest publication, featuring era-defining photography by, Craig R. Stecyk III, Glen E. Friedman, James Cassimus, Craig Fineman, Jim Goodrich, Ted Terrebonne, and others, responded with internal restructuring efforts to cut costs. In 1979, the publication got rid of "retainers" for its staff photographers, who from then on would only be paid for published photos. But that only helped forestall the inevitable. In 1980, the publishers behind *SkateBoarder* invited leading skateboard industry representatives to a meeting for the launch of a new editorial concept to keep the glossy well manicured and designed magazine in print. *Action Now* would branch out adding sports that were on the rise to mainstream fame such as BMX, Snowboarding and rollerskating, combined with a majority of skateboarding into one single, monthly publication starting with the August 1980 issue.

In a time before the cliche'd terms 'action' sports or 'alternative' sports were even created, before anything like the X Games, *Action Now* presented all of that, ahead of its time. In fact their mixed "extreme sports" angle created the blueprint for many later successful print magazine titles such *WARP, Strength, STANCE, Heckler, Super-X, LoDown* and others, as well as the ESPN television formula behind the X-Games. Despite obvious benefits from a business perspective they were banking on, the magazine's cross-over concept missed the mark with skateboarding's increasingly non-commercial, hardcore culture. "When skateboarding died and all the skate parks closed, it all went underground. *SkateBoarder* Magazine was going out of business and then *Action Now* came out, which had BMX… and all kinds of weird sports," said 1980s pro skateboarder Dave Duncan. Skateboarding still featured prominently in the premier August 1980 issue, including a Stacy Peralta interview, Gold Cup contest series preview, and a look behind the scenes of Devo's "*Freedom of Choice*" video shoot. But it only took a few issues of *Action Now* before the formula started looking cheesy, as skate content declined. "About 75% of the advertisers were skateboarding companies, and they were getting bummed because only 25% of the content was actually skateboarding!" said Dave Duncan.

EXTREME SPORTS 1.0

Looking back, the straw that broke the camel's back: "There was this horrible moment everyone remembers when there was a one-and-a-half page spread of a person jumping a horse over a some boulders on a beach. And everyone freaked out! They really were just trying to find advertisers to pay for this magazine." said photographer Glen E. Friedman. Mixing the equestrian scene with skateboarding did not go over well with core practitioners, or even some of the contributors such as Friedman and Stecyk who were up in arms. *Action Now* featured sports related to beach culture (where skateboarding originated) like cruiser bikes, and entire articles on BMX, early snowboarding, and music. Putting his finger on the magazine's biggest shortcoming, Friedman offered: "All these articles were watered down and written for a broader audience. And we had discussions where I told them that they still needed to keep it gritty and real, hardcore. Because even when people are not in the hard core, they like to read about the hard core. And they didn't. That's why it failed in my opinion, too watered down." Watered down or not, it's important to note that although the amount of skateboarding featured in *Action Now* was dwindling, it was quality coverage with an impact. "It was highly influential, most of the change that was going on in terms of tricks was going on in these issues. The stuff that skaters like Neil Blender or Cab were doing, it showed what was going on," said skateboard photographer Dave Swift, adding: "I was super bummed, because it would have only two, three [skate] tricks in the issue – but we soaked it up." For the record, photo editor "King James" Cassimus points out: "There was always skateboarding in the magazine and there was never an issue of Action Now that didn't feature skateboarding, even when there was virtually no skateboarding industry support." Ultimately, frustrations with *Action Now*'s extended focus on non-skate content inspired two counter-movements within the skateboard scene: First of all, *Action Now* unwittingly jump-started the DIY culture of home-made skate zines that soon began popping up at ramps and skate spots across the U.S. and places like Europe and Australia. And secondly, skateboard manufacturers decided that instead of blowing money on advertising in *Action Now,* they might as well get into publishing their own pure-play skateboarding titles. "Companies were saying, 'Why are we paying all this money to advertise in *Action Now*? Independent had just come out with their trucks and Santa Cruz [skateboards] was getting big. And they needed a magazine to promote their take on skateboarding culture, so that's how *Thrasher* came out," said Dave Duncan. So although it was discontinued after two short years in 1982, the failure that was *Action Now* inspired the birth of *Thrasher* magazine, which in turn eventually inspired *Transworld Skateboarding.*

AHEAD OF ITS TIME

In the bigger picture, the concept behind *Action Now* - namely clustering skateboarding with BMX, snowboarding, Freestyle bike riding, cross country country Mountain bike riding, rollerskating, and surfing among other activities - preceded the "action sports" approach behind the X Games by a solid 15 years. It was way ahead of the curve in many ways. The problem was that it wasn't the right time and people had such a strong bond to the original skateboarding " Bible", *SkateBoarder* Magazine. *Action Now* also tried to keep the scene alive by supporting major skateboard competitions such as 1980's Gold Cup Series events, dressing competitors in numbered bibs featuring the *Action Now* logo. As a fashionable gift to subscribers, the magazine offered single-color print logo tees with the magazine logo accompanied by the slogan, "i want action now!" The magazine also shared fashion advice from leading pros, including Steve Olson's primers on punk and rockabilly style as well as Stacy Peralta's Wear & Tear column, encouraging readers to break free from the mainstream's "uniform culture" by adopting vintage and military surplus pieces such as bowling shirts, "Bermuda" shorts, camouflage cargos, and skydiving pants. (Fashion designers, find that article, now!)

"King James" reminds us "One has to keep in mind the home grown Surfer Publications (who started *SkateBoarder*) had been around for decades, they had a deep love for skateboarding, and played a big part in its growth, so all the struggles incorporating other "action" and music in the magazine was just to try and keep it afloat. In the end, the magazine that promised "Progressive sports, people, and way more!" hit the wall with its February 1982 issue. "The industry went down and then the magazines followed. They went from over a million readers [as *SkateBoarder*] in July 1978 to under 100,000 readers. Because the skateboarding industry took a big dive" said Cassimus. Knowing that the end was near, *Action Now*'s editorial staff decided to go out in style and created a final issue with a heavy focus on hardcore skateboarding and culture: The cover featured an action shot of pro rider and artist Neil Blender, and Black Flag's iconic "bars" graphic, while the issue's content focused on backyard halfpipes, a full article on the punk band Black Flag, and snowboarding. Knowing that it was the last issue, the contributors all pushed going out with some integrity. Stories like the one on Black Flag made waves, and got them, who were primarily a Southern California band, known all across the country and internationally."

Many skateboarders welcomed the magazine's demise outwardly and still blame *Action Now* for branching out into non-core territory, but they would forever miss its design and quality that wasn't to be seen in a Skate publication for years to come. Glen E. Friedman said: "People were really disappointed and let down when *SkateBoarder* magazine left them in the dust with these other sports. Including me! Truth is *SkateBoarder* didn't leave them, they really tried to hold it together, but the industry couldn't afford it." According to Friedman, the editorial team briefly worked on relaunching their magazine under the original title in 1984, but ended up being shut down by a storm of animosity from new industry published competitor magazines. "People were stoked that the bible was coming back when I handed out *SkateBoarder* stickers again at a sparsely attended Upland contest, but it wasn't to be." End of story? Not quite, as *SkateBoarder* Magazine ultimately returned in the late 1990s as a skateboard-only title featuring the day's leading photographers and pro riders, plus some of the best writing ever seen in an action sports publication since the original in the 70's. But that's a chapter for Volume Two of this book.

DUANE PETERS: MASTER OF DISASTER

In the taxonomy of skateboard culture, Duane Peters is the kind of rider often labelled as an outlier. The kind of rider who stands alone, separate from the rest of the pack. The kind of rider that only comes along once every generation, set to blaze his own trail in terms of style and riding technique instead of falling in line with the others. Spearheading a new guard of pros in the early 1980s, Duane Peters forever changed skateboarding with the tricks he invented and the hard-charging style he cultivated. And skateboarding, in turn, changed him. Every bone broken, every inch of his body covered in scars and tattoos, his front teeth missing, Duane Peters is a walking testament to his ongoing skateboarding journey.

When Duane Peters barged onto the pool competition circuit as a gifted amateur in the late 1970s, they called him the "Master of Disaster" for his balls-to-the-wall style, always on the edge of losing control. (Landing an aerial at a late 1970s pool contest, Duane hung up on the lip with his front truck, still riding away and living to tell the story.) A fierce competitor and early adopter of punk rock culture, Peters became feared among his peers for psyching out opponents and dishing out abuse at skate events. "Duane would spit on certain people, like Tony Hawk," said pro skateboarder Eddie Elguera. Through it all, Duane "Nightmare" Peters made himself impossible to dismiss or ignore by virtue of the many tricks he contributed to skateboarding, including the Indy Air, and a new class of moves involving the deck or platform of the ramp, such as the Acid Drop, sweeper, layback rollout, and invert revert.

Beyond these groundbreaking tricks, the name Duane Peters represented style and attitude, best captured in a 1980 Skateboarder Magazine photograph shot by Ted Terrebonne: "My favorite photo of Duane Peters to this day is him just charging down the street. The striped socks, the Converse shoes, the Indy sticker on the truck, the short hair - from that moment on, everyone had to dye their hair," said pro skateboarder and musician Claus Grabke. Together with his Santa Cruz Skateboards teammate Steve Olson as partner-in-crime, Duane Peters injected punk rock culture into skateboarding, ready or not. "Duane Peters played a huge part in setting up this Fuck the World punk rock kind of attitude," said pro skateboarder Don Brown. Still skateboarding after hitting a few hard yards in life, Duane Peters has yet to slow down in his ongoing pro career, although the tattoo across his neck reads: KILL ME I NEED THE REST.

OVER THE EDGE

Duane Peters first picked up skateboarding in the early 1970s in Newport Beach, California, where he lived with his father after his parents had split up. Having cut his teeth sidewalk surfing and learning the basics, quickly, Peters got in on the front end of the backyard pool skating movement that spawned in Orange County and Los Angeles around 1975. On one of his pool hunting missions, Duane's apparent talent caught the attention of Brad Bowman, then a sponsored rider already well on his way to becoming pro. "I remember he had long hair back then, bleached down past his shoulders. And he was just a kid from Orange County.

DESTROY

Photo: Ted Terrebonne

He didn't surf that much – he was more of a skater. And Duane had talent," said Brad Bowman, adding: "There are certain people, the first time you see them you just know, there is something good planned for them. If they don't kill themselves they're gonna go somewhere." And go somewhere he did (although he would almost kill himself on several occasions). Duane Peters emerged as the hottest amateur – next to his rival Eddie Elguera – on the 1978 Hester Series pool contests. He gained notoriety as the first skateboarder to ever complete a full loop on a custom-built Plexiglas ramp behind Costa Mesa punk rock club, the Cuckoo's Nest, where he also dominated the mosh pit. Skateboard magazines stood in line for interviews and photos of the rookie talent.

The face of a new generation, Peters pioneered his own approach to vertical skateboarding, radically different from the surf-inspired style of his predecessors. Whereas surf-rooted riders approached the lip of a pool in a way that was light-footed and transitory – the way surfers quickly grace the break of a wave, keeping their weight below the edge, Duane Peters explored the concreteness of pool riding. Instead of floating or scraping lightly across the lip, Peters went over the edge, planting his foot on the pool's deck in new moves including the so-called sweeper. Even more reckless, he rolled off the deck into the pool – not carving sideways into the transition like a surfer, but plowing over the coping head-on – in a move called the Acid Drop; a full frontal death drop with survival instincts screaming in anticipation of certain whiplash into the deep end.

HARD YARDS

What's more, Peters not only looked at skateboarding with different eyes, he also looked different than the average skateboarder. With his chop cut hair, spiked wristband, and mad dog stare, the wild-eyed punker from Orange County resembled a new breed of skateboarder, even to his peers. "New cats were coming in, like the Eddies and Duane. And Duane was doing his thing. He had a solid goal. He did what he did. He made a name for himself and made up these tricks," said pro skateboarder Steve Olson, who was Duane's teammate on Santa Cruz in 1979 when the company turned the two pro. Instantly upon its release, the Duane Peters "Hazard Stripes" board – much like the Steve Olson "Checkerboard" model – became emblematic of the new wave of punk rock style, for which Olson and Peters were avid evangelists. "I remember Duane cutting people's hair in the parking lot at Big O skate park," said pro skateboarder Alan Gelfand. In 1980, Duane Peters had officially arrived after winning stop four of the Gold Cup contest series, besting Eddie Elguera and Steve Caballero. For a brief moment, the underdog was on top. Then skateboarding went off the deep end...

Ironically, the 1980 crash of the skateboard industry came at a time when riders like Duane Peters and cohorts were pushing the state of the art to brand-new heights, unrewarded. "The bummer for these skaters was that the money wasn't flowing for them, as it was in the '80s. These guys were superior athletes. I was always hoping to give riders the biggest check possible," said Santa Cruz Skateboards co-founder Rich Novak, who stacked his team with punk rockers such as Steve Olson, Steve Alba, and Duane Peters in the late 1970s. When skateboarding went underground, Duane stayed on, soon finding a new home on the punk rock-minded Skull Skates label while getting more serious about the musical aspects of punk. Over the years, his time spent skateboarding was only rivaled by hours clocked on stage as singer for punk bands like Exploding Fuck Dolls, US Bombs, and Die Hunns.

Speaking of stage appearances, Peters cultivated his own iconic persona dressed in German SS general hats, leather trench coats with Maltese cross emblems, and stove pipe pants. "Duane just is punk rock style, the way he puts outfits together, the way he wears a hat. He's just got that punk rock fashion," said Eddie Elguera.

But despite all these creative pursuits, Peters had also taken a destructive path early on. At the age of 18, he had started using heroin - inspired by Sid Vicious of the Sex Pistols, he told OC Weekly in an interview - and spent his career drifting in and out of rehab, in and out of jail, in and out of consciousness. Several times, he overdosed and almost died. "Duane was a great skater and a great kid. He just was one of those guys who always had his foot in a bucket of shit. But as fucked up as he was, he always skated really good. So all this stuff was just around his personality. It was the punk era," said Rich Novak.

Ultimately, all the hard living left its mark - beyond the scars and knuckle tattoos reading STAY AWAY across both hands - on Duane Peters. "If you're a drinker and a drugger and you do that shit all the time, you can just see it. You wear that shit like a fucking leather jacket. It just gets older and more beat up. The real leather jacket shows on your face and your body," said pro skateboarder Tony Alva, adding: "Take one look at some of the old punk rock skaters like Duane Peters and you can see it. He's the Keith Richards of skateboarding. Keith Richards used to be the most handsome man in rock 'n' roll. Look at him now. I'm not saying he's ugly, but he's weathered. And all the make-up and all the fancy clothes in the world are not going to change that, man."

One thing that has not changed over the years, however, is Duane's commitment to skateboarding. Still pro in 2018, the outlier stayed the course through the ups and downs of the skateboard industry and his own life. "He almost died a few times and he still went somewhere which is pretty amazing. And the fact that he is still here, is even more amazing. Duane is having a long and challenging journey," said Brad Bowman. For his 2015 induction into the Skateboarding Hall of Fame, Duane Peters took the stage walking on a cane, looking pale while leaning on his son, Clash Peters, and hiding behind large wayfarer sunglasses and a fedora hat. But the next day, in true Master of Disaster style, Duane Peters ditched the cane to attack the Combi Pool in the Master's Division of the Vans Pool Party Contest, rising to the challenge once again. How he does it, only Duane Peters knows. He's just not like the rest.

DUANE
PETERS

Hey Pal, Need a truck?
FIRE DEPT. OR POLICE
THE RELIABLE AUTOMATIC SPRINKLER CO. INC MT. VERNON N.Y.
INDEPENDENT
P.O. Box 1127 Capitola, CA 95010

A strong contender for the most frequently tattooed skateboard company logo of all time, the Independent Trucks Cross was recently named the #1 among The 50 Greatest Skate Logos by Complex magazine. All across the world, the "Indy" logo has come to represent 100% skateboarding and gnarly, punk-inspired lifestyle, subsumed by the battle cry "Ride the best, fuck the rest!" Co-founded by Richard Novak, Jay Shiurman, Fausto Vitello, and Eric Swenson, the San Francisco-based company released its inaugural truck, the Stage 1 model, on May 23, 1978, starting a long legacy of technical evolution and hardcore spirit.

But let's set the record straight: The Indy Cross is by no means associated with the Iron Cross worn by the German army during World War II – just the opposite. "The logo came from [artist] Jim [Phillips] who wanted to do the Iron Cross. And Jay and I didn't wanna do the Iron Cross because of the Nazi thing," said Independent co-founder Rich Novak, who was convinced by a 1978 magazine cover featuring Pope John Paul II. "Then Jimmy comes running into the office one day with *Time* magazine with the pope's picture on it – and there's the Iron Cross! And we said, Fuck it, let's do the Iron Cross! If the pope can do it, we can do it!'" (Actually, the pope-inspired cross is a variety of the mediaeval Cross pattée; or "footed cross" used in royal crowns throughout European history.)

Iron Cross or not, the company's aluminum trucks have since become the world's #1 selling skateboard hardware brand. And what's more, Independent was also among the first companies to master the leap from hardware into softgoods. At a time when skate-branded clothing options were limited, Independent apparel provided skateboarders with a way to dress as part of their tribe. "We didn't wanna wear jock stuff – we wanted our own gear. So when you had a company shirt, like a Powell shirt or an Indy shirt, it was like, 'Fuck yeah! I'm a skateboarder!'" said photographer and skateboard company owner Mark Oblow. The brand's image went from notorious to world-famous once its founders created *Thrasher* magazine in 1981 as a marketing tool for their trucks, endorsed by a team of early punk rock pioneers including Rick Blackhart, Steve Alba, Steve Olson, and Duane Peters under the slogan BUILT TO GRIND.

BUILT TO GRIND

Although Independent Trucks would become a driving force behind the rise of street skating – also aggressively promoted on the pages of *Thrasher* magazine – the beginnings of the brand lie with downhill racing: "When Jay and I started out, it was called 'Independent Suspension' and it was for racing. The name came about because we figured we would design a truck that had a Formula 1 suspension system," said Rich Novak. Looking for feasible designs, Novak and Shiurman came across the San Francisco operation run by Vitello and Swenson, who already had a line of trucks in stores. "Fausto and Eric were doing Stroker [trucks], which really sucked, and another truck called Rebound which really sucked."

At the time, the main truck brands on the market included Tracker, makers of the world's first skateboard-specific truck, as well as Bennett and Gullwing Trucks. Each of these trucks had their challenges, none presented the ultimate solution – especially when it came to offering the precise and responsive turns associated with the new breed of vertical pool skating that became a focus in the late 1970s. "So we said we needed a truck that's shaped like a Tracker and turns like a Bennett.

INDEPENDENT
TRUCK COMPANY

TIME
TO
GRIND

And that was the creation of Independent," said Rich Novak. Straight out the gate, the Stage 1 truck created the mold for current skateboard trucks with an all-metal baseplate holding a covered kingpin and a T-shaped hanger balanced on a pivot. Crucial input also came from first-generation team riders such as Steve Olson: "I did figure 8 carves in pools and needed new trucks that can turn. I told them which truck to steal from so they would turn." Olson's Santa Cruz Skateboards teammate Steve Alba told the designers, "to make them a bit wider so they grind better. And around the time OJs [wheels] came out and I put longer axles on my [Tracker] Fultracks. Fausto [Vitello] saw it and he wanted me to ride Indy's." Steve Alba seamlessly transitioned from early test pilot to full-fledged Independent team rider, all the while making history as one of the first pro skaters receiving a paycheck from their truck sponsor. "I could figure eight carve in the pools both ways. Fausto said, 'I will pay you 100 bucks a year!' That went to $250 a year, I was stoked I was making $250. Nobody on the team this day makes more than $250," said Steve Alba, who appeared in classic Independent ads skating with sunglasses and checker-patterns inked on his Chuck Taylor sneakers.

MADE IN AMERICA

Speaking of advertisements, the Independent brand found the perfect forum for cultivating its rugged aesthetic once *Thrasher* magazine got going in 1981. One of the first ads featured a gritty black and white photo of team rider Rick Blackhart, who also penned a regular column in *Thrasher* called "Ask the Doctor," smashing in the window of a dilapidated building. An equally classic Duane Peters ad shows the punk rock icon charging down a hill next to the slogan "Free on the Streets." Bridging the gap into the kindred world of punk rock music, an Independent ad shot by photographer Glen Friedman features Henry Rollins of skate punk trailblazers Black Flag declaring, "Yeah, I ride 'em!" Some more subversive messages included "Stop skate harassment," next to a crossed-out police officer, or a lofty Christian Hosoi aerial accompanied by, "Some get air, others get high" (see what they did there?).

As the Independent Truck line evolved from Stage 1 through subsequent updates and improvements, the brand's apparel collection also expanded to include more than just T-shirts. Over the years, Independent became known for quality sweatshirts, flannels, beanies, socks, pants, and even outerwear bearing the iconic Cross logo. "One of the only companies that I have seen do well in clothing, and I do wear some of their stuff, are the guys at Independent. They have a line of jackets and shirts that go with the truck line. Quality is high, prices are competitive and they are successful," said skateboard icon Tony Alva, adding: "There are some other people who have tried to branch out like that and have not had much success. I don't know too many people that had success with that kind of venture."

Today, Independent apparel is available across the globe either directly via NHS or through a number of license agreements to international vendors. But despit the global appeal, one thing remains unchanged almost 40 years after barging onto the scene: Look under the baseplate of any Independent Truck, and find the words Made in USA. The trucks are still made in San Francisco by Ermico Enterprises, the only remaining foundry in the US dedicated skateboard trucks. And of course, the Independent Cross Logo still shines bright on each baseplate, as well as the T-shirts and tattoos of hardcore skateboarders across the world as one of the most widely recognized and beloved brand icons of all time. "The idea behind the logo was to really stay basic, and that's what we did. It's still the number one truck – so it worked!" said Rich Novak.

FUN TEES
INDEPENDENT
RIDE THE BEST
INDEPENDENT
TRUCK COMPANY
!☆‡@? THE REST

PAINT
WALLS
NOT TRUCKS
INDEPENDENT

PAINT
WALLS
NOT TRUCKS
INDEPENDENT

HI CRU
by STEDMAN
L
VARIFLEX
M

LANCE MOUNTAIN: MR. SKATEBOARDING

Hardly any other skateboarder represents the early 1980s spirit of individual style, boundless creativity, and do-it-yourself ingenuity like Lance Mountain. In an era when Big Money and mainstream audiences had abandoned skateboarding for greener pastures, Robert Lance Mountain from Pasadena, California, set an example by rolling up his sleeves to keep what little was left of the skate scene going on a grassroots level: Building ramps, hosting skate contests, printing band T-shirts, publishing Zines, customizing clothes, playing in bands, inventing new moves, exploring the streets, taking photos, painting on shoes and griptape, designing board graphics, dressing in costumes for social commentary – Lance Mountain did it all, hands-on style, and then some.

Speaking on Lance Mountain's legacy, pro skateboarder and frequent creative collaborator Neil Blender said: "If there was a frontside invert contest, he would make people cry. His alley oops are the best also. One of the funnest to watch. His frontside airs are beyond people's thoughts. He's a rad drummer, too. He's been known to play trumpet, too. Great dude all around." One of the earliest pioneers of street skating, Mountain created the first rewind-the-tape moments in skateboard video history by acid dropping from a slanted roof in 1984's *The Bones Brigade Video Show*. "Lance was the first guy I ever saw street skating in a video part in the Powell video. He showed us that what's cool about skating is going from point A to B, and you are just having fun, out there hitting a curb with a slappy or sliding a rail and it's this whole new adventure," said skateboard artist Mark Oblow.

Most of all, Lance Mountain became living proof that skateboarding is forever rooted in fun and personal enjoyment, even at a pro level. In his 1983 *Thrasher* magazine interview, Mountain is shown goofing around rolling into a water-filled pool and beaming into the camera, *Blue Steel* style, on a fakie handplant. In the interview text, Neil Blender half-jokingly asked what the then 19-year-old intended to do about getting old. "I try to help prevent it by messing around, having fun, skating's probably going to prevent it the best," said Mountain, in a statement now bordering on prophecy. Because almost 35 years later, skateboarding has proven a literal Fountain of Youth as Lance Mountain goes *Benjamin Button* on the skateboard industry by still inventing never-been-done tricks and pushing the limits beyond the age of 50, as recently shown in a headline video part in 2015's *Nike Chronicles* Vol 3. video that cemented his status as one of the most influential skateboarders of all time.

NOT FULLY SERIOUS (UNLESS I'M SERIOUS)

It's a little known fact that Lance Mountain maintains an almost encyclopedic collection of skateboard apparel, including many pieces he has fashioned with his own hands throughout the years. But asked about the importance of fashion and apparel in skateboarding, the Skateboard Hall of Famer maintained: "I don't know if I can ever take it serious, like, 'This is the dress code and what you have to look like as a skater.'" Upon closer inspection, many pieces in Mountain's collection are just that, not fully serious; not actual components of a personal style or wardrobe, like pro skateboarder Christian Hosoi's immense closet during the 1980s, but part of an ongoing tongue-in-cheek commentary on skate style dating back to Mountain's early days.

LANCE
MOUNTAIN

Photo: Glen E. Friedman

Photo: Glen E. Friedman

Even before he picked up a skateboard in 1974 at the age of 10, Mountain enjoyed dressing up and fashioning his own outfits, not just for Halloween, and gravitated towards things that moved fast. When he received a clay-wheeled board as a hand-me-down from childhood friend Enrique Esparza, a world of DIY-fun opened up. "There was a revival of a lot of kids in the neighborhood skateboarding. But it was not very trick-oriented at the time, we played tag, played basketball on skateboards, built catamarans and rode boxes down the hill on our boards. So it was very play-oriented." But once Mountain received his first "serious" skateboard set-up with urethane wheels and started localizing nearby Montebello and Lakewood skateparks, he started exhibiting serious talent, quite quickly. Meanwhile, his clothing style had some ways to go, as an old photograph shows the gangly teenager posted up at the skatepark in shabby safety gear, DIY-gloves, and mall store jeans and sneakers. "I love that photograph!" said Lance Mountain, "I had all the wrong stuff. But I was dreaming I had all the right stuff!"

The dream would soon come true as Mountain worked his way up the amateur competition ranks. During the Gold Cup pool skateboarding contest series in 1980, Lance turned heads by winning first place in the amateur division in comps at Big O skatepark in Orange, and Upland Pipeline skatepark. It was time to get serious. "People told me I should get a sponsor, I never wanted to, I never thought about it really," said Mountain in his 1983 *Thrasher* interview. His first sponsor was Variflex, a successful manufacturer of complete skateboards with a team known for innovative, boundary pushing skateboarding, including riders such as Eddie Elguera. But although the Variflex team proved a force to be reckoned with at skate competitions, they were ridiculed by punk rock-minded skateboarders as "Varibots" for their focus on tricks over style. By the time Lance's interview finally went to print, most of the riders on Variflex had already quit as the company scaled down its skateboard division. And while Lance made sure to screen-print the company's logo on a Pepsi jersey to wear in the interview, the writing was on the wall: the Varibots had run out of batteries.

SKATER BRIGADER

The timing for Mountain's pro debut could not have been more unfortunate. The demise of Variflex was a canary in the coal mine for skateboarding's fall from mainstream glory. The industry had flat lined. There was no money to be made in the sport anymore. Most headline pros from the 1970s boom period had left the scene. And at the age of 19, Lance Mountain's shelf life as a pro rider had already gone past its expiration date by early 1980s standards. For a moment, he even considered alternative careers in his 1983 interview: "I've done some ads for Skate City and Variflex, hopefully that will help me get a job later, but I'm not interested in looking right now." Fortunately, he would never have to look for a "real" job, because around the same time, Lance's mother approached Stacy Peralta, team captain and ringleader of Powell-Peralta's prestigious Bones Brigade skateboard team – advertised as Energy in an Empty Tank World – to see if he could offer something more than the folks at Variflex. As it turned out, he did...

Something life-changing happened to Lance Mountain in late 1983 upon joining the Bones Brigade, Stacy Peralta's type-cast crew of trailblazing skateboarders connected by a quasi-military one-for-all ethos. First of all, skateboarding was slowly building momentum for a new growth spurt, a new boom in which Powell-Peralta would be a main driver. And secondly, Mountain joined a fresh team of upcoming pros like Tony Hawk and Steve Caballero that were heralded as the new faces of skateboarding and known for spearheading new trick innovations.

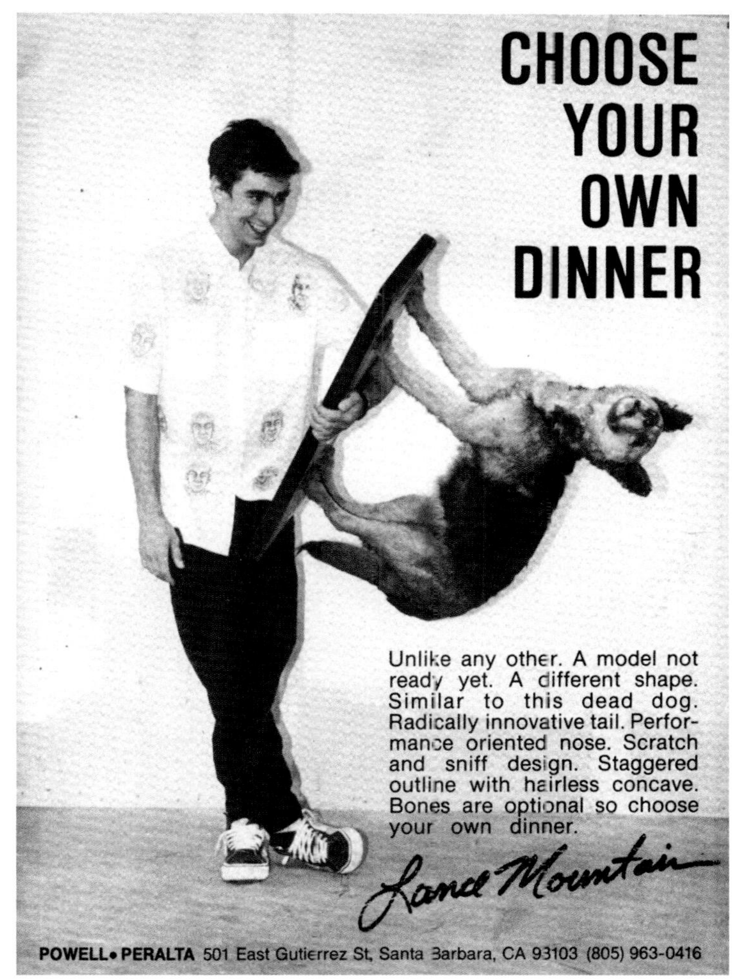

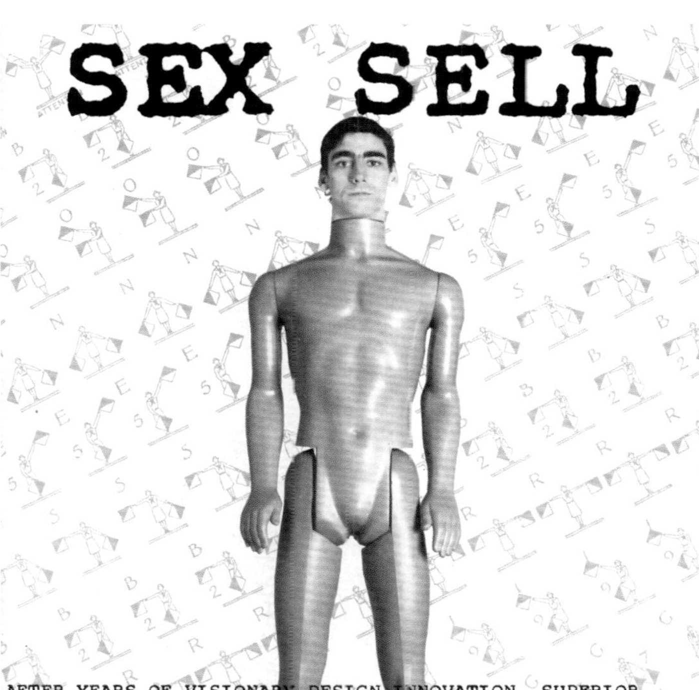

In the carefully orchestrated choreography of the Bones Brigade, Lance's role was more than skate hard and do well in competitions. It also consisted of making skateboarding appear fun and relatable - not exclusive and alienating by demanding a supernatural skill level. As echoed in documentaries such as Stacy Peralta's *Bones Brigade: An Autobiography*, not every kid could relate to the high-flying antics of a Hawk or Caballero - but every kid could go out on the street and have fun without taking it all too seriously, like Lance Mountain. Where other pro skateboarders grew super-sized egos, Lance led by being humble and down-to-earth, another reason for his lasting, positive influence.

"The good thing about Lance is that he was never the type of guy who would be out drinking or drugging or doing the whole womanizer thing and all of that. He never lived that part of the lifestyle and I don't think he looks back on it like he missed a thing. He's a straight arrow, and it shows in his choices in life. He's been a father for his son, he is spiritual and his religious beliefs are deep, and he never let mood-altering substances get in the way of his passion and desire to be a good skateboarder, and I think a lot of other guys have," said skateboard legend Tony Alva.

RISE OF THE UNDERDOG

In a little-known aside, Lance Mountain's rise to fame almost didn´t happened. When he joined the Bones Brigade and signed a contract to ride 36 demos a year and star in promotional video productions for the company, Powell-Peralta had no intention of giving Mountain, considered an "old man" at 19, a pro model board. But after the first-ever full-fledged skateboard video, the Stacy Peralta-directed *The Bones Brigade Video Show*, released in 1984 to critical acclaim - and with Lance's street segment among the biggest conversation points - skate shops began receiving inquiries for a Mountain pro board. Finally, Powell-Peralta obliged, and the rest is history: The 1985 Lance Mountain pro model with its stone age-inspired cave paintings of skateboarding became a classic piece of skateboard artwork and launched one of the longest-running pro careers in skateboard history.

Speaking of classic pieces, one of Mountain's early fashion choices was ridiculed at first, then blew up into a major trend: sweatpants. "One of the first contests that I won, I was wearing sweatpants. It was the Combi [pool] contest at Upland," said Mountain about the beginning of the trend. But he cited early fatherhood - his son Cyril was born in 1985 - as the main catalyst. "Sweatpants is what you wear when you have a baby and you don't get out of the house for three years." When Powell-Peralta released pro-graphic sweatpants that year, they instantly became major sellers, but drew some ire within the skateboard scene. "[Pro skater] Steve Olson has a quote in the new Powell documentary, and they ask him, 'What did you think about the Bones Brigade?' And he just says, 'I didn't like what they wore!' And it cuts to us and we are all in sweatpants," said Lance Mountain, who admitted that some fashion choices happen out of spite. "I kept the sweater I wore on the cover of the [1987] *Animal Chin* [video], because it was paisley, it was just the worst thing."

Also in the *Search For Animal Chin* video, Mountain appeared wearing a Scottish kilt, actually taken from his private wardrobe. "I was in a bagpipe band when I was a kid, so I've had hundreds of kilts when I was young. I just wore stupider stuff, almost even purposefully."

FUTURE·PRIMITIVE

Photo: Carol Beckwith

Photo: C.R. Stecyk

The future-primitive masters his environment by understanding it directly with his body-mind. The equipment he devises complements and enhances this understanding.

The Mountain deck reflects this mastery. It is a vehicle designed for those who realize that the challenge exists anywhere and everywhere.

If you already are the master of your environment, then you are ready for the latest innovation from the cranium of Mr. M.

The HEEL-BONE™...a precision engineered implement designed to increase leverage and grip on the tail. (see insert)

It is immediately adaptable. Are you?

POWELL• PERALTA...functional art for future-primitives, not the masses.

POWELL PERALTA

501 East Gutierrez Street, Santa Barbara, CA 93103

FUTURE·PRIMITIVE
FUTURE
PRIMITIVE
POWELL+PERALTA
© 1985
LANCE'S
RAMP JAM
1985
LANCE
MOUNTAIN
POWELL PERALTA COPYRIGHT 1985

LOCK
At
LANCE'S
Just Another Mystery
Dec. 29, 1984
Mystery
At
Lance's
Oct. 22
THRASHER

QUIKSILVER
MOUNTAIN
QUIKSILVER
LANCE
subtle variations.
MOUNTAIN
SKATE RAGS
SKATE RAGS

NOW
FULL FORMAT
STREET
LANCE 19½"
WHEELBASE
30" LENGTH
10" WIDTH
4" NOSE...
ALSO NEW
FINE ART!
POWELL PERALTA
LANCE MOUNTAIN

Lance
Mountain
Powell Peralta

At a late 1980s vert contest when the man to beat was Christian Hosoi, arguably the most fashionable skateboarder of all time and notorious for adorning his kit with all kinds of bandanas and drapery for flair, Mountain mimicked the overload of flair items with Ernie and Bert dolls dangling from his body. "Christian was draping a lot of stuff that he had hanging off of him. And I just went and thought, 'Let's have more junk, more draping hanging off!' So I had Ernie and Bert [dangling from my clothes]. I just think things are funny and I am having fun with it still," said Lance Mountain.

DIY CLOTHING STYLE

Before his sweatpants stage, Lance Mountain was notorious for customizing his own clothes, hunting down treasures in thrift stores and screen-printing his own shirts and jackets. "What happened for me was I got married and when you get married, you get lazy. You go straight to the sweatpants. And you don't go to the thrift stores anymore and you don't dress up. You're focused on having a family and you are tired. So your consciousness on what you are wearing went out the door," said Lance Mountain, who also started playing in bands - including The Republic with Neil Blender - and customizing band jackets early on. As inspiration, Mountain cited JFA and pro riders such as Steve Olson and Duane Peters who started their own punk bands in the late 1970s. It was the perfect storm of music, lifestyle, and skateboarding - and would define the look and feel of skateboarding in the early 1980s. "Bands like the Descendants and Black Flag and Minor Threat came in and that started to combine and form the Skate Rock movement with Caballero and Lance at the forefront," said pro skateboarder Don Brown.

But although his home-made jackets, hand-crafted bondage pants, and custom-printed T-shirts created an influential DIY, music-inspired look that trended hard in the skateboard scene, Mountain said the inspiration came from elsewhere. "Skaters took the punk look from early punk. Skaters get their influence from somewhere as well, and then regurgitate it out. Like, that whole skater baggy stuff, rave was going on at that time. Did the skaters come up with it, or did the ravers come up with it?" Mountain rode the DIY punk rock look well into the mid-1980s, and in hindsight said it made him miss out on possible clothing sponsors. "After the punk look and scene was dying, clothing sponsorships came around and Stacy told me, 'Just keep wearing what you're wearing. You should just keep wearing the Levi's and the Dickies.' So I passed on clothes sponsorships," said Lance Mountain.

At the same time, Mountain with his "dad rock" look was also flying under the radar when other skateboarders on the Bones Brigade received "The Talk" about failing to wear their sponsor's clothing and rocking band T-shirts or other music-inspired gear instead. Some industry insiders even mentioned a Bones Brigade Style Manual prescribing how team riders should dress and conduct themselves on and off the board, but Mountain maintained: "I think that came out to the new guys, like the Mike Vallelys... the later ones. I never got the booklet on how to perform and everything. I think this was right at the end [of Powell-Peralta]." After Stacy Peralta left the company to pursue a career in filmmaking around 1991, Lance Mountain also parted ways with the Santa Barbara-based brand to start his own company, The Firm, which provided the perfect outlet for all his artistic talents. Also in the 2000s, when cities in the US started getting kids "off the streets" by perching them into small public skate parks, Mountain printed his own prison-style shirts as a statement: "They were like little jails, little jails for kids. They were fenced in, like little juvenile halls, and that's where you could skate. So I thought it would be funny to make a jail shirt!"

STUSSY
e
Stüssy
dition 2001
NO. 53748

PROPERTY OF
SO.CALIFORNIA
SKATEPARKS
NO.53749

KEEPING THE FAITH

When Mountain launched The Firm in 1991, skateboarding was undergoing major stylistic changes, most prominently the influx of ultra-baggy pants and a more urban, hip-hop inspired vibe. Although a punk rock pioneer such as Lance Mountain would probably be last on anyone's list to be caught in parachute-sized denim jeans, he not only wore those garments, he even designed and marketed them through The Firm. "We made baggy pants, so I wore them. Basically, I never bought stuff, so I rode what was there. We made baggy pants, but ours probably weren't as baggy as everyone's," said Lance Mountain, adding: "Some people say, 'I don't follow trends, I just wear what I want!' And I'm like really?! You're wearing Levi's and a white shirt, and now the striped shirt is in. At least I can go and say that I wear whatever."

Speaking of wearing "whatever," while Lance Mountain was the host of the popular mid-1990s *411 Video Magazine* series, he also hit the streets in athletic pants tailored from synthetic materials, otherwise the domain of skateboarding's most thugged-out riders. "I was wearing swooshy pants when everyone was wearing them. I thought it was funny!" said Lance Mountain, adding: "I have video footage of me skating a skate park wearing plastic pants, dripping wet. This was back when people were wearing plastic pants and didn't sweat. And I'm skating like I normally skate and sweating like a pig into plastic pants. I just thought it was funny." On that note, Lance has never been a stranger to "fresh" style: He remains a team rider and design collaborator for original street wear brand, Stussy, and recently proved he can frontside crooks a bench and kickflip a picnic table, even at age 51.

But whether Lance Mountain is considered hesh, or fresh, or artsy, or gnarly, or punk, or street, or vert, or straight edge, or Old School, or New School - these are just labels bound to fall short of describing a much bigger truth. Because having been through all the highs and lows, all the trends and fashions and fads and gimmicks, Lance Mountain represents more than just an era in skateboarding - he single-handedly stands for everything that is positive and creative in skateboarding. Period. And speaking on the adoption of fashion trends and labels in skateboarding, Mr. Lance Mountain left us with an important piece of advice: "Everyone was born this innocent baby and then they become this thing that they want to back so hard like, 'I've always been this!' And then they change the next day: 'This is really who I am now!' To me, that's why I like to dress up, because it's all passing and it's all fading and in the end, you're still just that same innocent kid."

FLIP
RIDE FLIP!

THRASHER
BLACK
FLAG

Photo: Tom Boyle

PUNK: REBELS WITHOUT A CAUSE

The arrival of punk rock in skateboarding propelled the entire culture into a darker, grittier direction. Bright neon board graphics gave way to black-on-black designs with skulls and daggers. Windbreakers turned into studded leather jackets with band artwork patches as baggy board shorts became pegged stove pipe jeans worn with military boots. Mellow beachside get-togethers turned into punk shows with raging mosh pits. And the V-fingered flower power peace sign turned into a defiant middle finger. Because fuck rules, fuck authority, and fuck all the mainstream customers who walked out and left skateboarding for dead in 1980 when it was no longer trendy.

With punk rock, skateboarders had finally found a subculture that was commensurate to their underground status and defiance for society at large. "It all went together. I think the energy behind punk really correlated with skateboarding," said Scott Radinsky, singer in punk rock bands Ten Foot Pole and Pulley, plus co-founder of Skatelab skate park in Simi Valley. Something changed in the late 1970s when the first bars of Mink Deville's bass-heavy "Cadillac Walk" played at skateboard contests, or when The Ramones or Dead Boys came blaring out the speakers. "It created this intensity. That was the last time I remember when music was exciting," said 1970s pro skateboarder Brad Bowman, who was among the early adopters of punk rock into skateboarding.

Whereas to many observers, rock 'n' roll had gone soft and lost a good deal of its rebellious edge in the hippie-infused 1970s – keep in mind that Chuck Berry and cohorts initially caused public outrage with their music in the '50s – punk reignited the flames of rebellion and controversy. Punk single-handedly reinstated a voice for restless youths, which resonated with skateboarders. "When punk rock came along – it was OUR music. And it was just hopped-up '50s music, really. It was hopped-up rock'n roll but it had a bit of a different attitude to it all," said pro skateboarder Steve Olson, the man widely credited for ushering in the punk revolution in skateboarding.

LEADING THE CHARGE

Speaking of a different attitude, skateboarding's early punk rockers such as Tony Alva, Steve Olson, Jay Adams, and Duane Peters sent shocks to the system with their antics – sometimes bordering on antisocial behavior – at skateboard competitions and scene gatherings. Battle cries like "Skate and Destroy" and the by no means politically correct "Skate Nazi" movement pushed the boundaries of socially acceptable taste, but hey, shock value goes a long way in punk rock. Think of Sex Pistols frontman Sid Vicious, wandering around a Jewish neighborhood in France, where the majority of the population vividly remembered the horrors of Nazi occupation during World War II, wearing a swastika t-shirt with spiked up hair and a leather jacket.

Not for political reasons – the "Skate Nazi" movement also had no idealogical footing other than fanatical devotion to skateboarding – but for the sake of shock and defying societal rules of acceptable conduct. "Skateboarding at the core is antisocial – and deep down, that's what punk rock is," said skateboard photographer Skin Phillips. For the record, punk rock was not universally loved or openly embraced within the ranks of pro skateboarding when the music spilled into California via the New York underground in the late 1970s.

DANZIG

DEVO

Photo: James Cassimus

DEVO
duty now for the future
© 1979 DEVO, INC.

Photo: Ted Terrebonne

BLACK
FLAG

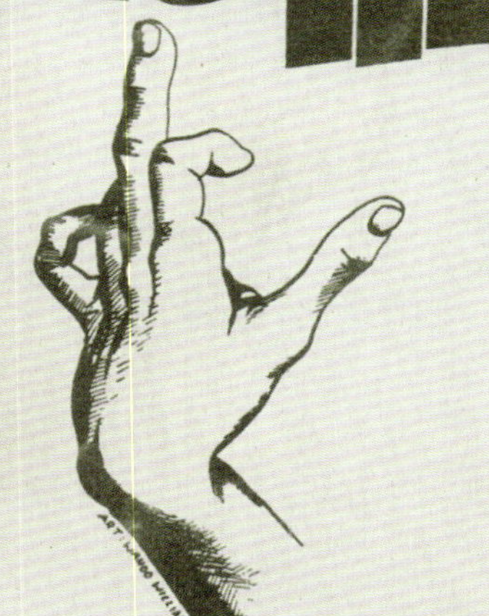
MY RULES

AGENT
ORANGE

Far from it. "I don't remember punk rock being a big issue in the skate scene. I remember Tony [Alva] was like, one of the first guys to dye his hair when the Ramones came out and all that. But I don't remember it being a big movement," said 1970s pro skater and graphic artist Wes Humpston. The rise of punk was spearheaded by a small cabal of skateboarders, who adopted the look and music as their own. "Only a handful of skaters really got it. The ones who really got it right away and ran with it was Steve [Olson], myself, Salba, Mickey Alba, Bert Lamar, Jonny Ray Bartel, and Skate Master Tate – there were 20 to 25 of us that really got into it," said Brad Bowman.

Then there was "the incident," also known as Steve Olson's punked-out appearance at the 1978 Skateboarder Magazine Awards. First of all, Olson's outfit was a clear departure from usual board sports regalia. "For the *SkateBoarder* Awards, some of the guys had broken into a bondage and S&M store in Garden Grove and they gave me some leather pants. And I had on these black and white shoes that were way too small but they looked too cool so you had to suffer through the pain and I had a shirt and a polka-dotted tie and a white dinner jacket, which I pulled from Sid Vicious in '*My Way*,'" said Steve Olson, who ended up winning the Reader's Choice category as Best Skateboarder and brought a bit of Sid Vicious of his own to the stage. "Winning it was just bizarre. We were doing what we were doing and they wanted a speech! Instead I just thought it was time to pick your nose and flick buggers at them. Juvenile delinquent shit. It really tripped the people out in the industry, like, 'This punk rock stuff is no, no, no! It's a bad scene.'"

But once the industry came to terms with the fact that punk rock was not about to disappear anytime soon, skateboard manufacturers began incorporating punk into their brand image. Tangible connections between the realms of skateboarding and punk rock started emerging on a product level, most notably with board graphics like the legendary Checkerboard and Hazard Stripes designs endorsed by Santa Cruz Skateboards pro riders Steve Olson and Duane Peters, respectively.

By dressing the part of the punk rocker in magazine appearances and playing in their own bands – Steve Olson even penned a fashion advice column in *Action Now* magazine on new looks like 'The Rockabilly' – these two pros opened the floodgates. "Steve Olson and Duane Peters can be credited for being very early in connecting the punk revolution with the skateboarding revolution. They both embraced that aesthetic early and acted almost as a bridge in connecting the two cultures because by the very early '80s punk and skateboarding would become synonymous," said skateboard icon Stacy Peralta.

Around 1981, skateboarding had gone completely underground and, in the process of losing its mainstream appeal and surviving at a grassroots level, had become inseparable with punk culture. Although still a teenager at the time, pro skateboarder Christian Hosoi remembers: "My dad set up these punk shows at the Marina [Del Rey] skate park. On the cover of a magazine they had a Circle Jerks concert and Jay Adams doing a front flip into the crowd. And Tony Alva was getting in fights in the parking lot. It was crazy." Within a few years, punk rock had gone from fringe phenomenon to center stage, and major manufacturers used the rebel aesthetic to market products, including the Rector "Punk Rock Protector" advertising featuring pro rider Rick Blackhart lounging in front of San Francisco punk rock venue Mabuhay Gardens in full safety gear. Punk was everywhere. "Back in the day you either liked metal, dirt rock, or Hendrix, or Ted Nugent, but then it just skipped to punk. There was nobody in skateboarding that wasn't into punk," said pro skateboarder Lance Mountain, adding: "It was just really broad, because skateboarding is broad."

AS8502
999
the CLASH
SHAM 69
SHAM 69
SHAM 69
NEVER MIND
THE BOLLOCKS

NO FUTURE
SMASH
XTC

MADE IN ENGLAND
DAKS
SIMPSON TAILORED

Paulo Due
Made in England
By HOYSENS

PUNK ROCK 101

Definitions of what constitutes punk rock music ran a wide gamut within the skate scene, at least initially. The scope of "punk" bands reached from originators of the movement such as the Sex Pistols and Ramones all the way to New Wave acts like California's Devo. "I was into the Ramones and the Dickies. Everyone's got different definition of them now, but back then all the bands that were new and coming up were lumped into the punk scene. Doesn't matter where they were from - Australia, Japan, Germany - all these bands, if they wore funky clothes and had screwed-up hair cuts, they were considered punk rock," said Brad Bowman. As it turns out, mainstream observers also "lumped" together their definition of what punk was, even years later. To hear Brian Brannon, singer of hardcore punk band JFA (Jodie Foster's Army) remember the early days: "Devo was first when punk rock started. We were in Arizona, and when we were getting into punk, all the jocks and cowboys did not know what punk rock was, but they did know Devo! So when they saw a punk rocker they started to shout out, 'Hey Devo! Come over here!' or, 'What's up Devo?! Whip it Devo! Shut up Devo!'"

Once the music gained a foothold in skateboarding and the club and concert scene had grown roots - with legendary venues in San Francisco, Los Angeles and Orange County - the entire scene became more specialized. "Around 1981, people really started segregating the music machine, because it was a giant machine, and really branched out into all these sub categories. Punk went into Hardcore, then there was Skinhead, there was Raw and Death Punk and New Wave, Old Wave, Screwy Wave. Everyone defined it however their neighborhood did at the time," said pro skateboarder Brad Bowman.

This local aspect of punk can hardly be overstated, especially once the music hit the birthplace and epicenter of skateboarding, California. The clash between skateboarding and punk in California created any number of permutations, from pro skateboarders who also played in punk bands all the way to marquee punk bands whose members also happened to skate. Ultimately, "skate rock" even became its own genre, born and raised in the Golden State. "I grew up in Southern California with Black Flag, the Circle Jerks and X. Northern California had Fear and Dead Kennedys and New York had the Ramones. England had the Clash and Sex Pistols," said pro skateboarder Dave Duncan. "All this together created a new vibe of short songs, like one or two minutes long, and just BAAAH! And it really fit skateboarding's aggression."

THE PUNK LOOK

In terms of clothing styles, the four members of mid-1970s UK phenomenon The Sex Pistols created the mold for punk apparel with their penchant for leather jackets and bondage gear, as well as their use of paint markers to customize clothing. Skateboard artist Ron Cameron traces the band's beginnings to a fashion boutique. "There was a shop called SEX in England, run by Malcolm McLaren and Vivian Westwood that was selling this weird bondage gear and crazy stuff that became Punk Rock That shop is where the Sex Pistols came from in 1975, they were kind of like a boy band, because they were put together by Malcolm. And he had the three guys and needed a frontman, so one day Johnny Rotten walks into the shop and said he wants to be the singer, and that was it. The Sex Pistols couldn't have lasted long because they were just put together."

SKATE BOARDS

JFA

Photo: JFA Brian Brannon

Photos: Mofo

But although the Sex Pistols disbanded within less than three years, their fashion influence became deeply ingrained within punk rock culture, where it morphed and spawned new iterations that marked a clean break from how people dressed during the previous decade. "In the '70s it was all about disco and people dressed up like Saturday Night Fever. Punk was the exact opposite. You were not trying to pick up on chicks, you were just trying to hang with your buddies and be gnarly. That's where a lot of punk fashion came from," said Dave Duncan. Among California skateboarders, punk rock clothing evolved into a more everyday look; more subtle and less costume-oriented than the 'Pistols with their over-the-top accessories and hair styles. " The Ramones had leather jackets on and torn jeans and that was kind of an image that just stayed with skateboarding. The Ramones were just regular dudes with leather jackets, not like in England with crazy spiked hair where it was a point to look different from everybody else," said Dave Duncan.

The desire to look different inspired another prominent look in the California punk scene: Paisley, a psychedelic motif based on ancient Persian vegetable style patterns became a popular theme on shirts and pants. "The Paisley era," remembers JFA singer Brian Brannon, "was when we were influenced by slam dancing. That was a big thing!" Delving into the inspiration for wearing Paisley shirts and sweaters, Brannon offered: "I like 1960s music, all kind of psychedelic music. The Leaves, the Animals, Jimi Hendrix, they all wore a lot of paisleys back then. And we wanted to be different, different from a lot of the hard core bands." At the time, Brannon noticed a standard, cookie-cutter style emerging in the punk scene. "T-shirt, ripped Jeans, boots and short hairs - that was the look, that was the uniform. And it's not punk rock if you all look the same! So that's why I came up with the Paisley!" Even years later, pro skater Lance Mountain would appear on the cover of 1987's *The Search for Animal Chin* video in a paisley sweater, which he now calls his "ugliest sweater ever". (See the sweater on the left.)

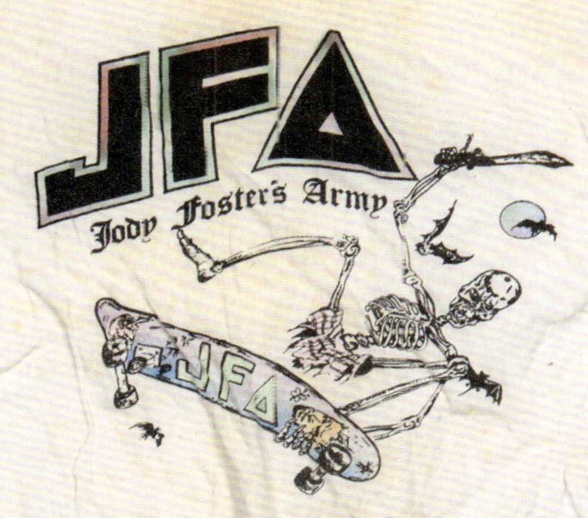

Musically, bands such as JFA were strongly influenced by UK punk rock. "The Sex Pistols, the Damed! We were playing fast an loud," said Brian Brannon of JFA. "We always said we were faster then any other band in the West. We were short, fast and loud!" Pro skateboarder Steve Olson also drew inspiration from what UK punk bands wore on stage. "The Ramones had their uniform. That was really, really cool to me. I had already seen punk rock and the Sex Pistols and I was influenced and down with it. I liked the Clash, I liked Johnny Thunders and the Heartbreakers, all of it." As another major influence, Olson named musician and 1980s punk icon Terry Nails, who customized clothing for the day's leading pros and worked with the founders of Independent Trucks in San Francisco. "Terry Nails really is one dude that flipped up the whole fashion thing for me. He comes from a musician's family and played with the Pointer Sisters and Ozzy [Osbourne]. He was already dressing in the new style that was happening within the new wave and punk rock, and played a big part in changing the way it was in skateboarding."

In 1980, the former Skateboarding World Champion bottled his own blend of punk rock attitude into an eponymous brand, Steve Olson Skates, replete with its own gritty advertising campaign featuring a leather-clad Olson next to runway models, as well as punk-inspired board art that spoke to the new lifestyle.

SPERMBIRDS
MY GOD RIDES
A SKATEBOARD

GangGreen
SKATE TO HELL

THIS IS THE FAMOUS GANG GREEN WE KNOW OF
NO OTHER BAND WHO CAN DRINK SO MUCH
THIER CONDUSIVE BEECH PARTY ATTITUDE
IS A NEW THREAT TO THE WORLD'S YOUTH
GG
GangGreen
KING OF BANDS
GENUINE
GENUINE
SKATE ALL DAY, DRINK ALL NIGHT
DRUNK AND DISORDERLY IN BOSTON, MA.
GangGreen
SAY NO TO DRUGS
PARTY MACHINE

"The whole punk thing fit. You would go into the [mosh] pit and your shirt's all jacked and jeans all trashed and you don't care. It just became a more Grunge-type of lifestyle, before Grunge even became popular. Skate all day and go right to the punk show. You don't need to get all fixed up for a night club or anything," said Dave Duncan.

DIY CULTURE

But when it came to sourcing apparel pieces for their punk rock outfits, skateboarders were largely left to their own devices. Skateboard manufacturers sold mostly hardware, and the only forays into soft goods included the usual branded T-shirts, sweatshirts, and shorts; not the elaborate cut-and-sew pieces such as leather jackets or fitted pants worn by punk rockers. Options remained slim even outside the skate universe, skateboarders could not just hit the local mall and get decked out at lifestyle stores like Hot Topic or Tilly's. Which placed the focus on another strong similarity between punk and skateboarding: do-it-yourself culture.

Punk rockers relied on home-brewed recording equipment and guerrilla promotion tactics such as flyers and xerox'd concert posters to keep their scene going. In the early 1980s, skateboarders also employed DIY tactics such as ramp building, zine publishing, and grassroots events to keep things rolling. Ever since the late 1970s, skateboarders like Brad Bowman and Tony Alva had been rummaging through thrift stores in search of new elements of their outfits, and the punk rock revolution kicked the home-spun clothing scene into high gear.

"It was fun to go and dress up. And it was fun to make your own stuff," said Steve Olson, adding. "My brother made shirts, painting them, and they were beautiful shirts. He was a huge influence and he showed me that you could do whatever." One of the most popular DIY-styles saw skateboarders brandishing their outfits with the logos and names of punk bands by all means available. "When punk rock came up in the 1980s, we would draw the band names on our shirts with ink pens and spray paint, stencils and anything we could. I would always write Black Flag or Dead Kennedys or whatever," said skateboard artist Ron Cameron, whose professional fashion merits include the logo artwork for SoCal brand RVCA.

Regularly featured in *Thrasher* magazine, these bands became part of the official skate soundtrack – also because band members such as Black Flag's Henry Rollins skated (he appeared in a 1982 Independent Trucks advertisement). Ideologically, these underground bands shared skateboarding's no-holds-barred, never-ask-for-permission DIY aesthetic.

Black Flag even ended up being sued by the manufacturers of Black Flag Insect Spray – marketing claim: "Kills Fast!" – over the rights to their band name. But while punk band names make perfect sense within the tightly knit context of punk and skateboarding, they tend to elicit interesting responses once clothing becomes walking signage. Pro skateboarder and punk musician Mike Vallely, currently the singer in Black Flag, found this out while in high school in New Jersey. "My buddy was a really good artist and he drew all the band logos on my pants. Typical bands like Circle Jerks, Black Flag, Suicidal Tendencies, Misfits. So I'm sitting in class and I have this woman teacher tell me, 'I need to talk to you after class.' And then she said to me, 'I see your pants, they say Circle Jerks. She says 'Do you know what a circle jerk is?' And I was so naive and innocent – I was 14 – so I said, 'It's a band!' And she's like, 'It's a bunch of guys jerking each other off in a circle. And I was like, What? That is a terrible band name!'" said Vallely, adding: "I know it is offensive, but that's exactly what they were going for."

Most skateboarders had only limited resources when it came to adding a punk edge to their clothes. "All we had in the early '80s was splashing bleach, stencils." But in the bigger picture, that also created a look on a broad scale – the "skate punk look," if you will of bleached clothing and pencil artwork. "One of the first things I did was I bleached my jeans. I had school jeans and I went in the laundry room and just poured bleach on them, and I took my shoes and poured bleach on them as well," said Mike Vallely.

Photo: Glen E. Friedman

The first official Suicidal Skate graphic by Wes Humpston aka Buldog Art - released as board and shirt graphic.

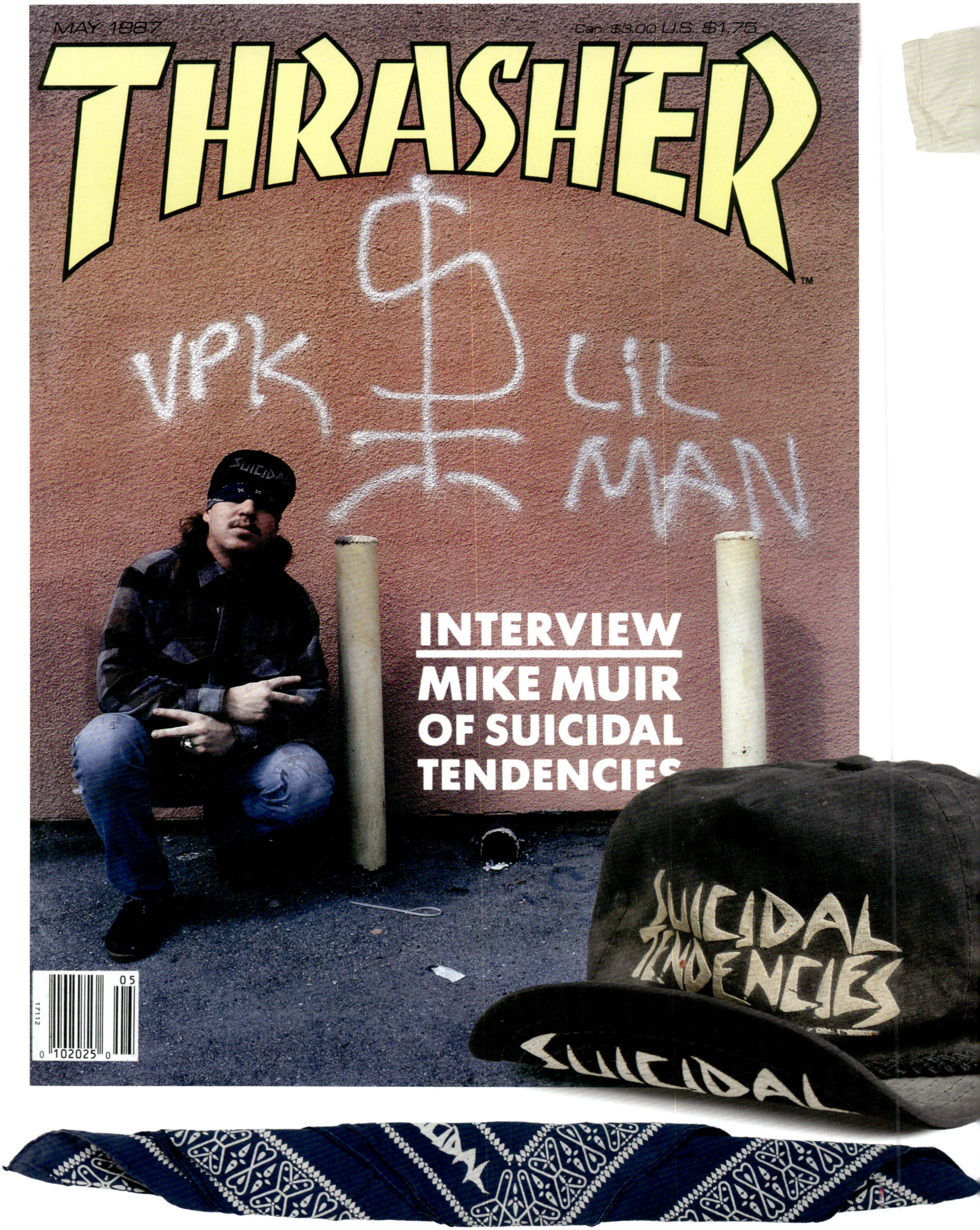

MAY 1987
Can. $3.00 U.S. $1.75
THRASHER
VPK
LIL
MAN
INTERVIEW
MIKE MUIR
OF SUICIDAL
TENDENCIES
SUICIDAL
TENDENCIES
SUICIDAL

Suicidal Tendencies graphic by Lance Mountain

Circle Jerks
ONE, AND... ...TWO, AND... ...THREE, AND...
...FOUR... ...AND...
REST.
Circle Jerks
GROUP SEX

Other DIY-tactics included drawing the punk-inspired checkerboard pattern onto sneakers - picked up by footwear company Vans in 1982's Style 98 slip-on famously featured in the *Fast Times at Ridgemont High* movie - and also appropriating colorways otherwise deemed "uncool" - most of all pink. "The punk rockers brought in pink! Skating in bright, fluorescent pink was definitely part of the whole punk and New Wave thing," said Santa Cruz Skateboards artist Jim Phillips. And bringing the punk rock look full-circle, gnar-approved footwear choices included rugged boots and Chuck Taylor basketball high tops, also for skating. "All these little punkers like Olson and Duane Peters were all wearing those gay basketball shoes like Converse. Those nasty punk rock pieces of shit. It's just fashion over function, there's no padding in the bottom," said Wes Humpston.

SON, CUT YOUR HAIR

Although California skateboarders deemed the Sex Pistols style of spiked, pointy hair too hectic for everyday use, punk rock attitude ultimately affected a sea change in hair styles. Again, Steve Olson emerged as a trailblazer, although largely unnoticed at first. "I kept my hair short and pierced my ear and they were like, 'Okay he lost his mind!' I was just going on with what was happening. But it wasn't really that big at the time," said Steve Olson. But before long, the look caught on among pro skateboarders, who then became role models for the skateboard public at large by ways of magazine and film appearances. But Lance Mountain clearly traces back the moment when short hair replaced long surfer hair. "It was Olson! He was the first to introduce that, dying the hair and cutting the hair and all these other guys did it. There was punk in skateboarding before people started cutting their hair. But in 1980, it was you have to cut your hair to say that you're punk."

Almost overnight, the short hair trend went viral. While on tour on the East Coast with Steve Olsen, skateboard photographer Ted "T-Bone" Terrebonne perfected his own "chop cut" hair cut technique. "You used your fingers and cut the hair short with scissors, which have it this punkish frazzled look." When Terrebonne returned to California, he passed on his learnings to Duane Peters and other California skaters, which started a trend. "I remember Duane Peters giving people hair cuts in the parking lot at Marina [Del Rey] skate park," said Christian Hosoi. "It went wild! Everyone started cutting hair and getting chop cuts," Terrebonne laughs. And the ironic part: "Parents loved it, because we were cutting our hair short." At the time, parents and teachers considered hair "long" when it came down to the collar of the shirt. "So although this was a punk look, they liked it, no matter how messy it looked," said Terrebonne.

Pro skateboarder and entrepreneur Steve Rocco remembers when the trend hit his neck of the woods. "Hermosa Beach was a hippie place and I had long hair down to my shoulders. And my dad would give me crap about it all the time. 'Cut your hair, son! Cut your hair!' So when I was 19 years old, I got into punk and Rodney [Mullen] was into Joy Division. So I had my hair shaved and I come home and my dad was like, 'What did you cut your hair for?! It looks so stupid!' Because by then, long hair had become normal and mainstream. So skaters wore really short hair for a while." Steve Olson and Duane Peters added some extra flair by dyeing their hair entirely or in just a few places, and rocking long sections of hair together with a short top. Jay Adams, deep in the throes of the Venice hardcore punk scene, rocked a full mohawk - still a major shocker at the time, much like neck tattoos. "Jay Adams went from surfer guy to a mohawk, doing backflips into the slam pit. And you would just go, 'This guy is crazy!'" said Christian Hosoi.

by Garry Scott Davis

YESTERDAY IS GONE

When a conversation delves into the subject of banks that skate, the names of certain groups, like J.F.A., the Necros, and the Faction, will undoubtedly pop up. The Faction, a band of skaters from Northern California, was formed on Halloween night, 1982 somewhere within the vicinity of Skaterville (San Jose), California, and it is there that they presently reside.

The Faction plays a brand of music that is so fast paced and flying that I don't even want to bother attempting to stick a label on it. All I know is that I like it! But if you are hung up on tags, I guess maybe you could call the Faction's music "Skate Rock", as they have written numerous songs relating to the typical hard-core skater situations, such as the song *Black Balled:* "Parents, teachers, police, do we need them? Action, myself, attitude, I claim in mayhem." Although all of the members of the Faction skate at one time or another, not all of their songs dwell on the subject of skateboarding. The cuts on their new and first 45 record will attest to that. The disc, released several weeks ago, kicks off with *Room 101,* a ghastly tale of man's inhumanity to man, derived from a scene in George Orwell's classic novel of future shock, *1984.* "A place for you if you do what's wrong" is the hopeless reality of *Room 101,* a chamber of torture for dissenting non-conformists in a futuristic totalitarian government. The second song, *Eternal Plan,* deals with the current trend of mercilessly attacking religion, a trend highly prevalent among some individuals in various underground music sects: "6-6-6 upon your head . . . you get caught up in the eternal fad. The way you dress is not enough, so you go one step beyond. Gotta be cool, gotta be tough, worship all that's wrong. Bottom's up for the Crucifix, real cool thing to do, burning forever in a fire pit, it's not for me but it's for you!" The aforementioned *Black Balled* ends side 2 and proves to be a perfect hard-core skater's tune: "The masses, they can't relate, blind as a bat." Enough said.

Flipping the disc over, you come across side 22 and the song *Yesterday is Gone.* It simply puts down those who, rather than taking action, mentally dwell in the past, desiring a different reality that the one in which they reside: "Yesterday was here, and you're still there!" A political number, *Bullets are Faster than Words,* is the second and last song of side 22. The cut very accurately admits the total impossibility of world peace—at least as long as man is on the earth: "You're dead set against killing, you'll never go to war. Peace in our time is thrilling, but your reality door is closed."

All in all, San Jose's Faction proves to be a very tight musical unit that, thanks to their lyricist Gavin O'Brien, possesses the ability to communicate various well-founded ideas pertinent to the society of the 1980's. TWS

CABALLERO
POWELL PERALTA
THE
FACTION

FACTION
THE FACTION
MARCH 3RD

TOTALLY UNMARKETABLE

Now, if these punk rock antics seemed crazy to fellow skateboarders, just picture the general public. Skateboarding was far from a mass-marketed sport at the time, but nevertheless, once riders had caught the punk rock virus, they were branded outsiders almost instantly. "The thing about discovering punk rock when I did, was it was so against the grain and it was so... especially in a small town in New Jersey... it was so radical! I came across a lot of animosity that was mostly from my peers," said Mike Vallely. "People looked at you, like 'What's up with your haircut? Is that bleach?!" said skateboard apparel designer Chris "Slappy" Sutherland, adding: "Being a skateboarder and having a skateboard meant something at the time. It made me realize that I was different from the general public. Heck, we even used to get beat up for it!" This would happen frequently, said Todd Huber, proprietor of Skatelab skate park. "If you wore these kind of clothes around my school, you would get your ass kicked. Here in Simi Valley there were jocks walking around with T-shirts that said 'Fuck Punk!'"

Then again, skateboarders, or the skateboard industry, were not looking for acceptance from outsiders. Actually, some observers argue that punk rock is still the reason why skateboarding is still not fully embraced by mainstream culture today, despite efforts such as the X Games or skateboarding as a potential Olympics event. "The whole skateboard industry is trying to become mainstream, but they are still fighting their history of the whole punk environment. It was just not ready to make that mainstream leap. Like Duane's name, Master of Disaster. Those two things are still fighting each other," said Cris Dawson.

But on a positive note, skateboard culture in the early 1980s had managed to become self-contained and autonomous in its orientation and underlying message, sometimes with destructive effects, as an entire generation of previous big-ticket pros dove into the deep end of alcohol and drug abuse. "Punk rock came in when people started getting into the cocaine and later the crystal meth," said an anonymous observer. As drugs emerged as a major part of the punk scene, they would claim the careers and lives of several skateboard legends. But there was a counter-movement, even within punk rock, the "Straight Edge" wave of bands such as Minor Threat with the conscious messages penned by singer/frontman Ian MacKaye, as well as bands such as 7 Seconds and later Fugazi.

SKATE ROCK

Straight edge or not, the early 1980s marked a time when punk and skateboarding rode together as one, quite literally. "A lot of the guys in the bands were skateboarders, so we would see them in the skate parks or at the backyard pool. But they wouldn't be like, 'Hey I'm the bass player of Mötley Crüe, come to my gig.' You wouldn't even know their names. Back then it was just, 'What's up, good to see you.' If you were a skateboarder, it didn't matter who you were or where you were from. You were just part of a group," said Brad Bowman. Skateboard brands such as Skull Skates, Zorlac, Alva Skates, Dogtown and a wave of other manufacturers embraced the punk aesthetic, most notably through the inflationary use of skulls in board graphics.

The intersection of music and skateboarding is especially apparent in the Dogtown Skates company, founded in Venice Beach by Jim Muir, the brother of Mike Muir, the frontman of hardcore mainstays Suicidal Tendencies. Co-produced by skate photographer Glen E. Friedman, Suicidal's 1983 premiere album Join the Army featured the song "*Possessed to Skate,*" accompanied by a video in which a pack of skateboarders demolishes an entire house. In 1984, the connection even led to the formation of a new brand based on music: "We started SUICIDAL SKATES and ran an ad in *Thrasher*, which was related to my brother's band Suicidal Tendencies," said Jim Muir.

Speaking of *Thrasher*, the San Francisco-based magazine founded by the makers of Independent Trucks celebrated the bond between punk and skateboarding right from the start, with regular features including band interviews, album reviews, and playlists of bands that were deemed part of the skate music canon. Meanwhile, punk artists such as Glen Danzig appeared on *Thrasher* covers, together with artwork by Zorlac Skateboards graphic artist Pushead, who allegedly inspired James Hetfield and Kirk Hammet of Metallica fame to ride skateboards. In 1983, *Thrasher* made the musical connection official by launching the first in an ongoing series of cassette tapes under the heading SKATE ROCK.

The first SKATE ROCK tape featured music from skater-run and skate-inspired bands such as The Faction, Minus One, The Big Boys, Riot, and Jody Foster's Army (JFA) with the tape cover featuring a punk singer wielding a microphone while skating a vert ramp. The connection between *Thrasher* and JFA, advertised in the mag as "A BAND OF SKATERS" runs especially deep. Three of the band's members – namely singer Brian Brannon, guitarist Don "Redondo" Pendleton, and bassist Michael Cornelius – regularly contributed their writing to the magazine throughout the 1980s and all band members skated.

JFA's tour shirts and merchandise were also a hand-in-glove fit for the budding punk scene: Standouts included a skating, sword-wielding skeleton or the portrait of President Ronald Reagan in the crosshairs of a rifle (JFA was named after 1981's failed attempt on Reagan's life and the would-be assassin's obsession with actress Jodie Foster). Another subversive JFA T-shirt design featured an Apache warrior known as Geronimo. "We had a lot respect for the native Americans and Geronimo was like the last bad ass of the Indians. He led the last band of Apaches to be caught," said JFA singer Brian Brannon about the design with its garish psychedelic colorway, adding: "That shirt was a tribute with kind of psychedelic colors, because we all listened to psychedelic music. We tried not to look like posers, like trying to pretend to be someone we are not."

Far from a poser, Brannon even appeared on *Thrasher*'s cover several times – including a fakie thruster in a full pipe shot by Kevin Thatcher for the April 1989 issue – and took up a full-time staff position in 1990, serving as music editor and art director until 1997.

BIG BOYS

DIRTY ROTTEN IMBECILES

Over the years, bands featured on SKATE ROCK samplers included the likes of Adolescents, Agent Orange, Aggression, Bad Brains, Big Boys, Black Flag, Circle Jerks, Dead Kennedys, Descendants, Gang Green, Hüsker Dü, Jody Fosters Army (JFA), LOS Olvidados, Meat Puppets, Minor Threat, Minutemen, Misfits, Poison Idea, Reagan Youth, Septic Death, Seven Seconds, Social Distortion, Toxic Reasons, T.S.O.L., and Steve Caballero's band The Faction, among others. These bands would also supply the soundtracks for key skateboard videos throughout the 1980s, as the music scene and skateboarding culture formed a symbiotic relationship that helped both sides survive through the lean years.

KEEPIN IT REAL

But even though skateboarding would emerge from the gutters as a hot craze once again in 1985, the hard yards spent walking in the shadows of the underground, rejected by society and mass market audiences, would prove invaluable in the bigger picture: "The punk rock connection to skateboarding cannot be overstated in how important it was. Why was it important? Because the embracing of punk rock is what allowed skateboarding to finally cut its ties to its surfing heritage and develop its own look, feel, tone and fashion. It wasn't until the early 80s that skateboarding began to develop its own voice, its own aesthetic and its own look and the punk rock connection was one of the things that made that happen," said skateboard icon Stacy Peralta.

It's a lasting connection, still riding strong today, especially since the late 1990s brought a major punk rock revival stirred up by the Huntington Beach-based skateboarding crew fondly remembered as the Pissdrunx. Notorious for their antisocial antics and close attention to detail in resurrecting the punk rock outfits from the halcyon days of the Sex Pistols and Ramones, the Pissdrunx inspired an entire generation of skateboarders to channel their inner Johnny Rotten. But here lies a major rub: At what point does punk rock lose its meaning and subversive implications and become nothing more than just a costume? Because really, as skateboard artist Mark Oblow puts it: "You dress punk rock because you're into punk rock."

Then again, such distinctions have always played a role for pro skateboarders with a strong sense of individuality, including Mike Vallely. "I wasn't into being some kind of radical punk, because I found out early on that it's a costume. And if you didn't have the right costume, you weren't cool. So I started to go into punk and as soon as I realized it was the same as being on the football team, I reacted to that too! And it made me go into my own skating, my own clothing, my own music," said Mike Vallely. Ultimately, dressing punk rock is perfectly acceptable, as long as you walk the walk and wear it as more than just an outfit, or uniform, or costume. "There is this underlying feeling in skateboarding that you are core or rowdy or tough and all these things go with it. Which is totally fine, if you can back it. But just being that and not backing it, that's fake!" said Lance Mountain.

ZORLAC
ZORLAC
THRAS

DIY-STYLE: DO YOUR OWN THING

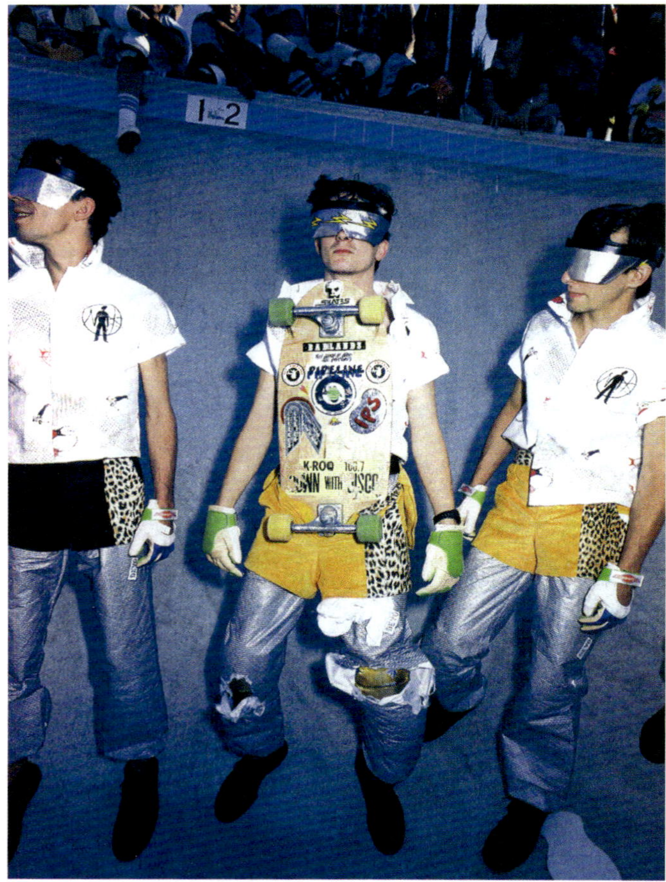

When the going gets tough, the tough get going. When skateboarding crashed in 1980, the remaining skateboarders refused to remain in the gutter and responded with boundless creativity in a true do-it-yourself spirit. No more skate parks with pristine concrete pools? Break out building plans by Rampage Ramps and *Thrasher* and build your own backyard halfpipe! No more big-ticket contest series with five-digit price money? Host your own ramp jams to keep the fire burning – first prize: one icy cold six-pack! No more glossy magazines covering the scene? Get crafty with Sharpie pens, typewriters, and photo copy machines and publish your own 'zines! Plus, make some flyers for that new punk band you started while you're at it! And no more skateboard apparel companies pushing stylish outfits? Hit up the local thrift store in search of hidden treasure and create your very own look – easy on the wallet, heavy on personal style!

After the big crash had cleaned the slate, the 1980s marked the start of a new era as skateboarders took charge of molding the culture's public image from the ground up. "Once the DIY artistic mentality came in – it exploded. Skateboarding turned the page on a chapter. All the old, matching team stuff was out – and every skater, even on the same team, was trying to look different from his teammates," said pro skateboarder Brad Bowman, who introduced skateboarding to thrift store treasure hunting in the late 1970s. Every skateboarder – from top pro to up-and-coming amateur – began exploring new stylistic horizons, including Powell Peralta team rider Lance Mountain, who would show up at contests wearing hand-dyed, distressed pants painted with the names of punk rock bands, adorned with all manners of patches and spikes, and paired with leather jackets, spiked hair, and skull-print bandanas worn as belts.

Skateboard companies also embraced the DIY aesthetic, allowing team riders access to in-house screen-printing presses to create their own photo print shirts or one-of-a-kind multi-logo tees. As a result, the variety of outfits and looks worn at skate spots and competitions skyrocketed. "It was an interesting time because it was so unique. You could look at someone and say, 'Wow, that's a skateboarder!' It was very '80s, that whole Xerox graphics, ruby cut-out thing... It was not very computerized and clean – but a real rugged thing," said 1980s pro skateboarder Don Brown. As Brian Brannon, singer in hardcore punk band JFA said: "Sometimes there are mistakes – and the mistakes are what makes it cool!" Most of all, skateboarders discovered their individuality in the early 1980s and weathered the tough times as a community of like-minded enthusiasts, who all dared to be different.

TAILORING 101

When punk rock emerged as a strong fashion influence, the trend of building outfits from thrift store purchases – started by Bowman and Steve Olson in the late 1970s – came to a rolling boil. Everywhere across the US, skateboarders were popping thrift store tags, finding stylish gems among other people's hand-me-downs at places like Goodwill or the Salvation Army. And since most thrift store purchases still required extra work and adjustments, skateboarders were forced to hone their DIY-tailoring skills in order to look sharp. "In the early '80s it was all about thrift store clothes. So we really had to learn how to work with clothes. We had to learn how to sew the pants so we could peg them and hem them at the right height, especially when punk rock came in. And we learned how to make Bermuda shorts longer and take the sleeves off the shirts," said skateboard artist Ron Cameron, who at the time also hand-painted his classmates' shoes with checkerboard prints and other designs (for a small fee).

The Republic
The Faction
Noise for the Needy
JFA
Jody Foster's Army
Out of school tour

When Jim Muir and Wes Humpston co-founded Dogtown Skates and released their first boards on the market, Skot Werner-Longo sent a money order that same day. His family owned a skatepark and shop called Playland in Flint, Michigan but he had no patience for the order to be delivered. So in a moment of DYI history, he asked resident artist Howard Field III to hand-draw Red Dog's graphic on the back of this rare t-shirt. Howard also applied his signature style to this unique piece of DIY skateboarding history. Loved, worn and faded - the shirt lost the sleeves in the 1980s due to typical Midwest humidity.

DOG
SKATES

Photo: Glen E. Friedman

it's
the real
thing!
Enjoy
Coca-Cola
Trade mark ®
Enjoy
Coca-Cola
Trade mark ®
it's
the real
thing!
it's
the real
thing!
Enjoy
Coca-Cola
Trade mark ®
Enjoy
Coca-Cola
Trade mark ®
it's
the real
thing!

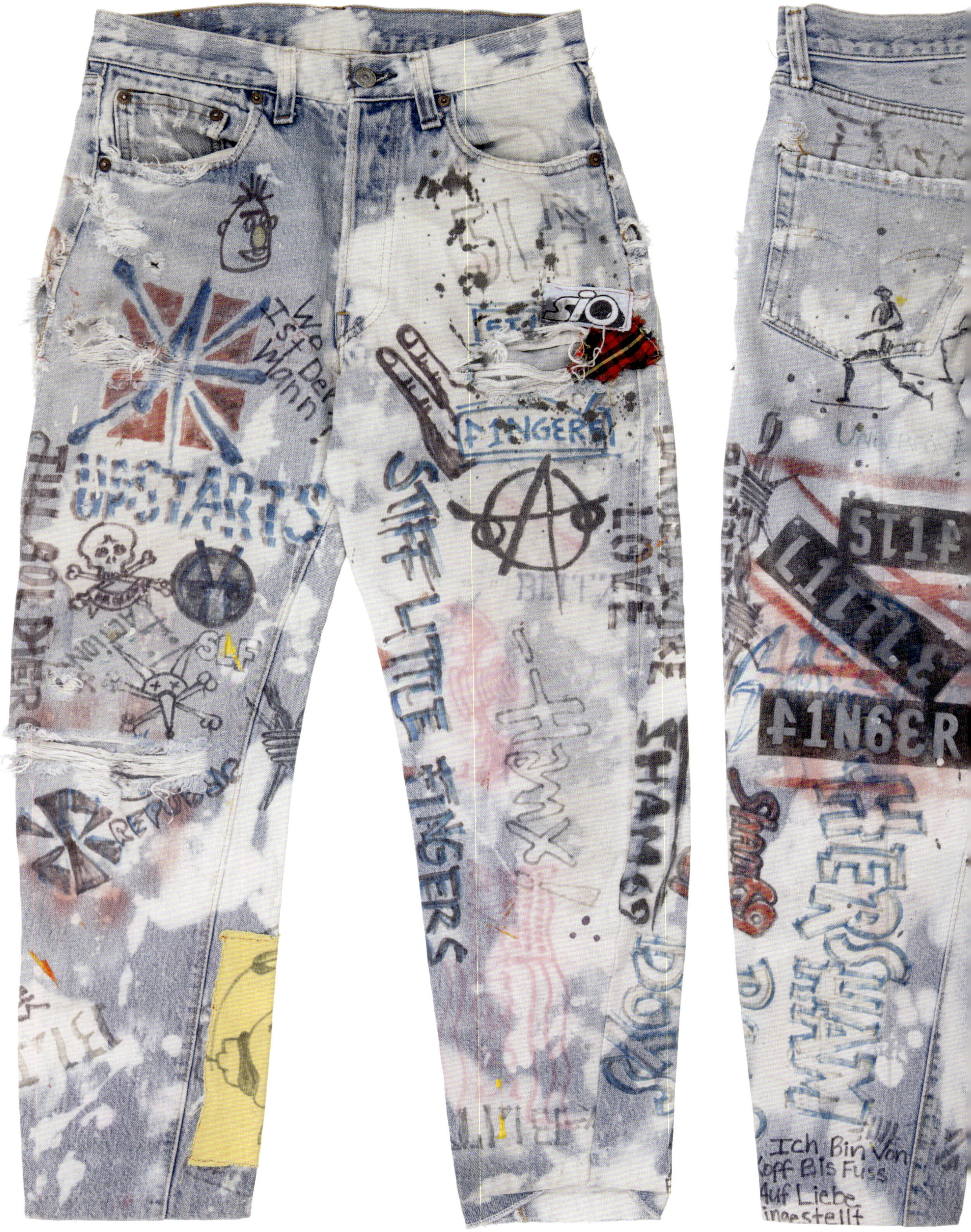

L1TTLE
Ich Bin Von
Kopf Bis Fuss
Auf Liebe

Photo: Swank

Soon enough, skateboarders went beyond merely adjusting their thrift store finds for fit and length. Creating full-blown mash-ups of clothes into entirely new creations became the new frontier of individual dress code. "Everyone was just doing things themselves, chopping up clothes or having their mom sew them. People were cutting up Levi's jeans and having their mom sew pads in them. It was pretty cool," said Brad Bowman. Some pro skateboarders crafted their own signature clothing items out of appropriated wardrobe pieces. "I always skated in bondage pants. I would make them myself. I sewed them up and put little things on them, like patches," said Lance Mountain. It's also worth noticing that even today, many pieces of skate apparel officially marketed by skateboard clothing brands continue to be modeled on something a team rider picked up at a thrift store. From Goodwill to the skate shop, the skateboard fashion cycle works in mysterious ways.

GRAPHIC STATEMENTS

As a next step, skateboarders added another layer of significance to their threads by ways of graphics and slogans. "Then it became about graphics on T-shirts because punk and New Wave were inspiring everyone. Even if you weren't an artist – just do it yourself. DIY! You can do it!" said Brad Bowman. Pro skateboarders such as Neil Blender penned the graphics to their own pro models, while griptape art emerged as a major outlet for creativity. At every skateboard contest, spray-painted skate art added new layers of meaning to ramps and obstacles – Neil Blender even famously spray-painted a face onto a wallride during his run in an early street competition.

With trigger fingers this loose on spray cans, painting on shoes and clothes was just a logical extension, said skateboarder and rapper Gerry "Skatemaster Tate" Hurtado: "You were wearing your thrift store pants and your Hawaiian print shirt or T-shirt and then have somebody draw on it. Or have them paint on your hat." The basic idea was for skateboarders to wear their heart, or passion for skateboarding, on their sleeves – or the back of their jackets. "In 1983-'84, I hand-painted several thrift store jackets with skate-related words, drawings, collaged stickers and other junk," said 1980s pro skateboarder and artist Gary Scott Davis.

Another skateboard artist even managed to convert his signature style DIY-graphics into official skate company artwork: While attending high school in Florida around 1981, Vision team rider John Grigley began "painting clothes and boards for friends. And after a trip to New York City in 1982, I started shipping spray-painted, dyed, and bleached clothes to a small boutique in the West Village." One of Grigley's most famous recurring graphics – first painted and later silk-screened on shirts, shorts, pants, and leather jackets – was the "Old Ghost" design, which he says was musically inspired: "I had an NME interview with Siouxsie & The Banshees taped to my door, titled 'Disturbing Old Ghosts,'" said Grigley, who now sells his clothes via the oldghostsdesigns website. The DIY evolution came full-circle when Vision used the Old Ghost artwork on 1984's Vision Guardian board – featuring a skull and the lettering OLD GHOSTS – as one of skateboarding's first pro rider-designed boards. In 1987, the graphic would return as the official pro model for Grigley, who contributed numerous designs over the years, including the spin-off Street Ghost graphic.

BONES
STIFF
UPSTARTS
BONES★BRIGADE
POST NO BILLS

LANCE
MOUNTAIN
POWELL*PERALTA

CLAUS GRABKE

SPREAD THE MESSAGE

The DIY-graphic trend also cross-pollinated the budding scene around home-made skateboard magazines – photocopied, black-and-white paper booklets called zines – that popped up on a local level as platforms for underground culture. Started as a hobby, the grassroots zine movement went viral once *SkateBoarder* magazine turned into a multi-sports title – severely limiting its skateboard coverage in the process – in August 1980. "When it was called *Action Now*, that's when we started making zines. Gary Scott Davis thinks that he made the first skate zine. I remember going to Sweden in 1981 for skate camp and GSD had made a Xerox'd magazine called RAMP LOCALS," said pro skateboarder Steve Caballero, who started his own zine named *SKATE PUNK* after he returned to the States that same year. "My zine didn't just cover skateboarding but also music and skim boarding. We started that zine together with my friend Gavin O'Brien, the singer from [Caballero's punk band] The Faction. *Thrasher* was already out at the time, I even had a *Thrasher* advertisement in my zine."

Thrasher magazine's signature blend of hardcore skateboarding with underground music – including a new wave of skater-founded bands – reflected what was happening in the early 1980s on a cultural level. Music became a major influence for skateboarding – and vice versa – and the powerful mix ultimately found an expression in DIY clothing by adding sew-on patches embroidered with band names, spray paint art of stenciled music group logos, and full-sized T-shirt art cut out and sewed on the back of denim and leather jackets (extra style points for cutting off the sleeves).

And while this kind of intersection between band artwork and personal clothing styles became commonplace in skateboarding's free-flowing DIY scene, the outside world could prove a bit of a contrast. "Inspired by [punk band] The Misfits, I wore my hair in a devil's lock and painted all of my pants so it looked like I was walking around on skeleton legs. That kit really offended a lot of random strangers out in public, who verbally abused me on a daily basis. I usually flung their crap right back in their faces," said Gary Scott Davis.

Some of the more notoriously punk-inspired skate companies, including Zorlac from Texas, took a page out of the motorcycle gang playbook by crafting their own blend of team jackets: Zorlac riders would show up in full force at contests rocking sleeveless leather jackets covered in spikes, rivets, hand-painted music artwork and the company's logo across the back. Fanning the flames, skate manufacturers gave their team riders free reign in using their printing presses for DIY projects. "All these great graphics started coming out of the SIMS warehouse," said Brad Bowman, who hand-screened his own photograph onto blank T-shirts. "One of them was a backside air shot of me with the BB logo on the board showing." And when skate teams visited magazines or other brands, the resulting DIY printing sessions would produce one-of-a-kind gems like *Thrasher* X Zorlac cross-branded T-shirts.

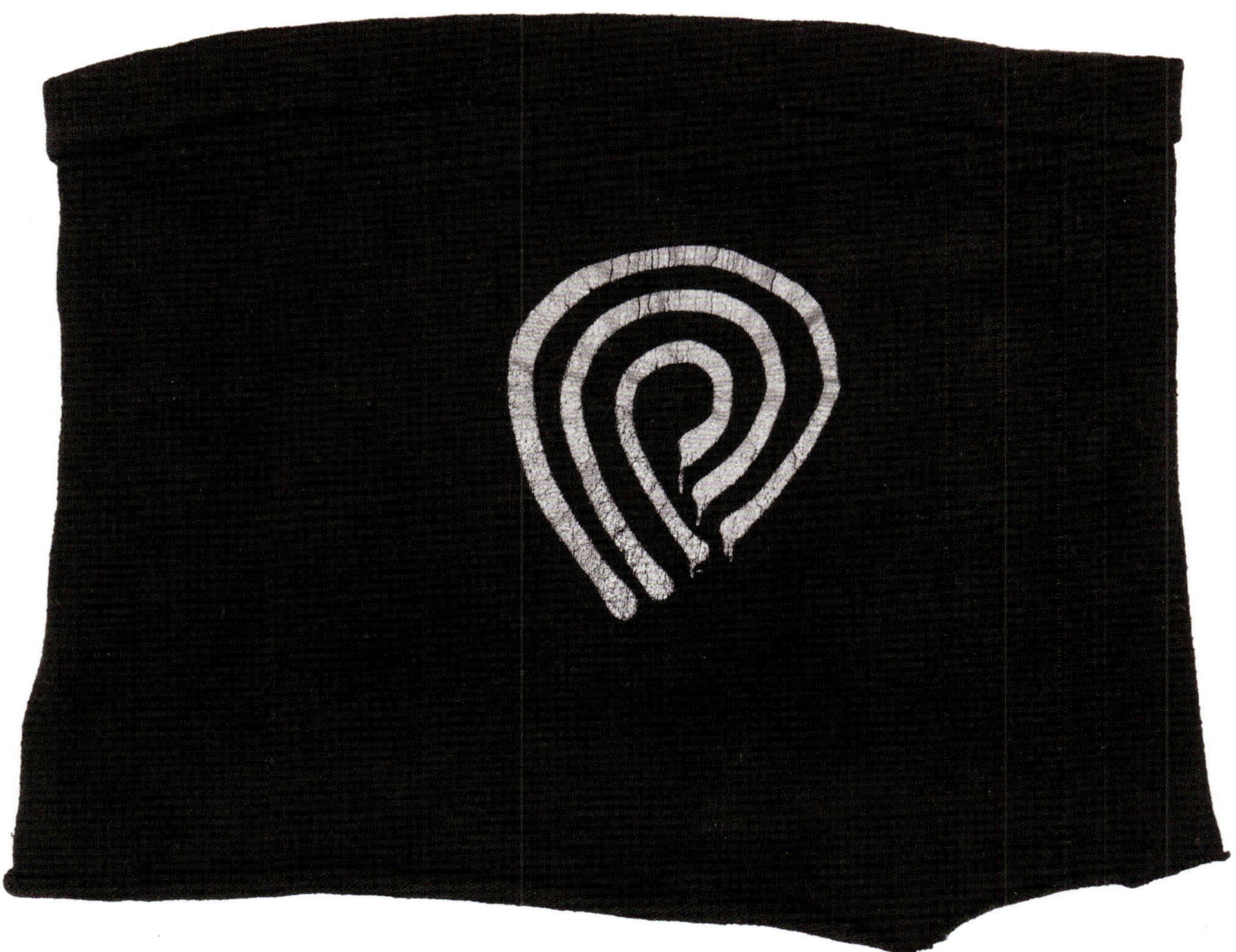

ON-POINT WITH OFF-PRINTING

It was only a matter of time before skateboard manufacturers would recognize the DIY phenomenon as more than just a fleeting trend, but an integral part of skateboard culture worth embracing on an official level. A growing number of companies paid attention to their riders' creative forays, sometimes turning DIY accessories into official products. Case in point: The Powell-Peralta head gasket, a wrap-around sleeve worn under the helmet for soaking up sweat that had its start organically as a DIY-item.

"In the '80s, skaters began to assert their individuality and to develop some unique 'skater fashion' items, as they modified and altered their standard T-shirt and shorts or jeans attire. The head gasket is a good example, as is cutting off the sleeves of a printed tee," said engineer and skateboard entrepreneur George Powell of Powell-Peralta fame.

Also at Powell-Peralta, the art department – mainly Craig R Stecyk III, Cris Dawson and Stacy Peralta – began evolving what Peralta calls "off-printing" of silk screened logos. "As you are probably very aware, company logos and graphics usually appeared on the back of tee-shirts dead center, very straight and conservative, and then a smaller pocket logo and graphic on the front of the shirt. The first Bones Brigade shirt we did, we printed images of bombs on the sleeve and then as the decade progressed we began offering shirts with graphics on the side of the shirts in cockeyed positions," said pro skateboarder and influential Bones Brigade founder Stacy Peralta, adding: "Then we printed Rat Bones logos and skeletons down the legs of our sweat pants, and so on. I believe these fashion trends began in skateboarding as I don't recall seeing them anywhere else."

Photo: Grant Brittain

THRASHER
ZORLAC
G&S TRUCKS
G&S
BILLY RUFF
SKATEGEAR
BAM
BAM
G&S
SKATEWHEEL
OFF THE WALL
THE PIPELINE
UPLAND, CA.

ZORLAC
SKATEBOARDS
zorlac
CRAIG JOHNSON
JOHN GIBSON
NEIL BLENDER
G&S

The first Suicidal Tendencies album featured lots of hand-drawn shirts by Rick Clayton, photographed by Glen E. Friedman. Fun trivia: Aside from creating the cover pictures and design, Friedman was also the producer of this first Suicidal Tendencies album.

DIY, ALL THE WAY

Before long, many skateboard manufacturers embraced off-center, chaotic print applications of their corporate art on all manners of clothing, while also tinkering with the fundamentals of their printing processes. At Santa Cruz Skateboards, resident artist [Jim] Phillipps came up with a color-over pattern, "so you could have a four color shirt that was actually eight colors. Because you would lay one color over the next and, let's say, a green and a yellow would turn purple. So then we started coming into some more exotic prints that were pretty far down the line from the original one-color prints we started with," said Santa Cruz co-founder Rich Novak. "A lot was done 'silk-screen' wise in skateboarding during the '80s. It was kind of a free-for-all in who could come up with the newest way and the newest thing to print," said Stacy Peralta.

The hands-on DIY-mentality became a defining aesthetic of 1980s skateboarding by encouraging skateboarders to build their own, print their own, and rock their own unique creative products. What's more, the DIY-mentality would inspire skateboarders to master new skills as autodidacts, all the way into carving out full-fledged second careers after pro skateboarding, with notable examples including Stacy Peralta's success as a filmmaker, Mark Gonzales' forays into the art scene or Jason Lee's path as a Hollywood actor.

Even today, practically all the trendsetters in skateboard are DIY enthusiasts, all the way. The long list includes pro skateboarder and self-taught DJ, music producer, visual artist, and clothing and footwear designer Chad Muska. Asked about the role of DIY in skateboard fashion, the multi-hyphenate urged skateboarders to blaze their own trail in pursuit of their own individual clothing styles: "It's okay to be influenced by somebody, but it's also important to always do things the way you wanna do them and never be scared to experiment with fashion," said Chad Muska. "Don't be scared of what your friends are going to say and make it fun – make it your own!"

SUICIDAL
TENDENCIES
RxCx

Early DIY t-shirt with hand-drawn "Old Ghost" graphics by John A. Grigley. In the mid-1980s, Vision Skateboards released a series of official "Old Ghost" decks, including the famous Vision Guardian. Grigley later created his own New York City-based fashion label Old Ghost Designs Inc. in the same style.

Photo: Chuck Hults

S.S.G. BY GSD!

FRAGILE
NO SMOKING!
SSG
SCURBS SKATE GANG
the FACTION
SKATE
THEN DIE!!
THE SSG
SAN JOSE
SANO-LAND
TRENCH
LIFE KILLS

YEAH TRACKER
YEAH TRACKER
SKATEBOARDING
KENTS IS FUNNER
THAN BUILDING BLOCKS
USED TO BE.
I NEED
BOOKS
NO YOU
SEIKO
DUCT TAPE
COULD FIX JUST
ABOUT ANYTHING
YOU COULD IMAGINE

UNDERGROUND STYLE: GARRY SCOTT DAVIS

issue no. 1

SKATE-FATE

SKATEBOARD MAG.

Ask any pro skateboarder from the mid-1980s about the skaters doing something boundary-pushing in terms of fashion style and DIY creativity during that era. The conversation will inevitably turn to Gary Scott Davis. Also known as GSD, the early street skateboarding pioneer from Cincinnati, Ohio, left his mark as a driving force in DIY and punk rock style after relocating from the Midwest to Oceanside, California in 1982. Officially recognized as the inventor of the Boneless One skate trick, Davis became a pro skateboarder for Tracker and made history as the first rider sponsored solely for street skating. And that's just one of many firsts credited to GSD...

As the publisher of the first homemade skate zine, Skate Fate, from 1981 onwards, Gary Scott Davis exerted tremendous cultural influence and later joined the editorial staff at TransWorld Skateboarding Magazine. His pro model board on Tracker is the first street-specific pro model, still revered for its progressive shape. Surrounding himself with skateboard luminaries and innovators such as Neil Blender and Lance Mountain, GSD gave voice of skateboarding's DIY movement and trick innovation in his writing. He also stirred the pot in skate fashion by customizing anything from pants to shirts and jackets, thereby inspiring an entire generation to do things their own way.

While his fashion style was loud, GSD preferred remaining quietly behind the scenes as somewhat of a dark horse. "I introduced fashion concepts from inside my head into my own personal world of skateboarding, which definitely never started any trends!" said Gary Scott Davis, who nowadays refuses to be photographed and shuns the media spotlight while still working as a creative in the skateboard industry. But a quick look at magazine photos featuring GSD in his prime paints a different picture, composed of ahead-of-the-times stylistics like customized pants paired with punk rock t-shirts and dyed hair. It's a look that would still ring true to core skateboarders today, much like other DIY outfits introduced by the enigma behind the three-letter acronym.

DOING THINGS YOUR OWN WAY

Growing up in Cincinnati, Gary Scott Davis first discovered skateboarding in 1973. Asked about the first specific 'skate outfit', Davis remembers: "Long hair, short shorts and tube socks in the mid-1970s, when I started skateboarding." But instead of settling into a pre-existing mold, GSD started doing his own thing early on: "Around 1980, I wore a long sleeve sweatshirt with one arm cut off completely at the shoulder. I don't know what the hell I was thinking, 'Hey, look at me! I'm different!'" Cutting off sleeves soon turned into full-on painting, writing ('Scurbs Skate Gang') stenciling and sewing patches on jackets for a customized look: "In 1983 to '84, I hand-painted several thrift store jackets with skate-related words and drawings, collaged stickers and other junk." GSD's creative output also included a home-made skateboard hard-goods brand, Sun Skates.

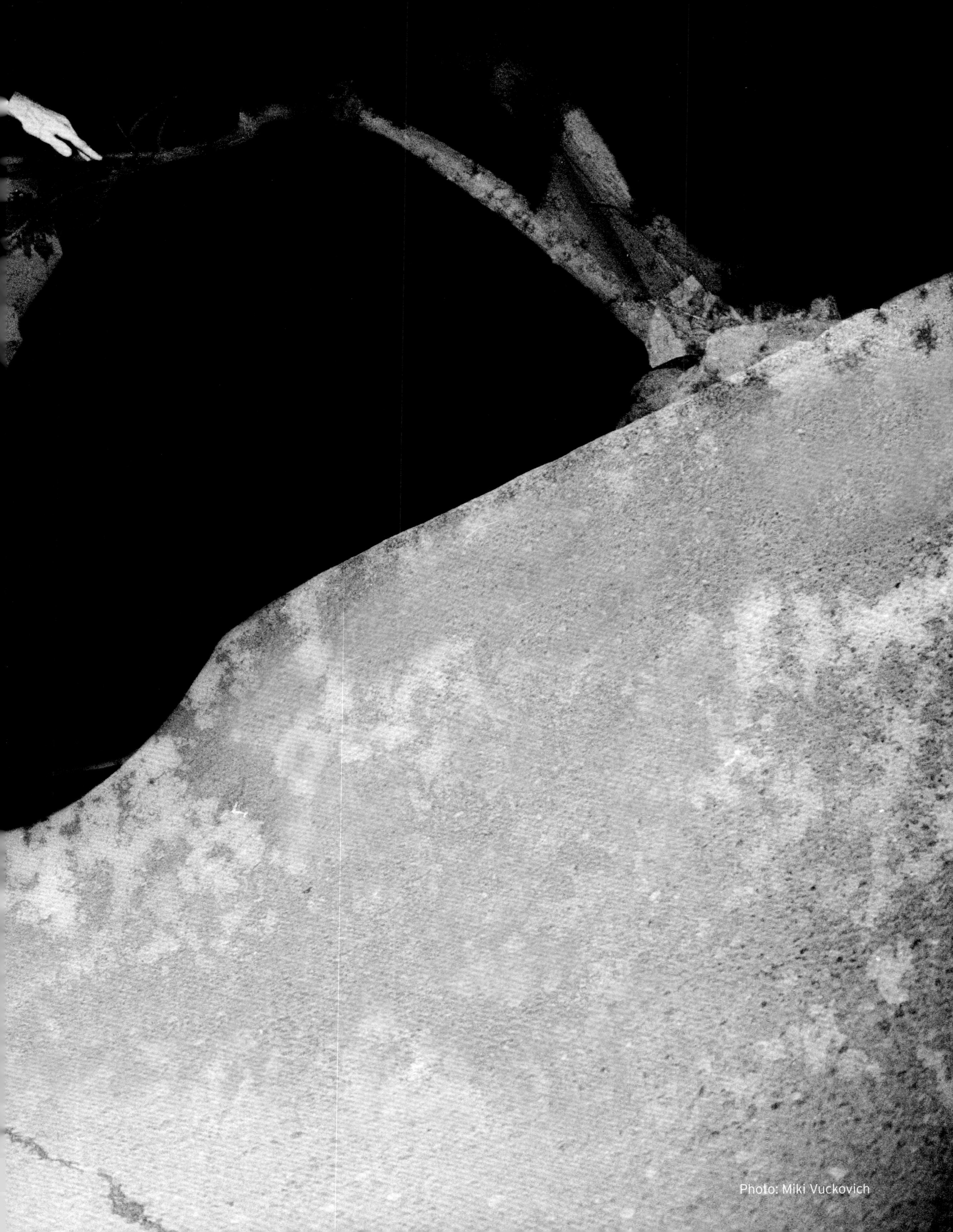

Photo: Miki Vuckovich

Davis built the boards himself and hand-painted the graphics individually, in the style of early skate graphic pioneers like Wes Humpston of Dogtown Skates fame. Hand-painted advertisements for Sun Skates depicted a blond-haired California-style surf skater reminiscent of Stacy Peralta.

SKATEBOARDING MISFIT

GSD appeared as a sponsored rider in ads and magazine features, using the spotlight to showcase his own homespun aesthetic. His 'goth' look remains burned into collective skate memory to this day. "In 1985, inspired by the Misfits, I wore my hair in a devil's lock and painted all of my pants, so it looked like I was walking around on skeleton legs.

That kit really offended a lot of random strangers out in public, who verbally abused me on a daily basis. I usually flung their crap right back in their faces." But once the rest of the (skate) world adopted the punk and goth look, Davis instinctively pivoted. "Around 1988, I tried to be super unpredictable by going in the polar opposite direction with a bright orange shirt, a straw hat and duct tape on my face. Around 1990, I fancied thrift store gas station jackets, the kind with the big racing stripe down one side on the front."

After his pro skate career officially ended, GSD took a step back. "I pretty much gave up on any semblance of fashion originality when the huge baggy clothes era took over skateboarding in the early Nineties," said GSD, although he was unsurprised when the trend ended as sudden as it started. "I guess skaters need to move on to the next big thing before most other people do." Next, GSD worked as a designer for skate labels such as Altamont clothing while playing music in bands like Custom Floor. Today, the OG dark horse of the industry is still at it, stirring the pot while watching from the sidelines. On that note, GSD would like to see more originality in current skate fashion: "Now it seems like skateboarding is ruled by a great big mish-mash of trends derived from the never-ending, standard teenage lifestyle templates of hesh, punk, hip-hop, rap, and so forth."

Photo: Miki Vuckovich

THRASH
THRASHER
SKATE
AND
DESTROY

THRASHER
MAGAZINE
PUS ZONE
©PUSHEAD

CINEMA
THRASHER
THRASHER
THRASHER
THRASHER
THRASHER
THRASHER

Photo: Doug Bigger

THRASHER

SKATEBOARD MAGAZINE

Name:

Address: City:

State: Zip:

T-SHIRTS $6.95

(Calif. residents add 6% sales tax.)

Postage & handling. ($1.00)

send your name, address and a check or money order to:

THRASHER, P.O. Box 24592, S.F., CA 94124

MORE DIRTY LAUNDRY FROM THRASHER

THRASHER MAG: SKATE AND DESTROY

Hundreds of skateboard magazines have come and gone over the years, but only one is revered as The Bible of Skateboarding. Since 1981, San Francisco's *Thrasher* magazine has gone beyond merely documenting skateboarding by providing the culture with its own unique voice, its own underground aesthetic, and its own hardcore vision. Right from the start, the gospel of *Thrasher* charted a radical new course into unexplored territory, all the while breaking with established conventions – most notably the widely held belief that skateboarding needed skateparks to survive. "At the height of the skatepark explosion, the skaters have been virtually swept off the streets and deposited in the parks, where the action is radical but lacks the inspiration of a knock-down, drag-out backyard pool session or a skate cruise down the boulevard with the crew," wrote editor Kevin Thatcher in the January 1981 issue's TALKING ED segment.

This search for inspiration in run-down places would become integral to the mindset of devoted followers the world over, united by the same faith: Thrashing. As Kevin Thatcher explained in the mag's inaugural issue: "Thrashing is an attitude, a skate attitude. Thrashing is part of a lifestyle, a fast-paced feeling to fit this modern world. Thrashing is finding something and taking it to the ultimate limit – not dwelling on it, but using it to the fullest and moving on. Skateboarding has not yet reached its maximum potential, and who can say what the limits are?" As the next frontier for pushing the limits, *Thrasher* pointed its faithful to the rugged city streets, widely unexplored wilderness at the time. "They started *Thrasher* to get street skating going. [Publisher] Fausto Vitello and the guys knew that skate parks were coming to an end so they were promoting street skating," said skateboard photographer Ted Terrebonne. Accordingly, *Thrasher*'s first issue tackled topics such as "In the Streets, Today." Quote: "A Curb is an obstacle until you grind across it." – and "Semi-Secret Spots" up for the taking.

Equally at home in the streets and backyard pools as much as dimly lit punk rock shows and raging mosh pits, *Thrasher* presented a new image of skateboarding – and skateboarders. Going out were the 1970s surfer-haired sunny boys in color-coordinated safety gear. Coming in was a loose affiliation of authority-defying punk rockers with torn jeans, bleached hair in Duane Peters-inspired chop cuts, and *Thrasher* T-shirts as emblems of their tribe. "We kind of patterned it after *Rolling Stone* [magazine] and the Oakland Raiders. With a music section and all this other shit," said *Thrasher* co-founder Rich Novak at Santa Cruz Skateboards and Independent Trucks about the formula behind the magazine. And the formula worked: As skateboarding emerged from the early 1980s crash, *Thrasher* became the hymn sheet for the global skate scene, cherished by skaters from the US to Australia. The mag shone a light on up-coming bands on the verge of blowing up, including Black Flag, Misfits, Metallica, Slayer, Beastie Boys, and Public Enemy – and added them to the skate soundtrack. "There was an explosion of skateboarding, and *Thrasher* was supplying a vision of what skateboarding looked like to millions around the world," said pro skater Don Brown. In 1986, the term *Thrashin'* went mainstream by ways of a Hollywood movie of the same name – and the rest is history.

Cultural relevance and hardcore credentials aside, the birth of *Thrasher* magazine can be attributed to a smart business decision: When Skateboarder magazine changed names to *Action Now* in August 1980 – and began covering the whole wide gamut of "action sports" with a dwindling share of skateboarding – the day's leading skate companies found themselves without a print title dedicated 100% to skateboarding.

THRASHER
Mag
THRASHER
Mag

SPORTSMASTER
BONES
THRASHER
THRASHER
THRASHER
THRASHER
THRASHER
BONES
THRASHER
THRASHER
THRASHER

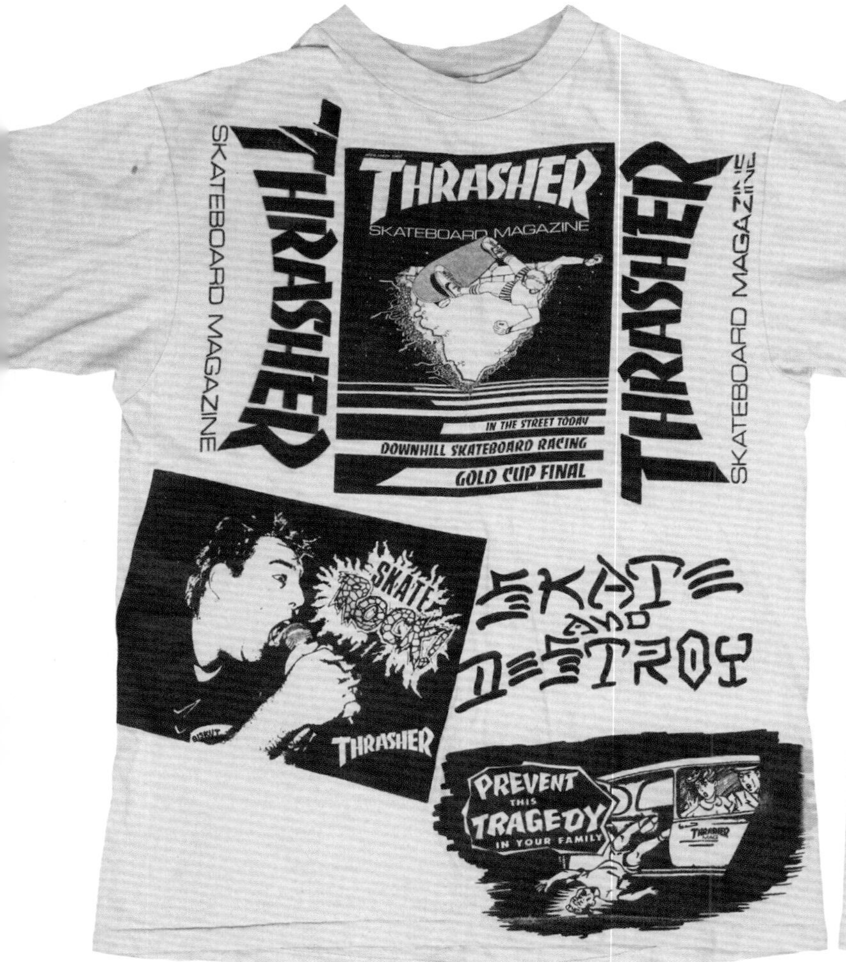

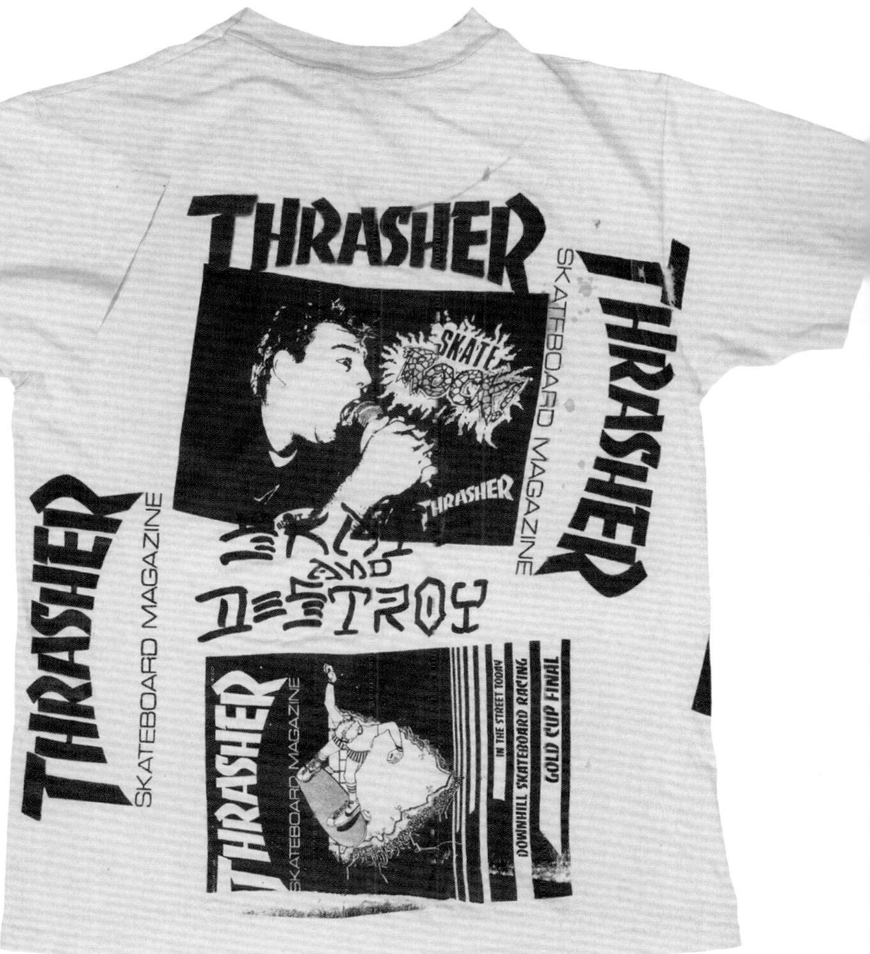

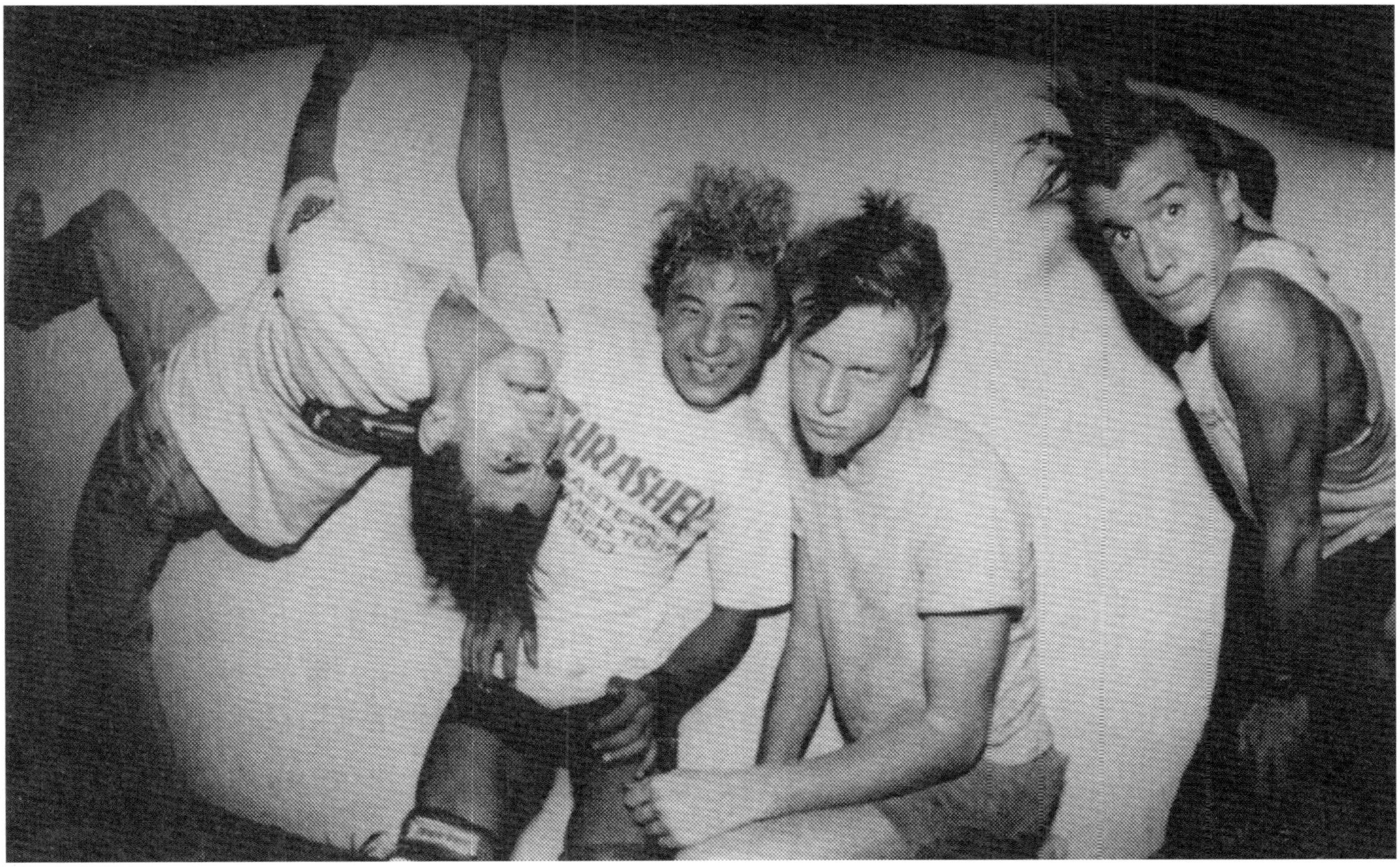

VOICE OF THE UNDERGROUND

What's more, the publishers of *Action Now* still wanted skate companies to pick up the majority of the cost, explained Rich Novak at Santa Cruz Skateboards, who was called into a meeting together with other company representatives in 1980: "The guys from *Action Now* were explaining that we are paying for 70% of the advertising but we are only going to get 30% of the coverage [with skateboarding]. And so I went, 'Fuck, this sucks!'" Far from thrilled about this kind of taxation without representation, Novak reached out to Fausto Vitello and Eric Swanson, the co-founders of brand-new truck company Independent Trucks in San Francisco. In a meeting that would mark the beginning of publishing company High Speed Productions, the three decided to cut ties with *Action Now* and start a new title of their own. "We said, 'This is stupid, we are pumping money into these guys and they're just gonna fuck us in the end. So that's how we created *Thrasher* Magazine," said Novak. "I got the money together to do it. We were all three doing Independent together. And we took [over] the workload Fausto had and let Fausto do the magazine." For editorial support, Fausto Vitello enlisted Edward Riggins as publisher and Kevin Thatcher as editor, together with a staff of writers with deep hooks into skateboarding and underground culture, including pro skateboarder and Independent teamrider Rick Blackhart and skater/musician Gerry "Skatemaster Tate" Hurtado.

In the bigger picture, Novak and cohorts knew that although skateboarding was going through a major down period in the early 1980s, it had the potential to rise into a global phenomenon again, just like it had during the mid-1970s boom period. With *Thrasher* as the voice for the new, radical style of skateboarding, advertisers had the chance to get in on the ground floor of the next revolution. "We knew that if we did *Thrasher* and *Thrasher* became a success, everything else would just follow suit," said Novak, citing the magazine's circulation numbers as a major indicator for the health of the industry. "It worked because at one point we were doing 325,000 copies a month worldwide, which is a lot. Because nowadays barely any of these magazines do more than 40,000 [per issue], which is why things are shifting to social media."

RAIDERS AND MISFITS

Before social media and the internet kept skateboarding's faithful connected, the early 1980s saw the rise of DIY skateboard magazines on a local level; many of them featuring a mix of skateboarding with lifestyle elements such as live music and punk rock. These regional bush drums kept the skateboard tribes on the same page on new skate spots, concerts, and get-togethers. "A lot of kids were making their own zines with photo copiers and Xerox'd pictures. It was kind of what the internet is now, everybody had their own little zines in all these places in the Midwest and Florida. Zines were cool to keep in touch with a lot of people and find out what was going on in these scenes up there," said 1980s pro skater Dave Duncan, adding: "*Thrasher* was a bit like a zine at first, no glossy paper and just printed. It also brought the punk scene into the mix because *Thrasher* featured music. And punk was big at the time!" Punk rock proved a perfect fit for *Thrasher* also because the magazine was modeled to reflect the brand image of Independent Trucks and its team of counter-culture, punk rock-inspired skateboarders such as Rick Blackhart and Steve Alba. These riders were also high-performers and part of a relevant set; an elite segment of skaters that represented their sponsors via regular coverage in the magazine.

THRASHER
SKATEBOARD MAGAZINE
IN THE STREET TODAY
DOWNHILL SKATEBOARD RACING
GOLD CUP FINAL
THRASHER
Mag
THRASHER
Mag
THRASHER
Mag
THRASHER
Mag
THRASHER
Mag
BUILT TO GRIND
INDEPENDENT
THRASHER
Mag
THRASHER
Mag
THRASHER
GRIND!
THRASHER
THRASHER
MAGAZINE
SKATE AND DESTROY
THRASHER
MAGAZINE
THRASHER
MAGAZINE
SKATE AND DESTROY
SKATE AND DESTROY

SKATE AND DESTROY

"When we started *Thrasher* we figured we would have 20 stars - we didn't care who they were - and they would always be featured as the best skaters. It was up to us as manufacturers to get the best teams together and choose the image we wanted to project," said Rich Novak, explaining the vibe behind some of the day's top companies as follows: "Powell [Peralta] chose the goody two shoes, Vision [Industries] got the nut balls from Orange County in tight shirts, and we took the Oakland raiders, all the misfits that wanted to be fuck-ups. Because we were fuck-ups and that's how we created this thing."

Joining *Thrasher*'s merry band of outcasts was easy: All skaters needed was a propensity for Thrashing, and perhaps some *Thrasher*-branded swag including stickers and T-shirts, which were offered via mail order right from the mag's early issues. Initially, the color schemes and logo designs - which would get more artistic and elaborate as the magazine grew - followed closely in the minimalist, bold graphical footprints laid down by Independent Trucks. "The whole pattern for *Thrasher* was modeled after Independent where you could have any color you want as long as it was silver. The same thing with *Thrasher* - it was going to have a red logo so we would just have the *Thrasher* name on a white T-shirt or black T-shirt," explained Rich Novak. While this strategy kept wardrobe choices manageable, not everyone was down with *Thrasher*'s focus on punkers and bad boys. In sunny Southern California, the makers of Tracker Trucks decided it was time to start a publication with a cleaner, more athletic focus in 1983: *TransWorld Skateboarding.*

SKATE ROCK

But clean and athletic was never *Thrasher*'s gig. Right from the start, *Thrasher* resonated with America's budding underground music scene, with new acts featured in the regular, full-page installment Notes from the Underground. These music pages allowed the magazine to curate a set of bands and tunes that fit the spirit - much the same way *Thrasher* continues to cultivate a set of skateboarders that fit the vibe of the mag, including the infamous Hellride crew. In those days before iTunes playlists, the *Thrasher* editors compiled their own mixes of music - the perfect soundtrack for Thrashing - in every issue under the title *Thrasher* World Chart. Early mentions included bands on the make such as The Clash, Madness, Police, Sex Pistols, and XTC. But it wasn't all music from angry young white adolescents - true to *Thrasher*'s broad underground leanings, the World Chart also featured reggae firebrands like Burning Spear, The Wailers, and Jimmy Cliff (because you can't spell "*Thrasher*" without spelling "hash"). And then there was the "Club bands" segment, a who-is-who of defining voices of America's mosh-pit punk rockers, including Circle Jerks, Adolescents, and Black Flag.

Speaking of Black Flag, the California punk rock icons are emblematic of the many touch points between *Thrasher*, skateboard brands, and the hardcore music scene: A 1982 Independent Trucks advertisement shot by Glen E. Friedman in Redondo Beach features Black Flag singer Henry Rollins skating with the slogan: "Yeah I ride 'em!"

THRASHER

Punk and music cross-pollinated with *Thrasher*'s skateboard aesthetic in countless ways, including the work of resident *Thrasher* artist Pushead, who would also design skateboard graphics for Texas-based Zorlac Skateboards as well as rising heavy metal stars Metallica. In turn, Metallica band members such as Kirk Hammett and James Hetfield appeared in the mag rocking *Thrasher* tees and riding Zorlac skateboards - bringing the countercultural mix full circle.

Over the years, *Thrasher* magazine's graphical style grew more diverse, as more artists submitted their works to what was a graphics-driven title from day one, when the first issue featured a stylized smith grind penned by Kevin Thatcher. Every issue showcased skateboard comics, depicting everything from pool sessions to gnarly punk rock clubs, and the column became a revolving door for skate-inspired graphic artists. The sheer amount of artwork also bolstered the magazine's T-shirt output, advertised as MORE DIRTY LAUNDRY FROM *THRASHER*. On the backend, High Speed Productions implemented an ingenious strategy to avoid overstock of unsold T-shirts: Some T-shirt designs would be advertised for sale in the magazine, but the publishers held out on actually printing them until a sufficient number of T-shirt orders came in. As a result, some T-shirt designs - even from reputed skate artists - never happened in real life or went beyond the sample stages.

Other iconic tee designs were simply poached - in true DIY-style - from outside sources, including the popular Prevent This Tragedy (in Your Family) graphic. Depicting an infant splashing head-first onto the pavement out of a moving car's rear door, the image originated from a safety device discovered by *Thrasher*'s publishers at a swap meet. "Fausto [Vitello] found this thing to keep the doors locked on old cars. And 'Prevent This Tragedy' was on the box like an advertisement, so we made a T-shirt out of it," said *Thrasher* co-publisher Ed Riggins, adding: "It was just so cool! It was such a bitchin' old thing, you could do anything with it, just the way it was." Even decades after its initial release, Prevent This Tragedy remains one of the most iconic *Thrasher* T-shirt designs and slogans of all time, right next to "Skate and Destroy" and "Why Can't My Boyfriend Skate?" Over the years, the magazine also allowed visiting pro skaters - including Santa Cruz Skateboards rider Claus Grabke - to freely use its screen printing facilities at the Hunter's Point offices, which resulted in a whirlwind of one-of-a-kind multi print tees featuring adapted *Thrasher* designs.

GLOBAL INVASION

The graphics engine kicked into high gear when *Thrasher* began curating and selling SKATE ROCK tapes - audio cassettes at 60 to 90 minutes play time, played in stereos or a portable device called a Walkman - replete with cover art by the likes of Pushead and other underground artists. Skate Rock tape cassettes kept the small underground skateboarding scene stoked and rocking out to tunes through the lean years between 1981 and 1984, when the number of get-togethers was small, and the major big ticket skateboard events of the 1970s had faded into distant memories. Keeping the ball rolling, *Thrasher* supported grassroots gatherings such as the "backyard bashes" at pro skateboarder Lance Mountain's halfpipe, for which the mag screen-printed a series of T-shirts handed out on the big day. Naturally, *Thrasher* would also cover these contests, sometimes applying a larger-than-life spin for good measure. "That introduced us.

THRASHER

We would do all these contests, where in the magazines it appeared to be thousands of people watching, but there were ten. But we would make it appear to have all these people watching these vert contests in the desert," said Rich Novak, happy with the way things turned out. "That's how all this energy got rolling. And all the artists got rolling and all the riders got rolling and this whole industry started rolling again. We just pushed it down the street to get it bigger and we knew we can only get it so big before it blows up again," said Rich Novak. Blowing up to bigger and better proportions, skateboarding ultimately emerged from the long drought in 1985 to catch a third wave; an international skateboard boom with *Thrasher* as a leading voice, known and recognized as the gospel of gnarlyness around the globe.

Fast forward to 2018, and everyone from mainstream bloggers to high fashion icons wants to sing from *Thrasher*'s hymn sheet. In February 2016, *Vogue* fashion magazine ran a story detailing "How the *Thrasher* Tee Became Every Cool Model's Off-Duty Staple," illustrated with the day's top-grossing super models strutting their stuff in *Thrasher* T-shirts. As the best way to score a chic *Thrasher* tee, the story suggested: "Opt for a one-year subscription to *Thrasher* magazine for $17.95 instead—it comes with a free T-shirt and it's a start to earning the street cred to back it up." (Not such a bad idea, actually!) Speaking of street cred, upper echelon rappers and singers such as ASAP Rocky, Kanye West, Rihanna, and Future are also out in those mean streets, representing the Bible of Skateboarding. More than 35 years have elapsed since *Thrasher* saw the light of day in Northern California, and skateboarding has become a broad church. But in reality, there are only so many true believers.

THRASHER

VANS
VANS
VANS

Designed By
VANS
VANS
VANS

VANS: CLASSIC CALIFORNIA STYLE

Whoever said "function before fashion," may have been talking about company policy at California footwear manufacturers Vans in the early 1980s. Because even when major fashionistas adopted the shoes as hot style statements, the company maintained its focus on making shoes for skateboarding. Nevertheless, Vans shoes were hot fashion items – even beyond the core skateboarding arena – celebrated as emblems of casual California style. The comfortable shoes with the wavy sidestripe logo were openly embraced by artists, musicians, and members of counter culture. "After punk rock came in, it became the stoner look, with the hat backwards, the Town & Country shorts, and Vans," said pro skateboarder Christian Hosoi, adding: "We wore Vans with Rectors [pads], Pro-tec [helmets], and Mad Rats to skate the skate park. That was all we skated back then."

But despite deep hooks into hardcore skate style and mainstream fashion – a rare combination, and ever so marketable – Vans management had little to no interest in dressing skateboarders beyond footwear – or taking their product offering head-to-toe with the addition of apparel. "I just think we had blinds on. Apparel was not something we focused on. It wasn't in the sweet spot. And my father didn't want to lose money," said Steve Van Doren, adding: "My dad only thought about shoes and that's what we did." Elaborating on the subject, Van Doren explained that the Vans business model was built around a core base of proven sellers with a limited count of SKUs. "If we had 100 styles and you wanted a 101st, we would take one out and put another shoe in. As my dad would always say, 'Make the shoe, put it in the store, sell the shoe, put the money in the bank,'" said Steve Van Doren, allowing that apparel was just an add-on, much like the toys his father would buy wholesale to resell at the store around Christmas time, knowing they attracted mothers shopping for their kids.

NO TIME FOR FASHION

In the late 1970s and early 1980s, Vans hardly produced any apparel beyond logo tees and the occasional team jersey. "Apparel was just that not that big then, I would say our business was 90 percent shoes and 10 percent apparel. Every store would have a [clothing] rack, but it didn't push 10 percent of sales. In the Sixties it was even 99 percent [shoes] to 1 percent," said Steve Van Doren. "Today it's just the opposite – our stores are 65 to 70 percent apparel, and 25 percent shoes." Asked about specific pieces of apparel from the 1970s skateboard boom, Van Doren pointed out: "In the skate area we always had some Off the Wall T-shirts and that kind of stuff. The printing was done in-house. We silk-screened our own stickers and shirts right at the factory." As a marketing device, Steve Van Doren also created Vans-branded cardboard boxes for the company's socks – little-known fact: Vans was a major seller of plain white socks in the late 1970s – that sold for $1 per pair. "The sock box was a gimmick we used for promos. You could put stickers and patches in there to hand out to people," said Steve Van Doren. While apparel remained a niche pursuit in the Van Doren's skateboard offering during the 1970s, the company made its most serious forays into apparel in the world of BMX, where Vans shoes had gained serious traction amidst a growing number of participants. Vans catered to the racing and dirt jump-oriented culture with long-sleeve, meshed nylon jerseys featuring racing-style checkerboard prints, and a number of tees and long-sleeves in various colorways.

VANS

VANS
"OFF THE WALL"
®
WORLD'S #1
SKATEBOARD
AND BMX
SHOE
VANS
VANS
VANS Keeps Up Its Winning Streak . . .
Athletes sponsored by VANS continue their winning
streak with first and second place finishes in BMX.
VANS
"OFF THE WALL"
"Pistol" Pete Loncarevich —1st Place winner, Pro
Class, at the NBL Easter Classic in Sarasota, Florida.
free-spirited California scene.

"What happened in BMX was a lot more colorful. Skaters were just wearing darker stuff. BMX and its teams were more responsible than skateboarding for all the colors coming in. You had the Haro team, the Diamond Back team, you had all these different teams with their signature colors. Gray and black, red and white, all these different things. Our riders, like Stu Thomsen and Eddie Fiola always had red, white, and blue - so that was driven by BMX." Also driven by BMX, Vans released the Style 98 slip-on shoe in 1979, which - unbeknownst to the team at Vans - was about to have its moment in the sun as the film industry shone a light on the shoe.

FAST TIMES AT VANS HIGH

In 1982, Vans received a major boost by ways of Hollywood, when actor Sean Penn played prototypical California stoner/surfer dude Jeff Spicoli in the teenage comedy *Fast Times at Ridgemont High*. And Spicoli, a perpetual stoner living the California dream - "All I need are some tasty waves, a cool buzz, and I'm fine." - didn't wear just any shoes. He wore Vans Style 98 slip-ons in a black-and-white checkerboard pattern that, following the blockbuster movie's $2.5 million opening weekend, soon emerged as the coolest shoes for hip teens across the world. "What happened was Sean Penn went into the Santa Monica store and bought a pair [of Style 98s]. And then the studio said, 'What are those?' and called the store manager," said Steve Van Doren. The rest is classic Vans company lore: Store manager Betty Mitchell, who later headed the Vans PR department, personally delivered several different pairs of Vans shoes to Universal Studios for the actor to choose from. But Sean Penn already knew: For Spicoli, the checkerboard slip-ons were the only way to go in true California Cool Dude Style.

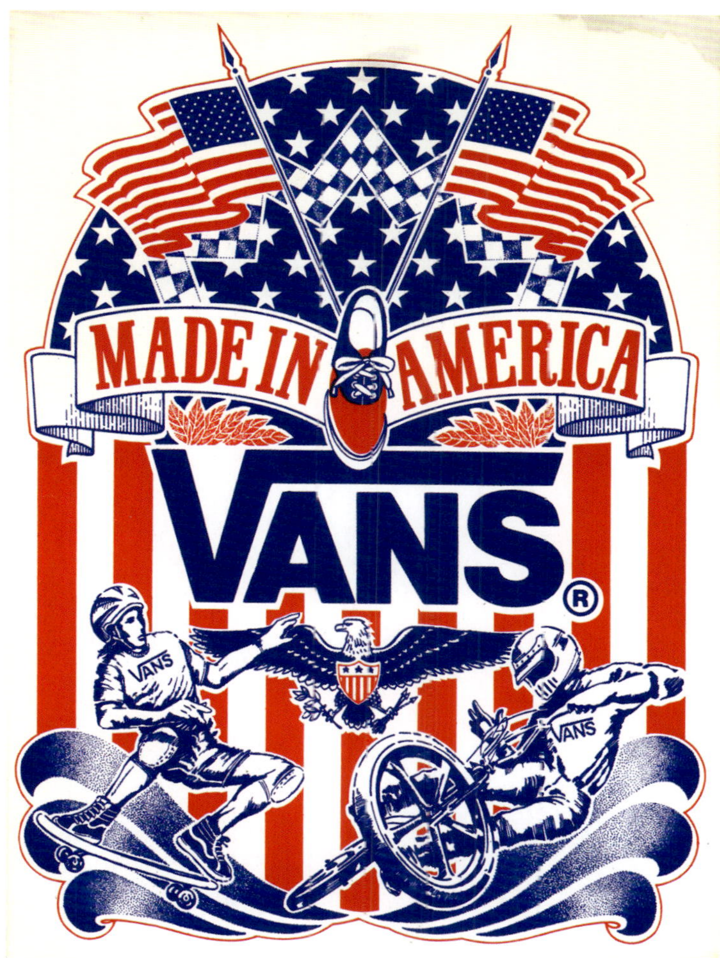

Asked about the origins of the checkerboard pattern, Steve Van Doren explained that kids would doodle on the white foxing tape surrounding the shoe's sole when they were bored in class. "The very bottom piece of the shoe was called the friction. So kids would sit in school draw a lines on their shoes and fill in the checkers." True to the Vans tradition of keeping an ear to what was happening on the streets, the organic trend soon featured as official products: "We saw what kids were doing, so we started making friction in checkerboard. Not the fabric, only the friction at first. And when kids started coloring on the toe of their shoe and on the fabric, I finally said, 'Okay let's do the fabric in checkers as well!'" said Steve Van Doren.

Skateboard artist Ron Cameron - the man behind the 1980s "Nothing is Cool" graphic - also recalls organically adopting the checkerboard pattern into his wardrobe as a kid. "I used to do draw checkers on Converse high-tops, the canvas ones, because I saw [pro skateboarder] Steve Alba do it in an Independent ad. I did it all meticulously with paint," said Ron Cameron, who set up a lucrative side business before checkered shoes officially sold at stores. "I used to charge kids $5 at school and draw checkers on them. That was before the Vans checkers came out."

The Fast Times movie blew the checkerboard pattern into the stratosphere, turning Jeff Spicoli into a household name, and Vans into *the* California lifestyle brand. "Sales absolutely took off!" said Steve Van Doren. "Every kid that saw them in the movie had to have a pair of checkered Style 98s. We went from being a chain with about 60 stores in Southern California and some wholesale in Northern California to all of a sudden getting calls from places like Oklahoma City, Florida, New York. With all these people calling in to get the shoes, all our sales reps were busier than ever. And we made everything in our own factories, so it was all taking off." The checkerboard pattern, also made famous by punk rock-minded skateboarders such as Steve Olson and Duane Peters would become an enduring brand emblem for Vans.

ASSASSINATE
LINCOLN

VANS
"Off The Wall"
FAST TIMES
VANS

In the early 1980s, the checkerboard print logo appeared on jerseys and shorts - mostly for the BMX crowd - and continues to be featured on the inside lining of Vans shoes and apparel today. Also never going out of fashion, the checkered Style 95 has proven an evergreen for Vans. "The nice thing is that every six or seven years there is a rebirth and a fashion of the checkerboard 95. And it gets bigger and bigger and bigger," said Steve Van Doren, adding: "I saw a story on The Greatest Sneakers of all Time, where the Air Jordan is number one, and the slip-on Checkerboard is number 6."

CHECK MATE?

Boosted by the cultural phenomenon that was *Fast Times at Ridgemont High*, Vans sales were poised to double in 1982 as the Style 98 became the first model to sell over 1 million units. But ultimately, things did not quite turn out as expected. "Sales went up to around $40 million and when the Checkerboard [Style 98] came out, we had the projection it was going to be $75 million. We never quite made it there, because my uncle was spending the money as fast as we made it. It was all going to our athletic shoes we started, the Serio line. That really slowed us down," said Steve Van Doren.

Ultimately, the Serio collection of performance sports footwear would prove the downfall of Vans shoes in the mid-1980s. Introducing runner-style shoes with a variety of different soles and uppers built from suede and nylon panels, Serio was a bold chess move, with fatal consequences: In the run-up to the 1984 Olympics in Los Angeles - heralded as the sports event of the century and a major opportunity for the struggling U.S. economy - Vans attempted to cater to a wide variety of mainstream sports such as soccer, baseball, wrestling, basketball and even skydiving. The Serio line launched amidst a major - meaning costly - marketing campaign and tremendous investments in manufacturing capacities.

VANS
DON'T GET PINNED
GET VANS
• OLYMPIC MEDALIST
• HEAD WRESTLING COACH OF ATHLETES IN ACTION
AVAILABLE IN SCHOOL COLORS
Van Doren Rubber Co., National Sales, P. O. Box 729, Anaheim, CA 92805, (714) 772-8270
KONA U.S.A.
8739 Kona Avenue
Jacksonville, Fla. 32211
(904) 725-8770
Orders outside Jax., Fla.
Call: (714) 937-0541
I ♥ AMERICA
and We're #1
VANS
Merry Christmas
& good luck in the new year from VANS
VANS
HANDCRAFTED AMERICAN-MADE ATHLETIC FOOTWEAR
VAN DOREN RUBBER CO., INC.
P.O. BOX 729, ANAHEIM, CA 92805
714/772-8270
DEALER INQUIRIES INVITED EXCEPT IN SO. CA
Combination of colors available. Narrow, medium and wide widths.
For additional information, see your local dealer or you may write VANS.
I LIKE
Classic
VANS

But despite positive reviews from magazines such as Runner's World, the collection flopped, straying too far from Vans core demographic, and loads of unsold Serio inventory began piling up at stores and warehouses. With so much riding on the success of Serio, Vans stumbled into financial disaster – and not even booming sales from Fast Times fans could soften the blow. "We went into Chapter 11 bankruptcy in 1984. We got into trouble and had to build it back up," said Steve Van Doren. With over $12 million in debt, Vans president Paul Van Doren had to make a decision: Throw it all away over a misplaced bet, or rebuild the company by focusing on its core strength – skateboarding?

Obviously, Vans was far from finished, and found unwavering support in the skateboard scene, which was also going through a rough stretch of underground survival in 1984. But as the second book of Skateboarding Is Not a Fashion will show, Vans ultimately managed to turn the tide through a renewed focus on making shoes that resonate with skateboarders – not mainstream athletes, lifestyle customers, or fashionistas – and drawing on its strong roots in skateboard culture. As Vans team rider Ray Barbee said on the eve of the company's 50th brand anniversary: "Vans has been in skateboarding since the beginning. Vans can say that. There's no other shoe brand that can say that. This ain't no fashion brand. This is a skateboard brand." To be continued...

Thunder from VANS™
MARTIN
APARIJO
WOODY
ITSON
EDDIE
FIOLA
BEATLE
ROSECRANS
KELE
ROSECRANS
#98-36
#36-18
#38-67
#98-25
#98-35
Combination of colors
For additional information

live to skate!
TWS
skate or die!
SION
TRANS-WORLD
SKATEBO

Photo: Grant Brittain

TWS MAGAZINE: GOOD, CLEAN FUN

Universal law maintains that for every action, there is an opposite and equal reaction. When skateboarding's most popular print magazine, SkateBoarder, changed its name to *Action Now* in 1980 and broadened its focus to mixed action sports, the resulting fallout gave rise to the underground-driven *Thrasher* magazine. And when *Thrasher*'s portrayal of skateboarding veered too far from family-friendly territory for some tastes – all the skulls, tattoos, nudity, and bleeding head wounds from stage diving at punk rock shows – the response was yet another new magazine, cultivating a more sportsmanlike vision: Started in 1983 by Peggy Cozens and Larry Balma, owner of Tracker Trucks, *TransWorld Skateboarding (TWS)* emerged as the yin to *Thrasher*'s yang, the sunny blue skies antithesis to *Thrasher*'s gritty gutter wastelands.

"The San Diego guys thought we were fucked up, so they created *TransWorld*. They wanted more of a mom-and-pop operation," said Rich Novak at Santa Cruz Skateboards and NHS, who co-founded *Thrasher* in 1981. Stating his side of the story, *TransWorld* founder Larry Balma, who named the magazine after his commercial fishing company, explained in a 2003 interview with *The San Diego Union-Tribune*: "They were pretty harsh, sex and drugs and using four-letter words and all that. And in the early '80s, the sport started growing and *[Thrasher]* wasn't the best magazine for young kids." Accordingly, the first issue of *TransWorld* featured an article by Peggy Cozens, deriding the punk rock aesthetic pushed by *Thrasher:* "I have become increasingly concerned about a new skate attitude being pushed on skaters: Skate and Destroy." As the antidote, *TransWorld Skateboarding* offered the mantra of "Skate and Create," supplemented by articles teaching readers how to organize a backyard skate contest, clean their griptape, and build their own skate scenes.

"Join us in a united effort to show the world our awesome sport. They haven't seen anything yet!" wrote the editors behind TransWorld Skateboarding, calling themselves THE UNITED SKATE FRONT, in the first issue's editorial. Photographers featured from day one included J. Grant Brittain, who picked up skate photography while working at Del Mar Skate Ranch and during his tenure as a photo editor of two decades became a defining force in *TransWorld's* photographic aesthetic. Over the years, *TransWorld's* pool of photographers included the likes of Spike Jonze, Dave Swift, Daniel Harold Sturt, and Skin Philips. And by virtue of documenting skateboarding in crisp color photos, *TWS* also exposed generations of kids to the importance of clothing styles: "Skateboard fashion is bigger than we had any idea, because when you are a kid, it's one of the only fashions you can really identify with," said longtime *TWS* photo editor, Skin Phillips.

GRAPHICALLY INSPIRED

Next to inspiring photography, *TWS* also delivered on its "Skate and Create" ethos by offering editorial space to the artistic pursuits of pro skateboarders. Starting with the magazine's second issue, pro rider Lance Mountain curated the "Ramp Locals" segment, serving the blossoming underground scene of home-made halfpipes with ramp plans and DIY-guides. Mountain would also visit backyard ramps and shoot photos of ramp builders and local skateboarders for "Ramp Locals" features.

TRANS-WORLD SKATEBOARDING

MAY/JUNE 1983

VOL. 1 NO. 1

$1.75

TRANSWORLD
SKATEBOARDING
MAGAZINE
SKATEBOARDING

TUFF ONES
PiL
ONEITA
POWER-T
TWS

AGGRO ZONE

Another popular installment included the "Aggro Zone" segment with words and illustrations by pro skateboarder Neil Blender, whose artwork featured all over the magazine as well as T-shirts and stickers. The prolific creative output from big name pros would inspire an entire generation of young artists to pursue their own illustrations, including Ron Cameron, one of the major artists at 1980s skate company Blockhead. "I was aware of that trinity of artists at TransWorld - GSD, Lance [Mountain] and Neil Blender. And Blender was the king of it all," said Cameron, for whom the magazine was a real eye opener. "In 1984 I was in junior high school and copied photos and replicated them as drawings to win awards. But the TransWorld guys made this light bulb go off in my head. You could just draw whatever comes in your mind - and it's better, you invented it! You invented this whole reality."

Over the years, artists featured in *TWS* included Andy Jenkins (Mel Bend), Lance Mountain, and Ed Templeton, among countless others. Their graphic designs, next to the TransWorld logo, would also feature on magazine merchandise and apparel such as T-shirts, sweatshirts, and windbreakers in the 1980s. At the time, skateboard apparel choices were far and few, so rocking a *TransWorld* logo T-shirt offered a welcome opportunity for skateboarders to wear the colors of their tribe without having to make their own clothing DIY style. *TWS* T-shirt styles were also heavily influenced by the magazine's longtime art director, influential graphic designer David Carson, who was at the forefront of blending clean typography with "dirty" photography techniques and organic design elements.

SKATE AND LOOK GREAT

Across the world, issues of *TransWorld Skateboarding* allowed skateboarders to catch up on the latest advancements in riding technique, just as much as the latest in clothing styles. The only catch lay in the inherent lag associated with print publications: "You would look at *Thrasher* or *TransWorld,* but it was sporadic to get your hands on those in Europe. So there was always a delay back then, six months or a year before trends would get over there," said 1980s pro skateboarder Don Brown, while adding some perspective: "Right now you can look on Instagram and see what [Eric] Koston is wearing today - and you can go out and buy it."

During *TWS* photo shoots, photographers would often take charge and encourage skateboarders to wear certain colors, a practice dating back to the 1970s. Grant Brittain would ask skateboarders to wear shirts in bright tones of red or yellow, which contrasted nicely against blue skies when caught on Fuji Velvia color film stock. After all, outfits and wardrobe choices would affect the entire aesthetics of a photo, explained Skin Phillips: "How the photos looked and how the skaters dressed was really important. And if you look at all the 1980s stuff, some of it is really kind of wild." Speaking of wild, the cover of *TransWorld Skateboarding's* premiere issue featured a young Steve Caballero floating an aerial at the 1983 Great Desert Ramp Battle wearing a thick wool sweater that's more Big Lebowski than Big Air - a fashion choice he still regrets. "That sweater was just a sweater I had because it was cold," said Caballero, adding: "There is also a sequence of me in that first issue wearing plaid pants with zippers in the back."

Skin Phillips looks at such fashion faux pas with a smile. "There are a lot of skeletons in the cupboard. The '80s were an awesome, brilliant time, but I don't know what was going on in terms of fashion. It was crazy. Skateboarding was finding itself and some people looked pretty crazy. Then again, you throw shit on the wall and see what sticks - and if it sticks, you go with it!" On that note, TransWorld's focus on covering the bright side of skateboarding also stuck, and the magazine remains one of the leading publications in 2018, still acting as the polished counterpart to *Thrasher's* grit in a universal balance of opposites.

SANTA MONICA AIRLINES: BADDEST CATS IN TOWN

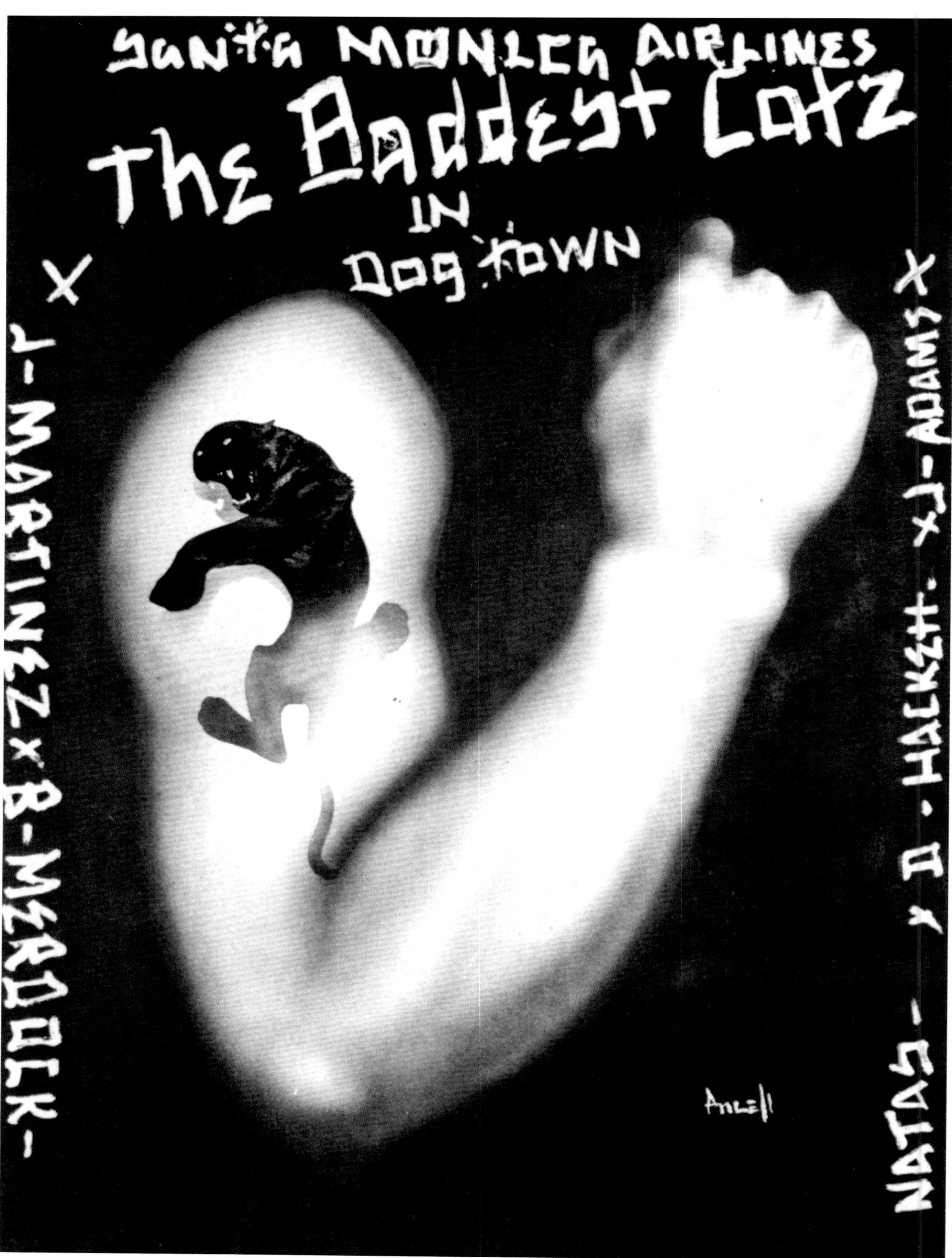

One of the defining brands of 1980s skateboarding took flight at a time when skateboarding was at an all-time high. Santa Monica Airlines started in 1978 as the brainchild of influential surf shaper and skateboard pioneer Skip Engblom, notorious co-founder of Jeff Ho and Zephyr Productions surf and skateboard shop, in a small warehouse in Santa Monica, California. Asked about the origins of the company name and iconic airplane logo, Engblom offered: "We were across the street from Douglas Aircrafts at Santa Monica Airport. And I always wanted to own an airline. I always liked the water-based planes on that run to Catalina [Island]."

Aside from these lofty ambitions, Santa Monica Airlines was also the culmination of some turbulence at ground level. First of all, the entire Zephyr shop operation – home of the Z-Boys skate team and Dogtown school of skating and surfing – did not end with an amicable split (Jeff Ho and Engblom are still not on talking terms). Secondly, Engblom's hand was forced into making his own skateboards by a negative experience with a new retailer, Skateboard Shop of Dogtown, whose proprietors were making skateboards using the Dogtown name. "I went to the shop and tried to buy boards and they wouldn't sell me any. And I had come up with the Dogtown name! These idiots had nothing to do with us or our people," said Skip Engblom.

Ultimately, Engblom decided to use the experience from crafting skateboards in the back of the Zephyr store to start his own business. "I was like, 'Fuck it! I'll just compete with them!' So me and this guy Jim Schulte started making our own skateboards, and I paid this girl I was living with at the time some money to roughly design the [Santa Monica Airlines] logo. We changed it five times, then registered the trademark and went forward," said Engblom about the brand's origins. But right when the company was getting off the ground, the skateboard industry spiraled out of control, crashing severely in 1980. This could have well spelled the end of the freshly launched brand, but Engblom and cohorts kept their airline running, keeping a close ear to the streets, where a revolution in skateboard style was brewing.

STREET STYLE REVOLUTION

On a trip to San Francisco in 1981, Skip Engblom made the acquaintance of a businessman and publisher who was about to take skateboarding in a new direction: Fausto Vitello, co-founder of Independent Trucks and publisher of *Thrasher* magazine. "The entire skate industry was in the toilet and I had gone to SF to sell skateboards, at Skates on Haight [shop]. Fausto had just started *Thrasher* and the guy said, 'You need to check out this magazine!'" On the pages of *Thrasher*, editor Kevin Thatcher and writers including Rick Blackhart presented a new, explosive mixture: progressive skateboarding, not within the confines of designated skate parks, but anywhere in the urban environment, blended with the anarchic attitude of punk rock music. Seeing a way for skateboarding – and his company – to move forward, Engblom set up a meeting with *Thrasher*'s enigmatic photographer, Mörizen Föche, aka "Mofo". "I met Mofo at Hunter's Point [skate park], and he and I became friends," said Engblom, who returned to Santa Monica inspired to start a new run of skateboards.

The connection to *Thrasher* went a long way during this underground period in skateboarding. One of the first *Thrasher* ads for Santa Monica Airlines, a gritty black-and-white half-page in the classifieds section, shows Engblom lounging next to an assortment of handcrafted skateboards in front of a graffiti-splattered wall that read BIG SM GANG.

SANTA MONICA
AIRLINES

SANTA MONICA AIRLINES
AVAILABLE THROUGH A.W.H. SALES
JAY ADAMS
SMA
MODEL
SANTA MONICA
AIRLINES
Buchinsky

SANTA
MONICA
AIR LINE
JAY ADAMS
S M A
MODEL

Now that things were running at next level capacities, Engblom had the freedom to branch out into apparel, injecting SMA's style into a clothing line. "I was the first guy who ever did an embroidery program in the skateboard business. I did sweat pants and sweatshirts, and letterman jackets. I made embroidered letterman shirts for SMA," said Skip Engblom. On that note, a letterman jacket - from "man of letters," or student - is an American varsity jacket worn by collegiate sports teams. The jacket features banded sleeves crafted out of leather, while the body is usually constructed of wool, embroidered with the name of the wearer and insignia of the team or school. "Natas and I went into a marketing deal for clothing with a company called Goldstone Brothers out of Texas that was later sold to Wrangler Jeans." The SMA apparel line also featured a number of board graphics as T-shirt designs, including one of the most iconic designs of 1980s skateboarding: The Natas Kaupas Panther graphic.

BADDEST CATS IN TOWN

As a little-known aside, Engblom reveals the origins of the Natas Panther graphic. "I came up with the panther. I was painting this arm with a panther on and the tattoo was coming alive. It was an ad that said The Baddest Cats in Dogtown. Because a dog has no chance against a panther." The advertisement featured team riders Jesse Martinez, Dave Hackett, and Brandon Murdock next to the panther artwork. As the next iteration, graphic artist Kevin Ancell framed the panther inside a triangle and added the name NATAS on the pro skater's 1986 SMA pro model, which became an instant bestseller on the heels of an iconic *Thrasher* cover photo depicting Natas on one of the first wallrides ever documented.

Over the next runs of the Natas graphic, artist Scott Brezinsky added foliage surrounding the panther, and Wes Humpston of Dogtown fame created what may be the best-known Natas Panther in 1985. Asked whether the Black Panther was a political statement, Skip Engblom explained: "I don't tell people what design to make their skateboards. My stuff is not political. Why not just do something that's fun? Sometimes people do things to piss other people off. Most of the artwork we made was from having a great time."

With the addition of street skating pioneers Jim Thiebaud and Julien Stranger to the team, Santa Monica Airlines emerged as a force to be reckoned with during the mid-1980s skateboard boom. Fast-forward to 2018, and SMA is up and running, sold at skate shops such as Santa Monica's Rip City, which went into business the same year as SMA. "I've been in business about 38 years. That means you must be doing something correctly. The only people who are still around since the '70s are only me, Dogtown, Santa Cruz and Powell. The rest of these guys come and go. So that's what is called weight... the totality of what's going on," said Skip Engblom.

JIMMY'Z
E-Z-IN, E-Z-OUT
hackett

JIMMY'Z: SURF, SKATE, RELATE!

Do your own thing. One of the most iconic 1980s surf and skateboard apparel brands, Jimmy'Z is emblematic of the do-it-yourself spirit at the heart of board sports culture. The L.A.-based clothing company started in 1984 when its namesake, artist and surf enthusiast Jimmy Ganzer began selling home-made surf shorts out of the back of his Buick "Woody" station wagon to surfers on the beaches of Malibu. Ultimately, the brand would take board sports apparel to new heights as the darling of Hollywood stars and forays all the way into the world of high fashion. "It was big fashion! That's what made it so unique. Surf fashion. No other brands did that," said original Jimmy'Z team rider, pro skateboarder Christian Hosoi.

As a signature performance feature, Ganzer's shorts offered a freely adjustable velcro waistband, maintaining a tight fit even in choppy waters. This invention instantly hit home with hardcore surfers, especially since big-name apparel companies had nothing to offer by ways of competition. "The people really dug them, especially the really cool people were buying my shorts. Soon the word got out and it was great to have an instant demand for my product," says Jimmy Ganzer. He also gave a pair to pro skater Dave Hackett. "A few days later he came back and said, 'You really have something there!' That encouraged me to make more."

BUILDING THE PERFECT BOARD SHORT

In search of materials, Ganzer would browse the Garment District in Downtown Los Angeles, where exotic and colorful fabrics were widely available at attractive price points. The quintessential mix of Downtown LA's international vendors strongly impacted the characteristic Jimmy'Z look. "I just used what I liked, a lot of the time I bought fabrics that weren't even meant for clothing." At the time, it cost Ganzer about $15 to make a pair of shorts, which he sold for around $30 by the beach. Keeping in mind that surfers need to move about freely while carrying equipment such as board wax, the self-taught designer put an emphasis on pocket space: "I made sure you could fit two tennis balls in there." Ganzer's magic number for leg length was 16 inches. "I never liked shorts to be too long, because they would catch your knees when you bent down too much. It's also about economy of material. You get more shorts out of your fabric at 16 inches length," Ganzer said, adding that he also experimented with hooks for sunglasses and a velcro'd fly on the front of the shorts.

From a lifestyle point of view, the easy-to-open, buttonless belt line also continued the liberated spirit of the previous decade: "The sound of velcro straps opening was the mating call of the 1970s," says Jimmy Ganzer. But the signature *E-Z-IN,E-Z-OUT* velcro belt also had its risks: "In high school you really had to watch out for people sneaking up from behind trying to rip your shorts off," remembers Todd Huber, co-owner and proprietor of Skatelab skate park and museum in Simi Valley.

SERIOUS BUSINESS

As more surfers kept asking for Ganzer's board shorts, the business soon outgrew its roots as a roadside operation. To make things official, Ganzer visited a lawyer to register a trademark for his clothing brand. "He told me I couldn't protect 'Jimmy's' with an 's' at the end because it was too generic. But with a 'Z' we could get protection," said Jimmy Ganzer.

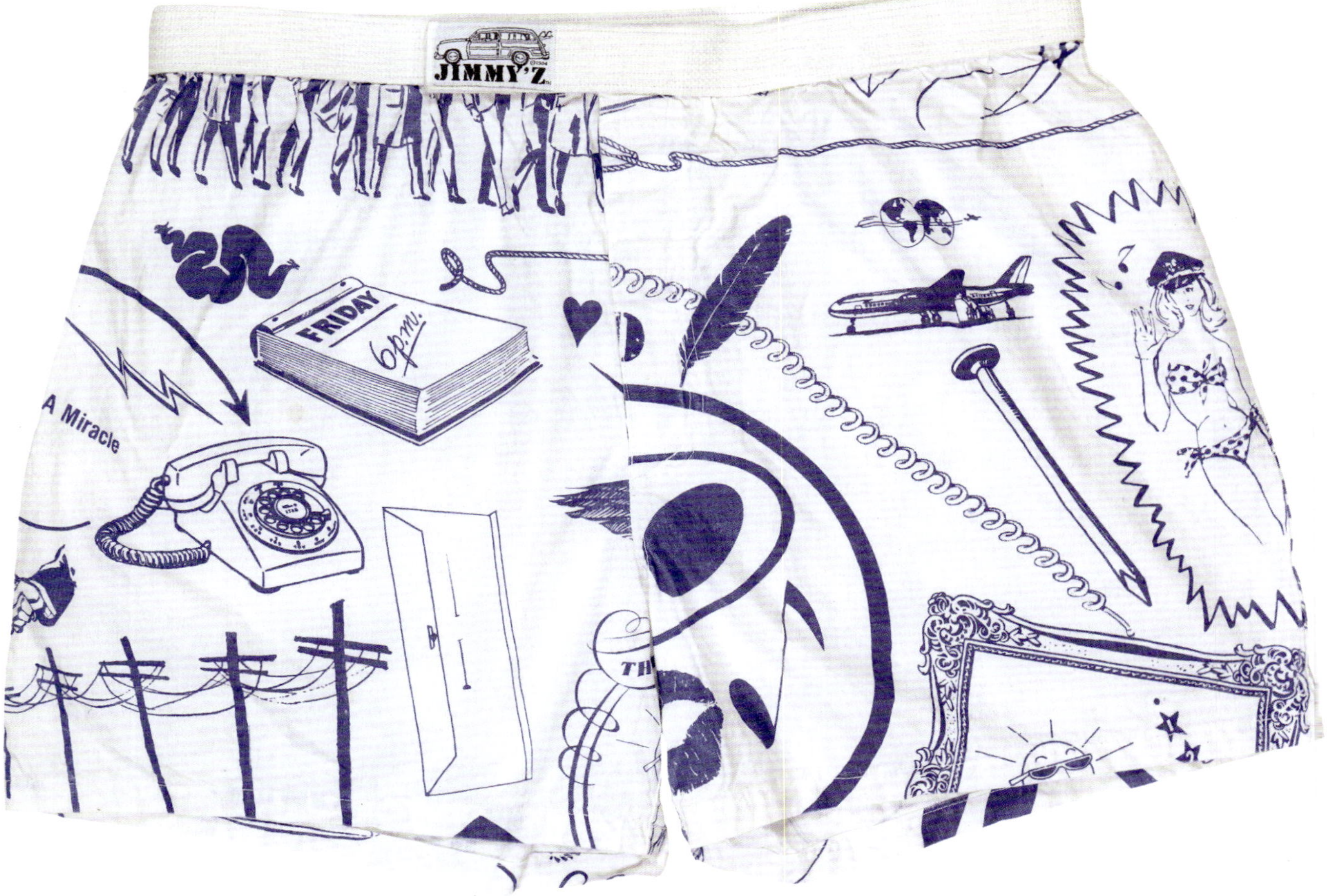
JIMMY'Z
FRIDAY
6p.m.
A Miracle

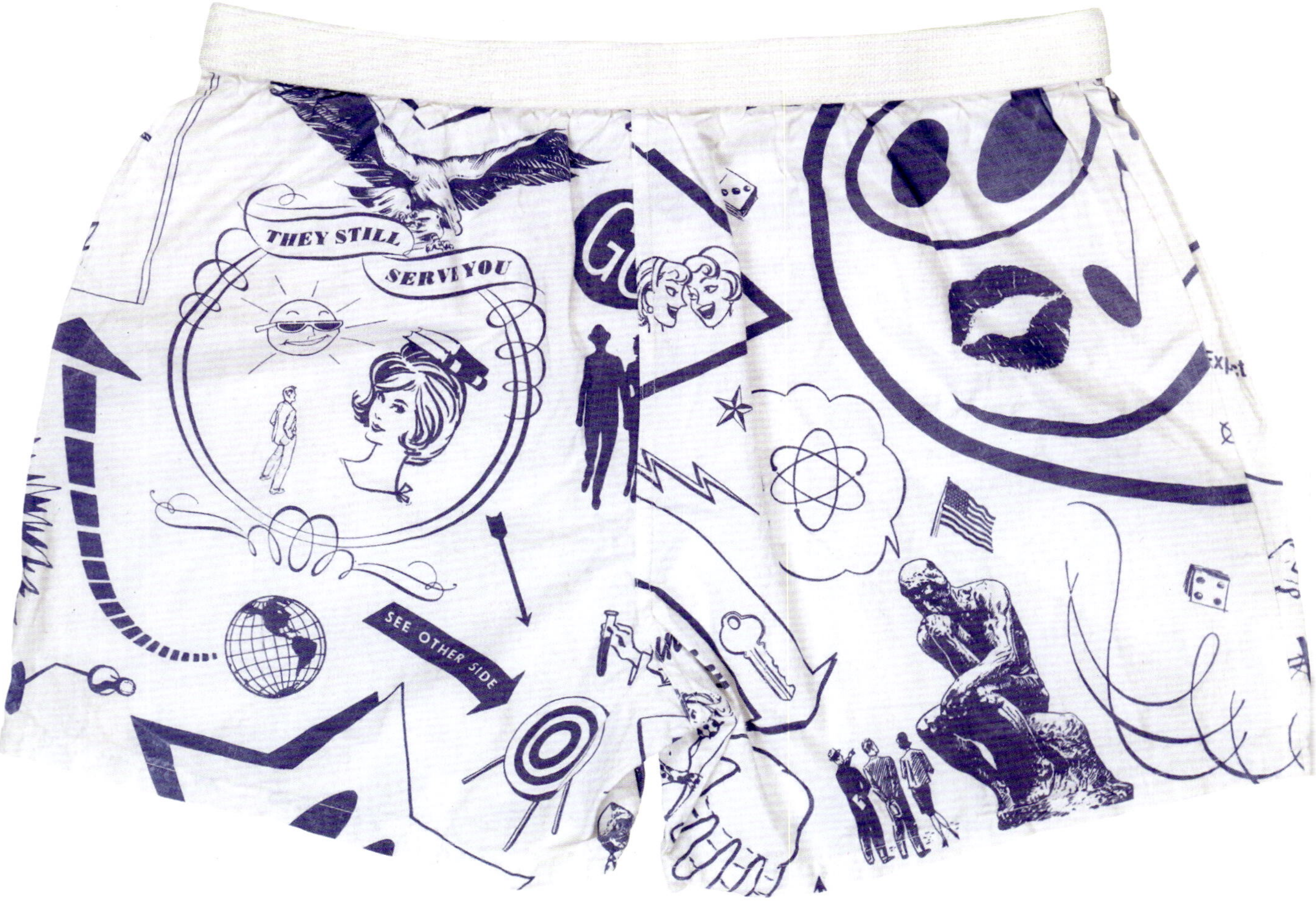
THEY STILL
SEE OTHER SIDE

JIMMY'Z
"SHOOTING THE CURL"
"Z SLAM-STAND"!
THE "JACK LA-LAME"
THE "BUDDHA STAND"
"HANG TWENTY"!
THE "SKID MARK"!
"SEMI-LAYBACK WITH FULL KNEE TWEAK".
THE "ATOMIC".
THE "INVERTED PRETZEL".
THE "CHEATER TEN".
FLOP A "BELLY GRIND"!

JIMMY'Z
LIFEGUARD

Z

JIMMY'Z MALIBU
DUKES

BIG-SPENDING
KING WITH
300 WIVES
JIMMY'Z

JIMMY'Z
What happened over the next few days
was typical of a whirlwind wartime
romance.
"'Hello', she said, 'wasn't that won-
derful'."
He took one of Sweden's top models.
He popped the question, and was accepted.
"The strange thing is," he told a
magazine interviewer,
She was only 25."
It was called The Pink strength
DRILL SARGE

SKATE
THIS
JIMMY'Z

This marked the birth of the Jimmy'Z brand name, and the logo immortalized its humble beginnings, depicting Ganzer behind the wheel of his "Woody" surf wagon. On the product front, Ganzer went deep into the materials and fabrics aspect of board sports apparel. "Jimmy'Z experimented with all that, iridescent materials, plastic looking fabrics, patent leather stuff, rayon, polyester - they did it all," said Christian Hosoi, who made the brand's spandex stretch pants - initially designed for women - a staple of his signature style during his reign as the world's most competitive vert skater in the mid-1980s.

By 1986, Jimmy'Z had grown into a hot-ticket brand offering far more than just shorts, riding high on the new wave of skateboarding's massive popularity. "We were witnessing the explosion of a culture and everyone wanted to be part of skateboarding and surfing. It was all going together at the time - surf, skate, relate!" says Jimmy Ganzer. "That was a time when skateboard fashion really took off," says skateboard photographer Skin Phillips, adding: "Everyone wanted Jimmy'Z and Vision and everyone wanted a Powell shirt."

STREET CRED ON FIFTH AVENUE

Having built an international reputation for comfortable clothes with loud prints and a laid-back California vibe, Jimmy'Z branched out into offering clothing for women and kids. But although women's swimsuits and lounge wear began selling at prestigious stores such as Saks Fifth Avenue, Ganzer and cohorts never compromised the brand's signature style. "One of our ads said, 'Loose clothes for loose people' and folks in the New York art scene looked at me and said, 'Wow, you're really living that lifestyle!' And I was... totally," says Jimmy Ganzer.

While many surf brands struggled to gain acceptance in the increasingly urban-oriented skateboarding community, Jimmy'Z managed to cross over. A great portion of the necessary street credibility came from top-notch riders featured in Jimmy'Z ads, including skateboard luminaries such as Natas Kaupas, Tommy Guerrero, Jesse Martinez, Scott Oster, Dave Duncan, Chris Cook, Eric Dressen and, most prominently, skateboard superstar Christian Hosoi - the son of Ganzer's friend from art school. "Although Jimmy'Z did not really come from skateboarding, people thought it did, because Christian [Hosoi] was in there," said skateboard photographer Dave Swift.

The Jimmy'Z art department was stacked with skateboard legends Dave Hackett and Steve Olson, keeping the company closely aligned with what was cool - and what was going to be next - in the skate and surf scene. Print advertisements alternated between crisp skateboard action shots of pro riders sessioning pools under blue California skies and elaborate, black-and-white fashion imagery by Venice-based photographer Philip Dixon. Not to forget high-concept creative exploits like Christian Hosoi street-planting on top of the globe, or the Jimmy'Z "Woody" surf mobile parked by a pleasant beach while a mushroom cloud from an atomic explosion rises ominously in the background.

JIMMY'Z
Hot n' Glassy Crystal Chambers Pumping Outside Slippery When Wet Coastal
Cruising First Break Surf Safaris Cutback Kickout Goofy Foot Spinner Head
Dip Sideslip Soul Arch Quasimoto Nose Tweak El Telephono Mysterioso Evening
Glass Off Barefoot Adventure Rollercoaster Flyaway Hot Doggin' Bitchin'
Spoonmeat Stoked n' Hooting E-Z in E-Z out Team Jimmy'z Sportwear

NATAS
JIMMY Z
JIMMY'Z®

Photo Chuck Katz
JIMMY'Z

JUST BACK FROM EVERYWHERE...TRY JIMMY'Z!

JIMMY'Z
E-Z-IN, E-Z-OUT

The art department also saw an internal explosion over a particularly captivating photograph: An early Jimmy'Z advertisement that ran in *LA Weekly Magazine*, *Surfer Magazine* and *TransWorld Skateboarding* Magazine depicted Dave Hackett performing a Hang Ten nose manual on the edge of a cliff accompanied by the slogan: "Just Back from Everywhere - try Jimmy'Z!" The photo soon found its way onto Jimmy'Z tees and sweaters in a far-out montage connecting Hackett's nose manual to the back of a swordfish. But when Hackett asked to be paid royalties for the zany design, Jimmy'Z not only allegedly declined, but recreated the photo with a young rider on their team. "They took me off the T-shirt and sweatshirt and put Hosoi on it and never paid me my royalties! Very uncool," said Dave Hackett. A bit later, Christian Hosoi was also featured in a similar T-shirt design in which he is being pulled by a hammerhead shark as a nod to his infamous Hammerhead pro model board.

FROM MALIBU TO HOLLYWOOD

Internal differences aside, the buzz surrounding Jimmy'Z soon spread beyond Ganzer's quiet beach community of Malibu and into the glamour and glitz of Hollywood. Celebrities wanted a slice of board sports cool and fashion-forward stylistics. "We were offering the Los Angeles perspective, the Hollywood style which is entirely different from the Orange County way in terms of morality and lifestyle," says Jimmy Ganzer. Hollywood style also meant exploring the realms of high fashion and music. "It was art, music, surf, skate - the entire lifestyle coming together," Ganzer explains. Standout pieces of Jimmy'Z "high fashion" period include a yellow banana pattern dress shirt ("I wanted the banana to look like a pecker," Ganzer revealed), a leopard print blazer, fragmented black-and-white photo prints as well as Matrix-style black trench coats.

Movie stars and pop culture icons including Hunter S. Thompson, the godfather of Gonzo-style journalism, made public appearances wearing Jimmy'Z threads. In 1988, Grammy-winning American guitarist Ry Cooder appeared in a Jimmy'Z advertisement cross-promoting his guitar sponsor with the slogan "Slide Guitars and Woody Cars." Actor Jack Nicholson wore the "banana print" T-shirt at a televised Laker's championship game and, 20 years later, in the Hollywood blockbuster The Bucket List.

BACK ON BOARD

The popularity of Jimmy'Z peaked in 1990, when Ganzer received an offer to sell the brand to an international surf company for a substantial payday. "You kind of want to take the carrot, but no one likes you for it," Ganzer said. The big deal fell through, however, and Jimmy'Z went through a series of ownership changes. Finally, Richard Harrington, a successful businessman and owner of surf label Maui and Sons bought the rights to Jimmy'Z. The brand remained dormant for years, leaving behind a storied legacy - and a couple of unanswered questions. Even today, many of the brand's followers still wonder about the proper pronunciation of Jimmy'Z: Is it pronounced like the genitive case, *Jimmy's*, or with a hyphenated break, *Jimmy-Z*? Pressed on the issue, Ganzer offered: "Actually, it's any way you want - we like a good mystery!"

The good news is that fans can keep guessing: Jimmy'Z has officially returned to skate and surf shops worldwide after Jimmy Ganzer and Blake Harrington of Maui and Sons fame relaunched the brand in 2011. The athlete team consists of proven rippers Steve Caballero, Giorgio Zattoni, Eddie Elguera, and Jocke Olsson, while Jimmy'Z is branching out beyond apparel into cruisers and longboards.

American
Apparel
JIMMY'Z

ROCK
JIMMY'Z
JIMMY'Z

DAWN OF A NEW ERA

As the year 1984 turned into 1985, the skateboard industry was seeing the light at the end of a long, dark tunnel. Skateboard hardware sales started picking up again, as skateboarding once again became a darling of Hollywood films and main- stream TV commercials. This new boom would mark the rise of New School skateboarding - a new school in the sense that skateboarding had once and for all cut all ties to surfing and emerged from the early 1980s slump with a new-found sense of identity and purpose. In terms of skateboard apparel, the mid-1980s also marked the arrival of a new school of clothing company, spearheaded by Brad Dorfman's Vision Street Wear label - a new type of company created solely for the purpose of designing clothes for skateboarding and the streets - where the focus of skateboarding's evolution was shifting at the same time. This sole focus on apparel was a stark contrast to clothing designed as an afterthought by companies primarily focused on manufacturing hardware. Also a new type of company without cross-over aspirations into surfing, but built on a strict "skater's only" policy.

Most of all, skateboard fashion was about to get wild and crazy in the mid-1980s. "The 1980s were an awesome, brilliant time in skateboarding - but it was fucking crazy. Skateboarding was finding itself and some people looked pretty crazy. But then again, you throw shit on the wall and see what sticks and if it sticks... you go with it!" said skateboard photographer Skin Phillips, adding: "There are a lot of skeletons in the cupboard, definitely. If you wore a beret in Europe you would get punched for it. The 1980s had a lot of tight clothing going on and a lot of weird haircuts and strange shorts! It changed a whole lot!" Speaking of skeletons, skateboard photographer J. Grant Brittain said: "Whenever you see photos of people from the Eighties, and people make fun of them... the excuse is always, 'Well it was the Eighties!' Always! People make fun of someone's hair... 'It was the Eighties!' And that's the excuse that sums it all up."

TO BE CONTINUED... IN BOOK 2!

All that madness - the painter caps, the neon, the super baggy pants, the lady's stretch denim and VSW berets - and much more will be featured in book two of *Skateboarding is Not a Fashion: The Illustrated History of Skateboard Apparel*. In Book 2, we chronicle the ongoing story of skateboard fashion from the year 1985 onwards. And with all the craziness, remember it was our craziness that we collectively own as skateboarders.

It's an ongoing story of fashion at the intersection of flair, style, and performance, with skateboarders leading the charge where others tend to follow. As skateboard artist Mark Oblow puts it: "Sure it's necessary to let the outside world in and sell skateboard products, but we also need to keep in mind that we are the ones that they are looking at. We are the ones that are controlling fashion!"

Photo: Chuck Katz

JIMMY'Z
JIMMY'Z

SKATEMASTER TATE

1959 - 2015

IN LOVING MEMORY - YOU WILL NEVER BE FORGOTTEN!

TO ALL AMAZING CONTRIBUTORS!

We would like to thank everyone who has supported *SKATEBOARDING IS NOT A FASHION* with their contributions, time and input! Also a big "Thank You!" for your courtesy in allowing us to use photos or words, other creative input and of course let us shoot your apparel, collections and dirty laundry.

We would never have been able to tell the story of skateboard apparel without your knowledge, suggestions, comments, photos and donations. Most of all, we want to thank you for believing in this project!

We have endeavored to attribute all work contained in this book.

Any omissions brought to our attention will be corrected in future editions!

Stay tuned - We will be back with Vol. 2

Help to

PRESERVE SKATEBOARD HISTORY

If you want to support the SKATEBOARD MUSEUM / SKATEBOARDING IS NOT A FASHION archive and exhibition:

PLEASE DONATE YOUR
stories, shirts, pants, socks etc.

YOU CAN CONTACT US ANY TIME:
:
info@SKATEBOARDMUSEUM.Berlin

"ENJOY LIFE, RIDE A SKATEBOARD!"

Photo: Glen E. Friedman

PHOTOGRAPHERS:

Doug Biggert
Warren Bolster
Tom Boyle
Grant Brittain
James Cassimus
Ron Chruch
tom & Rick Corombes
Bill Eppridge
Glen E. Friedman
Jim Goodrich
John Hudson
Chuck Katz
Wynn Miller
Mofo
Ralph Morse
Stan Sharp
Tom Sims
Craig B. Snyder
C. R. Stecyk III
Ron Stoner
Tod Swank
Ted Terrebonne
Steve Wilkings
Miki Vuckovich

INTERVIEWS:

Tony Alva
Neil Blender
Brad Bowman
Brian Brannon
Grant Brittain
Don Brown
Steve Caballero
Ron Cameron
James Cassimus
Michael Chantry
Cris Dawson
Garry Scott Davis
Titus Dittman
Steve Van Doren
Steve Douglas
Dave Duncan
Ed Economy
Eddie "El Gato" Elguera
Skip Engblom
Jeremy Fish
Brian Flynn
Glen E. Friedman
Jim Ganzer
Tim Gavin
Alan "Ollie" Gelfand
Patti McGee
Claus Grabke
John Grigley
Mark Gonzales
Dave Hackett
Jeff Ho
Christian Hosoi
Andy Howell
Todd Huber
Keith Hufnagel
Chuck Hults
Wes Humpston
Gerry Hurtado
Tom "Wally" Inouye
Jeremy Klein
Robin Logan
Jörg Ludewig
Marc McKee
Patti McGee
Lance Mountain
Jim Muir
Chad Muska
Rich Novak
Mark Oblow
Dave Olson
Steve Olson
Jodi Omaha
Stacy Peralta
Tim Piumarta
Jim Phillips
Skin Phillips
George Powell
Nathan Pratt
Scott Radinsky
Alphonzo Rawls
Mark Richards
Ed Riggins
Steve Rocco
Pierre André Sénizergues
Chris "Slappy" Southerland
Craig R. Stecyk III
Dave Swift
Ted "T-Bone" Terrebonne
Alaric Valentin
Mike Vallely
Damon Way

MAGAZINES:

Thrasher Magazine
TransWorld Magazine
The Skateboard Mag
Juice Magazine
SkateBoarder Magazine
BigBrother Magazine
Monster Magazine
Limited Magazine
KingPin Magazine
Slap Magazine
Solo Magazine
the quarterly Skateboarder

SHOOTING SHRITS / COLLECTIONS, LETTING US CRASH ON THE COUCH AND ANY KIND OF SPECIAL SUPPORT WE CAN THINK OF:

Markus Angerer
Larry und Luise Balma
Ray Barbee
Javier Sánchez Barrantes
Jochen Bauer
Matthias Bauer
Johannes Bethge
Harry Blitzstein
Kongo Boehmfeldt
Bod Boyle
Ralf Braitling
Markus Brilling
Partick "Bärty" Bruns
Simon Burlo
Jason Callaway
Jose Cerda
Steve „Scuba" Chalme
Mike Chantry
Ron Chatman
Rick "RxCx" Clayton
Dan Clements
Daniel Clemente
Gabe Clemens
Sean Cliver
Mo Cohen
Jason Cohn
Christopher Connelly
Eladio Correa
Henry Davis
Stefan „Slow" Dietrich
Martin Dockenfuß
Laura Doherty
Kristy Van Doren
Julian Duval
Lynn Downey
Emma und Peter Ehlert
Mackenzie Eisenhour
Filip Elerud
Pitt Feil
Arne Fensky
"Foley" & Civilist Crew Berlin
Marc Flammer
Ray Flores
Mike Folmer
Ciaro Foster
Dave Freil
Michael Furukawa
Kristian Gärtner
Sharon Gelfan
Bernhard Glimm
Joel Gomez
Konstantin Gräfner

Tommy Guererro
Martin Grüb
Tony Hallam
Stanton Hartsfield
Trevor Hill
Markus Hoch
Jennifer Huber
Moose Huerta
Zsuzsanna Ilijin
Kevin Imamura
Mario Irrek
Dirk Jakobs
Andy Jenkins
Thomas Kalak
Uli Kattenstroth
Natas Kaupas
Fritz Klein
Alex „Starsky" Kleinhans
Karl Knoop
Jochen Küpper
Philippe Lalemant
Dan Levy
Gordy Lienemann
Kaspar van Lierop
Richi Löffler
David Lopes
Dimitir Lorin
John Lucero
Martin Magielka
Ben Marcus
Gianluca Mariani
Rick Markell
Oliver Marquis
Rick Marr
Danny Martin
Stefan Marx
Marc Mckee
Paul Merrell
Stephen Mills
Heiko Müller
Mike Muir
Timothy Nickloff

Doug Palladini
Sebastian Palmer
Jake Phelps
Jimbo Phillips
Michael Ralla
Larry Ransom
Dirk "Shorty" Rassloff
Gerd Rieger
Johannes Ritter
Gabriel Rodriguez
Christian Rothenhagen
Steve Saiz
Steve Salba
Grant Saltarelli
Jeff Samuels
Oliver Scheibler
Thomas Schiller
Daniel Schindler
Thorsten Schlossbauer
Daniel Schmid
Mark Schmid
Prof. Paul Schmitt
Jan Schoper
Lars Schulte
Dave "Chopper" Seraita
Dale Smith
Jack Smith
Nick Street
David Sypniewski
Laura Thornhill
Charlie Tidball
Chuck Treece
Daniel Trujillo
Bryan Ray Turcotte
Tony Vitello
Mirko Wagner
David Watson
Skot Werner
Mark Widmann
Bjoern Wiersma
Erik Wolsky
Steffi Wolter

DE MODE
JAMAIS
FONCTION
FASHION SIMULATOR MODEL 360 7XI
THE SEARCH FOR
FUTURE
PRIMITIVE
POWELL PERALTA

THE 7 INDEX

HARDBACK COVER

Jay Smith - Photo by C.R. Stecyk III
1980 Powell-Peralta advertisement "A Man and His Models"

HARDBACK BACK

Tony Alva - Photo by Stan Sharp

Page 5 Skateboardmania
1979

Page 6 Hobie Team "Night Rallies" - Photo by Ron Stoner
1964 *the Quarterly Skateboarder Magazine* Vol.1 No.1

Page 11 DogTown Wheels advertisement - Photo by: D.T. Designs

CHAPTER - THE INTRO

Page 17 Art by Rick Griffin - "The Well dressed skateboarder"
1964 *the Quarterly Skateboarder Magazine* Vol.1 No.1

Page 18 Boy skateboarding in New York City's Central Park -
Photo by Bill Eppridge
(Getty Images - The *LIFE* Picture Collection)

Page 20 Young boy nailing Skateboard - Photo by Ralph Morse
(Getty Images The *LIFE* Picture Collection)

CHAPTER - THE ROOTS

Page 22 August 1959 Los Angeles - Photos by Tom Corombes

Page 26 Val Surf advertisement "Surf ´s Down"
Mark Richards / Val Surf Archive

Page 34 1965 Foxtail Park pool - skaterboarder unknown
Photo by Ron Stoner

CHAPTER - THE SIXTIES

Page 37 1964 Jim Phillips pointing finger at Long Bar
Photographer: Unknown

Page 40 Danny Schaffer 1964
the Quarterly Skateboarder Magazine Vol.1. No.1
Photo by Ron Stoner

Page 42 Dave Rochlen in his Vita Pack blazer "The Kick Turn"
1965 *the Quarterly Skateboarder Magazine* Vol.1 No.2

Page 46 60s Hobie Team patch from Cris Dawsons Archive

Page 50 Hobie National Team 1966 At the Santa Monica Civic Auditorium
Photographer unknown

Page 52 1969 Makaha Team Ty Page, Rusty Henderson,
Brad and Bruce Logan - Photo by ©Makaha, LLC

Page 58 Phil Edwards skateboarding - Photo by Ron Church

Page 65 Pat McGee Skatelab /
Skateboarding Hall of Fame Archive

Page 68 Danny Bearer "Skateboard Superstar"
Photo by James Gregory 1965 *Skateboarder Magazine* Vol.1 No.3

Page 72 1965 International Skateboard Championships
Photo by Ron Stoner 1965 *Skateboarder Magazine* Vol.1 No.3

CHAPTER - THE SEVENTIES

Page 86 Gregg Weaver aka the Cadillac Kid - Photo by Warren Bolster

Page 117 D. David Morin aka Krypto Team Captain
Photo by Glen E. Friedman

Page 130 1975 Zephyr Team Bahne/Cadillac National Championships
Photo by C. R. Stecyk III (upper row L-R) Shogo Kubo,
Bob Biniak, Nathan Pratt, Stacy Peralta, Jim Muir, Alan Sarlo
Chris Cahill, Tony Alva (bottom row L-R) Wentzle Ruml IV,
Peggy Oki, Jay Adams, Paul Constantineau

Page 137 Jeff Ho at the Bahne/Cadillac National Championships
Photo by C. R. Stecyk III

Page 144 Marty Grimes at Skatopia - Photo by Glen E. Friedman

Page 156 Steve Salba at Upland skatepark - Photo by Jim Goodrich

Page 158 Steve Evans at Carson Skatepark - Photo by Thibodeaux

Page 164 Tom "Wally" Inouye - Photo by Stan Sharp

Page 178 Santa Cruz Aptos Team - Photo by John Hudson

Page 182 Steve Olson at the Marina Pro Banked Slalom
Photo by James Cassimus

Page 200 Lonnie Toft riding the eight-wheeler Photo by Craig Fineman

Page 207 Howard Hood in home turf - Photo by James Cassimus

Page 208 Dough - Photo by Craig Fineman

Page 210 1978 Competition meeting at Clearwater, Florida
Photo by Craig B. Snyder

Page 216 Brad Bowman at Oasis banks - Photo by James Cassimus

Page 218 Brad Bowman doing an early-release air at Del Mar
Photo by James Cassimus

Page 222 Vicki Vickers at Marina Del Ray - Photo by Glen E. Friedman

Page 224 Laura Thornhill at Montebello - „Hot Shot"

Page 230 Tony Alva at Wallos ditch - Photo by Steve Wilkings

Page 234 The Free Former team riders Ty Page, Mark Bowden and
Bryan Beardsley jumping a car at La Costa
Photo by Jim Goodrich

Page 252 Eddie "El Gato" Elguera - Photo by Jim Goodrich

Page 257 Tom Sims at the Anaheim Bowl - Photo by Warren Bolster

Page 262 Sims Skateboardteam at the Paramount Skate Park
Photo by Tom Sims

Page 265 Tom Fain in Oxnard - Photo by Craig Fineman

Page 272 Dale "Sausage Man" Smith - Photo by Glen Miyoda

Page 280 Jay Adams at Del Mar - Photo by Grant Brittain

Page 285 Nathan Pratt DogTown - Photo by C. R. Stecyk III

Page 286 Nathan Pratt Horizon West "California Gun" ad
Photo by C. R. Stecyk III

Page 299 Shogo Kubo tail tap at Cherry Hill - Photo by Glen E. Friedman

Page 300 Shogo Kubo at Cherry Hill - Photo by Glen E. Friedman

Page 303 Gremlins - Artwork by Jim Phillips

Page 304 TonyAlva at Adolphs pool - Photo by C.R.StecykIII

Page 305 Tony Alva flipping the finger at an conest in Long Beach
Photo by Jim Goodrich

Page 310 Jay Adams Pro-File Skateboard World - Photo by Stan Sharp

Page 311 Tony Alva demo in Sweden - Photo by Wynn Miller

Page 313 Shogo Kubo at Tower Pool

Page 316 Tony Alva - Photo by Glen E. Friedman

Page 322 Tony "Mad Dog" Alva SkateBoarder interview
Photo by C. R. Stecyk III

Page 325 Tony Alva in Caracas 1979 - Photo by Jim Goodrich

Page 334 Tony Alva - Photo by Wynn Miller

Page 334 Stuttgart Main Trainstation - Photo by Mathias Bauer

Page 336 Jay Adams at Dog Bowl - Photo: Glen E. Friedman

Page 350 Tony Alva - Photo: Glen E. Friedman

Page 352 Chris Strople at Upland - Photo: James Cassimus

Page 354 Steve Rocco powerslide - Photo: Unknown

Page 365 Pepsi Team private photo - Photo by Gordy Lienemann

Page 374 Jana Payne at Concrete Wave - Photo by James Cassimus

Page 382 Stacy Peralta Upland 1978 - Photo by Jim Goodrich

Page 388 Stacy Peralta spinning - Photo by C. R. Stecyk III

Page 392 Stacy Peralta at Marina - Photo by Glen E. Friedman

Page 400 C. R. Stecyk III - Photo by C. R. Stecyk III

Page 409 Bones Brigade - Photo by Powell Peralta

Page 415 Eddie "El Gato" Elguera - Photo by Jim Goodrich

Page 428 Wentzle Ruml at Stokers - Photo by D. Kau

Page 440 Brad Bowman SkateBoarder Interview Photo by James Cassimus

Page 444 Brad Bowman handplant at Del Mar - Photo by James Cassimus

Page 446 Salba and Brad Bowman - Photo by Craig Fineman

Page 449 Salba over Dunlop at Pipeline - Photos by James Cassimus

Page 449 Salba at Boulder - Photos by James Cassimus

Page 454 Variant freestyle in Venice -Photo by James Cassimus

Page 456 Steve Olson at Long Beach - Photo by Ted Terrebonne

Page 462 Steve Olson at Kenter -- Photo by Glen E. Friedman

Page 467 Steve Olson at Pipeline - Photo by James Cassimus

Page 468 Steve Olson at Marina -- Photo by Craig Fineman

Page 483 Salba pointing finger - Photo by Steve Zirwas

Page 484 Steve Olson Brooklyn Banks - Photo by Christian Lepanto

CHAPTER - THE EIGHTIES (PART 1)

Page 494 Duane Peters at Del Mar - Photo by Glen E. Friedman

Page 496 Duane Peters - Photo by Ted Terrebonne

Page 498 Duane Peters styling Ted Terrebonne - Photo by White

Page 510 Lance Mountain TWS interview - Photo by Glen E. Friedman

Page 512 Lance Mountain at Lances Ramp - Photo by Glen E. Friedman

Page 526 Steve Caballero and Tommy Guerrero O'ahu, Hawaii
Photo byTom Boyle

Page 530 Steve Alba - Photo by James Cassimus

Page 533 Devo - Photo by Ted Terrebonne

Page 540 Tracy Gates - Photo by Lance Mountain

Page 542 JFA Band - Brian Brannon JFA Archive

Page 544 Brian Brannon at Pflugerville ditch - Photos by Mofo

Page 550 Mike and Jim Muir - Photo by Glen E. Friedman

Page 566 Devo / Brian "Pushead" Schroeder

Page 568 The Surf Punks - Photo by Glen E. Friedman

Page 573 Lance Mountain - Photo by Swank

Page 584 Record cover and RxCx Shirt - Photos by Glen E. Friedman

Page 580 Tommy Guerrero at San Pasqual Photo by Grant Brittain

Page 587 Chuck Hults - Photo Chuck Hults Archives

Page 592 GSD Skully Photo by Miki Vuckovich

Page 598 Christian Hosoi and Eddie Reategui at Tower Mags
Photo by Doug Biggert

Page 626 Subscribe TWS ad "Catch the Fun" Photo by Grant Brittain

Page 653 Natas Kaupas Photo by Chuck Katz

Page 658 Gerry Hurtado "Skatemaster Tate" Photo by Chuck Katz

Page 661 Gerry Hurtado "Skatemaster Tate" BEWARE flyer
Photo by Skateboarding Hall of Fame

Page 663 Jay Smith backyard ramp - Photo by Glen E. Friedman

Page 670 Jay Smith - Photo by Glen E. Friedman

Photo: Glen E. Friedman

INDEPENDENT
SCHLITZ
MALT LIQUOR

"This is the end
of the age of Aquarius and
the dawn of the SKATEBOARD!"
Ghost Rider
SKATEBOARDMANIA

mellow cat
BY TED RICHARDS
G&S
SANTA CRUZ
SKATEBOARDS
variflex
variflex
variflex
MAD RATS
SKATEBOARDER
VAL SURF
the Faction
SUMMER TOUR 84
VANS
POWELL
TEAM
PARK